Variations in the Expression of Inka Power

Participants in the "Variations in the Expression of Inka Power" symposium, October 1997. FRONT ROW, LEFT TO RIGHT: María Muñoz, John H. Rowe, John V. Murra, María Rostworowski de Diez Canseco, Tom Zuidema, and Lucy Salazar. SECOND ROW: Albert Meyers, Rebecca Rollins Stone, Tom Cummins, Susan Niles, and Richard Burger. THIRD ROW: Gary Urton, Verónica Williams, Brian Bauer, Charles Stanish, Ana María Lorandi, and Ramiro Matos. BACK ROW: Robert Batson, Jeffrey Quilter, Craig Morris, Terence D'Altroy, Heather Lechtman, Carmen Arellano, and Julián I. Santillana.

Variations in the Expression of Inka Power
A Symposium at Dumbarton Oaks
18 and 19 October 1997

Richard L. Burger, Craig Morris, and Ramiro Matos Mendieta, *Editors*
Joanne Pillsbury and Jeffrey Quilter, *General Editors*

Published by Dumbarton Oaks Research Library and Collection, Washington, D.C.
Distributed by Harvard University Press, 2007

Copyright © 2007 Dumbarton Oaks
Trustees for Harvard University
Washington, D.C.
All rights reserved.
Printed in the United States of America

Library of Congress Cataloging-in-Publication Data

Variations in the expression of Inka power : a symposium at Dumbarton Oaks, 18 and 19 October 1997 / Richard L. Burger, Craig Morris, and Ramiro Matos Mendieta, editors ; Joanne Pillsbury and Jeffrey Quilter, general editors.
    p. cm.
 Includes bibliographical references and index.
 ISBN 978-0-88402-351-7
 1. Incas—Antiquities—Congresses. 2. Andes Region—Civilization—Congresses. 3. Incas—Social life and customs—Congresses. I. Burger, Richard L. II. Morris, Craig. III. Matos Mendieta, Ramiro. IV. Pillsbury, Joanne. V. Quilter, Jeffrey, 1949-
 F3429.V377 2007
 985'.019—dc22

                      2007007522

Contents

vii **JOANNE PILLSBURY**
Foreword

xiii **RICHARD L. BURGER, CRAIG MORRIS, AND RAMIRO MATOS MENDIETA**
Preface

1 **CRAIG MORRIS**
Andean Ethnohistory and the Agenda for Inka Archaeology

11 **CARMEN ARELLANO AND RAMIRO MATOS MENDIETA**
Variations between Inka Installations in the Puna of Chinchayqocha and the Drainage of Tarma

45 **CHARLES STANISH AND BRIAN S. BAUER**
Pilgrimage and the Geography of Power in the Inka Empire

85 **TERENCE N. D'ALTROY, VERÓNICA I. WILLIAMS, AND ANA MARÍA LORANDI**
The Inkas in the Southlands

135 **CRAIG MORRIS AND JULIÁN IDILIO SANTILLANA**
The Inka Transformation of the Chincha Capital

165 **LUCY C. SALAZAR**
Machu Picchu's Silent Majority: A Consideration of the Inka Cemeteries

185 **SUSAN A. NILES AND ROBERT N. BATSON**
Sculpting the Yucay Valley: Power and Style in Late Inka Architecture

223 **ALBERT MEYERS**
Toward a Reconceptualization of the Late Horizon and the Inka Period: Perspectives from Cochasquí, Ecuador, and Samaipata, Bolivia

255 **MARÍA DE LOS ANGELES MUÑOZ**
     The Kallanka at Samaipata, Bolivia: An Example of Inka Monumental Architecture

267 **TOM CUMMINS**
     Queros, Aquillas, Uncus, and Chulpas: The Composition of Inka Artistic Expression and Power

313 **HEATHER LECHTMAN**
     The Inka, and Andean Metallurgical Tradition

357 **GARY URTON AND CARRIE J. BREZINE**
     Information Control in the Palace of Puruchuco: An Accounting Hierarchy in a Khipu Archive from Coastal Peru

385 **REBECCA R. STONE**
     "And All Theirs Different from His": The Dumbarton Oaks Royal Inka Tunic in Context

423 **RICHARD L. BURGER**
     The Archaeology of Inka Power: Concluding Thoughts

438 Notes on Contributors

443 Index

Foreword

Joanne Pillsbury

CONVERSATIONS LEADING TO THE CREATION OF A SYMPOSIUM ON THE Inka Empire began in 1995 when Richard Burger, Craig Morris, and Ramiro Matos Mendieta remarked to Jeffrey Quilter, then director of Pre-Columbian Studies at Dumbarton Oaks, that despite a number of successful roundtables, colloquia, and symposia on Andean archaeology, there had yet to be a major meeting devoted to the Inka, the last and perhaps best known of the Prehispanic Andean cultures. The Inka Empire, one of the ancient world's most extraordinary political entities, once stretched across the spine of the Andean cordillera from what is now southwestern Colombia, south through modern-day Ecuador, Peru, and Bolivia, and into central Chile and northwestern Argentina. The traditional view holds that their conquest of this vast territory was remarkably fast, occurring essentially in the last century or so before the arrival of Francisco Pizarro and his army in 1531. As Burger, Morris, and Matos point out in their preface, and as the contributors of this volume so elegantly demonstrate, this model, and other received ideas about the Inka (formed largely on the basis of historical documents), need to be reevaluated and debated in light of the wealth of new archaeological data uncovered in the past few decades.

For many years, Inka archaeology suffered from the same bias that once affected Aztec archaeology: as these two cultures were dominant at the time of the arrival of the first Europeans in the sixteenth century, they loom large in the earliest European historical accounts of the Americas. Such was the impact of these texts that it was felt that the need for the archaeological study of Inka culture was less urgent, because the documents provided a reasonably complete record. Fortunately this view has changed, and we have come to recognize that documents and archaeology tell us different things. Archaeology can provide a check on the accounts of writers who did not fully understand what they were encountering, or who had reason to embellish and invent for audiences in Europe and the Americas. Archaeology can also provide data of the sort not generally covered in the historical accounts. As Terence D'Altroy, Verónica Williams, and Ana María Lorandi note in this volume, the southern reaches of the Inka Empire receive scant attention in the historical sources, for reasons relating to Spanish interests, or more properly in this case, a lack of interest. And, as a number of contributors to this volume have illustrated, archaeology provides a means for studying populations and individuals who do not customarily appear in the historical records, records so often written by, and for, a very small sector of society.

The symposium, "Variations in the Expression of Inka Power," was held from 18 to 19 October 1997, and dedicated to four pioneering scholars of Inka culture: John V. Murra, María Rostworowski de Diez Canseco, John H. Rowe, and R. Tom Zuidema. While these authors are perhaps best known for their historical work, throughout their careers they remained open to and interested in archaeology (and in the case of Rowe, very active in field archaeology, particularly in the 1940s) and well aware of the importance of examining different lines of evidence in the creation of models of Inka culture. As the editors of this volume write in the Preface, their historical studies have had a major impact on archaeological research design in the last twenty years. And so it is fitting that these four be recognized as intellectual pioneers of a new generation of archaeologists. Sadly, the symposium in 1997 was the last time these four gathered together. John H. Rowe died in May of 2004, and John V. Murra in October of 2006. They are both greatly missed in the field of Andean studies. We particularly mourn their loss here at Dumbarton Oaks, as both men participated in numerous seminars, symposia, and other scholarly meetings over the years. In addition, John Rowe served as an advisor to the Pre-Columbian Program as a Senior Fellow from 1984 until 1990.

I must also note with great sadness that Craig Morris, one of the editors of this volume, died shortly after the papers were submitted to Dumbarton Oaks in 2006. He was a frequent participant in the scholarly activities here at Dumbarton Oaks, and his untimely death was a tremendous loss for our field.

I would like to thank the editors of this volume for suggesting the symposium, and for their vision and hard work in shaping the present volume. Thanks are also due to the contributors for their fine papers at the meeting and for their patience in the various editorial stages in the production of the volume. Jeffrey Quilter was integral to both the meeting planning and the subsequent transformation of symposium to publication. In the early stages he was assisted by Janice Williams, and later by Kristy Keyes. I am particularly grateful to Jai Alterman and Emily Gulick, assistants to the director of Pre-Columbian Studies, who contributed in numerous ways to the preparation of the volume. Juan Antonio Murro and Miriam Doutriaux, both archaeologists active in Andean research, took time away from their curatorial responsibilities here at Dumbarton Oaks to advise on aspects of the volume. Hélène Bernier, Augusto Oyuela-Caycedo, Karen Rasmussen, and Johan Reinhard were also helpful in the preparation of illustrations. Finally, I would like to thank Lynne Shaner and her staff in the Publications Office of Dumbarton Oaks for their work on this volume, in particular Grace Morsberger, Mariana Reynolds, and Hilary Parkinson.

This volume offers a range of perspectives on Inka power, with contributions by scholars writing about distinct parts of the empire, deploying different methodological approaches. As one might expect in a volume devoted to "variations in expressions" there is not necessarily a uniform voice in the representation of Inka culture. Diversity is reflected in everything from orthography to chronology. The editors chose to strive for a certain degree of consistency in major names and terms (for example, "Inka" over the more traditional "Inca," in keeping with official Peruvian orthography for Quechua), but a plurality of voices is still apparent in the different contributions. Diversity of opinion was particularly apparent when it came to chronology, and it is clear here that more research and debate are needed. While this may be the first volume dedicated to the Inka at Dumbarton Oaks, it will certainly not be the last, and we look forward to continuing the conversation at future opportunities.

— Joanne Pillsbury
　Director of Studies, Pre-Columbian Program, Dumbarton Oaks

FIG. 1 The Inka Empire at its greatest extent. The Inka themselves called their realm Tawantinsuyu ("The Four Parts Together") (drawing by Karen Rasmussen, Archeographics, based on data from Terence N. D'Altroy)

Joanne Pillsbury

FIG. 2 The Inka Empire, with sites mentioned in the volume indicated (drawing by Karen Rasmussen, Archeographics)

Preface

WE ORGANIZED THE DUMBARTON OAKS SYMPOSIUM "VARIATIONS IN THE Expression of Inka Power" in 1997 to take advantage of emerging research and to call attention to the extraordinary potential that archaeological investigations had for our understanding of the Inka period. This focus highlighted a change in attitude toward Inka research, which traditionally received less attention from archaeologists than earlier epochs of Andean prehistory. Although we considered casting the conference more broadly or choosing a specific theme that encompassed the work of both ethnohistorians and archaeologists, the wealth of new documentary studies made it impractical to attempt to cover adequately work in both sub-disciplines.

In dedicating the symposium and this volume to John Howland Rowe, John Murra, María Rostworowski, and Tom Zuidema, four giants of Inka research, we recognize both their individual contributions and the impact of their work, and of ethnohistory in general, on archaeological research. The approaches they developed are a vital source of models and specific hypotheses, providing the basis for interpreting the archaeological record. Moreover, each of these leaders of Inka research has shown an abiding fascination with the potential of archaeology for testing and expanding upon historical accounts of Inka culture and society. We hoped that the conference would serve as an appropriate commemoration of their remarkable accomplishments. In this light, we were especially delighted that all four of the honorees were able to attend the conference and provide their own insights during the lively discussions that followed each talk.

One of the primary contributions of archaeology has been to demonstrate the great regional diversity of the Inka realm, as strategies of expansion beyond Cusco were shaped to a bewildering variety of local situations. The approaches that archaeologists have taken to their investigations have also varied with the local situations, as well as with methodological and theoretical orientations. The result of both of these conditions is a diverse set of studies that illustrates the range and complexity of the field.

The selection of speakers for the symposium upon which this volume is based attempted to achieve geographic coverage of the Tawantinsuyu while also incorporating different levels of analysis and approaches to the Inka world. Dumbarton Oaks is one of the few institutions that encourage the interaction of art historians, with their distinctive humanistic perspective; archaeologists working within a social science framework; and scientists engaging in the laboratory study of material culture remains. All three perspectives are intentionally represented in this volume, although the reader will note that all of the authors transcend these narrow typologies. The examples published here have now been joined by a great wealth of new archaeological research on the Inka in all five of the modern Andean republics they once partially controlled, and prospects for the future are extremely bright.

We would like to thank Jeffrey Quilter, the former director of Pre-Columbian Studies, for his unflagging assistance in the organization and preparation of this volume and Joanne Pillsbury, current director of studies, for her enthusiasm and willingness to see this project through to completion. We would also like to acknowledge the staff support that we received from Sharon Rodriguez and Kira Cassel at Yale University and Sumru Aricanli at the American Museum of Natural History.

—Richard L. Burger
—Craig Morris
—Ramiro Matos Mendieta

Andean Ethnohistory and the Agenda for Inka Archaeology

Craig Morris

UNTIL THE MID-TWENTIETH CENTURY, INKA STUDIES FOCUSED PRIMARILY on the written sources compiled in the sixteenth century by Spanish chroniclers, administrators, and eyewitnesses to the invasion. Information from first-hand observations and access to participants in events prior to the arrival of Europeans appeared to be the best route to understanding the remarkable empire that flourished in the Andes before 1532. Scholars did not regard the limited and fragmentary archaeological record to be a viable source of substantive information on the nature of the Inka Empire. Locating and identifying sites mentioned in the written sources provided more in the way of interesting visual information than an increased understanding of the Inkas and the peoples they ruled. Scholars viewed the archaeological sites as adjuncts to the accounts of the early European observers, rather than sources of significant new data in themselves. Nevertheless, nineteenth-century explorers such as E. George Squier (1877), Johann von Tschudi (1860, 1918), and Alexander von Humboldt (1813, 1968) provided important verification of some aspects of the written sources and data on sites that would serve future archaeology. Perhaps the early archaeologists' greatest contribution, through their reports and illustrations, was to erase any doubt of the monumentality of the Inka achievement.

A few early studies, however, combined exploration with archaeological excavations that were systematic, and even problem oriented. Perhaps most notable were those of Bandelier (1910) and Bingham (1913, 1930). Bingham's work at Machu Picchu and Bandelier's research on the Islands of the Sun and Moon went well beyond exploration, as both excavated within specific architectural contexts, and both focused on the space-time frameworks characteristic of archaeology at that time. But they did not make significant progress on what are perhaps the two major emphases of present-day Inka archaeology: studies of the origins and expansion of the empire and coordinated research on architecture and excavated artifact assemblages to reconstruct activity patterns that elucidate Inka culture and society. The work of Max Uhle and, later, of Julio C. Tello went well beyond the early emphasis on exploration and illustration. Their long careers and prolific research provide important bridges to the present. Both understood the great depth of Andean civilization and recognized the Inkas as merely the last and, territorially, the largest of its manifestations. They conducted systematic archaeological field work and devoted serious analytical thought to the Andean past.

Uhle understood the importance of architecture to understanding the past, and invested much effort in producing accurate plans of several important Inka sites, including Pachacamac (Uhle 1903; Shimada 1991), La Centinela (Uhle 1924), and Tambo Colorado (Wurster 1999). While many of his excavations focused on cemeteries and formed the basis for later extremely important chronological studies (Menzel 1966, 1976), he was also very interested in linking written records and other evidence with architecture to reconstruct activities (e.g., 1903: 81–83).

Tello's primary interest was in tracing the origins of Andean civilization and demonstrating its deep pre-Inka roots (1929, 1942). Nevertheless, as a museum director and Peru's most eminent archaeologist, he was involved in cleaning (e.g., Tello 1943) and conservation work on Inka sites and on innovative exhibitions involving models of Inka settlements. As in all of his work, he was not interested in sites and objects for their own sake, but in the people and cultures that produced them.

The mid-twentieth century witnessed a virtual revolution in our understanding of the Inkas. Many scholars contributed to the new information, ideas, and perspectives that emerged during the period, but the four with greatest impact are those honored by this volume and the symposium on which it is based. The works of John V. Murra, María Rostworowski de Diez Canseco, John H. Rowe, and R. Tom Zuidema are based primarily on the written sources, and their numerous publications established new benchmarks for our understanding of Tawantinsuyu, as the Inkas called their realm. Each also trained important students who have gone on to make additional and substantial contributions of their own. The focus of this volume is archaeology, and the kinds of research each of the four did in his or her own quite different way has provided the stimulus and inspiration for the current wealth of archaeological research. Although the four are essentially contemporaries, a sequence can be noted in their impact on the field.

The work of John H. Rowe began to appear in the 1940s. His long article "Inca Culture at the Time of the Spanish Conquest" in the

Handbook of South American Indians (1946), was the most widely read of his early contributions. It is a highly cogent and encyclopedic account of an empire that was still virtually unknown to most readers. The field of archaeology, however, was more influenced by his *Introduction to the Archaeology of Cuzco* (1944) and "Absolute Chronology in the Andean Area" (1945). The latter, based on the lists of Inca rulers in chronicles, provided the chronological framework considered definitive for decades. The former, based on his archaeological fieldwork, gave the baseline definitions for the major features of Late Inca ceramics and architecture associated, in regional variations, with the expansion of the empire throughout the central Andes and beyond. It also established the Killke series as a predecessor ceramic style associated with the Inkas before their imperial expansion. More recently, he published (Rowe 1990) ethnohistorical evidence showing that Machu Picchu and other important sites in the Urubamba Valley served as "royal estates" of important Inka rulers, raising issues vital to our understanding of Andean principles of control over property and resources.

In 1955 John V. Murra completed his doctoral dissertation "The Economic Organization of the Inca State" (Murra 1978, 1980). Based on a thorough analysis of the then-known sixteenth- and seventeenth-century written sources, it contained a multitude of new insights. As an anthropologist well schooled in the ethnography of Africa, Oceania, and North America, Murra was less influenced than earlier scholars by ideas derived from European nation-states. The scarcity of references to substantial markets in the early accounts of the Inka began to make sense, in Murra's analysis, in an economy based on labor and reciprocity. He linked the economy with political power and with a series of unusual Inka institutions such as *mit'a* (Murra 1982), *mitmaq* (Murra 1972), *yana* (Murra 1966), and *aqlla* (Murra 1962a) that lay at the heart of the creation of wealth and the expansion of the empire. In the 1960s Murra initiated benchmark inter-disciplinary research in the Peruvian central highlands that brought together ethnohistorians, archaeologists, ethnologists, and a botanist to "re-study" an area detailed in a sixteenth-century Spanish administrative survey (Murra 1962b). The project gave archaeology a central role in a coordinated approach to the study of Inka issues and institutions that remains a model of interdisciplinary research design. One of the most significant ideas to emerge during that research was Murra's (1972) concept of "vertical ecological complementarity" in which sociopolitical units of various scales exploited environmental zones at different altitudes by distributing members of their own groups, archipelago fashion, across the landscape.

María Rostworowski (1953) began her career with an innovative account of an Inka ruler, Pachacutec Inka Yupanqui, based on the traditional sixteenth-century chronicles. An important article on Inka succession and royal marriage (Rostworowski 1960) introduced her work to an English-speaking audience. The bulk of her long and exceptional career, however, has focused on bringing to light new written sources from archives in Europe and Peru to form the basis of a series of distinguished studies (Rostworowski 1961, 1970, 1977, 1983, 1989) of local-level societies, particularly along the Peruvian coast. These publications have given us a new view of political and economic leadership in the great variety of regional polities that the Inkas incorporated into Tawantinsuyu. They also underline basic differences between the coast and highlands of the Andes, both as parts of the empire and prior to its formation. Her *Historia del Tahuantinsuyu* (Rostworowski 1988) brought an important synthesis of her ideas on the Inkas to readers of both Spanish and English (Rostworowski 1999).

In his 1964 publication, *The Ceque System of Cuzco*, R. Tom Zuidema presented a radical new way of looking at the Inkas using models derived from French and Dutch structuralism. His initial analysis focused on the structural relationships of the shrines near Cusco (Cobo 1964 [1653]; see also Rowe 1979), but he extended the principles he derived from those relationships to many realms of Inka social and political organization. His work on kinship (Zuidema 1977a, 1983), the calendar (1977b, 1982a), and Inka understandings of astronomy (Zuidema 1981a, 1981b, 1982b) have been especially influential. Initially, Zuidema's structural approach to the written sources did not seem amenable to archaeological applications. But it contributed to an understanding of the divisions within both Cusco and Tawantinsuyu as a whole and provided archaeology with an impetus to step beyond its typical concerns with economics, status, warfare, and ancient political systems. His research established a theoretical framework in which the material manifestations of religion and conceptual systems could be investigated by archaeologists (Bauer n.d.; also Morris 1987; Hyslop 1990).

The seminal contributions of these four scholars came at a propitious moment for archaeology. Archaeological methods and ambitions had advanced to the point that archaeologists could begin to reconstruct human activities as a route to understanding the economic, political, and religious organization of ancient societies. It could now work on the issues the ethnohistorians had raised. The basis was in place for a new partnership in which the written and material records, each incomplete and biased in its own way, could be coordinated to improve our understanding of one of the world's most fascinating peoples.

As work intensified on the archaeology of the Inkas, surveys and excavations revealed that the Cusco empire had left an unusually rich material record. Part of this has to do with the excellent preservation on the desert coast, but it also relates to customs of the Inkas themselves. In the highlands the Inkas built well-made constructions, largely of stone. The frequent Inka strategy of building major new centers on virgin soil, rather than occupying or modifying existing settlements, resulted in many sites with a single, rather short occupation. This simplified the design and execution of research projects. Depopulation and hasty abandonment of sites in the wake of the European conquest also tended to leave artifacts near their locations of use, making activity-pattern studies feasible.

The last three decades or so have seen an explosion of field research and a real transformation from an Inka archaeology primarily focused on chronology to an archaeology that works with other disciplines to achieve substantive cultural understandings. Much of the new work has been carried out by archaeologists from the Andean republics themselves, giving a new breadth of coverage for the vast area ruled by the Inkas. One of the most notable results of this new research is a greater appreciation of regional variation within the Inka realm. The monolithic Cusco-centric viewpoint of most of the chronicles has been replaced with a new vision of a flexible empire that responded to the challenges of diverse peoples and environments with varying strategies of conquest and rule.

John H. Rowe, John V. Murra, María Rostworowski de Diez Canseco, and R. Tom Zuidema have made numerous and outstanding contributions to Inka studies. That does not mean, of course, that they have agreed on all issues; after all, they grew out of differing intellectual traditions. Indeed, the tensions between their ideas and approaches have contributed to the excitement of their work—and of the research that continues in the Andes. Their differing emphases have influenced the varied approaches of the current archaeological agenda, and a coordinated diversity of ideas, like the coordinated diversity of Tawantinsuyu, lends itself to creative growth.

One can see Rowe's imprint in the renewed attempts to understand the history and process of Inka development. Rostworowski's focus on varying local scenarios and reciprocal patterns of political growth and administration have steered us away from mechanistic dependence on European-based models of social and economic complexity. Murra's emphasis on nonmarket exchange and ecological complementarity has directed archaeologists to look beyond individual settlements and standard regional surveys toward the systematic social and political links that wove complex ecological and economic patterns, creating groups that were dispersed in multiple, coordinated settlements—settlements that were sometimes interspersed among those of other groups. He also understood the importance of recruiting and encouraging Andeanist scholars who live permanently in the Andean countries, resulting in an explosion of high-quality research. Zuidema's attention to Andean symbolism and his efforts to understand dualism and other structural features have given us new ways to look at settlement patterns, architecture, and site planning as keys to the divisions and structure of Inka-period societies—and to the ways the various parts interacted.

Increasingly, we can see a rich interplay between the various ideas that have shaped the interpretations of the written sources and the evidence now emerging from the material record. Archaeology no longer seeks merely to verify and illustrate the sixteenth- and seventeenth-century sources, or even to evaluate competing interpretations of them. We now scour the written sources seeking confirmation of ideas and interpretations that are emerging from archaeology itself. The archaeological record is even more fragmentary than the written record, but material remains are less biased by a foreign worldview than were the accounts of the European observers, especially the "standard" chronicles. In trying to reconstruct a full and accurate understanding of the Inkas, it is the constant cross-checking of independent written and archaeological sources that is most likely to lead to success.

The brilliant accomplishments of twentieth-century Andean ethnohistory have thus set a sharply varied and challenging agenda for continuing research in which archaeology asks new questions, collects new kinds of information, and formulates new levels of substantive understanding. Although the relationship has been less evident to this point, it is important to underscore the role that ethnology also plays in the Andean partnership. The native Inka state is gone, but continuities at the local level between past and present offer the opportunity for ethnohistorians, ethnographers, and archaeologists to coordinate research. One of the most significant outcomes already emanating from the interplay of the three sub-disciplines is a better comprehension of the biases in early European observations. Ethnology has revealed characteristics of Andean communities and patterns of thought that sixteenth-century observers were not trained to detect. While the silent testimony of the material record cannot directly observe behavior or reveal patterns of thought as ethnography can, it is unaffected by foreign attitudes, and the impact of later activities can usually be detected and evaluated. When rigorously researched, archaeology can provide keys to the ways households, local groups, and even the vast empire as a whole lived and evolved.

This volume presents a small sample of the potential of archaeology to make the material world a source of information that corrects misconceptions and builds new understandings of the nature and growth of Tawantinsuyu. The stage is set for an interdisciplinary collaboration that will greatly diminish the enigma that has so long enveloped the Inkas.

References cited

BANDELIER, ADOLPH F.
- 1910 *The Islands of Titicaca and Koati*. Hispanic Society of America, New York.

BAUER, BRIAN S.
- n.d. Pacariqtambo and the Mythical Origins of the Incas. Paper presented at the 46th International Congress of Americanists, Amsterdam, 1988.

BINGHAM, HIRAM
- 1913 *In the wonderland of Peru: The work accomplished by the Peruvian Expedition of 1912, under the auspices of Yale University and the National Geographic Society*. National Geographic Society, Washington, D.C.
- 1930 *Machu Picchu, a citadel of the Incas: Report of the explorations and excavations made in 1911, 1912 and 1915 under the auspices of Yale University and the National Geographic Society*. Pub. for the National Geographic Society, Yale University Press, New Haven, Conn.

COBO, BERNABÉ
- 1964 [1653] *Obras* [*Historia del Nuevo Mundo*]. Biblioteca de Autores Españoles 91–92. Atlas, Madrid

HUMBOLDT, ALEXANDER VON
- 1813 *Vues des Cordillères, et monumens des peuples indigènes de l'Amèrique*. F. Schoell, Paris (see Spanish translation, 1968).
- 1968 *Sitios de las Cordilleras y Monumentos de los Pueblos Indigenas de America* (Bernardo Giver, trans.). Solar/Hachette, Buenos Aires (translation from French, 1813 edition).

HYSLOP, JOHN
- 1990 *Inka Settlement Planning*. University of Texas Press, Austin.

KROEBER, ALFRED L., AND WILLIAM DUNCAN STRONG
- 1924 *The Uhle Collections from Chincha*. University of California Publications in American Archaeology and Ethnology 21 (1): 1–54. University of California Press, Berkeley.

MENZEL, DOROTHY
- 1966 The Pottery of Chincha. *Ñawpa Pacha* 4: 77–144.
- 1976 *Pottery Style and Society in Ancient Peru: Art as a Mirror of History in the Ica Valley, 1350–1570*. University of California Press, Berkeley.
- 1977 *The Archaeology of Ancient Peru and the Work of Max Uhle*. R. H. Lowie Museum of Anthropology, University of California, Berkeley.

MORRIS, CRAIG

1987   Arquitectura y estructura del espacio en Huánuco Pampa. *Cuadernos Instituto Nacional de Antropología* 12: 27–45.

MURRA, JOHN V.

1962a   Cloth and Its Functions in the Inca State. *American Anthropologist* 64: 710–728.

1962b   An Archaeological "Restudy" of an Andean Ethnohistorical Account. *American Antiquity* 28: 1–4.

1966   New Data on Retainer and Servile Populations in Tawantinsuyu. In *XXXVI Congreso Internacional de Americanistas, Spain 1964*, 2: 35–45. ECESA, Seville.

1972   El "control vertical" de un máximo de pisos ecológicos en la economía de las sociedades andinas. In *Visita de la Provincia de León de Huánuco en 1562, Iñigo Ortiz de Zúñiga, visitador* (John V. Murra, ed.): 2: 427–476. Universidad Nacional Hermilio Valdizán, Huánuco, Peru.

1978   *La organización económica del Estado inca* (Daniel R. Wagner, trans.). Siglo Veintiuno, México, D.F. (doctoral dissertation 1955; publication in English, 1980).

1980   *The Economic Organization of the Inka State*. JAI Press, Greenwich, Conn. (doctoral dissertation, 1955).

1982   The Mit'a Obligations of Ethnic Groups to the Inka State. In *The Inca and Aztec States 1400–1800: Anthropology and History* (George Collier, Renato Rosaldo, and John Wirth, eds.): 237–262. Academic Press, New York.

ROSTWOROWSKI DE DIEZ CANSECO, MARÍA

1953   *Pachacutec Inca Yupanqui*. Editorial Torres Aguirre, Lima.

1960   Succession, Cooption to Kingship, and Royal Incest among the Inca. *Southwestern Journal of Anthropology* 16 (4): 417–626.

1961   *Curacas y sucesiones*. Costa Norte, Lima.

1970   El repartimiento de Doña Beatriz Coya, en el Valle de Yucay. *Historia y Cultura* 4: 153–267.

1977   *Etnía y sociedad: Costa peruana prehispánica*. Instituto de Estudios Peruanos, Lima.

1983   *Estructuras andinas del poder: Ideología religiosa y política*. Instituto de Estudios Peruanos, Lima.

1988   *Historia del Tahuantinsuyu*. Instituto de Estudios Peruanos, Lima.

1989   *Costa peruana prehispánica*. Instituto de Estudios Peruanos, Lima.

1999   *History of the Inca Realm* (Harry B. Iceland, trans.). Cambridge University Press, Cambridge.

ROWE, JOHN H.

    1944 *An Introduction to the Archaeology of Cuzco*. Papers of the Peabody Museum of American Archaeology and Ethnology 27 (2). Harvard University, Cambridge, Mass.

    1945 Absolute Chronology in the Andean Area. *American Antiquity* 10: 265–284.

    1946 Inca Culture at the Time of the Spanish Conquest. In *Handbook of South American Indians*, vol. 2, *The Andean Civilizations* (Julian H. Steward, gen. ed.): 183–330. Bulletin 143. Bureau of American Ethnology, Smithsonian Institution, Washington, D.C.

    1979 An Account of the Shrines of Ancient Cuzco. *Ñawpa Pacha* 17: 2–80.

    1990 Machu Picchu a la luz de documentos de siglo XVI. *Histórica* 14 (1): 139–154.

SHIMADA, IZUMI

    1991 Pachacamac Archaeology: Retrospect and Prospect. Introduction to *Pachacamac: A Reprint of the 1903 edition by Max Uhle*. University Museum Monograph 62, part 1, s. 15–66. The University Museum of Archaeology and Anthropology, University of Pennsylvania, Philadelphia.

SQUIER, E. GEORGE

    1877 *Peru: Incidents of Travel and Exploration in the Land of the Incas*. Harper and Brothers, New York.

TELLO, JULIO C.

    1929 *Antiguo Peru, primera epoca*. Editado por la Comisión organizadora del segundo Congreso sudamericano de turismo, Lima.

    1941 La Ciudad Inkaica de Cajamarca. *Chaski* 1 (3): 2–7.

    1942 *Origen y desarrollo de las civilizaciones prehistóricas andinas*. Librería e imprenta Gil, s.a., Lima.

    1943 Memoria Sucinta sobre los Trabajos Arqueológicos Realizados en las Ruinas de Pachacamac durante los Años 1940 y 1942. Memoria de la Junta Departamental Pro-Desocupados de Lima (1939, 1940 y 1941). Lima.

TSCHUDI, JOHANN JACOB VON

    1860 *Reise durch die Andes von Süd-Amerika, von Cordova nach Cobija im jahre 1858*. J. Perthes, Gotha.

    1918 *Contribución a la historia, civilización y linguistica del Perú antiguo*. Colección de Libros y Documentos Referentes a la Historia del Perú (Horacio Urteaga, ed.), vols. 9–10. Sanmartí y ca., Lima (originally published in German in 1881).

UHLE, MAX

1903 *Pachacamac: Report of the William Pepper, M.D., LL.D., Peruvian Expedition of 1896.* University of Pennsylvania, Department of Archaeology, Philadelphia.

1924 *Explorations at Chincha.* University of California Publications in American Archaeology and Ethnology 21 (2): 55–94. University of California Press, Berkeley.

WURSTER, WOLFGANG W. (ED.)

1999 *Max Uhle (1856–1944). Pläne archäoligischer Stätten im Andengebiet. Planos de sitios arqueológicos en el área andina.* Materialien zur allgemeinen und vergleichenden Archäologie 56. Verlag Philipp von Zabern, Mainz am Rhein.

ZUIDEMA, R. TOM

1964 *The Ceque System of Cuzco.* International Archives of Ethnography, supplement to vol. 50. E. J. Brill, Leiden.

1977a The Inca Calendar. In *Native American Astronomy* (Anthony F. Aveni, ed.): 219–259. University of Texas Press, Austin.

1977b The Inca Kinship System: A New Theoretical View. In *Andean Kinship and Marriage* (Ralph Bolton and E. Mayer, eds.): 240–292. A Special Publication of the American Anthropological Association 7, Washington, D.C.

1981a Inka Observations of the Solar and Lunar Passages through Zenith and Anti-Zenith at Cuzco. In *Archaeoastronomy in the Americas* (Ray Williamson, ed.): 316–342. Ballena Press, Los Altos, Calif.

1981b Anthropology and Archaeology. In *Archaeoastronomy in the Americas* (Ray Williamson, ed.): 29–31. Ballena Press, Los Altos, Calif.

1982a Catachillay—The Role of the Pleiades and of the Southern Cross and Alpha and Beta Centauri in the Calendar of the Incas. *Ethnoastronomy and Archaeoastronomy in the American Tropics* (A. Aveni and G. Urton, eds.): 203–229. Annals of the New York Academy of Science 358. New York Academy of Sciences, New York.

1982b The Sidereal Lunar Calendar of the Incas. In *Archaeoastronomy in the New World* (A. F. Aveni, ed.). Cambridge University Press, Cambridge, England.

1983 Hierarchy and Space in Incaic Social Organization. *Ethnohistory* 30 (2): 49–75.

Variations between Inka Installations in the Puna of Chinchayqocha and the Drainage of Tarma

Carmen Arellano
Ramiro Matos Mendieta

THE CENTRAL HIGHLANDS OF PERU[1] ARE A PART OF A QUADRANT OF THE Inka Empire called Chinchaysuyu. Within this region, we know at least nine large sites and numerous ones of second and third rank. The large sites are well documented, some of them with ethnohistoric data complementing the archaeological data. Settlements of lesser rank are known, for the most part, by the presence or absence of Inka-style architecture and ceramics in each site, settlement-pattern analysis, and the function of domestic and communal spaces. The archaeological data reveal at least three types of Inka settlement: 1) in a previously unsettled area, as in the case of Pumpu; 2) in an area where there was a pre-existing village, as in Tarmatampu; and 3) in an area nearby, as we observed in Warawtampu. Geographically, the territory that we identify as the Inka province (*wamani*) of Pumpu includes two main and complementary ecological zones: the altiplano, with a pastoral economy, and the drainage, with an agricultural economy.

The nine largest Inka installations from south to north are Vilcashuaman (Ayacucho), Ushkus (Huancavelica), Acostampu (Huancavelica), Sausa (Junín), Tarmatampu (Junín), Chakamarka (Junín), Pumpu (Junín), Warawtampu (Pasco), and Huánuco Pampa (Huánuco) (fig. 1). A visual inspection reveals that no two sites are alike, and not even the royal roads that lead to each site are the same. Most of these settlements have been characterized as provincial "administrative" centers of the Inka state or *tampu*, even though we do not know the exact meaning of the word tampu (Matos, Arellano, and Brown 1998: 185), the administrative functions of such centers, and their socioeconomic role in Inka politics.[2] What factors influenced the Inka's selection of sites as administrative centers? Did

FIG. 1 Location of Inka sites in the Central Highlands of Peru

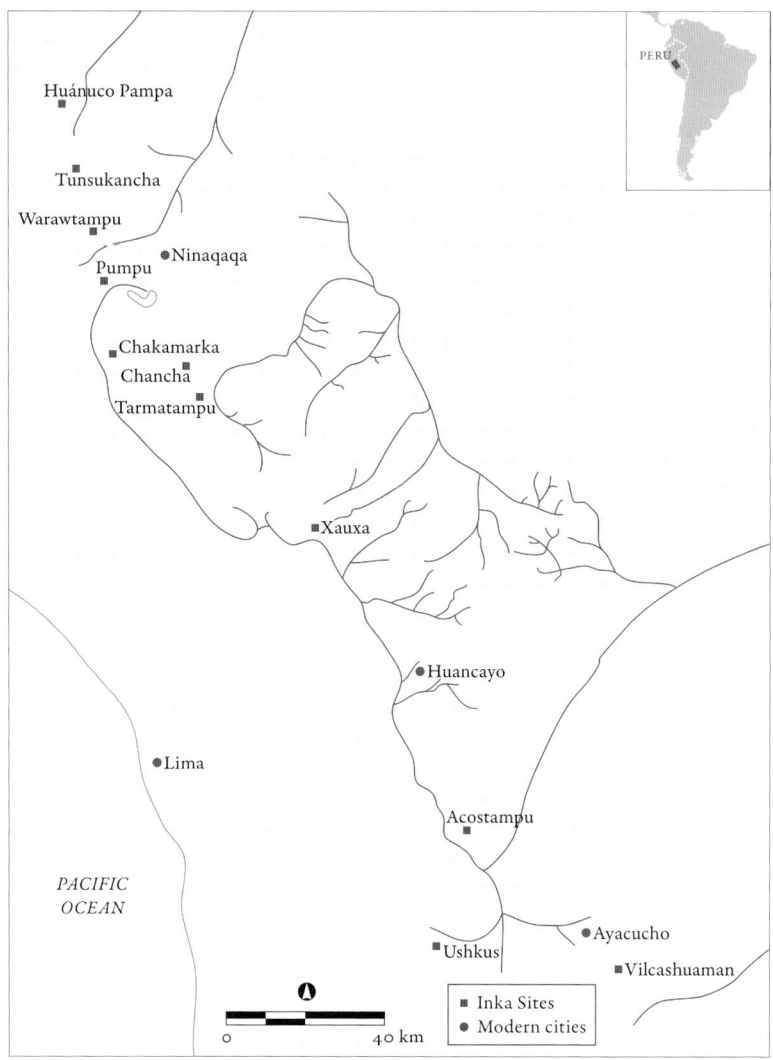

these fulfill the role of administrative centers only, or were they also centers of production? How did the Inka succeed in securing the cooperation of the subjugated local lords? These questions can be more fully answered by studying local sites and Inka sites, and by documenting how the local population utilized their natural resources and organized themselves. On the basis of archaeological data obtained in the last thirty years[3] at several Inka sites, we are now able to make regional comparisons and to provide answers to the above questions.

Area of Study

Our first task is to delimit a region of study. Here we are aided by information in sixteenth-century Spanish chronicles that sketch how the Inka organized their territory. Unfortunately, we must rely on a single source—

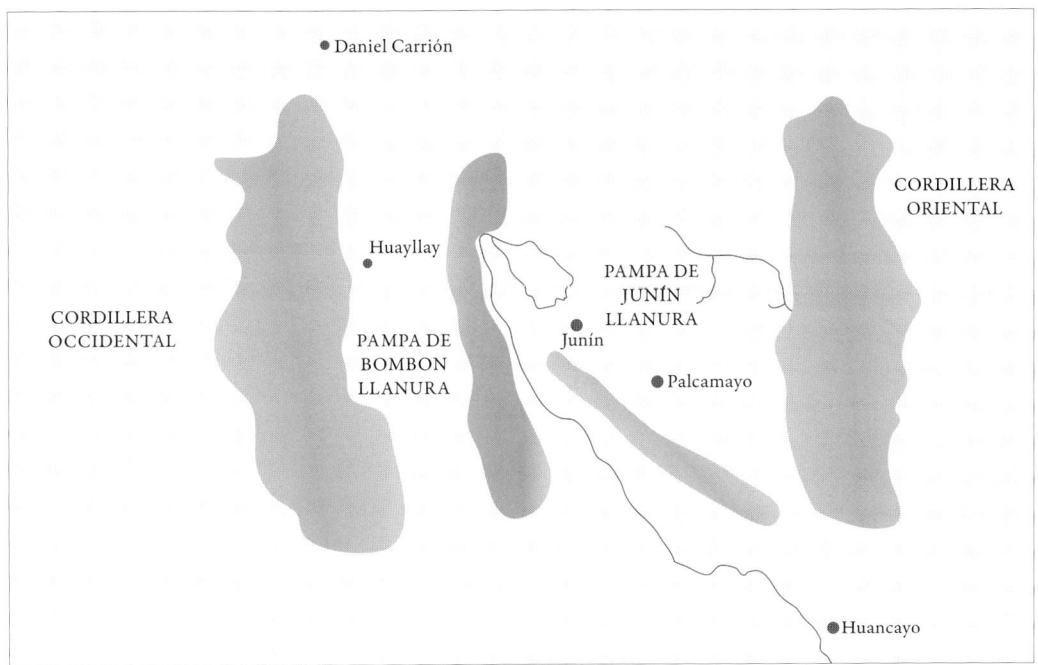

FIG. 2 Plains of Bonbon with modern names: Pampa de Bombon and Pampa de Junín (after Matos 1994: 194)

the chronicle of Pedro Pizarro—for information on this highland region, an area that comprised an Inka province or wamani. In his list of Inka provinces, Pizarro (1978 [1571]: 221) mentions that "Tarma and Atauillos and Bonbon is another province,"[4] which we interpret as forming an Inka province or wamani. We do not know if Pedro Pizarro knew with certainty what a wamani was and if by the Spanish word "provincia" he meant a wamani, but we think that archaeological and ethnohistoric data can confirm Pizarro's information.

The names Tarma and Atauillos also refer to ethnic groups; we do not know precisely what Pizarro meant by the term Bonbon. The Spaniards used the word to designate the Chinchayqocha plateau (today called Junín), and to designate the Inka administrative center located in that place (Cieza de León 1967 [1553] chap. 20: 65; Arellano 1988: 54; Matos 1994: 115–117; Nowack 1991: 29).[5] We have assumed in our study that when the Spaniards used the term Bonbon, they were referring to the plateau of the central highlands, which includes both the basin of Lake Junín (formerly known as Lake Chinchayqocha) and the Bonbon plateau with Lake Punrun as well as the puna that extends to the junction of two cordilleras in the modern department of Pasco (fig. 2; Matos 1994). The data from colonial documents indicate that this plateau was inhabited by several ethnic groups: the Atauillo (Atapillu[6]) to the northwest of Lake Chinchayqocha, the Chinchaycocha (Chinchayqocha) in the lake basin, and the Yaru (Yarush) in the northern part of the plateau, which includes the Upper Huallaga drainage (Lakes Punrun or Yanamate and

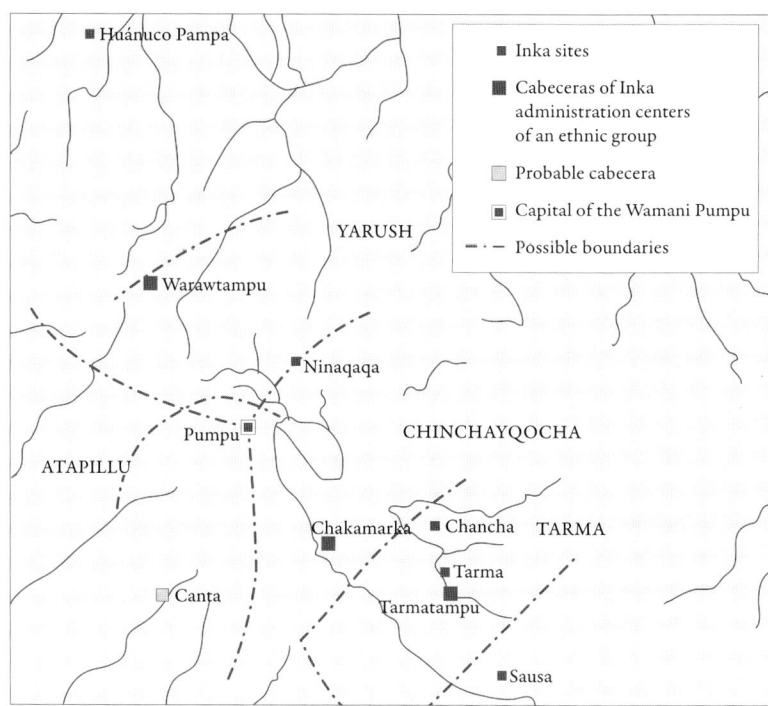

FIG. 3 Locations of the ethnic groups in the wamani of Pumpu

Lauricocha) (fig. 3; Arellano 1988: 54–55; Matos 1994: 73). Because the Yacha, Chupachu, Q'ero, and Mitmaq paid tribute to Pumpu (Ortiz de Zúñiga 1967 [1562] 1: 37, 47, 59 passim), they may have belonged to the Pumpu province, as Matos (1994) suggested for the Yacha. This information from Ortiz's *Visita* is reinforced by Pedro Cieza de León (1959 [1553]) chap. 50 [ii: XX]: 166)[7] who states that Pumpu and other provincial capitals (*cabeceras*) received tribute: "[. . .] and from every so many leagues around the tributes were brought to one of these capitals, and from so many others, to another."

Tribute-paying status vis-à-vis Pumpu should not be the only criterion for inclusion in this wamani, since these ethnic groups also paid tribute to Huánuco Pampa and Cusco. This leads us to ask why Pedro Pizarro does not mention the Yacha, Chupachu, Q'ero, and Mitmaq in his account. Pizarro's account is incomplete; he omits many ethnic groups, including large ones such as the Yawyus. Although Pizarro (1978 [1571]: 221) states that the Sawsa and the Wanka formed a province, he does not mention the Yawyus, whom Margarita Gentile Lafaille (1976) has shown belonged to the Wanka province.

Pedro Pizarro's document is extremely important, and the information it contains is supported by additional archaeological and ethnohistoric data. Relying on his account and the information of Gentile Lafaille, we suggest that the Inka province of Pumpu included four ethnic groups: Yarush, Chinchayqocha, Tarma, and Atapillu. The exact territory

FIG. 4 Locations of Inka settlements in the wamani of Pumpu

occupied by each group remains to be determined. Arellano (1994) is working on an approximate reconstruction of these territories on the basis of community land titles. Roughly, it can be said that the Pumpu province covered the altiplano of Junín and Pasco, the gorges of Tarma (Tarma drainage) and Upper Huallaga, all of modern Yauli province, and part of Canta province.[8]

Archaeological data permit the identification of four Inka administrative centers within this wamani: Pumpu, Warawtampu, Chakamarka, and Tarmatampu (figs. 3 and 4).[9] Pumpu is the largest settlement in the region and has been extensively described by Brown (n.d.) and Matos (1994). Its size indicates its importance, as does Cieza de León's account (1967 [1553] chap. 20: 65), which describes it as the *cabecera*. Warawtampu was the cabecera of the Yarush, Chakamarka the cabecera of the Chinchayqocha,

Variations between Inka Installations

and Tarmatampu the cabecera of the Tarma. No administrative center has yet been identified for the Atapillu.

Another way to assess the validity of Pizarro's account, using ethnohistoric data, is to determine the population density of a wamani. According to the sources, a wamani was made up of 40,000 households. This number should be taken only as an approximation, and we cannot confirm that the number of households in our region of study was 40,000 (Matos et al. 1998: 183). Arellano is currently evaluating whether the Inka decimal system was established in this area.

Geography and Natural Resources

An interesting feature of the Pumpu province is the existence of two complementary ecological zones: the puna of Chinchayqocha, suitable for raising camelids, and the hillsides and valleys of Tarma and Huarautambo, ideal for agriculture.[10] The puna is a high plateau with rolling hills covered with high-altitude grasslands. A prominent feature is Lake Junín, Peru's second largest after Lake Titicaca. The total area of the altiplano is approximately 9,000 km^2, with elevations that range between 3,900 and 4,600 m above sea level. It is sometimes called the "sweet puna," owing to its good climate and bountiful natural resources. While the altiplano of Titicaca often suffers from droughts lasting several years followed by torrential rain, the puna of Chinchayqocha is free of such catastrophic cycles. Two large Inka settlements can be found in this region: Pumpu and Chakamarka.

The second ecological level consists of a series of valleys that are natural routes to the eastern slopes of the Andes and the Amazon. The most important of these are the valleys of Huarautambo and Tarma. The valley of Tarma is formed by four creeks or streams that merge into the Chanchamayo River: the Huasahuasi, Palcamayo, Jacahuasi, and Tarma. This river basin extends approximately 5,000 km^2, with a topography broken up by deep gorges and narrow valleys, in which Andeans have historically attempted to maximize agricultural production. Cultivation extends between the *suni* and *quechua* ecological zones, from 2,500 to 3,800 m, alternating between canal- and rain-irrigation farming (Brown 1998). The Inka sites of Tarma and Chancha are found in this zone.

Huarautambo is located halfway between Huánuco Pampa and Pumpu, on the Upper Huallaga valley, where the Huarautambo or Lauricocha River flows. This site is over 3,650 m in elevation. It is one of the best potato production zones.

Inka Sites within the Pumpu Province

Archaeological studies show that Inka administrative cabeceras had standardized layouts and buildings, located along the Inka royal road (Morris

1973, 1982; Hyslop 1990). Certain buildings are always present—the *kallanka*[11], the main plaza, the *ushnu*, the *akllawasi*, residential *kanchas*, and *qollqas*. These structures enabled the functions of the state to be performed, and they are the primary indicators that suggest we are looking at an administrative center. The four sites we mentioned as being part of Pumpu province have many of these special public buildings. The apparent lack of some kinds of public buildings is due to the massive destruction of the ruins.

In spite of the fact that there was a general concept of what a cabecera should be, we see important differences in the general architectural plan and design (Inka state planning and construction technique); in the construction materials used (*sillar*, local not carved stone, adobe, and *champa*); in the types of residential kanchas (Inka kanchas with patio and rectangular rooms, irregular patio with rectangular rooms, kanchas with patio and circular rooms, kanchas with multistory houses); in the location of the settlement (on level ground, in a narrow quebrada, or on the side of a mountain); and in the type of settlement (built on unoccupied land, over pre-existing villages, or near pre-existing villages); and variation in settlement size.

There were also Inka sites of secondary and tertiary political rank in the wamani of Pumpu. They are considered to be of lower rank because they are smaller than cabeceras and they lack most of the standardized state buildings described earlier. Some of the lower-ranked sites are Chancha, Telarnioc, Pukatampu, Qochas, Ingapirca, and Ninaqaqa (fig. 4). Most of these Inka sites are linked by the *hatun ñan*, or royal Inka road, which links Cusco to Quito.

To assess the validity of Pizarro's account about the Pumpu wamani we must know which criteria were used by the Inka to delimit a province, considering the geopolitical and geoeconomical unit of the region. To understand the Inka conquest and the variation in their political domination of the province of Pumpu, we must consider the socioeconomic organization of the pre-Inka ethnic groups or *señoríos*, and their use and management of resources.

Pre-Inka Ethnic Groups and Lordships

Knowledge about the pre-Inka ethnic groups is based almost entirely on archaeological records. The predominant style of pottery found throughout the study area is called Late San Blas. We find other contemporaneous local styles associated with villages in the valleys of Tarma, Palcamayo, and Yanahuanca. The center of the San Blas style is found in the Junín altiplano, where it is associated with dwellings of puna pastoralists. Although the exact area of the San Blas style is unknown, it is interesting that its distribution coincides with the territory known during colonial

FIG. 5 Possible distribution of late prehistoric ceramic styles in the Central Highlands

times as the Chinchayqocha *repartimiento* or ethnic group (fig. 5). This style has wide distribution from the highlands of Junín to the adjacent valleys of Tarma, La Oroya, Huasahuasi, Palcamayo, and Chanchamayo, which is to say, in the basin of Tarma and Yauli. The distribution of San Blas ceramics throughout the Tarma basin should not be interpreted as an indication that the highland culture expanded to these regions, since the presence of other local ceramics in the Tarma basin indicates interaction between local and puna cultures (Parsons et al., 1997, 2000).

Another ceramic style of importance is the Mantaro, associated with agricultural settlements of the Quechua (ecological zone) valleys, which were part of the Wanka polity or señorío. The center of the Mantaro pottery style was in the Mantaro and Yanamarca Valleys. This ceramic style extended from the northeast to Tarma and the altiplano of Junín, and to the west, to the Yawyus and Atapillu territory. Since we have no evidence of military or political occupation to the north of Tarma, we

FIG. 6 Examples of San Blas pottery

assume that the Mantaro ceramics found in areas outside of the Wanka territory are a product of socioeconomic interaction. These two pottery styles—San Blas and Mantaro—do not appear suddenly. On the contrary, they are the product of long traditions strongly rooted within their territories, whose antecedents go back to the Early Intermediate period (Parsons et al. 2000).

The Late San Blas pottery is simple, abundant, and almost monotonous. It can be light brown, beige, or smoky white, and decorated with irregular red lines (sometimes curved) or with spots. Its shapes include hemispherical bowls, cooking pots (*ollas*) with short necks and everted rims, and jars with wide necks and mouths (fig. 6). As mentioned earlier, this pottery is associated with the villages and houses of pastoralists on the altiplano, mountain peaks, mountain slopes, the rocky moraines, and the lands around the lake. The size of these pastoralist villages varied between 25 and 30 ha, as is the case of Yanacancha and Marcacocha on the southern area of the altiplano. In the altiplano, the most prominent villages (Yanacancha, Marcacocha, Juninjirca, and Marcapunta) are situated on hilltops, as well as on the shore of the lake. Inhabited lakeside villages include Ondores, Ucu, and Ninacaca. San Blas pottery is associated with camelid herders who raised vicuña for their wool, and bartered it for other goods such as salt. San Blas ceramics were found in important *salinas* (salt deposits) like Kachiqocha (San Blas) and Qaqas (San Pedro) (Matos 1994: 35–36). The puna was also a zone where fresh products could be converted into dehydrated goods (such as *chuño*, *charki*, and *caya*), which were then easier to store and transport. The presence of Mantaro pottery in the altiplano suggests long-distance interaction, and the domestic trash suggests that these people had a stable household economy.

Variations between Inka Installations

FIG. 7 Mantaro-style pottery (Lighter Colored Base)
FIG. 8 Mantaro-style pottery (Red Base)

The Mantaro pottery style has two varieties: Mantaro Lighter Colored Base (fig. 7) and Mantaro Red Base (fig. 8). Both were produced using the same technology. The most common form are ollas with short necks, and oblong or globular jars with short necks. One variety is red-slipped and the other beige. The decoration of Mantaro-style pottery is geometric, with simple or parallel lines. Sometimes the decoration is stamped circles or incised lines. There are numerous zoomorphic and anthropomorphic figurines with anatomic characteristics such as eyes, teeth, and tongues.

Settlements associated with the Mantaro style are more nucleated than those associated with the San Blas style. These nucleated villages can have hundreds of circular houses, without streets or plazas, but the majority of the sites are surrounded by a defensive wall. Nucleated villages of circular houses have been called "beehive villages." The principal concentration of beehives sites is in the Mantaro and the Yanamarca valleys, but they also extend to the southern Tarma region (Pachacayo and Huaricolca). For this reason we deduced that the southern part of Tarma belonged to the Wanka señorío (figs. 5, 9). This was also suggested by Arellano (1998a: 49), who concluded that half of Hatun Sawsa (called Uchuy Sawsa) may have been located in the southern part of Tarma, and that this area was probably divided politically and integrated into two separate wamani of the Inka administration: Hatun Sawsa into the wamani of the Wanka and Uchuy Sawsa into the Pumpu wamani.

There were other, smaller ethnic groups, identified by local pottery styles, and by their modest size. Among the sites we have been studying between Pasco, Junín, and Tarma, we have identified at least three

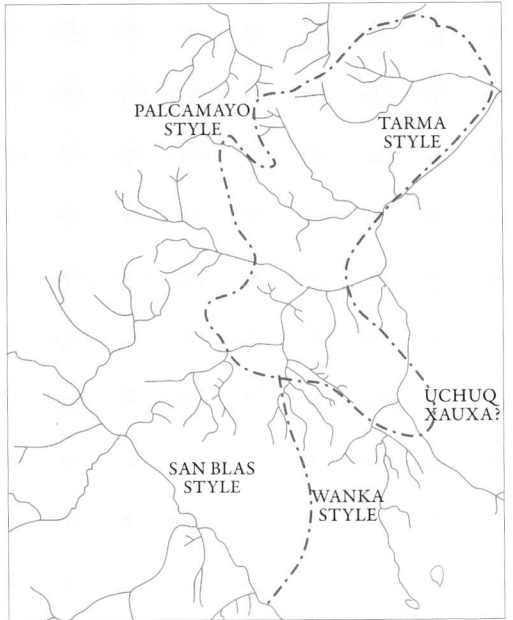

different local pottery styles, each with a limited geographic distribution within one valley or area of the altiplano (fig. 9). The first group appears in Tarmatampu and neighboring areas. The type of pottery is simple, generally utilitarian, brown, gray, or reddish, sometimes natural or brick red in color, and others are decorated with simple black or red lines, apparently without any standard designs (fig. 10). This style, tentatively called Tarma, is associated with the Tarma ethnic group, but that name probably was not in use prior to the arrival of the Inka.[12] This Tarma group occupied the western side of the Tarma Basin and the adjacent puna to the west and northeast.

Within the same basin, we find a second local pottery style, called Palcamayo, described by Bonnier and Rozenberg (1978a, b). The Palcamayo style is distributed from the source of the Palcamayo River, which is on the southeastern slope of the altiplano to the area northeast of the Tarma River (fig. 9). The Palcamayo style seems to coincide with an ethnic group that, according to colonial sources and to the present day, is known as Palcamayo (Arellano 1988: chap. 4, map 4).

The third pottery style, equally simple and utilitarian, is characterized by striations on the surface, and some vessels without any decoration at all. The most common shapes are ollas with narrow necks and flaring rims and jars with short necks and wide spouts. Numerous anthropomorphic and zoomorphic figurines were also found. This type of pottery is mostly distributed in the northern part of the altiplano and it extends to the Upper Huallaga. Given its spatial and temporal distribution, it seems to define part of the area of the ethnic group called Yarush. The style is related

FIG. 9 Possible distribution of ceramic styles in the province of Tarma

FIG. 10 Tarma-style pottery

Variations between Inka Installations

to pottery samples collected in Yacha territory, however, and this suggests an earlier expansion of the Yacha ethnic group into this area (fig. 5).

Colonial sources mention that the Atapillu extended to the northeast side of the lake. Unfortunately, no archaeological study exists of the Atapillu as well as of the territory occupied by the Yarush.

In summary, before the arrival of the Inka, the Pumpu wamani was occupied by seven ethnic groups with different territories—Yarush, Chinchayqocha (with San Blas–style pottery), Tarma (Tarma style), Pallqamayu (Palcamayo style), Atapillu, Yacha (Upper Huallaga style), and Wanka (Mantaro style). The ethnic groups with the largest territories were in the altiplano. These polities can be delimited not only by their different pottery styles, but also by the presence or absence of shrines and by differences in their dwellings and their burials (Matos et al., 1975).

The ethnic groups of the Pumpu province were not as strong or centralized as the Wanka, but the location of the majority of the villages on hilltops suggests that they were concerned with either defense or special religious rituals. These mountaintop settlements were enclosed by walls and ditches, which suggest that they had external struggles. It is unknown if they were organized into señoríos, but they were politically solid enough to permit the productive organization and distribution of goods, and the defense of their territory.

Small ethnic groups coexisted with larger, more powerful polities of the altiplano and Mantaro Valley. Tarma is ideally situated, almost equidistant from the Chinchaycocha puna, the Mantaro Valley, and the Chanchamayo or Andean eastern slope—allowing for the exchange of products with all three areas—a geographic setting that benefitted the later Inka. Palcamayo benefitted from the Qaqas salt-mine, which seems to have belonged to this ethnic group before the arrival of the Inka (Arellano 1988: 54), as well as from direct access to the eastern slope of the Andes and the Amazon Basin (fig. 4; Arellano 1988; Hastings n.d.). The Tarma Valley people built terraces and plots, expanding the area under cultivation with canals between the altiplano (4,100 masl [meters above sea level]) and the low valleys (2,500 masl). The domestic camelid population was also improved (Browman 1974). Bone remains found in later settlements confirm the importance of the vicuña within the local economy, especially for the production of textiles. At present, there are more than 1,000 vicuñas in the modern district of Tarmatambo and more than 3,000 vicuñas in the altiplano.

It is precisely among these small late señoríos that we observe the expanded production and distribution of goods. Stone tools, pottery, storehouses (*qollqas*), and a local network of roads, still poorly known, are associated with pre-Inka agriculture (Parsons et al. 2000). We have also seen pre-Inka storage units in diverse contexts—some associated with dwellings, others communal, and still others isolated from population centers (Angashmarca). The other qollqas may have been used for ritual purposes (offerings of the Pachamama), as we have seen in Pachacayo. In addition, the storage units may have been a place where interregional interaction took place.

The Impact of the Inka Conquest

All available documents state that Pachakuteq was the first Inka to conquer this area (Betanzos 1987 [1551] chap. 24: 123; Cieza de León 1967 [1553]: 165; Cobo 1964 [1653] 2: 81; Garcilaso de la Vega 1963 [1609]: 246; Herrera 1952 [1601] 9: 236; Pachacuti Yamqui 1993 [1640?]: 222; Salinas y Córdova 1957 [1630]: 18; and Vásquez de Espinoza 1969 [1629]: 383). Only one document, known as the declaration of the *khipukamayoq* (keepers of knot records) (*Discurso sobre la descendencia y gobierno de los incas* 1920: 15), mentions Wiraqocha Inka as the leader of the conquest. This would not be unusual, if the khipukamayoq traced their descent from the lineage (*panaka*) of Wiraqocha Inka. However, we cannot reject this information because we cannot identify the informant(s) of Cieza de León and Betanzos on Pachakuteq, and because—with the exception of Cieza de León, Betanzos, and the *Discurso*—all colonial sources cited are from the seventeenth century. The origin of this information is largely unknown. Moreover, recently obtained radiocarbon dates from the Mantaro region suggest an earlier Inka presence than that suggested by John Rowe (Matos personal communication, June 1996; Williams and D'Altroy 1998; D'Altroy, Williams, and Lorandi in this volume; Rowe 1944–45).

Cieza de León describes the Inka conquest of the region in this manner:

> The inhabitants of Bonbon, according to what they relate, had heard of the events [ruin][13] of Xauxa, and how the Huancas had been defeated, and, suspecting that the conquerors intended to continue their march, they determined to be prepared, so that they might not be taken unawares. Putting their women and children, with the property they could collect, on a lake which is near their abode, they waited for what might happen. The Inca captains, when they had arranged the affairs at Xauxa, set out and advanced as far as Bonbon, but as the people had taken refuge on the lake, they were unable to do other harm than eat their provisions. [As the Inkas saw this] they passed onwards and came to Tarama, where they found the people in arms. There was a battle, in which many of the people of Tarama were killed and taken prisoner, and those of Cuzco remained victors. As it was the will of the king that those of Tarama should pay tribute and serve like the people of other provinces, in return for which they

would be favoured and well treated, they agreed to all that was demanded of them. An account was then sent to Cuzco of all that had been done in this province of Tarama.

The Inca captains, after what has been written had come to pass, returned to the valley of Xauxa, where already great [lords and] presents and many women had been gotten together to be sent to Cuzco, and the people of Tarama did the same. (Cieza de León 1883 [1553] chap. 50: 156–157)

Cieza de León's account of the Inka invasion leads us to believe that Tarma, and possibly Pallqamayu, were overthrown by military force. But the Inka considered it more important to subdue the altiplano before Tarma. Immediately after the conquest, the natives of Tarma were forced to offer their women and goods as tribute. María Rostworowski called this type of military campaign "instant conquests" because there were no drawn-out battles with the subjugated inhabitants. What strategy was followed by the Inka to annex the altiplano? The hypothesis we have is that this region was annexed not by military force, but by diplomacy and reciprocity, concepts firmly rooted in Andean ideology.

According to Sarmiento de Gamboa, there was another conquest under the government of Thupa Yupanki, son of Pachakuteq:

although many of those defeated were conquered by his father, all or almost all of them carried arms, some to insure their freedom and others to defend themselves. (Sarmiento de Gamboa 1960 [1572]: 249; translation ours)

Despite Sarmiento's account, the subjugation of the Junín plateau does not seem to have been by military force, because Cieza de León, as he indicated in his first and second chronicle, said that Thupa Yupanki:

arrived at Xauxa, where the Huancas prepared a solemn reception. Thence he sent messengers in all directions, announcing to the people that he desired to win their friendship, without giving them offense or making war. He said that [therefore] they must have heard how the Incas of Cuzco exercised no tyranny and imposed no exactions on those who were their allies and vassals, and that, in exchange for the service and homage they gave, they received much good from their sovereign [and that they should send their ambassadors in order to make the peace with him]. In Bonbon they knew the great power with which the Inca came, and, as they expected great things from his clemency, they came to do him homage [. . .]. (Cieza de León 1883 [1553] chap. 56: 178)

The lay of this province of Bonbon [Pumpu] makes it strong, and this is the reason why its inhabitants were very warlike. Before the Incas could dominate them, they had great difficulties and many battles, until finally (according to many of the older Indians) they won them over to their rule by gifts and promises. (Cieza de León 1959 [1553] chap. 32 [LXXXIII]: 111)

The first description of the capture comes from the second chronicle *El Señorío de los Incas*, which is based on information collected in Cusco. It should not surprise us that there is no mention of the Inka sending gifts to the people of Bonbon before they were subjugated, whereas in the first chronicle, which was based on data supplied by inhabitants of the altiplano, such details are present. The altiplano informants also state that there were battles between themselves and the Inka, which may indicate there was more than one military invasion into the zone.

Upon introducing Inka administrative reforms, Pachacuti Yamqui relates that Thupa Yupanki ordered a general inspection:

he sent Collacchaguay, curaca of the Tarama of the Chinchaysuyos, to all the kingdom so that he should try to eat and drink with the curacas. (Pachacuti Yamqui 1993 [1640?]: 238)

It is notable that Pachacuti Yamqui used the word "try" (prouase), leading us to believe that the subjugation of the neighboring curacas was tenuous. These curacas could have been those of the altiplano. The curaca of Tarma therefore acted as ambassador for a region not yet or only weakly incorporated into the empire.

It is interesting to note that on the one hand, although there were military raids by the Inka—first by Pachakuteq, then by Thupa Yupanki and Wayna Qhapaq, as we shall see—this does not explain the constant campaigns of conquest or why Inka soldiers did not permanently besiege the zone. As Cieza de León remarks, the lake was a "force" for the Chinchayqocha, who hid in it.[14] We obviously cannot imagine that the entire population of Chinchayqocha hid in the lake. Who did hide then from the Inka? We suggest that those who hid among the reeds of the lake were the curacas and lords of the señoríos in order to avoid making the *mocha* or gesture of submission. According to Polo de Ondegardo (1917 [1571]: 117), it was an Andean custom that the conqueror of a region could only designate himself as lord of the conquered area when he possessed the body and domain of the lord he conquered. Although they made raids against the population, did the Inka ever conquer the Chinchayqocha?

Although the topography permitted the lords of the altiplano to maintain control of their territory, Inka domination of the neighboring señoríos of Tarma, Wanka, and others would have forced the Chinchayqocha—and probably the Yarush too—to submit to or accept a partial Inka occupation of their territory. Otherwise, it would have meant that the Chinchayqocha had limited access to the natural resources of the zones with which they traditionally interacted. As Nowack (1991: 76) points out, this was part of Inka military strategy. The Inka would conquer or amicably annex the neighbors of their enemies, in order to force them to capitulate. This occurred with the neighbors of Chinchayqocha; Tarma was conquered by military force and Yarush was annexed.

Because the Inka constructed the administrative center of the Yarush (Warawtampu) next to, but not on top of, the main village of Astupampa, as they had other centers in the province of Pumpu, and because cut-stone architecture is present in Warawtampu, we conclude that the Inka had special regard for the Yarush. We suggest that in the altiplano of Junín, the population's resistance to the Inkas could not long have been maintained without economic loss, since the Inka controlled the ethnic groups with which they traditionally interacted. This situation must have led to internal political problems, which forced them to adopt pragmatic relations with the Inka.

While the Yarush were likely in favor of annexation, the Chinchayqocha were probably not. The Yarush's decision to accept reciprocal relationships with the Inka must have been based on various things, one of which was the offering of important political posts by the Inka (which suggests that Guaman Poma's data with respect to this could be considered trustworthy). We see another reason for the annexation: it would be difficult for the Yarush lords to withdraw or hide in Lake Punrun, which is deeper and smaller than Lake Junín, and has no reeds. They also hoped to annex—maybe with the help of the Inka—part of the territory of the Upper Huallaga, which was possibly occupied by the Yacha ethnic group. We will not elaborate here about the possible alliance between the Inka and the Yarush. This will be the subject of future studies.[15]

We cannot ascertain which conditions led to Chinchayqocha's annexation to the Inka state; nor can we determine whether it was subjugated peacefully, violently, or not at all. We think the subjugation was partially violent because the Inka administrative center of the zone Chakamarka was constructed over a local village, as was the case for Tarmatampu, the center of the Tarma ethnic group, which was also conquered by force, according to Cieza de León.[16] The hostility against the Inka seems to have continued under the rule of Wayna Qhapaq, who, in a journey to Quito,

> sent embassies to the Yauyos [sic] and Yuncas, and some gifts to the chiefs of Bonbon, for, as they had a force in the lake, in parts where they swam, they spoke loosely, and he did not wish to converse with them until he saw their intentions [until he saw the manner in which to conquer Bonbon]. (Cieza de León 1883 [1553] chap. 63: 206)

From Cieza de León's citation we understand, on the one hand, that the Inka are sending gifts to Bonbon, and on the other, that he does not want to talk to the lords of Bonbon because they used the lake as a hiding place and spoke ill of the Inka. We interpret that the gifts were for the lords of Yarush, already incorporated into the empire, and for the lords of Chinchayqocha, whose territory probably suffered another military raid under this Inka. This may indicate again that the subjugation of Chinchayqocha was never complete under the government of Thupa Yupanki or Wayna Qhapaq.[17] In other words, they were likely never conquered because the Inka were not successful in capturing the lord(s) and the domain of Chinchayqocha. The fact that Chakamarka is placed over the village of a minor lineage group (*ayllu*) in Chinchayqocha (Arellano n.d.), leads us to believe that the conditions under which they were conquered were not satisfactory to the Inka. This is to say that with the construction of Chakamarka, the Inkas simulated that they had conquered the ethnic group when that was not the case.

Other components of the Inka infrastructure support this hypothesis. A stretch of the main Inka road crossed Chinchayqocha's territory as little as possible along the lake's left side. On this shore we also found another Inka site (Ingapirca), at the frontier between the Chinchayqocha and Atapillu ethnic groups. Chakamarka is located south of Chinchayqocha's territory, near Tarma. We interpret this as a military strategy. As Nowack (1991: 79) notes, it was very important for the Inka to safeguard the main roads against their enemies.

Inka Domination and Influence

As soon as the local population was dependent on the Inka state and had accepted the new policies, the Inka proceeded to build administrative centers and other infrastructure. We assume that, due to its early integration into the empire, the Tarma administrative seat was created before the rest of the wamani. We also assume that the creation of the wamani was only possible after the integration or conquest of the other ethnic groups and after the new Inka province had established its geopolitical and geoeconomic importance.

The province of Pumpu must have been formed under Thupa Yupanki, known as the political reformer (Guaman Poma 1936 [1615]: 111, 182, 193, 949; Pachacuti Yamqui 1993 [1640?] 238; Polo de Ondegardo 1917 [1571]: 116), who ordered the implementation of decimal divisions of the population and the territorial divisions of each ethnic group. We suggest that it was Thupa Yupanki who annexed the Wanka zone (located south of the Tarma River basin) to Tarma. We deduce this from the fact that during the colonial period (and today) the ayllus of Tarma (Collana, Congas, and Tapo) were under the jurisdiction of the curaca of Tarma, as their territory belonged to the colonial division (*corregimiento*) of Tarma (Arellano 1988, chap. 4, see map).

Tarmatampu is probably the oldest administrative center of the wamani. It was probably built under Pachakuteq, because before he conquered this region he had a policy of tampu building:

> He ordered that the captain who is taking soldiers order them to build the tambos every forty leagues from the city of Cuzco until they reached the limits of the empire, great deposits of all types of goods like corn and chuño and potatoes and quinoa and hot pepper and salt and dry meat and fish and live llamas. And this food should be used to conquer or pacify some province which had rebelled; as much food and deposits as necessary should be given to these soldiers until they reached the other tambo and from there another forty leagues where another portion would be given to them. And the distance between these tambos where this food would be given them was ordered to be called Xuco Guaman, which means flight of a falcon and each year the tambo's local caciques took care of these storehouses and supplied them in order to provide for said purpose and for their benefit. (Betanzos 1987 [1551] chap. 22: 114; translation ours)

The disposition of the great administrative centers in the wamani differs from Betanzos's description. For example, none of the administrative centers were forty leagues, or approximately 252 km, from each other.[18] Tarmatampu is about forty km from Chakamarka, which is thirty-five km from Pumpu, which is in turn forty km from Warawtampu. We suspect that various regulations were put into effect after Pachakuteq's rule, during which other types of tampu were established. Cieza de León's observation at the time of the Spanish invasion is of importance in this case. He states that tampu and storehouses (*qollqa*) were built between ten and twenty leagues apart in the Inka governor's holdings (Cieza de León 1986 [1553] chap. 44). The distances of ten or twenty leagues correspond to approximately fifty km or one hundred km.[19] He also states in another chapter that tampu were about four leagues apart from each other; that is, twenty km (Cieza de León 1986 [1553] chap. 82). The evidence would suggest that Cieza de León was referring to two kinds of tampu. The first type are fifty to one hundred km apart and may have served as both a tampu and a cabecera of the ethnic group. Several of them could have been part of a wamani, because Cieza de León says that they were in the "comarca" of an Inka governor. According to the *Diccionario de Autoridades* [1976 [1726] 1: 426), "comarca" means "neighbor land and next to a land, or place in the boundaries or confines of a land" (translation ours). The distances between the tampu of the province of Pumpu almost coincide with Cieza de León's descriptions. The second type of tampu coincides with small Inka sites found in the province, which are described below (fig. 4).

We do not know whether we should credit the construction of these new provincial seats to Thupa Yupanki or to Wayna Qhapaq. Under Pachakuteq, it seems that the tampu had a primarily military function—to supply the needs of the troops. We did not find any special features at Tarmatampu, however, that would support this assumption. Nevertheless, the presence of public buildings characteristic of other administrative centers leads us to believe that Tarmatampu was remodeled according to later Inka reforms.

To establish that important variations existed among administrative centers in the Inka domain, we will briefly describe Tarmatampu, Chakamarka, Pumpu, and Warawtampu.

TARMATAMPU (fig. 4): The Inka found extensive lands under cultivation, an agreeable climate and landscape, sufficient water for irrigation (Brown 1998), and a village in a strategic location. Because of its similarity to Cusco, the Tarma Valley could also grow the same variety of corn as that grown in the Cusco Valley. Tarmatampu was probably the residence of the principle curaca of the Tarma ethnic group, because Cieza de León indicates that it was conquered by the Inka. Our excavations reveal that the Inka constructed a new provincial administrative center over a local village.

According to Cieza de León (1959 [1553] chap. 32 (LXXXIII): 112), "In bygone days there were great lodgings and storehouses of the Lord-Incas in Tarma." These buildings occupied an area of firty-five ha with three clearly marked sections: Marka-Marka, San Juan Pata, and qollqas. The provincial administrative seat must have been installed in Marka-Marka, because still preserved are a complete kallanka, the center for textile production (*kumpi wasi*), a probable building for the chosen women (*aklla wasi*), and five residential compounds (*kancha*s). Standing walls indicate that there were two-story and three-story houses in the Inka kanchas of this sector, with internal compartments, plastered and painted in red, yellow, and white. The kallanka must have also been painted because the description by Fernández de Oviedo (1959 [1557] 5: 74), who cited Miguel de Estete referring to Hernando Pizarro's observation about this place, noted that "a good painted house and good lodgings" existed. At the eastern side of the kallanka is an open space that may have been a plaza. There is a wall along the side of another plaza in San Juan Pata, with traces of eighteen trapezoidal niches. This plaza is now a modern soccer field. This settlement seems to have been a provincial Inka installation with two large plazas, like at Cusco, which are not common in this type of center. The third sector was reserved for the qollqa, which were divided into two subdivisions: lower Pirwa-Pirwa (halfway up the mountain slope) and upper Pirwa-Pirwa (on the mountaintop). Unfortunately, the site has been destroyed and rebuilt with modern constructions, limiting the study of this area.

FIG. 11 Inka settlement of Chancha

Inside the territory under the jurisdiction of Tarmatampu, we found other Inka installations. One is Chancha (fig. 11), in the valley of Jacahuasi, a territory that was under an *ayllu* with the same name in the colonial period (Arellano 1988). It covers about fifteen ha (Parsons et al. 2000), and is somewhat smaller than Chakamarka. In Chancha, the Inka settled over a pre-existing village. No archaeological work has been done here. In the Cochas community, we also found the remains of an Inka building. On the altiplano we found two other settlements: Telarnioc and Pukatampu. Telarnioc has twelve qollqas not associated with other constructions, and is located off the main road. In Pukatampu, whose place name indicates it was a tampu, we found a stone enclosure of an apparent platform (*ushnu*) built of stone (*sillar*). While we do not know of any Inka installation in Pallqamayu, Inka-style ceramics appear in some pre-Inka villages as an intrusive cultural element. The salt deposits (*salinas*) of Qaqas in part belonged to Pallqamayu, but it was populated by individuals resettled by the Inka (*mitmaq*) (Arellano 1988).

The concentration of Inka installations in the Tarma area does not compare to the number found in other ethnic territories of the wamani. We suspect that their presence had to do with the supply and assistance of Inka troops that were needed to quell a rebellion of the Chinchay-qocha at any moment. This supports Cieza de León's view of the tense relations between the Inka and Chinchayqocha. We did not find evidence,

FIG. 12 Qollqas at the Inka site of Chakamarka

however, that Tarma's population could have caused problems such as those of the Chinchayqocha noted by Cieza de León (1959 [1553] chap. 32 (LXXXIII): 112) "whose natives were no less warlike than the natives of Bombón."

CHAKAMARKA (fig. 4): The Inka occupied a pre-existing village. Here the Inka implemented two strategies: political and economic. The Inka state planners decided to create an administrative center here because they saw the economic potential—the great expanse of the high plateau and the abundant resources. They settled next to the large raised fields and straw production areas (Parsons 1998). The abundant water was used to process dehydrated goods in the cold. The proximity of the hills facilitated the ventilation and storage of agricultural products in the qollqas (fig. 12). This was a politically strategic place because it was close to the border with Tarma. Its location supports our hypothesis that Inka installations in Tarma served as support for the Chakamarka political center.

In Chakamarka there is a plaza with an ushnu, a kallanka, an *aklla-wasi*, residential kanchas, qollqas, canals, and an Inka bath. This ushnu is one of the smallest ones known, scarcely measuring 2.10 x 1.20 m. The main road (fig. 13) crosses the plaza on the western side and access to the installation is by way of three wide causeways. Three state Inka roads come from Tarma and two of them reach Chakamarka.

Variations between Inka Installations

FIG. 13 Inka road (Inka ñan) at Chakamarka

Inside the Chinchayqocha territory there is another Inka installation known as Ingapirca. It is on the shores of the lake and close to the territory of Atapillu. It seems to be a kind of harbor or port. There is also the tampu of Ninaqaqa, which is located on the frontier with the Yarush ethnic group and the Amuesha group that live on the Eastern slope of the Andes (Smith n.d.). This tampu is crossed by a secondary Inka road that bounds the coast on the west side of the wamani located on the eastern side of the Andes in the Amazonian region. In summary, we can conclude that although we found Inka ceramics in some pre-Inka villages, the politically insecure situation in Chinchayqocha was reflected by the presence of only three Inka settlements, all located in frontier regions.

FIG. 14 Inka settlement of Warawtampu

PUMPU (fig. 4): In this case, the state officials chose unoccupied land at the junction of three rivers (*tinkuy pata*) to build this settlement. In Quechua *tinkuy* means "union" or "meeting place for individuals, ethnic groups, mountains, and roads." Given the use of the words *tinkuy pata*, we can assume that Pumpu must have had special social and political significance and/or symbolism (Topic and Topic 1997). Pumpu also marks the junction of two plains: Junín and Bombón (Matos 1994: 302). Although Pumpu was in Atapillu territory, it was a meeting point for three ethnic groups: Atapillu, Chinchayqocha, and Yarush. Pumpu also seems to have been located in the middle of the wamani, and it was crossed by the north-south road and the east-west Inka road.[20] Finally, this location also gave Pumpu direct access to the coast.

Pumpu is a good example of a new, exclusively Inka, administrative installation. Officials from Cusco participated in the planning, although the construction reveals the work of local masons following local stone-working traditions. Pumpu is a site identified almost exclusively with provincial Inka administration. Our archaeological data (Matos 1994; Brown n.d.) indicate that it was constructed primarily to fulfill three purposes: 1) to manage the resources of the area (wool, meat); 2) to process local products, such as wool for distribution to weavers, and foods that needed to be dehydrated before storage; and 3) to store and redistribute goods. Both Pumpu and Chakamarka show evidence of having been

Variations between Inka Installations

built to fulfill these three functions. Pumpu has 325 qollqas and Chakamarka has 120.

In Pumpu we found a main plaza with an ushnu, two kallankas, and an akllawasi; located nearby were a textile production center, residential kanchas, qollqas, canals, an Inka bath, and bridges (Matos 1994; Brown n.d.).

WARAWTAMPU (fig. 4): The Inka settlement of Warawtampu is the smallest administrative center in the region. It covers barely twelve ha. At Warawtampu, the Inka found a well-planned village known as Astupampa with public buildings two and three stories high, and elaborate residences with square rooms and funerary chambers. The pre-Inka village occupied an area three times bigger than the Inka settlement and the Inkas did not attempt to build a new installation over the pre-existing settlement. Instead, the Inkas decided to preserve the old village of Astupampa on the right bank of the river and build their new Inka settlement on the left bank, an area apparently without pre-existing houses. In the Inka settlement of Warawtampu, the most attractive buildings are those of sillar or cut stone, with trapezoidal doors and niches similar to those of imperial Cusco (fig. 14). These have sadly been almost completely destroyed by the modern inhabitants, but what remains is indicative of their former magnificence. The art and technology of stone carving was well developed in Inka society and it never ceased to have a religious and ideological significance. We suggest that the cut-stone buildings in Warawtampu and Pukatampu (Tarma) were used to display Inka religious and political power in this area.

At Warawtampu we also found residential kanchas, an Inka bath, and canals as well as bridges that serve as entrances into the Inka settlement. From our modern point of view, the site chosen for the Warawtampu settlement does not offer better ecological and economical potential than the others. We therefore believe that the most important factor for the foundation of Warawtampu was sociopolitical. It is in the neighborhood of smaller ethnic groups to the north such as the Yacha, Q'ero, Chupachu, and Mitmaq.

The different sizes of the administrative headquarters within the wamani of Pumpu apparently have to do with their position in the political and administrative hierarchy, as some scholars have suggested (Hyslop 1990; Matos 1994). Pizarro's document also supports this hypothesis. In 1534 Pizarro granted a group of villages to the care of a Spainard (*encomienda*):

> We entrust the treasurer, Alonso Riquelme, with the cazique taparas [*Tapraq*], principal cazique of Tarama y Porbo [*Pumpu*], with the caziques and principals of the said province and of the

villages of Chacamarca and [*Waraw*]Tambo with all his yndios, and villages of the land of Caxaconde, who was the cazique of that said province. The said trust is understood as the natives called it: Horna [*hanan*] and Hurca [*hurin*], which means to go down and up, [we also entrust] whichever villages are found [in the province], which apparently were not entrusted to any other persons; and moreover, we entrust the cazique chumbis [*of Atapillu?*] with his villages and yndios until his Majesty provides for them. (Pizarro 1942 [1534]: 10–11. See also Arellano 1988: 58–59; translation ours)

This document suggests that at the time the Spaniards arrived, the curaca of Tarma, whose name was Tapraq (Arellano 1988), was not only the curaca of the Tarma ethnic group, but also the Inka governor of the wamani of Pumpu. If this is correct, it would explain why the chronicler Pachacuti Yamqui says that the curaca of Tarma was an inspector of the region during the reign of Thupa Yupanki. In the document we find the name of another curaca named Caxaconde, who seems to have been the governor of the Yarush.[21] Through these documents, we have also gleaned the name of another governor of the province of Pumpu: Collacchagua, who governed under Thupa Yupanki.

In Pizarro's document we find a statement that the wamani was divided into two halves or moieties, called *hanan* and *hurin*. The fact that only the names of the curacas of Tarmatampu and Warawtampu were mentioned leads us to suppose that we might have the names of two governors of two moieties. Tapraq was probably the curaca of hanan and Caxaconde was the curaca of hurin. Based on this division, we suggest that Tarmatampu and Chakamarka constituted hanan, and the Yarush and Atapillu constituted hurin. This division was introduced by the Inka with a special purpose (Arellano 1998a), and can therefore explain why the administrative center of Tarmatampu is the second largest one in the wamani, after Pumpu.

The Collapse of the Wamani

Ultimately, all administrative centers of the wamani were partially or totally abandoned. Pumpu was important as an administrative center only as long as the Inka government lasted. When Vaca de Castro visited in 1542, Pumpu was already depopulated and, as a consequence, Pumpu does not appear in his list of tampu. Chakamarka was also deserted. Warawtampu was partially abandoned, but it is difficult to determine the details because of the destruction of the place. In some buildings of Tarmatampu there are traces of continued use, evidently of the textile workshops, during colonial times. However, the buildings, which represented Inka power and government such as the kallanka, were abandoned. The partial or total abandonment of administrative centers did not mean that Inka governors abandoned their duties as curacas. From the persistence of the name Tapraq in colonial documents of 1562 and 1566, we deduce that the same curaca or his descendant continued to be in charge (Arellano 1988).

In our efforts to define an Inka wamani in the Chinchaysuyu, the well-known chronicles of Felipe Guaman Poma de Ayala (1615–1980) and Cristóbal Vaca de Castro (1543–1908) did not provide the information we expected. Both authors established a list of tampus, which remain the most well known today. These include ranked social distinctions such as those indicated by Guaman Poma for Bonbon, which he defined as a "royal tambo." However, these two chronicles failed to take into consideration the political division of Tawantinsuyu and the sociopolitical characteristics of the provinces, even though these are mentioned as "conquered provinces."

Conclusion

By integrating ethnohistoric and archaeological data, we can begin to understand one of the provinces of Tawantinsuyu. Scarce data from documents can be confirmed through archaeological data. Pizarro's information about the existence of the province of Pumpu also seems to be correct. The geopolitical, geoeconomical, and geosocial situation of our region of study was understood by the Inka and incorporated into a new political structure, called wamani.

Cieza de León's account of the differences in the Inka conquest of the ethnic groups is confirmed through the variations between Inka installations in the region. The Inka state used a variety of strategies to incorporate and maintain subjugated peoples. Since those subjugated had been organized in different ways prior to domination by the Inka, each area constitutes a specific political and economic case, and it is important to develop as many case histories as we can. Some groups were incorporated by force while others were not. It appears that the Tarma groups had to be militarily subdued (probably because they were so centralized and powerful), while the less politically complex groups along the lake could be incorporated by means of diplomacy and reciprocal exchanges. We have seen that each Inka installation constitutes a different case study. One of the fundamental differences was whether the Inka were establishing a new settlement or constructing an installation on a pre-existing settlement. We also saw that Inka domination could be manifested on two levels: at the state level, with the construction of public buildings; and at the household level, where the inventory of vessel types and foods may have been affected.

Some sites display many Inka buildings with Inka-style architecture; others do not. Local traditions were often maintained alongside new styles introduced by the Inka. Although documents have been an enormous help in determining the events that took place in each region, it is now time for the archaeologists to meet the challenge of creating individual site-by-site histories from meticulous archaeological excavations.

Acknowledgment
We want to thank Joyce Marcus for her useful comments on and editing of the text.

Notes

1. For an archaeological definition and geographical demarcation of the central sierra see Matos (1998) and Lumbreras (1981).
2. Due to the widespread description of Inka expansion politics in the chronicles, the military use of tampu for storage, supplies, and as rest places for the soldiers is very well known. This partial description of the use of a tampu leads also to a partial definition of what a tampu is. Information about the use of tampu as administrative centers is also available, but much less so than the data about military campaigns.
3. See Matos (1998) for a review of archaeological investigations of Inka sites.
4. "Tarma y Atauillos y Bonbon es otra prouinçia." We prefer to use our own translation here. Philip Means's (Pizarro 1921[1571], 1: 231) edition reads: "we went to Atabillos, Tarama and Bombon, which is another province."
5. Duviols (1974–76: 287–288) pointed out that the Spaniards called the plateau "Bombón," which was not its real name.
6. The Quechua names of historical ethnic groups are in parentheses and will be used henceforth. The spelling of Atapillu follows Guaman Poma's usage (1936 [1615]: 110, 138).
7. Roman numerals in brackets in citations of Cieza de León refer to the chapter number in Markham's translation.
8. The *hatun curaca* of the Atapillu governed not only his own people but also those living in Canta, Huamantanga, and Piscas y Socos (Rostworowski 1978).
9. Based on archaeological data, Hastings suggested (n.d.: 195–196) that the Inka installations of Warawtampu (Yarush), Pumpu, Chakamarka (Chinchayqochan), and Tarmatampu (Tarma) may form part of a wamani.
10. Historical place names are written in Quechua, modern place names preserve the Spanish orthography.
11. There is currently some debate about whether kallanka is the correct name for the Inka complex's main building (Meinken 2005). colonial documentation seems to refer to the main building as tampu, while kallanka is used for a sacred space or plaza (Sergio Barraza, personal communication, February 2007).
12. As the word Tarma is not of Quechua origins but Aymara, Arellano (1998a: 23–26) doubts the existence of this name before the arrival of the Inkas. As a matter of fact, there are no Aymara toponyms in this region.
13. Corrections and additions to the original translation of Clements Markham (1883) are in brackets.
14. They hid among the reeds, although we do not know under what conditions or how long they stayed there. Contary to what Nowack

(1991: 77) has stated, there are no islands in the lake to which they could retire.

15   Arellano (1997: 49) has already suggested the possibility of an alliance between the Yarush and the Inka.

16   Nowack (1991: 77, 87) attests that the population of Pumpu may have had relative independence or a special status due to the possibility of hiding in the lake.

17   Nowack (1991: 33) suggested that the Inka's frequent raids against the Bombón population were due to the Inka's doubts about their loyalty.

18   We do not know which kind of league Betanzos used. We based our calculations in kilometers on the *Diccionario de Autoridades* (1976 [1726] 2: 380), where one league of Castilla's is approximately 6.3 km.

19   Our measurement of distance is based on Nowack's understanding of Cieza de León's use of the word "league." The distance measure was determined by a day's march and it depended on topography and the individual. Nowack (1991: 73), who based her calculation in part on the experience of Hyslop (1984), concluded that Cieza de León's league is about five km.

20   We thank Richard Smith who called our attention to this.

21   Arellano (1998a: 78) suggested that Caxaconde could have been a former curaca of Tarma. But a new interpretation of the text does not confirm this assumption.

References cited

ARELLANO, CARMEN

1988 *Apuntes históricos sobre la provincia de Tarma en la sierra central del Perú*. Bonner amerikanistische Studien 15. Bonn, Germany.

1994 Los títulos de comunidades como fuentes para una reconstrucción histórica de límites de las antiguas etnias andinas: El ejemplo de Tarma en la sierra central del Perú. *América Indígena* 4: 99–132.

1997 Kosmovisionen prägten die Politik. *Agora* 13 (2): 45–49.

1998a Hanan y Urin: Aspectos de la aplicación de un concepto dual andino en la administración inca de la sierra central. In *50 Años de Estudios Americanistas en la Universidad de Bonn: Nuevas contribuciones a la arqueología, etnohistoria, etnolingüística y etnografía de las Américas* (Sabine Dedenbach, Carmen Arellano, Eva König, and Heiko Prümers, eds.): 473–493. Bonner amerikanistische Studien 30. Verlag Sauerwein, Möckmühl, Germany.

1998b Los Inkas en la sierra central del Perú. Balance crítico desde la perspectiva etnohistórica. In *Actas del 49. Congreso Internacional de Americanistas*, Quito 1997. *Tawantinsuyu* 5: 18–22.

n.d. Pastores y tejedores del cacique principal de Chinchaycocha (1599). Paper presented at the 46th International Congress of Americanists, Amsterdam, 1988.

BETANZOS, JUAN DE

1987 [1551] *Suma y Narración de los Incas*. Atlas, Madrid.

1996 [1576] *Narrative of the Incas* (Roland Hamilton and Dana Buchanan, eds. and trans.). University of Texas Press, Austin.

BONNIER, ELISABETH, AND CATHERINE ROZENBERG

1978a L'Habitat en village, a la epoque préhispanique, dans le bassin Shaka-Palcamayo (Département de Junin, Pérou). *Boletín del Instituto Francés de Estudios Andinos* 7 (1–2): 49–71.

1978b Note complementaire sur l'habitat en village, à l'epoque préhispanique, dans le bassin Shaka-Palcamayo (Département de Junin, Pérou). *Boletín del Instituto Francés de Estudios Andinos* 7 (3–4): 59–60.

BROWMAN, DAVID

1974 Pastoral Nomadism in the Andes. *Current Anthropology* 15 (2): 188–196.

BROWN, DAVID

1998 Water and Power in the Provinces: Water Management in Inka Centers of the Central Highlands of Peru. *Tawantinsuyu* 5: 23–36.

n.d. Administration and Planning in the Inka Empire: A Perspective from the Provincial Capital of Pumpu, Central Peru. Ph.D. dissertation, Department of Anthropology, University of Texas, 1992.

CIEZA DE LEÓN, PEDRO DE

1883 [1553] *The Second Part of the Chronicle of Peru* (Clements R. Markham, trans. and ed.). Hakluyt Society, London.

1959 [1553] *The Incas* (Victor von Hagen, ed.). University of Oklahoma Press, Norman.

1967 [1553] *El Señorío de los Incas*. Instituto de Estudios Peruanos, Lima.

1986 [1553] *Crónica del Perú. Primera parte*. 2nd ed. Pontificia Universidad Católica del Perú, Lima.

COBO, BERNABÉ

1964 [1653] *Obras: Historia del Nuevo Mundo*, vol. 2. Biblioteca de Autores Españoles 92. Atlas, Madrid.

DICCIONARIO DE AUTORIDADES

1976 [1726] *Real Academia Española* 1–2. Editorial Gredos, Madrid.

DISCURSO SOBRE LA DESCENDENCIA Y GOBIERNO DE LOS INCAS

1920 [1540–1544] In *Informaciones sobre el antiguo Perú*. Colección de libros y documentos referentes a la historia del Perú, series 2, vol. 3. Sanmartí y ca., Lima.

DUVIOLS, PIERRE

1974–1976 Une petite chronique retrouvée: Errores, ritos, supersticiones y ceremonias de los yndios de la provincia de Chinchaycocha y otras del Piru. *Journal de la Société des Américanistes* 63: 275–297.

FERNÁNDEZ DE OVIEDO, GONZALO

1959 [1557] *Historia general y natural de las Indias*, vol. 5. Biblioteca de Autores Españoles 121. Atlas, Madrid.

GARCILASO DE LA VEGA, EL INCA

1963 [1609] *Comentarios reales de los Incas*. Ministerio de Instrucción Pública y Previsión Social, Montevideo, Uruguay.

GENTILE LAFAILLE, MARGARITA

1976 Distintos aspectos del tributo entre los Yauyos de Chaclla (siglos XV–XVIII). *Boletín del Instituto Francés de Estudios Andinos* 5 (3–4): 77–89.

GUAMAN POMA DE AYALA, FELIPE

1936 [1615] *Nueva corónica y buen gobierno*. Travaux et Mémoires de l'Institut d'Ethnologie, Paris.

HASTINGS, CHARLES

n.d. The Eastern Frontier: Settlement and Subsistence in the

Andean Margins of Central Peru. 2 vols. Ph.D. dissertation, Department of Anthropology, University of Michigan, Ann Arbor, 1985.

HERRERA, ANTONIO DE

1952 [1601] *Historia de los hechos de los castellanos en las Islas y Tierra Firme del Mar Oceano*, vol. 9. Academia de la Historia, Madrid.

HYSLOP, JOHN

1984 *The Inka Road System*. Academic Press, Inc., Orlando.

1990 *Inka Settlement Planning*. University of Texas Press, Austin.

LUMBRERAS, LUIS GUILLERMO

1981 *Arqueología de América Andina*. Editorial Milla Batres, Lima.

MATOS, RAMIRO

1975 Prehistoria y ecología humana en las punas de Junín. *Revista del Museo Nacional* 41 (37–74).

1994 *Pumpu: Centro administrativo inka de la puna de Junín*. Editorial Horizonte, Lima.

1998 Arqueología de la sierra central del Perú: Balance de las investigaciones. In *Actas del 49. Congreso Internacional de Americanistas*, Quito 1997. *Tawantinsuyu* 5: 113–119.

MATOS, RAMIRO, CARMEN ARELLANO, AND DAVID BROWN

1998 Asentamientos inka en Chakamarka y Tarmatambo (Dpto. de Junín): Problemas y criterios de interpretación para la reconstrucción de una provincia inka. In *I Encuentro Internacional de Peruanistas: Estado de los Estudios Histórico-sociales sobre el Perú a fines del siglo XX*: 181–193. Universidad de Lima, UNESCO, Fondo de Cultura Económica, Lima.

MEINKEN, ANJA

2005 Sobre el problema de definición de los edificios incaicos llamados kallanka. *Sequillao: Revista de Historia, Arte y Sociedad* 15: 57–70.

MORRIS, CRAIG

1973 Establecimientos estatales en el Tawantinsuyu: Una estrategia de urbanismo obligado. *Revista del Museo Nacional* 39: 127–141.

1982 The Infrastructure of Inka Control in the Peruvian Central Highlands. In *The Inca and Aztec States 1400–1800* (George Collier, Renato Rosaldo, and John Wirth, eds.): 153–171. Academic Press Inc., New York.

NOWACK, KERSTIN

1991 Das Kriegswesen der Inka nach Pedro de Cieza de León. In *Die Inka und der Krieg*: 1–141. Bonner amerikanistische Studien 17. Seminar für Völkerkunde, Bonn.

ORTIZ DE ZÚÑIGA, IÑIGO

1967 [1562] *Visita de la Provincia de León de Huánuco en 1562*, vol 1.

Universidad Nacional "Hermilio Valdizán." Facultad de Letras y Educación, Huánuco, Peru.

PACHACUTI YAMQUI, JUAN DE SANTA CRUZ
1993 [1640?] *Relación de antigüedades deste Reyno del Pirú*: 179–268. Centro de Estudios Regionales Andinos "Bartolomé de las Casas," Institut Français d'Etudes Andines, Cusco and Lima.

PARSONS, JEFFREY
1998 A Regional Perspective on the Inka Impact on the Sierra Central, Peru. *Tawantinsuyu* 5: 153–159.

PARSONS, JEFFREY R., CHARLES M. HASTINGS, AND RAMIRO MATOS
1997 Rebuilding the State in Highland Peru: Herder-Cultivator Interaction during the Late Intermediate Period in the Tarama-Chinchaycocha Region. *Latin American Antiquity* 8 (4): 317–341.
2000 *Prehispanic Settlement Patterns in the Upper Mantaro and Tarma Drainages, Junin, Peru*, 2 vols. Memoirs of the Museum of Anthropology, University of Michigan 34. Museum of Anthropology, Ann Arbor.

[PIZARRO, FRANCISCO]
1942 [1534] Provisiones de Don Francisco Pizarro, Gobernador del Perú años 1534–1540. *Revista del Archivo Nacional del Perú* 15: 9–24.

PIZARRO, PEDRO
1921 [1571] *Relation of the Discovery and Conquest of the Kingdoms of Peru*. 2 vols. (Philip A. Means, trans.). The Cortes Society, New York.
1978 [1571] *Relación del descubrimiento y conquista de los reinos del Perú*. Pontificia Universidad Católica del Perú, Lima.

POLO DE ONDEGARDO
1917 [1571] Traslado de un cartapacio a manera de borrador que quedó en los papeles del] Lcdo. Polo de Ondegardo, cerca del linage de los Ingas y como conquistaron. *Informaciones acerca de la Religión y Gobierno de los Incas*, part 2. Edición por Horacio Urteaga. Colección de Libros y Documentos referentes a la Historia del Perú, vol. 4. Lima.

ROSTWOROWSKI, MARÍA
1978 *Señoríos indígenas de Lima y Canta*. Instituto de Estudios Peruanos, Lima.
1988 *Historia del Tahuantinsuyu*. Serie Historia Andina 13. Instituto de Estudios Peruanos, Lima.

ROWE, JOHN HOWLAND
1944–1945 Absolute Chronology in the Andean Area. *American Antiquity* 10: 265–284.

SALINAS Y CÓRDOVA, BUENAVENTURA DE
1957 [1630]   *Memorial de las historias del Nuevo Mundo*. Universidad Nacional Mayor de San Marcos, Lima.

SARMIENTO DE GAMBOA, PEDRO
1960 [1572]   *História Índica*. In *Obras completas del Inca Garcilaso de la Vega*. Biblioteca de Autores Españoles 135. Atlas, Madrid.

SMITH, RICHARD
n.d.   Caciques chinchaycochas, funcionarios incas y sacerdotes amueshas: Los caminos antiguos de Chinchaycocha hacia la selva central. Paper presented at the conference "La Cultura de Pasco." Universidad Nacional "Daniel Alcides Carrión," 1999.

TOPIC, JOHN, AND THERESA LANGE TOPIC
1997   Hacia una comprensión conceptual de la guerra andina. In *Arqueología, Antropología e Historia en los Andes: Homenaje a María Rostworowski* (Rafael Varón Gabai and Javier Flores Espinoza, eds.): 567–590. Instituto de Estudios Peruanos, Banco Central de Reserva del Perú, Lima.

VACA DE CASTRO, CRISTÓBAL
1908 [1543]   Ordenanzas de Tambos. *Revista Histórica* 3: 427–492.

VÁSQUEZ DE ESPINOZA, ANTONIO
1969 [1629]   *Compendio y descripción de las Indias Occidentales*. Biblioteca de Autores Españoles 231. Atlas, Madrid.

WILLIAMS, VERÓNICA, AND TERENCE D'ALTROY
1998   El Sur del Tawantinsuyu: Un dominio selectivamente intensivo. *Tawantinsuyu* 5: 170–178.

Pilgrimage and the Geography of Power in the Inka Empire

Charles Stanish
Brian S. Bauer

HIGH IN THE SOUTH-CENTRAL ANDES OF SOUTH AMERICA, IN THE GREAT lake called Titicaca, lie two small islands (fig. 1). According to ancient Andean traditions, the heavenly bodies first rose to the sky from these two islands, and we know that during Inka times (AD 1450–1532) these islands were dedicated to the Sun and the Moon. As the origin point of the sky deities, the islands were among the most sacred locations of the Inka Empire and were visited by pilgrims from across the realm. Bernabé Cobo (1990: 94 [1653: bk. 13, chap. 18]) visited the islands in 1616 and noted that the veneration of the shrines was "so widespread that people came to this place on pilgrimage from everywhere." The word Titicaca itself may derive from a theological concept. Stanish and Bauer (2004) and Stanish (2003) note that Bertonio's Aymara dictionary defines the term "Thaksi Kala" as *piedra fundamental* (foundation stone). In this sense, "foundation" most certainly refers to some kind of creation belief.

In this paper, we address the role that this and other pilgrimage centers played in the Inka Empire. However, we also use the Titicaca sanctuary complex as an example of the powerful role that the manipulation of ideology and the conscious creation of "great traditions" played in imperial expansion. The Islands of the Sun and Moon, plus additional state-controlled installations on the nearby Copacabana Peninsula, comprised a culturally altered landscape of profound ritual and political significance. Beginning at the town of Yunguyu, pilgrims from around the empire walked through a series of increasingly sacred places and ultimately arrived at the Sacred Rock of Titikala located on the northern side of the Island of the Sun.

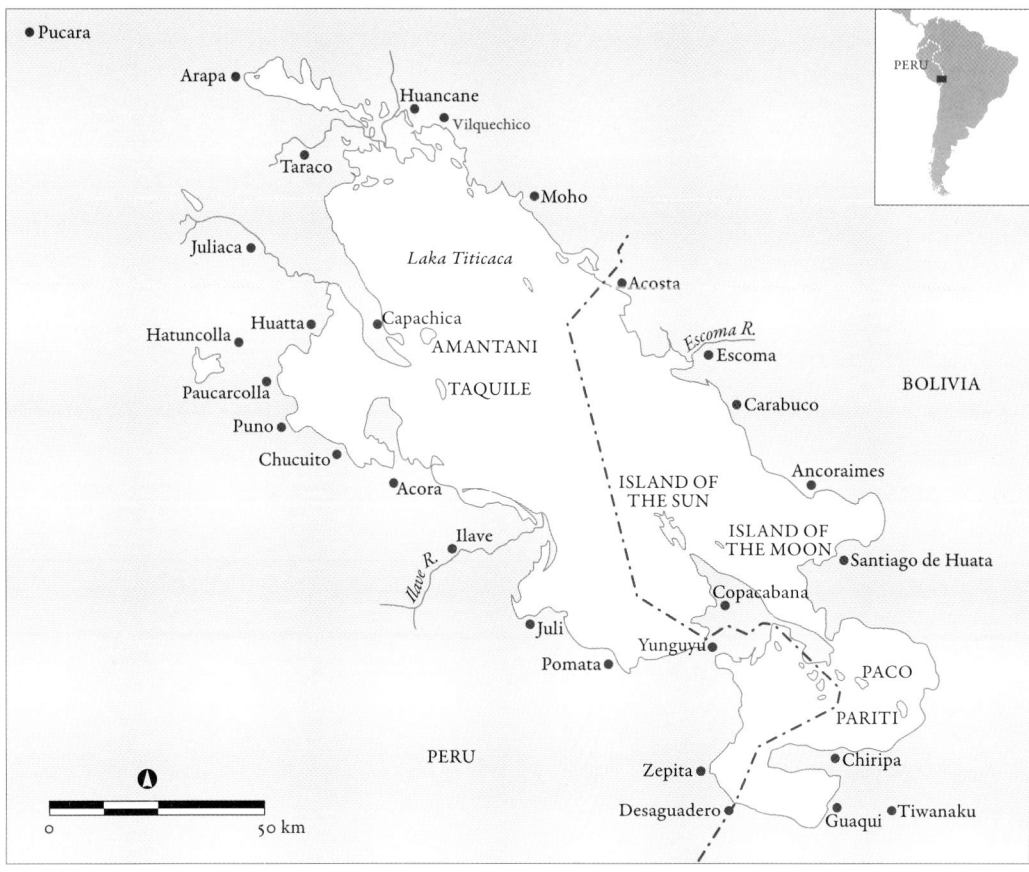

FIG. 1 The Lake Titicaca region

We argue that while the Lake Titicaca pilgrimage complex was culturally significant on several levels, the most prominent was the way in which it served the imperial interests of the Inka state. By conquering, incorporating, and enhancing the island sanctuaries, the Inka consciously achieved several ideological goals. The pilgrim route and state installations built on the islands were intentionally designed to co-opt ideological legitimacy from the local Aymara elite. The Inka altered the landscape in the southern Titicaca region to create a vast pilgrimage center where these politically useful ideological concepts were reinforced by the participation of both commoner and elite. In addition, as the holders and protectors of the origin place of the Sun and Moon, the Inka legitimized their authority on a pan-Andean basis. Finally, Inka control of the sanctuaries most likely served to link the Inka elite to the earlier Tiwanaku state, which had built the first pilgrimage center on these islands.

A Theoretical Perspective

Ideology is at once the most elusive and powerful of tools used by ancient states to project their authority. It is elusive because it is intensely personal and is imbued with different meanings, making it difficult to control. At the same time, precisely because it is so personal, ideology can be one of the most powerful means to assert imperial control. Viewed in this way, pilgrimages and large state-controlled shrines can be seen as playing important roles in defining and legitimizing the power of the elite within ancient states. From the Delian League and Rome in the classical Mediterranean world to the fragmented states of medieval Christendom in Europe to pilgrimages in Hindu and Muslim states, elites continuously reworked a "sacred" area into the endpoint of a physical and spiritual journey that transformed a pilgrim from a member of a local ethnic group or village into a participant in a larger state system.

The Inka were experts at this type of ideological manipulation, drawing on earlier traditions and creating new ones to suit the needs of their empire. The Inka use of the Islands of the Sun and Moon and the adjoining Copacabana area for state ideological purposes has to be understood on several levels. The appropriation of this renowned shrine complex from the local population in the late fifteenth century was a political statement of the authority of Inka rule. Furthermore, the use of gendered symbols such as the Sun (male) and the Moon (female) and the sanctification of natural features of the landscape, such as outcrops and springs, were consistent with "traditional" Inka conceptions of proper ritual that developed prior to the expansion of their empire. Moreover, the actual pilgrimage and ritual acts performed had both political and personal meanings.

The act of participating in the pilgrimage reinforced the political status of the pilgrim, whether commoner or elite. In this sense, it was a profoundly political act. On the other hand, there is little doubt that for many pilgrims the journey held deep religious meanings that were not consciously perceived as political. These ideological levels, from the overtly political and conscious that reinforced cultural values of the Inka state to the deeply felt religious sentiment by some participants, represent the range of meanings associated with this great ritual complex.

Pilgrimages and pilgrimage centers worldwide have been understood by two broad classes of theory. One theoretical perspective begins with Emile Durkheim. As John Eade and Michael Sallnow (1991: 4) note, the "Durkheimian approach to pilgrimage is sometimes given a Marxist slant. Here, the cults are implicated in the generation and maintenance of ideologies which legitimize domination and oppression." In this conception, pilgrimage centers are constructions used by elites to perpetuate class distinction, political authority, ideological legitimacy, and divine sanction of the existing social order. One of the great examples of a state creating a pilgrimage center to aid in the maintenance of an empire is that of Constantine after his conversion to Christianity. Glenn Bowman

(1991) demonstrates how the first pilgrimage center in Christendom was "consciously created as such by the emperor Constantine to provide physical anchorage for the written texts of the newly adopted state religion with which he hoped to unify the empire" (Eade and Sallnow 1991: 1). Another salient example is the cathedral of Santiago de Compostela in northwest Spain. Santiago (St. James) was renowned as a fighter against the Moors, and the ideological power of his supposed remains in the cathedral were intimately tied into Christian efforts to retake the Holy Land during the Crusades (Coleman and Elsner 1995: 106). A pilgrimage to this shrine most certainly served to immerse the pilgrim in the ideology of anti-Islamic expansion and western European military campaigns.

The second class of theory is what Eade and Sallnow refer to as the Turnerian approach. For Victor Turner, such religious constructions actually served to subvert the established social order (Eade and Sallnow 1991: 5). Turner viewed cults not as hegemonic devices that reinforced the existing status quo, but as counter-hegemonic institutions. From this perspective, shrines challenged the authority of the state by setting up alternative and competing religious icons that superficially conformed to religious orthodoxy but that were outside of the direct control of a hierarchy.

There are hundreds of examples of such counter-hegemonic shrines in history and ethnography. Medieval European Christianity is replete with cases of pilgrimage shrines that were created outside of, and in many cases antithetical to, the interests of the official Church. In the Americas, many pilgrimage centers developed in a context of popular dissatisfaction with the social order. The famous late-nineteenth-century case of Father Cícero Romão Batista, an indigenous Roman Catholic priest from northeast Brazil, illustrates how a shrine that threatens the social order can be created by individuals who have official sanction but work against ecclesiastical and state authorities. Father Cicero, a low-level member of the church hierarchy, who befriended socially unacceptable people, was close to expulsion by the ecclesiastical authorities when a "miracle" occurred during mass. He was dismissed by the church and essentially lost official ideological sanction. He then began a career in politics where he pursued policies contrary to the interests of the clergy.

Years after his death, the town where he conducted his ministry attracted thousands of pilgrims. The pilgrimage was outside the control of the church authorities, and it served to counter the interests of the status quo. As related in Martin Robinson (1997: 42), Father Cicero's town "remains a Holy City, the new Jerusalem, the centre of the world, the land of Salvation" for the thousands who travel there. This "Holy City," endowed with official Christian icons, actually functioned as a political challenge to the status quo.

Numerous local pilgrimage destinations and shrines around the Andes can also be interpreted as popular expressions of resistance against political forces beyond their immediate control or, at the very least, as local shrines controlled by nonelite populations. There were a multitude of sacred places in the Andes at the time of the Spanish invasion. Known as *huacas*, these varied in size and significance from local places or objects venerated by a single family to regionally important shrines worshipped by most of the people who lived around them (Bauer 1998). These huacas may have been pilgrimage destinations in a limited sense, but they were respected and maintained by a relatively small and culturally homogeneous group of people in a confined geographical area. In these instances, the Turnerian model works well and explains the varied social, political, ideological, economic, and cultural forces that revolve around the shrines.

Among the multitude of huacas in the Andes at the time of European contact, a few select ones represented centers of pan-Andean religious importance that were profoundly different from the local shrines understood within a Turnerian perspective. While these great huacas also served as local shrines for the people who lived near them, they were principally famous as the destination for long-distance pilgrimages. The fact that long-distance pilgrimages were made to these shrines distinguished them as fundamentally different from local huacas. The shrine complex in the southern Titicaca Basin is an example of these great huacas. It was essentially a state institution, with local nonstate roots. The ritual complex was designed to project a set of unambiguous meanings associated with Inka culture, the Inka state, and most importantly, Inka political ideology.

We believe that a Durkheimian framework is the most appropriate theoretical tool for understanding such a huge and important pan-Andean pilgrimage center as the shrine complex on the Islands of the Sun and Moon. We approach the problem of the origin and maintenance of the sacred islands as one tied into the development of complex polities in general. We argue that the Lake Titicaca shrine complex was more akin to Constantine's efforts in the Holy Land and the cathedral of Santiago de Compostela than to the worship of a local shrine. From this perspective, the development of pan-regional pilgrimage complexes (with temples, support buildings, attendants, and so forth) only occurs in the context of state levels of organization. This is because only states have the capacity to mobilize labor, provision the attendants, and maintain the infrastructure of such a large complex. Furthermore, these kinds of pilgrimages serve huge regions and integrate numerous ethnic groups, and therefore fit precisely into the ideological needs of multiethnic, regional state organizations.

Great Shrines of the Empire

A pilgrimage center provides an ideal opportunity to materially depict state ideology. Selected natural features, architecture, artifacts, and rituals can be combined into a comprehensive metaphor for transmitting the ideals of the state religion. The significance of a local shrine is magnified substantially when it is co-opted by a state. The mere fact that the pilgrimage center, now associated with the dominant state, exists on or near an older sacred site sends a powerful message of cultural dominance and legitimate succession.

The Inka were masters at converting local shrines into centers of great ideological importance. At the time of European contact, several notable shrines controlled by the Inka were found across the empire. The three most important sanctuaries were the Coricancha in Cusco, Pachacamac on the coast, and the Islands of the Sun and Moon in Lake Titicaca. Each of these shrines was of pan-Andean importance and intimately connected with state authority.

THE CORICANCHA

The most important sanctuary in the Inka state was the Coricancha, called Templo del Sol (Temple of the Sun) by the Spaniards. The Coricancha, which means "enclosure of gold" in Quechua, was located on a slight rise in the heart of Cusco, near the confluence of two small rivers that flowed through the city. According to some early founding legends, it was here that the first Inka couple built their household and began the process of creating an empire.

The Coricancha was originally a local shrine of the pre-imperial Inka peoples. A number of separate archaeological excavations have been conducted in and around the temple during the past four decades by Luis Barreda Murillo, Arminda Gibaja Oviedo, Alfredo Valencia Zegarra, and Raymundo Béjar Navarro. These Cusco archaeologists have each recovered exceptionally high-quality Early Inka (i.e., Killke) pottery (ca. AD 1000–1400), indicating that the special nature of the site extends back before the establishment of the empire.

From the Coricancha radiated the spatial divisions, or *suyus*, that divided the Inka Empire into four quarters. The northwest quarter of the empire was referred to as Chinchaysuyu and the northeast was named Antisuyu. The two southern quarters included Collasuyu to the southeast and Cuntisuyu to the southwest. The Inka Empire was seen as the summation of these four parts and the Coricancha marked the center of the empire and their world.

Because the Coricancha contained the finest gold and silver objects of the empire, it was sacked by the Spaniards even before they established a secure rule over the Andes. Nevertheless, we know a great deal about the organization of the temple and the activities that occurred there from the many Spaniards and natives who lived in Cusco during the Conquest period. The Coricancha is said to have held a set of temples dedicated to various deities: the Sun, the Moon, the Stars, the Thunder, the Rainbow, and the creator god Viracocha. The most important shrines in the complex, however, were those of the Sun and the Moon. These images were housed in separate chambers that were adorned with gold and silver respectively. Cobo offers the following description of the Temple of the Sun:

> The most important and most sumptuous temple of this kingdom was the one located in the city of Cusco; this temple was held to be the chief center or capital of their false religion and the most venerated sanctuary that these Indians had, and for that reason, it was visited by all of the people of the Inka Empire, who came to it out of devotion on pilgrimages. This temple was called Coricancha, which means "house of gold," because of the incomparable wealth of this metal which was embedded in the temple's chapels and walls, its ceilings and altars. (Cobo 1990: 48–49 [1653: bk. 13, chap. 12])

After the fall of the Inka Empire, the monastery of Santo Domingo was built on the site of the temple and much of the original compound was destroyed. Nevertheless, the remains of the former structures, and the superb Inka stone work, can still be seen (Bauer 2004).

PACHACAMAC (MAKER OF THE WORLD)

Another important sanctuary, called Pachacamac, was located on the coast a short distance south of modern-day Lima. This large center is consistently described in the chronicles as an area of immense religious importance.[1] For example, Cobo writes:

> In magnitude, devotion, authority and richness, the Temple of Pachacama[c] was second only to the magnificent [Cusco] Temple of the Sun. Since it was a universal sanctuary, people came to the Temple of Pachacama[c] on pilgrimages from all over the Inka Empire, and there they made their votive offerings. (Cobo 1990: 85 [1653: bk. 13, chap. 17])

In the center of the complex was a series of massive adobe platforms. The largest platform held a temple that housed the idol of Pachacamac. Pilgrims, both noble and common, made offerings and received advice at this universally recognized oracle.

After the incorporation of Pachacamac into the Inka Empire, the oracle remained an important huaca. The chronicles suggest that Topa Inka, Huayna Capac, Huascar, and Atahualpa each visited the shrine seeking advice. The Inka constructed a number of state installations at Pachacamac including a Temple of the Sun and lodgings for the priests, attendants, and guards of the complex. Quarters were also constructed for the chosen women of the state who served in the temple. There were also additional buildings to house the pilgrims who arrived at the sanctuary (Cieza de León 1967: 334–337 [1554: pt. 1, chap. 72]; Cobo 1990: 85–90 [1653: bk. 13, chap. 17]).

Within months of establishing himself in Cajamarca, Francisco Pizarro sent his brother, Hernando Pizarro, to investigate the Pachacamac shrine. On his arrival at the oracle, Hernando learned that pilgrims from as far as 300 leagues (approximately 1,600 kilometers) visited the principal idol and that the lords of the surrounding polities came annually to make sacrifices (Xérez 1985: 130–148 [1534]). The official report from this expedition tells of Hernando Pizarro's encounter with the principal huaca at the site:

> The captain talked with them and said that he wanted to see that idol that they had. . . . It was in a good house well painted in a very dark, smelly, very closed room. They have a very dirty idol made of wood. They say it is their god, the one which nurtures and supports and maintains them. At the foot of it they had offered some gold jewels. It is so venerated that only its pages and servants, that they say that the idol selects, serve him; and no other dares to enter, or is worthy of touching the walls of its house. . . . They come to this devil in pilgrimage of 300 leagues with gold and silver and clothes, and those who arrive go to the watchmen and request the idol's servant, and he enters, and speaks with the idol, and he says that entrance is granted. (Xérez 1985: 136–137 [1534]; translation ours)

Hernando spent almost a month in the town and temple area looking for gold. He then returned to the highlands with the spoils and added them to Atahualpa's ransom.

Archaeological research at Pachacamac began in 1896 with Max Uhle's (1906) investigations. Historical and archaeological work on this pilgrimage center has continued throughout the twentieth century. It is now known that the occupation of Pachacamac is of great antiquity, and it is widely speculated that the site was already a pilgrimage center during the period of Wari (AD 600–900) control of the coast (Schreiber 1992: 106; Morris and von Hagen 1993: 121). If Pachacamac was a pilgrimage center in Wari times, then it is a good example of the Inka state appropriating an important religious shine for its own purposes.

Islands of the Sun and the Moon

Upon initial contact with the Inka Empire, the Spaniards were told that the Sun first emerged from a Sacred Rock on an island in Lake Titicaca. They also learned that the founding couple of the Inka Empire rose from this great island. Furthermore, informants told the Spaniards that the island housed a series of temples that was part of a religious complex on the southern shores of the lake and that the largest temple stood beside the revered rock.

The first Europeans to view Lake Titicaca were two members of Francisco Pizarro's forces. They arrived at the shores of the lake in late December 1533 or early January 1534. According to their report, and others that followed, there were indeed two sacred islands, one called Titicaca (Island of the Sun) and the other Coati (Island of the Moon).

Following these initial visits, the shrine complex was described by chroniclers who lived in the region. The two most important are Bernabé Cobo and Alonso Ramos Gavilán. Both of these authors furnish extensive eyewitness accounts of the Inka remains on the islands and describe how the pilgrimages were conducted. Most importantly, Ramos Gavilán and Cobo provide detailed descriptions of the Inka shrine complex on the Islands of the Sun and Moon in the century following the Spanish conquest. These two chroniclers represent what we believe to be the most accurate and essential sources for the early history of the islands.

Cobo visited the islands about eighty years after Pizarro's explorations and interviewed many of the local inhabitants. He described the islands and noted that they were one of the three great sanctuaries of the Inka:

> On the basis of its reputation and authority, this sanctuary was the third most important one for these Peruvian Indians. Actually, it comprised two magnificent temples, which were located on two separate islands of Lake Chucuito [Titicaca].[2] And since both islands are close to the town of Copacabana, we use this name to make reference to the sanctuary. One of these islands was called Titicaca, and the other Coata [Coati]. The former was dedicated to the Sun, and the latter to the Moon. (Cobo 1990: 91 [1653: bk. 13, chap. 18])

Cobo's descriptions of the Islands of the Sun and the Moon are supported by, and partially derived from, those of Ramos Gavilán (1988 [1621]). Cobo and Ramos Gavilán visited the Lake Titicaca region during the same decade, although they belonged to different religious orders and lived in separate towns. Ramos Gavilán resided in Copacabana, a town that was controlled by the Augustinians. Cobo spent time in Juli, a major Spanish religious center initially established by the Dominicans but later taken over by the Jesuits.[3]

According to Ramos Gavilán and Cobo, the religious complex on the Island of the Sun included the Sacred Rock called "Titikala," a temple to the Sun and other sky deities, and a large labyrinth-like structure that housed the "chosen women" (also called Mamacona) of the state who

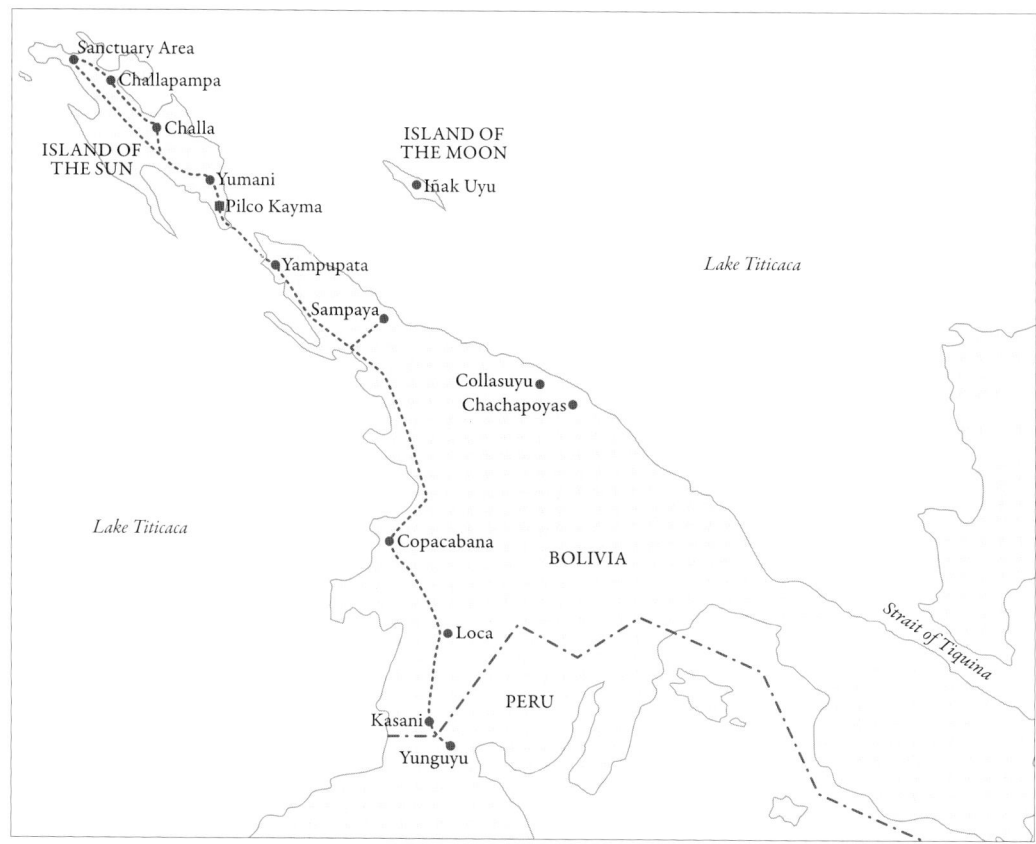

FIG. 2 The Copacabana mainland and the Islands of the Sun and the Moon

attended the shrine. There was also a large temple complex, which is now called Iñak Uyu, on the Island of the Moon. The political and ideological importance of these islands was immense, and the Inka Empire invested huge resources in maintaining various temples, storehouses, and roads on the islands, as well as on the Copacabana mainland (fig. 2).

Lake Titicaca and the Origins of the Inka

A large number of Inka myths have been passed down to us in fragmented form. Two myths are central to understanding the Inka sanctuary of the Titicaca Basin: the Lake Titicaca origin myth and the Pacariqtambo origin myth. Although the accounts about Lake Titicaca are of primary interest to us, many early writers provide hybrid versions, combining elements of both myths into a single narrative.

The Pacariqtambo origin myth was the central narrative of the foundation of the Inka state as promulgated by their own historians and intelligentsia. It was recorded in over twenty separate chronicles. This myth begins with the emergence of Manco Capac, the first Inka, and his royal brothers and their sister/wives from a cave, called Tamputoco, south of Cusco in the region of Pacariqtambo. The myth describes Manco Capac's northward journey from Pacariqtambo to the Cusco Valley and his battle with the indigenous people of the region. It recalls the triumphal occupation of the valley by Manco Capac and the establishment of a new dynastic order (Bauer 1992a, 1996). Through the Pacariqtambo origin myth, the ruling elite of Cusco were seen as the direct descendants of Manco Capac.

Numerous chroniclers also indicate that the Inka and other peoples of the Andes believed that the creator god, known as Viracocha, caused the Sun and the Moon to rise from Lake Titicaca. This momentous event ended a prolonged period of darkness. Sarmiento de Gamboa records one such account:

> Viracocha went to this island and ordered the sun, moon, and stars to emerge and rise up into the sky to give light to the world, and so it was done. They say that he made the moon much brighter than the sun and that because of this the jealous sun threw a handful of ash into its face as they were about to rise into the sky. From then onwards [the moon] has the darkened color that it has now. (Sarmiento de Gamboa 2007: 49 [1572: chap. 7])

Other writers, especially those who visited the Lake Titicaca region, record even more details about this myth. For example, Cobo provides another version of the creation myth:

> The shrine of the Sun, which was on the Island of Titicaca, was a large solid crag. The reason it was consecrated to the Sun and worshipped can be traced to a ridiculous story. It is said that in this province the people of ancient times tell of being without light from the heavens for many days, and all of the local inhabitants were astonished, confused and frightened to have total darkness for such a long time. Finally, the people of the Island of Titicaca saw the Sun come up one morning out of that crag with extraordinary radiance. For this reason they believed that the true dwelling place of the Sun was that crag, or at least that the crag was the most delightful thing in the world for the Sun. Thus a magnificent temple, for those times, was constructed there and dedicated to the Sun, although it was not so magnificent as it was after the Inkas enlarged it and enhanced its fame. (Cobo 1990: 91–92 [1653: bk. 18. chap. 18])

The early writers also commonly combined the Pacariqtambo origin myth with the Lake Titicaca origin myth. They speak of the first Inka and his sister/wife appearing on the Island of Titicaca and link this appearance with the parallel emergence of the Sun and the Moon on that same island. The writers then relate how the first Inkas left the Titicaca region and traveled to Cusco via Pacariqtambo. In these accounts, rather than simply explaining the origin of the heavenly bodies, the Lake Titicaca origin myth is transformed to explain how the first Inka (analogous to the sun) and his sister/wife (analogous to the moon) emerged from the island. In other words, Inka intellectuals successfully linked the ruling elite of Cusco with that of the principal shrine of one of their most important highland provinces. The origin place of the Quechua-speaking Cusco elite was mythologically merged with the most sacred place in the Aymara-speaking Titicaca Basin. The Islands of the Sun and Moon became the ideological beachhead of Inka expansion to the south.

Incorporation of the Islands into the Inka Empire

There is some ambiguity in the historical sources as to when the Lake Titicaca region was incorporated into the Inka Empire and who built the structures that now stand on the islands. Among the sources that refer most extensively to the arrival of the first Inka to the Island of the Sun are Cieza de León (1554), Ramos Gavilán (1621), and Cobo (1653).[4] Cieza de León, the earliest of these writers, traveled through the Lake Titicaca region in 1549, and finished his memoirs only five years later in 1554. He suggests that while Viracocha Inka may have established an alliance with the Lupaca, his son Pachacuti was the first of the noble Cusco clan to visit and construct buildings on the sacred islands of Titicaca. Elsewhere, Cieza de León (1967: 277 [1554: pt. 1, chap. 101]) says that Pachacuti's visit was followed by those of later Inkas as the territory of the empire extended southward into modern-day Bolivia, Chile, and Argentina.

Ramos Gavilán (1988: 32, 36 [1621: bk. 1, chap. 3]), resident of Copacabana in 1618, challenges the information provided by Cieza de León, stating that Pachacuti's son, Topa Inka, was the first Inka to arrive at the islands. Ramos Gavilán indicates that Topa Inka was so impressed by the Island of the Sun that he ordered its entire population to be resettled in the village of Yunguyu, outside the larger Copacabana sanctuary. He then repopulated the mainland area and the island with people selected from across the Inka Empire. Topa Inka is said to have constructed a series of buildings on the island, including a royal palace for himself about a league from the rock. Ramos Gavilán (1988: 171 [1621: chap. 27]) states that after completing his work on the Island of the Sun, Topa Inka traveled to the island of Coati to build a shrine dedicated to the Moon, the wife of the Sun.

Ramos Gavilán (1988: 120 [1621: chap. 18]) states repeatedly that Huayna Capac, the son of Topa Inka, also played an important role in developing Inka installations on the sacred islands. Not wanting to have been outdone by his father, Huayna Capac visited both of the islands and improved their facilities (Ramos Gavilán 1988: 120 [1621: chap. 18]). Huayna Capac is also said to have sent two of his daughters to serve in the Temple of the Sun near the Sacred Rock (Ramos Gavilán 1988: 185 [1621: chap. 31]).

The Pilgrimage to the Sacred Islands of Lake Titicaca

A state-controlled pilgrimage is more than a trip to a sacred place. It is an orchestrated series of acts, propelled by natural or man-made objects and places along the way, that leads the pilgrims to a greater awareness and appreciation of an abstract concept. Unlike visits to smaller shrines that are developed by individuals or groups outside of a political or social hierarchy, a pilgrimage to a state-sponsored center takes place across a carefully constructed ritual landscape. Pilgrims are forced to follow a prescribed pathway that is inevitably characterized by a series of specific, state-serving, religious icons and representations. By participating in a state-controlled event, the pilgrims implicitly or explicitly recognize the sanctity and authority of the ideology embodied in the shrine. The Lake Titicaca shrine complex represents a clear case of a state-altered landscape, with a prescribed pathway through a series of sequentially more sacred spaces that ultimately arrives at the most powerful destination point, the birthplace of the Sun. Using historical and archaeological data, we are able to reconstruct this pathway and parts of the cultural landscape.

ARRIVING AT COPACABANA

The sacred complex began at the town of Yunguyu, about an hour's walk from Copacabana. Cobo notes that a wall was constructed near Yunguyu and that guards were stationed at the gates to inspect travelers wishing to enter the Copacabana area:

> Since the area starting from the straits or isthmus which I mentioned above between Yunguyu and Copacabana was considered to be a sacred place, the Inka had this entrance closed off with a wall which he had made from one beach to the other. He had gates put along the wall with watchmen and guards to look over the people who came to the sanctuary on pilgrimages. (Cobo 1990: 94 [1653: bk. 13, chap. 18])

Later in his account, Cobo (1990: 96 [1653: bk. 13, chap. 18]) states that to gain access to Copacabana, the pilgrims spoke with a confessor and did penance. Ramos Gavilán (1988: 127 [1621: chap. 20]) describes a public building that the Inka built for the pilgrims to stay in. The pilgrims also abstained from salt, meat, and chili peppers. Interestingly, nearly four and a half centuries later, the Copacabana peninsula is still separated from the rest of the mainland by the national border of Peru and Bolivia. A modern wall and arch stands on a ridge at the border just outside of Yunguyu, and visitors must pass through immigration guards and seek permission to continue their journey.

Ramos Gavilán (1988: 127 [1621: chap. 20]) relates that as the pilgrims passed from Yunguyu to Copacabana they were provided with food and supplies from the royal storehouses at a place called Loca. The social and political status of the pilgrims apparently determined the nature of these gifts. The community and storehouses of Loca are probably those mentioned in a 1548 Copacabana *encomienda* document (Espinoza Soriano 1972: 10) that describes "another small town in which there are certain storehouses, that is between the town of Copacabana and Yunguyu, with seventeen Indians of service and nine widows and elders." According to Espinoza Soriano (1972: 5), the village of Loca still exists between Yunguyu and Copacabana. The Inka storehouses, however, have disappeared.

After arriving at Copacabana, the pilgrims rested for several days and prayed at the local temples and shrines before proceeding to the Island of the Sun (Ramos Gavilán 1988: 171–172 [1621: chap. 28]). A second confession was made in Copacabana before they departed for the island. Today, Copacabana is a major Christian shrine and one of the most important Catholic pilgrimage destinations in South America. It is no coincidence that the Catholic priests constructed such a shrine in this city (MacCormack 1991; Sallnow 1987). Archaeological evidence, as indicated by large quantities of Inka pottery, suggests a substantial Inka occupation under the city, and the town layout conforms to an orthogonal grid pattern as defined by John Hyslop (1990). There is a typical plaza that probably follows the Inka one, and the famous Christian church next to the plaza was probably constructed over an Inka structure (fig. 3). Likewise, near the town there are a number of Inka-style cut stones typical of Inka ritual places.

From Copacabana, the pilgrims walked toward the port of Yampupata, three to four hours away, on a well-paved Inka road. According to Ramos Gavilán (1988: 127 [1621: chap. 20]), while en route from Copacabana, the pilgrims passed through two additional checkpoints, with warehouses holding corn, other crops, and freeze-dried meat (*charqui*). Today, a major Christian shrine is found in a valley near a section of Inka road. This shrine was most likely patterned after Inka ones in the area. There may have also been a place at Yampupata for the pilgrims to spend the night before crossing over to the Island of the Sun (Squier 1877: 327).

The crossing of the strait from Yampupata to the Island of the Sun was an integral part of the pilgrimage process. Here, the Inka authorities were able to exert absolute control on the movement of pilgrims (fig. 4). Ephraim Squier made the two-kilometer trip across the strait in 1865 and provides a vivid description of the journey:

> Leaving behind the little playa or beach [of Yampupata], our Indian boatmen pushed along under a steep, rocky cliff, until they reached the point where the strait between the main-land

FIG. 3 Copacabana is a major Christian shrine, and is one of the most important Catholic pilgrimage destinations in South America (anonymous photograph, ca. 1900, private collection).

FIG. 4 For millennia reed boats have been used to transport people and goods from the Copacabana mainland to the Island of the Sun (photograph by William H. Rau, ca. 1900, private collection).

FIG. 5 The ruins of Pilco Kayma have long attracted the attention of tourists to the region (photograph by Luis D. Gismondi ca. 1920, private collection).

and the island is narrowest. The water at the foot of the cliff is very deep, but wonderfully transparent. We were more than two hours in propelling the balsa across the strait, a distance which an ordinary oarsman in a Whitehall boat would get over in fifteen minutes, and landed on the island under the lee of a projecting ledge of rocks, full in view of the Palace of the Inka [Pilco Kayma] and the terraces surrounding it, half a mile to our right. (Squier 1877: 329)

Squier traveled in a particularly small boat, but he notes that there were larger vessels on the lake, some of which could be rigged with a sail and were capable of carrying as many as sixty people.

The former landing place on the Island of the Sun is simply called Puncu (entrance). It is at the extreme southeastern tip of the island, the point of land closest to the mainland. The remains of a prehistoric road that began at this landing point and ran across the southern slope of the island towards the modern village of Yumani can still be seen on the hillside. Squier describes the remains of Inka structures at Puncu. Thirty years later these structures were barely visible (Bandelier 1910: 187, 191), and today only a few walls and a light scatter of Inka pottery remain to mark this important debarkation point.

From this landing place the pilgrims began their trip to the opposite end of the island. They soon passed the impressive site of Pilco Kayma. This two-story, multichambered structure was surrounded by a set of terraces. Its function is unknown, since none of the early colonial writers mention it. This silence is surprising, since Pilco Kayma is one of the most prominent and accessible Inka complexes on the island (fig. 5).

As the pilgrims journeyed towards the Sacred Rock area, they reached the summit of the island and walked along the ridge for approximately seven kilometers. Along the route they passed one of the largest Inka villages on the island, a site now called Apachinacapata. From the ridge, the traveler could have walked directly to the sanctuary area at the far end of the island, or have taken a lower trail that led past several Inka villages along the northwest lakeshore. Our survey work on the ridge between Apachinacapata and the Sacred Rock identified a series of low, rectangular platforms with light scatters of Inka pottery along the main trail. Although their exact function is unknown, these platforms may have served as offering spots along the pilgrimage route.

During Inka times, the two most important lakeside settlements on the island were Challapampa and Kasapata. Challapampa is on a narrow spit of land between two large bays, and surface collections indicate that the site was built during Inka times. It may have been the town that Cobo (1990: 94 [1653: bk. 13, chap. 18]) credits to Topa Inka Yupanqui: "He made a moderate-sized town one league from the temple, and the majority of the inhabitants were *mitimaes* [colonists] of Inka blood and lineage. And he had a dwelling built there for them to live in."

Kasapata is on a wide and extensively terraced isthmus, a short walk from the rock sanctuary at Titikala. During Inka times, it was larger and perhaps more important than Challapampa. Ramos Gavilán (1988: 87 [1621: chap. 12]), refers to this site when he writes that Topa Inka Yupanqui "founded a moderate sized town, half a league, or almost, before the rock and shrine, and built his royal palace in it." It is also referred to by Cobo (1990: 93 [1653: bk. 13, chap. 18]), who states that "one quarter of a league before one reaches the temple, there was an impressive tambo or inn for the pilgrims to stay in."

Surface collections and excavations at Kasapata by both Bandelier (1910: 203–213) and by our project have yielded elegant Inka ceramics as well as evidence of large trash middens (Stanish and Bauer 2004). Work at the site has also documented the remains of various Inka buildings, including one that measures approximately forty meters long. The building has five doorways and may be the structure mentioned by Ramos Gavilán (1988: 176 [1621: chap. 29]) when he discussed the December and June solstice celebrations that took place on the island.

The Entrance to the Sanctuary Area

A paved trail heading north from Kasapata leads directly to the sanctuary area, which is separated from the rest of the island by a low wall. The Sacred Rock area is a zone of minimal agricultural potential relative to the island as a whole. Today, it is uninhabited as it was in the nineteenth century (Squier 1877; Bandelier 1910). Nevertheless, we know that during the Inka period it housed one of the most important shrines of the ancient Andean world.

Both Ramos Gavilán and Cobo provide similar, although not identical, observations about the sanctuary area. Cobo states that there was a single entrance to the sanctuary, a gate called Intipuncu (Door of the Sun), that was located some 200 paces from the Sacred Rock. According to Cobo, it was at this portal that Topa Inka Yupanqui removed his sandals, a custom that was followed from then on. Cobo implies that most pilgrims were not allowed to approach the rock directly, traveling only as far as the Intipuncu where they handed their offerings to the attendants who resided in the sanctuary. He also provides a detailed description of a set of footprints and Inka structures that were near this gate. The footprints, in fact, are natural inclusions in the bedrock and can still be seen today.

Ramos Gavilán's description of the sanctuary entrance is more extensive than Cobo's. Although somewhat confusing, Ramos Gavilán suggests that the pilgrimage route passed through three closely spaced gateways to enter the sanctuary, and that at each door they held an audience with a priest. Ramos Gavilán indicates that the first door was called Pumapuncu (Door of the Puma). The second door, Kentipuncu (Door of the Hummingbird), was located some 200 paces from the rock and was covered with hummingbird feathers. We know that this is the same door that Cobo calls Intipuncu (Door of the Sun), since both authors indicate that there were Inka structures and footprints near it. The third and final door, Pillcopuncu (Door of the Pillco), was adorned with pillco feathers.[5]

Although differing in details, Ramos Gavilán's and Cobo's accounts of the entrance to the sanctuary area on the Island of the Sun are not unlike those provided by Garcilaso de la Vega for priests entering the Coricancha in the heart of Cusco. Garcilaso de la Vega (1966: 186, 187, 359 [1609: pt. 1, bk., 3, chap. 23; bk. 6, chap. 21]) notes several times that those visiting the temple had to remove their sandals when they were within a 200-step radius of the Coricancha. Furthermore, only the highest Inka royalty could enter the temple area itself, accompanied by the priests of the Sun. Visitors of lower status could only approach the entry gate of the temple, where they passed their offerings to the priests.

FIG. 6 The Sacred Rock of Titikala

The Sanctuary

The Inka constructed a number of features in the sanctuary area. The most important of these included an offering area near the Sacred Rock, a Temple of the Sun and other sky deities, a storehouse, and living quarters for those who served the shrine. We are fortunate that both Ramos Gavilán and Cobo described some of these facilities in detail.

The Sacred Rock, from which the sun rose, is a large exposed slab of reddish sandstone that lies near the center of the sanctuary area (fig. 6). It was believed that the sun left from a small hollow in this rock (Ramos Gavilán 1988: 164 [1621: chap. 26]). The far side of the rock descends down the eastern hillside toward the lake. Ramos Gavilán (1988: 115–116, 149 [1621: chap. 17, 24]) suggests that this side was covered with fine Inka cloth (*cumbi*), "the most subtle, and delicate, that never was seen in Indies." The plaza side, which is notably convex, was faced with plates of silver and gold (Ramos Gavilán 1988: 115–116, 150 [1621: chap. 17, 24]).

A plaza adjoins the Sacred Rock. Ramos Gavilán (1988: 93 [1621: chap. 13]) indicated that many gold idols, ceramic vessels, and other items had already been looted by treasure hunters in this plaza. Furthermore, he stated that there was a round stone in front of the rock into which corn beer (*chicha*) was poured as an offering to the Sun. He added that there were still traces of chicha vessels on the surface of the plaza. Ramos Gavilán (1988: 116 [1621: chap. 17]) also noted that the round offering stone had been used as a base for a cross that was erected in the plaza (fig. 7).

Pilgrimage and the Geography of Power

FIG. 7 The northern end of the Island of the Sun. The Sacred Rock and its adjacent plaza area can be seen on the right (photograph by Luis D. Gismondi ca. 1920, private collection).

FIG. 8 The ruin of Iñak Uyu is widely believed to be the remains of the Temple of the Moon (anonymous photograph, ca. 1900, private collection).

There were other structures in the sanctuary area as well. Ramos Gavilán (1988: 93 [1621: chap. 13]) writes that some thirty steps from the rock, toward the south, were located the Houses of the Sun, Thunder, and Lightning. Cobo provides a more detailed description of the temple, suggesting that it was an elaborate structure containing windows, cupboards, or niches along the walls. He also indicates that it was located some forty paces from the rock, near a maze-like storehouse. The labyrinthine storehouse that Cobo refers to is a large architectural complex called the Chinkana. Ramos Gavilán (1988: 93 [1621: bk. 1, chap. 13]) correctly places this majestic site on the southern slope of the island, in a gully facing the Peruvian shore to the west, and he indicates that it was already deteriorating when he visited the island.

The Return Home

Ramos Gavilán (1988: 170–171 [1621: bk. 1, chap. 28]) indicates that after visiting the Island of the Sun, many pilgrims traveled to the Island of the Moon (fig. 8). Cobo concurs and adds the following information: "Upon finishing their prayers and offerings at this sanctuary of Titicaca, they continued on to Coati Island, which was considered to be the second station. And since a visit to these sanctuaries was sold to them at such a high price, the result was that such visits were held in higher esteem"

Pilgrimage and the Geography of Power

(Cobo 1990: 96 [1653: bk. 13, chap. 18]). There is a large ruin on the Island of the Moon, called Iñak Uyu, which is widely believed to be the remains of that temple (Stanish and Bauer 2004).

After attending the Island of the Moon, the pilgrims began their homeward journey. Unfortunately, little is known of the status of the pilgrims after their return to their homeland. We can only speculate that it must have been great, since Garcilaso de la Vega (1966: 191 [1609: pt. 1, bk. 3, chap. 25]) notes that: "any Indian who could get a grain of that maize [of the Island of the Sun] or any seed to cast in this barn thought he would never want for bread for his whole life." Surely a person who had journeyed to the origin place of the Sun would have held considerable stature within the community.

Inka Settlement Patterns on the Island of the Sun

Recent archaeological research indicates a huge Inka presence on the Islands of the Sun and the Moon. All of the sites mentioned by the early documents have been located, and several dozen other smaller sites were discovered. The settlement system on the Island of the Sun, the larger of the two islands, is the most striking (fig. 9). The Inka may have relocated some people from existing settlements on the Island of the Sun to the mainland, and most likely imported mitimaes from across the empire, as described in the early historical documents, to repopulate it.

The Inka roads on the island were built on earlier trails that had crossed the island for millennia. The Inka were adept at formalizing earlier road systems throughout the Andes, and they did the same on the Island of the Sun. There were two principal roads that led from the southern side of the island to the Titikala area. The first begins in the Yumani area and leads north on the high ground on the west side of the island past Apachinacapata. It continues on the high ridge past some small platforms and then descends down to the Titikala area. The second road also begins in the Yumani area and continues on the east side to Apachinacapata as well. This road then descends down past the Challa Bay and follows the east side of the island past Challapampa and Kasapata, and finally the Titikala area. Inka sites are located along these roads and were constructed in part to service and/or have access to them.

One of the most striking characteristics of the Inka settlement pattern is the plethora of small sites. On the Island of the Sun, more than sixty of the sites were less than one hectare, while the largest habitation site was only a few hectares in size. This settlement distribution is characteristic of an imperial control strategy: a generally bimodal distribution of a few moderately sized administrative sites with a large number of small villages and hamlets. A similar Inka settlement pattern has also been documented on the mainland in the Juli-Pomata region (Stanish et al. 1997).

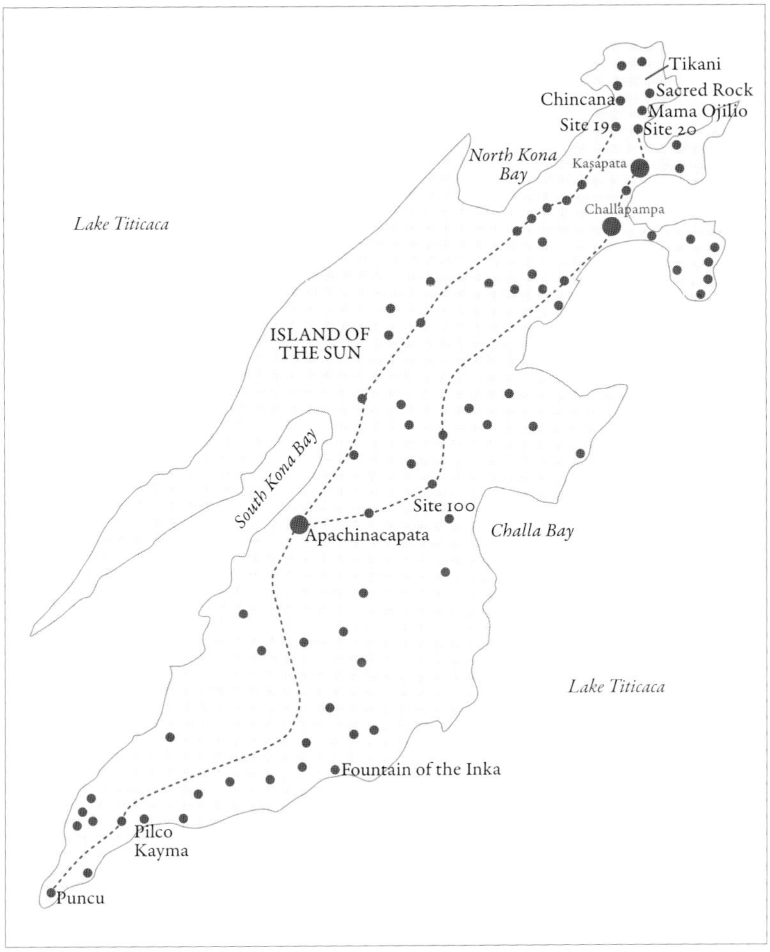

FIG. 9   Inka settlement pattern on the Island of the Sun

Apart from the lack of large administrative centers like those on the mainland such as Hatuncolla and Chucuito, it is significant that the Inka state utilized the same strategy on both the island and the mainland, scattering the bulk of the population into small settlements. Alongside these small settlements were a few larger ones that also functioned as minor administrative sites. One plausible hypothesis is that the native populations of the island were scattered into these small hamlets, while the state-dependent groups, particularly the mitimaes, were concentrated into the larger settlements. This proposition, of course, remains to be tested.

It is important to note that almost all nonritual sites on the island were located in optimal agricultural or fishing areas.[6] This settlement choice suggests that the island itself was converted into an economically productive area designed to provision the ritual specialists that were housed at the shine complex. In other words, the Island of the Sun was indeed a major ritual and pilgrimage center, but the settlement data indicate the Inka organized the populations to provide for the island's subsistence. It seems that many of the goods that sustained the people on the island, including the priests, Mamacona (female attendants), and other ritual specialists, were produced on the island.

There are three important exceptions to this pattern of economic optimization. On the southern side of the island in the natural "bowl" or small valley above the Fountain of the Inka there is a large concentration of agricultural terraces. Unlike other parts of the island, there are no Inka hamlets or villages on, or between, the terraces. The habitation sites were located on either side of the valley to the east and west, where they were concentrated in great numbers along with less formal agricultural terraces. This kind of clustering of fields and settlements is the typical pattern for the Titicaca Basin in the Inka period: a set of agricultural fields and a series of sites that housed the peasant population that worked those fields (Stanish et al. 1997). The unusual settlement pattern in and around the Fountain of the Inka demands explanation.

We explain this distribution as a function of ritual settlement determinants. That is, the Inka state forced populations to live away from this particular valley for ritual and/or aesthetic reasons. There is a large stone stairway that ascends from the lake edge up to the Yumani community. The entire valley section would have been built with beautiful terraces, perhaps housing gardens of special maize or other plants. The peasantry who worked these fields may have been forbidden to live in the valley itself.

The second area that does not conform to the optimal pattern of agricultural land use is the western part of the island. Along the lower portions of the hillside there are large terraces without any evidence of habitation sites; this possibly was an area used to grow special crops. The climate in this area is distinct due to the strong sunlight and a topography that protects the terraced areas from wind. These features create a warmer environment that could have been used to grow non-altiplano crops.

The third area that has substantial human settlement without any appreciable agricultural sustaining land is, of course, the Titikala area. A number of sites discovered in the northern section of the island are not associated with good agricultural land. Most of these are small sites located adjacent to the sanctuary area. Further north, away from the ritual area, are several small sites on the Tikani Peninsula. These are associated with modest terracing and probably housed farmers who cultivated maize and other crops for the use and maintenance of the sanctuary's religious specialists. Therefore, the Titikala area proper was not an agricultural zone and the settlement determinants in this region were largely ritual.

Our survey work on the island also identified an unusual cluster of settlements and agricultural features in the southern Kona Bay, which deserves description. This cluster is composed of a major Inka site characterized by a walled platform, which contains several niches. The site is located between two *quebradas* (ravines). Each quebrada was canalized with water diversion walls. These walls narrowed and formed the neck of a larger, oval depression located at the base of the pampa. This depression most likely functioned as a tank or reservoir. Below the tank are a series of relict raised fields. These fields do not cover an extensive area (a few hectares at most) but were used to intensively grow agricultural produce.

Finally we note that the number of sites and the total size of the habitation area during the Inka period is extremely high relative to the earlier periods, and this increase cannot be accounted for by natural population growth alone. Even accounting for some minor methodological problems, there is little doubt that people were brought into the area from elsewhere. In the case of the Island of the Sun, documentary evidence indicates that the Inka imported colonists from the mainland and elsewhere in the empire. The archaeological evidence supports these historical data.

The Antiquity of the Pilgrimage Center

One of the most fundamental questions that we addressed in our archaeological research on the Islands of the Sun and Moon concerns the antiquity of the shrine complex. The question can be framed as: did the Inka create a shrine *de novo* or did the empire appropriate an already existing ritual complex? To answer this question we must examine the pre-Inka remains on the island.

THE ALTIPLANO PERIOD SETTLEMENTS OF THE ISLANDS (AD 1100–1450)

The time immediately prior to Inka expansion in the Titicaca Basin is referred to as the Altiplano or Late Intermediate period (Hyslop n.d.; Lumbreras 1974; Stanish et al. 1997). It is defined as the time after the collapse of the Tiwanaku state (ca. AD 1100) and prior to the control of the area by the Inka (ca. AD 1450). The fall of the Tiwanaku polity led to an era of conflict in the Titicaca Basin. During this period, the former political organization shifted from a centralized state to a series of smaller entities, and the region witnessed the development of the Aymara polities (*señoríos*).

By far, the two largest polities of the lake region during the Altiplano period were the Lupaqa and the Colla. The Lupaqa capital was at the town of Chucuito, on the Peruvian side of the lake. They controlled territories as far south as the Desaguadero River, and possibly even further. To the north, they controlled the Puno Bay, and possibly up to the town of Paucarcolla. The Colla were located in the northwestern and northern basins. Their capital was Hatuncolla, near Sillustani. Their territory abutted the Lupaqa to the south, and extended north well away from the lake region.

Cieza de León suggests that the Island of the Sun was conquered by either the Lupaqa or the Colla. But he is ambiguous about which group conquered the islands. In the same section of his book, however, Cieza de León relates that there was subsequent fighting with the Canas and Canchi, and then the famous meeting of Viracocha Inka with the Lupaqa king in Chucuito (Cieza 1976: 232–235 [1554: pt. 2, chap. 52]). If we take the sequence of events as generally chronologically correct, then the Island of the Sun could have been conquered by either polity. However, if we assume that the death of the Colla paramount at the hands of the Lupaqa at Paucarcolla meant that the Colla lost regional influence, then it would be likely that the Island of the Sun would have fallen under Lupaqa control.

The evidence that the island was part of the Lupaqa polity immediately prior to the conquest of the area by the Inka is indirect at best, but it is compelling. In the first instance, the island is located close to the core Lupaqa territory. The pottery diagnostics on the island fit into the general southern tradition of the Titicaca Basin as a whole. These pottery styles are typical of Lupaqa area sites along the southwest side of the lake (Stanish et. al 1997). Furthermore, the Inka may have continued the tradition of Lupaqa presence in the Copacabana area by sending representatives of the Lupaqa within their mitimae program (Diez de San Miguel 1964 [1567]: 81; Ramos Gavilán 1988: 84–85 [1621: chap. 20]).

The settlement pattern of the Island of the Sun during the Altiplano period indicates a population size substantially lower than that of the Inka period and only marginally higher or equal to the earlier Tiwanaku period. These data conform to the general patterns of the region as a whole (cf. Stanish et al. 1997; Stanish 1997). Average site sizes reverted to pre-Tiwanaku levels as well, also typical of the region. Sites were scattered over the island, clustering in the richest agricultural areas such as the Challa Bay and the Kalabaya Peninsula (fig. 10).

During the Altiplano period in the Titicaca Basin, people built fortified sites called *pukaras*. On the Island of the Sun, there was one major fortified site (Kurupata) that had been occupied since pre-Tiwanaku times. This hilltop site, still called a pukara today, is surrounded by a fortification wall. During the Altiplano period, this site was most likely used as the principal fortified site on the Island of the Sun.

The status of the Sacred Rock area during the Altiplano period remains ambiguous. Settlement in the northern Titikala area (the entire part of the island in the sanctuary area) was reduced to only a few sites. The sites are not large and there is no evidence for any special constructions or elite/ceremonial artifacts. Excavations adjacent to the Sacred Rock itself indicate only an Inka occupation. There is no evidence of a special ritual site, nor is there any evidence that the Tiwanaku site of Chucaripupata

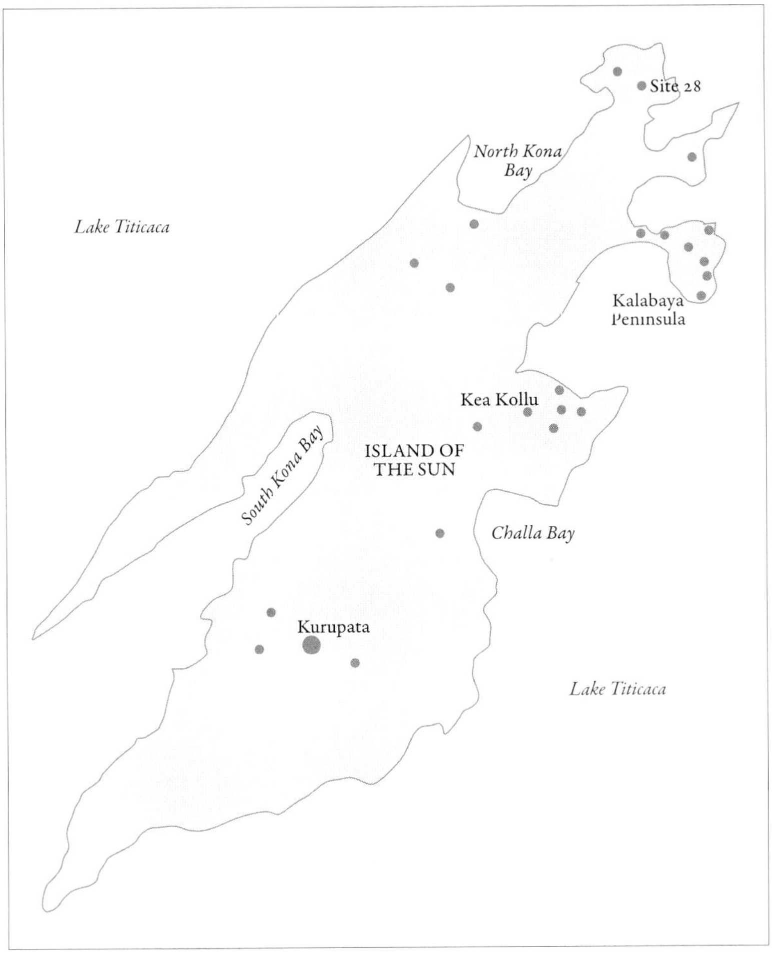

FIG. 10 The Altiplano-period settlements of the Island of the Sun

continued to be occupied in the Altiplano period in the entire Titikala area. In short, there is no evidence of a regional shrine during this period.

It is nevertheless significant that people continued to live in this agriculturally poor but ritually rich area. The main Altiplano-period occupation in the Titikala area is Site 28, a moderately sized settlement in the region. This site has no evidence of corporate or ritual architecture, but is located in an area that is not economically rich. Likewise, documentary evidence suggests that there was a shrine at the time of Inka conquest. Finally, the fact that the shrine was appropriated by the Inka also implies continuity from the Tiwanaku period. The settlement, excavation, and historical data therefore suggest that the Sacred Rock area was a local huaca of the Altiplano-period polity on the island. In other words, this would have been a pattern of shrine worship in the absence of large-scale political authority. While there is little doubt that a regional shrine did not exist, the question as to whether there was a local shrine remains open.

Pilgrimage and the Geography of Power

THE TIWANAKU OCCUPATION: THE FIRST PILGRIMAGE CENTER

Sometime in the middle of the first millennium AD, the peoples of Tiwanaku began to expand from their homeland in the Tiwanaku Valley to create the first indigenous state of the Andean altiplano. At its height, Tiwanaku would control a large territory throughout the Titicaca Basin. The Islands of the Sun and Moon were one of the first areas to be controlled by this expanding polity around the sixth or seventh century AD (Seddon n.d., 2004).

Evidence of Tiwanaku occupation on the Islands of the Sun and Moon was found more than one hundred years ago. In 1895 Bandelier recovered a number of Tiwanaku pottery vessels from the islands and the nearby mainland. He also recovered various Tiwanaku gold and silver objects. Likewise, work by Johan Reinhard and associates discovered Tiwanaku pottery and metal objects off the island of Koa (Ponce Sanginés et al. 1992; Reinhard 1992a, b).

Our survey and excavation work provides additional information on the Tiwanaku occupations on the Islands of the Sun and Moon. The survey located twenty-eight Tiwanaku sites on the Island of the Sun, and two on the Island of the Moon. The total number of sites decreased from the earlier period, but the mean site size of the Tiwanaku settlements was larger, averaging over one hectare. Tiwanaku continued the process of settlement nucleation that began in the previous period and reached the highest average site size in the history of the Island.

The survey data make it clear that the islands were a fundamental part of the Tiwanaku polity, and we interpret them to indicate that the island was incorporated into the Tiwanaku state around AD 600. Two sites emerged as the principal settlements on the Island of the Sun during this period: Chucaripupata and Wakuyu. The site of Wakuyu has no remaining architecture. However, several observations suggest that Wakuyu was a major site with elaborate architecture. The site is located on a low hill, surrounded by terraces. The terraces have a high density of pottery on the surface, indicating that they were domestic terraces and were used at one point as floor surfaces for houses. Since excavations in other Tiwanaku sites have revealed wall enclosures and a small sunken court in similar flat areas, we believe that this site may also contain elaborate structures beneath the modern ground surface (Stanish et al. 1997). Alberto Perrin Pando (1957) excavated at the site and discovered several Classic Tiwanaku pottery vessels. He also noted that the hill was artificial, and he discovered at least one major wall at the site.

The site of Chucaripupata is about the same size as Wakuyu and there is also no evidence of corporate architecture on the surface. However, excavations by Matthew Seddon indicate that there were indeed substantial architectural constructions at the site. He discovered a series of large

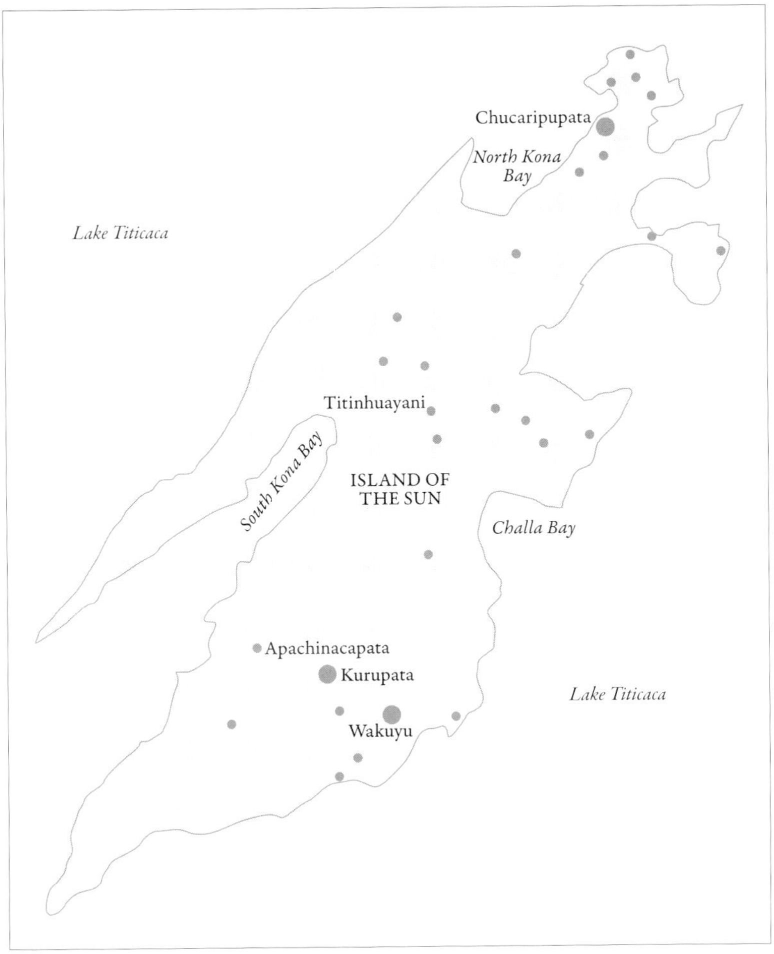

FIG. 11 Tiwanaku settlement pattern on the Island of the Sun

walls, domestic areas, and terraces. Furthermore, Seddon's excavations recovered a large number of elite ceramic vessels not typical of simple village sites (Seddon n.d., 2004). In short, there were at least two major Tiwanaku settlements on the Island of the Sun, one located near the richest economic area, the Challa Bay, and the second located near the Sacred Rock.

Settlement and excavation evidence suggests that the Sacred Rock area was first utilized in a systematic manner as a pilgrimage destination by the Tiwanaku state. The survey data, as seen in figure 11, reveal several Tiwanaku sites in a line along a road between Apachinacapata and Chucaripupata. The two-meter-wide road begins at least at Apachinacapata, continues along the ridge above Challa and Kasapata, and drops down to the site of Chucaripupata within the sanctuary area. This pattern constitutes the first evidence for any kind of formalized pilgrimage route from the historically known landing place in the south of the island to the sanctuary in the north. Curiously, there is no line of Tiwanaku sites

Pilgrimage and the Geography of Power

along the low, eastern side of the island where the Inka road and a series of Inka settlements were constructed much later.

It is during the Tiwanaku period that we see the first construction of a major site with corporate construction in the Titikala area. This, of course, is the site of Chucaripupata. It is also significant that the population of the northern end of the island increased along with a simultaneous aggregation of population into Chucaripupata. In the Tiwanaku period, therefore, there were two principal population centers on the Island of the Sun. One can be interpreted as the political and economic center, located in the Challa area. Chucaripupata, in contrast, is best interpreted as the focus of political and religious ritual (Seddon 2004).

Survey and excavation work on the Island of the Moon indicate that its ceremonial center, the temple site of Iñak Uyu, was occupied in the Tiwanaku period as well (Bauer, Covey, and Terry 2004). At this site, there is solid evidence of a major Tiwanaku occupation lying beneath the Inka complex. The fact that substantial numbers of ritually significant objects dating to the Tiwanaku period (for example, *incensarios*, finely made queros [drinking vessels], and gold and silver objects) were recovered at Iñak Uyu supports the hypothesis that a ritual pilgrimage complex was established on the islands by the Tiwanaku state.

In summary, the Islands of the Sun and Moon were incorporated into the Tiwanaku state around the middle of the first millennium AD. The first formalized pilgrimage route to the Titicala area was created at the same time that control of the islands was established. Prior to this time, the Sacred Rock area and the Island of the Moon may have been important local huacas, but there is no evidence of a pan-regional significance. In the Tiwanaku period, a ritual complex, complete with major architectural constructions and possible attendant populations, was established on both the islands. The incorporation of the Islands of the Sun and the Moon, and the creation of a pilgrimage route, would have been an integral part of the process of Tiwanaku imperialism as it expanded throughout the Titicaca region and beyond.

Shrine Worship and Regional Control in the Inka Empire

We take a modified Durkheimian perspective to understand the religious complex in the southern Titicaca Basin. The shrines of the Islands of the Sun and Moon were maintained by the Inka state to impart a sense of legitimacy to their rule in Collasuyu in particular, and throughout the empire in general. The overriding purpose of the complex was to impart a sense of political legitimacy in their control of the region. By controlling the Islands of the Sun and the Moon, the Inka were able to compete successfully with local elites, specifically the Lupaqa nobility, for ideological hegemony in the region. At the same time, they converted the islands into a great pilgrimage center that profoundly affected their attempts to create and exert control over the ideology of the conquered provinces throughout their empire.

There is a tendency in contemporary scholarship to downplay the role of hierarchies, or at the very least, to inflate the role of nonelite in various forms of resistance to state authority. There is no question that commoner populations can successfully resist elite hegemony, particularly ideological hegemony in state and imperial contexts. That resistance often takes its most successful form as "unofficial" or "illegal" religions. We recognize that such resistance took place in the Inka state, alongside that of overt political resistance to state control. However, we locate that ideological resistance to state control not in the pan-regional pilgrimage centers under the control of the state, but rather in the local huacas and shrines maintained by nonelite populations under Inka authority.

The later Spanish Catholic domination provides a useful analogy. Overt resistance to Spanish ideology did not take place in the large Jesuit or Dominican urban centers, but in the countryside where people continued to worship "pagan" shrines. The extirpation of idolatry by Spanish religious authorities, backed by the power of the state, did not concentrate on large cities as much as it focused on rural and semirural communities where such practices persisted. The most significant resistance to ideological hegemony was not concentrated in the large centers like Lima, Cusco, or even Copacabana, but rather in the rural countryside where unofficial religious ideological practices continued to be practiced.

We reject a Turnerian perspective that sees pilgrimage centers as counter-hegemonic phenomena. Rather, the Island of the Sun and its sister shrine, the Island of the Moon, were state constructions designed and perpetuated to maintain state ideological and political control. The Inka appropriated a ritual center of earlier cultures, and they expanded and elaborated it on a scale previously unseen in Titicaca Basin history. In other words, a religious center was not only taken over but it was turned into a pan-Andean center of unprecedented scale and importance.

This pan-Andean aspect represents a level achieved by the Inka that the Tiwanaku state and its immediate successors did not, and could not attempt. At the time of the European invasion, the Islands of the Sun and Moon were ritually and politically significant not only for the Aymara-speakers of the Titicaca Basin, but for all the peoples of the Inka Empire. The Inka converted what was a regional shrine into an imperial pilgrimage destination. A shrine of significance to an earlier and smaller state (Tiwanaku) and later a conflict-ridden local polity (the Lupaqa), it was converted into the birthplace of the cosmos and origin of the founding lineage of Tawantinsuyu. In this master stroke, the Inka intellectuals not only co-opted a shrine of regional importance in what was arguably their richest highland province, Collasuyu, but converted it into a center that sanctified the very founding and existence of their state in Cusco.

The shrine complex on the Islands of the Sun and the Moon was a fundamental element of the expansion process of the Inka Empire as it incorporated the heartland of Collasuyu. As such, the journey to the islands served both overt and covert political ends. The pilgrimage complex was also of profound religious significance to the thousands of people that visited each year. During Inka times, and most likely in the earlier Tiwanaku period, these islands were the final destination point of pilgrims on a religious journey. Although this journey was through an Andean landscape, many aspects of the trip mirrored elements of pilgrimages worldwide. This ritualized movement from the ordinary to the divine is especially clear in the pilgrim's progress to the Islands of the Sun and the Moon. It was a structured passage through a series of gates, ports, and landings of greater and greater sanctity. The pilgrims entered the Copacabana Peninsula through the guarded Yunguyu gates and spent several days journeying across mitimae-controlled lands to the port of Yampupata. After traveling by boat to the southeast tip of the Island of the Sun, they traveled on foot to the sanctuary area at its northwest end. The fact that the pilgrimage destinations were islands served to physically, and perhaps spiritually, separate them from the mainland. In this sense, the use of an island as a pilgrimage destination provided a clear separation between the most sacred and the less sacred, with the act of crossing the lake mediating this divide.

The pilgrims approached the area of the Sacred Rock by passing through one or more doorways, where they handed their offerings to the resident priests. It is not by chance that the final destination of the pilgrims was on the point of land furthest from the mainland at the northwest end of the island. Like many pilgrimage centers of the world, the sanctuary was situated in a remote location that served to emphasize its other-worldliness. A trip to the island sanctuary was to leave behind the recognizable shores of the mainland, and the ordinary, and journey to the point of cosmic origins.

Travel through the sacred landscape of Copacabana and the islands was not casual or incidental, but it reflected a regulated set of movements that stressed the special nature of the journey. Pilgrims gave confessions and abstained from certain foods as they passed though the various entrances, thereby physically and spiritually cleansing themselves. As the pilgrims trekked across the Copacabana region, they were supervised and monitored by the priests and attendants of the shrines. Through the tightly controlled access to the Copacabana area and the preparatory rites that the visitors underwent, the pilgrim's journey was transformed beyond simple travel and became a ritual itself (Coleman and Elsner 1995: 25).

Furthermore, by controlling access to the region and the sanctuaries, and by dictating the manner in which the pilgrims passed through each of the various entrances, the state was able to impose its own ideological character on the shrines. By imposing conformity on the ritual actions of the pilgrims, the state constrained, if not largely determined, the visitors' experiences at the shrines (Eade and Sallnow 1991: 11).

The Inka state was heavily invested in the maintenance of the island sanctuaries. The Inkas performed a number of annual rites, including the December and June solstice rituals, on the Islands of the Sun and the Moon. They presented a wide range of offerings, from maize beer (*chicha*) to children, to the Sacred Rock. The Inka removed the existing population of the islands and the surrounding mainland, replacing them with as many as 2,000 colonists from across the empire. They also established groups of elite women on the islands whose role was to serve the sanctuaries. Furthermore, they built a number of state facilities on the mainland and the islands, including temples, storehouses, specialized housing for the attendants, and lodging for pilgrims.

The Sacred Rock and the surrounding sanctuary were extensively modified by the Inka state. The convex side of the rock held an elaborate metal altar and a stone offering place, while the opposite side was covered with fine textiles produced by the servants of the state. A plaza area was built in front of the rock and a series of state structures were constructed in the sanctuary. With each of these additions the state altered the contents of the sanctuary area and asserted its authority. Likewise, the trip to the rock was also controlled and shaped by the state. Pilgrims were granted permission to enter the Copacabana area by official guards, and once inside they were fed and clothed from state warehouses and housed in state hostels. Although the pilgrims traveled through a sacred landscape, the panorama, both physical and ideological, was filled with symbols of the state. The powers of the state and those of the sacred locations, points of intense religious devotion, became intermixed and inseparable.

Notes

1   Among the many descriptions of Pachacamac are: Hernando Pizarro (1959: 82–83 [1553]); Pedro Cieza de León (1976: 334–337 [1554: pt. 1, chap. 72]); Hernando de Santillan (1950: 58–59 [1563]); Pedro Pizarro (1921: 244 [1571]); Cristobal de Albornoz (1984: 214 [ca. 1582]); Miguel Cabello Valboa (1951: 338 [1586]); and the Huarochirí manuscript (1991 [ca. 1608]).

2   In some early records, Lake Titicaca is called "Lake of Chucuito," after the capital of the nearby Lupaqa kingdom.

3   See Meiklejohn (1988) for a discussion of the relationship between the Church and the Lupaqa peoples in the colonial period.

4   Because Cobo incorporated a number of different sources into his chronicle, including those of Cieza de León and Ramos Gavilán, the work is at times contradictory. This is certainly the case for his accounts of the Inka conquest of the Lake Titicaca region and his descriptions of the Island of the Sun.

5   A pillco or pillku bird is described by González Holguín (1989: 285 [1608]): "Apillco ppichu. Un pájaro de los Andes colorado preciado por las plumas [A colorful Andean bird prized for its feathers]."

6   There is a similar pattern on the mainland as evidenced by the settlement data from the Juli-Pomata survey (Stanish et al. 1997).

References cited

ALBORNOZ, CRISTOBAL DE
    1984 [1582]   Instrucción para descubrir todas las guacas del Pirú y sus camayos y haziendas. *Albornoz y el espacio ritual andino prehispánico* (Pierre Duviols, ed.). *Revista Andina* 2 (1): 169–222.

BANDELIER, ADOLPH
    1910   *The Islands of Titicaca and Koati*. The Hispanic Society of America, New York.

BAUER, BRIAN
    1992a   *The Development of the Inca State*. University of Texas Press, Austin.
    1992b   Ritual Pathways of the Inca: An Analysis of the Collasuyu Ceques in Cuzco, Peru. *Latin American Antiquity* 3 (3): 183–205.
    1996   Legitimization of the State in Inca Myth and Ritual. *American Anthropologist* 98 (2): 327–337.
    1998   *The Sacred Landscape of the Inca: The Cuzco Ceque System*. University of Texas Press, Austin.
    2004   *Ancient Cuzco: Heartland of the Inca*. University of Texas Press, Austin.

BAUER, BRIAN, AND CHARLES STANISH
    2001   *Ritual and Pilgrimage in the Ancient Andes: The Islands of the Sun and Moon*. University of Texas Press, Austin.

BAUER, BRIAN, R. ALAN COVEY, AND JOSHUA TERRY
    2004   Excavations at the site of Iñak Uyu, Island of the Moon. In *Archaeological Research on the Islands of the Sun and Moon, Lake Titicaca Bolivia: Final Results from the Proyecto Tiksi Kjarka* (Charles Stanish and Brian S. Bauer, eds.): 139–173. Cotsen Institute of Archaeology, University of California Press, Los Angeles.

BERTONIO, LUDOVICO
    1984   *Vocabulario de la lengua Aymará*. Centro de Estudios de la Realidad Económica y Social, Cochabamba, Bolivia.

BOWMAN, GLENN
    1991   Christian Ideology and the Image of the Holy Land: The Place of Jerusalem in the Various Christianities. In *Contesting the Sacred: The Anthropology of Christian Pilgrimage* (John Eade and Michael Sallnow, eds.): 98–121. Routledge, London.

CABELLO VALBOA, MIGUEL
    1951 [1586]   *Miscelánea antártica; una história del Perú antíguo con prólogo, notas e índices a cargo del Instituto de Etnología (Seminario de Historia del Perú-Incas)*. Universidad Nacional Mayor de San Marcos, Instituto de Etnología, Lima.

CALANCHA, ANTONIO DE LA
    1982 [1638] *Corónica moralizada del orden de San Augustín en el Perú* (I. Prado Pastor, ed.). Universidad Nacional Mayor de San Marcos, Lima.

CIEZA DE LEÓN, PEDRO
    1967 [1554] *El Señorío de los Incas: Segunda parte de la crónica del Perú* (C. Araníbar, ed.). Instituto de Estudios Peruanos, Lima.

COBO, BERNABÉ
    1979 [1653] *History of the Inca Empire* (Roland Hamilton, trans.). University of Texas Press, Austin.
    1990 [1653] *Inca Religion and Customs* (Roland Hamilton, trans.). University of Texas Press, Austin.

COLEMAN, SIMON, AND JOHN ELSNER
    1995 *Pilgrimage: Past and Present in the World Religions.* Harvard University Press, Cambridge, Mass.

DIEZ DE SAN MIGUEL, GARCI
    1964 [1567] *Visita hecha a la provincia de Chucuito.* Ediciones de la Casa de la Cultura de Perú, Lima.

EADE, JOHN, AND MICHAEL J. SALLNOW (EDS.)
    1991 *Contesting the Sacred: The Anthropology of Christian Pilgrimage.* Routledge, London.

ESPINOZA SORIANO, WALDEMAR
    1972 *Los Huancas, aliados de la Conquista: Tres informaciones inéditas sobre la participación indígena en la conquista del Perú, 1558–1560–1561.* Universidad Nacional del Centro del Perú, Huancayo.

GARCILASO DE LA VEGA, EL INCA
    1966 [1609] *The Royal Commentaries of the Incas and General History of Peru*, parts 1 and 2 (H. V. Livermore, trans.). University of Texas Press, Austin.

GONZÁLEZ HOLGUÍN, DIEGO
    1989 [1608] *Vocabulario de la lengua general de todo el Perú llamada lengua Quichua o del Inca.* Presentación de Ramiro Matos Mendieta. Prólogo de Raúl Porras Barrenechea. Universidad Nacional Mayor de San Marcos, Editorial de la Universidad, Lima.

HYSLOP, JOHN
    1990 *Inka Settlement Planning.* University of Texas Press, Austin.
    n.d. An Archaeological Investigation of the Lupaqa Kingdom and Its Origins. Ph.D. dissertation, Department of Anthropology. Columbia University, New York, 1976.

LUMBRERAS, LUIS G.
   1974   *The Peoples and Cultures of Ancient Peru* (Betty J. Meggers, trans.). Smithsonian Institution Press, Washington, D.C.

MACCORMACK, SABINE
   1991   *Religion in the Andes: Vision and Imagination in Early Colonial Peru.* Princeton University Press, Princeton, N.J.

MANNHEIM, BRUCE
   1991   *The Language of the Inka Since the European Invasion.* University of Texas Press, Austin.

MEIKLEJOHN, NORMAN
   1988   *La iglesia y los Lupaqas de Chucuito durante la colonia.* Centro de Estudios Rurales Andinos "Bartolomé de las Casas," Instituto de Estudios Aymaras, Cusco, Perú.

MORRIS, CRAIG, AND ADRIANA VON HAGEN
   1993   *The Inka Empire and Its Andean Origins.* Abbeville Press, New York.

PERRIN PANDO, ALBERTO
   1957   Las tumbas subterraneas de Wakuyo. In *Arqueología Boliviana* (Carlos Ponce Sanginés, ed.): 173–205. Alcaldía Municipal, La Paz.

PIZARRO, HERNANDO
   1959 [1553]   Carta a la Audiencia de Santo Domingo. In *Cartas del Perú (1524–1543)* (Raúl Porras Barrenechea, ed.): 77–84. Colleción de documentos inéditos para la historia del Perú 3. Sociedad de Bibliófilos Peruanos, Lima.

PIZARRO, PEDRO
   1921 [1571]   *Relation of the Discovery and Conquest of the Kingdoms of Peru* (Philip Ainsworth Means, trans.). Cortes Society, New York.

PONCE SANGINÉS, CARLOS, JOHAN REINHARD, MAX PORTUGAL, EDUARDO PAREJA, AND LEOCADIO TICLLA
   1992   *Exploraciones arqueológicas subacuáticas en el Lago Titikaka.* Editorial La Palabra Producciones, La Paz.

RAMOS GAVILÁN, ALONSO
   1988 [1621]   *Historia del santuario de nuestra Señora de Copacabana* (I. Prado Pastor, ed.): Gráfico P. L. Villanueva S.A., Lima.

REINHARD, JOHAN
   1983   High Altitude Archaeology and Mountain Worship in the Andes. *American Alpine Journal* 25: 54–67.
   1985   Sacred Mountains: An Ethno-Archaeological Study of High Andean Ruins. *Mountain Research and Development* 5 (4): 299–317.

1992a Investigaciones arqueológicas subacuáticas en el lago Titikaka. In *Exploraciones arqueológicas subacuáticas en el Lago Titikaka* (Ponce Sanginés, Johan Reinhard, Max Portugal, Eduardo Pareja, and Leocadio Ticlla, eds.): 421–530. Editorial La Palabra Producciones, La Paz.

1992b Underwater Archaeological Research in Lake Titicaca. In *Ancient America: Contributions to New World Archaeology* (Nicholas Saunders, ed.): 117–143. Oxbow Books, Oxford, England.

ROBINSON, MARTIN

1997 *Sacred Places, Pilgrim Paths: An Anthology of Pilgrimage.* Marshall Pickering, London.

SALLNOW, MICHAEL J.

1991 Pilgrimage and Cultural Fracture in the Andes. In *Contesting the Sacred: The Anthropology of Christian Pilgrimage* (John Eade and Michael J. Sallnow, eds.): 137–153. Routledge, London.

1987 *Pilgrims of the Andes: Regional Cults in Cuzco.* Smithsonian Institution Press, Washington, D.C.

SALOMON, FRANK, AND GEORGE C. VRIOSTE

1991 [1608] *The Huarochirí Manuscript: A Testament of Ancient and Colonial Andean Religion.* Translation from the Quechua edition by Frank Salomon and George L. Urioste. University of Texas Press, Austin.

SANTILLÁN, HERNANDO DE

1950 [1563] Relación del origin, descendencia política y gobierno de los Incas. In *Tres relaciones de antigüedades peruanas* (M. Jiménez de la Espada, ed.): 33–131. Editorial Guaranía, Asunción, Paraguay.

SARMIENTO DE GAMBOA, PEDRO

2007 [1572] *History of the Incas* (Brian S. Bauer and Vania Smith, trans. and eds. Introduction by Brian S. Bauer and Jean-Jacques Decoster). University of Texas Press, Austin.

SCHREIBER, KATHARINA

1992 *Wari Imperialism in Middle Horizon Peru.* Anthropological Papers of the Museum of Anthropology, University of Michigan, Ann Arbor.

SEDDON, MATTHEW

2004 Excavations at the Site of Chucaripupata: A Tiwanaku IV and V Temple and Domestic Occupation. In *Archaeological Research on the Islands of the Sun and Moon, Lake Titicaca, Bolivia: Final Results of the Proyecto Tiksi Kjarka* (Charles

Stanish and Brian S. Bauer, eds.): 93–137. Cotsen Institute of Archaeology, University of California, Los Angeles.

　n.d.　Ritual, Power, and the Development of a Complex Society: The Island of the Sun and the Tiwanaku State. Ph.D. dissertation, Department of Anthropology, University of Chicago, 1998.

SHIMADA, IZUMI (ED.)
　1991　*Pachacamac: A Reprint of the 1903 Edition.* And, *Pachacamac Archaeology* (Max Uhle). University Museum Monograph 62. University Museum of Archaeology and Anthropology, University of Pennsylvania, Philadelphia.

SQUIER, EPHRAIM GEORGE
　1877　*Peru; Incidents of Travel and Exploration in the Land of the Incas.* Harper and Brothers, New York.

STANISH, CHARLES
　1997　Nonmarket Imperialism in a Prehispanic Context: The Inca Occupation of the Titicaca Basin. *Latin American Antiquity* 8 (3): 1–18.

　2003　*Ancient Titicaca: The Evolution of Complex Society in Southern Peru and Northern Bolivia.* University of California Press, Berkeley.

STANISH, CHARLES, AND BRIAN S. BAUER (EDS.)
　2004　*Archaeological Research on the Islands of the Sun and the Moon, Lake Titicaca, Bolivia: Final Results of the Proyecto Tiksi Kjarka.* Cotsen Institute of Archaeology, University of California, Los Angeles.

STANISH, CHARLES, EDMUNDO DE LA VEGA, LEE STEADMAN, CECÍLIA CHÁVEZ, J., KIRK LAWRENCE FRYE, LUPERIO ONOFRE, MATTHEW SEDDON, AND PERCY CALISAYA CHUQUIMIA
　1997　*Archaeological Survey in the Juli-Desaguadero Area of Lake Titicaca Basin, Southern Peru.* Fieldiana Anthropology, new series, 29. Field Museum of Natural History, Chicago, Ill.

XÉREZ, FRANCISCO DE
　1985　*Verdadera relación de la conquista del Perú.* Edición de Concepción Bravo. Historia 16, Madrid.

The Inkas in the Southlands

Terence N. D'Altroy
Verónica I. Williams
Ana María Lorandi

WHEN THE INKAS DREW THE REGION SOUTHEAST OF CUSCO INTO Tawantinsuyu, they took possession of a breathtakingly variegated land inhabited by an equally diverse populace. Over time, they created Kollasuyu, the largest of the four parts (*suyu*) of the realm, from the rich, populous altiplano, the more temperate valleys of the intermontane south and flanking piedmonts, Atacama's perennial desert, and America's most commanding peaks (fig. 1).[1] Today, that region takes in a corner of Peru, much of Bolivia, northwest Argentina, and half of Chile. Notwithstanding a century's research, we know much less about the Pre-Hispanic societies south of Lake Titicaca and Cusco's reign than elsewhere in Tawantinsuyu. A number of factors have contributed to that imbalance, but the limited interest shown by the Spanish Crown and its agents surely played a crucial role. The major chroniclers, with rare exception, wrote little about the empire's southern 1,500 km, in part because the conquest of the north allowed the Spaniards to extinguish Inka rule in the south. With the striking exception of Potosí's silver deposits, discovered in 1544, the conquistadores also found that the south held fewer people or riches than Peru. Some societies also resisted Spanish domination for a century and a half, so that the Inkas were a distant memory by the time many subjects were drawn into the viceroyalty. The relatively meager historical coverage these conditions fostered—not just in the chronicles, but also in detailed inspections and court records—has tended to magnify our vision of the region's marginality within the Inka realm.

The respite between Inka and Spanish rule has created a different challenge for archaeology. The shifts in material culture that marked the end of Cusco's power in the north are not readily evident in the south, and

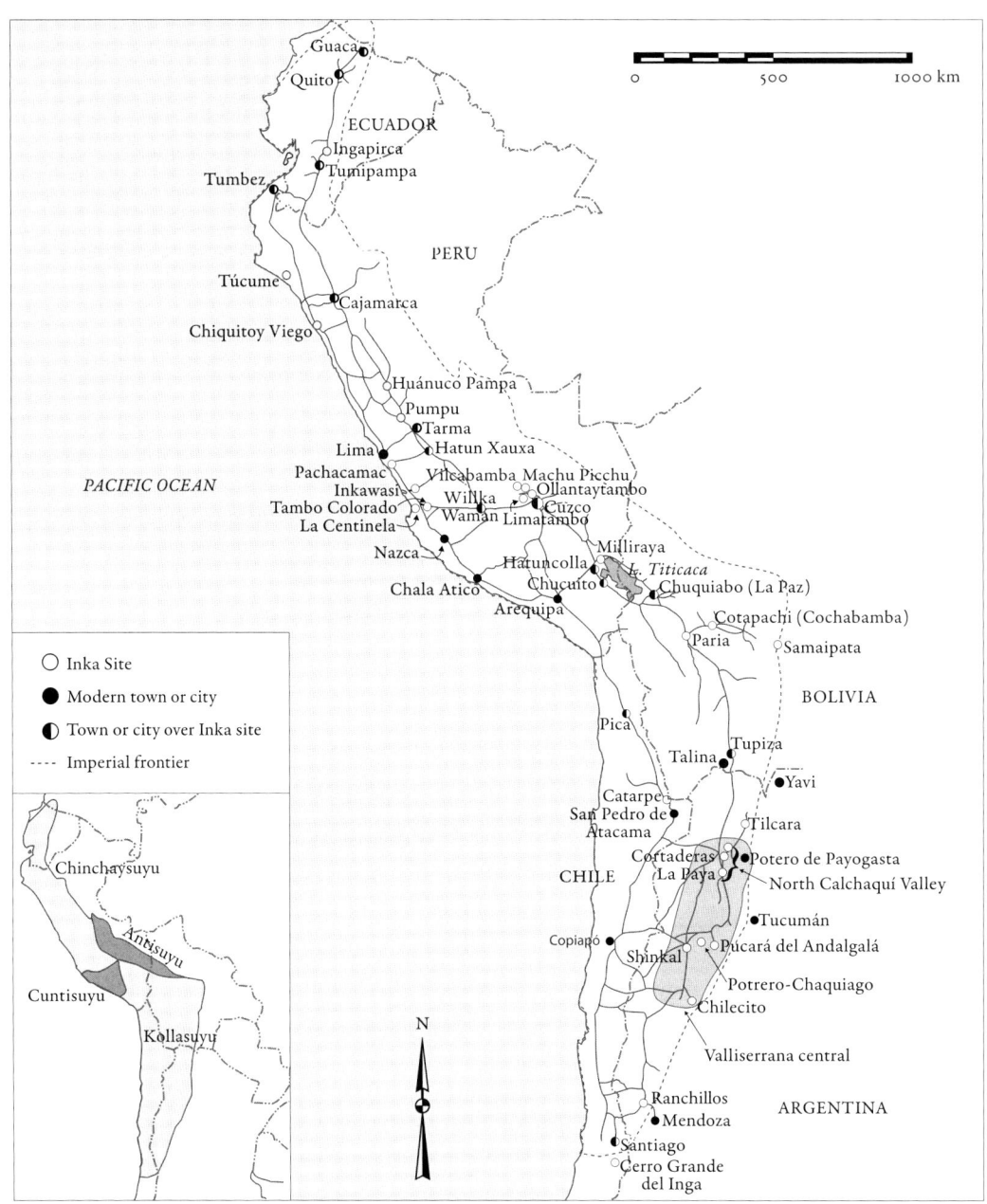

FIG. 1 The southern Andes, showing the main highways and trunk routes of the Inka road system (after Raffino 1983: inset map; and Hyslop 1984: frontispiece)

there is no temporal archaeological marker comparable to the inception of the Spanish historical record. Moreover, the south was enormous, but its population was generally sparser than that of the central Andes and it lay far away from the Inka heartland. Agricultural lands were limited and the imperial infrastructure boasted neither provincial centers nor roads that could rival the impressive facilities built between Lake Titicaca and Quito. Modern archaeological research has also been less intense than in the central Andes, and much of the region remains to be systematically surveyed. As a result, archaeology has added to the perception that the southern Andes were marginal to Inka interests (González 1983).

Even so, there is widespread evidence for substantial Inka involvement in the region. In fact, the intensity of state activities—as judged from the density of state installations—was notably higher than on Peru's north coast and in southern Ecuador, both regions that drew a great deal of imperial attention. Just as in the north, the Inkas clearly had a grand strategic view in organizing their southern domain, which they adjusted to the social and natural conditions of each area. Throughout the south, the Inkas built installations to conduct their activities and resettled colonists at strategic locations where the occupation had previously been scant. Two major highways linked those installations, paralleling the high mountains, and a series of routes joined the major routes of transit or provided access to the flanking lowlands. Raffino (1983b; 1993) and his colleagues have catalogued over 300 Inka installations or local sites with intrusive Inka sectors from the edge of the altiplano on south. Although the major centers have probably all been recorded, recently intensified research has recorded scores of new Inka sites. The frontier from central Bolivia southward contains numerous fortifications, many of which appear to have been erected late in Cusco's reign. The evidence for the exploitation of mineral wealth is plentiful, corroborating the rationale for Inka interest often expressed in the early documents. State managers also intensified other forms of production, creating farms that were comparable to those farther north and a major step upward in production from indigenous agriculture. In addition, the known high-elevation Inka ceremonial sites are heavily concentrated in the southern cordillera.

In short, the Inkas seem to have reorganized the south following policies like those applied in the north but at a scale proportionate to the region; that is, appreciably less extensive than in Peru, but equally significant for the region's peoples. The apparent modesty of the Inka presence is thus a product both of reality and of the ways in which information has been accrued and assessed. Under these circumstances, understanding the southern empire requires both a macroregional perspective and a comparative assessment of divergent local situations. It also requires that we draw inferences from a sketchier database and rely more heavily on archaeology than scholars do elsewhere. Our goal in this paper is to summarize the broad picture, while noting that our information is drawn from an uneven and probably not fully representative cross-section of evidence.

The Pre-Inka Setting
Despite the slim documentary record, we know that the ethnic composition of the southern Andes was variegated. As is the case elsewhere, the

FIG. 2 The principal ethnic groups of the southern Andes, according to early colonial sources (16th–17th c.)

Inka demographic reshuffling and Spanish misrepresentations of the native societies complicates our understanding. Typically, the identities historically attributed to particular peoples depended a great deal on who was doing the naming and under what circumstances. In the early colonial period, the peoples of northwest Argentina were often subsumed under very broad terms such as the Diaguitas, Calchaquíes, and Tucumanos. That practice may have been a convenient shorthand for administrators, but it simplified a complex social landscape of which the Inkas were well aware (Lorandi and Boixadós 1987–88; Lorandi 1988). In figure 2, we present the locations of the major ethnic groups of late prehistory. The native societies probably comprised several score distinct groups, whose distribution did not necessarily correspond neatly with the organization of political entities. The polities of the main valleys were far more complex and grander in scale than those of the eastern plains, even though the *etnías* (ethnic groups) of the mountains occupied smaller territories.

A brief review of settlement organization, public architecture, agriculture, and mortuary treatments from an archaeological perspective will help to sketch out the nature of the pre-Inka societies living in the region. To judge from the available information, those societies ranged from acephalous, semisedentary groups to mid-range polities that exhibited some degree of political ranking, but no evidence of social classes. González (1983) has estimated that the largest polities of the Regional Developments period encompassed no more than 20,000 people, and most of the political entities may well have been substantially smaller. Nevertheless, ranked or perhaps even incipiently stratified societies were present in some locations, notably in the valliserrana of northwest Argentina.

The Quebrada de Humahuaca, and the Calchaquí, Santa María, Hualfín, and Abaucán valleys all exhibited hierarchical settlement patterns with several town-sized communities. Among the largest of the settlements were Quilmes and Fuerte Quemado in the Santa María Valley; the complexes around Valdéz and Borgatta in the northern Calchaquí Valley; and Tilcara, Los Amarillos, and Volcán in the Quebrada de Humahuaca. Each town probably housed several thousand people and was surrounded by smaller villages (Tarragó and Díaz 1972, 1977; Tarragó 1978; Díaz 1983; Nielsen 1997; Cremonte and Garay de Fumagalli 1996). The largest sites of the era contain evidence for public construction, in some cases large central plazas flanked by nonresidential buildings, and in others probable civic-ceremonial architecture and terracing. The scope of influence or power of the leaders in the centers may have been restricted, however, as more than one town-sized settlement existed in each major drainage.

One of the more striking aspects of the regional settlement pattern in northwest Argentina is a significant shift in settlement location that occurred around AD 1300. In the Quebrada de Humahuaca, the Santa María, Cajón, and northern Calchaquí valleys, people moved into larger, nucleated settlements, whose locations and construction often suggest that the inhabitants were concerned with defense (Nielsen 1997; DeMarrais n.d.). At the same time that local conflicts may have been escalating, interregional interaction was apparently increasing. Contacts across the Andes with Chilean societies appear to have grown, for example, as exhibited by an increase in the use of similar ceremonial paraphernalia that may have been associated with drug consumption (Nielsen 1997).

Major land improvement projects were also undertaken during the late pre-Inka era. In Cachi Adentro, a lateral valley feeding eastward into the Calchaquí River, the residents of Las Pailas and vicinity lived adjacent to about 500 ha of irrigated, drained, and terraced fields thought to have been largely developed during the Regional Developments period (Tarragó and Núñez Regueiro 1972). Similarly, the residents of Fuerte Quemado in the Santa María Valley lived next to about 500 ha of irrigated agricultural enclosures (Kriscautzky n.d.). In some cases, it is not clear how much of the intensification was indigenous and how much was stimulated or sponsored by the Inkas, since there were important Late Horizon occupations at some sites. Even so, the scale of the pre-Inka populations suggest that notable land improvements and water management were needed to sustain life in the towns that had developed.

Significantly, the mortuary record from the region shows marked variations in the treatment of individuals after death. None of the tombs discovered yet has boasted the wealth of the richest contemporary people of Peru, but labor-intensive and finely made goods were concentrated in a limited number of tombs. Whether the societal reorganization of ca. 1300 resulted from conflict over resources, social competition, political maneuvers, or other causes remains to be determined. What seems clear, in any case, is that the major societies of the southern Andes were in a dynamic phase during the century or two before the advent of Inka rule.

The Inka Incorporation

For half a century, most scholars have followed John Rowe's (1944: 57) lead by accepting the late imperial chronology proposed in 1586 by the Jesuit chronicler Miguel Cabello Valboa (1951). Cabello wrote that AD 1438 was a pivotal year in Inka history, for that was when the ruler's son, Prince Inka Yupanki, led a successful resistance to a Chanka attack on Cusco. The prince then usurped the throne from his father Wiraqocha, assumed the honorific name Pachakuti, and began to expand his domain through diplomacy and conquest. The southern Andes fell to his son Thupa Inka Yupanki, who assumed military command in 1463 and the throne in 1471 (see also Betanzos 1996: 148–149). Cabello judged that the Inkas annexed the Chilean and Argentine territories ca. AD 1470–1480. Later, during Wayna Qhapaq's rule (1493–1526), the Chiriguanos (Guaraníes) took advantage of the emperor's preoccupation with the north Andes to penetrate the southeastern frontier, accompanied by the Portuguese explorer Alejo García. Wayna Qhapaq responded by dispatching the commander Yaska to reassert control and strengthen the frontier with a cordon of forts (Cieza 1967: 211–212). In 1535, when Diego de Almagro made the first Spanish visit through the region, some of the Inka centers were still functioning, but that situation had changed by 1545, when Diego de Rojas passed through. From Cabello's historical perspective, therefore, Inka dominion in the southern Andes lasted about fifty to sixty-five years.

Archaeological evidence is beginning to call that chronology into question. In the Cusco heartland, settlement survey, excavations, and radiocarbon dates taken by Alan Covey and Brian Bauer collectively indicate that the Inka were emerging as a local power by the thirteenth century

AD and had likely formed a regionally dominant, state-level society by the early fourteenth century (Bauer and Covey 2002; Covey 2003). If that assessment is correct, it is at odds with Cabello's more compressed historical framework.[2] For this discussion, it opens the possibility that important developments in provincial Inka history occurred somewhat earlier than has conventionally been accepted.

Intriguingly, a suite of radiocarbon dates suggests that the Inka presence in the south may have begun in the first half of the fifteenth century, rather than between 1470 and 1480. As of 1998, fifty-seven radiocarbon assays had been reported from Inka occupations from the southern Titicaca basin to the southern imperial margins.[3] Forty-three of those are from Argentina and northern Chile, a figure that reflects archaeologists' intense concern with dating the Inka presence, partly because of the thin historical record. Many of the dates fit the historical conception of the imperial expansion as a mid-to-late fifteenth-century phenomenon. However, quite a few assays antedate the presumed date of the Inka occupation of the region by several decades, which has made a number of the region's archaeologists skeptical of the utility of the historical chronology. Such early dates come from recently excavated contexts that cover the core region for the Inka occupation in Argentina: the Quebrada de Humahuaca (La Huerta, Peña Colorada, Volcán), the Calchaquí Valley (Potrero de Payogasta), the Bolsón de Andalgalá (Potrero-Chaquiago), La Rioja (Cerro Negro Overo), and Mendoza (Ciénaga de Yalguaraz) (Bárcena 1979; Múñoz and Chacama 1989; Bárcena and Román 1990; Stehberg 1991–92; D'Altroy and Williams n.d.; Williams 1996; Williams and D'Altroy 2000; D'Altroy, Williams, and Bauer n.d.; cf. Pärssinen and Siiriäinen 1997).

We may cite our own data as examples of the coeval early occupations of important Inka settlements in two adjacent provinces (fig. 3; table 1; Williams and D'Altroy 1999). The Proyecto Arqueológico Calchaquí obtained five radiocarbon assays from stratigraphic deposits associated with habitation and craftwork at the Inka center of Potrero de Payogasta. The five dates, from two superimposed levels of Inka architecture, exhibit probability distributions that span the fifteenth century. The highest probabilities for four dates are earlier than the accepted chronology for the Inka occupation of the region, and three have 2σ brackets ending before AD 1460.[4] Farther south in Catamarca, we have twelve dates from Potrero-Chaquiago and Agua Verde. The materials from eight of those dates are contextually associated with Inka architecture and ceramics. Eight of those dates correspond to Inka-period occupations, because of their contextual associations with Inka architecture and ceramics (table 1, fig. 3). Two additional early dates with doubtful depositional contexts fall in the thirteenth century, and a final date is modern.

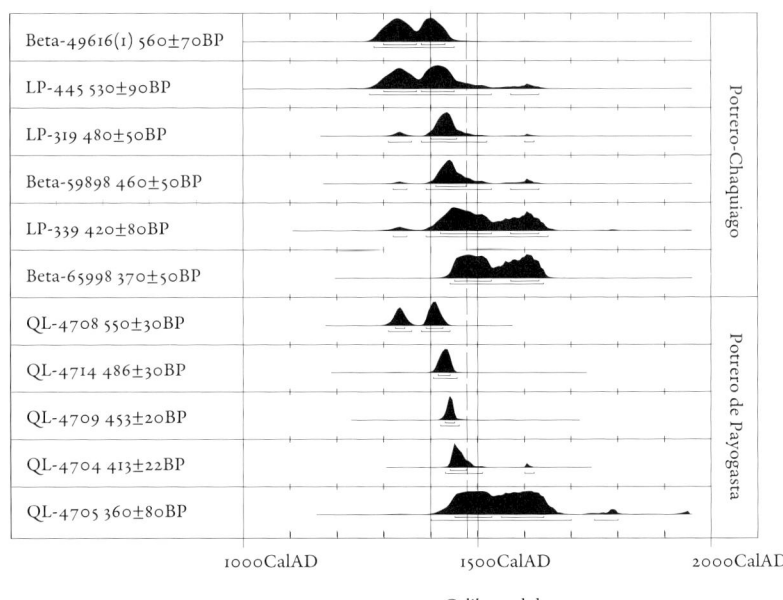

FIG. 3 Calibrated radiocarbon dates from the Inka installations of Potrero de Payogasta, in the northern Calchaquí Valley, Salta, Argentina and Potrero-Chaquiago, in the Bolsón de Andalgalá, Catamarca, Argentina. The dashed line corresponds to the conventional historical date for the Inka conquest of the region, ca. AD 1460–1470.

Table 1 Calibrated radiocarbon ages from Inka-context deposits at Potrero-Chaquiago and Potrero de Payogasta, Argentina, sorted by radiocarbon age; calibrated using OxCal V. 3.10 © Bronk Ramsey 2005

Location	Site	Lab ID	Uncalibrated age (BP)	Calibrated dates 68.2% (1σ) probability
Catamarca, Argentina	Potrero-Chaquiago	Beta-49616 (1)	560 70	1300 AD (37.7%) 1370 AD 1380 AD (30.5%) 1430 AD
Calchaquí Valley, Argentina	Potrero de Payogasta	QL-4708	550 30	1325 AD (24.3%) 1345 AD 1390 AD (43.9%) 1425 AD
Catamarca, Argentina	Potrero-Chaquiago	LP-445	530 90	1300 AD (30.6%) 1370 AD 1380 AD (37.6%) 1450 AD
Calchaquí Valley, Argentina	Potrero de Payogasta	QL-4714	486 30	1415 AD (68.2%) 1440 AD
Catamarca, Argentina	Potrero-Chaquiago	LP-319	480 50	1400 AD (68.2%) 1455 AD
Catamarca, Argentina	Potrero-Chaquiago	Beta-59898	460 50	1410 AD (68.2%) 1475 AD
Calchaquí Valley, Argentina	Potrero de Payogasta	QL-4709	453 20	1430 AD (68.2%) 1450 AD
Catamarca, Argentina	Potrero-Chaquiago	LP-339	420 80	1420 AD (49.5%) 1530 AD 1570 AD (18.7%) 1630 AD
Calchaquí Valley, Argentina	Potrero de Payogasta	QL-4704	413 22	1440 AD (68.2%) 1475 AD
Calchaquí Valley, Argentina	Potrero de Payogasta	QL-4705	360 80	1450 AD (33.3%) 1530 AD 1550 AD (34.9%) 1640 AD
Catamarca, Argentina	Potrero-Chaquiago	Beta-65998	370 50	1450 AD (41.4%) 1530 AD 1570 AD (26.8%) 1630 AD

We wish to emphasize the need to be very cautious in interpreting these dates. In addition to the intrinsic error involved in radiocarbon dating, the possible reuse of construction materials and dates taken from long-growing plants could lead to misleadingly early interpretations of the dates of occupations. Even so, the calibrated dates collectively suggest that the southern Andes may first have come under Inka rule in the first half of the fifteenth century, not midway through the second half (D'Altroy, Williams, and Bauer n.d.; Adamska and Michczyski 1996). Although the case is not closed on the issue of dating the formation of the Inka polity, the evidence from both Cusco and the south makes it difficult to accept the historical position that the south first fell to Cusco's armies only half a century before the Spanish invasion. Instead, the archaeological data suggest that Inka dominion lasted closer to a century. While that situation may force us to rethink the nature of Inka history, it also opens the door to understanding the different stages of Inka annexation of the region and consolidation of control.

Calibrated dates 95.4% (2σ) probability	Material analyzed	Associations and comments	Date taken	Citation
1280 AD (95.4%) 1450 AD	burned maize	hearth; C-13 calibrated	1987	Williams 1996
1310 AD (40.2%) 1360 AD 1380 AD (55.2%) 1440 AD	wood	surface inside structure	1993	Williams and D'Altroy 1999
1270 AD (91.5%) 1530 AD 1570 AD (3.9%) 1630 AD	charcoal	medium density midden with ash	1992	Williams 1996
1405 AD (95.4%) 1455 AD	wood	cultural fill below floor level	1993	Williams and D'Altroy 1999
1310 AD (7.9%) 1360 AD 1380 AD (85.7%) 1520 AD 1600 AD (1.8%) 1620 AD	carbonized trunk	floor level	1989	Williams 1996
1320 AD (2.2%) 1350 AD 1390 AD (86.3%) 1530 AD 1570 AD (6.9%) 1630 AD	charcoal	medium density midden with ash	1992	Williams 1996
1420 AD (95.4%) 1460 AD	wood	occupation zone, soil laid down during use	1993	Williams and D'Altroy 1999
1320 AD (1.5%) 1350 AD 1390 AD (93.9%) 1650 AD	carbon	medium density midden with ash	1990	Williams 1996
1430 AD (90.8%) 1510 AD 1600 AD (4.6%) 1620 AD	wood	occupation zone inside structure	1993	Williams and D'Altroy 1999
1400 AD (94.0%) 1700 AD 1750 AD (1.4%) 1800 AD	dung	cultural fill on floor	1993	Williams and D'Altroy 1999
1440 AD (95.4%) 1640 AD	charcoal	floor level (a)	1992	Williams 1996

Imperial Rule in the South

Kollasuyu, the empire's southeastern part, was geographically its largest. The documentary record provides enough information to know that the area south of the altiplano was divided into four or five provinces. In the eastern ranges, the province called Chicoana included the area from Talina, Bolivia, to just south of the settlement called Chicoana, Argentina, which probably lay at Puerta de La Paya. To the south lay the province of Quiri-Quiri, which encompassed the remaining Calchaquí Valley, and the Santa María, Andalgalá, Hualfín, and Abaucán valleys. The province of Tucumán included the valleys of the eastern border and sub-Andean mountains. The southernmost province, probably considered part of Chile, extended from modern La Rioja to Mendoza, and westward across the Andes through the valley of Uspallata to central Chile (Lorandi and Boixadós 1987–88). Northern Chile was incorporated within a region known as Tarapacá.

Most of the southern Andes were apparently less intensively administered than many of the societies from Lake Titicaca to Tumipampa, but the region may well have been more directly ruled than the Peruvian north coast and the eastern Andean slopes. Unfortunately, we lack detailed written descriptions of the relations between southern leaders and the Inkas. In the central and northern provinces, Inka rule ranged from intensive and direct, in which the decimal hierarchy was installed and some native leaders were granted the title of honorary Inka, to destructuration and almost total depopulation (Malpass 1993). The lord of Chincha, for instance, was accorded a status that placed him fatally at Atawallpa's side when the latter was captured in Cajamarca by the Spaniards. In the Upper Mantaro Valley, Peru, a region favored by rulers from Thupa Inka Yupanki through Waskhar, the previously decentralized Xauxa and Wanka were organized into three *saya*, each of which was headed by a native lord, or *kuraka* (D'Altroy 1992). Conversely, the Chimú polity was taken apart and its leader held honorary hostage in Cusco (Rowe 1948). In more punitive acts, the greater part of entire etnías were massacred or resettled, as in the case of the Guarco of Peru's central coast, the Ayaviri (southern Peruvian highlands), and Ecuador's Kañari, who had sided with Waskhar's losing cause against Atawallpa. In an alternative approach, in highland Ecuador the Inkas provided special status to selected chiefs, who became the state's clients (Salomon 1986).

Where particular areas of the southern Andes fell within this array of Inka approaches is still largely unknown. It seems reasonable to assume, but hard to demonstrate, that the upper tier of Inka administration followed the northern blueprint. If the situations were parallel, the provincial governor would have been an ethnic Inka, supported by indigenous elites responsible for implementing state policies, but not making them.

Considering the small scale of the pre-Inka polities, the administration for many people was likely centralized in a form analogous to central Peru. The prominence of *mitmaqkuna* (colonists resettled by state mandate) in several southern provincial centers makes it probable that some important positions were filled by outsiders (see below). Intriguingly, evidence for the renowned decimal administration is missing from the south Andes, but we do not know if that lacuna stems from state policy or if the hierarchy vaporized between the Inka collapse and the assertion of Spanish rule. If the decimal structure was not installed, some other way to mobilize labor must have been used, but we do not know what that may have been at present.

The archaeological evidence fills in the picture considerably and suggests that the Inkas applied five main policies in the region. A key concept was to create pockets of state settlements at strategic positions. Among them were the upper Quebrada de Humahuaca, the northern and mid-Calchaquí Valley, the Lerma Valley, around the confluence of the Santa María, Hualfín, and Abaucán valleys, and around Santiago de Chile. Conversely, the area that is now northern Chile was governed from state installations placed high in the mountains, in a manner that at least topographically paralleled the indirect approach applied to the north coast of Peru. The imperial occupation, as assessed from the distribution of those Inka sites, was selectively intensive (Williams and D'Altroy 1999). A second policy, linked to the founding of provincial installations, was to intensify nearby activities in mining, farming, herding, and artisanry. Third, military security was improved by erecting fortresses behind the perimeter of political and economic control and by building defensive features at key provincial centers, such as Puerta de La Paya in the Calchaquí Valley and Pucará de las Pavas in the Aconquija Massif. On both sides of the Andes, those forts were placed fairly high in the mountains, even though Inka settlements and farms were founded well below the piedmont along the east. Fourth, the region's peoples were moved around extensively, with some groups such as the Tucumanos and Pulares receiving notable benefits, and others, such as the recalcitrant Calchaquíes, losing in the bargain. Finally, the Inkas laid claim to the sacred landscape through the construction of shrines and thus positioned themselves between the indigenous peoples, nature's powers, and the local societies' own ancestral histories. Although we may surmise that the mix of policies varied over time, at present we lack the information to determine a chronological sequence for their application. In the sections that follow, we examine some of the evidence for these aspects of Inka rule.

The Imperial Infrastructure

The most outstanding similarity between the southern and central Inka-period infrastructure is the network of state installations constructed along the main highways and on smaller routes that joined them or linked the mountains with the lowlands (Raffino 1983b; Hyslop 1984; Raffino 1993; Gifford n.d.; Acuto n.d.). Many southern centers shared features of plans, architectural detailing, and activities with those of the north. Even so, the major settlements diverged in crucial ways from the major sites between Cusco and Quito and on the Peruvian coast. One significant distinction was in scale. The Peruvian highland centers—such as Willka Wamán, Hatun Xauxa, Pumpu, and Huánuco Pampa—were on a scale of magnitude larger than their southern counterparts. Huánuco Pampa, the grandest of the Inka provincial sites, contained over a thousand buildings, while the complexes at Shinkal or Cortaderas contained only about one to two hundred, excepting storehouses. The central ceremonial plazas in the heartland sites could hold 10,000 people, many times more than those of the south.

The emphasis given to defensive considerations also varied by region.[5] The Inkas did not maintain a fixed border like modern states, but were flexible in their external relations and often maintained pacific ties with external societies. Even where they hardened the frontier, the effective limits of Inka rule often lay well behind the farthest explorations of expeditionary forces. Along the southeastern perimeter of Kollasuyu, many Inka settlements were situated in a defensible position, fortified, or both. In that respect, the southern Andes are more comparable to northern Ecuador than to the heartland. The distribution of protected frontier settlements suggests that the Inkas were more concerned with physically regulating relationships with societies outside their control at the northern and southern margins of the empire than near the heartland (fig. 4; Hyslop 1990: 146–190; D'Altroy 2002: 209–213). The known forts are usually found in locales where Wayna Qhapaq campaigned, where Inka expeditions failed or were heavily resisted, or where incursion was a realistic threat. Because imperial expansion was an irregular process, however, many parts of the empire lay near a frontier at some point (Morris 1988). The forts in northern Chile and Argentina's Calchaquí Valley, for example, were probably at the front lines at one point but eventually lay almost 1,000 km behind the empire's southern limits (Raffino 1983a; Niemeyer and Schiappacasse 1988; Stehberg and Carvajal 1988; Williams et al. 1998).

The fortified frontier sites seem to have been intended to contain traffic into and out of Inka lands, not to form an impermeable wall. Typically situated at natural points of constriction, such as mountain passes, they were not heavily staffed. Major walled sites, such as Inkallajta (Bolivia),

opposite page
FIG. 4 The distribution of the principal known fortified Inka sites in the southern Andes

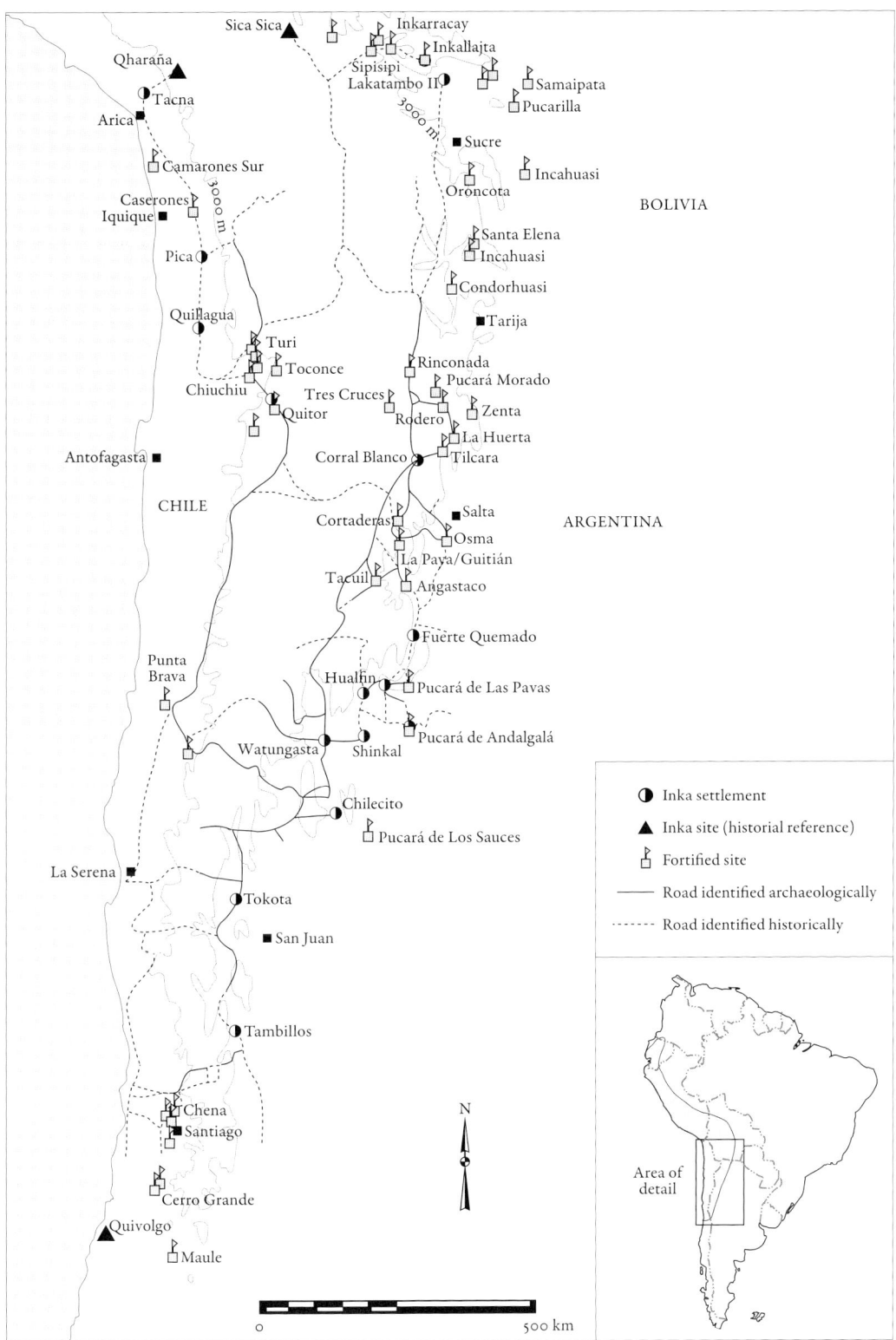

The Inkas in the Southlands

Pucará de Andalgalá (Argentina), and Cerro Grande del Inga (Chile), consisted of enclosures with broad open areas and spare architecture, set on hilltops or at the crest of steep slopes. The largest forts enclosed only about ten ha, which limited the personnel who could seek refuge, but kept the perimeters fairly short. Many had several concentric walls, moats, or revetments. The encircling walls were often built with bends, interior platforms, and salients that granted multiple options for casting projectiles at approaching troops (Hyslop 1990: 163–190). Regularly dispersed piles of sling stones are still visible in the salients at Cerro Grande del Inga.

Bolivia's southeastern periphery illustrates the lack of a fit between historic recorded explorations and archaeological evidence of Inka military control. One of Thupa Inka Yupanki's expeditions reportedly advanced to Paititi, a lowland settlement along the Río Madre de Dios about 800 km east of Cusco, but the forts along that perimeter lie about 400 km behind that position. Thierry Saignes (1985: 18) interprets a series of Inka sites on the upper Beni River as part of an Inka effort to take direct command of the Llanos de Mojo (see also Denevan 1980: 51). Samaipata (1,700 m), which lies a bit farther south, is the easternmost major Inka settlement in the region (see the articles by Meyers and Muñoz, this volume). Its elaborate animal and geometric imagery cut into stone is reminiscent of Cusco's best artistry in stone, and it may have represented a conceptual demarcation between the civilized empire and the chaos beyond. The Inkas used gifts to help maintain friendly relations with some peoples even farther onto the lowlands, an effort made worthwhile by the discovery of gold about one hundred km to the southeast. They installed 1,000 miners there, along with 5,000 other mitmaqkuna to support them (Alcayaga 1961; Saignes 1985: 20; Pärssinen 1992: 130–131).

Despite their efforts, the region was restive. As noted earlier, about 1520, an unknown number of Guaraníes made the only known serious penetration of an Inka frontier once rule had been established (Saignes 1985: 14–17; Hyslop 1988: 42; Pärssinen 1992: 110). The commander Yaska, dispatched from Ecuador by Wayna Qhapaq, mobilized an army and retook the perimeter, hardening it with a series of fortresses. Among the ethnic groups installed to protect the border in the valleys around Tarija in southern Bolivia were Carangas, Chichas, Churumatas, Tomatas, Juries, and Moyo-Moyo. Most—excepting the Tomatas who possibly came from the Copiapó (Chile) area—were from the southern Bolivian altiplano or adjacent plains (Lorandi 1997: 168).

A similar situation existed in what is now Argentine territory. There, the Inkas hardened the perimeter in the eastern cordillera, beyond which Inka expeditions advanced onto the plains. They asserted little control, however, beyond the piedmont. In Jujuy, the easternmost array of small forts, *tampu*, and ritual sites lie along or just below the crest of the mountains: Cerro Chasquillas, Cerro Amarillo, Pucará Morado, Puerta de Zenta, Pucará Tres Cruces, and Pueblito Calilegua (Raffino 1993: 213–234; Nielsen 1997). In modern Salta province, the Inkas attained enough security over the piedmont between the mountains and the plains to set up farms and associated facilities with hundreds of storehouses (*qollqa*). Several state sites were built in the Lerma Valley, including 1,700 qollqa at Campo de Pucará, probably to house the produce of a state farm (Boman 1908; Fock 1961; González 1983; Mulvany de Peñaloza 1986).

Farther south, the lands above Tucumán were guarded by the walled settlement now called the Pucará de Andalgalá, but Inka expeditions may have penetrated one hundred km beyond that, into Lule territory.[6] In Pärssinen's (1992: 129) view, Inka control extended as far as Santiago del Estero, but he concludes that effective rule did not extend far into the plains. Taking a more conservative view, Lorandi (1988) concludes that Tucumán was the eastern limit of the Inka advance and that the Quechua spoken farther to the east arrived when colonists who had been situated in the highlands went home. She notes that the natives of the Tucumán piedmont allied themselves with the Inkas against other eastern peoples and, for their pains, were resettled as military and economic mitmaqkuna various places within the southern empire. Several major sites in Argentina's intermontane valleys were also fortified, among them the site known as Pucará de las Pavas or Nevados de Aconquija in the Aconquija Massif, and the provincial center at Puerta de La Paya and Guitián in the Calchaquí Valley. At the valley head, the Inkas also established an administrative complex at Cortaderas to strengthen their hold on the valley (Hyslop 1984: 175–177; González and Díaz 1992; DeMarrais n.d.; Williams et al. 1998; Gifford n.d.; Acuto n.d.).

The southern limit of the empire has never been determined. The chroniclers Pedro de Cieza de León, Juan de Betanzos, and Hernando de Santillán all placed the limit at or near the Maule River (Valdivia 1960: 13; Bibar 1966: 137–138; Mariño de Lobera 1960: 254; Olaverría 1852), a judgment that is often accepted today (Medina 1952; Silva Galdames 1986; Hyslop 1988: 44). Even so, authors ranging from the earliest chroniclers to modern historians have placed it as far north as the Maipu River, outside modern Santiago, and 300 km farther south, at the Bío Bío River. The most southerly known Inka fort is Cerro Grande del Inga, located in the Cachapoal drainage about 80 km south of Santiago (Planella et al. 1991; Planella and Stehberg 1994). Like Cerro Chena, in the Maule River drainage, Cerro Grande del Inga was an existing settlement that the Inkas took over (Stehberg 1976). Inka copper axes and pottery have been found beyond those sites however, as far south as Valdivia, 700 km beyond Santiago. As Dillehay and Gordon (1988: 220) observe, different authors' choice of locale for the imperial limits may thus stem from their sources of information and analytical criteria. They note that if we accept the idea that different forms of Inka relations with other peoples varied in geographic extent, the problem of fixing an imperial border disappears, since the Inkas seem to have formed economic and cultural ties with the Araucanians far beyond the empire's military or political reach.

Frontier relations in Kollasuyu were complicated by many factors, because they met diverse imperial needs that changed over time and because overtures were met with differing responses. It is especially interesting that the Inka advances to the south, like those of the far north, stopped at locations that were not natural geographic termini. Instead, progress halted at the beginnings of expanses of temperate lands occupied by the Mapuche, lands that were agriculturally far richer and more densely populated than those farther north in Chile. It seems likely that logistical obstacles, the great distances from Cusco, and formidable local resistance combined to halt the progression of Inka rule much beyond the regions that were already controlled by the beginnings of the sixteenth century.

Provincial Installations

Given the diversity of Inka facilities in the southern Andes, it will not be possible here to provide a comprehensive review of their character and distribution (Debenedetti 1908; Mostny 1949; De Lorenzi and Díaz 1977; Hyslop 1984, 1990; Niemeyer 1986; Bárcena 1988). Instead, we will focus our attention on two regions in which we have conducted field research, the northern Calchaquí Valley (Salta Province) and the Bolsón de Andalgalá (Catamarca Province) to afford a more detailed understanding of how Inka rule was applied at a local level.

NORTHERN CALCHAQUÍ VALLEY

Inka-related sites in the northern Calchaquí Valley include provincial centers, way stations, and local communities with state precincts (fig. 5). The Inkas followed two distinct approaches in building their settlements in the valley's north and central sectors. Two major branches of the Inka highway entered the valley from the north (Hyslop and Díaz 1983). Seven state sites line a fifty km stretch of the eastern highway from the upper valley to Tastil, uninterrupted by any major Santamariano community. Along the Potrero River are Cortaderas, Potrero de Payogasta, and Ojo de Agua, above which lie Corral Blanco, Capillas, Apacheta Ingañan, and Corralito. Just east of the main Potrero River lies Belgrano, another extensive settlement associated with a broad expanse of irrigated fields.

Important Inka sites also lie along the western road branch in the La Poma sector of the main Calchaquí River drainage: Pucará de Palermo, Río Blanco, Los Graneros, La Encrucijada, and Apacheta Acay. On the

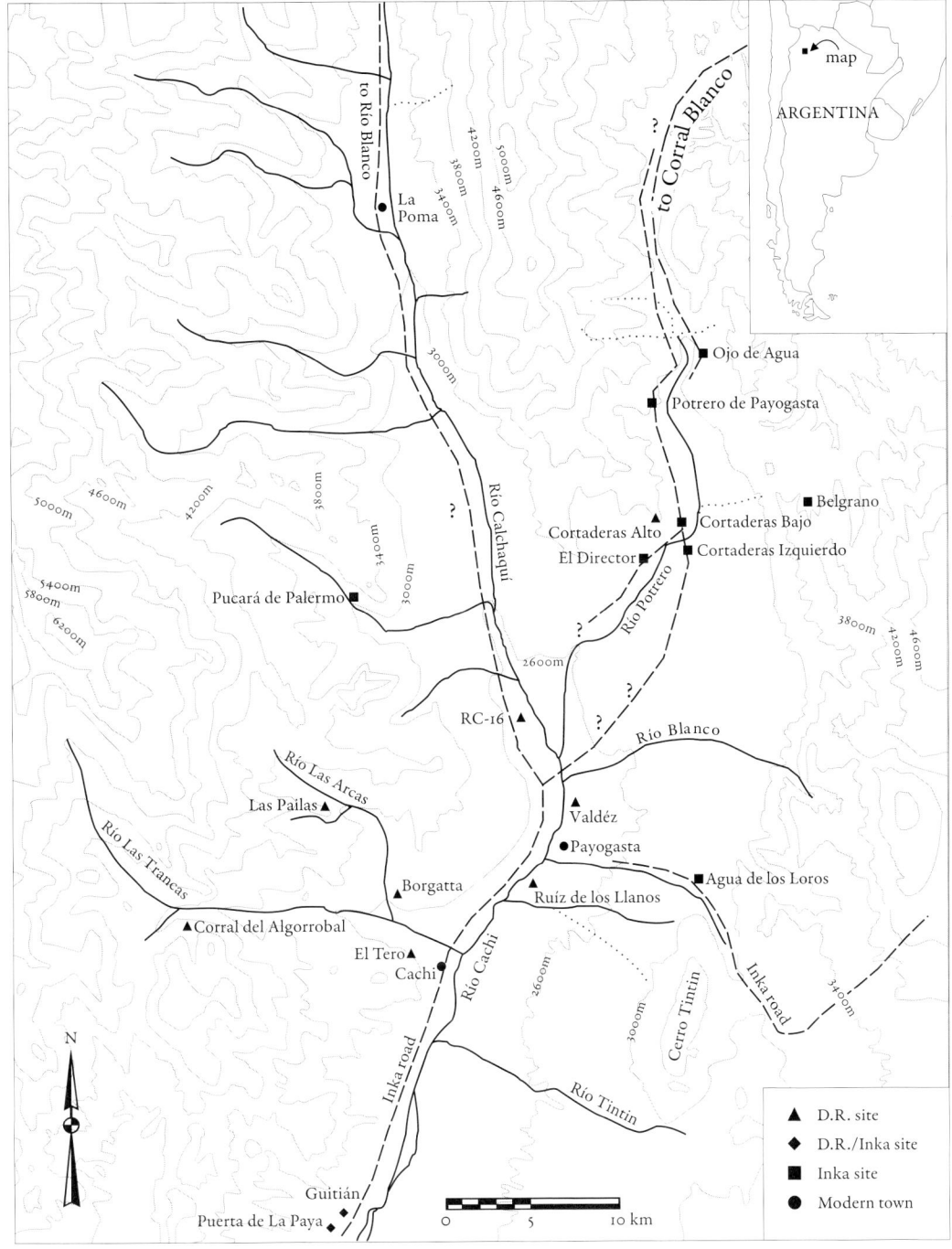

FIG. 5 The distribution of major late Pre-Hispanic sites in the northern Calchaquí Valley

road running eastward to the Valle de Lerma are Agua de los Loros and Tin Tin, at exit points from the valley. In contrast, the mid-valley occupation contains state and local components intermixed in the same sites. The paired sites of Puerta de La Paya (12 ha) and Guitián (6 ha) stand out as major settlements with intrusive Inka sectors in existing local communities. Provincial Inka or Inka-related pottery is also found at many local sites, in both the main and the productive lateral valleys.

Puerta de La Paya (12 ha) was the central valley's main Inka installation and has tentatively been identified as Chicoana, the provincial center visited by Almagro in 1535 (González 1983; see Lorandi and Boixadós 1987–88). Hermann Ten Kate (1893) and Juan Ambrosetti (1907–08) began research there around the turn of the century and work has continued intermittently since. Surface remains consist of irregular, Santamariano residential architecture, into which a complex of Inka-style rectilinear structures was intruded. A thick, zig-zag wall encloses the site, apparently for defensive purposes. The most prominent building in the Inka sector is the Casa Morada, a rectangular structure (13.55 m EW x 4.24 m NS) built of blocks of reddish sandstone, with quadrangular niches typical of Inka buildings (González and Díaz 1992). Ambrosetti's (1902, 1907–08) 202 exhumed burials form the most spectacular array of Inka grave lots found in Argentina. The materials recovered include Inka-style ceramics, bead strings, and thirty-five metal objects. The site of Guitián (6 ha; fig. 6), across a quebrada from Puerta de La Paya, exhibits a similar layout of an Inka sector intruded into a Santamariano settlement. Its principal features include a central plaza with a small platform mound, bordered by a long hall (*kallanka*) and rectilinear residential compounds. Like Puerta de La Paya, it is surrounded by a fortification wall and access was restricted to three entryways.

In contrast to the architecturally mixed sites of the central valley, the state sites of the north Calchaquí Valley exhibit constructions that were more characteristic of the Inka. Cortaderas was a multipurpose settlement about forty-five km up valley from Puerta de La Paya (fig. 7). It contains several sectors, including an upper fortified Santamariano settlement (Cortaderas Alto, 9 ha) that may have been appropriated or evacuated by the Inkas. Around the base of the hill are an Inka residential settlement, a storage facility, a small fort, an administrative and ceremonial facility, and assorted other small constructions (fig. 8; Gifford n.d.; Acuto n.d.). The main Inka highway passes through one of the lower sectors, called Cortaderas Bajo (4 ha). Just to the south of Cortaderas lies an area of irrigated fields, within which are the remains of residential buildings from which Inka pottery has been recovered. When considered together, the array of facilities at Cortaderas indicates that the Inkas made a considerable investment in the occupation of this location—a pivotal point joining

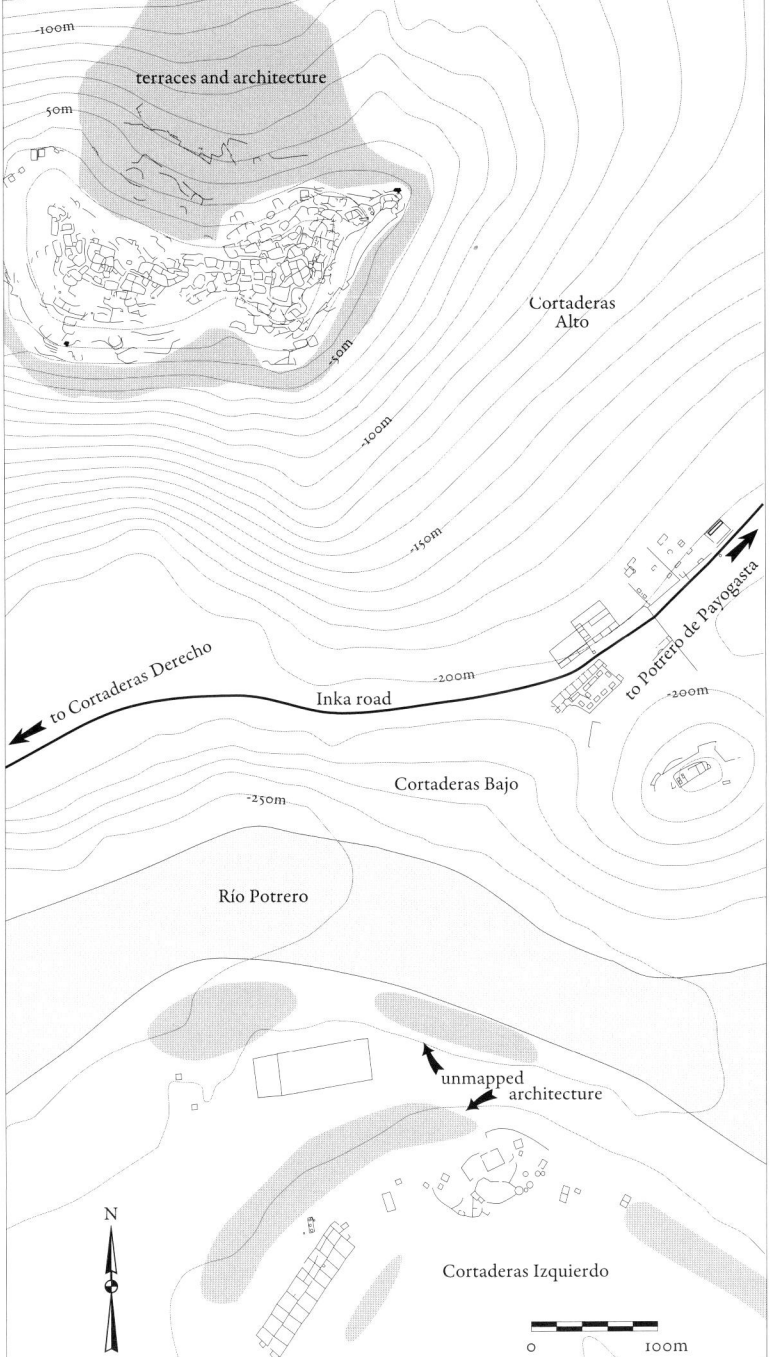

FIG. 6 The complex of sites at Cortaderas, in the Río Potrero drainage of the northern Calchaquí Valley

FIG. 7 The Inka site of Guitián, in the central part of the northern Calchaquí Valley

FIG. 8 Reconstruction of the roadside tampu at Cortaderas Bajo (courtesy C. Gifford)

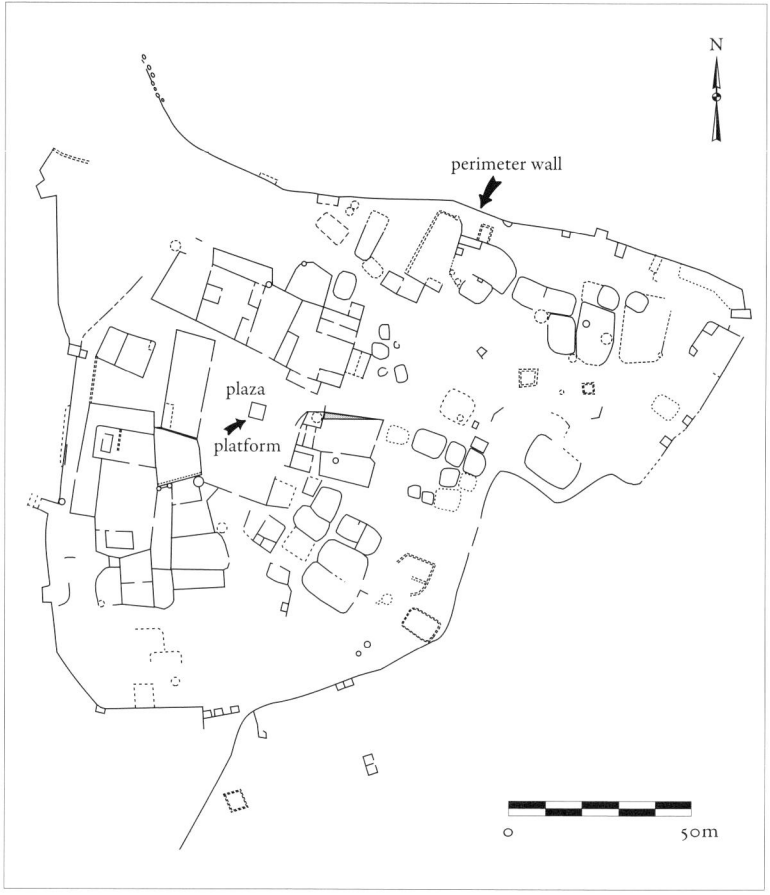

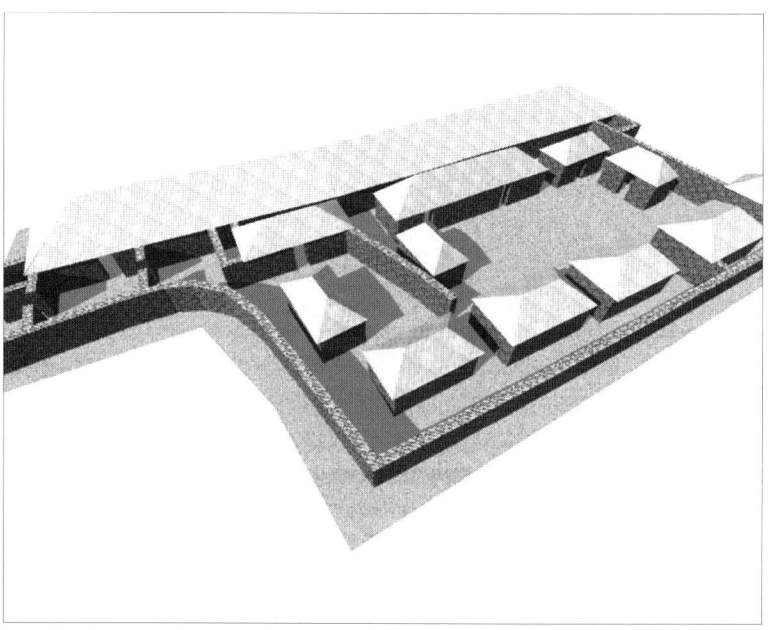

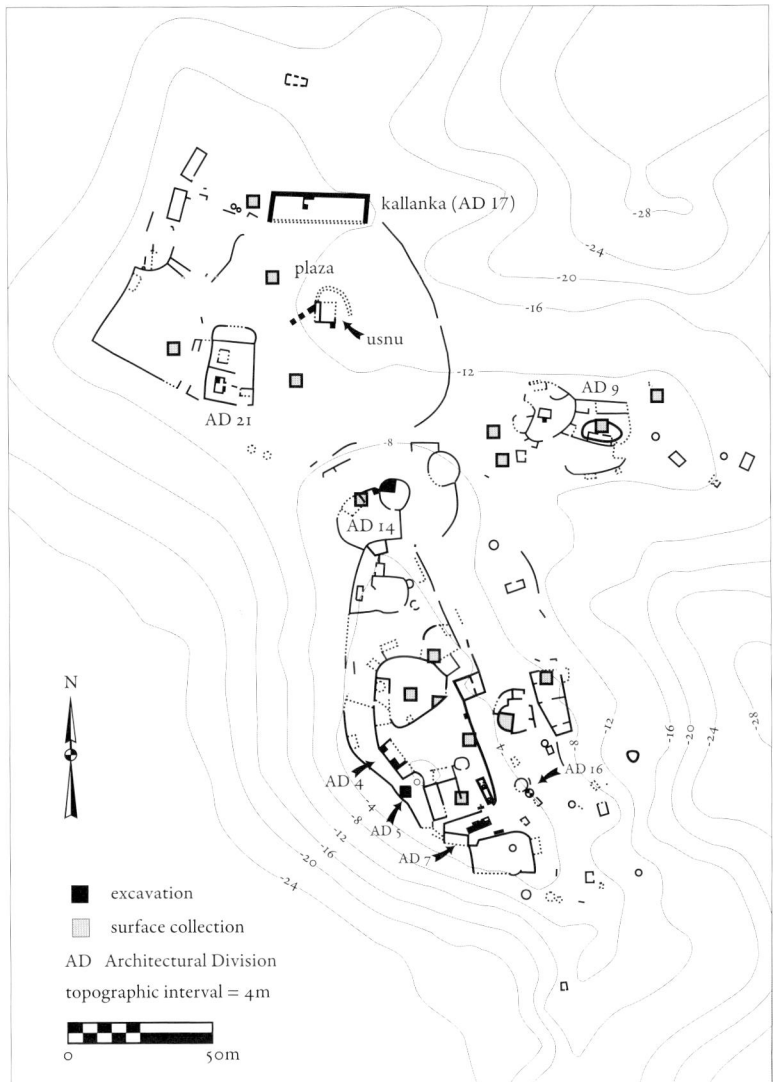

FIG. 9 The Inka site of Potrero de Payogasta, in the Río Potrero drainage of the northern Calchaquí Valley

the Calchaquí Valley with the puna and Quebrada de Humahuaca that lie to the north.

About five km to the north lies Potrero de Payogasta (9 ha; fig. 9), another multipurpose state installation at the head of the Potrero Valley adjacent to the main Inka road (Difrieri 1948; Schávelzon and Magadán 1992). The settlement contains seven principal architectural sectors distributed along a low ridge crest. An additional fortified hilltop sector, about 1 km NW, contained storehouses and residences. Inka architectural forms include a platform mound, the largest standing kallanka in Argentina, and building complexes, all arranged around two plazas. Excavations in fourteen locations, up to two m in depth, yielded evidence for

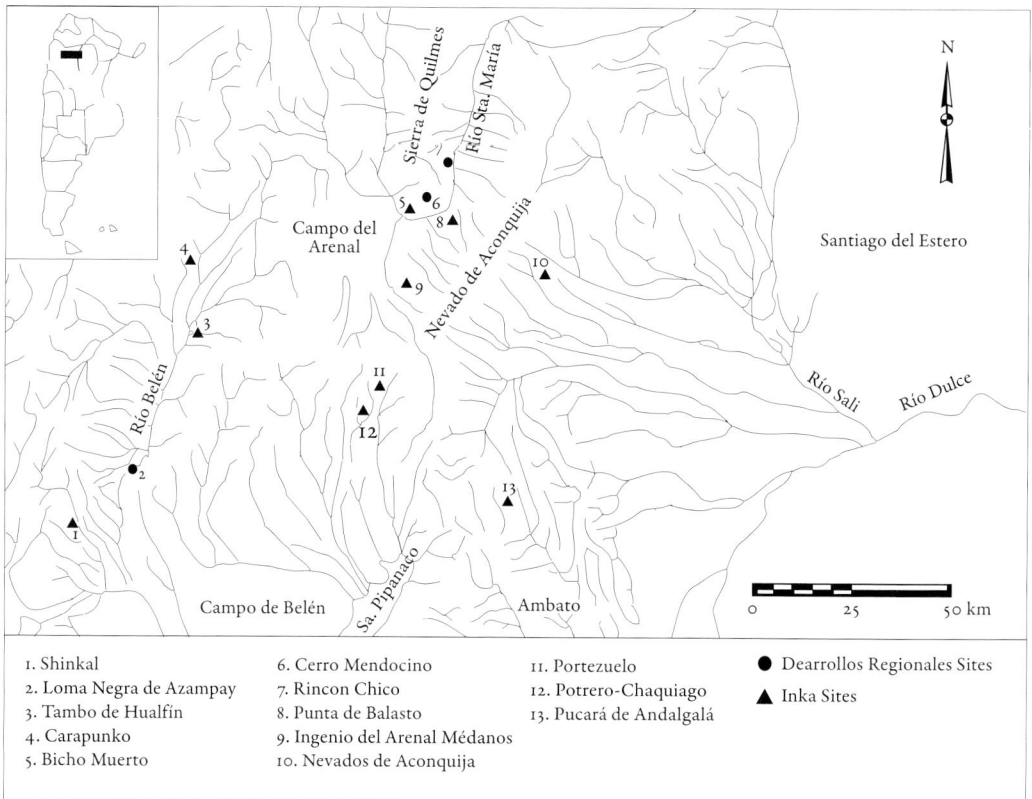

FIG. 10 The distribution of major Inka sites and Inka-era local sites in central part of the modern province of Catamarca

habitation, storage, production, and ceremonial activities. The present surface architecture was apparently planned; it overlies a burned layer and an earlier Inka component with a different orientation, dated to the first half of the fifteenth century (fig. 3, table 1). We infer that an initial Inka occupation was followed by a major burning event and that the settlement was later rebuilt.

SANTA MARÍA VALLEY AND THE BOLSÓN DE ANDALGALÁ

The Inkas also undertook a considerable building program in the Santa María Valley and its vicinity, about 250 km south of Cortaderas and Potrero de Payogasta. The more southerly region contained a much sparser indigenous population, but the Inka presence was nonetheless impressive and diverse. It included administrative centers, smaller tampu, and fortified redoubts, all joined by the major road system (fig. 10). As was the case farther north, there is abundant evidence for agricultural and craft production conducted by personnel working for the state (see below), and for the movement of colonists from their native lands to new locations designated by the Inkas.

The major Inka sites within the Inka province of Quiri-Quiri lie close to one another, near the juncture of the Hualfín, Santa María, and

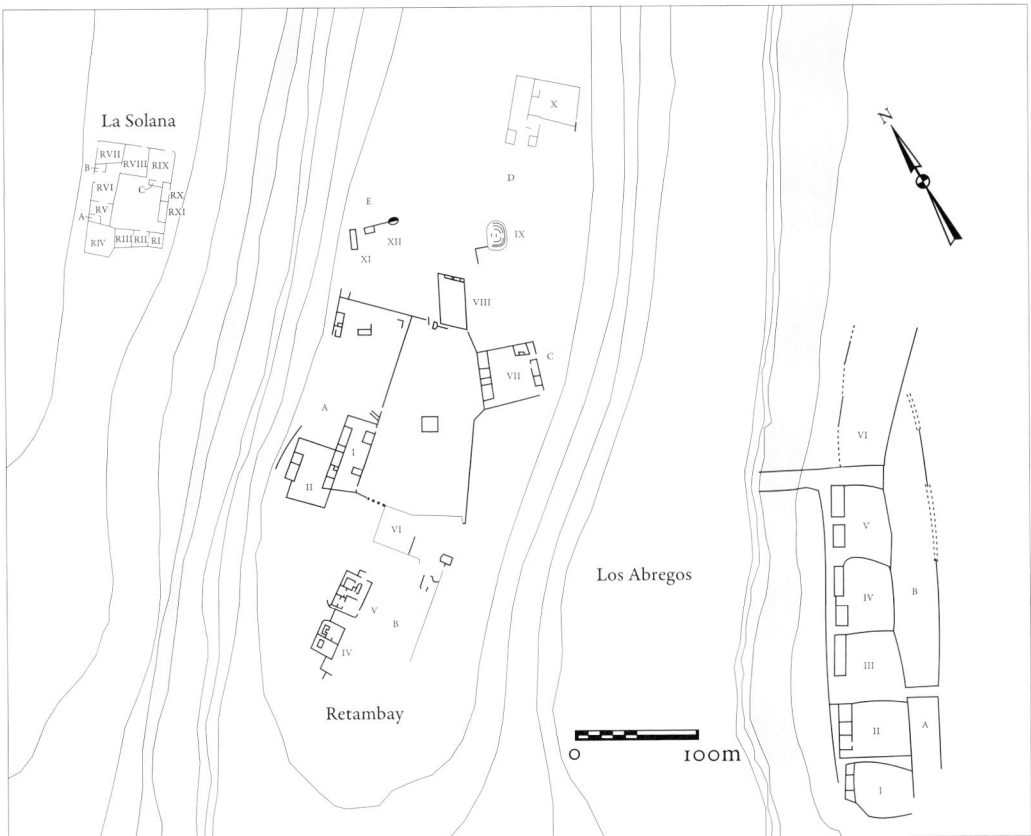

FIG. 11 The Inka installation of Potrero-Chaquiago, in the Bolsón de Andalgalá (province of Catamarca)

Abaucán Valleys. In an area that extends no more than about thirty km lies an impressive array of state installations. Among the most important settlements is Shinkal, in the southern part of the Hualfín Valley. Shinkal (12 ha) lies on the left bank of the Simbolar River near the modern town of Londres de Quinmivil, on a meseta, the piedmont, and the valley bottom (Raffino 1983b: 437). The main sector of the site consists of a large enclosure containing several kallanka and smaller structures (Raffino 1983b). Placed along the crest of a small hill are two to three lines of circular qollqa, which together total about sixty buildings (Snead 1992). González (1983) cites documentary evidence that suggests that as many as 20,000 mitmaqkuna were committed to the supervision of Shinkal, but the archaeological evidence to indicate where they might have lived has yet to be found. Under any circumstances, it appears that the settlement was the principal center for the region.

Potrero-Chaquiago is a smaller Inka installation that probably lay at an administrative level below Shinkal (Williams 1983, 1991, n.d.). Its five sectors are distributed over only 4.3 ha, but it has yielded considerable evidence for craft production of various kinds (fig. 11; see below). Like many of the planned Inka sites along the main routes of the south Andes,

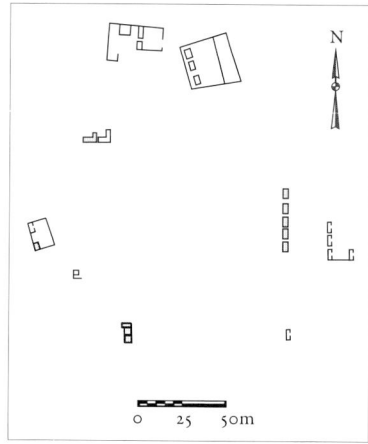

FIG. 12 The Inka tampu of Ingenio del Arenal Médanos, in the Campo del Arenal to the south of the Santa María Valley (Province of Catamarca) (after Márquez Miranda and Cigliano 1959) *opposite page*

it contains rectangular architectural compounds (RPC), internal plazas, and a small platform mound. Because it was a previously uninhabited locale, its location at the transition from the eastern subtropical zone to the Andean puna was probably crucial to its establishment. Also, like many of the sites in the south, Potrero-Chaquiago retains evidence that the Inkas intensified agricultural production for local use through construction of terraces and small irrigation systems that watered fields near the settlement. It also contains a small number of enclosed storehouses (15 circular qollqa in two groups) whose contents were probably intended for local use.

Watungasta, composed of two sectors, is located at the confluence of the Abaucán Valley and the La Troya quebrada. The entire complex covers about 15.6 ha, spread out over the riverbank and adjacent piedmont. One of the sectors, which was also occupied during the Hispanic period, contains rectilinear and circular compounds built of adobe. The other sector, occupied during the Regional Developments and Inka periods, has both Inka residential architecture and agricultural constructions. An additional important Inka tampu in the Santa María Valley lies at Fuerte Quemado. Within a major pre-Inka settlement are found a series of nine Inka-related compounds and sets of qollqa, some with diameters up to six m. Drawing from excavations in eleven enclosures, Kriscautzky (n.d.: 212) reports finding considerable evidence for weaving and metallurgy (see below). South of Fuerte Quemado is the site of Punta de Balasto (10 ha) and, on the western piedmont of Aconquija, lies the site called Ingenio del Arenal Médanos (3.5 ha; fig. 12). Punta de Balasto contains a large plaza with a platform (*usnu*), next to which are eight storage structures and fifteen architectural compounds, some of which were apparently residential (Carrara et al. 1960; Raffino 1983b). Ingenio del Arenal Médanos, which lies on the plain of the Aconquija Massif, is composed of thirty-five rooms arrayed around the plaza. The site also contains more than twenty rectangular compounds and a platform mound associated with a road (Márquez Miranda and Cigliano 1961: 126). Its location in the lower sector of Campo del Arenal, adjacent to a modern road from Santa María to Capillitas, suggests that Ingenio del Arenal Médanos could have controlled transit and communications between the Cajón, Santa María, and Hualfín valleys and the Capillitas range, and from there to the Bolsón de Andalgalá.

In the Quebrada de Yocavil, five km southwest of Punta de Balasto, lies Bicho Muerto. It consists primarily of fifty rectangular and trapezoidal architectural compounds, interconnected by a series of passageways; some circular constructions are also present. The compounds form two major sectors, one on either side of the drainage that forms the quebrada. An additional fortified sector of the site, called Bicho Muerto Fortaleza, is formed by thirty-five rectangular, circular, and trapezoidal compounds and open spaces (González 1995: 98).

Pucará de las Pavas (2.5 ha) lies on the slopes of Aconquija at 4,300 masl (meters above sea level) in the modern province of Tucumán. It is composed of two sectors situated adjacent to a road. In the northwestern sector of the main plaza lies a six m high, stepped platform mound (Hyslop and Schobinger 1991: 21–22). Without going into further detail, it is worth observing that these sites constitute only a fraction of the Inka constructions in the region. Many smaller sites, such as Huehuel, Campo Colorado, Portezuelo, and Los Choyanos, also lie along the road network.

DISTINCTIVE ARCHITECTURAL CONSTRUCTIONS

We would like to draw attention here to a particular kind of architecture that characterized numerous Inka installations from Lake Titicaca south, but is absent farther north. This form consists of an elongated building divided into two parallel rows of cells. Constructions of this form are known as far north as Hatunqolla (Catherine Julien, personal communication, July 1997), and were erected in at least nine important Inka sites throughout Kollasuyu, including locations in the Quebrada de Humahuaca, the Cajón Valley, and the Calchaquí Valley. Among those sites are Calahoyo Grande on the frontier between Argentina and Bolivia; Corral Blanco and Cortaderas Izquierdo in the Calchaquí Valley; San Antonio del Cajón, Corralitos, La Maravilla, La Lagunita, and Campo de Huasamayo in the Cajón Valley; and Ranchillos in Abaucán Valley. There is a noticeable concentration of this kind of building in the Cajón Valley.

As an example, we may cite Cortaderas Izquierdo, which dominates the principal space of the administrative sector of this important Inka complex. This structure measures about 130 m long and 35 m wide and is oriented north-south. It contains twenty interior cells, with entrances at both the north and south ends and a few doorways crossing over from one row of cells to the other. Some of the cells also contain interior architecture, which appears to have defined small rooms and platforms.

A variety of interpretations has been suggested for these buildings, among them storehouses, protected farm plots, and craft production centers. Lack of excavations in such buildings, however, makes it difficult to choose the correct one. Even so, given their central location in important sites, their distribution south along the length of the Inka highways from Bolivia, and their great size, they appear to have been a critical part of the standard Inka repertoire at state installations in Kollasuyu. Whether they were related to production, administration, or military activities remains to be determined.

Demographic Transformations

Under Inka rule, the Andean social landscape was transformed by the resettlement of much of the population into new locations. This process was both a local phenomenon and a result of the Inka colonization program. Before Cusco's rule brought a forced tranquility to the land, many highland societies had been embroiled in regional hostilities for decades, if not centuries. For protection, they often agglomerated into larger communities built in high-elevation, defensible positions. Many of those towns, whether in the Peruvian sierra, the altiplano, or the southern Andes, were inconveniently placed for access to water, croplands, and expansive pastures. On a broad scale, the goals and many particulars of the Inka colonist program have been well described (Espinoza 1970, 1973, 1975, 1987; Lorandi 1991; D'Altroy 2005). Waldemar Espinoza, who has provided a wealth of useful information on resettlement, has identified two principal state goals: economic production and military security. Further goals lay in the political and ideological arenas. As we will describe below, the Inkas appear to have used colonists as part of a treaty relationship, whereby some groups received favorable treatment, in the form of lands and elevated political power, in exchange for serving the state. Certain enclaves, such as Copacabana on Lake Titicaca, seem to have been designed to imprint the imperial ideology at sacred locales. As a result, several factors acted to disperse populations, often to lower, smaller settlements: the attraction of easier access to productive resources, an interest in being closer to the wealth and power focused at state installations, and the Inkas' interest in managing subject societies to their own ends. These resettlement processes radically, but selectively, transformed the ethnic landscape of the southern Andes.

Because we cannot discuss local shifts with much precision in the south, except in a few cases, we focus here on the colonists. The mitmaqkuna in the region came from various parts of the empire. In the north, in the Quebrada de Humahuaca and the Calchaquí Valley, colonies were installed of the peoples who lived in the south-central part of the altiplano (Espinoza 1981). The ethnic composition of the Calchaquí Valley appears to have been modified substantially under Inka rule. The earliest sources suggest that the Pulares were the most important, if not sole, ethnic group (Lorandi and Boixadós 1987–88). They likely shared the settlements of Cachi, Payogasta, and Atapsi with members of other groups. The last of those towns lies at the northern border of lands held by the Calchaquíes, who fiercely resisted Inka rule and suffered displacement as a consequence (Matienzo 1967: 280–281). A number of the key state settlements in the valley, such as Chicoana and Tolombón, were settled by mitmaqkuna from Chicoana or Sicuani, in the province of Canas, to the south of Cusco. They most likely were installed to exercise a strong state hand in particularly intransigent parts of the valley.

On the lower slopes of the eastern Andes in Jujuy and Salta, the Inkas resettled Chicha and Churumata nobles (*orejones*) (Doucet n.d.). The latter were also installed in Tucumán (Lorandi 1984; Presta and del Río n.d.). Toward the south, in the Yocavil and Hualfín valleys, the Bolsón de Andalgalá, around Londres, and in part of Abaucán, the Inkas installed colonists taken from the Tucumán-Santiago piedmont. On occasion, their settlements were known as Tucumanao or Tucumangasta, meaning "town of the Tucumanos." Such colonies, which probably rendered rotating labor service, introduced Quechua to their homelands on the plains of Santiago del Estero when they returned home after the empire's demise. In the far south, from La Rioja (Chilecito) to Mendoza, the mitmaqkuna seem to have come from the other side of the Andes, from central Chile (González 1982: 339).

In short, there is a strong possibility that the entire south lay under the control of imported state agents—a situation brought on by the unsettled frontier nature of the region. The difficulties of integrating small-scale chiefdoms into a state system, as well as resistance both from within and beyond Tawantinsuyu's lands, may have required more direct means of rule than might otherwise have been appropriate for a geographically distant zone.

High-Elevation Ceremonial Sites

One of the most striking features of Inka ideology is the reverence paid to the sacred landscape, a practice which is apparent in a variety of situations, most notably the more than 328 places of veneration (*wak'a*) on forty-one to forty-two conceptual ritual (*zeq'e*) lines emanating from central Cusco and the "New Cuscos" erected at six different locations, such as Tumipampa, Ecuador, and Inkawasi, Peru. More modest homage paid to the deities of the natural environment can be found in the carved stones scattered across the landscape, the canalized springs, and the mountain peak sites containing ceremonial caches and the more rare human sacrifices. That combination of ideas involved both an animistic religion and concepts of the cosmos that had specific geographic and spatial referents.

As Juan Schobinger, Antonio Beorchia Nigris, Johann Reinhard, and María Ceruti describe, more than fifty high-elevation (above 5,000 m) ceremonial sites have been identified in the Andes (Schobinger et al. 1966; Beorchia Nigris 1987; Reinhard 1985; Ceruti 1997). Regrettably, relatively few have been found intact by professionally trained archaeologists. Such high-elevation ceremonial sites are concentrated in the southern Andes, along the highest mountain ranges separating Argentina and Chile (fig. 13). Among the locations that have been explored is Llullaillaco, the world's highest known archaeological site, situated on an active volcano at 6,739 m. Other high peaks with important offerings include Aconcagua,

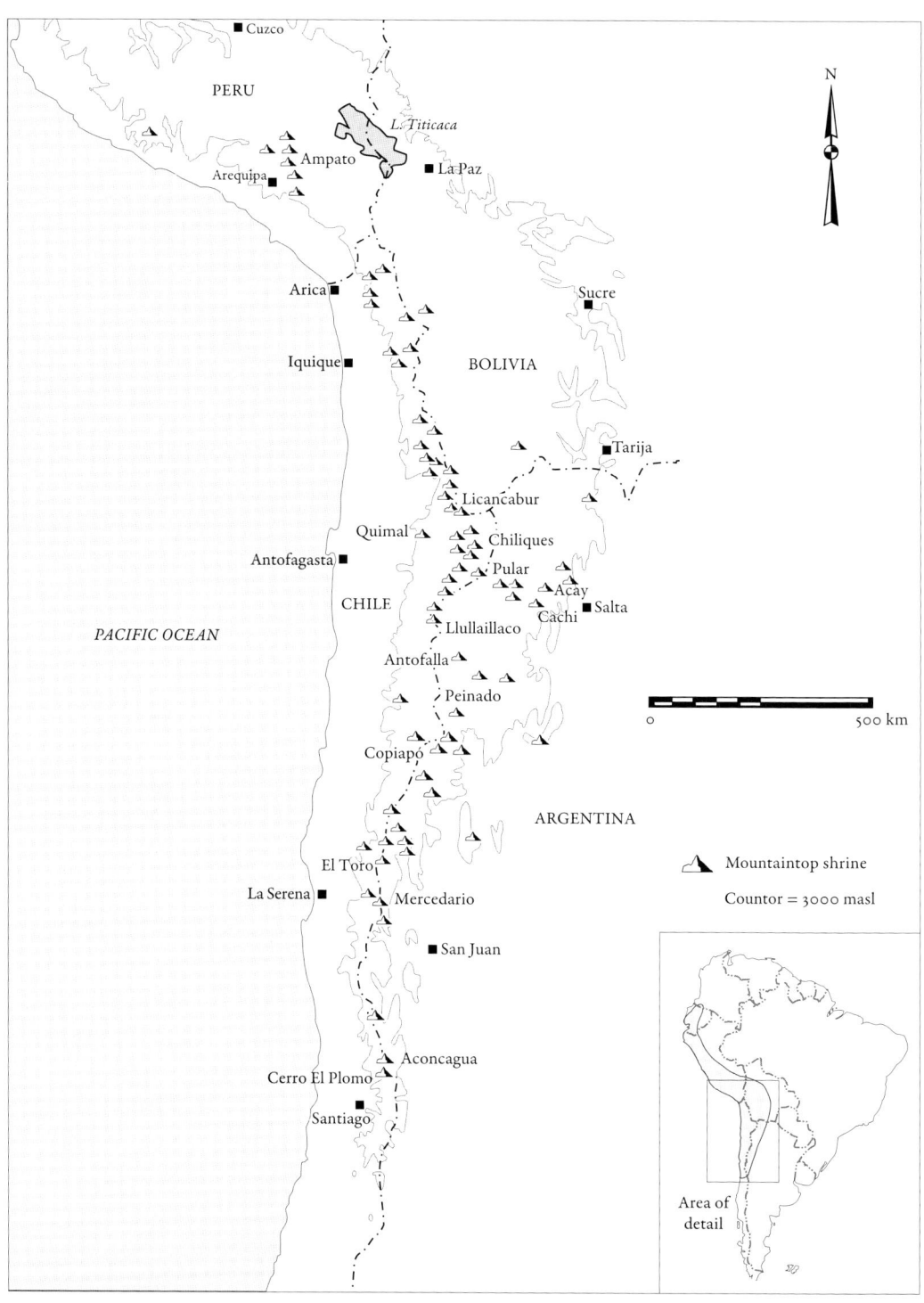

Cerro El Toro, Cerro El Plomo, Copiapó, Cerro Mercedario, Chiliques, Pular, Licancabur, and Quimal. The sites usually consist of small buildings and platforms, or rows of stones, in a slightly sheltered location, sometimes at the end of a string of staging or stopping posts along a path up to the mountaintop.

The most elaborate artifacts recovered from the mountain peak sites include paired human statuettes and llama figurines modeled in gold and silver or carved in *Spondylus* shell from Ecuador's coastal waters (Reinhard 1985). The material caches also include human hair, camelid bones and dung, pottery, wood, grass, coca leaf, rope, carbon, and feathers. Strikingly, but rarely, the sites contain the frozen bodies of children, adolescents, and adults of both sexes. It seems most likely that all were sacrificed in the ceremony called the *qhapaq ucha,* which was reserved for the most important occasions or activities, such as the ascension or death of a ruler. Examples of such sites in the south include Cerro el Plomo and Volcano Copiapó in Chile, and Cerro El Toro and Mt. Aconcagua in Argentina.

Reinhard (1985, 1992) suggests that the Inkas had religious, political, and economic motivations for creating the sites. A core reason was to pay homage to the mountain deities, called *apu* or *wamani*, who were envisioned as the owners of the flocks. The weather and sea deities were also intimately linked to the peaks and their sources of water in Inka cosmology. By building these ceremonial sites, the Inkas interposed themselves as the mediators between human society and the supernatural world. Since people in many Andean regions believed that particular mountain peaks were their ancestors' places of origin and that their prosperity depended on maintaining good relations with the spirits who resided there, the Inkas' actions claimed primacy over the genealogical foundations of the peoples who lived in the vicinity of the peaks. Thus religious and political goals could be neatly meshed. Raffino (1983b: 243) has also emphasized the high correlation of Inka sites with mineral exploitation in Argentina, with the implication that the mountains were seen to be the sources of the ore, one of the main causes of Inka penetration into the region.

There is some debate over the antiquity of many high-elevation sites in the south. Both Beorchia (1987), a pioneer of high-elevation studies, and Ceruti (1997) argue that several of the sites could well antedate the Inka occupation of the region, although the proof is not yet available. If that were the case, the Inkas claimed a regional custom as their own, with modifications appropriate to their own beliefs and practices. Reinhard (1985), while not discounting the possibility of pre-Inka mountain peak sites, nonetheless maintains that the securely dated offerings belong to the Inka era. Whatever the antiquity of the earliest mountaintop sites, it appears that the Inkas made considerable efforts to propitiate the deities that lived there and thus to interpose themselves between the

FIG. 13 The distribution of known high-elevation ceremonial sites in the southern Andes (data drawn from Reinhard 1985, 1992 and Ceruti 1997)

inhabitants of the region and the ancestral and supernatural powers that resided therein.

Economic Intensification under Inka Rule
AGRICULTURAL PRODUCTION

In broad terms, agricultural production in most of the southern Andes was markedly lower than in the central Andes because of climatic and topographic limitations. Even so, output may have been comparable with respect to the region's productivity. After the Inkas secured new territories, state personnel set about ensuring that food was available to people working on state business. That end was accomplished by reserving lands for state farms, which local workers cultivated as part of their labor service. It appears to have been standard practice to grant the mitmaqkuna usufruct rights on lands they used to support themselves. The farms were often located near provincial centers, but some immense farms were established in especially favorable agricultural locations. The best-known of the farms lay in the temperate Cochabamba Valley, Bolivia, where Wayna Qhapaq ordered the valley vacated to make way for 14,000 agricultural workers, both permanent colonists and corvée laborers (Wachtel 1982). The lands were reportedly dedicated to growing maize for the Inka's armies.

State farms have been identified archaeologically in several locations, the most impressive at Coctaca in the upper Quebrada de Humahuaca, Argentina (Albeck 1992–93; Albeck and Scattolin 1991; Casanova 1934; Nielsen 1997). There a vast terraced field system covers about six km^2 on the alluvial fans and piedmont (3,700 m) just below the fringe of the altiplano. The identification of this field system as an Inka construction is based on, among other evidence, the lack of antecedent occupation by local populations, the scale of the project, and the presence of Inka residential settlements in the midst of the terrace systems. There may have also been extensive state farms on the lowest piedmont of the Lerma Valley (1,200 m), where a string of Inka sites runs along the edge between the Andes and the eastern plains (Mulvany de Peñaloza 1986, n.d.). The most expansive of those farms may have lain at the Campo de Pucará, which reportedly contained 1,700 storehouses (Boman 1908; Fock 1961; González 1983).

In the northern Calchaquí Valley, the Inkas appear to have expanded the territory of the nearby Pular ethnic group at the expense of the native Calchaquíes, and may have imported Yavi mitmaqkuna from southern Bolivia or northwest Argentina (Lorandi and Boixadós 1987–88). State agricultural production was apparently focused in several locations associated with state settlements. The far northern valley has two branches, along the Potrero and Calchaquí rivers, respectively, each of which contains a series of Inka installations. In the Potrero drainage, the Inkas intensified production by building canals on both sides of the river in association with the state settlements described earlier. In the other branch, expanses of irrigated land are associated with multiple state installations at Palermo and La Poma. The modern extent of irrigated lands at Palermo covers 1,000 ha although we cannot be sure that an area that large was under cultivation during the Late Horizon. About forty km farther to the south, the Inkas constructed a canal several kilometers long that expanded the irrigated lands in front of the paired installations at Puerta de La Paya and Guitián, the main center for the Inka province of Chicoana. Even farther to the south, in the Molinos area, there is also evidence for Inka occupation in association with field systems, but evidence for Inka-related agricultural projects in the area has not yet been reported.

Although there is substantial evidence for intensified production in the longitudinal Calchaquí Valley, the most productive lands in the vicinity were the lateral valleys, most of which lie to the west. Fed by runoff from the Andes and protected from the most extreme elements, these valleys provide more temperate, moister microclimates than the main valley (Tarragó 1978). There is considerable evidence for Inka-period occupation and extensive field systems in those lateral valleys (Tarragó and Díaz 1977; DeMarrais n.d.), but the nature of Inka production there remains to be worked out in detail. Although the Calchaquí production was intensified under Inka dominion, the agricultural products were likely intended for consumption in activities that were locally focused, as the storehouses at all Inka settlements in the region probably number in the low hundreds (Acuto n.d.).

In the more southerly part of the *valliserrana* of northwest Argentina, in the modern province of Catamarca, there is substantial evidence for intensified agricultural production resulting from Inka dominion. For example, in the Santa María Valley, Myriam Tarragó has identified areas of intensified farming in the region from Rincón Chico to Fatamanca. Large open enclosures, with associated residential occupations, stretch along five km of the valley. The largest individual area, at Medanitos, covers about thirty ha of the land surface (Tarragó 1978: 182). At Quilmes, also in the Santa María Valley, Raffino et al. (1983–85) estimate that an extensive zone of agricultural production to the south of the settlement may have covered as much as 500 ha. That area includes expanses of terraces irrigated by a reservoir with the capacity to hold about 7,000 m^3 of water. Similarly, at the nearby site of Fuerte Quemado, Kriskautzky has identified large areas enclosed by stone walls, which may have been committed to agriculture (de Hoyos and Williams 1994). In each of those latter two centers the Inkas appear to have taken over existing settlements, and it is not yet clear how much of those extensive agricultural land improvements were a consequence of state intervention or how much was already in place by the advent of Cusco's rule.

Farther to the south, however, at Potrero-Chaquiago and in the Quebrada El Totoral, there are substantial remnants of enclosed cultivated fields, terraces, canals, and reservoirs associated with Inka settlement (Williams and Lorandi n.d.: 136). The occupation at Potrero-Chaquiago is distinctive in that the center was established in a location that was previously unoccupied. The farms developed there were purely a consequence of state projects.

In several of these cases—the Quebrada de Humahuaca, the northern Calchaquí, and Potrero-Chaquiago—the Inkas appear to have appropriated much of their land from areas that were lightly used, if at all, during the period immediately preceding. That approach may well have ameliorated the impact on the agricultural productivity of the local populace and taken some of the sting out of being exploited for labor and other resources. Elsewhere, as in the mid-valley Calchaquí, the Inkas appear to have partially displaced indigenous populations and supplanted them with colonists. That stratagem seems to have been related to the Inkas' difficulty in pacifying the Calchaquíes and the use of mitmaqkuna from the more compliant Pular and Yavi etnías. At Fuerte Quemado and Quilmes, a third approach may have been put into action—installation of a relatively small Inka presence and the possible intensification of food production for state use.

CAMELID PASTORALISM AND HUNTING

There is less information on the nature of pastoralism under Inka rule in the southern Andes than for areas from Lake Titicaca north. The altiplano, which runs from far northern Argentina to the Titicaca Basin, was a prime locale for herding before and under Inka rule, but documentary sources on practices in the south are notably scant. Archaeological work in the region has identified a number of late prehistoric high-elevation settlements, especially in the Argentine pre-puna and puna, that contained corrals. The area around San Antonio de Los Cobres, for example, and the upper Quebrada de Humahuaca contain significant numbers of herding sites. As Raffino (1983b) has catalogued as well, complexes of corrals are almost invariably an element of the architecture at Inka sites.

Faunal materials recovered from archaeological sites consistently show a preponderance of large camelids (llama, guanaco) as the principal meat source, but bones from the smaller camelids (vicuña) are also frequently present (Pollard 1981, 1983; Sandefur and Daniels n.d.; Kriscautzky n.d.). Faunal remains from local sites with Inka components from the Quebrada de Humahuaca and the eastern valleys of Jujuy suggest that herding was a main source of meat but there is ample evidence for the exploitation of wild camelid and cervid hunting as a dietary complement to domestic meat sources. Whereas Inka sites such as Papachacra and Hornaditas in Jujuy show a preponderance of wild camelids (vicuña and guanaco), at La Huerta llamas dominate the faunal assemblage. The information available on herd management practices suggests that the Inkas may have slaughtered adult animals after they had finished their fertile cycles (Madero n.d.a).

The limited information available on herd management practices in the Calchaquí Valley suggests that the Inkas may have slaughtered animals at their prime meat age for consumption at provincial centers, whereas the indigenous residents allowed some animals to live out close to their natural life spans (Sandefur and Daniels n.d.; D'Altroy et al. 2000). There is ample evidence for hunting in the archaeological record of the late Pre-Hispanic periods, largely in the form of obsidian projectile points (Russell n.d.). However, there is little specific information on Inka-related hunting practices or restrictions placed on the local populations, such as a ban on vicuña hunting, which was generally reserved for royalty.

Potrero-Chaquiago's faunal remains show an almost exclusive reliance on domesticated camelids. Both adults and juvenile animals were slaughtered (Madero n.d.b), indicating that there was an ample supply of animals available to the population for food, textiles, and transportation. This suggests that the residents of the settlement and vicinity practiced careful herd management.

EXTRACTION OF RAW MATERIALS AND CRAFT PRODUCTION.
Thus far, the discussion of the economy has focused on relations of production in the agro-pastoral sector. However, the southern Andes under Inka rule are known best for their mineralogical and craft activities. Early chroniclers such as Juan de Betanzos (1996), Pedro Sarmiento de Gamboa (1960), and Pedro Pizarro (1986) wrote that the central purpose of the Inka ventures into the southern Andes was to obtain mineral wealth. Both Chile and northwest Argentina are rich in copper minerals and there was a considerable industry in mining and bronze metallurgy many centuries before the birth of the Inka state (González 1981). The south also had a long history of lapidary production in copper minerals such as turquoise, malachite, and atacamite, and gold objects have been recovered from graves from the Formative period onward.

Archaeological surveys in the southern Andes substantiate the view that the Inkas took ample advantage of the mineral wealth of the region. Raffino's (1983b: 250–252) compilation of Inka-related archaeological sites enumerates sixty-eight sites in Argentina and fifty-eight in southern Bolivia and Chile that were involved in mining gold, silver, copper, galena, lead, zinc, tin, and other minerals. Overall, he estimates that about seventy-five

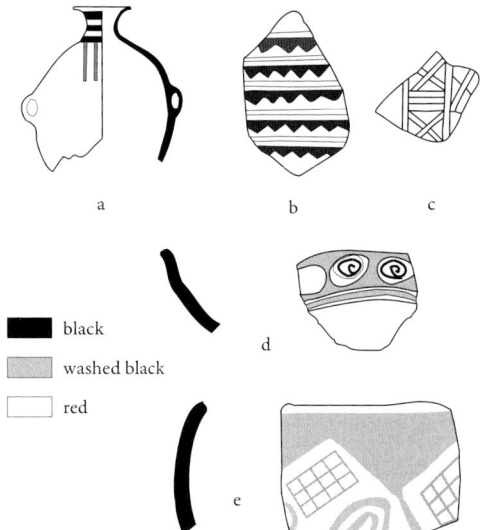

FIG. 14 Ceramics from Potrero-Chaquiago: a–c) Provincial Inka polychromes; d) Yavi Chico Polychrome; e) Altiplano Chicha

percent of Inka sites in the south were involved in mineral extraction or processing (Raffino 1983b: 243). Among the sites mentioned, eighteen are associated directly with extraction, ore processing, and smelting locations (Quillay and perhaps la Encrucijada, Argentina), and workshops that produced either ingots or finished products (Potrero de Payogasta and Potrero-Chaquiago, Ingenio del Arenal Médanos, and Rincón Chico, Argentina). Granted that the proportion of activities dedicated to such efforts at many sites may have been limited and that quite a few of the sites mentioned were small, this is still an impressive commitment of human resources to the industry.

Both historical and archaeological lines of evidence attest to specialized state craft production in the south, some in enclaves of specialist producers, or mitmaqkuna. Perhaps the best-documented craft center was at Potrero-Chaquiago in northwest Argentina (Lorandi 1984; Williams and Lorandi n.d.; Williams 1996). There, archaeological evidence of state-supported ceramic manufacture, weaving, and metallurgy has been found. The ceramic industry provides some especially interesting features, as several distinct types of pottery were apparently made locally. In addition to the provincial variant of Cusco polychrome (fig. 14), potters made ceramics in styles that were similar to those of the Yavi and Santiago del Estero regions, but with local materials. Ceramics in styles that suggest a Tucumán origin are also found in many of the Inka sites of the southern Calchaquí, Santa María, Hualfín, Andalgalá, and central Catamarca valleys (Lorandi 1988: 242). Lorandi and Williams have argued that the evidence points to the presence of colonist potters, installed by the state, who made pottery both in the state style and that of their homelands.

This evidence is part of a broader pattern of the production and distribution of pottery under Inka dominion. Unlike the major Inka installations of the central Andes, even the most prominent Inka sites in the south often exhibit ceramic assemblages of which state polychromes form less than fifty percent. The remainder of the assemblages consist of local types, such as Santamariano Bi-Color and Tri-Color or Belén Black-on-Red and a series of fine wares that appear only in Inka sites. Among the last are Averías and Famabalasto Black-on-Red in imitation of styles east of the Andes, Pacajes and Yavi Chico Polychrome from the altiplano, and Black Polished and Inka Paya from both the Calchaquí Valley and Catamarca. Overall, the pattern seems to point to a system in which both local quotidian and fancy pottery styles were used to supplement the Inka wares. Such a practice was notably different from that found in the central Andes, where state personnel seem to have gone to great lengths to ensure that the material goods used to sustain activities at the state centers were made in a distinctive style so that manufacture and circulation could be controlled. Whether the more southerly pattern was a consequence of lower state interest in such control, support of a different array of activities, or a more flexible organization for mobilizing goods remains to be determined.

FIG. 15 Manufacturing debris of mica, including unworked pieces, small debris with cut marks, and partly finished disks, from Potrero de Payogasta (composite image courtesy Timothy Earle)

The archaeological evidence for craft production of various kinds suggests that it was organized into workshops. At Potrero-Chaquiago, different kinds of production were focused in particular architectural compounds, suggestive of close state control over workshop activities. There is evidence of metalworking in bronze and manufacture of adornments made of mica, marine shell, and malachite (Williams 1983, n.d.; Williams and Lorandi n.d.). At Fuerte Quemado as well, Kriscautzky reports a metallurgical workshop with remains of gold and copper metallurgy. Similarly, artifacts from a lapidary workshop have been recovered from the site of Pucará de Tilcara in northern Argentina (Krapovickas 1981–82). At Potrero de Payogasta, evidence has been found of metalworking in bronze and gold and manufacture of a range of adornments out of mica, marine and land snail shell, bone, and atacamite (Earle 1994). The craft production there included all stages of work, from raw material and ore processing, to rough shaping of objects, to finishing details. Mica manufacture, for example, is indicated by plentiful waste, including unworked pieces, small debris with cut marks, and partly finished disks and other pendants that were probably damaged during manufacture (fig. 15). All of the craft activities were concentrated in one protected sector of the settlement, at a distance from the main plaza, kallanka, and associated buildings. Even so, it is intriguing that virtually all of the highest-quality and imported ceramics recovered in excavations were found in the same architectural complex, suggesting that craft activities were given some degree of status but were not associated directly with ceremonial locations. Although metallurgical production was present, the scale of smelting was far lower than that at Valdéz, a large Pular town occupied before and after the Inka occupation. At that town, crucibles and molds were found in high densities, sometimes with copper encrustations.

Perhaps the strongest evidence for the importance of camelid use in the south lies in the textile industry. Ambrosetti's (1907–08) excavations of 202 tombs at Puerta de La Paya turned up over 1,000 spindle whorls and numerous other tools used in shearing wool and weaving cloth (Calderari n.d.). At Chivilme, in the Lerma Valley, Mulvany (n.d.) has even found a workshop that manufactured spindle whorls. An interesting find, from the excavation of eleven compounds at Fuerte Quemado, is a great concentration of vicuña bones, implying that there was an important industry in weaving the finest of camelid wools (Kriscautzky n.d.: 212). At Potrero-Chaquiago 151 spindle whorls, 297 *fichas* (disks, possibly spindle whorls), five combs, and three awls were recovered (Williams n.d.).

Overall, archaeological investigations into the extraction of raw materials and the production of craft objects indicate that the Inkas committed a significant proportion of their available labor to such activities throughout the southern Andes. In contrast to the heartland, however, the evidence for access to the products is limited. Nowhere in the south have any subject settlements been registered that contain the array of Inka polychrome ceramics found in some of the sites of the Upper Mantaro Valley in the central Peruvian highlands. Even at the main state installations of the south, the Inkas made considerably more use of local materials and limited the contexts within which state-style material culture was employed. In the northern Calchaquí Valley, for example, the finished ceramic, metallurgical, and other objects in the Inka style recovered in excavations have been concentrated in burial contexts. Ambrosetti's (1907–08) burials from Puerta de La Paya stand out as the principal example of that practice.

Conclusions

In closing, we would like to return to a point made at the outset. The appearance of a limited application of Inka power in the southern Andes, in comparison to areas farther north, is a consequence of both real patterns and the nature of the available evidence. It is true that the state infrastructure was not as ambitiously developed as it was from Lake Titicaca north. None of the state centers in the south was as large as the main settlements between Cusco and Quito, nor were the native societies nearly as populous or wealthy. Even so, the Inkas built a wide array of provincial centers and smaller tampu, protected by fortified installations that defended both the southern extension of the empire and its eastern flanks. They also extensively reorganized the indigenous societies through resettlement, while intensifying mineral extraction and agricultural and craft production at numerous locations.

The scope of those investments and transformations has been partially masked, primarily by the meager early documentary record and the limited scale of archaeological research. As a result, we still have a far less nuanced understanding of this vast region than has been developed for the northern half of the empire. An additional contributing factor lies in the modern Andean nations' visions of their prehispanic pasts. In Peru and Bolivia, national identities owe much to the great civilizations of the indigenous Americas, especially the Inkas and Tiwanaku. Such links are far more tenuous in Argentina and Chile, where the Inkas are seen largely through the eyes of academics and museologists. That historical schism between native past and modern society has added to our vision of the Inka occupation in the south as having been more marginal that it was in actuality.

As research has intensified over recent years, our knowledge of Kollasuyu has increased proportionally. Two of the most significant advances for the southern lands described here concern the potential expansion of the empire's time line and the intensity of Inka rule. The chronology, extent, and diversity of the state installations indicate that the Inkas may have been present earlier and certainly invested far more effort in ruling the south than is usually recognized (cf. Raffino 1983b; Hyslop 1990). When considering the variations in Inka power expressed throughout the empire, it seems best to view Inka rule in the southern Andes as appropriate to the peoples and resources—that is, more restricted than in the central Andes, but no less significant for the region's indigenous peoples and comparably challenging for the Inkas.

Notes

1   The authors of this paper would like to thank the organizers of the Dumbarton Oaks symposium "Variations in the Expression of Inka Power" for inviting us to present the paper on which this chapter is based. We would also like to thank Columbia University, Universidad de Buenos Aires, Universidad de La Plata, Universidad Nacional de Salta, CONICET, the U.S. National Science Foundation, the Dumbarton Oaks Research Library and Collection, Dow Chemical, La Fundación Antorchas de Argentina, the provincial and municipal authorities of Salta and Catamarca, and the Museo Arqueológico de Cachi for their support of our research. A special thanks is owed to all of our colleagues who have shared their research information and who have worked together with us in the field. We also thank Liz DeMarrais and Kirsten Olson for their comments on an earlier draft of this paper.

2   There is a considerable literature on the discrepancies among historical sources on the Inka chronology, and scholars are divided on the utility and accuracy of Cabello's sequence. We do not wish to enter into an extended debate on that issue here, but will note that there are several other Inka-era chronologies in the Spanish sources, all of which give imperial history more time depth than Cabello, usually implausibly so. Generally speaking, scholars have accepted Cabello's sequence as the best estimate available, but few take his dates literally.

3   In the time since the original compilation of this paper, a number of additional radiocarbon dates have been accumulated for the southern Andes, but we have not incorporated them into this paper.

4   The earliest of those dates is significantly different at the 95% level from the earlier of the two dates falling within the historical time frame: $T'=11.14$; $\Pi^2=3.84$.

5   Material in this section is partially distilled from or expanded in D'Altroy (2002: 209–213, 260–262).

6   Matienzo (1967 [1567]: chap. 34) wrote that an Inka road reached Santiago del Estero; Betanzos (1987 [1551]: chap. 35, p. 160) stated that Thupa Inka Yupanki conquered the Zuries; and the khipu kamayuq (Qhapaq Ayllu in Rowe 1985 [1569]: 226]) said that Wayna Qhapaq used Juri soldiers in his northern campaigns. For descriptions of Pucará de Andalgalá, see González and Núñez Regueiro (1958–59: 116–119) and Hyslop (1990: 182–186).

References cited

ACUTO, FÉLIX A.
n.d. Landscapes of Ideology and Inequality: Experiencing Inka Domination. Ph.D. dissertation, Department of Anthropology, SUNY Binghamton, 2004.

ADAMSKA, ANN, AND ADAM MICHCZYSKI
1996 Towards Radiocarbon Chronology of the Inca state. *Andes: Boletín de la misión arqueológica andina* 1: 35–58.

ALBECK, MARIA ESTHER
1992–93 Areas agrícolas y densidad de ocupación prehispánica en la Quebrada de Humahuaca. *Avances en arqueología* 2: 56–77.

ALBECK, MARIA ESTHER, AND MARIA CRISTINA SCATTOLIN
1991 Cálculo fotogramétrico de superficies de cultivo en Coctaca y Rodero: Quebrada de Humahuaca. *Avances en arqueología* 1: 43–58.

ALCAYAGA, DIEGO F.
1961 [1605] Relación cierta que el padre Diego Felipe de Alcaya... In *Cronistas cruceños del alto Perú virreinal* (Hernando Sanabria Fernández, ed.): 47–68. Publicaciones de la Universidad Gabriel René Moreno. Santa Cruz de la Sierra, Bolivia.

AMBROSETTI, JUAN B.
1902 El sepulcro de La Paya últimamente descubierto en los valles Calchaquíes, Provincia de Salta. *Anales del Museo Nacional* 8: 119–148.

1907–08 Exploraciones arqueológicas en la ciudad prehistórica de "La Paya" (Valle Calchaquí, Provincia de Salta). *Revista de la Universidad de Buenos Aires* 8 (Sección Antropología, 3), 2 vols. Facultad de Filosofía y Letras. M. Biedma é hijo, Buenos Aires.

BÁRCENA, J. ROBERTO
1979 Informe sobre recientes investigaciones arquelógicas en el NO de la Provincia de Mendoza, Argentina (Valle de Uspallata y zonas vecinas). In *Actas del VII Congreso de Arqueología de Chile* 2: 661–692. Ediciones Kultrun, Santiago de Chile.

1988 Investigación de la dominación incaica en Mendoza: El tambo de Tambillos, la vialidad anexa y los altos cerros cercanos. *Espacio, tiempo y forma: Prehistoria* 1: 397–426. UNED, Madrid.

BÁRCENA, J. ROBERTO, AND ALICIA J. ROMÁN
1990 Funcionalidad diferencial de las estructuras del tamo de Tambillos. *Anales de arqueología y etnología* 41/42 (1986/87): 7–81.

BAUER, BRIAN S., AND ALAN R. COVEY
    2002   Processes of State Formation in the Inca Heartland (Cuzco, Peru). *American Anthropologist* 104 (3): 846–864.

BEORCHIA NIGRIS, ANTONIO
    1987   *El enigma de los santuarios indigenas de alta montaña.* Revista del C.I.A.D.A.M. 5 (1985). Centro de Investigaciones Arqueológicas de Alta Montaña, San Juan, Argentina.

BETANZOS, JUAN DE
    1996 [1557]   *Narrative of the Incas* (Roland Hamilton and Dana Buchman, trans. and eds.). University of Texas, Austin.

BIBAR, GERÓNIMO DE
    1966 [1558]   *Crónica y relación copiosa y verdadera de los reynos de Chile* (Irving A. Leonard, transcription). Fondo Histórico y Bibliográfico José Toribio Medina, Santiago, Chile.

BOMAN, ERIC
    1908   *Antiquités de la région andine de la République Argentine et du désert d'Atacama.* 2 vols. Imprimerie Nationale, Paris.

CABELLO VALBOA, MIGUEL
    1951 [1586]   *Miscelanea antártica: Una historia del Perú antiguo.* Universidad Nacional Mayor de San Marcos, Facultad de Letras, Instituto de Etnología, Lima.

CALDERARI, MILENA
    n.d.   Asentamiento y dinámica cultural en La Paya, Valle Calchaquí medio. Beca Doctoral. Informe Final. CONICET. Buenos Aires, 1992.

CARRARA, MARÍA T., ANA MARÍA LORANDI, S. RENARD, AND MYRIAM TARRAGÓ
    1960   Punta de Balasto. In *Investigaciones arqueológicas en el Valle de Santa María* (Eduardo M. Cigliano et al., eds.): 4: 13–41. Publicación del Instituto de Antropología. Facultad de Filosofía y Letras, Universidad Nacional del Litoral, Rosario.

CASANOVA, EDUARDO
    1934   Observaciones preliminares sobre la arqueología de Coctaca (provincia de Jujuy). *Actas y trabajos científicos del XXV Congreso Internacional de Americanistas (La Plata, 1932).* Vol. 2. "Coni," Buenos Aires.

CERUTI, MARÍA CONSTANZA
    1997   *Arqueología de Alta Montaña.* Editorial MILOR, Mendoza, Argentina.

CIEZA DE LEÓN, PEDRO DE
    1967 [1553]   *El Señorío de los Incas: Segunda parte de la Crónica del Perú.* Instituto de Estudios Peruanos, Lima.

COVEY, ALAN R.
  2003 A Processual Study of Inca State Formation. *Journal of Anthropological Archaeology* 22 (4): 333–357.

CREMONTE, MARIA BEATRIZ, AND MERCEDES GARAY DE FUMGALLI
  1996 Estado actual de las investigaciones arqueológicas en el sector meridional de la Quebrada de Humahuaca y su borde oriental. In *Congreso en Investigación Social:* 379–393. Universidad Nacional de Tucumán, Tucumán, Argentina.

D'ALTROY, TERENCE N.
  1987 Transitions in Power: Centralization of Wanka Political Organization under Inka Rule. *Ethnohistory* 34: 1: 78–102.
  1992 *Provincial Power in the Inka Empire.* Smithsonian Institution Press, Washington, D.C. and London.
  2002 *The Incas.* Blackwell Publishers, Malden, Mass.
  2005 Remaking the Social Landscape: Colonization in the Inka Empire. In *The Archaeology of Colonial Encounters* (Gil Stein, ed.): 263–295. SAR Press, Albuquerque, N. Mex.

D'ALTROY, TERENCE N., ANA MARÍA LORANDI, VERÓNICA I. WILLIAMS, MILENA CALDERARI, CHRISTINE A. HASTORF, ELIZABETH DEMARRAIS, AND MELISSA B. HAGSTRUM
  2000 Inka Imperial Rule in the Northern Calchaquí Valley, Argentina. *Journal of Field Archaeology* 27 (1): 1–26.

D'ALTROY, TERENCE N., AND VERÓNICA I. WILLIAMS
  n.d. Informe sobre Fechados de Radiocarbono en Potrero de Payogasta y Valdéz Valle Calchaquí, Pcia. de Salta, Rep. Argentina. Submitted to the Ministerio de Educación y Cultura, Provincia de Salta, Republica Argentina, 1994.

D'ALTROY, TERENCE N., VERÓNICA I. WILLIAMS, AND BRIAN S. BAUER
  n.d. Inka Expansionism: A Comparison of Radiocarbon and Historical Dates, 1998.

DEBENEDETTI, SALVADOR
  1908 *Excursión arqueológica á las ruinas de Kipón (Valle Calchaqui—provincia de Salta).* Publicaciones de la Sección Antropología 4. Imp. M. Biedma é hijo, Buenos Aires.

DE HOYOS, MARIA, AND VERÓNICA I. WILLIAMS
  1994 Un patrón de asentamiento estatal para propósitos especiales. Resumenes. Actas y Memorias del XI Congreso Nacional de Arqueología Argentina. *Revista del Museo de Historia Natural de San Rafael* 1: 196–199. Museo de Historia Natural, Dirección Municipal de Cultura, Mendoza, Argentina.

DE LORENZI, MÓNICA, AND PIO PABLO DÍAZ
  1977 La ocupación incaica en el sector septentrional del Valle Calchaquí. *Estudios de Arqueología* 2: 45–59.

DEMARRAIS, ELIZABETH

n.d. Materialization, Ideology, and Power: The Development of Centralized Authority among the Pre-Hispanic Polities of the Valle Calchaquí, Argentina. Ph.D. dissertation, Department of Anthropology, University of California, Los Angeles, 1997.

DENEVAN, WILLIAM M.

1980 *La geografía cultural aborígen de los Llanos de Mojos.* Juventud, La Paz, Bolivia.

DÍAZ, PÍO PABLO

1983 Sitios Arqueológicos del Valle Calchaquí. *Estudios de Arqueología* 2: 93–104.

DIFRIERI, HORACIO

1948 Las ruinas del Potrero de Payogasta (Provincia de Salta, Argentina). In *Actes du XXVIIIe Congrès Internacional des Americanistes:* 599–604. Musée de L'Homme, Paris.

DILLEHAY, TOM D., AND AMÉRICO GORDON

1988 La actividad prehispánica de los Incas y su influencia en la Araucania. In *La frontera del estado inca.* Proceedings of the 45th International Congress of Americanists, Bogotá, Colombia, 1985 (Tom D. Dillehay and Patricia J. Netherly, eds.): 215–234. First published as BAR International Series 442. British Archaeological Reports, Oxford, England.

DOUCET, B. GABRIEL

n.d. Acerca de los churumatas, con particular referencia al antiguo Tucumán. Paper presented at the 1st Congreso Internacional de Etnohistoria. Buenos Aires, 1989.

EARLE, TIMOTHY K.

1994 Wealth Finance in the Inka Empire: Evidence from the Calchaquí Valley, Argentina. *American Antiquity* 59 (3): 443–460.

ESPINOZA SORIANO, WALDEMAR

1970 Los mitmas yungas de Collique en Cajamarca, siglos XV, XVI, y XVII. *Revista del Museo Nacional* 36: 9–57.

1973 Las colonias de mitmas múltiples en Abancay, siglos XV y XVI. *Revista del Museo Nacional* 39: 225–299.

1975 Los mitmas huayacuntu en Quito o guarniciones para la represión armada, siglos XV y XVI. *Revista del Museo Nacional* 41: 351–394.

1981 Un testimonio sobre los idolos, huacas y dioses de Lampa y Cajatambo, siglos XV–XVII: Supervivencias en Cajamarca. *Ciencia et Praxis: Revista de la Universidad de Limando* 15: 115–151.

1987   Migraciones internas en el Reino Colla: Tejedores, Plumeros, y Alfareros del Estado Imperial Inca. *Chungará* 19: 243–289.

FOCK, NILS

1961   Inca Imperialism in Northwest Argentina, and Chaco Burial Forms. *Folk* 3: 67–90.

GARAY DE FUMAGALLI, MERCEDES, AND MARÍA BEATRIZ CREMONTE

1997   Correlación cronológica del yacimiento de Volcán con sitios de los valles orientales (Sector Meridional-Quebrada de Humahuaca). *Avances de Arqueología* 3: 191- 212. Instituto Interdisciplinario de Tilcara, Jujuy, Argentina.

GIFFORD, CLARENCE H. III

n.d.   Local Matters: Encountering the Imperial Inkas in the South Andes. Ph.D. dissertation, Department of Anthropology, Columbia University, 2003.

GONZÁLEZ, ALBERTO REX

1981   Pre-Columbian Metallurgy of Northwest Argentina. In *Pre-Columbian Metallurgy of South America* (Elizabeth Benson, ed.): 133–202. Dumbarton Oaks Research Library and Collection, Washington, D.C.

1982   Las "Provincias" inca del antiguo Tucumán. *Revista del Museo Nacional* 46: 317–380.

1983   Inca Settlement Patterns in a Marginal Province of the Empire. In *Prehistoric Settlement Patterns: Essays in Honor of Gordon R. Willey* (Evon Z. Vogt and Richard M. Leventhal, eds.): 337–360. Harvard University Press, Cambridge, Mass.

GONZÁLEZ, ALBERTO REX, AND PÍO PABLO DÍAZ

1992   La Casa Morada. *Estudios de Arqueología* 5: 9–54.

GONZÁLEZ, ALBERTO REX, AND V. NÚÑEZ REGUEIRO

1958–59   Apuntes preliminares sobre la Arqueología de Campo de Pucará y alrededores (Dpto. de Andagalá, Pcia. de Catamarca). *Anales de Arqueología y Etnología* 14–15: 115–62.

GONZÁLEZ, LUIS R.

1995   Blues del Bicho Muerto: Observaciones arqueológicas en el sur del valle de Yocavil. *Palimpsesto: Revista de Arqueología* 4: 97–102.

HYSLOP, JOHN

1984   *The Inka Road System.* Academic Press, Orlando, Fla.

1988   Las fronteras estatales extremas del Tawantinsuyu. In *La Frontera del Estado Inca* (Tom Dillehay and Patricia Netherly, eds.): 35–55. International Series 442. British Archaeological Reports, Oxford, England.

1990   *Inka Settlement Planning.* University of Texas Press, Austin.

HYSLOP, JOHN, AND PÍO PABLO DÍAZ
    1983   El Camino Incaico: Calchaquí-Tastil (N.O. Argentina). *Gaceta Arqueológica Andina* 1 (6): 6–8.

HYSLOP, JOHN, AND JUAN SCHOBINGER
    1991   Las ruinas incaicas de los Nevados del Aconquija. *Comechingonia* 9: 17–30.

KRAPOVICKAS, PEDRO
    1981–82   Hallazgos incaicos en Tilcara y Yacoraite (una reinterpretación). *Relaciones de la Sociedad Argentina de Antropología* 149 (2): 67–80.

KRISCAUTZKY, NESTOR
    n.d.   Arqueología del Fuerte Quemado de Yokavil. Ph.D. dissertation, Facultad de Ciencias Naturales y Museo de la Universidad Nacional de La Plata, Argentina, 1994.

LORANDI, ANA MARÍA
    1984   Pleito de Juan Ochoa de Zárate por la posesión de los indios ocloyas. ¿Un caso de verticalidad étnica o un relicto de archipiélago estatal? *Runa* 14: 125–144.
    1988   Los diaguitas y el Tawantinsuyu: Una hipótesis de conflicto. In *La frontera del estado inca*. Proceedings of the 45th International Congress of Americanists, Bogotá, Colombia, 1985 (Tom D. Dillehay and Patricia J. Netherly, eds.): 235–259. First published as BAR International Series 442. British Archaeological Reports, Oxford, England.
    1991   Evidencias en torno a los Mitmaqkuna incaicos en el N.O. argentino. *Anthropológica* 9: 213–236.
    1997   *De quimeras, rebeliones y utopias: La gesta del Inca Pedro Bohórquez*. Universidad Pontificia del Perú. Fondo Editorial, Lima.

LORANDI, ANA MARÍA, AND ROXANA BOIXADÓS
    1987–88   Etnohistoria de los Valles Calchaquies en los Siglos XVI y XVII. *Runa* 17–18: 263–420.

LOZANO, PEDRO
    1873–74   *Historia de la Conquista del Paraguay, Río de la Plata y Tucumán*. Casa Editora "Imprenta Popular," Buenos Aires.

MADERO, CELINA
    n.d.a   Estudios económicos del pastoreo de camélidos en poblados prehispánicos del noroeste de Argentina: Una visión arqueológica. Informe Final Beca Perfeccionamiento CONICET, Argentina, 1993.
    n.d.b   Informe de la arqueofauna del sitio Inka Potrero-Chaquiago. Sector Retambay (provincia de Catamarca), 1995.

MALPASS, MICHAEL, ED.
　1993　*Provincial Inca: Archaeological and Ethnohistorical Assessment of the Impact of the Inca State.* University of Iowa Press, Iowa City.

MARIÑO DE LOVERA, PEDRO
　1960 [1580]　*Crónica del Reino de Chile.* Biblioteca de Autores Españoles 131: 227–562. Ediciones Atlas, Madrid.

MÁRQUEZ MIRANDA, FERNANDO, AND EDUARDO M. CIGLIANO
　1961　*Problemas arqueológicos en la zona de Ingenio del Arenal (Prov. de Catamarca)* [*Revista del Museo de La Plata*, new series, sección antropología 5: 123–169]. Facultad de Ciencias Naturales y Museo, Universidad Nacional de La Plata, La Plata.

MATIENZO, JUAN DE
　1967 [1567]　*El Gobierno del Perú* (Guillermo Lohmann Villena, ed. and preliminary study). Travaux de l'Institut Français d'Études Andines 11. Institut Français d'Etudes Andines, Paris and Lima.

MEDINA, JOSE TORIBO
　1952 [1882]　*Los aborígenes de Chile.* Fondo Histórico y Bibliográfico. J. T. Medina, Santiago, Chile.

MORRIS, CRAIG
　1988　Mas allá de las fronteras de Chincha. In *La frontera del estado inca.* Proceedings of the 45th International Congress of Americanists, Bogotá, Colombia, 1985 (Tom D. Dillehay and Patricia J. Netherly, eds.): 131–140. First published as BAR International Series 442. British Archaeological Reports, Oxford, England.

MOSTNY, GRETE
　1949　Ciudades Atacamenas—Norte de Chile. *Boletín del Museo Nacional de Historia Natural* 24: 125–204.

MULVANY DE PEÑALOZA, ELEANORA
　1986　Nuevas evidencias de la ocupación incaica en el valle de Lerma. *Runa* 16: 59–84.

MÚÑOZ, IVÁN, AND JUAN CHACAMA
　1989　*Cronología por termoluminiscencia para el Período Intermedio Tardío y Tardío en la Sierra de Arica.* Doc. de Trabajo 5: 1–40. Universidad de Tarapacá, Arica, Chile.

NIELSEN, AXEL E.
　1997　*Tiempo y Cultura Material en la Quebrada de Humahuaca, 700–1650.* Instituto Interdisciplinario de Tilcara, Facultad Filosofía y Lettras, Universidad de Buenos Aire, Buenos Aires.

NIEMEYER, HANS
　1986　La ocupación inkaica de la cuenca alta del Río Copiapó. *Comechingonia* 4: 165–294.

NIEMEYER, HANS, AND VIRGILIO SCHIAPPACASSE

1988 Patrones de asentamientos incaicos en el Norte Grande de Chile. In *La frontera del estado inca.* Proceedings of the 45th International Congress of Americanists, Bogotá, Colombia, 1985 (Tom D. Dillehay and Patricia J. Netherly, eds.): 131–40. First published as BAR International Series 442. British Archaeological Reports, Oxford, England.

OLAVERRIA, MIGUEL DE

1852 [1594] Informe de Don Miguel de Olaverria sobre el Reyno de Chile, sus Indios y sus guerras. *Documentos sobre la Historia la Estadistica y la Geografia de Chile* (Claude Gay, ed.), vol. 2, *Historia física y politica de Chile según documentos:* 13–54. E. Thunot, Paris.

PÄRSSINEN, MARTTI

1992 *Tawantinsuyu: The Inca State and Its Political Organization.* Societas Historica Finlandiae, Helsinki.

PÄRSSINEN, MARTTI, AND ARI SIIRIÄINEN

1997 Inca-Style Ceramics and Their Chronological Relationship to the Inca Expansion in the Southern Lake Titicaca Area (Bolivia). *Latin American Antiquity* 8: 255–271.

PIZARRO, PEDRO

1986 [1571] *Relación del descubrimiento y conquista de los reinos del Perú.* 2nd. ed. (Guillermo Lohmann Villena, ed.). Pontificia Universidad Católica del Perú, Fondo Editorial, Lima.

PLANELLA, MARÍA TERESA, AND RUBÉN STEHBERG

1994 Etnohistoria y arqueología en el estudio de la fortaleza indigena de Cerro Grande de la Compañia. *Revista Chungará* 26: 1: 65–78.

PLANELLA, MARIA TERESA, RUBÉN STEHBERG, BLANCA TAGLE, HANS NIEMEYER, AND CARMEN DEL RÍO

1991 La fortaleza indígena del Cerro Grande de la Compañía (Valle del Cachapoal) y su relación con el proceso expansivo meridional incaico. *Actas del XII Congreso Nacional de Arqueología Chilena:* 403–421. Sociedad Chilena de Arqueología, Dirección de Bibliotecas, Archivos y Museos, Santiago and Temuco, Chile.

POLLARD, GORDON C.

1981 The Bronze Artisans of Calchaquí. *Early Man* 33: 27–33.

1983 Nuevos aportes a la Prehistoria del Valle Calchaquí, Noroeste Argentino. *Estudios de Arqueología* 3–4: 69–92.

PRESTA, ANA MARÍA, AND MERCEDES DEL RÍO

n.d. Reflexiones sobre los churumatas del sur de Bolivia. Paper presented at the 1st Congreso Internacional de Etnohistoria, Buenos Aires, 1989.

RAFFINO, RODOLFO A.

1983a *Arqueología y etnohistoria de la región Calchaquí: Presencia hispánica en la arqueología argentina,* vol. 2. Museo Regional de Antropología e Instituto de Historia, Facultad de Humanidades UNE, La Plata, Argentina.

1983b *Los Inkas del Kollasuyu.* 2nd ed. Ramos Americana Editora, La Plata, Bolivia and Buenos Aires, Argentina.

1993 *Inka: Arqueología, historia y urbanismo del altiplano andino.* Corregidor, Buenos Aires.

RAFFINO, RODOLFO A., RICARDO J. ALVIS, LIDIA N. BALDINI, DANIEL E. OLIVERA, AND M. G. RAVIFIA

1983–85 Hualfín-El Shincal-Watungasta: Tres casos de urbanización inka en el N.o. Argentino. *Cuadernos del Instituto Nacional de Antropología* 10: 425–458.

REINHARD, JOHAN

1985 Sacred Mountains: An Ethnoarchaeological Study of High Andean Ruins. *Mountain Research and Development* 5 (4): 299–317.

1992 An Archaeological Investigation of Inca Ceremonial Platforms on the Volcano Copiapó, Central Chile. In *Ancient America: Contributions to New World Archaeology* (Nicholas J. Saunders, ed.): 145–172. Oxbow Monograph 24. Oxbow Books, Oxford, England.

ROWE, JOHN H.

1946 Inca Culture at the Time of the Spanish Conquest. In *Handbook of South American Indians,* vol. 2 (Julian Steward, ed): 183–330. Bureau of American Ethnology Bulletin 143. Washington, D.C.

1948 The Kingdom of Chimor. *Acta Americana* 6: 26–59.

RUSSELL, GLENN S.

n.d. Preliminary Report on the Lithic Remains from Potrero de Payogasta and Valdéz. In Final Report to the National Science Foundation (Terence N. D'Altroy, compiler), Washington, D.C., 1990.

SAIGNES, THIERRY

1985 *Los Andes Orientales: Historia de un Olvido.* Instituto Francés de Estudios Andinos, Lima.

SALOMON, FRANK

1986 *Native Lords of Quito in the Age of the Incas: The Political Economy of the North-Andean Chiefdoms.* Cambridge University Press, Cambridge, England.

SANDEFUR, ELSIE, AND ROBERT DANIELS

n.d. Preliminary Report on the Faunal Remains from Potrero de Payogasta and Valdéz. In Final Report to the National Science Foundation (Terence N. D'Altroy, compiler), 1990.

SARMIENTO DE GAMBOA, PEDRO

1960 [1572] *Historia de los Incas.* In *Obras completas del Inca Garcilaso de la Vega.* Biblioteca de Autores Españoles 135: 193–297. Ediciones Atlas, Madrid.

SCHÁVELZON, DANIEL, AND MARCELO MAGADÁN

1992 Potrero de Payogasta: La Arquitectura de una ciudad incaica del noroeste argentino. In *Ancient America: Contributions to New World Archaeology* (Nicholas J. Saunders, ed.): 173–188. Oxbow Monograph 24. Oxbow Books, Oxford, England.

SCHOBINGER, JUAN (ED.)

1966 *La "Momia" del Cerro el Toro,* supplement to vol. 21, *Anales de Arqueología y Etnología.* Universidad Nacional de Cuyo, Mendoza, Argentina.

SILVA GALDAMES, OSVALDO

1986 Los promaucaes y la frontera meridional incaica en Chile. *Cuadernos de Historia* 6.

SNEAD, JAMES E.

1992 Imperial Infrastructure and the Inka State Storage System. In *Inka Storage Systems* (Terry Y. LeVine, ed.): 62–106. University of Oklahoma Press, Norman.

STEHBERG, RUBÉN

1976 *La fortaleza de Chena y su relación con la ocupación incaica de Chile Central.* Publicación Ocasional 23. Museo Nacional de Historia Natural, Santiago, Chile.

1991–92 El límite inferior cronológico de la expansión incaica a Chile. *Xama* 4–5: 83–89.

STEHBERG, RUBÉN, AND NAZARENO CARVAJAL

1988 Road System of the Incas in the Southern Part of Their Tawantinsuyu Empire. *National Geographic Research* 4 (1): 74–87.

TARRAGÓ, MYRIAM N.

1978 Paleoecology of the Calchaquí Valley, Salta Province, Argentina. In *Advances in Andean Archaeology* (David L. Browman, ed.): 485–512. Mouton, The Hague.

TARRAGÓ, MYRIAM N., AND PÍO PABLO DÍAZ

1972 Sitios Arqueológicos del Valle Calchaquí. *Estudios de Arqueología* 1: 49–61.

1977 Sitios Arqueológicos del Valle Calchaquí (II). *Estudios de Arqueología* 2: 61–71.

TARRAGÓ, MYRIAM N., AND VICTOR NÚÑEZ REGUEIRO
    1972 Un diseño de investigación arqueológica en el valle Calchaquí: Fase exploratoria. *Estudios de Arqueología* 1: 62–85.

TEN KATE, HERMANN
    1893 Rapport sommaire sur une excursion archaeologique dans les provinces de Catamarca, Tucumán et Salta. *Revista Museo de La Plata* 5.

VALDIVIA, PEDRO DE
    1960 *Carta al Emperador Carlos V.* Biblioteca de Autores Españoles 131: 3–74. Ediciones Atlas, Madrid.

WACHTEL, NATHAN
    1982 The *Mitimas* of the Cochabamba Valley: The Colonization Policy of Huayna Capac. In *The Inca and Aztec States, 1400–1800: Anthropology and History* (George A. Collier, Renato I. Rosaldo, and John D. Wirth, eds.): 199–235. Academic Press, New York.

WILLIAMS, VERÓNICA I.
    1983 Evidencia de actividad textil en el establecimiento incaico Potrero Chaquiago (Provincia de Catamarca). *Relaciones de la Sociedad Argentina de Antropología* 15: 49–59.
    1991 La cerámica como indicador de áreas de actividad a través del análisis de los procesos de formación de sitio. *Shincal* 3 (1): 86–103.
    n.d. La ocupación inka en la región central de Catamarca (República Argentina). Ph.D. dissertation, Universidad Nacional de La Plata, Argentina, 1996.

WILLIAMS, VERÓNICA I., AND TERENCE N. D'ALTROY
    1999 El sur del Tawantinsuyu: Un dominio selectivamente intensivo. *Tawantinsuyu* 5: 170–178.

WILLIAMS, VERÓNICA I., AND ANA MARÍA LORANDI
    1986 Evidencias funcionales de un establecimiento incaico en el noroeste Argentino. *Comechingonia* 4: 133–148. Vol. Homenaje al 45⁰ Congreso Internacional de Americanistas (Bogotá), Córdoba.

WILLIAMS, VERÓNICA I., ANA MARÍA LORANDI, TERENCE N. D'ALTROY, AND CHRISTINE A. HASTORF
    n.d. Informe de avance del Proyecto Arqueológico Calchaquí (Campañas 1990–92). *Andes: Antropología e Historia* (m esp. Homenaje a Pío Pablo Díaz). Salta, Argentina (in press)

The Inka Transformation of the Chincha Capital

Craig Morris
Julián Idilio Santillana

FOR MANY YEARS NOW A MAJOR EMPHASIS IN INKA STUDIES HAS BEEN placed on the diversity of Tawantinsuyu. Older notions of a monolithic empire with a highly centralized government and a single set of political, economic, and religious principles have long since been abandoned. Some of us have even called into question the role of a strong army as the primary force in the creation and maintenance of the empire except in peripheral areas (Morris 1998; Murra 1986).

We continue, nevertheless, to search for strategies of rule that both explain the expansion out of Cusco and the apparently high level of coordination within the New World's largest native political entity. After all, there is the indisputable evidence of a particular, almost standardized, "Inka style" in architecture, ceramics, textiles, and metals—as well as the impressive network of roads and monumental settlements extending for thousands of miles over diverse terrain. What were the principles of governance that underlay such a remarkable domination of so many diverse peoples over such a vast and varied landscape?

Our best hope of identifying these common principles in Inka rule is through the comparison of regional studies of Tawantinsuyu such as those brought together in this volume and others published over the past two decades (e.g., D'Altroy 1992; Julien 1983; Malpass 1993). As a contribution to this developing catalog of diversity in Tawantinsuyu we offer evidence and analysis of material from the Chincha Valley—derived from the results of research we have carried out there intermittently since the mid-1980s.

As noted in summary form elsewhere (Morris and Von Hagen 1993: 145–146, 163–166), Chincha is of particular interest because it represents a large coastal kingdom brought peacefully into Tawantinsuyu. More than forty years ago, Menzel (1959) noted unusual patterns of change in the pottery of the Chincha region. Chincha pottery combined Inka and local Chincha forms and design elements in ways that suggested a real stylistic melding, not just the outright imitation of Cusco pottery or the borrowing of the occasional design element. Perhaps even more significant, the use of Inka-influenced pottery was not abandoned immediately after the European invasion, as happened in many other areas of the Andes, as local peoples threw off the yoke of Inka domination. The fusion of the local with the imperial—in pottery style at least—was more than an imposed and temporary condition.

The most prominent hypothesis offered in explanation of this apparently close relationship between the ruling Inka elite and their local counterparts is that of María Rostworowski in her classic article, "Los Mercaderes de Chincha" (1970; reprinted in 1977). Her argument, based on an account usually called simply "Aviso" (1977: 130–140) posits that the special relationship was based on Chincha's economic clout. That clout stemmed in part from the valley's wealth produced by its farmers and its fisherfolk, but what was special about Chincha were the merchants, *mercaderes,* reported to have engaged in long-distance trade by sea. Chincha traders linked the coast of what is now Ecuador to the southern highlands of Peru. In Rostworowski's reconstruction the key to Chincha trade was the warm-water *Spondylus princeps* (*mullu* in Quechua), which normally is found along the Peruvian coast only when relatively rare El Niño events bring its warm-water habitat south. By Inka times *Spondylus* was already sacred and extremely valuable. According to the *Spondylus* scenario the special importance of Chincha in the eyes of the Inka can be attributed to a desire to control this commodity so important in religion and in political ritual (Rostworowski 1977; see also Blower 2001; Murra 1975).

None of the research of several projects sponsored jointly by the American Museum of Natural History, Instituto Andino de Arqueología (Canziani 1992; Lumbreras 2001) and the Institute of Andean Research have found significant quantities of *Spondylus*. Even though there has now been considerable excavation at the Chincha capital, La Centinela, and the contiguous site of Tambo de Mora, the total study sample of the vast and rich valley remains quite small. It is, nevertheless, surprising that the seat of power has not yielded significant amounts of *Spondylus* in numerous excavated-use contexts. There is the possibility that the information of the "Aviso" document is somehow inaccurate or exaggerated. We, however, favor an alternative explanation—that "Aviso" merely reports an incompletely realized blueprint of Inka plans for eventually controlling the distribution of the important commodity through their Chincha allies. It would make sense for the Cusco rulers to seek alternatives to the north-coast centers that had probably managed most *Spondylus* redistribution in pre-Inka times (Pillsbury 1996). The close and friendly ties being forged with Chincha would have made that kingdom a logical alternative. There is at least a hint that this might be the case in the contents of the graves excavated by Max Uhle in Site E, near La Centinela. At least four high-prestige Late Horizon– or Early colonial–period burials contained whole *Spondylus* shells, and some *Spondylus* beads were also found (Kroeber and Strong 1924: 39, 46; Menzel 1966: 123). This contrasts markedly with earlier graves, suggesting that during Inka times an effort to increase the flow and use of *Spondylus* may have been under way in Chincha. In any case the *Spondylus* hypothesis remains intriguing, and the search continues in the Chincha Valley for additional evidence of long-distance *Spondylus* exchange. Marco Curatola (1997) has proposed an alternative, or supplementary, hypothesis related to the basis of Chincha's wealth. He notes the existence of important guano islands off the coast of Chincha, and the historical references to the importance of guano in several neighboring valleys. He also points out the importance of fish and birds in the iconography of pottery, wood, and architectural friezes. There seems little doubt that guano would have been a vital resource for Chincha, but the extent of its involvement in the area's external economy remains to be demonstrated by future research.

Whereas irrefutable evidence of long-distance trade in Chincha has so far not materialized, the evidence of the great wealth of the valley and of the intimate connection between Cusco and Chincha has been amply demonstrated. The archaeological survey by Luis Lumbreras and Jose Canziani (Canziani 1992; Lumbreras 2001) expanded on Dwight Wallace's (1971, 1991) earlier results, producing records of a great density of archaeological sites and demonstrating that Chincha was a major center of wealth for virtually all periods from the Early Horizon onward. In the Chincha Kingdom of the Late Intermediate Period major sites were built along the wide mouth of the valley and at several locations at its heart and upper neck (Canziani 1992: 110–118). Most of these sites continued to be occupied in Inka times.

Much of our evidence on the Chincha-Cusco interconnection comes from the architecture and excavations in La Centinela (fig. 1). That site was apparently the political and religious core of the Chincha capital, whose original name is unknown. We agree with Lumbreras (2001: 44–46) that the cluster of sites which includes La Centinela and Tambo de Mora is best thought of as a single settlement unit. Surface survey suggests that open space between them may have been covered with less substantial architecture, now obliterated.

The Inka had modified La Centinela in both obvious and subtle ways. The most obvious modification was the construction of a large

FIG. 1 La Centinela from the air. Note Sectors II and III in the foreground. Courtesy Department of Library Services, AMNH (photograph by Shippee-Johnson, 1931).

palace compound based on principles of Inka architectural planning and containing numerous features characteristic of Inka architecture in Cusco and throughout many of the provinces of Tawantinsuyu (Morris 2004). The subtle indications of Inka modification involve changes to the major architectural units based on truncated tapia pyramids that had been built at the site prior to Inka domination. Surface collections suggest that Inka-influenced ceramics were used in all of these architectural units, and two of them had witnessed substantial architectural renovations in Inka times.

The eleven architectural compounds into which we have divided La Centinela cover an area of approximately thirty hectares (fig. 2). They are separated by walls, passages, streets, and, plazas, and except for the major road that separates what we have designated Zone I from Zone II, there is little suggestion of strict overall planning. La Centinela probably grew up organically. The ten units or zones, built in Late Intermediate, Chincha times, are loosely grouped on three sides of a large truncated pyramid built of tapia walled cells filled with rubble. It is tempting to suggest that these compounds might have been built sequentially, as was apparently the case with the compounds (*ciudadelas*) at Chan Chan (Kolata 1990;

FIG. 2 Plan of La Centinela showing divisions into sectors (lines spaced 100 m)

Narváez 1989), but our chronological evidence is not sufficiently refined to confirm this. The largest of the pyramid mounds is that of Zone II, containing the great pyramid, which exceeds forty meters in height and near its top bears a wall with a deep-relief frieze (fig. 3). We propose below that this pyramid is associated with the Chinchacamac oracle referred to in the written sources (see below). Of the remaining nine pre-Inka sectors, VIII and XI had undergone substantial architectural modifications in Inka times.

The distinguishing features of Inka construction that allow it to be differentiated from the earlier Chincha architecture are (a) the use of parallel-sided adobe bricks as opposed to the earlier poured tapia (Wallace 1998), (b) the frequent incorporation of trapezoidal niches, and (c) the use of spacious plazas in a more "horizontal" form of architectural planning, in contrast to the vertical tendencies of local Chincha monumental architecture with its truncated pyramids. It is important to note that Inka planning and construction features did not completely eliminate local features. As we will see, there are several cases where adobes and tapia are combined in the same construction—and even cases where tapia lies on top of adobes.

FIG. 3 Frieze in Sector III, La Centinela. Courtesy Phoebe Hearst Museum of Anthropology, University of California, Berkeley (photograph by Max Uhle).

The combination of Inka and local features in Late Horizon Chincha ceramics is even more complex than in architecture. There are many examples of classic Cusco Inka style, such as A and B Polychrome (Rowe 1944: 47) on sherds and vessels (fig. 4). The typical Cusco Inka forms of plates, pots, and the so-called aryballoid jars are common. There are also a series of shapes and decorative features that we identify with local Chincha styles (fig. 5). These were probably produced prior to Inka domination, but some are found in later contexts, and part of the basic Chincha vocabulary of forms and designs continued into Inka times. However, classic Chincha pieces such as those published by Menzel (1977: 132, fig. 136) and others (Kroeber and Strong 1924: 17, 26) from the Uhle collection excavated in the La Cumbe cemetery are rare in La Centinela–use contexts.

A third group of pottery combines Chincha and Inka features. This group also includes some features, such as the use of somewhat sloppy red, black, and white lines and triangles that show Inka influence, although they do not copy standard Inka designs (fig. 6). These occur in many excavated contexts and possibly also continued into colonial times, although we emphasize that we do not yet have a fine-grained chronological sequence.

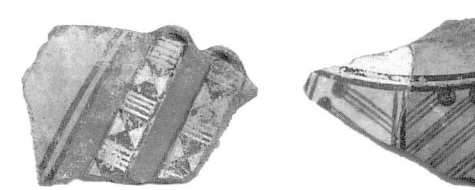

FIG. 4 Sherds from La Centinela showing typical Late (Imperial) Inka Polychrome decoration

FIG. 5 Sherds from La Centinela showing local Chincha decorations

FIG. 6 Sherds from La Centinela showing Inka-Chincha decoration

The Inka Transformation of the Chincha Capital

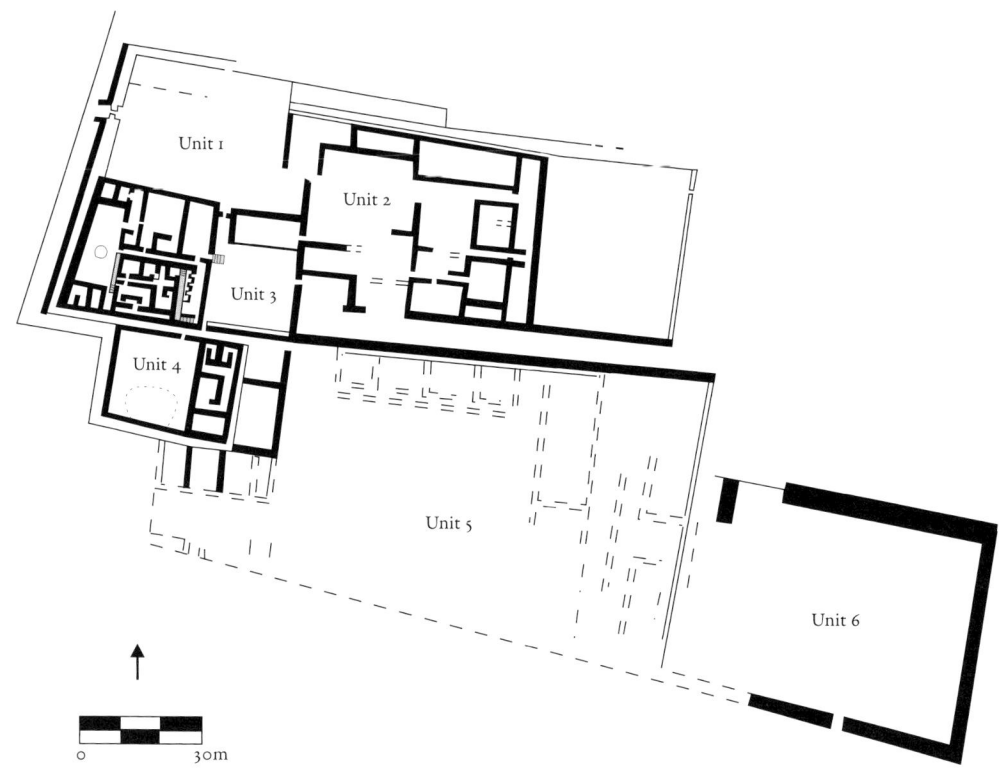

FIG. 7 Plan of Sector III showing Unit divisions

Sector III: The Inka Administrative and Religious Complex

The compound, mentioned above, that constitutes the most obvious evidence of an Inka occupation of La Centinela is Sector III (fig. 7). It was built at the southwestern edge of the site and constitutes the largest of its eleven sectors. The sector seems to have been planned as an administrative palace and religious complex using primarily Inka construction techniques and concepts of urban planning. It is based on plaza areas, large and small, enclosed by walls. In general it is not a pyramidal construction, but rather is based on horizontal themes, even though substantial parts of it are elevated. Our interpretation of the details of this section is still preliminary, and we excavated only a very small part of it. It is clear, however, that the sector includes a variety of elite and nonelite residential rooms with domestic refuse, as well as structures and open areas that probably served as locales of political and religious ceremonies.

Whereas its construction of adobes and the overall character of its architecture and planning bear a clear and easily recognizable Inka stamp, many of the details of this elaborate compound set it quite definitely apart from other Inka sites with which we are familiar in other parts of Tawantinsuyu. We believe these differences are explained largely by the fact that this was a compound built at the command of the Cusco rulers not on virgin land, as was so often the case, but as the most visible element

FIG. 8 Photo of Inka Palace (Sector III, Unit 3) taken from Sector II stairway

of the transformation of the capital of a close and vital ally. Thus, while its association with the Inka and their architectural vocabulary are its most notable feature, many of its details show respect for local stylistic traditions, and even more important, they suggest the incorporation of local people and officials—as well as the principal local shrine—into a revised sociopolitical order. Sector III was clearly *the* elite compound of the capital of the Chincha Kingdom during the Inka Period. Its design housed, symbolized, and helped direct the interactions between the two groups so as to achieve the intended alliance.

As can be seen in figure 7, Sector III can be subdivided into five major areas or units. To the east, Unit 1 is essentially an entrance plaza that serves as the main access to Sector II. A major gateway in the site's northern façade leads into the plaza and toward a long stairway that ascends the great Sector II pyramid. The stairway includes a large section built of adobes that modifies the side of the tapia pyramid and contrasts with the sloping ramps that are the common interconnections between the various levels of Chincha truncated pyramids. As one climbs the stairway a clear view of the Inka palace and the remainder of the Sector III complex can be seen spread out below to the south (fig. 8). A pile of back-dirt from very old *huaquero* activity in Sector II fills most of the Unit 1 plaza, covering evidence of other structures that might have been in it except for adobe benches constructed against the south and east walls. The major function of Unit 1 seems apparent: to re-interpret the Sector II pyramid complex by orienting its access through Sector III, the new, Inka seat of power in Chincha.

The centerpiece of Chincha religion prior to Inka control was Chinchaycamac, "the creator of Chincha," an oracular deity who may have been considered a son of Pachacamac, the great oracle in the Lurin Valley on the Peruvian central coast (Rostworowski 1992: 52; MacCormack 1991: 155; Castro and Ortega Morejon 1974 [1558]). According to Cieza (1959 [1553]: 346) the people of Chincha "did not give up worship in their ancient temple of Chinchay-camac" even though a temple of the sun was built. Max Uhle (1924: 67) suggested that the La Cumbe site about a kilometer and a half to the north was the locale of Chinchaycamac. We feel it far more likely to have been the massive Sector II pyramid, and that the Inkas had essentially co-opted it into their own strategy for the integration of Chincha into Tawantinsuyu.

South and east of the Unit 1 plaza is a complex of rooms and compounds that our excavations suggest may have served habitation, and possibly textile production functions. There is a possibility that parts of this area, which we designate Unit 2, may have been a compound of weavers, perhaps a group of *mamakuna* on a model similar to the one that we proposed for Huánuco Pampa (Morris 1972; Morris and Santillana 1978). However, because of the mixed contexts in these rooms, the evidence from the excavations must be regarded as inconclusive at this point. Unit 2's position in relation to the Sector II pyramid strongly implies functions related to religion, and the *mamakuna*'s potential association with such functions makes them prime candidates for residents of this area. We might speculate that Unit 2 in its entirety was an Inka religious area juxtaposed to and near the Chincha pyramid—perhaps even containing the temple of the sun referred to by Cieza de León.

We will provide a more exhaustive consideration of the excavations in the area at a later date, but it is worth noting that the ceramics indicate very strong Inka associations. All of the sectors we sampled had abundant quantities of both Inka material and non-Inka material. They vary, however, in the comparative quantities of the various Inka and non-Inka forms and decorative features. Considering painted decoration, about 32 percent of 566 sherds with painted decoration from Sector III have Inka designs, while about 21 percent have Chincha motifs, with the remaining 47 percent having mixed or uncertain stylistic associations. Looking at the 740 sherds with form diagnostics, about 46 percent are based on classic Inka forms. This is the highest proportion for any sector of the site except Sector I, where the small sample (32 sherds) is from a compound near the main road that is probably unrepresentative of that sector as a whole.

Polished blackware pottery with a fine paste constitutes about 6 percent of the pottery from Sector III. Earlier we noted references in the written sources to a relationship between the huacas of Chincha and Pachacamac. The relationships between the polished blackware ceramics of Pachacamac, Chincha, and other areas need to be evaluated to see if they might shed additional light on the ties between the various sites and regions where polished blackware ceramics occur.

The remaining three units of Sector III are interrelated and, in our interpretation, constitute the central sociopolitical element of Inka-period La Centinela. They probably provided residential space for the Inka and Chincha leaders and were the ceremonial settings in which these leaders interacted with each other and with parts of the populace of the capital and the Chincha kingdom as a whole. The interpretation of these units is fundamental to understanding the power structure of Chincha during the Inka period. Much of the interpretation and reconstruction that follows is based on models of spatial organization developed by Morris (1987; 2004) for Huánuco Pampa, derived in part from the observations of Fray Martín de Murúa (1946 [1590]: 165–166) on an Inka palace in Cusco.

To the south of the Unit 1 entrance plaza leading to the Sector II stairway is a compound (Unit 3) that constitutes what we designate an administrative palace (Morris 2004). Wallace (1998) has also described it as a palace, as has Uhle (1924: 75–80). Like Unit 2, the palace is built on the lower terrace of the Chincha-period Sector II (Wallace 1998: 14–16). Since the palace is treated in more detail in the just-cited articles, we will not provide a full description here.

The essential feature of Inka administrative palaces is that they were not only the residences of the ruler or his representative, but also contained spaces where the ruler's social group interacted ceremonially with the local group or groups. The palace was divided into two main parts. One (Sub-Unit 3a, see fig. 7) was associated with local people, presumably mainly the local elite, and the other (Sub-Unit 3b, fig. 7) with the Inkas. This latter part provided some restricted "public" space and private areas that contained the "royal" residential quarters and also apparently housed some activities of a sacred or religious nature.

It is important to note that while the administrative palace in Chincha certainly represents the seat of the Inka ruler or his representative, it is a much reduced and less emphatic palace complex than those we have studied at Huánuco Pampa and Tambo Colorado. Its relatively small scale, particularly in the more public outer courtyard area (Sub-Unit 3a), may suggest that direct interaction between local peoples and Inka officials in the palace itself involved smaller numbers of people than in Tambo Colorado or, particularly, Huánuco Pampa (Morris 2004).

The somewhat attenuated nature of the Inka palace is probably related to the fact that it shared prominence in Sector III with the architectural unit to its immediate south. Although similar in elevation to the Inka palace, that compound, designated Unit 4 (see fig. 7), was built up from the original ground surface, and is not located on the Chincha-period terrace of Sector II (Wallace 1998). It is separated from the Inka palace by a corridor that leads eastward to a relatively large rectangular plaza (Unit 5). The corridor thus links the rectangular plaza with both the Inka palace and Unit 4. We did not excavate or clear Unit 4, and it is heavily damaged by treasure hunters, making it impossible to determine most of its architectural details. It is essentially a small truncated pyramid built of adobes. It had rooms on its relatively flat top, but it is not possible to determine their exact number or form. There were also rooms on a lower forecourt to the east and south. Because of the destruction and lack of thorough study, we can say nothing of the activities that may have taken place in Unit 4. However, the overall form of an elevated pyramidal structure contrasts with the more horizontal feel of the Inka palace across the corridor—even though the two units have similar elevations and were built at the same time. With its adobe construction and its relationship to the corridor and the Unit 5 plaza, Unit 4 is clearly an integral part of the Inka-period, Sector III addition to La Centinela. Its form, however, refers to the Chincha truncated pyramid. These architectural clues and many of its details allow us to hypothesize that this may have been a residential palace for the Chincha lord—built on an Inka spatial model across from and connected with the Inka palace.

The suggestion, derived from architecture and archaeology, of a palace built by the Inka for the local lord is confirmed by Santillán (1927 [1563]: 14–15). In a passage relating to the Inka's treatment of the leaders of groups brought peacefully into Tawantinsuyu, Santillán states: "To them [the Inka] bestowed favors and gave gifts of gold cups and clothing from Cusco, and in honor of their obedience he ordered that in each of those provinces a house be built for the said lord beside that which he had built for himself, and those who did not obey of their own accord were forced into subjugation with all rigor and cruelty."

The formal relationships between Units 3 and 4 are among the most intriguing aspects of La Centinela's architecture. They also provide essential clues to the inter-relationships between the elites of the Inka Empire and the Chincha kingdom. Close examination of figure 7 reveals that the entrance off the separating corridor into what we suggest is the palace of the lord of Chincha is a classic Inka double-jambed doorway. At first we thought this clear Inka doorway was inconsistent with the hypothesized use of the compound as a palace for the local lord. Further inspection, however, reveals that the doorway off the same corridor into the Inka palace (Unit 3) has only a simple, single jamb. The placing of an Inka doorway into the Chincha compound and a simpler, local, doorway into the Inka palace is consistent with the sense of reciprocity in which the doorway is a sign of welcome to those intended to enter through it.

Furthermore, the entrances in both cases are *not* into the parts of the palaces that contain residences. Instead, they are into the open courtyard areas that constitute the more public parts of the overall palace compounds. In the case of Inka administrative palaces, as mentioned above, this more open area was likely associated with a local elite. In a local palace based on an Inka model, it is thus not surprising that there would be a similar more open and public area identified with the Inkas.

In terms of the spatial vocabulary of Inka palace architecture, the compound with the double-jambed doorway and that with the simple doorway are also in their appropriate positions. In the case of the local palace, the supposed Inka courtyard is at the northern edge of the compound, the same position as the "royal" residential area of the Inka palace compound across the corridor. The more restricted and possibly residential area of Unit 4 is in the "local" position to the south—the same position as the "local" courtyard complex with its simple doorway into the Inka palace. In terms of function, both palace compounds were apparently intended for use by the occupants of the more restricted "residences" and also by members of the elite of the other group. Thus, Inkas were admitted through their double-jambed gateway into the north courtyard of Unit 4, the Chincha palace, and the Chincha elite were admitted into the south courtyard of Unit 3 through the plain gateway. The spatial positions of the residential and more public areas in the two compounds are reversed. Functionally, however, they are quite similar. Each palace has its restricted residential compound and area limited to its own group, as well as an area into which were admitted members of the other group, as signified by the design of the gateway. The spatial positions demonstrate the differing sociopolitical levels, and the gateways confirm those identities by placing the design associated with each group in the appropriate position.

In sum, what we see here is the architectural expression of what anthropologists have called inverse dualism, in which structural positions are reversed in certain circumstances (Levi-Strauss 1967: 140–141). By looking at the functional aspects of the palaces' architectural units in the context of their positional structure we can begin to infer something of the social relationships between the leadership of the two groups. The buildings and open plazas provide settings for a carefully controlled interplay between opposition and collaboration.

This relationship of palaces is also consistent with the written account that has the Inka ruler and the Chincha lord riding near each other in their litters at Cajamarca (Pedro Pizarro 1916 [1571]: 32). Whatever the use of

Units 3 and 4, they were at least powerful architectural symbols of the sharing of authority implied in the written sources, providing new insights into the complexities of leadership in an important Inka province.

The large rectangular plaza (Unit 5) on the southern side of Sector III was not studied in detail, and many of its aspects are unclear because of destruction. The plaza, with a large gateway in its southern wall, was a major entrance plaza, perhaps serving the site as a whole during the Inka period. After entering the site through the gate (see fig. 2), one could presumably have proceeded ahead to enter a corridor between Sectors III and V or turned left into the main space of the plaza itself. This large plaza is reminiscent of the spacious public plazas that were a common feature in many Inka centers. Such open plazas frequently had one or more long buildings or "great halls" (Niles 1999: 274) on one or more of their sides. In La Centinela a long multiroom building is on the north side of the plaza, against and below Unit 2 (see fig. 2). The great plazas are often near a site's center and form one of its most prominent features. Pumpu (Matos 1994), Tambo Colorado (Uhle in Wurster 1999: 158–159; Gasparini and Margolies 1980), and Huánuco Pampa (Morris 1987) provide some of the best-known examples of these large plazas. They are obviously public spaces intended for the assembly of a large number of people. The incorporation of a main gate in this one, and its placement on the edge of the site, would tend to imply that many of the people admitted into the plaza may not have lived in, or otherwise pertained to, La Centinela itself. The fact that a course of tapia, the construction feature associated with pre-Inka Chincha, runs visibly on top of the adobes that constitute the greater height of its outer wall, seems an additional indication that this area was intended primarily for non-Inkas. This plaza was almost certainly a Chincha part of the Inka-built sector, as we will elaborate below, and it is appropriate that it incorporated local design and construction features.

Sector III as a whole represents the Inka's most elaborate and visible strategy for linking the Cusco rulers to their coastal subjects and allies. On its northern side, Unit 1, it cleverly re-orients and re-identifies the access to the site's most prominent religious monument through a new principal gateway and plaza. On its southern side the other new plaza, Unit 5, leads to the public and private architectural units that we believe were the dual palaces for the Inka and the Chincha lord, redefining the political order of the capital. Previously cited earlier work (Morris 1987, 2004) has used models of Inka organization developed from studies of the written sources (i.e., Zuidema 1964; Wachtel 1973; less directly Rostworowski 1993 [1977]) to derive architectural principles from studies of archaeological sites. On the basis of this work, we can propose a partial interpretation of how the three primary Units (3, 4, and 5) of this sector might have been used and what they meant in terms of Inka-Chincha political relations.

That interpretation takes the form of a three-part model in which public and private spaces can be identified architecturally with three major groups or classes: (1) the Inkas of the royal lineage groups (*panacas*); (2) an intermediate level of people, usually important local elites, related to the Inkas by marriage or possibly by fictive kinship; and (3) the non-Inka outsiders who made up the bulk of the subjects of Tawantinsuyu.

In Huánuco Pampa and some other Inka centers, the large central plaza space with ample egress and access to the outside was presumably the space intended for outside groups of non-Inkas (Morris 1987; Morris and Covey 2003). The housing facilities at Huánuco Pampa provided both temporary and longer-term shelter for these groups. Some of that housing was in the long rectangular great halls on the plaza; much of it was arranged in neighborhoods separated by radial "streets." These neighborhoods may even have been arranged by some now difficult-to-reconstruct hierarchical positioning that helped define the stratified sociopolitical relationships between the groups who used them. In other words, the settlements may have been designed essentially as sociopolitical maps that allowed the rulers to assign relationships by assigning space (Morris 1987: 36–41). The ritual apparatus, which was the central focus of places like Huánuco Pampa, of course, facilitated and underscored the definition and re-definition of intragroup relationships. Those relationships were further reinforced by gifts and state hospitality offered in ritual contexts.

In Chincha, this relatively simple tripartite model appears to have been adjusted and re-shaped. Both the public plaza for the "outsiders" and especially the part of the Inka palace (Sub-Unit 3a) that we believe was associated with the group of important locals are comparatively small in relation to the overall scale of the site. Test excavations in Sub-Unit 3a produced very small amounts of material, contrasting dramatically with Huánuco Pampa, suggesting that the spaces were little used. Most important, the Inka palace itself shares its position, in relation to Unit 5 (the "common" or non-Inka space), with the probable Chincha palace. This distortion of the simple hierarchical relationship seen in other Inka centers indicates that power was shared. It also suggests a certain ambiguity: there is an implied ability to take different perspectives on the power relationships in different situations. If we are correct that Unit 4 was indeed the palace of the Chincha lord, then his residence was in a slightly more direct line to the public area to its east than the palace of the Inka. The easternmost platform of the hypothesized Chincha palace even looks like an open stage designed to be viewed from the large plaza. The small and private outer courtyard of the Inka palace (Sub-Unit 3a) may indicate that in Chincha the functions of this part of the administrative palace were replaced by the preexisting, centralized pattern of local leadership, located in Unit 4. From most functional points of view, the middle level in the tripartite structure was probably supplanted by the dual relationship between the occupants of Units 3 and 4, as described above.

The specific relationships we read into the complicated sector the Inka had built to define their control over the Chincha kingdom are admittedly speculative. But we are convinced that Sector III does reflect a situation in which the Inka put into operation a genuinely dual system of leadership for Chincha. Dualism at the apex of the political hierarchy carries with it both ambiguity and tension, and over the long run it may be unstable. But from the shorter perspective of incorporating a valuable and powerful ally into an expanding empire, it was probably very effective. Its ambiguity allowed the lower levels of the Chincha populace to see shared power and the Inka to avail themselves of local leadership in managing resources they may not have understood fully; however, the entire Sector III architectural complex was built of adobes, and there seems little doubt that the Inkas had designed, and ultimately controlled it.

The Less Modified Sectors
Of the eight sectors (I, II, IV, V, VI, VII, IX, and X) that appear to have undergone relatively little architectural modification in Inka times, we tested only three, Sectors I, II, and IV. The unusual ceramic evidence for the Inka-period use of Sector I, where we excavated an area near the site's principal road, was mentioned above. The activities in the area primarily involved undecorated Form A (see Rowe 1944: 48) Inka jars and Inka plates. Two of the jars and one of the plates had classic Inka decoration. This is a ceramic assemblage we associate with the serving of food and drink, and it is not surprising in a context near a principal road, even if that context is not marked by characteristically Inka architecture.

The imposing Section II is the site's principal pyramid, and is our candidate for the shrine of Chinchaycamac as discussed above. The pyramid itself and the architecture of the sector as a whole were apparently changed relatively little by the Inka, although reorienting access to the pyramid through Sector III constitutes a fundamental alteration of its patterns of use. The ceramics in the small areas we tested were a rather unnoteworthy mix of Inka and local material. Fewer Inka feature sherds were found here than in Sector III, but more than in Sector VIII, described below.

Small excavations near the summit of Sector IV uncovered an apparent offering of hot peppers, but the pottery finds in the sector were inadequate in both number and features to shed any light on Inka-Chincha interrelationships.

Since our research focused on the relationships between Chincha and its new overlords, we concentrated our efforts in areas with notable Inka evidence on the surface. The study sample would have been quite

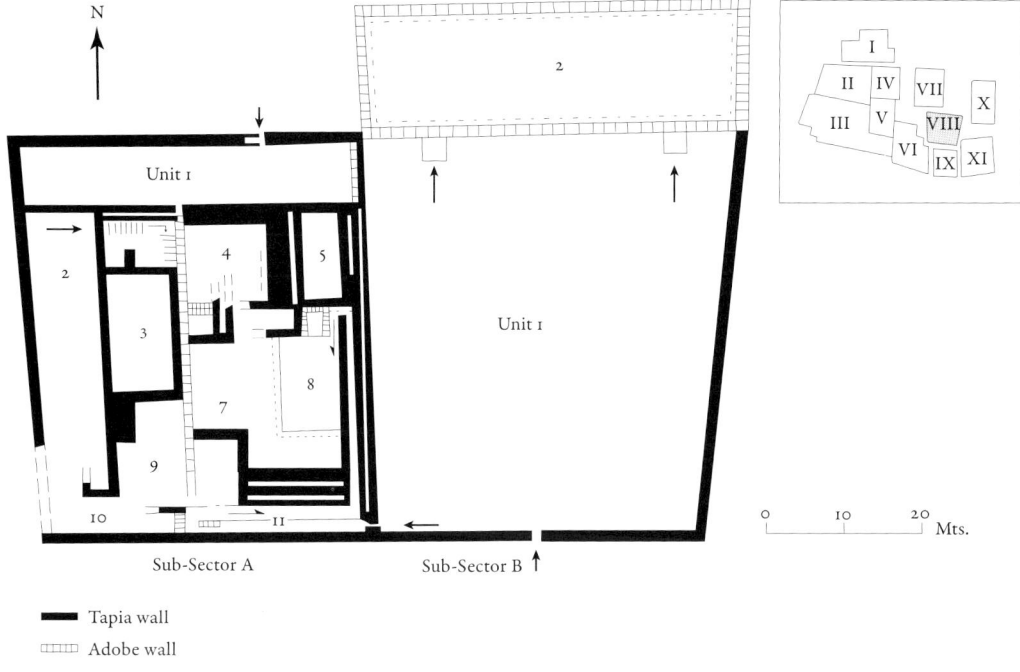

FIG. 9 Plan of Sector VIII showing Unit divisions and structure

different if our goals had been to gain a representative picture of the site of La Centinela as a whole. The problem, of course, is that our results give an inadequate picture of the Inka impact on those areas in which the Cusco overlords did not make architectural changes. We hope that future research will address this issue.

Sector VIII: The Transformation of a Local Compound

In many respects the most intriguing sectors of La Centinela are Sectors VIII and XI because of their extensive Inka-period modifications to existing architecture. The trapezoidal niches in Sector XI, in particular, stand out. Its extensive use and alteration in modern times, however, makes Sector XI a difficult candidate for study. Sector VIII, on the other hand, is one of the best preserved at the site. It is also interesting that Sector VIII lies directly along a sight line, and almost due east, from a gateway of the Inka palace (Sector III, Unit 3).

The sector divides into two sub-sectors, VIIIA and VIIIB (fig. 9). Sub-sector VIIIA consists of a truncated pyramid that originally must have reached about 20 m in height and measured about 68 by 90 m at its base. It was built using basic local architectural concepts, and almost certainly was constructed prior to Inka control. Sub-sector VIIIB is formed by a large enclosed courtyard or plaza; it is somewhat trapezoidal in form and appears to have been conceived and constructed using Inka patterns of planning and design. Although its enclosure walls were built primarily of tapia, along its north side a platform about 1.5 m in height was built of adobes. This obviously public space represents an expansion of the role of public ceremony in the compound during Inka times.

While Sub-Sector VIIIB was the principal Inka-period addition to the sector, VIIIA was also extensively modified. Although visually subtle, the modifications resulted in the redefinition of the entire sector. A main feature of this replanning was an extension of a wall built of adobes, running north to south, apparently added in Inka times. This wall, as extended, effectively cuts Sub-Sector VIIIA in two (see fig. 9). Because of the potential of Sector VIII to contribute to a better understanding of Inka-Chincha articulations, we devoted an entire field season to its excavation.

Sub-Sector VIIIA is formed of three superimposed vertical levels, the lowest being the largest and the highest being the smallest. All three of the levels support structures and open activity areas. Two large rectangular structures, about 10 x 40 m each, are found at the lowest level. These are numbered Structures 1 and 2. Such structures are not part of the Chincha architectural pattern and, although built of tapia, probably date from the period of Inka occupation. On the second level there are three small structures (nos. 3, 4, and 5) none of which was excavated. The top of the mound contains a platform structure (no. 8) and Structure 9.

In terms of access, Sub-Sector VIIIA is especially interesting. Its northern and western parts (west of the adobe wall and designated Unit 1) are accessed through an entrance in the north wall of Structure 1 (see fig. 9). This building then gives access to Structure 2 on the lower level, Structure 3 on the second level, and Structure 9 on the top level. Unit 2, to the east of the adobe dividing wall, lacks enclosed structures. Instead, that part consists of a series of entranceways, passages, and ramps that lead from the large Sub-Sector VIIIB enclosed courtyard up to Structure 8—which is a kind of balcony or platform overlooking the courtyard.

Architecturally, the western part, Unit 1 (including Structure 1) consists of groups of rectangular buildings, essentially Inka in form, accessed through a door in the north side of the complex. The eastern part of the Sub-Sector (Unit 2) adheres to a Chincha pattern of ramps and passageways leading to an open platform. Although both sub-sectors are adapted to the tapia pyramid, presumably built before the Inka arrived, they are quite different in feel and in traffic flow. The adobe wall accentuates and formalizes their separation. It appears that VIIIA was divided into two parts in Inka times. Its western part (Unit 1) was substantially modified by a series of enclosed rectangular structures, while its eastern part (Unit 2) retained a Chincha character of open ramps and platforms. The eastern section with its local character seems, curiously, to be oriented directly toward and accessed from the large courtyard of Inka-period construction. Essentially, the courtyard and platform space

(Sub-Sector VIIIB and Unit 2 of Sub-Sector VIIIA) were likely linked as ceremonial spaces.

The ceramic distributions from the excavations in VIIIA largely mirror the pattern of architectural division based on the forms of the structures, the access patterns, and the adobe dividing wall. The final studies of the ceramics from the Sector are not concluded; however, the material has been coded into a computer database using a combination of type and attribute analyses. Some of the preliminary results of that work are pertinent here. Structures 1 and 9, in the northern and western parts, showed 35.6% and 31.1% Inka vessel shapes; Structure 8, which is the principal feature east of the adobe wall, had only 8% Inka vessel shapes. The passageways along the perimeter contain vessels generally consistent with those from the structures, with No. 10 in the western part having several vessels of Inka shapes and No. 11 in the eastern part having none. We hasten to add, however, that there were fewer than 10 form diagnostic sherds in each passageway, making these results of questionable significance. In painted decoration, the entirety of Sector VIII has a low percentage of Inka-related decorated sherds. From Unit 1, Structure 1, 6.5% had Inka decorative motifs, whereas Structure 9 had 12.9%. In the eastern side (Unit 2), structure 8 had no sherds with Inka painted motifs.

In terms of both architecture and ceramics our data thus suggest a division of Sub-Sector VIIIA during Inka times. One side of the mound, the north and west (Unit 1), has a much stronger Inka association than the eastern side (Unit 2). The architecture also suggests a functional distinction. The north and west were probably devoted to more closed and restricted kinds of activities involving smaller numbers of people. The east, with its open platform spaces, was more closely associated with the large plaza of Sub-Sector B, and was thus more public.

A closer analysis and, eventually, additional excavations, may clarify the kinds of activities that took place. We would speculate that the large plaza may have been the scene of ceremonies with a largely local Chincha character. These might have included marriages, or other rites of passage, or events that were important in local sociopolitical or religious life. Although such determinations are beyond the scope of archaeologists, it seems plausible that Sector VIII may have related to some sub-unit of Chincha society—such as a descent group.

The evidence from the eastern side (Unit 2) of VIIIA suggests that any such ceremonies probably had a local character. The west and north side (Unit 1) suggest activities for a smaller, more closed group—one more closely identified with the Inka. Their relationship to the more public aspects of the compound are unclear, but we might speculate on power and control behind the scenes. The use of adobes in the platform of Sub-Sector VIIIB, the adobe facing on the VIIIA pyramid itself, and the presence of Inka-form vessels (about 22%) in the excavated remains from the plaza (VIIIB) show a notable Inka architectural and ceramic presence in the public plaza, although the platform above it, where the officials probably sat or performed, and the ceramics they utilized emphasized local characteristics.

We will probably never be able to determine the exact nature of the Inka presence seen in the north and west (Unit 1) of Sub-Sector VIIIA. Was there a presence of people from Cusco? We would guess not. Was a new group of people brought in associated with or related to the Inkas, perhaps by marriage? Was an existing local group bifurcated, much as the compound itself had been, with one part becoming more closely related to the Inkas? Were the contrasts between Unit 1 and Unit 2 related strictly to activities, with an Inka-associated group acting behind the scenes to control ceremonies while the participants in the plaza below were served from vessels that included numerous Inka elements—all in front of an architectural backdrop that featured both local and Inka features? Do we somehow have evidence here for the Inka's sanctioning of marriage and performing other roles in local ceremonial life? All of these alternatives remain in consideration.

What is beyond doubt is that in Sector VIII the Inkas had inserted themselves directly into one of the constituent units that made up the capital of the Chincha kingdom. This was not simple indirect rule whereby the Inkas were allied with the lord of Chincha and allowed him to continue to rule for a largely absentee imperial authority—monitored by frequent reports and occasional inspections. Furthermore, the signs of the Inkas and the indications of their presence were not limited to the complex relationships between the Inka and the local lord symbolized, and probably actualized, in Sector III. They were present also at least one level lower in the sociopolitical hierarchy—where a unit somehow identified with the Inkas was inserted into a local sociopolitical unit. They had divided a local compound and created a new dual structure, allowing them to participate in newly expanded ceremonies in Sector VIII and to influence and control the people who used it.

Dualism, Religion, and the Sharing of Power

This discussion of the archaeological information we recovered from La Centinela provides evidence that the Inka transformation of the Chincha capital was both subtle and radical. We see two major kinds of transformation, both visible in the architectural impact the Inkas had on the site.

The first, and most simple, was in the sphere of religion, where the major pyramid (Sector II) was reoriented to relate to the new Sector III that was added by the Inkas. If we are correct that the great pyramid was a shrine associated with the Chinchaycamac oracle, the Inkas now controlled public access to it through a new gateway, grand stairway, and entrance plaza. The plaza essentially brought together the site's most prominent architectural features: on the left, the great Chincha-period pyramid with access to its summit; to the front (Sector III, Unit 2), a smaller compound that may have been associated with Inka religion and, on the right, the new palace and administrative complex built by the Inkas. With the striking view of the Inka complex afforded from the access stairway, those who came to worship Chinchaycamac would be duly impressed that a new political order had been instituted. The role of religion in the new order was clearly prominent and, at least in terms of architectural mass, the emphasis was on the traditional Chincha religion more than on new elements introduced from Cusco.

The second transformation was in the sphere of sociopolitical structure and organization. In both Sector III and Sector VIII we found evidence suggesting that an Inka or Inka-affiliated unit had been added to the local sociopolitical hierarchy by creating units that were internally divided. An Inka or Inka-affiliated unit was placed in opposition to a local unit. The two were linked together in a dual architectural structure, which presumably also signified a dual sociopolitical structure. The case of Sector III represented the apex of authority. There the Inka ruler or his stand-in was linked to the lord of Chincha in what were probably dual palaces. The Inkas had obviously ordered the construction of the palaces, but, together, they represented both the local lord and the imperial ruler. The two were brought together in a manner that symbolized, and presumably also made operational, a form of unity that retained elements of opposition. Architecturally, we see only the stage set for what must have been a kind of dynamic ambiguity that could only be fully appreciated and analyzed by witnessing the performances and interactions that took place in the spaces. Nevertheless, the architecture does allow us to grasp the essentially dual nature of power that linked Chincha to Tawantinsuyu.

In Sector VIII an existing architectural unit was bifurcated, once again linking an Inka-affiliated segment with a local segment. In this case, the archaeological evidence alone permits us little insight into what kinds of groups may have been involved in using the architectural complex. There is, nevertheless, with the newly built large open courtyard, an added emphasis on public space, and presumably on ritual performance. As was the case in Sector III, it is the local side of the architectural complex that seems most directly related to the public space, with the Inka material somewhat behind the scenes.

While the two cases differ in scale and in detail, they suggest that a significant aspect of the Inka transformation of La Centinela was to introduce a dual system of organization through which the Inka could control Chincha by sharing power with local groups on at least two levels. They had used traditional principles of dual organization (e.g., Zuidema 1964; Isbell 1978; Mayer 1977; Urton 1997; Wachtel 1973), probably recognizable to the local polity, as a means of making themselves part of the local sociopolitical hierarchy. The highest level and one sub-ordinate unit had been modified to effect dual forms; how far down the local hierarchy this mechanism might have been used, of course, can only be guessed without additional research. In both levels for which we have evidence, there was also an increased emphasis on public gathering space, with the new open plaza areas of VIIIA and Unit III5. The role of public ceremony was thus apparently increasingly emphasized in Inka times. We have shown the Inka emphasis on ceremony in the rule of incorporated peoples in Huánuco (Morris 1982; Morris and Thompson 1985). In Chincha, however, the distribution of ceremony in terms of both space and sociopolitical hierarchy, was different. In Huánuco it was directed at a variety of non-Inka local elites from groups of varying sizes with the aim of building both obedience and a local hierarchical structure (Morris and Covey 2003). In La Centinela a newly increased role for ceremony was aimed at influencing an already well-established internal sociopolitical hierarchy by bringing Inka participation into it.

In evaluating the distribution of ceremonial space and the operation of dual leadership at the highest level of authority in Chincha, it is worth repeating the observation above relating to the small size and apparently minimal use of the outer courtyard of the Inka palace (Sub-Unit 3a in Sector III). We believe that in other cases of Inka administrative palaces (Morris 2004) this was the ceremonial area devoted to relationships between the Inka rulers or their representatives and the local elite. The equivalent outer courtyard (Unit IIB2) in the administrative palace at Huánuco Pampa was one of the most important and heavily used compounds in the city. Literally tons of material relating to feasting were found there. In Huánuco the Inka were not dealing with an already centralized kingdom. Instead they had to deal with a multiplicity of local leaders of small polities. They needed to organize these local leaders, define their relative positions, and chart their relationships to the ruler and the state. The activities in the outer courtyard of the palace were thus vital to state interests and the space and resources devoted to them were substantial.

In Chincha, the local level, headed by the lord of Chincha, was already relatively centralized and stable. The strategy seems to have been to elevate what would have been an intermediate level in a triadic political structure in other regions into an essentially dual relationship with the Inkas, allowing the intermediate level (localized in the outer courtyard in the administrative palace) to be reduced architecturally to a small facility for a few people. This arrangement of at least the strong semblance of dual rule is a remarkably sophisticated accommodation to local political realities, apparently permitting relatively harmonious and effective integration. It contrasts markedly with a model of simple imposed rule where an imperial official is brought in along with a garrison to support his authority. It is a model of political integration that was probably feasible only in circumstances where the events that led up to incorporation were relatively peaceful (Morris and von Hagen 1993: 169).

The emphasis on religion and the complex manipulation of dual political structures that we see in the archaeological evidence at La Centinela overshadow the initial working hypothesis on the importance of long-distance trade, probably in *Spondylus* shell, as the critical feature of Inka-Chincha relationships. Of course, our evidence deals primarily with the political mechanisms of rule—not necessarily the motivating factors that led to the Inkas' interest in gaining a controlling alliance with the Chincha Kingdom. Perhaps their interest in Chinchaycamac was a prime motivation for their efforts in the Chincha Valley? Our own lack of confidence in the power and predictive efficacy of oracles should not lead us to presume that the Inkas used them only as a self-consciously fictive device for persuading the populace.

We remain convinced, despite a lack of clear supporting evidence, that there were compelling economic motivations for the establishment of close Inka-Chincha relationships. The frequency of small-balance scales from Chincha, especially in the recently examined collections of Max Uhle at the Hearst Museum of the University of California, Berkeley, at least implies a preoccupation with weights and measurement (Kroeber and Strong 1924: 38–39). The measuring might have been involved in some sort of production activity requiring precision measurement of precious materials, rather than trade in finished products. The balance beams are quite small, and if *Spondylus* was the product they measured, it would have been in a very fragmentary form. In his famous observation of the balsa boat, often thought to have been from Chincha, Bartolomé Ruiz (Sámano and Xérez 1937 [1528]: 66) attributes the use of such balances to the weighing of gold: "They carried some small scales to weigh gold, like those of Roman manufacture." An analysis of the Inkas' participation in the Chincha Valley's wealth and economic activities must await new evidence and insights from future research, but the overall wealth—as seen in the potential of a lush irrigated valley and a bountiful sea—was certainly great. At the very least, participating in that wealth would have been vitally important in providing the economic resources essential for a rapidly expanding state.

Although the economic picture remains unclear, we feel that the political and religious dimensions of the Inka transformation of Chincha and its capital are largely in place. The Cusco elite carefully planned and executed a multilevel strategy of integration through dual control. The architectural evidence shows that it was a carefully planned attempt to influence local activities and structures—to govern in considerable depth. That strategy contrasts markedly with those in other areas where the Inkas located their administrative centers far from local settlements. The resulting impact, by the time the empire fell, was so superficial that local peoples rejected Inka decorative motifs almost immediately after Pizarro toppled Atahualpa, the last independent Inka ruler. Seeing some of these details of the Inka's efforts at religious and sociopolitical transformation at La Centinela provides us with a fuller understanding of Menzel's (1959) insightful observations on ceramic styles in the region. The Inkas had built a firm and enduring base for a new sociopolitical order in Chincha, an organic dual order in which they were direct participants.

References cited

BLOWER, DAVID
    2001 The Many Facets of Mullu: More Than Just a Spondylus Shell. *Andean Past* 6: 209–228.

CANZIANI A., JOSÉ
    1992 Patrones de Asentamiento en la Arqueología del Valle de Chincha, Perú. *II Curso de Prehistoria de América Hispana:* 89–123. Universidad de Murcia. Murcia.

CIEZA DE LEÓN, PEDRO DE
    1959 [1553] *The Incas of Pedro de Cieza de León* (Harriet de Onis, trans., Victor W. von Hagen, ed.). University of Oklahoma Press, Norman.

CURATOLA, MARCO
    1997 Guano: Una hipótesis sobre el origen de la riqueza del señorío de Chincha. In *Arqueología, antropología e historia en los Andes: Homenaje a María Rostworowski* (Rafael Varón Gabai and Javier Flores Espinoza, eds.): 223–240. Instituto de Estudios Peruanos, Lima.

D'ALTROY, TERENCE
    1992 *Provincial Power in the Inka Empire.* Smithsonian Institution Press, Washington, D.C.

GARCILASO DE LA VEGA, EL INCA
    1966 [1609] *Royal Commentaries of the Incas and General History of Peru,* parts 1 and 2. (H. V. Livermore, trans.). University of Texas Press, Austin.

GASPARINI, GRAZIANO, AND LUISE MARGOLIES
    1980 *Inca Architecture* (Patricia J. Lyon, trans.). University of Indiana Press, Bloomington.

ISBELL, BILLIE JEAN
    1978 *To Defend Ourselves: Ecology and Ritual in an Andean Village.* University of Texas Press, Austin.

JULIEN, CATHERINE
    1983 *Hatunqolla: A View of Inca Rule from the Lake Titicaca Region.* University of California Press, Berkeley.

KOLATA, ALAN L.
    1990 The Urban Concept of Chan Chan. In *The Northern Dynasties: Kingship and Statecraft in Chimor* (Michael E. Moseley and Alana Cordy-Collins eds.): 107–144. Dumbarton Oaks Research Library and Collection, Washington, D.C.

KROEBER, ALFRED L., AND WILLIAM DUNCAN STRONG
    1924 *The Uhle Collections from Chincha.* University of California Publications in American Archaeology and Ethnology 21 (1): 1–54. University of California Press, Berkeley.

LEVI-STRAUSS, CLAUDE
1963   *Structural Anthropology.* Balance Books, New York.

LUMBRERAS, LUIS GUILLERMO
2001   Uhle y los asentamientos de Chincha en el siglo XVI. *Revista del Museo Nacional* 49: 13–87.

MALPASS, MICHAEL (ED.)
1993   *Provincial Inca: Archaeological and Ethnohistorical Assessment of the Impact of the Inca State.* University of Iowa Press, Iowa City.

MATOS M., RAMIRO
1994   *Pumpu: Centro Administrativo Inka de la Puna de Junín.* Editorial Horizonte, Lima.

MAYER, ENRIQUE
1977   Beyond the Nuclear Family. In *Andean Kinship and Marriage* (Ralph Bolton and Enrique Mayer, eds.): 217–239. Special Publication of the American Anthropological Association 7. American Anthropological Association, Washington, D.C.

MENZEL, DOROTHY
1959   The Inca Occupation of the South Coast of Peru. *Southwestern Journal of Anthropology* 15 (2): 125–142.
1966   The Pottery of Chincha. *Ñawpa Pacha* 4: 77–144.
1976   *Pottery Style and Society in Ancient Peru: Art as a Mirror of History in the Ica Valley, 1350–1570.* University of California Press, Berkeley.
1977   *The Archaeology of Ancient Peru and the Work of Max Uhle.* R. H. Lowie Museum of Anthropology, University of California, Berkeley.

MENZEL, DOROTHY, AND JOHN H. ROWE
1966   The Role of Chincha in Late Pre-Spanish Peru. *Ñawpa Pacha* 4: 63–76.

MORRIS, CRAIG
1982   The Infrastructure of Inka Control in the Peruvian Central Highlands. In *The Inca and Aztec States, 1400–1800* (George A. Collier, Renato J. Rosaldo, and John D. Wirth, eds.): 153–171. Academic Press, New York and London.
1987   Arquitectura y estructura del espacio en Huánuco Pampa. *Cuadernos Instituto Nacional de Antropología* 12: 27–45.
1988   Más allá de las fronteras de Chincha. In *La frontera del estado inca* (Tom D. Dillehay and Patricia Netherly, eds.): 131–140. BAR International Series 442. British Archaeological Reports, Oxford.

1998   Inka Strategies of Incorporation and Governance. In *Archaic States* (Gary Feinman and Joyce Marcus, eds.): 293–309. School of American Research Press, Santa Fe.

2004   Enclosures of Power: The Multiple Spaces of Inca Administrative Palaces. In *Palaces of the Ancient New World* (Susan Toby Evans and Joanne Pillsbury, eds.): 299–323. Dumbarton Oaks Research Library and Collection, Washington, D.C.

MORRIS, CRAIG, AND ALAN COVEY

2003   La Plaza Central de Huánuco Pampa: Espacio y Transformación. In *Identidad y transformación en el Tawantinsuyu y en los Andes coloniales: Perspectivas arqueologícas y etnohistóricas,* part 2. Boletín de Arqueología PUCP 7.

MORRIS, CRAIG, AND JULIÁN IDILIO SANTILLANA

1978   Perspectiva arqueológica de la economía incaica. *Histórica* 2 (1): 63–82.

MORRIS, CRAIG, AND DONALD E. THOMPSON

1985   *Huánuco Pampa: An Inca City and Its Hinterland.* Thames and Hudson, London.

MORRIS, CRAIG, AND ADRIANA VON HAGEN

1993   *The Inka Empire and Its Andean Origins.* Abbeville Press, New York.

MURRA, JOHN V.

1975   El tráfico de mullu en la costa del Pacifico. In *Formaciones económicas y políticas del mundo andino:* 255–268. Instituto de Estudios Peruanos, Lima.

1986   The Expansion of the Inka State: Armies, War, and Rebellions. In *Anthropological History of Andean Polities* (John V. Murra, Nathan Wachtel, and Jacques Revel, eds.): 49–58. Cambridge University Press, New York.

MURÚA, MARTÍN DE

1946 [1590]   *Historia del origen y genealogía real de los reyes inças del Perú.* Superior de Investigaciones Científicas, Instituto Santo Toribio de Mogrovejo, Madrid.

NARVÁEZ V., ALFREDO

1989   Chan Chan: Chronology and Stratigraphic Contents. *Andean Past* 2: 131–174.

NILES, SUSAN A.

1999   *The Shape of Inca History: Narrative and Architecture in an Andean Empire.* University of Iowa Press, Iowa City.

PILLSBURY, JOANNE

1996   The Thorny Oyster and the Origins of Empire: Implications of Recently Uncovered Spondylus Imagery from Chan Chan, Peru. *Latin American Antiquity* 7 (4): 313–340.

PIZARRO, PEDRO

1916 [1571] *Relación del Descubrimiento y Conquista de los Reinos del Perú y del Gobierno y orden que los naturales tenían, y tesoros que en ella se hallaron: Y de las demás cosas que en él han subcedido hasta el día de la fecha.* Colección de Libros y Documentos Referentes a la Historia del Perú 6: 1–186.

ROSTWOROWSKI DE DIEZ CANSECO, MARÍA

1977 [1970] Mercaderes del valle de Chincha en la época prehispánica: Un documento y unos comentarios. In *Etnía y sociedad:* 97–140. Instituto de Estudios Peruanos, Lima.

1993 [1977] Estratificación social y el Hatun Curaca en el mundo andino. In *Ensayos de historia andina: Elites, etnías, recursos:* 41–88. Instituto de Estudios Peruanos, Lima.

ROWE, JOHN H.

1944 An *Introduction to the Archaeology of Cuzco.* Papers of the Peabody Museum of American Archaeology and Ethnology 27 (2). Harvard University, Cambridge, Mass.

SÁMANO, JUAN, AND FRANCISCO XEREZ

1937 [1528] La relación. *Cuadernos de Historia del Perú,* Paris.

SANTILLÁN, FERNANDO DE

1927 [1563] *Relación del origen, descendencia, política de los Incas.* Colección de libros y documentos referentes a la historia del Perú 9, second series. Imprenta y Librería Sanmarti y Ca., Lima.

UHLE, MAX

1924 *Explorations at Chincha.* University of California Publications in American Archaeology and Ethnology 21 (2): 55–94. University of California Press, Berkeley.

URTON, GARY

1997 *The Social Life of Numbers: A Quechua Ontology of Numbers and Philosophy of Arithmetic.* University of Texas Press, Austin.

WACHTEL, NATHAN

1973 *Sociedad e ideología: Ensayos de historia y antropología andinas.* Instituto de Estudios Peruanos, Lima.

WALLACE, DWIGHT

1971 *Sitios arqueológicas del Perú (segunda entrega), Valles de Chincha y Pisco.* Arqueológicas, Publicaciones del Instituto de Investigaciones Antropológicas 13. Museo Nacional de Antropología y Arqueología, Lima.

1991 The Chincha Roads: Economics and Symbolism. In *Ancient Road Networks and Settlement Hierarchies in the New World* (Charles D. Trombold, ed.): 253–263. Cambridge University Press, New York.

1998 The Inca Compound at La Centinela, Chincha. *Andean Past* 5: 9–33.

WURSTER, WOLFGANG W. (ED.)

1999 *Max Uhle (1856–1944): Pläne archäoligischer Stätten im Andengebiet. Planos de sitios arqueológicos en el área andina.* Materialien zur allgemeinen und vergleichenden Archäologie 56. Verlag Philipp von Zabern, Mainz am Rhein.

ZUIDEMA, R. TOM

1964 *The Ceque System of Cuzco.* E. J. Brill, Leiden.

Machu Picchu's Silent Majority:
A Consideration of the Inka Cemeteries

Lucy C. Salazar

Nací como lirio en el jardín, y ansí fui criado, y como vino mi edad, envejecí, y como había de morir, así me sequé y morí.

I was born as a lily in the garden, and like the lily was raised, as I grew old and death was coming, I withered and died.[1]

ON THE MORNING OF 24 JULY 1911, HIRAM BINGHAM III, THE DIRECTOR OF the Yale Scientific Expedition to Peru, accompanied by a Peruvian military escort, Sergeant Andrés Carrasco, and a young guide, made one of the major archaeological discoveries of the twentieth century in the high Andes of Peru: the majestic archaeological site of Machu Picchu. Although known to local residents and travelers, it had not been included in the written accounts of the Inkas (fig. 1). Since then Machu Picchu, the most regal of the surviving Inka palaces[2] or Inka royal estates, has become the symbol par excellence for Andean culture and Peruvian national identity. Machu Picchu was built by Emperor Inka Yupanqui, later remembered by his descendants as Pachacuti, the great king who built the city of Cusco and reformed Inka religion. To understand an Inka site it is necessary to contextualize it within the larger sociopolitical framework. Machu Picchu has often suffered by being treated without any such contextualization and consequently it has been viewed as a great mystery (Salazar 2004: 27). This has been true not only in works for the general public, but also in those produced by archaeologists and historians.

The burials allow us to observe aspects of life at Machu Picchu that are difficult to ascertain by studying monumental architecture alone. While the remains recovered in the central zone are associated with classic Inka

material, the tombs that Bingham located in the uneven terrain on the periphery of the site are characterized by grave goods whose style is not predominantly that of Cusco Inka. To understand this archaeological patterning, we must consider the identity of the individuals buried in the some 104 caves and rock shelters used as burial chambers that were studied by George Eaton and the other members of the 1912 expedition (fig. 3).

In this essay, I will consider Machu Picchu and its position within the structure of the empire, with a focus on the cemetery areas. I believe that my work sheds some light on the way power was exercised by the Inka elite, both in terms of their relations with the retainers (*yanaconas*) and the state-directed colonists (*mitimaes*) that served them and the factional tensions that shaped the power struggles between members of the elite Inka class. Although Machu Picchu is frequently utilized as a type site for the study of the imperial style of the Inka state, the investigations of the burial grounds reveal a more complex pattern, reflecting activities particular to a dynastic descent group—royal corporation—or *panaca*, as well as the multiethnic composition of the populations under its control. While the first can be appreciated in the well-known architecture and the materials associated with it, the second is most clearly reflected in the contexts of the tombs of the 174 individuals, buried at the site, that were documented by the 1912 investigations (Burger and Salazar 2003).

After a preliminary analysis of the documentation and archaeological materials deposited at the Yale Peabody Museum, we suggested that Machu Picchu should be considered a royal estate constructed by one of Cusco's royal *panacas* (Burger and Salazar 1993; Salazar 2004). A panaca was a kin group descended from a principal Inka ruler (known as a Sapac Inka) and this group included the male and female descendants of that individual, with the exception of his successor to the kingship, who went on to found his own panaca (Sarmiento 1942). The colonial written sources give us information on the landscape around the Inka capital and how these lands were granted to the Inka ruler, his panaca, and the royal lineages *(ayllus)* (Rostworowski 1988: 182). The royal estate was developed primarily to sustain an Inka king and his court during his lifetime

opposite page
FIG. 1 Machu Picchu among the peaks of the Andes (photograph by Richard L. Burger)
FIG. 2 Burial Cave (Gran Salón) (photograph by Hiram Bingham)

FIG. 3 George Eaton at Machu Picchu (photograph by Hiram Bingham)

and after his death (Niles 1988: 57). These royal corporations controlled lands around their royal estates and used the products from them for their own consumption and other purposes. In the case of Machu Picchu, the surrounding cultivatable area is relatively small but is well suited for maize agriculture.

From Spanish narratives written in the early colonial period, we know that members of the panacas and their guests used the royal estates in the areas near Cusco as places of rest and relaxation, and participated in activities such as hunting and feasting (Betanzos 1987: 189). Intensive agriculture was carried out in the Yucay Valley, especially the cultivation of maize; at other estates hot peppers and coca were the primary crops (Farrington 1995; Niles 2004: 55–57). Although we do not have a complete understanding of the functioning and organization of these royal estates, a consideration of the architecture of Machu Picchu indicates that in addition to agriculture, members of the panaca were preoccupied with the production of metal goods, astronomical observations, and ritual activities typical of the empire's religious system.

In 1986, John Rowe independently identified Machu Picchu as a royal estate based on sixteenth-century documents. Rowe associated the archeological site with the historical name of "Pijchu" or "Pichu," a term for mountains (Rowe 1987: 14). In these documents all the lands in the bottom of the valley belonged to Inka "Yupangui" (i.e., Inka Pachacuti Yupanqui) and his panaca—Inaca Panaca Ayllo (Sarmiento de Gamboa 1942: 141). Inka Pachacuti Yupanqui conquered this region in the course of his campaign into the areas of Vitcos and Vilcabamba (Cobo 1979: 135–137). He apparently took the land along the river for himself. Rowe's hypothesis that Machu Picchu was founded by Pachacuti is consistent with our preliminary ceramic analysis indicating the complete absence of the ceramic styles known as Killke, Lucre, and other styles immediately antecedent to the imperial style of Inka pottery.

It is also significant that a large number of architectural units, around thirty, appear to have been used for religious activities (Bingham 1930: 56–66; Buse 1978). This quantity is high when compared to the remains of other royal estates, such as Chincheros, Pisac, and Callachaca. This suggests that the panaca of Pachacuti from the outset may have played an exceptionally important role in the ceremonial life of the Cusco elite. According to Betanzos, one of Pachacuti's sons, Yamque Yupanqui Topa, was said to have devoted his life to Inka religious activities rather than political rulership (Betanzos 1987). If a special link existed between Pachacuti's panaca and the Inka religious cult, it might help to explain the presence of unusual ritual constructions like the Temple of the Three Windows, whose architectural reference to the Inka mythical origins is unparalleled at other royal estates (Salazar 2004: 36).

Given its apparent function as a royal estate of Pachacuti's panaca, it is not surprising that Machu Picchu was constructed utilizing the conventions of design and masonry associated with the Inka elite and still visible in many of the surviving examples of palaces and temples in Cusco. The finest architecture at Machu Picchu is concentrated in the portions of the site dedicated to ceremonial activities and the residences of the elite (Salazar and Burger 2004b). The residences utilized the classic architectural form known as a *kancha*. These rectangular compounds have a single entrance, a central open-air patio, and various roofed buildings with interior spaces for diverse activities. The kanchas pertained to the elite as evidenced by the use of double-jambed entryways and walls of finely cut and polished stone. Many also incorporate household shrines. The masonry in these domestic constructions and other exquisite buildings used locally available granite, but it is possible that specialists from the altiplano may have participated in their construction.

Bingham's 1912 excavations concentrated on the elite residential zone and the ceremonial sector. The ceramic remains found in these areas are dominated by the classic Inka stylistic conventions utilized in the empire's capital at Cusco (Salazar and Burger 2004a: 126–156). Thus, the architecture and the ceramics in the central sector of Machu Picchu are characterized by the classic Inka style that symbolized the identity of the Inka ethnic group that imperialized Tawantinsuyu. As Manuel Chávez Ballon (1971), Tom Zuidema (1990), and others have pointed out, the layout of Machu Picchu likewise shares many features with Cusco and some provincial Inka installations.

The ethnohistoric evidence available indicates that one of the prerogatives of an Inka panaca responsible for the conquest of new zones and populations was to assign a number of individuals in the conquered group for its own service or to give these individuals to other panacas as an act of generosity (Betanzos 1987: 50). I interpret the presence of non-Cusco materials in the cemeteries as an indicator of the residence of non-Inka ethnic groups at Machu Picchu in their capacity as yanaconas and mitimaes.

In the Inka sociopolitical structure, the yanacona was the term used for the retainers or dependents (*criados*) assigned to the governing elite (Betanzos 1987: 50). The category of *camayocs* was applied to specialists (Espinoza 1978: 231–247, 1987: 217–219; Spurling n.d.: 232). The social and economic status of people in these categories apparently varied according to the prestige associated with their individual roles, which included those servants of the elite, administrative counselors, and craftsmen, most notably metallurgists, potters, and weavers. The graves at Machu Picchu appear to correspond to yanacona of varying ethnic origin; some of whom it will be argued were probably camayoc.

Analysis of the human remains indicates that both men and women were represented at a ratio of 1:1.5 rather than the radically asymmetric 1:4 calculated by Eaton (1916). The skeletal evidence also indicates that some of the women had given birth. Moreover, there are numerous skeletons of fetuses, infants, and young children (Verano 2000: 143–152). These findings allow us to set aside Bingham's theory that Machu Picchu was a place for the "chosen women" (*acllahuasi*) and that the buried women had been dedicated to the cult of the sun.

Machu Picchu Burials

Most of the graves disclosed by Bingham's investigations are located among the clusters of boulders that are found in peripheral sectors of the site (fig. 2). The funerary contexts for the most part are modest, and there is not a great investment in the elaboration of the funerary environments. Rarely was there evidence of more than a simple stone wall closing off the natural cavity formed by an unmodified boulder (Bingham 1930; Eaton 1916).

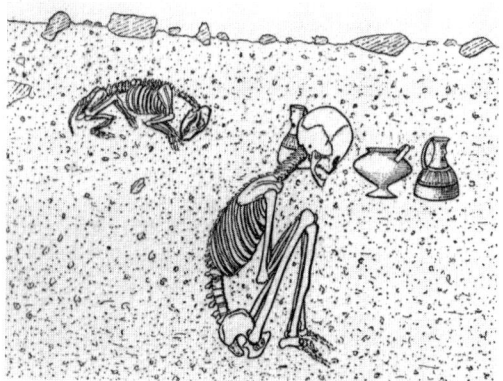

FIG. 4 Diagram of Burial Cave 26 at the terrace wall (after Eaton 1916)

The small burial chambers documented by the Yale Peruvian Expedition often contained skeletal remains, pottery, and other artifacts. The goods deposited with each individual, however, are few, and rarely more than four to six ceramic vessels and some artifacts of bone and metal in any grave. A large number of these funerary objects show evidence of having been heavily utilized, probably by the individuals during their lifetime. Many had been damaged and repaired prior to their interment.

The modest nature of the burial chambers and the associated goods, as well as the biological and cultural diversity of the population, and the suite of occupational illnesses evident in the human remains led us to conclude that these burials represented the interments of yanacona rather than of the elite members who occupied Machu Picchu's elegant kanchas (Gasparini and Margolies 1980). It is likely that those members of the elite who perished at Machu Picchu were returned to Cusco rather than entombed at the royal estate in Cusco's rural hinterland. While the absence of elite burials and the consequent paucity of precious metal objects at Machu Picchu created problems for Hiram Bingham at the time of his excavations, the existence of a large sample of graves of those who served the elite offer an unusual opportunity to focus on this group and their relationship with the dominant class.

The association of the burial objects and human remains offers us an opportunity to examine the ethnic identity and daily activities of the individuals buried there. It is well known from the sixteenth-century Spanish narratives that the yanaconas and camayocs were drawn from throughout the empire. The yanaconas and/or camayocs at Machu Picchu had been brought from diverse conquered provinces. They represent various ethnic groups that can be identified principally by their cultural material styles, funerary rituals, and cranial forms. By far the most common ethnic groups represented in the Machu Picchu cemeteries are from the area surrounding Lake Titicaca (Collas, Lupaqa, Pacajes); they constitute over half the sample. There are also significant numbers of Chimú and Cañaris, as well as a small number of Chachas and other groups. The number of burials of people from Cusco is quite small (Salazar 2001, n.d.a).

To visualize and characterize the ethnic variability and its implications from an archaeological perspective, I have selected four different burials for more detailed discussion: one with Cuzqueño identity, one from the altiplano area, one from Chachapoyas and the final one from the Chimú area of the Peruvian north coast. The first burial was located on a terrace of a rock shelter in the southeast section of the site; Bingham called this zone Cemetery 3 (Bingham 1930: 103). The remains in the burial belonged to a woman forty to fifty years old and roughly 1.64 m in height. She had evidence of vertebral arthritis, an occupational infirmity resulting from strain that her daily activities placed on her back (Verano 2003: 145). Her body was deposited in a fetal position some 1.20 m from a terrace wall; two short staircases led to the surface of this terrace, on which was located a large stone (fig. 4). Near the buried woman was the skeleton of a Collie-like dog (Miller 2003: 17). The other objects found in the burial were two face-necked jars, a pedestal vessel (*olla*), two pins (*tupus*), a pair of tweezers, a mirror, a coca lime spoon, a seed, and two cactus needles (Eaton 1916: 25; Bingham 1930: 110; Salazar 2001: 121). The metal objects are bronze rather than gold or silver, although the mirror-like object had a silver plated surface (Rutledge n.d.; Salazar and Burger 2004a: 187; fig. 5). In addition to these objects encountered in the interment itself, fragmented materials were found apparently linked to above-ground burial rituals at the gravesite.[3] The entire assemblage of ceramics recovered in the burial can be identified as fitting within the canons of forms and designs of the Cusco style of Inka pottery (fig. 6). Considering the available evidence from the skeleton and associated burial

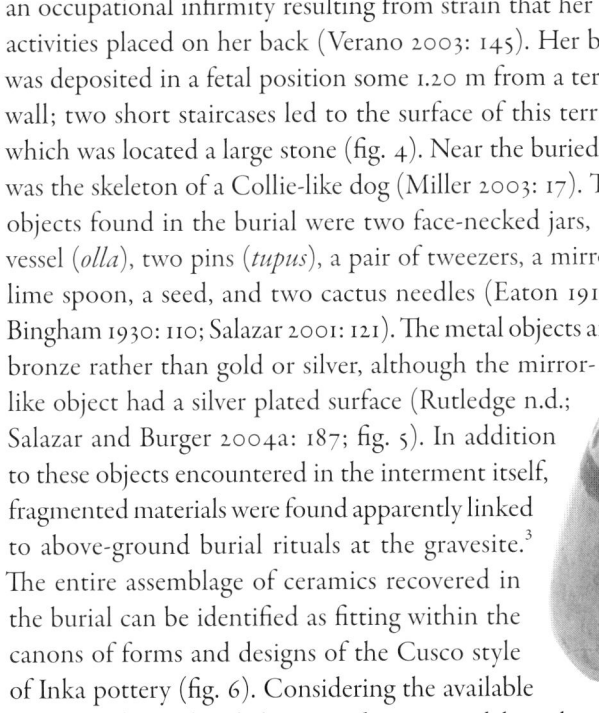

FIG. 5 A parabolic bronze mirror with silver plating, Cave 26

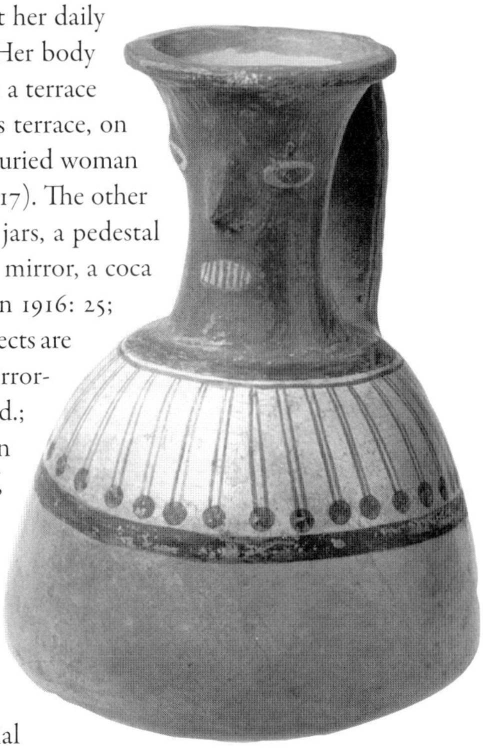

FIG. 6 A Cusco-Inca style face-necked jar with a half khipu decoration around the neck, Cave 26

objects, I would suggest that this woman might have been a Cuzqueña retainer who perhaps was charged with performing rituals and ceremonies associated with female deities (Salazar 2001: 122–123). These rituals, called Coya Raymi, occurred in September, the month of the Moon. These rituals, and their associated organizations, allowed Inka women an opportunity to display their strength (Silverblatt 1987: 54–65). Although the role of retainer is not prestigious within the vertical hierarchy of Inka society, the mortuary treatment suggests a degree of privilege, particularly if compared to members of the general rural population of the empire.

The second burial to be discussed here is located in cemetery 1 in the northeast extreme of Machu Picchu, midway along the path to Huayna Picchu and called Cave 59 (Eaton 1916). This grave presents the remains of two females; one was approximately twenty to twenty-four years old at the time of her death, while the other's age is difficult to calculate (Verano 2003: 149). The grave goods consisted of two serving vessels, two small plates, two jars, two cooking pots with pedestal bases, and two bronze tupus. There was also one repaired bottle, whose handle had been broken off; inside of this bottle were pieces of carbonized organic material, a piece of leather, fragments of burnt human crania, teeth, and a skull of a rodent of the genus *Abrocoma* (Miller 2003: 12–13; fig. 7). This funerary context holds an assemblage of vessels associated with an individual of relatively low status: two small cooking pots, two jars to hold chicha or some other liquid, and two decorated plates to serve food. It is significant that the jars, as well as the bottles and plates, are made in a style utilized by the Collas of Lake Titicaca during the Inka period (Julien 1983: pls. 20–21; Salazar 2001: 134). In contrast, the cooking pots are local both in their style and production. The inclusion of the remains of slaughtered camelids within the burial could reflect Colla funerary rituals as described by Pedro Cieza de León and other chroniclers (Cieza de León 1984 [1553]: 273). The unusual combination of items found inside the bottle is suggestive of traditional healing practices known today as *curanderismo* (Salazar n.d.a: 123–124; Sanchez 1989: 105).

FIG. 7 A jar with everted rim in a provincial Inca-Cusco style with a reworked handle, Cave 59

The third burial was located in Cemetery 3 two-thirds of the way up the Machu Picchu mountain, south of the city (Eaton 1916). The interment was found at Cave 71 and included the remains of a young male nineteen to twenty-four years old, with circumferential or mild annular cranial deformation (Verano 2003: 150). The offerings in this grave consisted of two cooking pots (pedestal ollas) and a decorated two-handled bowl

(Salazar 2001).[4] There were also four iliac llama bones, which had been worked into digging tools and bear the wear marks from their intensive use (Miller 2003: 56–57). On the basis of the form of the skull and the cultural offerings, I would like to suggest that this individual was from an ethnic group of the northern highlands.

The final burial to be considered in this essay was located in Cemetery 4, Cave 101 (Eaton: 1916) that is found in the western side of the site above the ceremonial sector. As Eaton noted, very little human material was collected (Eaton 1916). Among the funerary objects deposited with the interment was a two-piece mold stirrup spouted bottle with a stylized modeled bird (fig. 8) (Bingham 1930: 165; Burger and Salazar 2004: 133–134), a two-handled jar with cream slip painting (Salazar n.d.a: 163), and fragments of an aryballoid vessel and a jar. Other offerings are a small bronze pin and three figures of a soft greenstone, identified as schist, cut into the form of ritual knives and animals (Salazar and Burger 2004a: 160). Bingham found various schist objects like this one, including some that were only partially complete, suggesting that they were being produced at Machu Picchu itself. Julinho Zapata (personal communication, 2001) had carried out excavations at Machu Picchu in buildings associated with craft activities; in one such area he recovered worked schist fragments associated with ceramics in a Chimú-Inka style. This find is consistent with my interpretation of the individual from Cemetery 4 as a metal worker of the Chimú ethnic group who participated in the production of metal and stone objects, some of which appear to have had a ceremonial character. The pottery in this burial has forms and designs identifiable with a late variant of the Chimú-Inka style (Schjellerup 1985: 20, pl. 41). The place where this pottery was produced remains unknown and should be studied through sourcing techniques such as neutron activation. There were also animal bones belonging to a vizcacha (*Lagidium peruanum*), one of six identified in the burials at Machu Picchu (Miller 2003: 6).

In general, the pathologies of the skeletal remains from Machu Picchu's cemeteries suggest some differences in status and occupation of the buried individuals that served the elite residents of the site. While back problems, broken bones, and dental infections were the most common infirmities, many individuals lacked such occupational health problems. Scholars have recognized the diverse social positions held by yanaconas, noting that these differences were linked to their occupational specializations (Espinoza Soriano 1987, 1978; Murra 1978; Spurling n.d.; Villar Córdova 1982).

FIG. 8 Chimú-Inca stirrup spout bottle, Cave 101

The funerary contexts at Machu Picchu allow us to infer that despite the large number of ethnic groups represented in the burials, the mortuary practices basically conformed to those of the dominant group, the Inkas. There is little variation at Machu Picchu in the selection of natural caves and rock shelters for burial rather than creation of masonry *chullpas* such as those used in the altiplano or the painted mausoleums and funerary bundles found in Chachapoyas. Nor do we find the creation of pit burials or below-surface burial chambers that characterize the Late Horizon on the central and north coast. Another feature that characterizes the majority of the Machu Picchu burials, in those cases where preservation and documentation is adequate, is the fetal position of the bodies when they were originally placed in mummy-like bundles. This too suggests the dominance of the Inka burial pattern, at least in regard to the funerary environments (Rowe 1995: 33; Salomon 1996: 324).

As I have noted, the individuals interred at Machu Picchu appear to have been left above ground in fetal position, surrounded by food and liquid refreshments as well as a few personal objects of everyday life. This arrangement would have allowed them to be attended to long after their deaths. The dead had to be treated as the living: by being placed on the surface of these shelters, they could breathe and receive homage once a year, usually in the form of food and drink.

In the majority of the burials that Bingham analyzed, there was an area directly in front of the funerary environment where bone and ceramic remains were usually recovered. In contrast to the materials associated with the dead, this pottery is very fragmented and incomplete. The same is true of the faunal material belonging to camelids and other animals. These materials are best interpreted as evidence of postmortem rituals carried out at the burial site. It is significant that the ceramics found outside the caves and rock shelters include large jars, cooking vessels, and aryballoid vessels. Many of these were made to serve large groups of people and they contrast with the small vessels found as grave offerings, which were produced for individual use.

Discussion

What can we learn from the study of these and other Machu Picchu burials? On the one hand, the tombs offer a new vision of the lives of the yanacona and/or camayocs brought to Machu Picchu: their health, their diet, their life span, and their specialization. Analysis of the tombs allows us to begin to penetrate the multiple levels of individual identity and their real implications for understanding the daily lives of people in a way not possible even through a close reading of the Spanish narratives. The vision of retainers plagued by chronic back problems but with access to Inka metal mirrors, shawls pins, or tupus and tweezers not commonly available

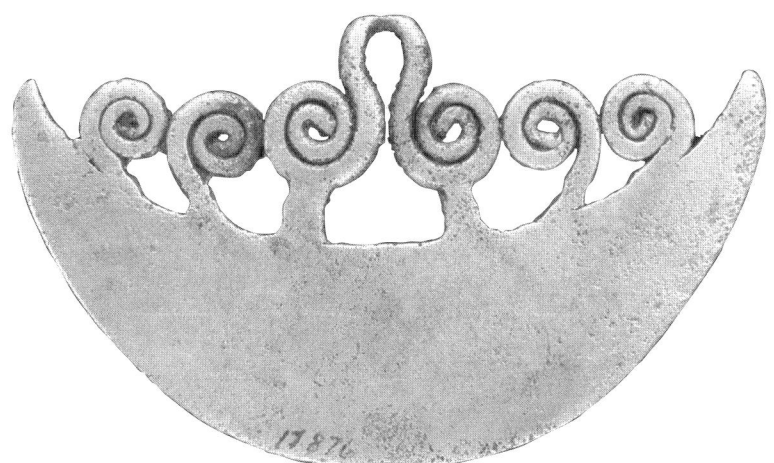

FIG. 9 Crescent-shaped bronze knife pendant with curvilinear adornment in a Cañari-Inca style

to farmers in the rural hinterland hints at the sacrifices and opportunities that came with being assigned as a retainer to a royal corporation, regardless of one's ethnic background.

It is fascinating that these individuals continued to retain their original ethnic identity within the context of the royal estate. Their use of personal pottery made in the style of their homeland was a public expression of this identity that would have been evident to those dining with them. Significantly, many of these non-Cusco vessels are serving vessels that are found in pairs, reflecting their use in entertainment. In this light, the frequent efforts to repair these vessels, often modifying broken rims through abrasion, takes on new symbolic significance (Salazar and Burger 2004a: 134, cat. no. 23).

At the same time, locally produced Inka pottery, especially cooking vessels, was also frequently included as grave goods, suggesting the integration of the foreigners into the local social and cultural context; moreover, as noted, the way in which they were buried corresponds to local patterns rather than those of their homelands. There is no reason why chullpa burials or below-ground interments could not have taken place at Machu Picchu. The conformity to the Cusco-style pattern of entombment suggests the degree of dominance in the asymmetric relations in which these people lived and died.

The study of the tombs can also affect our understanding of the Inka elite of a royal panaca that ultimately was responsible for the presence of the individuals buried at Machu Picchu. It is possible to ask why, at the royal estate of Inka Pachacuti Yupanqui, there are individuals from the area of Chimú domination and not from the Wanka? Why Collas and Cañaris (fig. 9) and not Ichma or Diaguitas? An explanation leads back to the historical evidence that Machu Picchu was founded by the Inka Pachacuti. It is reasonable to expect that members of the groups he conquered would be present, such as the Chimú or Colla. However, this is only a partial explanation, since many of the groups conquered during Pachacuti's reign are not represented at the site and, at the same time, several groups conquered by Pachacuti's successors, who founded other panacas, are present, such as the Chachapoyas who were conquered by Tupac Yupanqui. To understand this unexpected patterning, it is necessary to explore the ways in which panacas utilized particular specialists—especially metallurgists in the case of Machu Picchu—in order to maintain their political influence. This process continued after the death of the founder Inka Pachacuti Yupanqui through ties to other panacas. By way of these links the panacas continued to obtain specialized labor in the form of yanaconas/camayocs from newly conquered ethnic groups. In Machu Picchu the continued dynamism of the panaca after the death of Pachacuti is reflected not only in the ethnic makeup of the tombs, but also in the continued growth and construction at the site. Several projects, including an additional canal bringing water to Machu Picchu, were under way at the time the site was abandoned (Wright, Valencia Zegarra, and Crowley n.d.)

Recent discussions of the power struggles that characterize state societies have shown a renewed interest in struggles within the elite group rather than assuming solidarity within this group and conflict between it and the socioeconomic classes it dominated and exploited. These divisions within the elite can be conceptualized as competing factions. Their strategies often involved the creation of strategic alliances with less prestigous groups, thereby creating vertical fissures within the society that crosscut ethnic groups and social classes. Studies of factional competition have long been fashionable in ethnographic research, particularly in Africa, but their emergence as a focus of attention in anthropological archaeology is largely due to the efforts of Elizabeth Brumfiel, who has developed an interesting model of factional competition in her research on the Aztec empire (Brumfiel 1989). Among the Inka elite, the panacas constituted a formal organizational basis for factional competition within the elite and analyses such as those of Tom Patterson (1991) have used the historical records to trace how panacas competed to influence the selection of the new emperor and access to the resources this ruler would generate and channel. It is also evident that panacas developed special relationships with particular non-Inka ethnic groups with skills or natural resources that were especially valued. It is possible to hypothesize that the patterning of non-Inka groups at the royal estate of Machu Picchu reflects the particular pattern of alliances and linkages between Pachacuti's panaca and select ethnicities in the hinterland. It would be interesting to compare this patterning with that of royal estates belonging to the panacas of Pachacuti's successors. Thus, the study of royal estates such as Machu Picchu may provide an opportunity to explore the role played by individual panacas. This theme acquires increasing relevance in light of recent studies of factions as an important element in elucidating the process of development and the imperializing transformations produced by the creation of Tawantinsuyu.

One final sidelight on the role of the yanaconas and mitimaes at Machu Picchu concerns their activities above and beyond basic functions such as construction, site maintenance, and personal service. The artifacts recovered from the graves and refuse argue against their involvement in agricultural work, and there is likewise no evidence for ceramic production and most other kinds of craft activity. The production of small schist carvings of possible religious significance was undertaken on a small scale, as mentioned earlier, and appears to have been associated with people brought from the north coast. There is even stronger evidence that metalworking was carried out at Machu Picchu (Gordon 1985, 1986, 1987; Mathewson 1915; Rutledge n.d.). The materials excavated by Bingham indicate the creation of tin bronze alloys at the site, and he has suggested experimentation with bismuth in the casting of pins. Metalworking byproducts and raw materials for creating metal artifacts provide a strong indication of this unexpected component of daily life at a royal estate. Additional evidence of work in precious metals was recovered during the excavations at Machu Picchu by archaeologists Luis Watanabe (personal communication, 1987) and Elba Torres (Wright, Valencia Zegarra, and Crowley n.d.: 43), but the details of these finds have yet to appear in print.

It may be significant that most of the ethnic groups identified in the tombs are mentioned in the Spanish chronicles as having special metallurgical skills and some of them may have been brought to Machu Picchu particularly because of this technical knowledge. The creation of highly valued craft items may have been part of an intentional strategy by the panaca who could use these wealth objects as gifts in establishing or reinforcing alliances with other groups.

The link between metallurgy and magical transformation has been observed cross-culturally, and in the Andes the use of metals to represent supernatural forces is a feature not only of the Inka, but of many of their predecessors over two millennia. Thus the appropriateness of metallurgy at the royal estate may follow a religious as well as strategic logic. At the very least, it forces us to reexamine our conceptualizations of life at the Inka royal estates and the imperializing process.

Notes

1 Inka Pachacuti's fondness for flowers was recorded in the *cantares* or *haravec*, songs that memorialized the events of his life history. As he lay dying, he began to sing this cantar. It was recorded by Sarmiento de Gamboa (1947 [1572]: 140).

2 For the term *palace*, see discussion in Salazar and Burger (2004b).

3 These mirror-like artifacts have been found associated with Inca female burials and warfare (Salazar 2001: 122).

4 For a description of the ceramic vessel forms at Machu Picchu see Burger and Salazar (2004).

References cited

BETANZOS, JUAN DE

    1987 [1551–1557] *Suma y Narración de los Incas* (María del Carmen Martín Rubio, transcription, notes, and prologue). Ediciones Atlas, Madrid.

BINGHAM, HIRAM

    1930 *Machu Picchu, a Citadel of the Incas.* Memoirs of the National Geographic Society. Yale University Press, New Haven, Conn.

BRUMFIEL, ELIZABETH

    1989 Factional Competition in Complex Society. In *Domination and Resistance* (David Miller, Michael Rowlands, and Christopher Tilley, eds.): 127–139. Unwin Hyman, London.

BURGER, RICHARD, AND LUCY C. SALAZAR

    1993 Machu Picchu Rediscovered: The Royal Estate in the Clouds. *Discovery* 24 (2): 20–25.

BURGER, RICHARD L., AND LUCY C. SALAZAR (EDS.)

    2004 *Machu Picchu: Unveiling the Mystery of the Incas.* Yale University Press, New Haven, Conn.

BUSE DE LA GUERRA, HERMANN

    1978 *Machu Picchu.* Third edition. Librería Studium, Lima.

CHÁVEZ BALLON, MANUEL

    1971 Cusco y Machupijchu. *Wayka* 4–5. Universidad Nacional San Antonio de Abad Cuzco, Cuzco.

CIEZA DE LEÓN, PEDRO DE

    1984 [1553] *Crónica del Perú: Primera Parte.* Pontificia Universidad Católica del Perú. Fondo Editorial, Lima.

    1985 [1553] *Crónica del Perú: Segunda Parte.* Pontificia Universidad Católica del Perú. Fondo Editorial, Lima.

COBO, BERNABÉ

    1964 [1653] Historia del Nuevo Mundo. In *Obras* (P. Francisco Mateos, ed.). Biblioteca de autores españoles 91, 92. Ediciones Atlas, Madrid.

EATON, GEORGE F.

    1916 *The Collection of Osteological Material from Machu Picchu.* Memoirs of the Connecticut Academy of the Arts and Sciences 5. Tuttle, Morehouse, and Taylor, New Haven, Conn.

    n.d. Notes on Yale Peruvian Expedition. Folders 14–26, Yale University Archives, 1912.

ESPINOZA SORIANO, WALDEMAR

    1978 Los Chachapoyas y Cañares de Chiara (Huamanga), Aliados de España. In *Historia, Problema y Promesa* (Francisco Miró Quesada Cantuarias, Franklin Pease G. Y., and David Sobreville

A., eds.): 231–253. Pontificia Universidad Católica del Peru, Fondo Editorial, Lima.

1987 Migraciones Internas en el reino Colla. Tejedores. *Revista Histórica* 36: 209–305.

FARRINGTON, IAN S.

1995 The Mummy Palace and Estate of Inka Huayna Capac at Quispeguanca. *Tawantinsuyu* 1: 55–65.

GASPARINI, GRAZIANO, AND LOUISE MARGOLIES

1980 *Inca Architecture* (Patricia J. Lyon, trans.). Indiana University Press, Bloomington.

GORDO, ROBERT B.

1985 Laboratory Evidence of the Use of Metal Tools at Machu Picchu (Peru) and Environs. *Journal of Archaeological Science* 12(4): 311–327.

1986 Metallurgy of Bronze Tools from Machu Picchu. *Proceedings of the 24th International Archaeometry Symposium:* 233–242. Smithsonian Institution, Washington, D.C.

1987 Laboratory Evidence of How Metal Artifacts Were Used. In *Tecnologia Nell'Antichita* 7: 109–112.

HEYERDAHL, THOR, DANIEL H. SANDWEISS, AND ALFREDO NARVÁEZ

1995 *Pyramids of Túcume: The Quest for Peru's Forgotten City.* Thames and Hudson, New York.

JULIEN, CATHERINE J.

1983 *Hatunqolla: A View of Inca Rule from the Lake Titicaca Region.* University of California Press, Berkeley.

MATHEWSON, CHAMPION H.

1915 A Metallographic Description of Some Ancient Peruvian Bronzes from Machu Picchu. *American Journal of Science* 40 (240): 1–36.

MILLER, GEORGE R.

2003 Food for the Dead, Tools for the Afterlife: Zooarchaeology at Mach Picchu. In *The 1912 Yale Peruvian Scientific Expedition Collections from Machu Picchu: Human and Animal Remains* (Richard L. Burger and Lucy Salazar, eds.): 1–63. Yale University Publications in Anthropology 85. Peabody Museum of Natural History, New Haven, Conn.

MOLINA, CRISTÓBAL DE

1916 [1573] Relación de las fábulas y ritos de los Incas. In *Colección de libros y documentos referentes a la historia del Perú* 1 (Carlos Romero, ed.). Sanmartí y ca., Lima.

MURRA, JOHN

1975 *Formaciones economicas y políticas del mundo andino.* Instituto de Estudios Peruanos, Lima.

NILES, SUSAN A.

1988 Looking for "Lost" Inca Palaces. *Expedition* 30 (3): 56–64.

2004 The Nature of Inca Royal Estates. In *Machu Picchu: Unveiling the Mystery of the Incas* (Richard L. Burger and Lucy C. Salazar, eds.): 49–68. Yale University Press, New Haven, Conn.

PARDO, LUIS

1957 *Historia y arqueología de Cuzco.* 2 vols. Imprenta Colegio Militar Leoncio Prado, Lima.

PATTERSON, THOMAS C.

1991 *The Inca Empire: The Formation and Disintegration of a Pre-Capitalist State.* Berg Publishers, London.

PROTZEN, JEAN-PIERRE, WITH STELLA NAIR

1997 Who Taught the Inca Stonemasons Their Skills? A Comparison of Tiahuanaco and Inca Cut-Stone Masonry. *Journal of the Society of Architectural Historians* 56 (2): 146–167.

ROWE, JOHN HOWLAND

1982 Inca Policies and Institutions Relating to the Cultural Unification of the Empire. In *The Inca and Aztec States 1400–1800: Anthropology and History* (George A. Collier, Renato I. Rosaldo, and John D. Wirth, eds.): 93–118. Academic Press, New York.

1987 Machu Picchu: A la luz de los documentos del siglo XVI. *Kuntur* (4): 12–20.

1989 Machu Picchu: A la luz de documentos del siglo XVI. *Histórica* 14 (1): 139–154.

1995 Behavior and Belief in Ancient Peruvian Mortuary Practice. In *Tombs for the Living: Andean Mortuary Practices* (Tom Dillehay, ed.): 27–41. Dumbarton Oaks Research Library and Collection, Washington, D.C.

RUTLEDGE, JOHN W.

n.d. The Metals Artifacts from the Yale Peruvian Expedition of 1912. Master's thesis, Department of Anthropology, Yale University, 1984.

SALAZAR, LUCY C.

2001 Inca Religion and Mortuary Ritual at Machu Picchu. In *Mortuary Practices and Ritual Associations: Shamanic Elements in Prehistoric Funerary Contexts in South America* (John Staller and Elizabeth J. Currie, eds.): 117–127. BAR International Series 982. Archaeopress, Oxford.

2004 Machu Picchu: Mysterious Royal Estate in the Cloud Forest. In *Machu Picchu: Unveiling the Mystery of the Incas* (Richard L. Burger and Lucy C. Salazar, eds.): 21–48. Yale University Press, New Haven and London.

n.d.a Ritual, Politics, Death and Power at Machu Picchu. Master's thesis, Department of Archaeology, Yale University, 2001.

n.d.b Inca Religion and the Political Power of Sacred Space: Machu Picchu's Pachacuti Country Palace. Paper presented at the 50th International Congress of Americanists, July 2000, Warsaw, Poland

n.d.c Una revaluación de las Tumbas de Machu Picchu Excavadas por la Expedición Científica de la Universidad de Yale, 1912. Paper presented at the 49th International Congress of Americanists, July 1997, Quito, Ecuador.

SALAZAR, LUCY C., AND RICHARD L. BURGER

2004a Catalogue. In *Machu Picchu: Unveiling the Mystery of the Incas* (Richard L. Burger and Lucy C. Salazar, eds.): 125–217. Yale University Press, New Haven, Conn.

2004b Lifestyles of the Rich and Famous: Luxury and Daily Life in the Households of Machu Picchu's Elite. In *Palaces of the Ancient New World* (Susan Toby Evans and Joanne Pillsbury, eds.): 325–353. Dumbarton Oaks Research Library and Collection, Washington, D.C.

SALAZAR, LUCY, AND VUKA ROUSAKIS

2000 Tejidos y Tejedores del Tawantinsuyu. In *Los Incas: Arte y Símbolos* (Banco de Crédito, ed.): 269–303. Lima.

SALOMON, FRANK

1995 "The Beautiful Grandparents": Andean Ancestor Shrines and Mortuary Ritual as Seen through Colonial Records. In *Tombs for the Living: Andean Mortuary Practices* (Tom D. Dillehay, ed.): 315–353. Dumbarton Oaks Research Library and Collection, Washington, D.C.

SÁNCHEZ MACEDO, MARINO ORLANDO

1989 *De las sacerdotisas, brujas y adivinas de Machu Picchu.* M. O. Sánchez Macedo, Lima.

SARMIENTO DE GAMBOA, PEDRO

1944 [1572] *Historia de los incas.* Colección Horreo 10, 2nd ed. Emecé, Buenos Aires.

SCHJELLERUP, INGE

1985 *Chimu Pottery.* The National Museum of Denmark, Copenhagen.

SILVERBLATT, IRENE

1987 *Moon, Sun and Witches: Gender Ideologies and Colonial Peru.* Princeton University Press, Princeton, N.J.

SPURLING, GEOFFREY

n.d. The Organization of Craft Production in the Inka State: The Potters and Weavers of Milliraya. Ph.D. dissertation, Cornell University, 1992.

VALENCIA ZEGARRA, ALFREDO, AND ARMINDA GIBAJA OVIEDO

1992 *Machu Picchu: La investigación y conservación del monumento arqueológico después de Hiram Bingham.* Municipalidad del Qosqo, Cusco.

VERANO, JOHN W.

2003 Human Skeletal Remains from Machu Picchu: A Reexamination of the Yale Peabody Museum's Collection. In *The 1912 Yale Peruvian Scientific Expedition Collections from Machu Picchu: Human and Animal Remains* (Richard L. Burger and Lucy Salazar, eds.): 65–117. Yale University Publications in Anthropology 85. Peabody Museum of Natural History, New Haven, Conn.

VILLANUEVA URTEAGA, HORACIO

1971 Documentos sobre Yucay en el siglo XVI. *Revista del Archivo Histórico del Cuzco* 13 (1970): 1–148.

VILLAR CÓRDOVA, PEDRO E.

1982 *Arqueologia del Departamento de Lima.* Ediciones Atusparia, Lima.

WRIGHT, KENNETH R., ALFREDO VALENCIA ZEGARRA, AND C. CROWLEY

n.d. Archaeological Exploration of the Inca Trail, East Flank of Machu Picchu and Palynology of Terraces. Final Report. Instituto Nacional de Cultura. Wright Paleohydrological Institute, Denver, 2000.

ZUIDEMA, R. TOM

1990 *Inca Civilization in Cuzco.* University of Texas Press, Austin.

Sculpting the Yucay Valley: Power and Style in Late Inka Architecture

Susan A. Niles
Robert N. Batson

THE ARCHITECTURAL REMAINS IN THE REGION AROUND YUCAY AND Urubamba are unique among Inka constructions because we have detailed historical records that can be compared with the buildings to understand their construction, design, chronology, and use. The development is an example of late Inka construction, commissioned by the Inka king, Huayna Capac, as a royal estate around the year 1496. Starting with the natural resources available to him—alluvial fans, abundant water, high points for construction and low points that were problem areas for drainage—Huayna Capac sculpted a uniquely cultural landscape, one which was an expression of the personal power of its builder.

Introduction to the Site

The Yucay Valley is adjacent to the Inkas' home territory of the Huatanay Valley, and their capital, Cusco. Known today as the Urubamba or the Vilcanota Valley, the colonial documents use the Inka name of Yucay to refer to the narrow, temperate valley so favored by Inka kings for their country palaces (fig. 1).

The portion of the Yucay Valley developed by Huayna Capac included all the lands on the north side of the valley between the constriction of the valley at Acosca, and that above Pachar (fig. 2). The approximately fifteen km of valley that he claimed was an intentionally created space. Prior to the construction of this estate, there was only a minor Inka presence here; it was the homeland of four native groups, the Pacas, Cachis, Chichos, and Chaocas (Villanueva Urteaga 1971). Nearby, Topa Inca had developments in Chinchero, and in several valleys that abut the estate, at Urquillos and Taracachi, while Pachacuti had been active both above

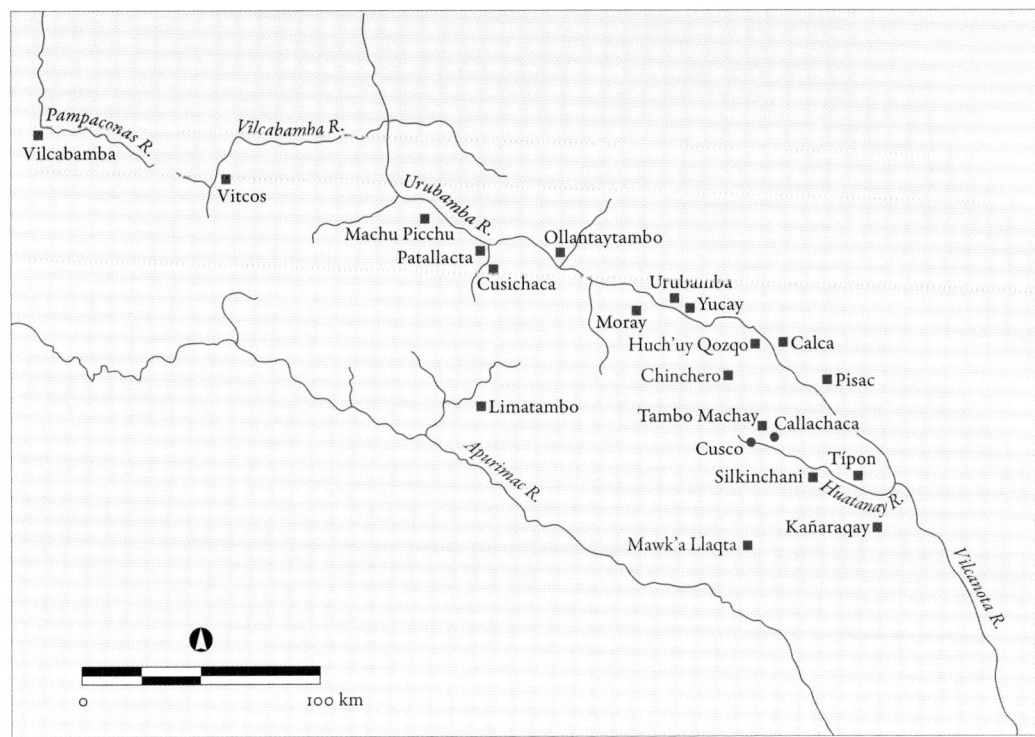

FIG. 1 Map of the Huatanay and Vilcanota-Urubamba Valley region, showing principal sites associated with royal Inka activity.

Urquillos and below Pachar. Prior to its development by Huayna Capac the land was probably very undesirable: it is swampy, and the Urubamba River meandered over much of the valley floor.

The first stage of the Inka reclamation of the region was to channel the river and build up terraces. Juan de Betanzos, writing in the mid-sixteenth century, cites an account that

> Huayna Capac ordered that one hundred thousand Indians, or as many as possible, come from all the land. Then his order was sent out to all the provinces, and within six months one hundred fifty thousand Indians assembled in the city of Cuzco. When the Inka saw them, he ordered the lords of Cuzco to go with those workers and take them to the Valley of Yucay. The Inka himself also went with them and started the work of improving the valley. He had the river moved along the side facing Cuzco, making it stronger and making a bed where it went. Along the path of the river the Inca had hills leveled. Thus he made the valley flat so that it could be planted and harvested. There he had houses built and lodgings where he could go to enjoy himself. In this valley he gave farmlands to the lords of Cuzco, both to the living and to the dead lords whose statues were there. They sent their yana-cona servants to cultivate their vegetables and other things for their enjoyment. There Huayna Capac had many small towns of

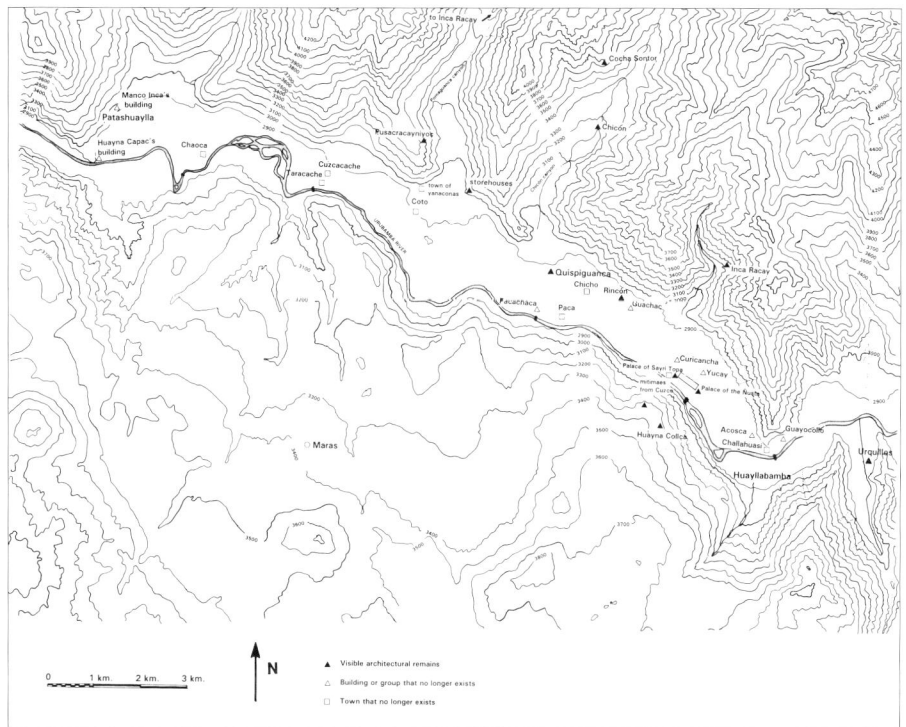

twenty, thirty, and fifty Indians built. In these towns he put many mitimae Indians from all the nations and all the provinces of the land. (Betanzos 1996 [1551–57]: pt. 1, chap. 43, 170)

The archaeological evidence matches the claim that the valley floor was completely reshaped in Huayna Capac's reclamation. The estate was provided with roads, bridges, irrigation and terracing systems, homes for farmers, temples, palaces, and parklands.[1] We will focus our discussion on one complex in the estate, the palace known as Quispiguanca, located on the northern edge of the modern town of Urubamba. We will also make some comparisons to other portions of the estate, most notably the terrace system at Yucay, the Inka-style buildings on the plaza of the modern town of Yucay, and Cocha Sontor, a hunting lodge high up in the Chicón Canyon.

The site had a complex history in the late fifteenth and early sixteenth centuries. Its rich lands and large population of resident farmers were carved up, handed out, and fought over by Spanish conquerors, displaced Inka royalty, and ambitious native lords (*caciques*) of other ethnic groups alike, and claims for pieces of the estate were launched in the courts from 1550 through 1615. Texts or discussion of some of the legal claims are presented by Horacio Villanueva Urteaga (1971), María Rostworowski de Diez Canseco (1962, 1970), Guillermo Lohmann Villena (1965), Juan Henríquez de Borja (n.d.), Susan Niles (1993, 1999), and Ken Heffernan

FIG. 2 Topographic map of Huayna Capac's country estate. The eastern limit of the estate is at Acosca. The western limit is at a constriction in the valley just west of Patashuaylla. The estate included all lands north of the Urubamba River, and had major architectural groups at Yucay, Quispiguanca, and Cocha Sontor.

Sculpting the Yucay Valley

(1995). The inspections and inventories (*visitas*) that supported the land claims in the Yucay Valley are rich sources of detail that allow us to identify the function and ownership of particular holdings. Because our goal in this paper is to focus on the archaeology of the site, rather than its history, however, we will simply note that, because of these legal documents, it is possible to reliably locate works of royal architecture on the estate, including the palace built for Huayna Capac.

His palace, identified in these documents as Quispiguanca, was set amid parklands, and there was a lake adjacent to it (Villanueva Urteaga 1971: 38). The complex is located near the midpoint of the estate, on a slight rise of land at the north edge of the valley. It is just to the east of the entrance to the canyon dominated by the imposing snow peak, Chicón. The compound is built on broad terraces that are part of a series of elegant agricultural terraces stepping north from the Urubamba River and upward into the mouth of the Chicón Canyon.

Overview of the Palace Compound

The site today is located within the San José neighborhood on the north edge of the town of Urubamba. Approximately a quarter of its area is within the boundaries of the modern cemetery; the rest is on land under active cultivation. The site is crossed by roads—ancient footroads as well as modern dirt roads used by vehicles and pedestrians. Figure 3 shows an overview of the plan of the site,[2] and its relationship to these features. In the following discussion, though, we will strip off the modern layers and look at the Inka work at the site (fig. 4), focusing on the standing remains that can be observed.

THE BUILDING TERRACE

The main building terrace at Quispiguanca is a broad rectangle approximately 189 m in length across its south face, and approximately 125 m wide, measuring to the face of the buildings that border its north edge. This terrace defines the space we consider to be the main plaza, and the main entryway to the site.

By examining changes in the quality of masonry near the base of the terrace wall, we determined its original above-ground height on the well-preserved south and east sides to have been at least 3.9 m, with a freestanding wall of less well-fitted stonework rising perhaps another 2 m above it (fig. 5). Although it is now only poorly preserved, we believe that this upper wall originally ran the full length of the south face of the terrace wall, and in the interstices between buildings on the east wall.

The visible faces of the terrace are made of carefully fitted stone, and the south face was provided with decorative niches (fig. 6). Poorly preserved now, the niches were double-jambed and had wide proportions:

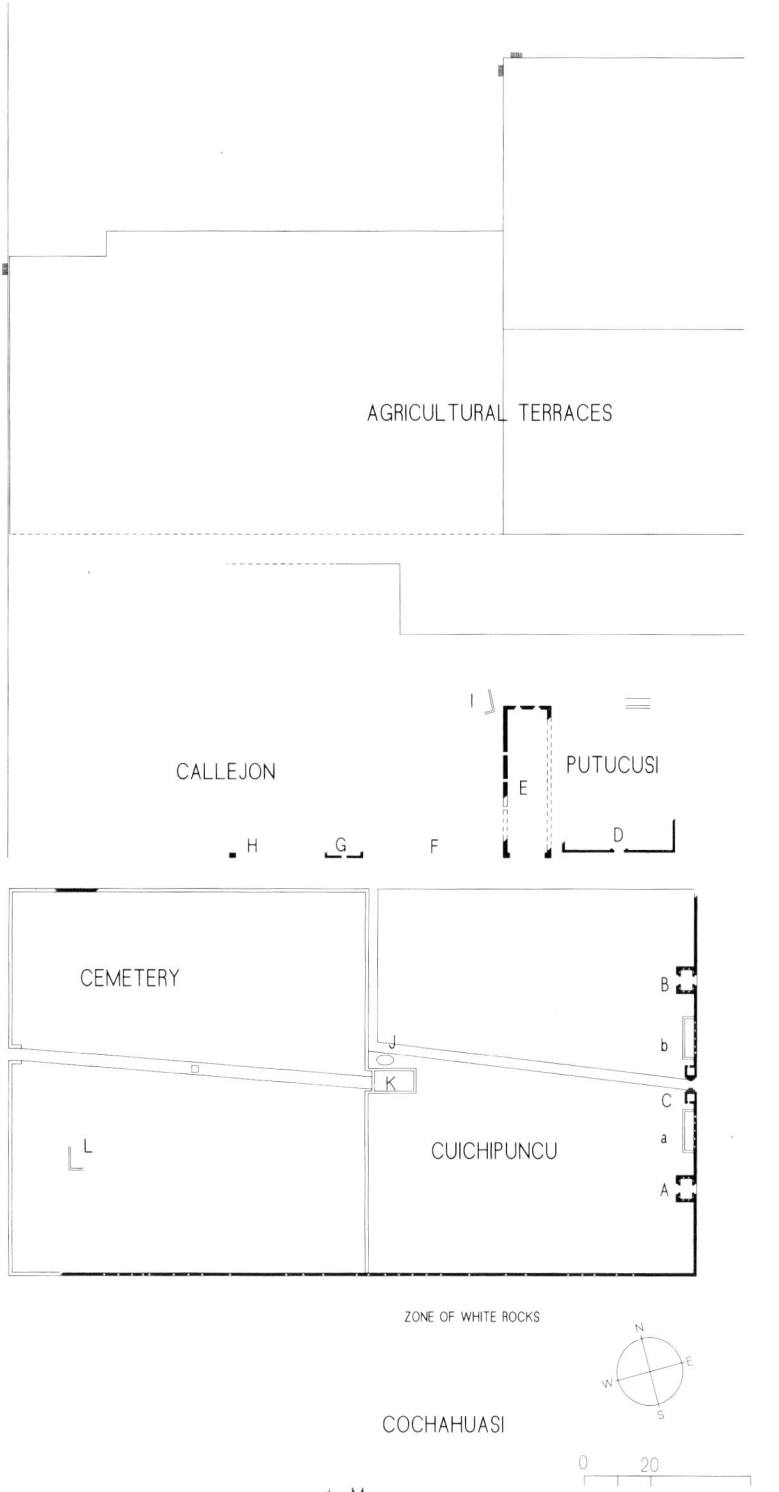

FIG. 3 Plan of Quispiguanca showing existing Inka walls (dark hatching), hypothesized Inka walls (dotted lines), and walls delineating ancient or modern fields, roads, or terraces (solid lines). A, B: gatehouses; a, b: rectangular buildings; C: portal; D: Putucusi courtyard compound; E, H: great halls; F, G, small buildings; I, wall stubs and canals; J: big white rock; K: cemetery chapel; L: terrace wall; M: reservoir wall stub.

Sculpting the Yucay Valley

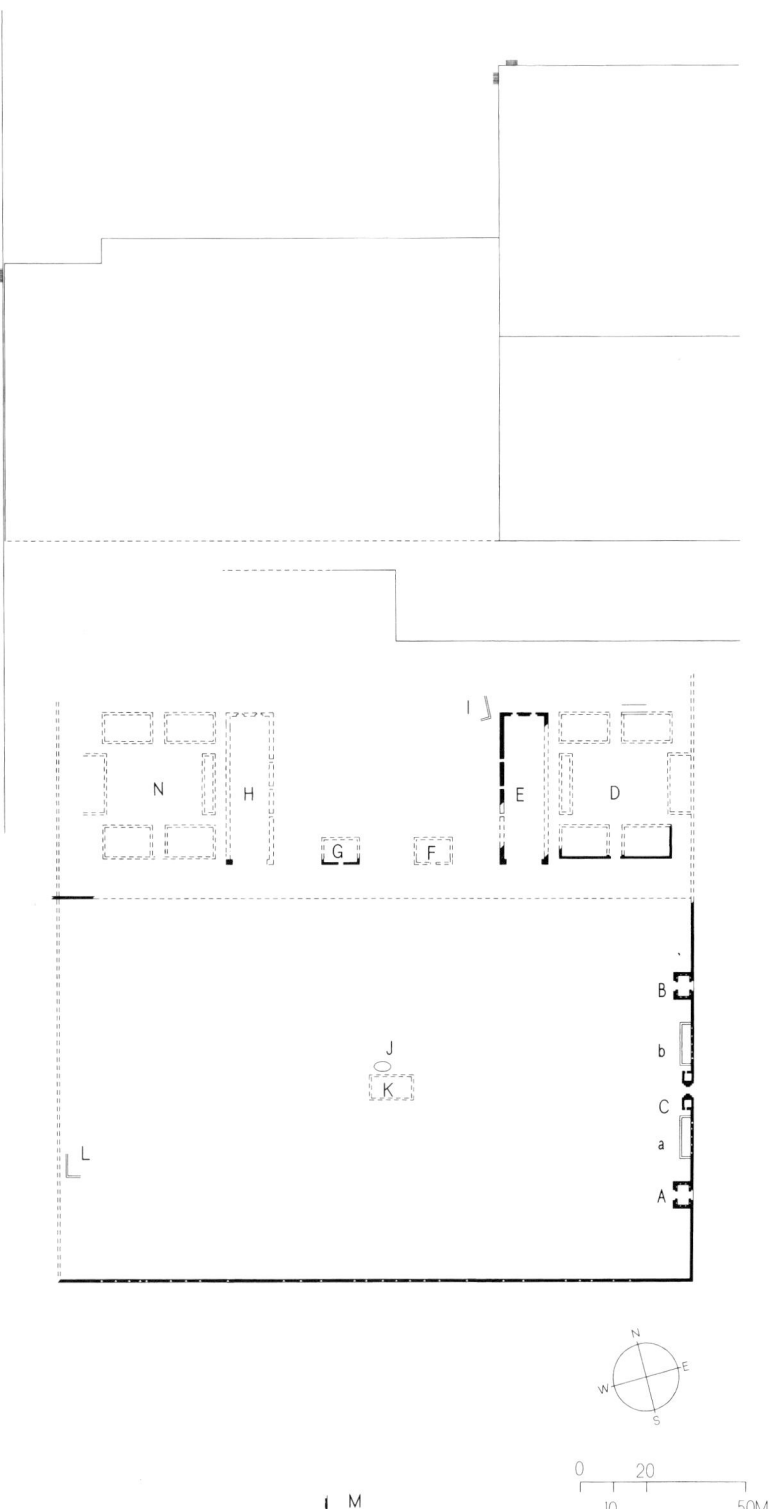

FIG. 4 Plan of Quispiguanca as it may have looked, including hypothetical reconstruction of the buildings of the north terrace groups.

FIG. 5 South terrace wall. The join of the well-fitted masonry and the less well-fitted masonry is clearly visible on the left side of the picture. The adobe portion of the wall is modern. Vegetation grows from the Inka niches. The lower terrace wall in the foreground is not ancient.

FIG. 6 Detail, double-jambed niche from the south terrace wall

Sculpting the Yucay Valley

FIG. 7 Detail, plan of the east entry wall. A, B: gatehouses; a, b: small rectangular buildings; C: central portal comprising two towers.

FIG. 8 The existing remains of the east entry wall; a: the view from the interior of the compound; b: the view from the exterior.

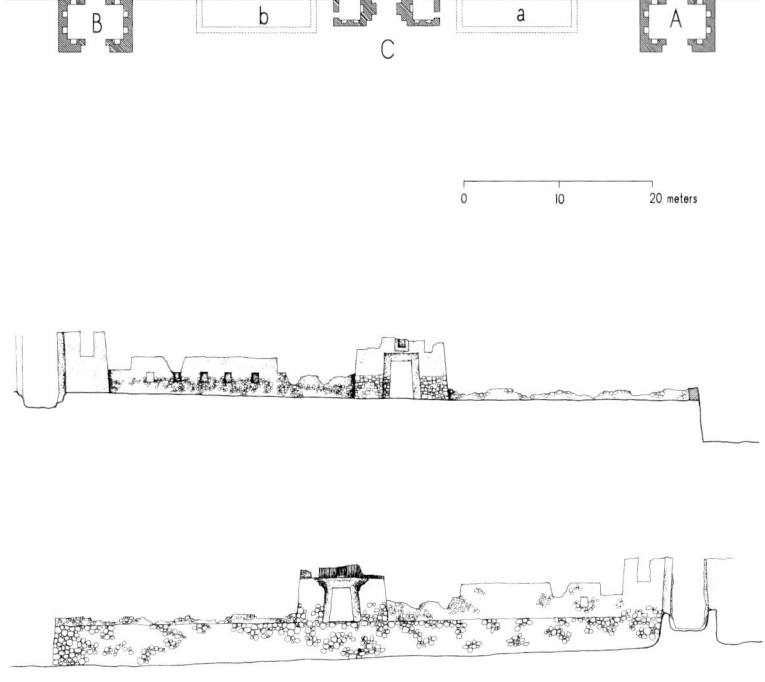

1.1 m wide at the base, 1.1 m at the height of the inner niches and, we estimate, 1.3 m as an overall height. A few of the niches preserve traces of red-mud plaster. Despite the poor preservation of this wall and the displacement of many niches by vegetation, it is possible to observe the remains of 28 niches. From their regular disposition on the wall, we are confident that this south-facing terrace wall originally had at least 40 niches along its length. There are no corresponding niches on the east terrace wall.

THE EAST ENTRY

The architecture of the east side of the site was designed to mark formal access into the interior space of the compound and to provide a decorative façade to define this enclosed space. The group consists of a symmetrical arrangement of structures that flank an ancient, and now modern, footroad. On each side of the road there are remains of a small square building, which we call a gatehouse (A and B on fig. 4); a narrow, probably rectangular building (a and b on fig. 4); and a tower with a square footprint (C on fig. 4, and see figs. 7, 8a, 8b).

The gatehouses (A and B) are small structures (7.9 m x 6.5 m, based on exterior measurements) with symmetrically disposed features. As is typical for this site, foundations are of stone and upper walls are of adobe;

external walls have better-fitted stone masonry than the interior ones. The walls have been preserved to a maximum height of 5.16 m. Each gatehouse has an oversized, double-jambed doorway facing in toward the plaza and opposite one that faces out, beyond the building terrace (fig. 9). These doorways are 3.2 m tall, with an inner-jamb width of 1.85 m. The doorways still preserve traces of their original lintels, which were composed of two tree trunks, approximately 30 cm in diameter, probably of locally available *aliso* wood. In all doorways, the double jamb is apparent from the outside wall of the building. Adjacent to the doors on the buildings' interiors are barhold devices (fig. 10). The interior of the building also includes eight niches at the ground-floor level. Like the doorways, most of the niches have wooden lintels and traces of mud plaster. The niches are 1 m in height, with 70 cm bases and 60 cm tops. One curious aspect of the niche construction here and at some other buildings on the site is that the top of the niche slants upward noticeably from front to back; this slant is about 5 cm over the 50 cm depth of the niches. We are not sure what this feature means, but it is characteristic of the site and is a feature also noted on the single completely preserved doorway into gatehouse A.

The building also has interior features in its upper walls (fig. 11). Centered about 80 cm above the top of the doorway on the west wall is a

FIG. 9 Gatehouse A seen from the west, with its oversized doorway framing archaeologist John H. Rowe.

FIG. 10 Northeast interior corner of Gatehouse A, showing an interior doorjamb, barhold device (at shoulder height), and niche. Traces of the thin mud-plaster finish are visible in the niche and on the edge of the doorjamb.

Sculpting the Yucay Valley

FIG. 11 Cross-section, Gatehouse A: left, south interior wall; right, west interior wall

FIG. 12 Detail, east entry wall from the interior of the compound. On the left, the south tower of portal C. To the right, remains of a modern building (still visible in 1986), built against the niched Inka wall.

small double-jambed niche flanked by two apparently standard-sized windows, now badly deteriorated. There is no evidence of a second story in the gatehouse structures, so we assume that the niche was meant to be viewed from the ground level. The exterior of the west wall of one of the buildings also has a double-jambed niche centered between the windows about 4.7 m above the modern ground level. There are also two small, double-jambed niches at this approximate height on the south wall of gatehouse A. Given the otherwise strict symmetry of the building, we assume that both walls of each gatehouse originally had the high windows and double-jambed niches on the front and rear interior and exterior walls, and the pair of double-jambed niches on the side walls.

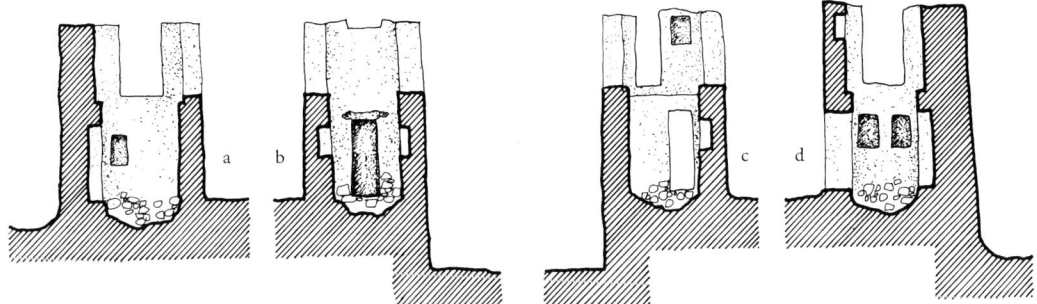

FIG. 13 Cross section, south tower of portal C; a: west interior wall; b: north interior wall; c: south interior wall; d: east interior wall.

A wall connects each gatehouse to its partner, the tower building (fig. 12). The wall is pierced with at least one window; niches on the wall define the rear wall of a narrow building that is no longer standing (a and b on fig. 4). The building was approximately 12.7 m in length and was no more than 3.4 m wide (traces of the side walls of one building were still visible in 1986). We can say no more with certainty about its construction or its design.

Perhaps the most intriguing structures on the site are the pair of buildings that flank the road (C on fig. 4). Seen from the inside of the compound, each appears to be a narrow tower with a single interior room that measures 2.4 m x 2.3 m on the ground floor. The best-preserved wall currently reaches a height of 5.3 m and we surmise that the building originally stood over 6 m, without considering the height of the roof. Each tower has a single, narrow, off-center doorway on the side facing its gatehouse, which provided access to the ground level, and a second similarly sized opening at the second-floor level gave access to an upper story that could have been reached by a ladder placed against the outside of the structure. The building interiors have asymmetrical arrangements of architectural features: at the first-floor level, two niches on one wall face a single niche on the opposing wall; the off-center doorway faces a centered niche that is 2.29 m tall (fig. 13). The support ledge for the second floor can be observed about 2.75 m above the base of the first floor on the east and west walls; there is no corresponding ledge on the north and south walls.

The second-floor interior features include wide openings centered on the east and west walls, narrow openings on the south and north walls, and a niche on the south wall that is not symmetrical with respect to any feature on the north wall. The first floor walls are made of mud-plastered stone; the second-floor walls are entirely composed of mud-plastered adobe brick.

Taken individually, the tower buildings are unusual and oddly proportioned. But it is important to view them as a pair. The two buildings flank

FIG. 14 View of the towers comprising portal C, seen from the east. Two jambs of the leftmost tower are clearly visible; the third jamb is barely discernible in the rubble core.

the roadway that gave access to the ancient plaza (fig. 14). The exterior walls of each, that is, the walls that bracket the roadway, define a triple-jambed portal with an opening of about 2 m. Traces of two of the three jambs are clearly visible today, and the third jamb is verified by discontinuities in the masonry, and by the way in which the wall has weathered. From the joins in the masonry at the base of the tower, it is possible to discern the line that we believe defined the ancient roadbed, too—approximately 1.3 m higher than the modern road level.

These towers seem out of place in Inka architecture because of their lack of symmetry and their relative height. If we consider them as independent units, and assume each had a roof to protect the adobe and the occupants, we come up with a rather un-Inka-like design; further, we are simply left with two towers that happen to flank a road rather than a clearly defined doorway. If we focus on the portal they define and posit a simple lintel over the opening, we face the problem of providing a rain-shedding roof to protect the adobe and the plaster. And in both cases, we still face the design problem that the buildings are asymmetrical if looked at individually.

In trying to make sense of the towers, it occurred to us to look at them as a single unit. They define the road symmetrically, and if they are viewed as a unit, they become two matching parts of a single structure.

We have imagined a structure above the lintel that would convert each tower, visually, into the lower portion of a single building. The structure would appear from the outside to be an upper story, and it would support the building's roof. The resulting structure would be a building grander than the two gatehouses that flank it, but like those structures, would have a central, great doorway that provides equally elaborated entry or exit.

In the elevation drawing of the eastern surrounding wall of the compound (fig. 15), it is possible to see the relationship—in design, proportion, and symmetry—of the gatehouses with the central portal building. As we have reconstructed them, the gatehouses are depicted with steeply pitched, hip roofs. This is a style that is appropriate for Inka buildings of these proportions and it is a style that would enhance the illusion of height, which we think is important to the appearance of these buildings—especially from outside the compound's walls. The relatively even weathering of the adobe walls strengthens our assumption that the

FIG. 15 Elevation of the east entry wall, viewed from the east. Roof styles are conjectural.

gatehouses had hip roofs, rather than gabled ones, but we note that we have no absolute proof for the style of roofing.

The elevation drawing also incorporates our observation of several critical construction details of the site. The architecture and, indeed, the upper portion of the terrace foundation, all show evidence of having been coated with mud plaster. Multiple layers, totaling around 5 cm in thickness, are still visible in places. Again, as is typical for Inka architecture, the plaster shows abundant use of grass to temper it, which helps it to adhere to the surface of the wall and to dry evenly without cracking.

The plastering seems to have been an integral part of the construction of the buildings. On the exterior wall of the north gatehouse, for example (B on fig. 4), it is possible to see that the initial coating of mud plaster was placed on the south and east wall faces before the surrounding wall was built against the gatehouse. Subsequent layers of plaster would have covered this join and given a smooth, overall surface to the buildings, thus obscuring this initial layer. The interior walls of buildings were plastered to the floor level, and the exterior walls facing the plaza seem also to have been plastered to the ground level. On exterior walls facing outward, however, there is no trace of plaster; we suggest these exterior-facing walls were probably plastered only above the level of the fitted masonry of the supporting terrace. It is possible to see intentionally made grooves just below the join of the fitted masonry with the less-well-fitted masonry above it. These grooves would have been necessary to have a smooth plane on the finished wall, taking account of the thickness of the mud plaster applied from the groove upward. This is a feature found at other Inka sites, and observed in other major architectural complexes on the estate, including the Palace of the Ñusta in Yucay (Niles 1999: 192, fig. 6.37), and the hunting lodge of Cocha Sontor in the Chicón Canyon. In these latter cases, the plaster groove appears on purely free-standing walls, and not just terrace walls, suggesting that the decision to plaster only the upper walls was an aesthetic one, rather than an artifact of constructing buildings on a terrace.

The observable plaster traces at the gatehouses of Quispiguanca are about the same color as the adobe walls—a pinkish brown that is similar to the nearby soil. Niles's field notes from 1986 record two relatively thick layers of a slightly browner plaster, topped by a thin layer of a pinker

Sculpting the Yucay Valley

FIG. 16 Rendering of Quispiguanca's exterior wall, as it may have looked if viewed from the southeast.

plaster. There is also a bit of nearly cream-colored, smoothed plaster on a protected jamb in gatehouse A, which we also believe is part of the base preparation, rather than a finish coat. It may be the pinkish upper layer visible on parts of the building that has led some researchers to claim the buildings were originally painted red (Gibaja 1982: 89; Farrington 1995: 61). We surmise that these layers formed the base coat, which would have had a final finish in a carefully selected mud plaster or paint.

On one of the double-jambed niches of the south terrace wall there are still traces of a dark red paint or plaster on top of the base coat. We have made the assumption that all of the niches—and all of the architectural contrasting details, such as doorjambs—were originally covered with this red plaster. For purposes of the reconstruction drawings (fig. 16), we have assumed that the background color of the buildings and terrace wall would have contrasted with the red. We have posited a cream color on the basis of a small ceramic house model from the University Museum in Cusco, which shows a cream-colored background and contrast features in a dark maroon-red and black. The result is a striking visual effect that contrasts the dark, textured, and organic appearance of the stonework on the base of the wall with the smooth, bright, and clearly human-created treatment of the plastered and painted surfaces of the buildings above.

The reconstruction drawing of the east-wall façade also shows the problem of access into the compound. There seems to be no possible access through either of the gatehouses, as their door openings are almost 4 m above ground level. Evidently the builders took the double-jambed

FIG. 17 Rendering of the central portal of the east entry wall, as it may have looked if approached from the east.

doorway—a marker of high prestige in Inka architecture—and squandered it, by converting it into a nonfunctional decorative feature. Entrance through the triple-jambed portal would have involved a climb of about 2.6 m from ground level, facilitated, we believe, by means of a ramp. Ramps can be seen at other sites associated with Inka royalty, among them in the Qellu Raqay complex at Ollantaytambo, and in the terrace system at Chinchero. Here, a ramp would solve the problem of access from ground level up to the plaza level (fig. 17). It would also enhance the illusion of hiding the architectural spaces and activities of the compound's interior from casual passersby (if there were such people on Inka royal estates), and would cause the view of that impressive space to unfold abruptly when visitors passed up the ramp and through the portal.

The east entry opens onto a broad, terraced expanse that contains no remains of ancient buildings above ground. We have assumed that this space would have been open and relatively flat in antiquity as well, which is why we characterize it as the main plaza for the palace compound. We will return to some tantalizing features of its design shortly, but first we will consider the architectural group that forms the north boundary of the plaza.

Sculpting the Yucay Valley

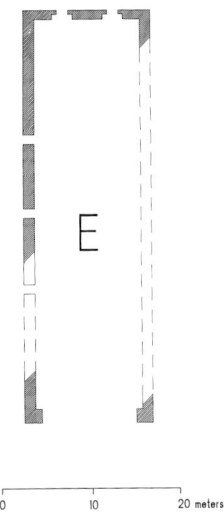

FIG. 18 Detail, plan of the great hall (E on fig. 3)

THE NORTH BUILDING COMPLEX. Bordering the north side of the plaza is a modern road that runs in front of ancient building foundations. Preserved now as very weathered wall stubs, four separate groups can be clearly seen (D, E, G, and H on fig. 4), and a fifth can be reliably posited (F on fig. 4). The group appears to be raised on a terrace that rose less than 1 m above the surface of the main plaza.

The best-preserved building in the group was a great hall (fig. 18). Measuring approximately 14.2 m x 43.8 m (based on exterior measurements), the structure had fitted stone foundations and adobe upper walls. The building is oriented with one of its short sides facing south, toward the site's main plaza. This side has a single, broad opening that provided entrance into the building; only the base of the foundation is visible today. Traces of the adobe gable at the opposite end are preserved to a height of 2.83 m. That end also has two double-jambed doorways (the doorways have widths of 2.06 m and 2.28 m, respectively, to the outer jamb), with the double jamb visible from the building's interior. The base of the long wall on the west side is preserved as a field boundary, and two door openings are clearly preserved. In the interest of symmetry, we posit that a third doorway would have been present in the portion of the wall that is no longer intact. The opposite long wall is no longer visible above ground, so we do not know whether it, too, had doorways. One interior corner of the building preserves traces of a bright orangish-red paint.

In analyzing the design of this building, we used references in various sixteenth- and seventeenth-century sources to identify the building type. Pedro Pizarro describes a building type he calls a *galpón*:

> A *galpón* is a very large building with an entrance in the end wall, from which you can see everything inside, because the entrance is so big, running from one wall to the other, and the ceiling is all open. The Indians have these *galpones* for their drunken festivals. They have others with closed ends, and with many doors on the side walls, and the whole building is of a single room. These were very big, without any divisions; rather, they are open and clear of obstacles. (Pizarro 1986: chap. 21, 160; translation by Niles)

Garcilaso adds that there were four such structures in Cusco, most inside palace compounds around the main plaza (1609: bk. 6, chap. 4, 132 r.). The Inka term for a building with three walls and one open side was *cuyus manco* (González Holguín 1952: 58). Guaman Poma depicts the cuyus manco as among the kinds of palaces built by the Inkas; he shows it as a building with a broad opening on one short, gabled end (fig. 19; Guaman Poma f. 330; 1980 [1614], vol. 1: 303). He also depicts a cuyus manco from Cusco being torched in the Inka rebellions; the building has been turned into a church, but its wide opening and thatched roof are clearly visible (fig. 20; Guaman Poma f. 401; 1980, vol. 2: 372).

The cuyus manco at Quispiguanca was probably paired with a building of identical form that is built 63 m west of its partner (H on fig. 4). This building is barely discernible: only one pier of its door opening is visible in the modern wall that borders the fields. Still, this bit of wall is identical in style and size to the pier of the other great hall, making our identification plausible. Further, the wall that edges a modern road runs exactly where the east long wall of the building ought to have been. Many field and architectural boundaries in and around Urubamba follow the walls of ancient buildings, a fact which strengthens our identification of the admittedly paltry remains as being of a second cuyus manco.

In the area between these two great halls there are remains of one, and possibly two, smaller structures. It is possible to discern the corners of a building 11.3 m in length with a door opening centered in the wall that faces the main plaza (G on fig. 4). A single building corner and a great deal of reused building stones continue in the modern wall that borders the road for an identical distance (F on fig. 4), leading us to posit a second, similar-sized building there.

The arrangement we model for this portion of the site is a small plaza defined on at least three sides by buildings. This small plaza is centered relative to the site's main plaza, which lies below it. The larger buildings that define its sides look out over the main plaza through the end-wall

FIG. 19 Guaman Poma's depiction of Inka palace types. On the far left, a building with a wide opening in its gable end wall, labeled "cuyus mango" (Guaman Poma f. 329; 1980, vol. 1: 303).

FIG. 20 Guaman Poma's depiction of Manco Inka setting fire to the cuyus manco of Cusco in 1536 (f. 400; 1980, vol. 2: 372).

FIG. 21 Remains of the exterior walls of the courtyard house complex (D on fig. 3). The irregularities in the adobe upper wall are due to weathering of the buildings' interior niches. The doorway giving access to the courtyard group is blocked with loosely piled rocks. The modern road in the foreground is the Inka terrace that supported the north terrace group.

doors, and toward the intimate plaza through the multiple doors in the long wall. Because of the slight grade of the site and the disposition of the buildings that define the small plaza, activities that took place in the small plaza may not have been visible from the main one.

The back wall of the best-preserved great hall (E on fig. 4) is 21.2 m from the beginning of high agricultural terraces. We believe that this space, too, was an important part of the site, though its design remains elusive. We start with the observation that the double-jambed doorways on the cuyus manco seem to point the wrong way. If they were marking the entrance into an important building, we would expect to see the elaborated side to the building's exterior (as is the case with similar doorways in the end wall at the Temple of Viracocha at Raqchi). Here, however, they seem rather to elaborate the exit from the building into the space behind it. There are remnants of Inka fitted stone wall stubs, canals, and out-of-context building stones in this region. Modern canals pass through this space, too, falling from the front of the agricultural terraces and crossing just west of the great hall. While we are far from understanding exactly what it looked like, we strongly suspect that these traces are remains of a water shrine of some sort: we believe it was a place where the canalized water was carefully managed and, perhaps, brought across the small plaza between the great halls.

In addition to the buildings that define the small plaza group, the northern building complex contains another compound, shown as D on fig. 4. Set back slightly relative to the great halls and small buildings, the poorly fitted stone foundations and adobe upper walls of its south-facing wall are still visible along the modern road, standing to a height of 3.15 m (fig. 21). The visible walls have traces of niches, and appear to have been the rear walls of two buildings, 15.65 m and 15.72 m in length, respectively, separated by a narrow passage with a formal doorway (the doorway may have been double-jambed, with the double jambs facing inward, away from the main plaza). Traces of the walling that surrounded this compound are visible on the east wall (where the wall is preserved for about 9 m) and the rear wall (a rear wall is found about 41.9 m from the front wall). Behind the rear wall of the compound is a narrow (1.9 m) passage separating the rear wall of the compound from the rear wall of the modern field boundary. We do not know whether the modern boundary wall follows an ancient wall course.

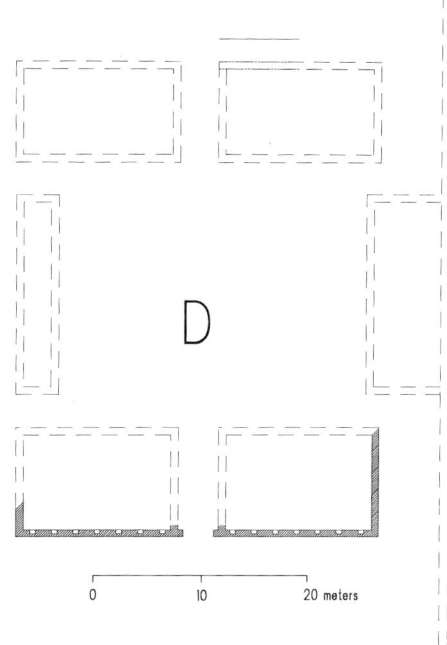

FIG. 22 Detail, plan of the courtyard complex (D)

The remains in this portion of the site are the exterior walls of a self-contained building group premised on the courtyard-house arrangement so favored by the Inkas. Farrington and his associates have excavated the field in which the compound was built. The plan resulting from their excavation indicates five buildings of varying size and plan, raised on a low platform and facing onto a courtyard 25 m on a side (Farrington 1995: 62; fig. 8).[3] We have based our plan (fig. 22) on Farrington's, but with changes where our observations of above-ground remains suggested a different plan. As we have reconstructed the complex, it is similar to subsidiary buildings at the Temple of Viracocha at Raqchi, which similarly have paired rectangular buildings that face across a courtyard that is 27 x 31 m and are separated by a 2.2 m passageway (Gasparini and Margolies 1980: 236, fig. 222).

We note that our site plan of the northern building complex includes one huge gap: we have no evidence of what might have been built on its west end. We believe that there had to have been something in this space originally, as it is well within the terraced area that delimits the built space of the site. The space "left over" after the verifiable buildings are put in is slightly larger in area than the zone in which the just-mentioned courtyard-house compound was built. We hypothesize that a group that matches its design might have been built there, too (N on fig. 4).

Sculpting the Yucay Valley

FIG. 23 Fitted Inka wall within the modern cemetery (L on fig. 3), probably part of the terracing that supported the now-vanished west boundary wall of the Inka site.

THE MAIN PLAZA

The overall plan of the site contains a great open area delineated on all three sides by terracing or architecture. We would like now to offer suggestions about the design of this space.

There is a great deal of symmetry at Quispiguanca, and an obvious devotion to mirroring buildings, groups, and spaces. This is seen most clearly in the mirror symmetry of the gatehouses, towers, and adjacent structures to the north and south of the entry road on the east wall. But it is also a principle that governs the design of the great halls, and that might have shaped the arrangement of the other compounds on the north edge of the plaza. There is also extraordinary regularity in the plan: the unit of 21 meters seems to be the building block of the large spaces at the site. Looked at this way, the great halls are about two units long; the small plaza is three units by two; the main building terrace is nine units by six.

In our initial thinking about the site, we assumed that symmetry and mirroring would govern its plan completely, and we operated on the assumption that its now-vanished west wall would have matched the elaborate gatehouses and portal of the east side. The only trace of the west wall is a bit of Inka wall stub of relatively nicely fitted masonry in about the right place for the terrace wall. One local informant claimed that there had originally been towers near where the modern cemetery wall had been built, a claim that, if true, is what we would have expected to have seen at the site.[4] However, there is a bit of walling at right angles to the support

FIG. 24 The white boulder near the center of the site (J on fig. 3). The gable stub visible behind the rock is from an old chapel (rebuilt in 1997 or 1998) located at the center of the Inka plaza (K on fig. 3). The boulder is about 2 m tall.

terrace wall within the cemetery (L on fig. 4) that shouldn't be there if the site had a completely symmetrical gatehouse and portal complex (fig. 23). We believe there had to be some sort of architectural elaboration of the west side of the site, but we are not convinced that it would have matched the arrangement of the east entry wall. Our site plan shows our reluctance to comment on the design of the west side of the site.

The road that entered the site through the triple-jambed portal on its east side presumably crossed the plaza, bisecting it. We sought a feature along its midpoint that might relate to the site's north-south axis. There is a large white rock rooted in the ground exactly at the middle of the east-west axis of the site, which would seem a logical candidate for the central focus of the space, but it is a few meters off of the north-south midpoint (fig. 24). However, at the exact midpoint of the terraced space are the crumbling walls of a Catholic chapel, tucked in the back corner of the modern cemetery, and adjacent to the imposing white boulder (fig. 25). If the east-west road went straight across the main plaza, it would have crossed the area where the chapel is built, just south of the large white rock. We posit that the chapel is built where the Inkas may have had a shrine or platform related to the rock and the center of the plaza. The name of the palace, Quispiguanca, is composed of the words *quispi* (shining or crystal) and *guanca* (boulder or upright standing rock). It is tempting to suggest that it took its name from the rock that stood near its central space.

Sculpting the Yucay Valley

FIG. 25 Old chapel in the Urubamba cemetery (K on fig. 3), rebuilt in 1997

WATER AND PARKS

The identification of the rock as a central focus of the site helps to explain something else that we believe was integral to its design: the movement of water across architectural spaces. We have noted the probability that there was an architecturally elaborated treatment of water moving into the site from the agricultural terraces above it, in the area behind the great halls and small plaza. Where did that water go? If we look at the course of the modern channel that provides water to fields and homes on and near the site, the water is moved from the zone of architecture down to the white rock, on a line bisecting the Inka plaza. Although the water now is redirected to nearby houses and fields, we believe that it must originally have moved around the rock and across the plaza. The terraced plaza slopes at a gentle, but consistent 1–2° grade from north to south, as evidenced by the clearly visible construction line that marks the top of the terrace. This is the same slope that is used in the modern canals in the area to assure the movement of water across spaces that appear to be flat.

Once it was moved around the rock and across the plaza, the water had to drop down the face of the terrace that defined its edge. Today it courses down the terrace where it pools up and is used as drinking water by farm animals and wash water by residents of the San José neighborhood. We believe that the water in ancient times also moved across the terrace face (though not at this same location), where it was collected not in a pool, but in an artificial lake.

Sixteenth-century sources describe the buildings of Quispiguanca as being built beside a park with a lake (Villanueva Urteaga 1971: 38). Ironically, Quispiguanca is located on a natural high point that is almost the only part of the estate that would not have been waterlogged. In contrast to other parts of the estate where we know that the natural water was managed into pools and fountains, here the lake that was made would have had to have been artificially constructed and maintained. The area adjacent to the face of the niched terrace wall is named Cochahuasi (*cocha*, "lake"; *huasi*, "house"), a name applied to a field that used to run from the terrace down to the area where a public co-ed school was built in the 1980s (the area is now full of houses). The area is used for adobe making by residents of the neighborhood; cursory observation of the many holes they have dug shows sterile, silty soil. All of these features lead us to suggest that this is where Huayna Capac's lake was located.

The identification of this area as a lake makes sense of several other remarkable features. Part of the area in front of the niched wall is full of enormous white boulders—similar to the white rock that is the apparent focus of the plaza, though some here are even larger (fig. 26). Boulder fields are found all around Urubamba, where landslides bring a great deal of rock and debris down from the Chicón Canyon and adjacent hillsides. But due to its proximity to undamaged Inka remains, we believe that this boulder field was present in Inka times and that the rocks were incorporated in the lake. The lake would have offered an attractive surface to reflect the rocks, and to reflect the red-painted niches arrayed on the impressive terrace wall above it (fig. 27). Because the view from the south would have been so spectacular, we suggest that there must have been a road or path from which the complex and its reflection could be seen, though any such features are now obscured by modern construction. There is a precedent for the identification of the lake as a surface designed

to reflect nearby features. Cocha Sontor, high in the Chicón Canyon, which is identified in historical sources as a hunting lodge, also includes a reflecting pond. There, it is a clearly identified, rectangular reservoir with well-fitted masonry (Niles 1999: 176–188; 2004).

We do not know the limits of any lake that might have been built at Quispiguanca. There is an L-shaped set of wall stubs at modern ground level located 72.3 m south of the niched terrace wall (M on fig. 4). Farrington excavated this feature and identified it as a small, L-shaped reservoir with maximum dimensions of 13.75 m x 25 m, with a depth of 2.05 m (Farrington 1995: 63). We suggest that this small reservoir could have been related to controlling the release of water from what we believe was a larger lake closer to the niched wall.

Discussion

The design of Huayna Capac's estate is unusual, but not completely without parallel. The extant architecture is based on relatively well-fitted stone foundations, with adobe brick upper walls and abundant use of clay plaster. Adobe architecture is common for highland Inka architecture, and is found in many important buildings, such as the Temple of Viracocha at Raqchi, and at buildings on the estate of Callachaca near Cusco. All of the original adobe that we were able to observe was well within the range of variation for Inka adobes (as outlined by Moorehead 1978), both in terms of size and in the way the bricks are laid. As is the case with other Inka sites, the adobes appear to have been made of locally available soils, and there is conspicuous inclusion of vegetal fiber. The use of thick mud plaster on the walls is typical of Inka architecture in adobe as it is on stone walls. Where the mud coating is to cover a wood lintel, the lintel is wrapped in fiber rope and is padded with grasses to help the covering adhere. Similar techniques are seen at such Inka sites as Calca (Niles 1988), Ollantaytambo (Protzen 1993: 163), and at other complexes on the site (the Palace of Sayri Tupac in Yucay and a niched wall at Cocha Sontor). We observed three extant layers of mud plaster on the gatehouses, visually similar in color to the adobes. The lower layers have a high proportion of vegetal inclusions, and the top layer is carefully smoothed, presumably to provide a good base for the paint that we believe was applied to the buildings. Painting walls is reported for other highland Inka sites, including the Temple of Viracocha at Raqchi (which still has stepped red triangles on its lower walls and had, at the time of Squier's visit, bright purple niches in subsidiary buildings; Squier 1877: 411) and Ollantaytambo (see Protzen 1993: 237). The Palace of Sayri Tupac in Yucay has brightly painted wall interiors, too, though probably of post-Conquest date.

Quispiguanca's stone foundations are more variable in style. The foundation wall of the supporting building terrace is typical of the fitted

opposite page
FIG. 26 View of the field called Cochahuasi, in front of the south terrace wall, seen from the west.

FIG. 27 Rendering of the niched terrace wall, southeast corner, as it may have looked

FIG. 28 Rendering of the east and north sides of the Inka plaza, as buildings may have looked if viewed from near the center point of the plaza

masonry Niles has elsewhere called "intermediate style" (Niles 1987), which is reported from royal estates near Cusco and from important provincial sites. The stone walls that were meant to be seen are generally better-fitted than are the walls that were meant to be covered with plaster. For example, we can contrast the fitted masonry from the lower walls and door jambs of the Cocha Sontor complex (which we believe from plaster grooves was meant to be seen) with the interior walls of a gatehouse at Quispiguanca (which retains traces of its thick plaster, and which we know was not meant to be seen). The only extant structure on the estate with Cusco-style fitted masonry is the Palace of the Ñusta compound in Yucay (Niles 1999: 190–192), and its relationship to the architecture at the rest of the site (chronologically and in terms of function) is unclear.

The plan of the palace compound is also of interest. Most striking is its arrangement around a huge plaza that is bounded on three sides by architecture (fig. 28). In another group on Huayna Capac's estate, Yucay preserves a massive plaza that has buildings on at least two sides and drops off on the lower edge (Niles 1999: 188–190).

Two additional close-at-hand examples are the main plaza in Inka Cusco, which similarly had buildings on three sides (see, e.g., Gasparini and Margolies 1980: figs. 36, 43, 44) and Calca, an estate some 19 km west of Yucay, which includes a plaza bounded by grand buildings on the upper three sides, and dropping off in a terrace on its lower edge (Niles 1988).

The size of Quispiguanca's plaza imposes a visual effect of shifting one's perspective on the relative volume of the buildings and walls that define it. Looming and forbidding from the exterior, the mass of the portal and gatehouses on the plaza's east side, and the great halls on its north side shrink into a visible, but hardly daunting, perimeter as the visitor's attention focuses on the vast plain of the plaza. The same effect would have been experienced in Cusco's plaza, which was even larger and was surrounded by even taller buildings (some roof peaks may have reached the height of a modern eight-story building; Protzen and Rowe 1994: 243). The effect of shifting the visitor's focus from vertical to horizontal space seems to have been an intentional part of Quispiguanca's design, which relates it to the important space of the Inka capital and, almost certainly, to other Inka sites built on or around plazas.

The focus on the center of Quispiguanca's plaza, which we posit to have been a site for rituals related to or involving the adjacent white rock, is also in keeping with Inka design, where rock and platform complexes or more ornate usnus may be found in the center of a plaza or on its edge (see the review by Hyslop 1990: 69–101). We have suggested, too, that water may have been coursed across the main plaza, and around the rock, as well as across the small plaza in the northern building complex. Our supposition is informed by the frequent association of water with rocks in Inka sites (examples are too numerous to mention), and by the reported examples of water used to bisect plazas (see, for example, Manyaraki at Ollantaytambo, in Protzen 1993: 66, as well as the Inka plaza of Cusco, in Gasparini and Margolies 1980: figs. 36, 43, 44).

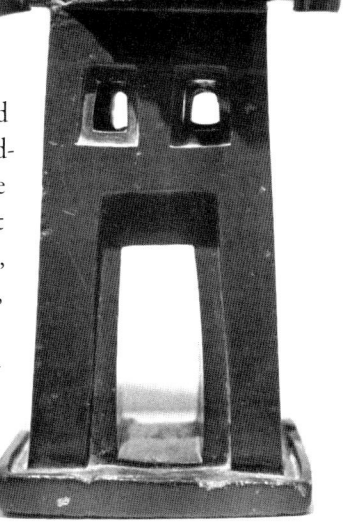

FIG. 29 Small stone architectural model from the University Museum (Museo Inka) in Cusco. The image depicts a tower with square footprint and double-jambed pass-through doorway. Approximately 40 cm tall.

The estate shows buildings of unusual, though not unprecedented forms. On the estate, the nearly square footprint, relatively tall walls, and oversized doorways of the paired gatehouses at Quispiguanca are echoed in the front view of the portal-building we suggest for the palace compound. They also have their parallel in the nearly square footprint, tall walls, and narrow niches of the associated hunting lodge in Chicón (Niles 1999: 177–182). Still on the site, but not discussed here, is the Palace of Sayri Tupac in Yucay, which Arminda Gibaja has discussed as a post-Conquest building (Gibaja 1982; and see Niles 1999: 192–194). Although it is much larger than the buildings of Quispiguanca, there are similarities in form: again, we note the roughly square footprint, the oversize exterior niches, and the giant doorway. The Water Temple at Ollantaytambo is another isolated, and probably late Inka, structure that shares these attributes. And, finally, the Qellu Raqay complex at Ollantaytambo shares the features of roughly square footprint, oversized exterior niches, and off-centered doorways on the first and second floors (Protzen 1993: 102–107; and Sawyer 1980). A small stone architectural model from the University Museum in Cusco clearly depicts this style of structure (fig. 29). The model shows a pass-through building

Sculpting the Yucay Valley

of the sort observed for the gatehouses at Quispiguanca, and posited for the portal structure.

The open-fronted great hall of Quispiguanca, like other great halls, has the rough length-to-width proportion of 3:1. In building form, we find parallels between Quispiguanca's great halls and the Temple of Viracocha at Raqchi, a building so large that it has a central wall and columns to support its roof (Gasparini and Margolies 1980: fig. 227). Its parallels to the cuyus manco at Quispiguanca are seen in the pair of double-jambed doorways in one short wall (although here the double jambs face the exterior of the building), in the abundant use of adobe in the upper walls, and in the evidence that the interior walls, at least, include designs rendered in red paint. Another parallel to Quispiguanca's great halls comes from the church in Chinchero, not far from Urubamba, built on the foundations of an Inka structure that had a wide opening on a short wall and proportions of 3:1 (Gasparini and Margolies 1980: fig. 203, structure A).

Chinchero was an estate built by Topa Inca, Huayna Capac's father, and may have provided a close-at-hand model of the building type.[5] At Chinchero, a cuyus manco incorporated into the foundations of the colonial church is arranged so that its wide open door faces out across an impressive terraced space, while the three side doors on its long side open onto a smaller terraced plaza, an arrangement reminiscent of Quispiguanca. This great hall is similarly partnered with another (Nair n.d.: fig. 10: 6), though in contrast to the pair at Quispiguanca, at Chinchero the buildings are oriented at right angles to one another. Although they are no longer standing, documentary evidence affirms that the northeastern side of Cusco's plaza also had two great halls, one with an end-wall doorway opening onto the plaza (Niles n.d.; Protzen and Rowe 1994: 242). The arrangement of paired great halls related to plazas at three sites so intimately associated with royal activity is intriguing, though we can't determine whether the arrangement is based on a requirement that certain spaces be provided for prescribed royal activities, or whether it simply reflects borrowing of a familiar or aesthetically pleasing architectural plan from nearby sources.

While we have argued that there are parallels for the unusual architecture we see at Huayna Capac's estate at Yucay, we do not mean to suggest that it is not distinctive. In contrast to the low walls, relatively narrow doorways, and dark interior spaces of most Inka buildings, Quispiguanca includes large buildings, tall walls, and wide doorways. There is a recognizable style at work here, one that grows from the canons of Inka architecture put in place two generations earlier and come to full flower in the revolutionary style of Quispiguanca. It is a style that the Inkas, too, found innovative.[6] The design of Quispiguanca was entrusted to Lord Sinchi

Roca, one of Huayna Capac's half-brothers and one of the few Inka architects who was named and associated with the construction of particular buildings. Sinchi Roca is also remembered as a clever and innovative man, especially good at geometry (Sarmiento 1960: chap. 58, 260; Murúa 1962–64: chap. 30, 76–77; and Cobo 1964: bk. 11, chap. 16, 89). He is the man who built Huayna Capac's town palace as well, including the paired towers that so captured the attention of Pedro Pizarro (1986: chap. 21, 161–162). Elsewhere Niles has argued that Sinchi Roca is most likely the man who built the Temple of Viracocha at Raqchi when Huayna Capac reendowed it (Niles 1999: 236–253); thus it is not surprising that the architecture of that site would provide a parallel to the design of Quispiguanca.

In building a palace for Huayna Capac, Sinchi Roca chose a kind of regularity to the plan. To a greater degree than is seen in most sites around Cusco, the plan of Quispiguanca embodies a nearly mathematical precision in its design (something that is admittedly much easier to do on a flattened terrace, rather than on the steep slopes often used for royal estates). The site is based on units of approximately 21 m, which form an invisible grid that certainly facilitated our understanding of the site and that surely governed its very precise design. On this grid, buildings are disposed in precise groups that, themselves, display internal symmetries, and that focus attention on the centerlines of the site. While royal Inka architecture is never haphazard, more than at other sites Quispiguanca seems a model of order, one that is focused inward, toward its various center points.

The buildings of the east entry wall, for example, and the cuyos manco buildings have openings onto the great plaza and offers views of whatever constructions or activities might have been at its center. Other compounds at Quispiguanca are oriented toward different central spaces: the courtyard group (D on fig. 4) faces its own central court, and the pair of great halls and adjacent smaller buildings likely also opened onto a small plaza. Garcilaso reports having seen a building in the Yucay Valley that still had a tall, pyramidal roof, because, unique among the Inka buildings in the region, "the Indians did not burn it in their general uprising against the Spaniards because their kings had sat in it to watch their principal festivals, which took place in an enormous square plaza, or rather, field, which was in front of it" (Garcilaso 1609: bk. 6, chap. 4, 132 v.). While we do not know that he was talking about the buildings of Quispiguanca, his comment gives a sense of the way such structures might have been used, and the meaning of their orientation toward a central space. It also hints at the social and political significance of such buildings and the views they afforded.

The architecture at Quispiguanca is also arranged to force an appreciation of its open spaces. For example, entering the site through the triple-jambed portal, a visitor would climb on the approach and receive a sudden view of the open plaza, and, particularly, its central space, which would be both above and in front of the visitor, and oriented so that it would be lit by the sun all day. That grand space could only be entered, though, after the visitor passed through the relatively dark and confining space of the portal. A similar effect would felt by a visitor to the great hall (E on fig. 3). The interior of that space would be fairly dark, as any opening on the east and west sides would be shaded by the walls and tall roofs of nearby buildings. Entering the building from the north side, through a double-jambed doorway, the visitor would be squeezed through that narrow entry, would experience the dark, but relatively open space of the building's interior, and would be rewarded with bright views of the wide space of the great plaza.

The trick of alternating narrow passages with open spaces is seen in a number of Inka constructions—indeed, it is at the heart of the design of the *cancha*, which squeezes visitors through a narrow opening in the surrounding wall to reward them with the experience of the courtyard's relatively open, and well-defined center. We argue that, at Quispiguanca, we see this principle of Inka architecture taken to its logical extreme. We also point out that the orientation of the site and its buildings is such that the contrast between bright and dark spaces is used to enhance the contrast between open and constrained ones, and works together with the shift in perspective from vertical to horizontal space that is imposed on the visitor who walks into the compound, and across its plaza.

In contrast to other Inka royal works that provide windows, thrones, and platforms to encourage the view of the natural or sacred features in the surrounding landscape, within the palace compound at Quispiguanca the high walls and looming buildings would have forced the attention of the visitors on the purely cultural space defined within its perimeter. Nature—in the form of rocks and water—is brought into the cultural space. And even the surrounding landscape is an artifact, including as it did an artificial lake and carefully planted trees and flowers. The importance of the architectural creation may have been reinforced by the duplication of its built features in their reflection in that lake.

Much of the design of Quispiguanca is about control. The provision of a surrounding wall with restricted architectural access suggests a desire to control the entrance into the royal precinct, and even to control views of that space. Approaching the triple-jambed portal, the visitor would have been dwarfed by its imposing walls, and would have been subject to constant scrutiny by the sentries that surely were positioned in its high openings. Historical sources remind us that the estate was maintained by a huge population of subject workers, most of them colonists redistributed by order of the state (*mitimaes*) (Villanueva Urteaga 1971; Rowe

1982; Niles 1993). The strict social hierarchy of the estate included recognition of workers' statuses as various kinds of low-level workers or overseers, and also included recognition of their status as natives of the valley, mitimae from the provinces, or ethnic Inka noblemen (*orejones*) from Cusco.[7] The control that is implicit in the social ordering of the estate has its parallel in the control expressed in the design of the estate. In its physical design—as in its social plan—spaces are rigidly defined, and access to the complexes' various parts was surely not universally granted.

We must also see the design of the estate as an expression of Inka power—in this case the power of an individual king. Huayna Capac did not come to office without a struggle: there were at least two attempts against him in the first few years following his father's death, as reported by Martín de Murúa (1962–64, vol. 1: chaps. 28–29, 70–75), Miguel Cabello Balboa 1951: chap. 20, 357–360), Pedro Sarmiento de Gamboa (1960: chap. 55, 259), Bernabé Cobo (1964: chap. 16, 88), and Joan de Santa Cruz Pachacuti Yamqui (1968: 305–308). In the first case, one of his father's concubines maneuvered to place her favorite son on the throne. A more serious attempt was launched by one of Huayna Capac's regents, who was scheming to put his own son on the throne, and had gained allies among several provincial governors. Quelling this attempt led to the execution of most of the conspirators and punitive raids on the provinces that had been implicated in the plot. When he finally took the throne, Huayna Capac had to show a lot of people who was boss.

The excess we see in the development of his estate and the building of his palace was a response to the historical circumstances that prevailed at the time of Huayna Capac's accession and the construction of the palace. By bringing in 150,000 workers from the provinces, Huayna Capac was showing the provincials, their governors, and the nobles of Cusco that he was in firm political control of the empire. The lavish use of labor and materials in his constructions similarly demonstrated that he had economic power, and the creation of an estate would help to consolidate that power. To an audience of nobles who knew how to read Inka architecture, his buildings would have reminded them that Huayna Capac was asserting his royal authority, too, by building the biggest buildings with the most elaborate portals. Their design is not subtle to an audience familiar with the canons of Inka architecture.

Conclusion

We offer our discussion of the standing remains at Quispiguanca as a model for how Inka architecture might be studied in the field, and how it can be read in light of the ethnohistorical record and the broader tradition of Inka architecture. We reiterate that in attempting to understand Inka architecture, it is important to observe details of construction so that one can characterize its style and technique fully; it has been our experience that even the smallest details of construction and architectural design can give insight into changes in Inka architectural style. Rather than considering Inka architecture as static and unchanging, we argue that Inka architectural style is dynamic. Late Inka architecture is the product of at least three generations of evolutionary development, punctuated by bursts of stylistic innovation. Some of the reasons for the changes in architectural style emerge from the social forces in play at the time particular sites were created, a claim that can be documented in the case of the commissioning of Quispiguanca by Huayna Capac. We hope that we have convincingly shown how the tension between adhering to a stylistic tradition while breaking with it can result in an especially interesting design, one that expresses the personal power of the king who ordered it built.

Acknowledgments

The research reported here was begun by Niles in 1986 and 1987, facilitated by a grant from the H. John Heinz III Charitable Trust and by a Summer Research Fellowship from Lafayette College. A final season carried out by Niles and Batson in 1997 was supported by a grant from the Advanced Research Committee of Lafayette College. Various friends and colleagues have shared their time or insights on Quispiguanca with us. We acknowledge, with thanks, the help and advice of Angel Mejía, Eloy Mejía, John H. Rowe, Jean-Pierre Protzen, Claire DeFoor, Cynthia Allen, Sarah Steck, and the late Ed Lamb.

Notes

1   The overall design of the estate is analyzed in Niles (1999). This paper focuses only on the palace compound that was part of that estate.

2   In previous publications, Niles presented partial plans of the compound (Niles 1988, 1993, 2004). The plans and drawings we offer here are based on additional fieldwork and include both corrections and extensions of earlier observations, and are identical to versions published in Niles's book on the estate (1999). Farrington (1995: 60, fig. 3) has also published a small plan of the site. Our observations were made independently of his, and our site plan differs significantly from his. In particular, we come to different conclusions about the western edge of the site. We are confident that the remains he calls J and H are post-Inka, and that the west wall of the Inka site was approximately 16.4 m east of the modern cemetery wall, where Farrington locates it. We did not see the remains Farrington labels as E7 and E8 on the eastern edge of the site, nor did our observations suggest the presence of the building he labels as G1 on his plan. Farrington's plan includes detail to which we defer in the northeastern courtyard and in a reservoir south of the site, zones where he excavated, and where we made our observations on the basis of surface remains.

3   While we base our discussion of this compound on Farrington's excavation results, we note that his published plan does not coincide with his description of the excavation (Farrington 1995). We have tried to reconcile the two in our consideration of the remains in this part of the site.

4   This comment was made to John Rowe in 1986 when he visited the site. We are grateful to him for sharing notes from that visit with us.

5   Farrington offers an independent comparison to Chinchero, though he posits a very different plan for the great hall at Quispiguanca (Farrington 1995: 63). He bases his claim not on the shared feature of a wide end-wall doorway at both sites, but on his belief that the great hall at Quispiguanca had a pair of high windows, a feature also found at a building at Chinchero.

6   Rowe (1990) offers an interpretation of the distinctive social design of the estate as a response to Huayna Capac's position as a man accustomed to leisure.

7   A full discussion of these social statuses is beyond the scope of this paper. Some of the important social identities of workers on the estate are noted by Rowe (1982). For additional detail on the social composition of the estate, see Niles (1999: 121–153). The population of workers on the estate included 1,000 households from Collasuyu, 1,000 from Chinchaysuyu, as well as the towns of the native residents of the valley (Pacas, Chaocas, Chichos, and Cachis), and ethnic Inkas from Cusco

(Villanueva 1971). There were also *mamaconas* in residence on the estate, though we do not know how many, nor do we know how many members of Huayna Capac's *panaca* may have lived on the estate to see to its maintenance.

References cited

Arte de la lengva general del Peru, llamada Quichua
    1603   Casa de Clemente Hidalgo, Sevilla.

BETANZOS, JUAN DE
    1996 [1551–57]   *Narrative of the Incas* (Roland Hamilton and Dana Buchanan, trans. and eds.). University of Texas Press, Austin.

CABELLO BALBOA, MIGUEL
    1951 [1586]   *Miscelánea antártica: Una historia del Perú antiguo.* Universidad Nacional Mayor de San Marcos, Facultad de Letras, Instituto de Etnología, Lima.

COBO, BERNABÉ
    1964 [1653]   *Historia del Nuevo Mundo.* Biblioteca de Autores Españoles 91–92. Ediciones Atlas, Madrid.

FARRINGTON, IAN S.
    1995   The Mummy, Palace, and Estate of Inka Huayna Capac at Quispeguanca. *Tawantinsuyu* 1: 55–65.

GARCILASO DE LA VEGA, EL INCA
    1609   *Primera parte de los commentarios reales, qve tratan del origin de los Yngas, reyes qve fveron del Perv, de su idolotria, leyes, y gouierno en paz y en guerra: de sus vidas y conquistas, y de todo lo que fue aquel Imperio y su República, antes que los Españoles passaran a el.* Officina de Pedro Crasbeeck, Lisbon.
    1966 [1609]   *Royal Commentaries of the Incas and General History of Peru* (Harold V. Livermore, trans.). University of Texas Press, Austin.

GASPARINI, GRAZIANO, AND LUISE MARGOLIES
    1980   *Inca Architecture* (Patricia J. Lyon, trans.). Indiana University Press, Bloomington.

GIBAJA, ARMINDA
    1982   La ocupación neoinca del valle de Urubamba. In *Arqueología de Cuzco* (Italo Oberti, ed.): 81–96. Instituto Nacional de Cultura, Cusco.

GONZÁLEZ HOLGUÍN, DIEGO
    1952 [1608]   *Vocabulario de la lengua general de todo el Perú llamada Qquichua o del Inca.* Imprenta Santa María, Lima.

GUAMAN POMA DE AYALA, FELIPE
    1980 [1614]   *El primer nueva corónica y buen gobierno* (John V. Murra and Rolena Adorno, eds.). 3 vols. Siglo Veintiuno, México, D.F.

HEFFERNAN, KEN
    1995   Paullu, Tocto Usica and Chilche in the Royal Lands of Limatambo and Quispeguanca. *Tawantinsuyu* 1: 66–85.

HENRIQUEZ DE BORJA, JUAN
n.d. [1614] *Por el Marqves de Oropesa, como marido de Dona [sic] Ana Maria de Loyola Coya. Sobre la satisfacción que pretende le haga su Magestad por los derechos y pretensiones en que viene informado por la Real Audiencia de Lima.* Biblioteca Nacional, Santiago.

HYSLOP, JOHN
1990 *Inka Settlement Planning.* University of Texas Press, Austin.

LOHMAN, GUILLERMO
1965 El testamento inédito del Inca Sayri Tupac. *Historia y Cultura* 1 (1): 13–18. Instituto Nacional de Cultura, Lima.

MOOREHEAD, ELIZABETH
1978 Highland Inca Architecture in Adobe. *Ñawpa Pacha* 16: 65–94.

MURÚA, MARTÍN DE
1962–64 [1590–1611] *Historia general del Perú, orígen y descendencia de los incas.* 2 vols. Edición de Manuel Ballesteros-Gaibrois. Colecciones Joyas Bibliográficas. Bibliotheca American Vetus, Madrid.

NAIR, STELLA
n.d. Of Remembrance and Forgetting: The Architecture of Chinchero from Thupa 'Inka to the Spanish Occupation. Ph.D. dissertation, Departments of Anthropology and Architecture, University of California, Berkeley, 2003.

NILES, SUSAN A.
1987 *Callachaca: Style and Status in an Inca Community.* University of Iowa Press, Iowa City.

1988 Looking for "Lost" Inca Palaces. *Expedition* 30 (3): 56–64.

1993 The Provinces in the Heartland: Stylistic Variation and Architectural Innovation near Inca Cuzco. In *Provincial Inca: Archaeologial and Ethnohistorical Assessment of the Impact of the Inca State* (Michael A. Malpass, ed.): 146–176. University of Iowa Press, Iowa City.

1999 *The Shape of Inca History: Narrative and Architecture in an Andean Empire.* University of Iowa Press, Iowa City.

2004 *Moya* Place or Yours? Inca Private Ownership of Pleasant Places. *Ñawpa Pacha* 25–27: 189–206.

n.d. Encountering Inca Architecture. CASVA Colloquium CXCV. National Gallery of Art, 4 November 2004.

PACHACUTI YAMQUI SALCAMAYGUA, JOAN DE SANTA CRUZ
1968 [early 17th c.] *Relación de antigüedades deste reyno del Peru.* Biblioteca de Autores Españoles 209: 279–319. Ediciones Atlas, Madrid.

PIZARRO, PEDRO
 1986 [1571] *Relación del descubrimiento y conquista de los reinos del Perú*. Edición de Guillermo Lohmann Villena. 2nd ed. Pontificia Universidad Católica del Perú, Fondo Editorial, Lima.

PROTZEN, JEAN-PIERRE
 1993 *Inca Architecture and Construction at Ollantaytambo*. Oxford University Press, New York.

PROTZEN, JEAN-PIERRE, AND JOHN HOWLAND ROWE
 1994 Hawkaypata: The Terrace of Leisure. In *Streets: Critical Perspectives on Public Space* (Zeynap Çelik, Diane Favro, and Richard Ingersoll, eds.): 235–246. University of California Press, Berkeley.

ROWE, JOHN H.
 1982 Inca Policies and Institutions Relating to the Cultural Unification of the Empire. In *The Inca and Aztec States, 1400–1800: Anthropology and History* (George A. Collier, Renato I. Rosaldo, and John D. Wirth, eds.): 93–110. Academic Press, New York.
 1990 Machu Picchu: A la luz de documentos del siglo XVI. *Histórica* 14 (1): 139–153. Lima.

SARMIENTO DE GAMBOA, PEDRO DE
 1960 [1572] *Histórica indica*. Biblioteca de Autores Españoles 135: 193–279. Ediciones Atlas, Madrid.

SAWYER, ALAN
 1980 Squier's "Palace of Ollantay" Revisited. *Ñawpa Pacha* 18: 63–73.

SQUIER, EPHRAIM GEORGE
 1877 *Peru; Incidents of Travel and Exploration in the Land of the Incas*. Harper and Brothers, New York.

VILLANUEVA URTEAGA, HORACIO
 1971 Documentos sobre Yucay en el siglo XVI. *Revista del Archivo Histórico del Cuzco* 13 (1970): 1–148.

Toward a Reconceptualization of the Late Horizon and the Inka Period: Perspectives from Cochasquí, Ecuador, and Samaipata, Bolivia

Albert Meyers

INKA ARCHAEOLOGY, LIKE THAT OF THE OTHER GREAT EMPIRES OF LATE Pre-Columbian America, suffers from the paradoxical situation that on the one hand we possess much more data than for earlier cultures and, on the other hand, this wealth of data has led us to neglect the study of material culture and its interpretation.[1] One reason is that archaeology has become an addendum to the interpretation of the written sources. This is problematic when dealing with nonliterate societies. In Mexico, where some original native textual documents exist, archaeological evidence has not only complemented, but also corrected ethnohistorical interpretations. One of the principal postulates is the strict separation of the analysis of the material remains from that of the textual material, combining them only when comparing the results (Meyers 1998a [1976]; Smith 1992; Pärsinnen and Siiriäinen 1997: 256).

Another misunderstanding in the treatment of the two different source materials is the tendency to verify through archaeology the historical data, such as the change of rulers, the conquest of the provinces, or the exchange of people throughout the empire. Such events are rarely reflected in the archaeological material and, in general, as has been stated (Sinopoli 1994), an archaeology of empire that concentrates too much on military conquests will run the risk of overlooking other factors such as exchange relations. Consequently, the distribution of imperial ceramic styles in time and space may not correlate exactly with military or political expansion.

In this chapter, I present two different loci of power of the Inka state, one in the northern and one in the southeastern periphery. In order to evaluate the style of Inka power, I shall briefly refer to the archaeology of Cusco. After a discussion of some manifestations of Inka power in the two cases, I shall draw some conclusions in terms of different superimposed religious power systems and try to interpret the evidence within the framework of an archaeological chronology for the Inka culture.

Cusco Archaeology: The "Bottling Up" of the Inka Style

In 1993, John Hyslop (1993: 351) posed a classic question: How did the Inka do so much in such a short time? The standard version of Inka history for more than sixty years, is that roughly in the decade between 1460 and 1470 all major provinces between Ecuador and Chile and Argentina were conquered (e.g., Rowe 1945). Here is not the place to discuss the methodological problems of this short version: the tendency of the informants to attribute the great deeds to their closest relatives; the logical, logistical, and organizational problems of such a rapid expansion and stabilization of the empire (see Meyers 1975, 1998a [1976]: 31–42). Rather, I maintain that an archaeological treatment of this phenomenon, separate from a study of colonial textual sources, can lead to different conclusions. From the perspective of art history, the supposed creation of such a sophisticated and stylistically well-balanced style as the Cusco Inka style can rarely be developed by one ruler and promoted in such a short time. This seems even more obvious if we consider the limitations of the proposed antecedents that have more in common with contemporaneous neighboring styles than with the Imperial Inka style. While I cannot agree with Hyslop's acceptance of the short chronology, I find more value in his statement that the "Inka horizon must be viewed as the mobilization of pan-Andean resources, not just Inka ones from Cusco" (Hyslop 1993: 351).

Whereas this statement has been applied to the imperial expansion only, it can be expanded to include the initial phase of the empire, which would begin earlier than the proposed date of 1438, as well as the formative phase of the Inka style. Geographically speaking, isolated development is unlikely not only for theoretical reasons, but also because of the various parallels that can be found in surrounding areas close to Cusco (Bauer 1992a, b) and more to the south, as Max Uhle (1912) and Philip A. Means (1931: 199) suggested long ago. Possible candidates to "compete" with Killke as precedent of the Inka style are Churajón, Chiribaya, San Miguel, Gentilar, and others in the southwest, and also the altiplano style called Kolla, and the Mollo style, east of Lake Titicaca (Ponce 1957). It is this latter style that shows the closest stylistic connection between Tiwanaku and Inka. This position represents a serious alternative to the "bottling up" of the Inka style in the Cusco area.

The same argument could be made for the architecture. Despite all differences, there exist clear reasons for postulating a stylistic line from Tiwanaku to the Inka, probably via the *chullpa* (burial structures) complex or the Mollo architecture as documented, for example, in Iskanwaya (Arellano 1985).

The Inka in the Province: The Style of Power, the Power of Style

It can be assumed that the Inka state exercised its powers in a variety of manifestations. What we know about the ruling principles shaping political, economic, social, and religious reorganization is primarily based on written evidence from the Spanish Colonists. Also, ethnohistorically defined principles of state dominance such as ethnic relocations and their replacement by Cusco people or Inkaized groups, not to mention general models such as economic complementarity (e.g., Hyslop 1993: 348), have not been convincingly verified by the archaeological evidence. The same is true of the military expansion of the Cusco people, headed by certain kings and generals, as assumed by the "standard version." No Inka fortress, civil or religious construction element, or any material object, especially in the provinces, can yet be convincingly attributed to a specific Inka emperor such as Tupac Yupanqui or Huayna Capac.

What we have is a general set of elements such as fortifications, storage and road systems, "Imperial Inka" architecture, and transportable cultural remains, whose careful examination over the last decades has advanced our knowledge considerably and has changed our view from a rather standardized to a much more differentiated one. By classifying all these features as manifestations of state power, however, we again run the risk of oversimplifying. What we can learn from the ethnohistorical record is that the Inka style of power was apparently a flexible one, with ruling principles changing from region to region. Consequently, one of the tasks of the archaeologist is to consider every element of the material culture separately in terms of style, geographical distribution, and chronology before drawing upon generalizations mostly based on ethnohistorical concepts.

In the case of ceramic styles, I would prefer not to speak of a symbol of state power (Morris 1995) or even that of a single ruler (Rowe 1996), but reformulate the problem as one of the power of the style itself. Given the high mobility of all sorts of goods in the Andes (staple and wealth), it would not be surprising to find the expansion and imposition of the Imperial Inka style around the Andes unsupported by military conquest or other sorts of political pressure. And, from another perspective, why should a Cusco Coya not prefer fine Chimú pottery in her household? Were there official prescriptions determining the forms and decoration of Inka ceramics and were they controlled by the state? Does the evidence of the existence of state potters in some places mean that there was no production for the "free market"?

Given a degree of self-regulation in the field of production and distribution, variety of use in functional sense, availability, and prestige

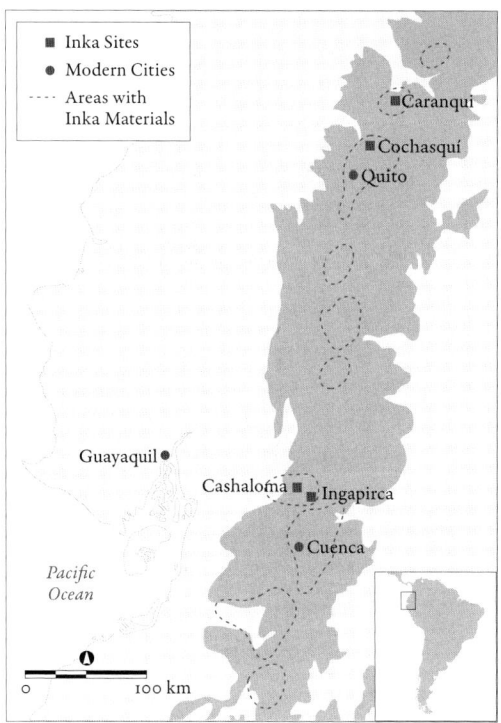

FIG. 1 Distribution of imperial Inka materials in Ecuador (drawing by Karen Rasmussen, Archeographics, after Meyers 1976: map 2)

and fashion of certain wares, it is difficult to distinguish between Cusco Inka pottery, state pottery, provincial pottery, and Inka pottery as Morris (1995: 426) has suggested. Drawing an analogy to Roman provincial archaeology, in an earlier article (Meyers 1975), I underlined the widespread phenomenon of a clear Inka influence on local wares, especially of domestic use. I called a second group "Inka imitation ware," a more or less crude imitation of the most typical forms and motives. The group of "mixed styles" is the privileged field for the study of power balance between all the elements of both styles (Meyers 1975). Their existence throughout the Inka Empire, not only in Peruvian territory, is evidence of the free contact between styles and probably also potters, and an argument against state regulation.

CASE I: THE RAMP PYRAMIDS FROM COCHASQUÍ

Inka culture in Ecuador is represented by a variety of features, including the different ceramic styles (influenced, imitation, and mixed) mentioned above particularly in the Cashaloma-Inka complex in the southern highlands (Fresco 1984). The distribution map of several elements of the Imperial Inka styles shows ten geographical units of findings, with a slight decrease in intensity toward the north (fig. 1). In contrast to Hyslop's interpretation (1993, citing Salomon and Fresco), however, the Inka frontier north of Quito clearly demonstrates a strong stylistic influence on local ceramics, as I have demonstrated elsewhere, based on an analysis of the ceramics from Cochasquí (Meyers 1989). Apart from the well-documented concentration of Inka fortresses in that area, a thin-section analysis by Tamara Bray proved that Inka-style pottery from this region is indistinguishable from the local Caranqui ware (Bray n.d.: 140, 1992: 227), suggesting that local pottery was produced along Inka lines. In the ceramics of Cochasquí's second phase, Inka influence is evidenced by the use of black as an additional color, and by a characteristic rim treatment (Meyers 1989).[2] Among the whole vessels found at Cochasquí, the prevailing vessel shapes are Form 1 ("aryballus"), mostly in imitation style; Form 10 (foot bowl); and cooking pots (*ollas*) with tripod legs instead of the common ring base.[3] The most curious specimen is the "fern pattern" on an Inka-Form 1-imitation vessel applied using the technique of resist painting (Oberem and Wurster 1989: figs. 96, 97).

FIG. 2 View of Pyramid E at Cochasquí during the 1964–65 excavations (photograph by Udo Oberem)

Cochasquí, in the Sierra Norte de Quito, consists of a complex of fifteen stepped earthen pyramids with up to 200 m long ramps that lead to the platforms (fig. 2). The same cultural and chronological complex includes a series of burial mounds and a habitation site. Excavations at the largest construction, Pyramid E, in 1964 and 1965, uncovered the lower section of the stepped structure, which was made up of walls constructed of big blocks of volcanic tuff (*cangahua*) with a pillow-like outside surface, resembling Cusco Inka stone walls (fig. 3). This same observation was made by Max Uhle in the 1930s, when he watched the work of grave robbers at the same building. He interpreted this huge building as an Inka sun temple (Uhle 1933).

The platform of Pyramid E as well as those of other similar excavated structures was consolidated with brick-hard burned clay. These structures contained a series of postholes that, together with small circular ditches, suggested the existence of round houses with conical roofs (fig. 4). Rectangular cavities up to 6 m long and 50 cm wide molded in clay were positioned symmetrically in relation to the central axis (fig. 5). Every cavity formed a rectangular area into which another rectangular area had been deepened in a concentric way with the sides a little bit inclined. On the platform of Pyramid E the excavators found a series of stone cones stuck in the cavities, always in groups of three, forming a triangle that could hold a cooking pot. The excavators interpreted the pyramids with the house

FIG. 3 Detail showing the blocks of cangahua, Pyramid E (photograph by Udo Oberem)

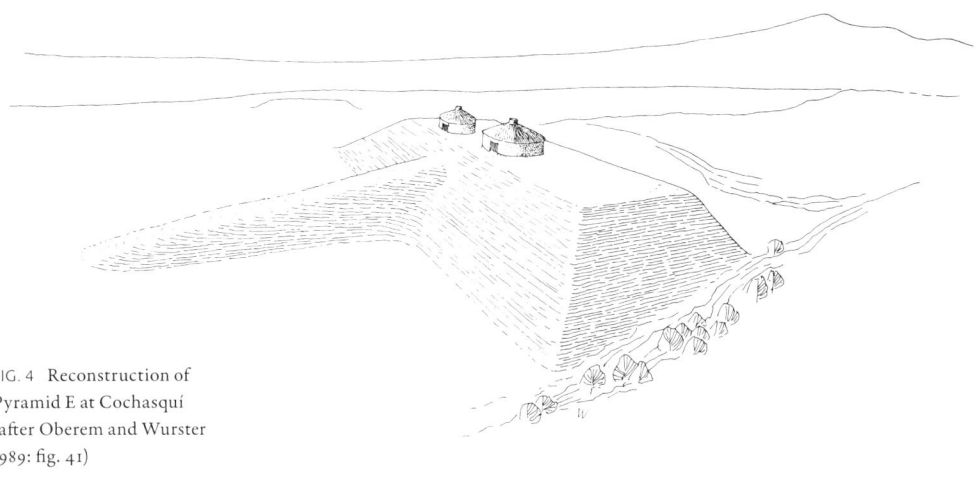

FIG. 4 Reconstruction of Pyramid E at Cochasquí (after Oberem and Wurster 1989: fig. 41)

constructions as seats of the Caranqui lords of the region, famous for their resistance to the troops of Huayna Capac. They assumed that the cavities served as domestic kitchens and did not consider a ritual function for these features, although they did not deny the possibility of other explanations (Wurster 1989: 58–60).

The documentation of an analogous cavity from the carved rock in Samaipata, eastern Bolivia, has led me to reconsider the function of this fairly rare element at Cochasquí. The feature at Samaipata has a striking similarity to those of Cochasquí, the major difference being that it is carved in the northwestern corner of the huge sandstone rock and is among hundreds of carved elements at that site (fig. 6). It lacks the stone cones, but it has the same dimensions (6 m long and 50 cm wide), running in an east-west direction. There is sufficient evidence to assume that they are the products of a common culture, while not necessarily assuming a contemporaneous origin for these features encountered across such a vast geographical distance. These have not yet been documented in other literature, so far as I know. My suggestion is that they served as recipients for liquids during libation and/or burning

FIG. 5 Cavities on the platform of Pyramid E at Cochasquí (photograph by Udo Oberem)

FIG. 6 Rectangular cavity near feline relief on the carved rock at Samaipata

FIG. 7
Location of Samaipata and other sites in the eastern Andes (drawing by Karen Rasmussen, Archeographics, after Meyers and Ulbert 1998b)

opposite page
FIG. 8 View of Samaipata from the southeast, with the carved rock outcrop visible above the semitropical vegetation.

FIG. 9 Sector 3 (Spanish House) of Samaipata, after consolidation

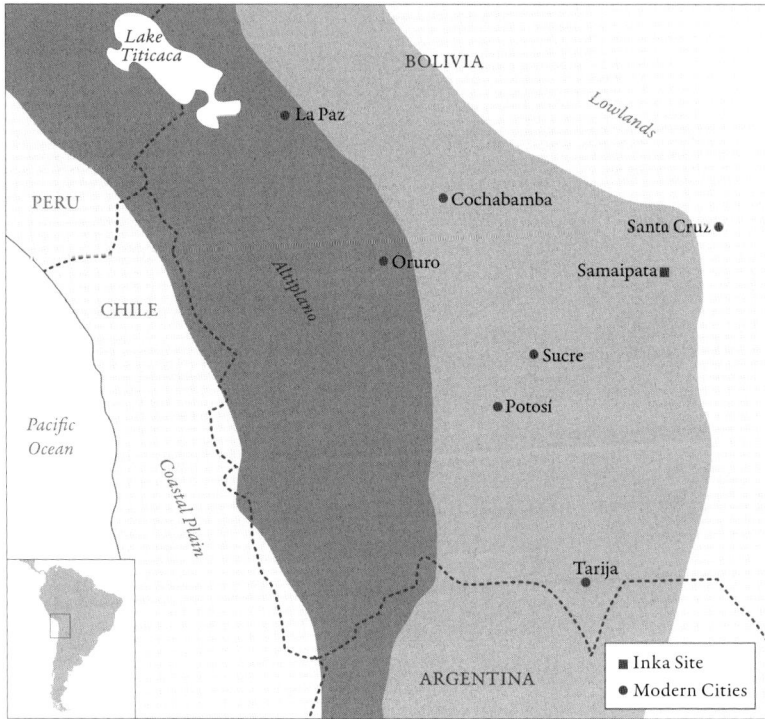

rituals. In contrast to Cochasquí, the carved rock of Samaipata can be dated to the Late Horizon. In the case of the Cochasquí cavities, my explanation would only be plausible if the house was burned and the cavities added after that event. This is technically possible. I therefore hypothesize a change at Cochasquí of the civil and perhaps ritual residence of the local lord into a place for the execution of state rituals. Practicing Inka public rituals on top of a former native elite residence not only provides a clear demonstration of power but also may have been intended as humiliation or punishment of those who resisted conquest by the Inka.

CASE II: THE CARVED ROCK FROM SAMAIPATA

The so-called Samaipata Fort ("Fuerte de Samaipata") is situated on one of the last flanks of the eastern Bolivian Andes, at an altitude of about 1,900 m, a little more than 100 km to the southwest of the modern city of Santa Cruz de la Sierra (figs. 7, 8). The site was visited by Thadäus Haenke at the end of the eighteenth century and described by the French traveler Alcide d'Orbigny some forty years later (d'Orbigny 1835–1847). His interpretation as a "lavage d'or des Incas" was rejected at the beginning of the twentieth century by the Swedish scholar Erland Nordenskiöld, who considered it the last outpost of the Inka Empire toward the eastern lowlands. He also placed more emphasis on its ceremonial character (Nordenskiöld 1924), as did Hermann Trimborn (1967).

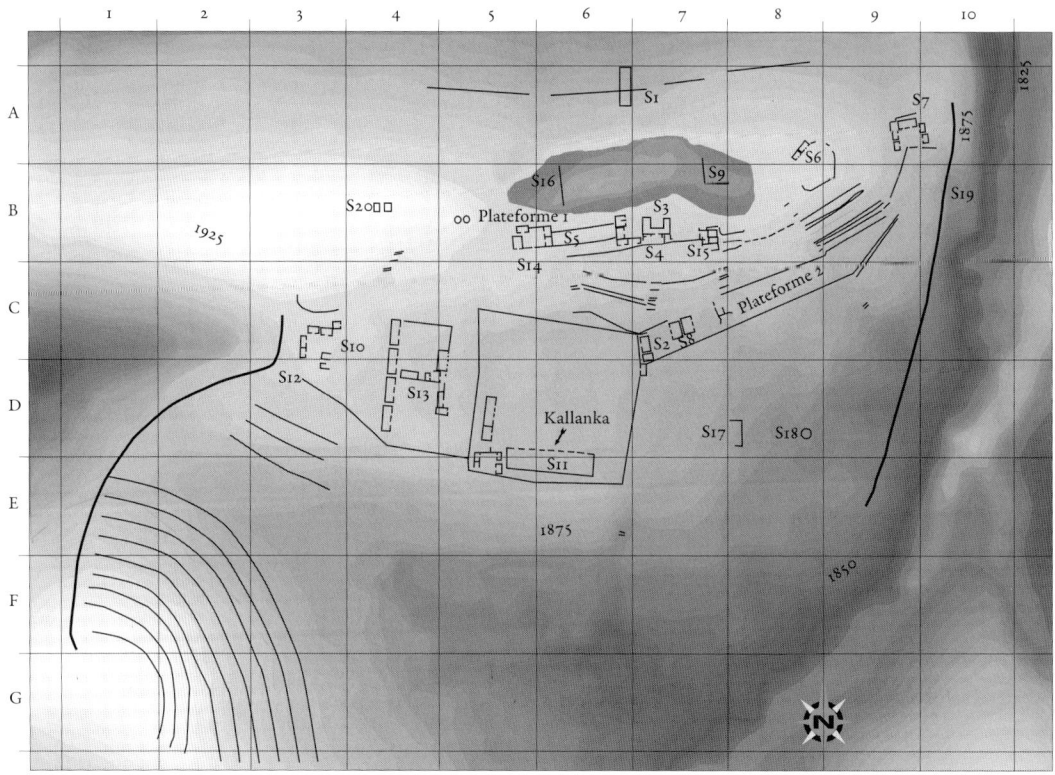

FIG. 10 Plan of the archaeological complex of Samaipata indicating the excavation sectors (drawing by Peter Pahlen, Cornelius Ulbert, and Rolando Marulanda)

Since then, Samaipata has been generally interpreted as one of the great fortresses that protected the eastern flanks of the empire against the continuous attacks of the savage forest peoples ("Chunchos salvajes") of the lowlands. An examination of the ethnohistorical material reveals, however, that these writings have more to do with a projection of the various armed conflicts between the Chiriguanos and the Spaniards during the viceroyalty of Toledo (Julien 1997), than a rejection of the time of the Inka. This vision is still manifested today by the common denomination of the site as "El Fuerte de Samaipata." Indeed, the Arabic-Andalusian style "patio-house" situated on top of the Inka ruins, almost attached to the carved rock (fig. 9), can be interpreted as the throne/headquarters of a Spanish captain from the time of these conflicts (Meyers n.d.). Furthermore, we identified at least one Inka fortress some 60 km southeast of Samaipata (Meyers and Ulbert 1998a, b), which would confirm the recent suggestions of a more eastern expansion of the Inka Empire in that region (Pärsinnen 1992; Saignes 1985).

D'Orbigny's map indicates a "village des Incas" to the south of the famous carved rock, and during our excavations between 1992 and 1994 we documented an extended complex of terraces, structures, and buildings of various sizes at the site (fig. 10; Meyers 1993, 1998b; Meyers and Ulbert 1998a, b).[4] The great hall (*kallanka*), with an extension of 68 m x

FIG. 11 Imperial Inka ceramics from the excavations in Sector 2 at Samaipata

FIG. 12 Ceramics of low-land origin (known locally as Chiriguano ware) found between the two Inka occupations in Sector 2 at Samaipata

16 m, that flanks the great plaza to the south is described by my colleague and codirector of the last field season, María de los Angeles Muñoz (see her chapter, this volume).

In four different excavation sectors, we documented two construction phases of Inka buildings, the later one evidencing two occupation floors separated by layers of destruction. This is not the place to describe the occupation sequence in detail or the diversity of the material recovered. The pottery assemblage includes at least three ceramic wares of Inka style (fig. 11) as well as local wares (fig. 12). The local wares show an affinity with a stylistic complex distributed along the eastern flank of the Andes and with wares found in the Amazonian region to the north and the Chaco

FIG. 13 View of the carved rock outcrop at Samaipata, from the west

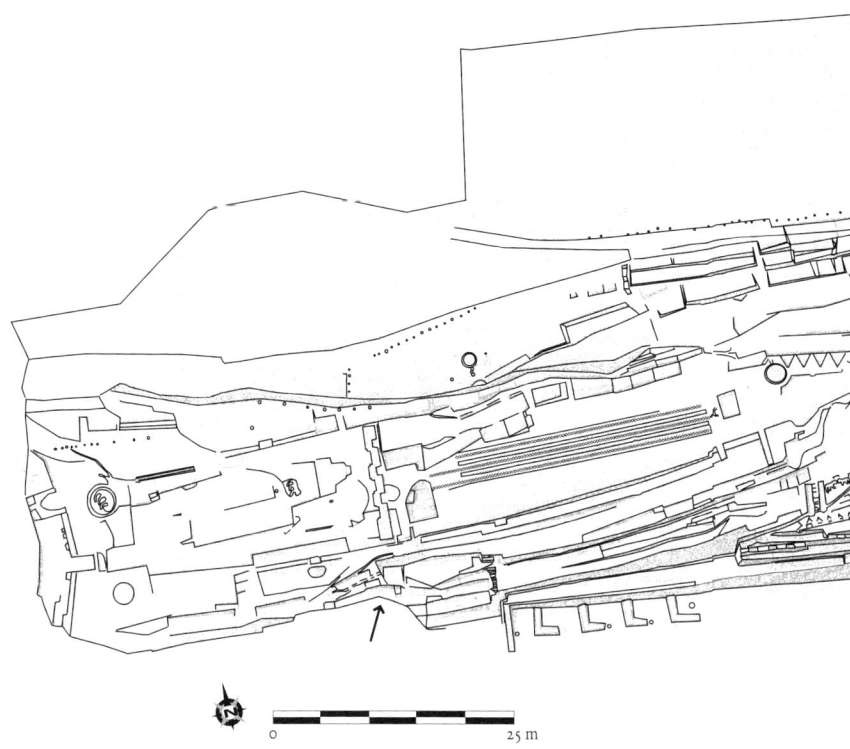

region to the south. Rather than focus on these artifactual remains, I want to consider the large rock-carving complex that reveals a heterogeneous combination of diverse motifs, multiple processes of carving, and stylistically different features, which could serve as a unique "quarry" of Pre-Columbian Andean and perhaps non-Andean ritual complexes (fig. 13).

The carved rock of Samaipata consists of a huge sandstone ridge with a 250 m east-west and 50 m north-south extension. It is covered by figurative representations of felines, serpents, and geometric figures such as rhombuses, meanders, triangles, rectangles, and circles (fig. 14). Several carved basins are distributed around the rock. A special unit appears to be formed by the steps and rectangular seats ordered in rows on the southern part (fig. 15). These give the whole complex the appearance of a sort of amphitheater. Other features on the top of the rock have been interpreted and named in the earlier literature, especially in the work of Leo Pucher (1945). For example, he interpreted the grooves of rhomboids paralleled by two canals (fig. 16) as the representation of a serpent (*el dorso de serpiente*). He called the complex of seats, carved in the form of a circle, "the choir of the priests" (*el coro de los sacerdotes*). Five niches were carved on the northern flank (fig. 17), part of a large temple building. Portions of the wall are still in situ (fig. 18). While not considering those elements clearly

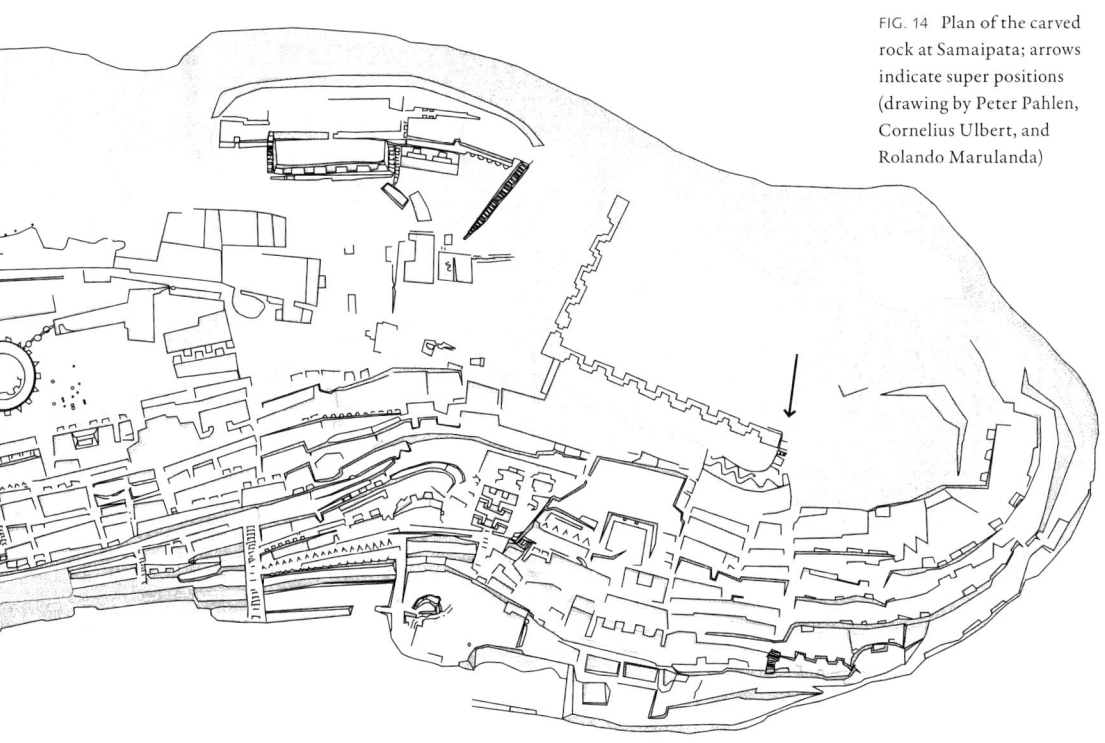

FIG. 14 Plan of the carved rock at Samaipata; arrows indicate super positions (drawing by Peter Pahlen, Cornelius Ulbert, and Rolando Marulanda)

added in a later phase of utilization and construction, I want to point out two cases of a clear superposition of Inka elements whose interpretation could not only provide a new vision of Inka presence in the provinces, but also shed new light on Inka development in the core area.

Two Religious Systems Superimposed in Samaipata?

In this section, we are concerned with two complexes of worked sandstone walls erected on top of the rock at Samaipata. On the western side, there is a transversal wall oriented in north-south direction and still conserved to a height of 80 cm (fig. 10, S16; see also fig. 13). It contains three double-jambed niches facing west and three single-jambed niches facing east toward the two long carved canals. Along its southern part, it cuts a 40 cm deep basin into two parts. The other complex lies at the eastern end of the carved rock and consists of two walls positioned in the form of an L (fig. 10, S9; see also fig. 14, arrows). The transversal wall contains six double-jambed niches arranged in a meandering form whereby three niches face alternately to the east and the west. It is separated by a small passage from the longitudinal wall, which has seven double-jambed niches facing south and six single-jambed niches facing north. The eastern end enters into a semicircle carved into the rock, which contains several triangular and quadrangular seats. The wall ends in front of one of these seats, leaving the semicircle structure dysfunctional.

opposite page
FIG. 15 Aerial view of the southern portion of the rock outcrop at Samaipata

FIG. 16 Aerial view of the two canals on the rock outcrop at Samaipata

FIG. 17 Aerial view of the temple structure with niches at Samaipata, from the northwest

this page
FIG. 18 Detail of the temple structure, with stone wall in foreground

FIG. 19 Carved stone outcrop (Throne of the Inka) on Rodadero Hill, Sacsayhuaman (photograph © Edward Ranney)

FIG. 20 The upper stone of Sahuite (photograph © Edward Ranney)

In both of the above cases, we are dealing not with buildings, but rather with niched galleries, which were superimposed on top of the rock carvings. The western gallery was probably connected to the two canals to form a ritual complex, especially considering that the canals are inclined toward the gallery. On the eastern end of the canals there is a basin positioned asymmetrically, which seems to be rendered dysfunctional in the same way as the eastern niche gallery.

What has attracted our attention at Samaipata is the apparent nonintegration of the previous system into the new ritual complex. Obviously, we have two different ritual complexes. Moreover, we interpret the two systems as opposed to each other, with the later one not respecting and perhaps even explicitly rejecting the earlier one. This impression could be extended to the majority of the other carvings, many of which have been interrupted and dismembered. For example, transversal staircases or niches are carved at the edges of the rock. These belonged to large roofed buildings built on the flank of the carved monument, whose reconstruction by computer simulation reveals that the elements of the carved rocks could no longer be seen from the adjacent platform or from the grand plaza with the kallanka down to the south. Thus, superposition of the late complex on top of the former one can be interpreted as a demonstration of power similar to that at Cochasquí at the other extreme of the empire.

Several conclusions can be drawn from the evidence. Three of them are presented here as hypotheses. Because of the methodological considerations explained above, only archaeological arguments based primarily on the traditional methods of stylistic comparison and stratigraphical superposition will be employed.

HYPOTHESIS 1: ALL ELEMENTS ARE OF INKA ORIGIN

All the complexes described at Samaipata are hypothesized to be of Inka origin, and the stylistic differences and superpositions related to different phases of occupation and use by the Inka. The style and technique of rock carving and of almost all the structural elements have parallels in the Cusco region. Analogues can be drawn to various carved boulders and rock outcrops, including the carved steps of Rodadero Hill at Sacsayhuaman (fig. 19) and the rock of Sahuite in Apurimac (fig. 20). These, and many other cases of such features, have until now mostly been interpreted as Inkaic in the archaeological literature. Consequently, at Samaipata, we have to define two stylistically and stratigraphically separate complexes, both created by the Inka.

In the phase Inka I, the rock would have been carved with canals, seats, and steps, as an aesthetic expression of Inka masonry art and for ritual use in making liquid and/or burnt offerings or other ceremonies. In the phase Inka II, the rock would have been cut at the edges to add

Toward a Reconceptualization of the Late Horizon and the Inka Period

the niched temples. The niched galleries were likely constructed at the same time, along with other elements such as the two canals. Cult activities would have been concentrated on the niches, which are carved on a smaller, more human scale. The result is a fundamental change in the orientation of the two complexes. The first is directed against the rock or toward the earth. This change is reflected at the level of action as well as at the site of contemplation. In the first phase, as seen from above, the rock appears as a giant sculpture of the earth, a sort of "sculptarchitecture" (Paternosto 1996: 60–61 and passim), so the whole rock looks like a single great temple reminiscent of other architectonic examples such as Malinalco in Mexico or Petra in Jordan.

The second ritual complex is oriented in another direction, no longer toward the earth but rather toward the horizon or even the sky. In some sense, it cuts off the vision to the earth, which is now covered by temples and galleries. Within these galleries, figurines, mummies, or other venerable things might have been displayed. Like the stones of the galleries, they represent transportable elements. The whole cult in the later phase appears to be one of portable things. Even the ancestors are transportable in the form of mummies and the Sun in the form of statues. Of course, mythology is transferable and can be symbolized in the form of the various groups of four double-jambed niches or little "windows," which appear on several parts of the rock. These appear to have symbolized the Inka origin myth of the four Ayar brothers and sisters.

The ritual system underlying these architectural elements does not seem to be concerned with, or respectful of, the static earth elements. On the contrary, it appears as a system of power, of subordination, and even of disdain. Some of the symbols of the previous ritual system can be imagined not just as ceasing to function, but as having disappeared. Several of the basins, for example, had been filled with sand so as not to disturb the new religious system in its symmetry and presentation to the subjugated people. This ritual perspective, cut off from the earth and directed to the horizon and to the peaks of the mountains, was reinforced, transforming the former platform steps into pillars that could serve as visual lines (*ceques*) that delineate the landscape to the horizon and even the sky, as a way of establishing possession. This is the view of a conquest society. It transforms the religious symbols and places of the conquered society into transportable state-owned goods applicable and redistributable to dissimilar conquered societies throughout the Andes.

My interpretation of this conjunction of elements is not that of an integration, as has been commonly suggested by those relying on written sources, but that of a clear superposition, with demonstrable public effects like the introduction of new transportable symbols to replace the existing chthonic elements. In the same way, the increasingly studied artificial altars (*ushnus*), sometimes built around or on top of a natural rock outcrop, can be seen not only as symbols of power and conquest but also as the incorporation of military and ritual elements into the complex of state religion. They can be observed especially on the periphery of the entire empire from Rumicucho to the north of Quito (Almeida 1984) through La Fortaleza, some 60 km east of Samaipata (Meyers and Ulbert 1998a), through El Shincal in Argentina (Raffino et al. 1998), and south of modern Santiago de Chile (Stehberg 1995).

Several consequences result from these considerations. Assuming that the two systems are manifestations of the same Inkaic culture, we calculate that a considerable amount of time would be necessary for the change from the one to the other. The history of religion tells us that in archaic societies, no religious system changes from one day to another. Myths, like the dream of a founder of a religion who claims to have received his orders from god ("sunturwasi legend"), can be interpreted as phenomena of etiology, that is to say, an explanation "ex post facto." Generally, they serve to legitimate a new cult created by the new state elite or its leader.

A search for archaeological explanations of these changes will hardly find local or closely related comparative elements, even in the eastern Bolivian Andes. One has to extend the area of research past Lake Titicaca to the Cusco Valley, as did other students of the carved rock of Samaipata, such as Nordenskiöld and Uhle (1910) early in the twentieth century. There is no doubt that the biggest concentration of elements of both religious systems exists in Cusco and its neighboring regions (Hemming and Ranney 1990). Considering this as the core region for the development of the Inka style, one should also assume a more or less "organic transition" from one system to the other. Again, here we are concerned with methodological problems and those of the presentation and interpretation of concrete and comparable data from Cusco.

Beginning with the most important transportable material, ceramics, we have to deal with the old and well-known "Killke problem," which has been treated in a rather dogmatic way since its first definition more than sixty years ago (Rowe 1944). This problem can only be resolved by more concrete archaeological work. It has been stated repeatedly that Killke ceramic production persisted through the Inka period (e.g., Lunt 1988: 494, 498) and there seems to be evidence of various contemporaneous "Killke-related" styles in the same region (Bauer 1992b; Rivera Dorado 1977). However, the problem in considering these new archaeological data is that the authors' interpretations are guided too much by historical preconception. Sometimes, a separate archaeological argument is promised and in the final discussion questionable historic data again are taken into consideration. However, one of the results in the field of chronology

FIG. 21 Torso of a zoomorphic ceramic vessel found in a looter's pit, Sector 4, Samaipata

is the modification of the "master-sequence" expanding the Inka to a period starting from 1400 AD (Bauer 1992a).

We also have various hints of the superposition of construction phases and probably construction styles, as has been argued even for Machu Picchu (Kendall 1988: 474).[5] A very serious problem, however, is represented by the mass of carved rocks and their association with standing architecture. It is difficult to establish a method to identify sequences or even modifications in these cases. But if we depart from the stark vision of a single, short phase of construction and distribution of Inka elements in the Cusco region, we become aware of the sequential processes that can be presumed for sites like Sacsahuaman, Ollantaytambo, Vilcashuaman, and, of course, Machu Picchu.[6] For the Andean flanks east of Cusco, we have documented several examples of boulders enclosed by walls, which are comparable to Samaipata (Fejos 1944).

HYPOTHESIS 2: MANIFESTATIONS OF TWO CULTURE COMPLEXES: INKA AND PRE-INKA

A second and alternative explanation would ascribe the rock carvings to two cultures: 1) the Inka and 2) pre-Inkaic cultures, whose origin could be the local Andean culture or even that of the eastern lowlands. Evidence of cult stones from the latter regions exists, especially in or near the rivers (Riester 1981). The presence of lowland ceramics at Samaipata (figs. 12, 21) demonstrates that the site might have been attractive to people from the "Oriente" or eastern lowlands. Among the authors who postulate a pre-Inkaic origin for Samaipata (Rivera Sundt 1979: 108), however, aside from the mention of the mythic importance of animals such as the jaguar and the boa constrictor (e.g., Pucher 1945), there have been no concrete elements to confirm such views. Nevertheless, the region of Moxos will have to be taken into account in future studies of this kind. The eastern Bolivian valley region was also a considerable source of the late ceramics recovered at Samaipata, but these have been too little studied to make serious comparisons.

So again we return to the nuclear region of the development of the Inka style. The stepped stones of Rodadero Hill in Cusco, the so-called Throne of the Inka from Intincala, Copacabana, Lake Titicaca (Paternosto 1996: 98, 99), and the stepped structures of the carved rock of Samaipata have a common stylistic and probably a common religious background. However, there seems to exist a closer relationship to the stepped stone carvings of the Pumapunku complex in Tiwanaku than to what has been specified as Inka architecture until now. Also, similar structures in Cusco,

Sacsahuaman, Ollantaytambo, and even the stepped stone of Machu Picchu and other elements in that area show this same pattern. To draw the conclusion that we have to concern ourselves with the Tiwanaku complex would not only be premature, but also inadequate. In the more or less 3000 m² excavated in Samaipata, we did not find a single ceramic sherd of the classic Tiwanaku style.

In any case, our understanding of the Tiwanaku culture complex in terms of the architecture as well as the ceramics suffers from the same general problems as in the Inka case. For example, we still do not have a convincing subdivision of the Tiwanaku style, which is supposed to have lasted more than a millennium in the altiplano, nor a definition of its patterns of expansion. What we can assume is that in the Cusco to Titicaca region there was a "creative climate" to forge a mixture of Wari and Tiwanaku styles that resulted in a new stylistic concept. It is my opinion that future studies of Inka origin that concentrate on the stylistic lines from these cultural complexes to the Imperial Inka style, via possible mediator styles, such as Churajón (Szykulski n.d.) and Mollo (fig. 22), will be very promising.

HYPOTHESIS 3: THREE OR MORE PHASES OF ROCK CARVINGS

A third explanation derives from the evidence of at least three phases of origin and use of the sacred complex of Samaipata. Given the fact that the veneration of rocks and working of stones is an old phenomenon in South America, beginning with Chavín, including San Agustín in Colombia, and ending with various cultural manifestations even in the lowland areas, one could conclude that the huge boulder of Samaipata could have played a role as a sacred hill (*loma santa*) since remote times (Riester 1976). However, at this moment we lack specific evidence for early rock carving, although we have found Formative-period ceramics, probably of lowland origin, in the excavations at Samaipata.

The second phase would be represented by the steps, seats, and similar carvings. Its most important characteristic would be the conversion of the rock into a giant "archisculpture." Whether we call it early Inka or pre-Inka is a question of definition of what is Inka in the core area. The third phase would include the niched elements, especially the niched temples and galleries, the libation canals, and probably also the cavity similar to those of Cochasquí. The Inka use of the rock seems to correspond to the two construction phases defined for the standing stone architecture in the excavations. Finally, we could add a fourth phase, which consists of the reutilization of the Inka houses after their destruction by the Chiriguanos

FIG. 22 Mollo-style ceramic vessel combining late Andean and eastern elements (Museo de Metales Preciosos, Colección Fritz Buck, La Paz)

and/or the Spaniards, and also the offerings of ceramics and seeds found in the niched galleries that date from the time of the Spanish Viceroyalty.

Toward a Reconceptualization of the Late Horizon and Inka Periods

The problems with the so-called "master-sequence" established for the Ica Valley by John Howland Rowe, when applied in the broader context of Peruvian archaeology, have already been alluded to in this chapter. But, given the lack of a convincing alternative to this chronological framework, it seems reasonable to modify the existing model rather than to reject it. In the south central Andes, especially in northern Chile and in Bolivia, there has been a tendency to adopt this framework, at least when referring to the Late Intermediate period and the Late Horizon.

The most important criterion for its application in these regions seems to be the existence of a Middle Horizon, here represented by the Tiwanaku style. As Tiwanaku is believed to have lasted longer than Wari, the period between the Middle and Late Horizon would be reduced considerably. The situation becomes more complicated if we consider two other Horizon styles mentioned in the literature, the Horizonte Tricolor del Sur (Ibarra and Querejazu 1986) and the so-called Black-on-Red Horizon (e.g., Pärsinnen and Siiriäinen 1997: 265). The first of these styles developed earlier than Tiwanaku and points to an independent formative cultural development in the southeastern Bolivian and the northwestern Argentinian Andes. The second style is a post-Tiwanaku phenomenon, which belongs to the complex out of which the Imperial Inka style must have originated. However, it must be clear that the application of the "master-sequence" in Bolivia only makes sense in terms of a mere periodization scheme that subsumes the different stages and periods of development in that geographical area. The start of the Late Horizon (LH) is understood not as the beginning of the military expansion, but as the spread of Inka cultural material throughout the later empire.

The problem of defining the Late Horizon in the core area is that we are still ignoring the origin of the Inka style—in cultural, temporal, and geographical terms. Until now, as has been stated, almost all scholars have searched for the origin of Inka culture in the Cusco region. Even though we have two Inka origin myths, archaeologists as well as ethnohistorians take into consideration only the "Paqaritambo version." No archaeologist until now has seriously examined the "Titicaca version" and considered possible Inka precursor styles in that area. Stylistically, in the same way Killke or Killke-related styles are called Early Inka, one could postulate that the late circum-Titicaca styles belonged to an early Inka ceramic complex. The "advantage" of Killke, of course, is its geographical closeness to the later Inka capital. But no clear transition from Killke to Cusco Inka and its expansion from Cusco to the Lake Titicaca area has been proven.

So there is still room for arguments for the development of Inka style in the Lake Titicaca area and its expansion to the Cusco Valley. Similarly, one could look for other foci in the "Inka core area."

My conclusions based on these considerations imply a two-phase vision of the development of Inka culture:

1) As discussed, I refer to the last two Pre-Hispanic cultural manifestations as Inka I and Inka II. Inka I is a cultural complex distributed throughout the core area and characterized by common cultural patterns inherited from the preceding Wari/Tiwanaku culture horizon. While there may not have been political unification, the cultural expressions demonstrate great similarity as exemplified by the stepped rock carvings, pottery with similar shapes and decorative patterns, and probably also a common domestic architecture. Inka II is a highly standardized cultural pattern that, up to now, is evidenced mainly in the public sphere, particularly in architecture, and in the other fancy art styles subsumed under the denomination of Imperial Inka.

While the appearance of Inka I is rather rural and noncentralized, devoting attention to the protection of the agricultural fields against bellicose neighbors, the Inka II complex is that of an organization with a highly developed public culture and technology and perhaps a stronger degree of political unity. Judging by the lack of Imperial Inka fortresses in the core area, one can assume that the process of state formation had been finished.

2) This leads us to the temporal question. I calculated a time span of 200 years for the Inka I period beginning in 1100 AD, the estimated date of the collapse of the center of Tiwanaku. As the Wari influence in Cusco is thought to have ceased about 200 years earlier, a middle date of 1000 AD for the beginning of the Late Intermediate period for the whole area could be acceptable (table 1). In the absence of reliable historical data for the military expansion of the empire during the Late Horizon, I correlate its beginning with the expansion of Inka Imperial style through military expansion, trade, or other exchanges. The problem lies in the definition of the area from which the expansion begins. In our case, where we assume a very large core area, we have to estimate a considerable time for the distribution of the style from one or multiple manufacturing centers and for the consolidation of the Horizon style in the entire area. This process would

TABLE 1 Chronology of the Late Horizon (LH), the Late Intermediate period (LIP) and the Inka periods

1550 AD–1600 AD:	Inka IIc	LH 3	(colonial Inka)
1400 AD–1550 AD:	Inka IIb	LH 2	(Cusco Inka, outside the core area)
1300 AD–1400 AD:	Inka IIa	LH 1	(Cusco Inka, in the core area)
1000 AD–1300 AD:	Inka I	LIP	(Formative Inka, in the core area)

represent the first phase of Late Horizon (LH 1) for which I calculate 100 years. Recent radiocarbon dates from sites at the periphery of the core area, that is to say, northern Chile, northwest Argentina, and Bolivia (altiplano and eastern slopes) (Adamska and Michczynski 1996) suggest that by about 1400 AD the Imperial Inka style had already spread beyond the frontiers of the core area. We accept this date for the beginning of LH 2, which does not end with the conquest by the Spanish but, depending on the remoteness of the area, probably some decades later. In some areas, as is well known and documented, the Imperial Inka style survived for a considerable time after the Spanish Conquest, integrating some Inka forms and decorative elements with certain techniques of the conquest culture. Consequently, it seems suitable to define a third phase (LH 3), which would last from approximately 1550 to 1600 AD.

In summary, we have a 300-year span for the Imperial Inka style, which, in comparison with the earlier elaborate art styles prior to the Inkas, is not very long. Of course, the styles' further development was brutally interrupted by the Conquest, but there is reason to believe that there was considerable time for the "maturing" of such a style. It was these and similar considerations that led me to reject the "short version" of Inka chronology more than thirty years ago (Meyers 1975). The recently presented C 14 measurements shed new light on the question, but have to be considered from a methodological perspective. It is my hope that future excavations in the Cusco and Titicaca areas, as well as on the periphery, will deliver stratigraphic and other evidence to provide a more differentiated picture of the development of the Inka style and its various manifestations through time and space.

Conclusions

In this essay, I have considered the methodological problems of handling the data with which Inka archaeology is concerned. It was my intention, perhaps a bit exaggerated in some places, to discuss and object to some preconceptions and scholarly traditions that have advanced our knowledge in some fields of study, but have been an obstacle to creativity and the development of alternative interpretations in others. In the case study of Cochasquí, I presented a different vision of the Inka domination in that northern periphery, one that was more intensive than generally presumed. In Samaipata, I identified two cultural-religious complexes, whose interpretation throws new light on the Inka culture in the core area. Many scholars will disagree with my denomination of the earlier phase as Inka I; this chronological framework is presented nonetheless in order to stimulate discussion and future studies. Its applicability and possible modification must be tested empirically. I am aware that the last word in this matter has not yet been spoken.

Notes

1   This essay is an attempt to combine some results of recent research projects with observations on the state of Inka archaeology dating back as far as the early seventies. Not all of the arguments are accompanied by citations from the literature, especially when there is agreement among most of the scholars. I am very grateful to Kerstin Nowack for the correction of the English text of an earlier version and for her detailed comments, although we disagreed on many of the points under discussion. I also thank the students of a seminar on Inka culture, held in 1996/97 at Bonn University, for their comments and collaboration. Finally, I would like to thank Joanne Pillsbury for her encouragement, and especially Grace Morsberger for her patience and great ability in editing the final version. Rolando Marulanda and Iken Paap kindly assisted in preparing the map of the carved rock (fig. 14) for publication. Of course, all shortcomings fall under my responsibility. Only minor changes to the original text and updates to the bibliography have been made.

2   The same has been demonstrated for Cayash, Central Peru (Krzanowski and Tunia 1986). This report is one of the best discussions of Inka influence on local ceramics written.

3   As a precondition for my doctoral dissertation on the Inka style in Ecuador in the seventies (Meyers 1976 [1998a]), I had to reconsider the existing classifications of Inka ceramics, mainly from Bingham (1915, 1930), Pardo (1938, 1939), and Rowe (1944). As I published the reasons for my new classification many years ago in Spanish (Meyers 1975), I will simply state here that I relied strictly on material coming from so-called "closed contexts," applying form and quantity as my method of analysis. The fourteen main shapes (*leitformen*) were organized into seven form classes, based mainly on the Sacsahuaman material (Valcárcel 1934–1935; Valencia 1970), the grave goods from Machu Picchu (Bingham 1915, 1930; Eaton 1916), and, to a minor extent, from Ollantaytambo (Llanos 1936). A similar classification of the decoration and rim profiles of materials from secure Cusco Inka contexts, excluding all possibilities of an earlier or later intrusion, is still a desideratum.

4   The "Proyecto de Investigaciones Arqueológicas en Samaipata" (PIAS) was carried out with the permission of and in coordination with the Instituto Nacional de Arqueología (INAR), La Paz. I am very grateful for the support of its directors, Oswaldo Rivera and Juan Albarracín-Jordán. I also thank Omar Claure, Willy Pantoja, Javier Gonzales, and María de los Angeles Muñoz, who acted as codirectors during the field campaigns. The project was supported by the Deutsche Forschungsgemeinschaft (DFG), Bonn and by minor grants. Thanks also to VARIG-Airlines for their assistance in resolving transportation problems.

5   Also here we have the intention of dating via historical deduction (e.g., when Machu Picchu is attributed to the epoch of Pachakuti). While I am not completely opposed to the method of identifying architectural structures as belonging to certain Inka lords at the time of the Spanish Conquest, this method can be a supplement to the main task of identifying architectural styles and differences.

6   I am convinced that Machu Picchu has a long occupation history, starting from pre-Inka times, comparable to the situation we found at Samaipata.

References cited

ADAMSKA, ANNA, AND RICHARD MICHCZYNSKI
1996 Towards Radiocarbon Chronology of the Inka State. *Andes: Boletín de la Misión Arqueológica Andina* 1: 35–58.

ALMEIDA REYES, EDUARDO, AND HOLGUER JARA CHÁVEZ
1984 Investigaciones Arqueológicas en el Pucará de Rumicucho. In *El Pucará de Rumicucho* (E. Almeida and H. Jara, eds.): 9–27. Miscelánea Antropológica Ecuatoriana. Serie Monográfica 1. Museos del Banco Central de Ecuador, Quito.

ARELLANO LÓPEZ, JORGE
1985 *Mollo: Investigaciones arqueológicas*. Impr. Nacional, La Paz, Bolivia.

BAUER, BRIAN
1992a *The Development of the Inca State*. University of Texas Press, Austin.
1992b *Avances en arqueológia andina*. Centro de Estudios Regionales Andinos "Bartolomé de las Casas," Cusco.

BINGHAM, HIRAM
1915 Types of Machu Picchu Pottery. *American Anthropologist* 17 (2): 257–271.
1930 *Machu Picchu, a citadel of the Incas: Report of the explorations and excavations made in 1911, 1912 and 1915 under the auspices of Yale University and the National Geographic Society.* Pub. for the National Geographic Society, Yale University Press, New Haven and London.

BRAY, TAMARA
1992 Archaeological Survey in the Northern Highlands of Ecuador: Inca Imperialism and the Pais Caranqui. *World Archaeology* 24 (2): 218–233.
n.d. The Effects of Inca Imperialism on the Northern Frontier. Ph.D. dissertation, Department of Anthropology, State University of New York at Binghamton, New York, 1991.

D'ORBIGNY, ALCIDE
1835–1847 *Voyage dans l'Amérique méridionale* . . . 6 vols. Pitois-Levrault, Paris.

EATON, GEORGE
1916 *The Collection of Osteological Material from Machu Picchu*. Memoirs of the Connecticut Academy of Arts and Sciences 5. Tuttle, Morehouse, and Taylor, New Haven, Conn.

FEJOS, PÁL
1944 *Archaeological Explorations in the Cordillera of Vilcabamba, Southeastern Peru*. Viking Fund Publications in Anthropology 3. New York, N.Y.

FRESCO GONZÁLEZ, ANTONIO
1984 *La arqueología de Ingapirca (Ecuador): Costumbres funerarias, cerámica y otros materiales.* Comisión del Castillo de Ingapirca, Consejo de Gobierno del Museo Arqueológico del Banco Central del Ecuador, Cuenca, Ecuador.

HEMMING, JOHN, AND EDWARD RANNEY
1990 *Monuments of the Incas.* University of New Mexico Press, Albuquerque.

HYSLOP, JOHN
1993 Factors Influencing the Transmission and Distribution of Inka Cultural Materials throughout Tawantinsuyu. In *Latin American Horizons* (Don Stephen Rice, ed.): 337–356. Dumbarton Oaks Research Library and Collection, Washington D.C.

IBARRA GRASSO, DICK EDGAR, AND ROY QUEREJAZU LEWIS
1986 *30,000 años de prehistoria en Bolivia.* Editorial Los Amigos del Libro, La Paz, Bolivia.

JULIEN, CATHERINE
1997 Colonial Perspectives on the Chiriguana. In *Resistencia y adaptación nativas en las tierras bajas latinoamericanas* (Maria S. Cipolletti, ed.): 17–76. Ediciones Abya-Yala, Quito, Ecuador.

KENDALL, ANN
1988 Inka Planning North of Cuzco between Anta and Machu Picchu and along the Urubamba Valley. In *Recent Studies in Pre-Columbian Archaeology* (Nicholas J. Saunders and Olivier de Montmollin, eds.): 457–488. BAR International Series 421 (iii). BAR, Oxford, England.

KRZANOWSKI, ANDRZEJ, AND KRZYSZTOF TUNIA
1986 Cerámica de la región Cayash. In *Cayash prehispánico: Primera parte del informe sobre las investigaciones arqueológicas de la Expedición Científica Polaca a los Andes, Proyecto Huaura-Checras (Perú, 1978)* (Andrzej Krzanowski, ed.): 84–186. Zakład Narodowy imienia Ossolińskich, Wrocław.

LLANOS, LUIS A.
1936 Trabajos arqueológicos en el Departamento de Cuzco bajo la dirección del Dr. Luis E. Valcárcel. Informe sobre Ollantaytambo. *Revista del Museo Nacional* 5 (2): 123–156.

LUNT, SARAH
1988 The Manufacture of the Inca Aryballus. In *Recent Studies in Pre-Columbian Archaeology* (Nicholas J. Saunders and Olivier de Montmollin, eds.): 489–511. BAR International Series 421 (iii). BAR, Oxford, England.

MEANS, PHILIP A.
　1931　*Ancient Civilizations of the Andes*. C. Scribner's Sons, New York.

MEYERS, ALBERT
　1975　Algunos problemas en la clasificación del estilo incaico. *Pumapunku* 8: 7–25.
　1976　*Die Inka in Ekuador: Untersuchungen anhand ihrer materiellen Hinterlassenschaft*. Bonner Amerikanistische Studien 6. Bonner Amerikanistische Studien, Bonn.
　1989　Análisis de la cerámica tosca. In *Excavaciones en Cochasquí, Ecuador, 1964–1965* (Udo Oberem and Wolfgang Wurster, eds.): 180–197. Verlag Phillip von Zabern, Mainz am Rhein.
　1993　Trabajos arqueológicos en Samaipata, Depto. De Santa Cruz, Bolivia. Primera Temporada 1992. *Sociedad de Investigación del Arte Rupestre de Bolivia (SIARB), Boletín* 7: 48–58. La Paz.
　1998a　*Los Incas en el Ecuador: Análisis de los restos materiales*. Colección Pendoneros 6–7. Ediciones Del Banco Central del Ecuador: Abya-Yala. Quito.
　1998b　Las campañas arqueológicas en Samaipata, 1994–1996. Segundo Informe de Trabajo. *Sociedad de Investigación del Arte Rupestre de Bolivia (SIARB), Boletín* 12: 59–86. La Paz.
　n.d.　La crónica de Alcaya y otros datos históricos sobre el Fuerte de Samaipata. Ms. on file. Seminar für Völkerkunde, University of Bonn, 1997.

MEYERS, ALBERT, AND CORNELIUS ULBERT
　1998a　Archaeological Explorations in Eastern Bolivia: The Samaipata Project. In *Past and Present in Andean Prehistory and Early History* (Sven Ahlgren, Adriana Muñoz, Susana Sjödin, and Per Stenborg, eds.): 19–31. Etnologiska Studier 42. Etnografiska Museet i Göteborg, Göteborg, Sweden.
　1998b　Inka Archaeology in Eastern Bolivia: Some Aspects of the Samaipata Project. *Tawantinsuyu* 3: 79–85.

MORRIS, CRAIG
　1995　Symbols to Power: Styles and Media in the Inka State. In *Style, Society and Person: Archaeological and Ethnological Perspectives* (Christopher Carr and Jill E. Neitzel, eds.): 419–433. Plenum Press, New York.

NORDENSKIÖLD, ERLAND
　1915　Incallacta: Eine befestigte und von Inca Tupac Yupanqui angelegte Stadt. *Ymer* 2: 169–185.
　1917　The Guarani Invasion of the Inca Empire in the Sixteenth Century: An Historical Indian Migration. *Geographical Review* 9: 103–121.

1924 *Forschungen und Abenteuer in Südamerika*. Strecker und Schröder, Stuttgart.

OBEREM, UDO, AND WOLFGANG WURSTER (EDS.)
1989 *Excavaciones en Cochasquí, Ecuador, 1964–1965*. Materialien zur allgemeinen und vergleichenden Archäologie 42. KAVA. Verlag Phillip von Zabern, Mainz am Rhein.

PARDO, LUIS A.
1938 Hacia una nueva clasificación de las cerámica cuzqueña del antiguo imperio de los Incas, Peru. *Revista del Instituto Arqueológico del Cuzco* 3 (4–5): 1–22.

1939 Arte peruano: Clasificación de la cerámica cuzqueña (época incaica). *Revista de la Sección Arqueológica de la Universidad Nacional del Cuzco* 4 (6–7): 3–27.

PÄRSINNEN, MARTTI
1992 *Tawantinsuyu: The Inca State and Its Political Organization*. Studia Historica 43. The Finnish Historical Society (SHS), Helsinki.

PÄRSINNEN, MARTTI, AND ARI SIIRIÄINEN
1997 Inka-Style Ceramics and Their Chronological Relationship to the Inka Expansion in the Southern Lake Titicaca Area (Bolivia). *Latin American Antiquity* 8 (3): 255–271.

PATERNOSTO, CÉSAR
1996 *The Stone and the Thread: Andean Roots of Abstract Art*. University of Texas Press, Austin.

PONCE SANGINÉS, CARLOS
1957 *La derámica Mollo*. Biblioteca Paceña, La Paz.

PUCHER, LEO
1945 *Ensayo sobre el arte pre-histórico de Samaypata*. Talleres tipográficos salesianos, Sucre, Bolivia.

RAFFINO, RODOLFO, DIEGO GOBBO, ROLANDO VÁZQUEZ, AYLEN CAPPARELLI, VICTORIA G. MONTES, RUBÉN ITTURRIZA, CECILIA DESCHAMPS, AND MARCELO MANNASERO
1998 El ushnu de El Shincal de Quimivil. *Tawantinsuyu* 3: 22–39.

RIESTER, JÜRGEN
1976 *En busca de la loma santa*. Editorial Los Amigos del Libro, La Paz, Bolivia.

1981 *Arqueología y arte pupestre en el oriente boliviano*. Editorial Los Amigos del Libro, Cochabamba and La Paz, Bolivia.

RIVERA DORADO, MIGUEL
1977 La cerámica inca de Chinchero, Peru. *Indiana* 4: 139–170.

RIVERA SUNDT, OSWALDO

1979 El complejo arqueológico de Samaipata. In *El Fuerte Preincaico de Samaipata* (H. Boero R. and O. Rivera S., eds.): 41–144. Editorial Los Amigos del Libro, La Paz, Bolivia.

ROWE, JOHN HOWLAND

1944 *An Introduction to the Archaeology of Cuzco.* Peabody Museum, Cambridge, Mass.

1945 Absolute Chronology in the Andean Area. *American Antiquity* 10 (3): 265–284.

1996 Inca. In *Andean Art at Dumbarton Oaks* (Elizabeth Hill Boone, ed.): 301–320. Dumbarton Oaks Research Library and Collection, Washington, D.C.

SAIGNES, THIERRY

1985 *Los Andes Orientales: Historia de un olvido.* Instituto Francés de Estudios Andinos, Lima, Peru.

SAUNDERS, NICHOLAS J., AND OLIVIER DE MONTMOLLIN

1988 *Recent Studies in Pre-Columbian Archaeology.* BAR International Series 421 (iii). BAR, Oxford, England.

SINOPOLI, CARLA

1994 The Archaeology of Empires. *Annual Review of Anthropology* 23: 159–180.

SMITH, MICHAEL E.

1992 Rhythms of Change in Postclassic Central Mexico: Archaeology, Ethnohistory, and the Braudellian Model. In *Archaeology, Annales, and Ethnohistory* (A. Bernard Knapp, ed.): 51–74. Cambridge University Press, Cambridge and New York.

STEHBERG L., RUBÉN

1995 *Instalaciones incaicas en el norte y centro semiárido de Chile.* Colección de antropología 2. Dirección de Bibliotecas, Archivos Museos, Centro de Investigaciones Diego Barros Arana, Santiago, Chile.

SZYKUSLKI, JOZEF

n.d. La cerámica de Churajon. Ms. on file, Seminar für Völkerkunde, University of Bonn.

TRIMBORN, HERMANN

1967 Der Skulptierte Berg von Samaipata: Archäologische Studien in den Kordilleren Boliviens III. *Baessler Archiv*, Beiträge zur Völkerkunde, NF 5: 130–169.

UHLE, MAX

1910 Zur Deutung der Intihuatana. In *Verhandlungen des XVI. Internationalen Amerikanistenkongresses*: 371–388. A. Hartleben, Vienna and Leipzig.

1912 Los orígenes de los Incas. In *Actas del XVII Congreso Internacional de americanistas*: 302–352. Impr. de Coni hermanos, Buenos Aires.

1933 Die Ruinen von Cochasquí. *Ibero-Amerikanisches Archiv* 7 (2): 127–134.

VALCÁRCEL, LUIS E.

1934 Los trabajos arqueológicos del Cusco: Sajsawaman redescubierto II. *Revista del Museo Nacional* 3: 3–36, 211–233.

1935 Los trabajos arqueológicos en el departamento del Cusco. Sajsawaman resescubierto III–IV. *Revista del Museo Nacional* 4: 1–24, 161–203.

VALENCIA, ALFREDO

1970 Las tumbas de Saqsaywaman. *Revista Saqsaywaman* 1: 173–177.

WEDIN, AKE

1963 *La cronológia de la historia incaica: Estudio crítico*. Insula, Madrid.

WURSTER, WOLFGANG

1989 Ruinas existentes. In *Excavaciones en Cochasquí, Ecuador, 1964–1965* (Udo Oberem and Wolfgang Wurster, eds.): 11–103. Verlag Phillip von Zabern, Mainz am Rhein.

The Kallanka at Samaipata, Bolivia: An Example of Inka Monumental Architecture

María de los Angeles Muñoz

THE SAMAIPATA SITE IS LOCATED IN WHAT HAS BEEN CONSIDERED THE border area between the Inka Empire and the territory of the people of the lowlands with whom they were often at war. Because of these military conflicts, a series of fortresses was built along this border in Kollasuyo. Examples of such fortresses are Incarracay, Inkallajta, Oroncota, Inkapirka, Manchachi, Inkahuasi, and Condorhuasi.

In 1994, during the second field season of the Samaipata project, clearing of dense forest vegetation in the small quebrada to the south of the carved "ceremonial" rock revealed a previously unknown complex of monumental architecture. The complex consists of a central, almost quadrangular plaza that measures 100 m on a side flanked by a long hall (*kallanka*) 68 m x 16 m, and, on a higher platform to the east, seven rectangular buildings, each measuring more than 30 m in length. The rock, the seven niched structures that border it, the terraces, and the other architectural elements together form a monumental complex that is the remains of an important Inka administrative and ceremonial center in the eastern Bolivian Andes.

The constructions in the area south of the ceremonial rock are an example of the so-called "architecture of Inka power" defined by Graziano Gasparini and Luise Margolies (1980: 71) and they display many of the distinctive elements set forth in the model proposed by these scholars: the presence of a main and secondary plaza, at least one kallanka on the plaza, a house of the "chosen women" (*aqllawasi*), a temple of the sun, and storehouses (*qollqas*). These features are found in almost all of the administrative Inka centers with some differences according to the region. Architectural evidence from Samaipata will

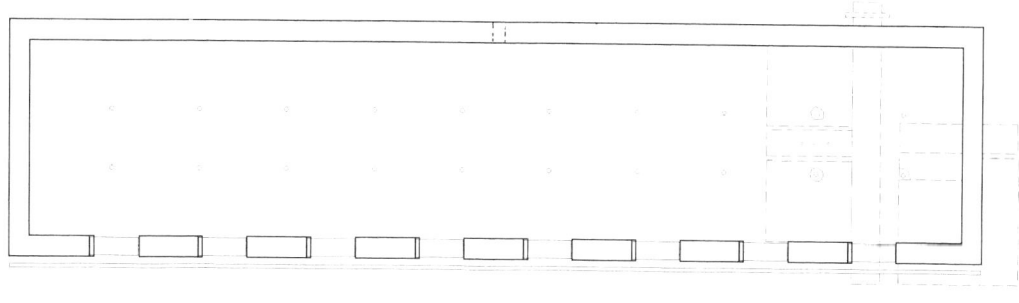

FIG. 1 Plan of the kallanka at Samaipata, Bolivia

be presented here and discussed together with details of the excavation of the western part of the kallanka, a structure comparable to the kallanka at Inkallajta in the neighboring Cochabamba region.

The kallankas are typical Inka buildings of great dimension, which are found in almost all of the Inka provincial capitals and they are, because of their size, a symbol of power. The kallanka is a large, long, rectangular, often two-story structure supported by a series of pillars along a longitudinal axis (Gasparini and Margolies 1980: 196). It has no inner divisions, only a space under a roof made of wooden frames and covered with straw. Generally, only one long wall has doors, the opposing or "rear" wall presenting a continuous series of niches or windows. The shorter sides of the building have gable walls of stone and, sometimes, adobe. Little is known of the function or functions of kallankas, although there have been many interpretations—it is speculated that the kallankas may have served as living quarters, covered markets or temples, palaces or lodgings for important individuals or lords (cf. Gasparini and Margolies 1980: 67–68, 196–219; Morris and Thompson 1985: 112).

The large architectural complex south of the sculpted ceremonial rock at Samaipata is built on three platforms at different levels, and it probably served as an administrative-religious center. The kallanka at Samaipata (fig. 1) is located on the lowest of the platforms, and thus makes up part of this ceremonial administrative Inka center. It is 68 m long and 16 m wide and, after Inkallajta, is the largest kallanka in Bolivia (Ibarra and Querejazu 1986: 322). Samaipata's kallanka is erected on the southern part of the main terrace and, together with other smaller buildings to the west, borders the great central plaza. Its northern wall faces this central plaza and has eight entryways. Two seasons of excavations in 1994 and 1995 focused on the western section of this kallanka, and the results of these investigations allow us, for the first time, to have an archaeological basis for the reconstruction of one important kallanka, that of Samaipata. In

FIG. 2 Channel at the foot of the kallanka at Samaipata

addition, the excavations in the kallanka at Samaipata allow us to compare it with similar structures at other major Inka centers.

In order to avoid confusion, the term *kallanka* will be defined here in terms of its large dimensions (40 m minimum) and its location within the larger architectural complex (windows or doors facing the plaza). Tumipampa, Chinchero, Huánuco Viejo, Tambo-Inga, Uchuy Cusco, Tunsucancha, and others share these characteristics. Inkallajta is the largest example of a kallanka, measuring 78 m in length and 26 m in width, and having twelve doors that lead to the main plaza. The kallanka at Inkallajta is the center around which the rest of the structures have been built. Similar constructions, though of lesser dimensions, are found throughout the Inca territory. Though not kallankas, per se, they were located in the plaza and had a more permanent nature. Samaipata's kallanka's (68 m x 16 m) northern walls face the central plaza and the sculpted rock, and each of its eight doors is 3.4 m wide. At the foot of the kallanka is a well-constructed slate channel that runs the entire length of the structure (fig. 2). It begins from a furrow in the bedrock. A similar channel also exists at the Chinchero kallanka (Alcina Franch 1976: 32).

Inka architecture in Bolivia is provincial. Walls are of unworked stone joined together with mud mortar and filled with clay and gravel. Their upper walls are usually built of adobe and there are internal and external niches. As a rule, the back walls have no openings. Inkallajta, which is a representative example of this style, has .85 m thick walls that were plastered and painted red, a common practice in the southern part of the empire. At Samaipata, the walls were built directly on the bedrock and they are 1.4 m thick. The lower section of the walls is made out of finely carved stone and the upper part is made out of more coarsely worked

FIG. 3 Schematic view of the excavations in Sector 11 of the kallanka at Samaipata, Bolivia

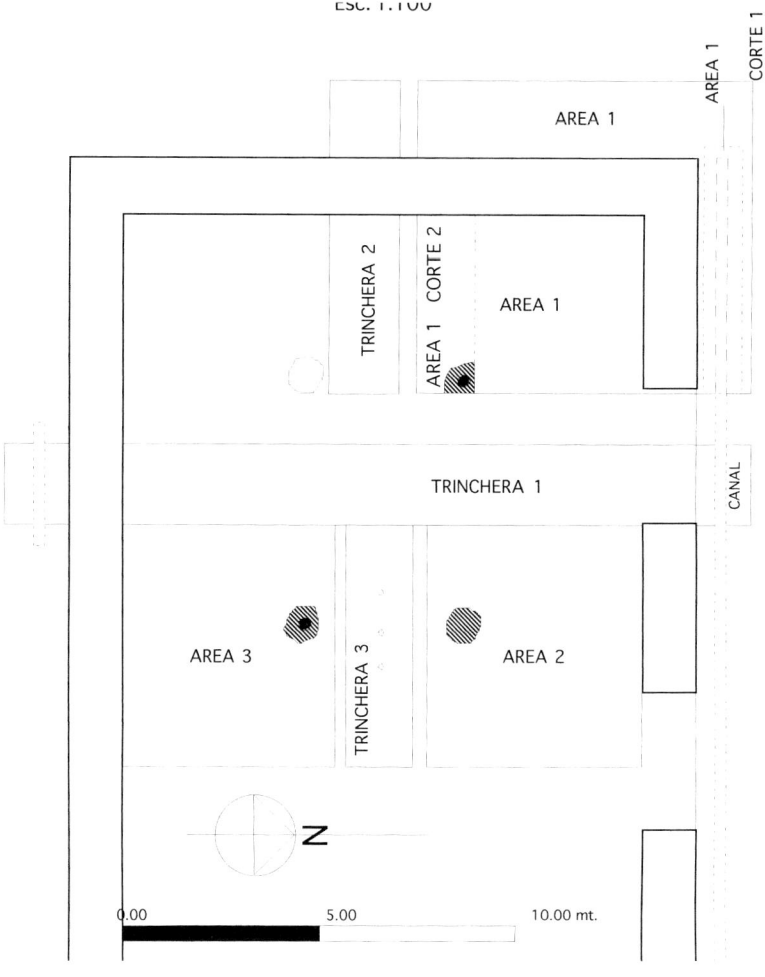

sandstone. The walls were plastered or burnished with a resinous material, and the adobe sections on top of the walls appear to be painted. The southern wall of the kallanka shows evidence of a doorway or a window. Based on the archaeological evidence, we have been able to determine that this enormous construction had a total height of 12 m.

The stratigraphy in the Samaipata's kallanka is uniform everywhere except in the section of the cave-in along the western wall. In general, the stratigraphic sequence consists of a thick layer of humus followed by a yellowish-red stratum that was underlain by a thin layer of gravel that apparently served as a make-shift floor. There are no remains of carefully prepared floors. A compact layer of sandstone fills in and levels the irregularities of the bedrock that supports the Samaipata's kallanka. Beneath the cave-in in the western section of the kallanka, a layer of tar or resin sealed off dozens of holes that may have been made to support ladders or scaffolds while the western wall was being built.

FIG. 4 Excavation of Areas 1, 2, and 3 in Sector 11 of the kallanka at Samaipata, Bolivia

The roofing system of large kallankas is a subject of special interest because of the inherent difficulty of spanning these large structures. In Inkallajta, the sidewalls show evidence of a two-story roof for the kallanka. In Samaipata, the most outstanding features that were found were three large postholes, each one m in diameter (figs. 3, 4). These had been carved 1.8 m into the bedrock itself. The excavated features allowed us to predict the location of the fourth posthole as well as the likely location of the rest of the posts in the eastern portion of the structure. The technique utilized at Samaipata was the following: a hole was made in the bedrock and its base and walls were lined with yellow clay and gravel. Wooden posts 30 cm in diameter were set into the clay, and then surrounded with gravel and sand; finally, the hole was filled up with plaster. The plaster thinned out until it reached the walls. Because the wooden posts were not wedged in with rocks, we think that the mortar and plaster was effective in holding them upright. There would have been a total of eighteen trunks in the Samaipata kallanka aligned in two lateral rows and separated from each other by 6 m. The result was a three-nave building. Small aligned holes were also found in the floor, as well as others that were close to the large post holes. Assuming that a similar technique was used at Inkallajta, which is 10 m wider than Samaipata, there could have been a four-nave construction with two aisles at the sides and one in the center.

On the system of the kallanka's roof, there are only hypotheses. In general, the roofs consisted of a framework of wooden posts covered with mats of hay and totora reeds. In the Samaipata case, it was made of palm leaves tied with ropes. If it seemed necessary, wooden props were created to bear the burden of the top covering at intermediate points. Sometimes, middle walls and even cylindrical columns were used, as at San Pedro de Cacha. At Samaipata, calculations made on a base of 12 m x 16 m long

FIG. 5 Hypothetical reconstruction of the roof system of the kallanka in Sector 11, Samaipata: Hypothesis 1 and 2 (drawing by Fernando Terrazas)

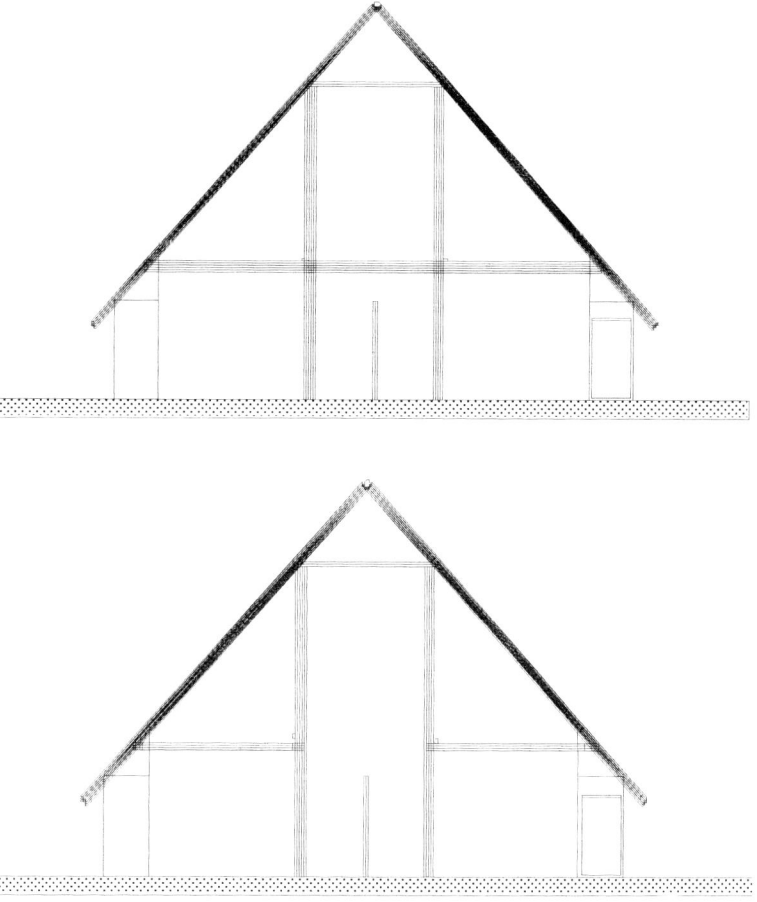

suggest that the roof had a 48-degree inclination. On the basis of these measurements, architect Fernando Terrazas has proposed two alternative hypotheses to explain the building's roofing system (fig. 5). The first one posits stabilizing trunks throughout the width (figs. 6, 7), while in the second hypothesis, as a possible result of influence from the eastern lowlands, the center of the building is freed of the stabilizer elements (figs. 8, 9). I believe that the second hypothesis is more plausible and that the three holes located between the larger ones could have been used to support wooden columns that served to stabilize the roofing in much the same way as in lowland malocas today; such a case was documented by Erland Nordenskiöld (1922) in 1911 among the Chacobo (fig. 10). In spite of the strong influence of Cusco Inka architecture, as seen at Tambo-Inga, the influence of the lowland or *yunga* cultures must also have played an important role in the spatial conception and the building techniques that were used in the Bolivian centers of Tawantinsuyu. Obviously, this included the roofing system.

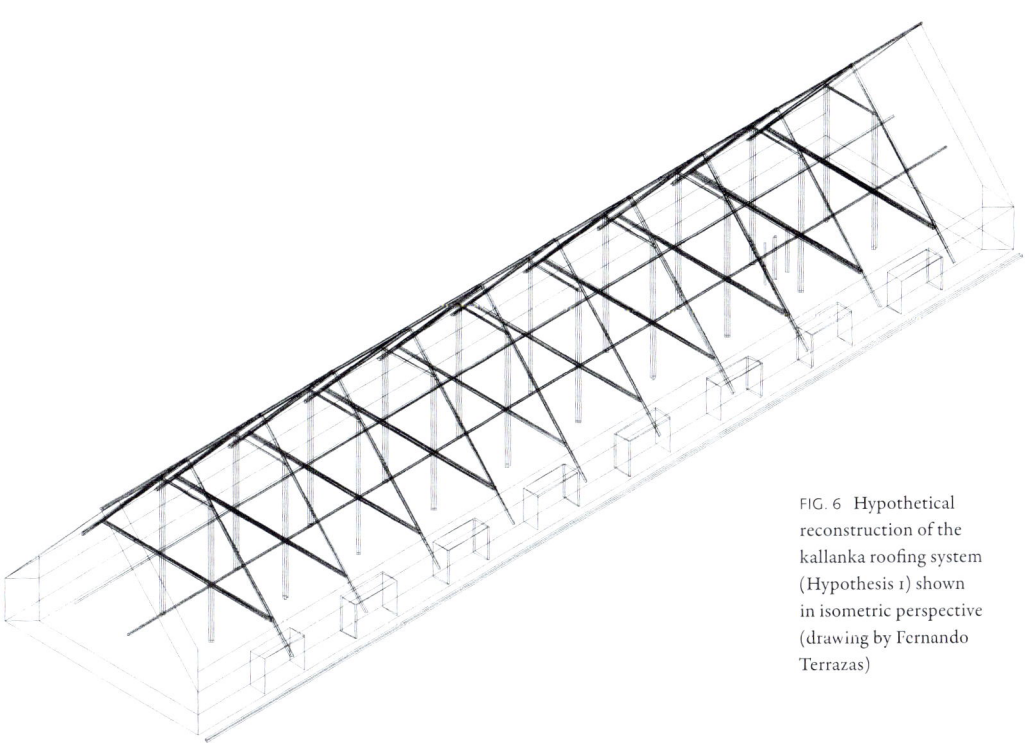

FIG. 6 Hypothetical reconstruction of the kallanka roofing system (Hypothesis 1) shown in isometric perspective (drawing by Fernando Terrazas)

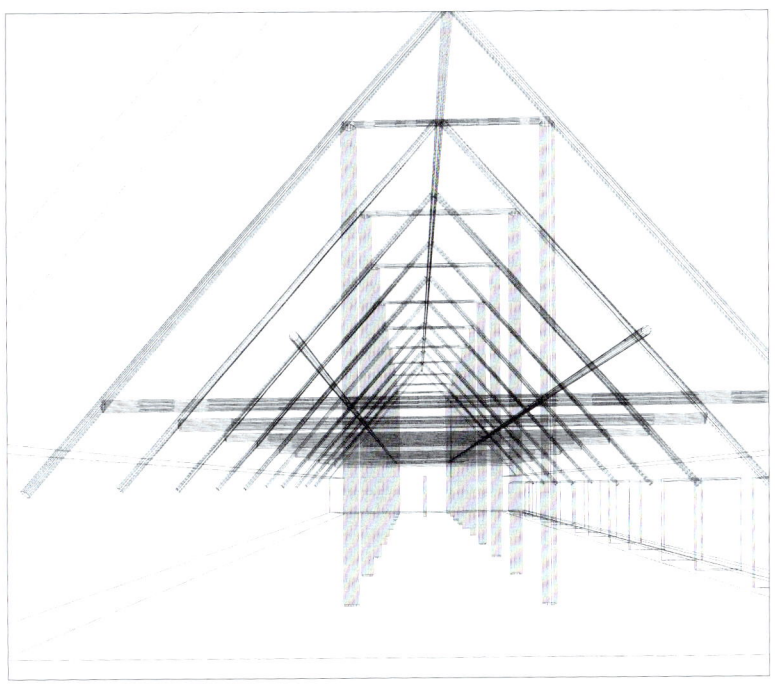

FIG. 7 Hypothetical reconstruction of the kallanka roofing system (Hypothesis 1) shown in an alternative isometric perspective (drawing by Fernando Terrazas)

FIG. 8 Hypothetical reconstruction of the kallanka roofing system (Hypothesis 2) shown in isometric perspective (drawing by Fernando Terrazas)

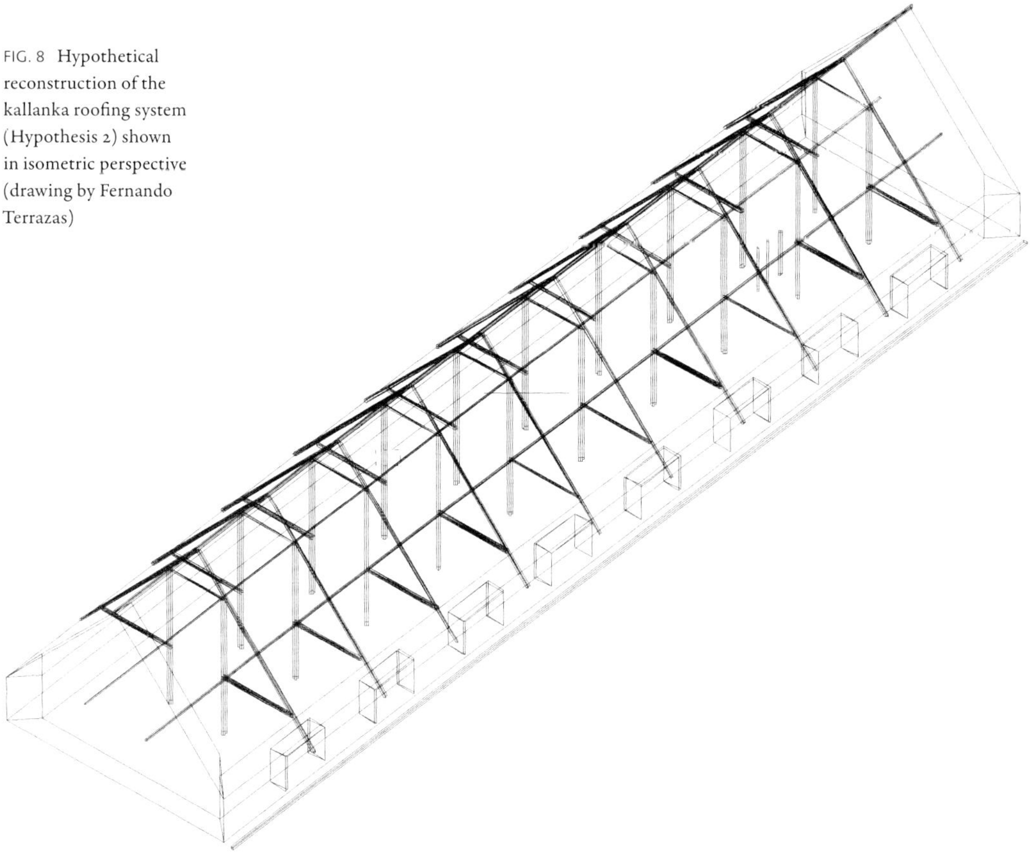

FIG. 9 Hypothetical reconstruction of the kallanka roofing system (Hypothesis 2) shown in alternative isometric perspective (drawing by Fernando Terrazas)

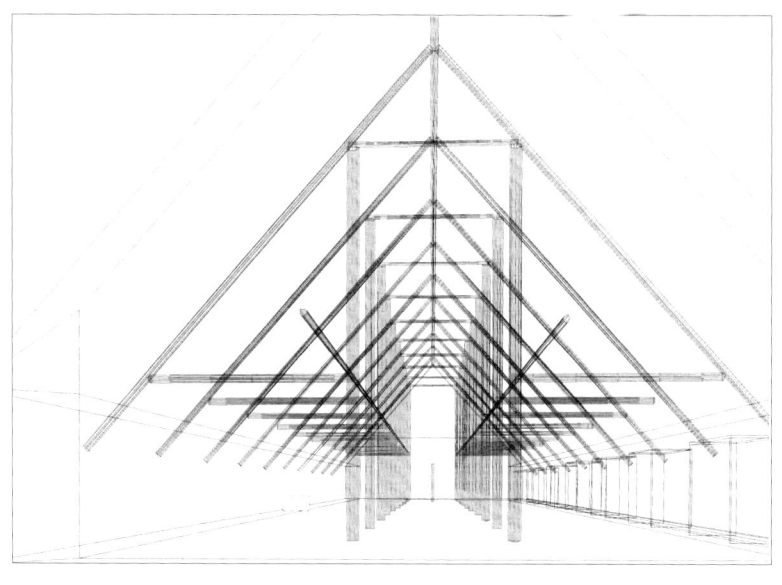

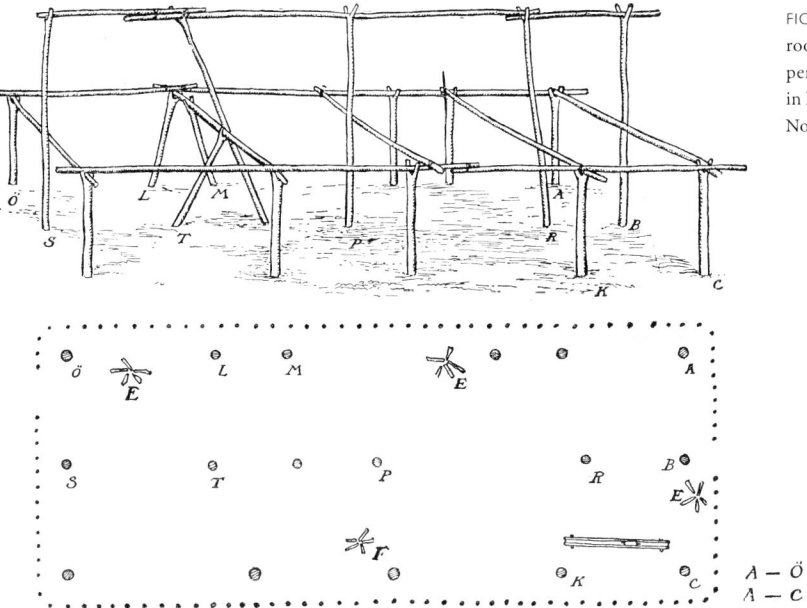

FIG. 10 Floorplan and roofing support system of a perishable Chacobo maloca in lowland Bolivia (after Nordenskiöld 1922)

Ceramics in the Santamaria, Chicha, Imperial Inka, and Paya-Inka styles were found in close association with the Bolivian kallankas. In Huánuco, at Tusuncancha and Huánuco Viejo, the layer with cultural material was very thin and held very little pottery (Morris and Thompson 1985). In contrast, Samaipata yielded large and thick pieces with better workmanship, as well as smaller pieces that were thinner and of poorer quality. Both provincial Inka and lowland ceramics were found together with pieces of pottery with textile impressions that are credited to intrusions by the Chiriguano. Polishers and bola stones are also abundant at the Samaipata kallanka.

Samaipata shows two clear phases of occupation: the first one being associated with the system of post holes and wooden posts just described. The wooden posts were broken and burned, evidence suggestive of a scene of destruction. In the second and later phase, the post holes were completely covered with gravel. There are also niches filled with ceramics that may be the result of a sporadic occupation after the Inkas were vanquished. According to historical sources, the Inkas eventually returned to the site, rebuilding it.

As to the function of the kallankas, it has been suggested that they were reunion chambers, temples, or civic buildings (Lara 1988: 40; Nordenskiöld 1957: 8); sometimes storehouses and, more frequently, military barracks. Furthermore, in the case of Samaipata, the presence of the ceremonial rock rules out the idea that the structure was a temple. Nevertheless, the fact that Inkallajta is the largest site discovered to date along the Chiriguano border makes us more inclined to the idea that the kallankas served as military barracks. In order to better understand the function or functions of these distinctive features, it will be necessary to more fully excavate kallankas in several sites.

If the kallankas are a basic element in the Inka architecture of power, then Samaipata can no longer be considered as a marginal zone or a last stand in the east but rather as an Inka provincial capital.

References cited

ALCINA FRANCH, JOSÉ

1976 *Arqueología de Chinchero*, vol. 1: *La arquitectura*. Memorias de la Misión Científica Española en Hispanoamérica 2. Ministerio de Asuntos Exteriores, Dirección General de Relaciones Culturales, Junta para la Protección de Monumentos y Bienes Culturales en el Exterior, Madrid.

GASPARINI, GRAZIANO, AND LUISE MARGOLIES

1980 *Inca Architecture* (Patricia J. Lyon, trans.). Indiana University Press, Bloomington.

IBARRA, GRASSO, D. E., AND ROY QUEREJAZU.

1986 *30000 años de prehistoria en Bolivia*. Editorial los Amigos del Libro, La Paz-Cochabamba.

LARA, JESÚS

1987 *Inkallajta Inkarraqay*. Editorial Los Amigos del Libro, La Paz-Cochabamba.

MORRIS, CRAIG, AND DONALD E. THOMPSON

1985 *Huánuco Pampa: An Inca City and Its Hinterland*. Thames and Hudson, London.

NORDENSKIÖLD, ERLAND

1922 *Indianer und Weisse in Nordostbolivien*. Strecker und Schröder, Stuttgart.

1957 Incallajta: Ciudad fortificada fundada por el Inca Tupac Yupanqui. *KHANA: Revista municipal de arte y letras* 1 (23–24).

Queros, Aquillas, Uncus, and Chulpas: The Composition of Inka Artistic Expression and Power

Tom Cummins

THE ICONOGRAPHY OF INKA POWER AS SOMETHING RECOGNIZABLE AND tangible lacks any sustained descriptive analysis. This is due, in part, to the want of a profound investigation of the nature of Inka power and its exercise as an expressive system in the visual field. On the other hand, it is also due to a lack of a critical understanding of Inka art in relation to Tawantinsuyu as a sociopolitical entity.[1] In regard to art history, this was once especially the case. George Kubler long ago sought to explain Inka art through its relation to Inka imperial power, writing that "the intrinsic meaning of Inca art reinforces the general impression of an oppressive state. It is as if, with the military expansion of the empire, all expressive faculties, both individual and collective, had been depressed by utilitarian aims to lower and lower levels of achievement" (Kubler 1975: 335). To Kubler then, Inka power had a devastating effect on the long tradition of Andean visual expression, both in terms of artistic skill (lower and lower levels of achievement) and artistic function (utilitarian).[2] Certainly, the Inka expression of power was never as visually exuberant as either the Maya or Aztec forms, cultures to which Inka culture is often compared. But this is a false comparison, as the Inka never intended to integrate architecture with a pictorialized mythical history of sculpture and painting so as to create stages for political/religious theater.[3] The few architectural sculptures at sites such as Huánuco Pampa only serve by their presence to underscore their general absence in Inka centers. This absence in the archaeological record finds resonance both in the textual descriptions of Inka sites and in the few depictions of Inka architecture in the sixteenth-century manuscripts of Martín de Murúa and Felipe Guaman Poma de Ayala. Both written accounts and the drawings concentrate on the architectonic and

FIG. 1 "Coricancha," color-wash on paper, Guaman Poma de Ayala, in Martín de Murúa's *Historia del origen y genealogía real de los reyes del Piru*, folio 64v, 1590–1605

FIG. 2 Inka stone in wall of "Sinchi Roca's Palace," commonly known as "Hatun Rumiyoc," Cusco, ca. 1520

masonry qualities of the buildings. Remarkably, even in the images of the most important buildings in Cusco such as the Coricancha, which is depicted housing the golden statue of the sun (Murúa n.d.: folio 64v), there is neither sculptural nor painted embellishment of the architecture itself (fig. 1).

There is, however, no evidence that the rise of Inka power correlates to a decrease in expressive facilities, at least not within the visual media and forms that were central to the southern Andean expressive tradition. Inka power was decidedly different, although perhaps no less "oppressive" than Aztec power, but this difference does not necessarily suggest a qualitative difference in the capacity to visually express power. In fact, one would be hard pressed to establish a causal relationship between forms of power (be they social, political, religious, military, or any combination) and expressive capacity. The capacity to express power, visually or otherwise, is a constituent part of power. Inka forms of visual expression may have been more difficult and much less accessible to recognize and to categorize for sixteenth-century Spanish chroniclers than those which they encountered in Mexico (Cummins 1994). Nonetheless, the Inka achieved a system of visual representation that was at once internally coherent yet expressive throughout the Andes such that it could successfully manifest the nature of Tawantinsuyu without supplanting that which already existed locally. And this system was different from those registered in Mesoamerica. The "unadorned" walls of Cusco, for example, articulated through the carefully beveled joins of multiangled stones not only the labor-intensive character of Andean social organization, but also the seeming pan-Andean metaphysical importance of light and shadow cast against the physical properties of a wall (fig. 2).[4]

The intractability of many Inka visual forms, both sculptural and two-dimensional, for Spaniards was in part due to their nonfigural nature, thereby rendering their references visually less immediate.

However, as I shall argue, it was also the relational signifying role between things in association with this abstraction that underlay a part of the Inka imperial system of representation, a system that was glimpsed only obliquely by the Spaniards. I will argue first that there are relationships between sets of Inka objects based on metonymy, and second that there are relationships between sets of Inka images, most especially *tocapu*. More importantly, these relationships are variously established through arrangements and ritualized engagements that create fields of meaning that are greater than any single image or object and are encompassed in the Andean "world of things."[5] This condition is certainly not particular to Inka art, and the isolation of the individual art object is part of modern aesthetics and archaeological practices. Nonetheless, the signifying relationship between Inka objects and the forms in which they appear (those categories considered by modern scholars to express an Inka aesthetic by their heightened visual characteristics through design, technique of production, or both) is a constituent element of their being and therefore a critical element of an Inka aesthetic.

FIG. 3 One male and two female Inka figurines, hammered gold, h: 5.2 cm, 5.5 cm, 5.2 cm, B-606.PG/B-607.PG/608, Dumbarton Oaks, Washington, D.C., ca. 1500

The range of Inka visual forms does, of course, include the figural, especially in sculptural forms, effected mostly in metal and in situ stone work and found most often away from urban areas (fig. 3).[6] In fact, I know of no abstract silver or gold sculptures, so that it seems that these metals were given over exclusively to the figural expression of the Inka, whereas stone could be carved in either style (figs. 4, 5). Some discrete and repetitive figural images occasionally appear on Inka ceramics (fig. 6). A few extant textiles have figural motifs, mostly butterflies, interspersed within a geometric design (fig. 7). In fact, it is probably best not to divide Inka style into figural and abstract in the sense of opposing means of expression and referentiality, but to see them as combining together in a meaningful relationship, one that is not yet fully understood.[7] This is a relationship that has a long tradition in the southern Andes, perhaps best recog-

FIG. 4 Inka llama figure (*conopa*), private collection, ca. 1500

The Composition of Inka Artistic Expression and Power

FIG. 5 Inka Waka, Machu Picchu, ca. 1520

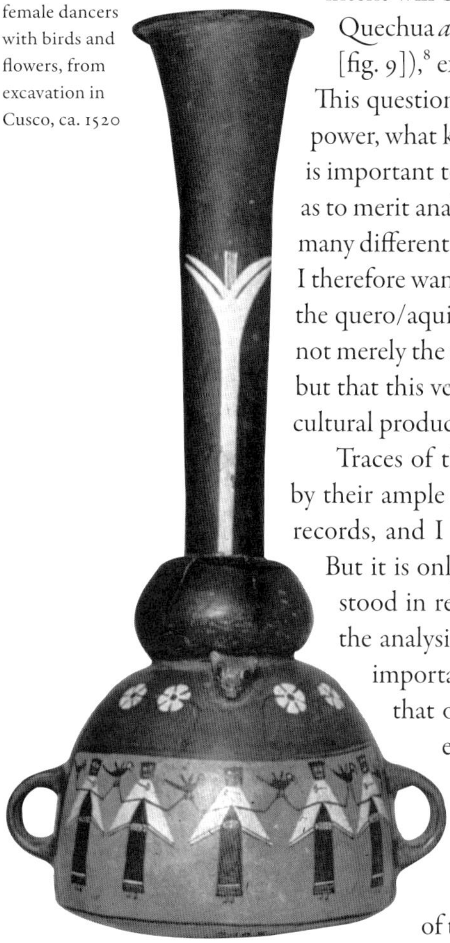

FIG. 6 One of a pair of Inka ceramic vessels with painted female dancers with birds and flowers, from excavation in Cusco, ca. 1520

nized in Wari/Tiwanaku textiles in which there is the increasing disaggregation of anatomical elements from the body as a whole. They become elements whose relationship is based not on an underlying naturalism, but on a visual structure that breaks down and reassembles parts within a patterned relationship (Sawyer 1963; Conklin 1986).

I will leave aside my last observation so as to concentrate in this essay on the meaningful relationship between Inka objects and images. Moreover, I will first focus on one specific type of object, a drinking vessel, and its greater field of meaning as one element in a composition of things and signs. More specifically, my intent will be first to ask how this type of Inka drinking vessel (in Quechua *aquilla* [fig. 8] if made in metal and *quero* if made in wood [fig. 9]),[8] expressed power in itself and in relation to other things? This question, however, begets two further questions: what kind of power, what kind of expression? Before addressing these questions, it is important to establish why this vessel form should be so privileged as to merit analysis of Inka power and its expression when there are so many different objects that the Inka created with great care and beauty. I therefore want also to suggest in this essay that the attention given to the quero/aquilla in a volume dedicated to the analysis of the Inka is not merely the arbitrary result of twentieth-century academic research, but that this vessel type did, indeed, occupy a privileged place in Inka cultural production and social interaction.

Traces of the aquilla's importance are immediately recognizable by their ample appearance in the archaeological and ethnohistorical records, and I begin with a general description of this object type. But it is only in looking at the aquilla/quero, as something understood in relation to other objects, that a number of issues about the analysis of Inka art might be reexamined. In fact, one of the important aspects of Inka artistic practice is the relational value that one type of object has to another. That relationship is established in various ways, but by whatever means that relation is produced it is a critical part of the object's significance. The aquilla/quero as an Inka object of heightened expressive value should not be studied in isolation and I therefore will not give a detailed analysis of the quero and aquilla. Such a study appears elsewhere in

FIG. 7 Inka military-style tunic (*uncu*), tapestry weave with checkerboard design butterfly, 36 x 29 in., private collection, ca. 1500

FIG. 8 One of a pair of aquillas, silver, h: 5 ½ in. (dia. 4 15/16 in.), private collection, ca. 1500

FIG. 9 One of a pair of queros, Inka, wood, The Metropolitan Museum of Art, the Michael C. Rockefeller Memorial Collection, bequest of Nelson Rockefeller, 1979 (1979.206.1074.), ca. 1500

The Composition of Inka Artistic Expression and Power

a book about Inka and colonial queros (Cummins 2002). Rather, I want to suggest what these vessels allow us to say more generally about Inka art as part of a symbolic expression that is as subtle and as coherent as any imperial referential system in world history.

Emblems of Inka Wealth and Power

To begin to understand the importance of the quero and aquilla in Inka culture, one can look to the historical residue of the Inka as it was represented to Quechua listeners more than one hundred years after the Spanish conquest. Francisco de Avila, in his sermon for the fourth Sunday of Advent published in 1648, explains the Christian metaphysics of the ephemeral and transitory nature of human history and material wealth for an Andean congregation. He refers directly to the fading memory of the Inkas and their lost power and wealth. In a translation of the Spanish version of the sermon he writes:

> And then, after all this everything is finished, nothing remains. What is there of the Inkas who were once so feared? What has become of their silver and gold? *Their garments of royal tapestry weave? Their cups for drinking?* Their fields? Their palaces? Their wives? Today, we can't even remember their names. (Francisco de Avila 1648: 43; emphasis mine)[9]

In the Quechua version, the objects of mention are nominalized according to their proper Quechua terms:

> Chaymantari llapam ymahInkacaccapas ppuchucan, manam yntallapas tacyanchu. Maymi cunan ñaupachica manchafcca Yncacuna? Maymi collqquen, ccorin? *Toccapuccompincuna, aqquillan, qquerun,* chacran, hatun huacin, huarmincuna? Mana ñam futillantapas yachachicchhtlu.

Avila conjures up for his mid-seventeenth-century Quechua listener only two types of specific objects that are directly associated with Inka power and wealth: *Toccapuccompi* (fine tapestry-weave textiles with a *tocapu* design) and the aquilla and quero. What is important, I believe, is that Avila's mention of these objects is not arbitrary, something he pulled out of the air so as to give local flavor to his metaphysical point. Nor do I think that his pairing of fine textiles and Inka drinking vessels is merely accidental, a point to which I shall return. It is important, however, to note first that Avila in his sermon calls upon the understanding that Andean memory for the Inka past can be evoked by these objects and their associations. It is through this memory that Avila can call upon these objects so as to be able to conjure up an image of Inka wealth and power for Andean listeners sitting in a church more than a hundred years after the Spanish conquest. This memory, moreover, is not connected necessarily to an oral narrative, but is intrinsic to the objects recounted and the structure of their relationship as they are placed in proximity to each other either in an ephemeral ritual or a permanent composition.[10]

Avila, of course, is not the only colonial author to ascribe such a role to aquillas and queros (Falcón 1918 [1567]: 144; Anonymous ca. 1580: 82; Cieza de León 1553: chap. 83, 24), and they appear in the chronicles almost from the beginning, being one of the first objects of exchange between Atahualpa and Pizarro at Cajamarca (Cummins 2002: 14–20). Normally, these vessels are called simply *vasos* in Spanish, a move that reduces them to a single category of thing without distinguishing between types within the category; that is, aquilla and quero. But what is important in the context of Avila's sermon is that these objects had a very clear resonance within Andean memory as markers of Inka imperial power and prestige. Furthermore, Avila's sermon, as well as other colonial texts, makes clear that the value of vasos is not predicated on an intrinsic value of material. That value comes first in Avila's sermon when he mentions the Inka's gold and silver, using a European notion of a universal equivalent. Nor is Andean prestige or value predicated on the technology of production. Queros are carved and aquillas are either hammered or molded and some may have been cast. What is significant for Avila and his listeners is the object type, the vessel, of which there are several different material manifestations: 1) metal, which is further compartmentalized into gold and silver; 2) wood; and 3) ceramic, a type that is not mentioned by Avila but that is present in the archaeological record. Another differentiating factor is size. Queros and aquillas range in height from an inch to nearly three feet, their size depending, in part, upon the significance of the particular ritual act of drinking. For example, Garcilaso de la Vega says that the paramount ruler, the Sapa Inka, kept a miniature pair of golden aquillas so that he could fulfill the obligatory act of exchanging toasts without having to drink too much. Joan de Santacruz Pachacuti Yamqui mentions the use of gigantic queros used in a festival in Cusco as a means to punish complaining lords (*curacas*) (Cummins 2002: 27, 73–74).

What is it then that ontologically links these vessels if it is not material or forming technology, criteria that we normally impose on Inka art to categorize various objects for an analytical framework?[11] First of all, queros and aquillas, regardless of their material, do have a commonality beyond their vessel shape. There is no such thing as an individually produced quero or aquilla. They are always made in pairs and they are almost always used in pairs because, as Garcilaso de la Vega, El Inca, explains:

> they had ... cups for drinking that were paired (*todos hermanos*), two by two: be they large or small, they had to be of the same size, of the same form, from the same metal, gold or silver, or wood. And this they did so that there would be equality in what they drank.[12]

Production in pairs is thus an intrinsic attribute of queros and aquillas. The pair must be made from the same material and perhaps from the same source. That is, the pair of queros seems to have been made from the same block of wood, and it may be that silver and gold aquillas may have been thought to be made from a single source of metal. As Garcilaso de la Vega makes clear, the production in pairs is based upon the social relations that are enacted through ritual drinking. That relationship is predicated upon the moiety division of *ayllu* communities, called *hanan* and *hurin*, such that each pair of vessels is a materialization of this social division: they are even personified as "hermanos." And although one could believe that Garcilaso is using the seventeenth-century understanding of the word,[13] he is actually referring to the Quechua term *yanantin yanantillan*, which Diego González Holguín translates as *dos cosas hermanadas*. Yanantin is a term and a concept critical to social identity in the Andes as discussed by Tristan Platt (1978) and it finds its materialization in the production of aquillas and queros.

The pair therefore can be used in different forms of exchange to enact the various metaphors generated from this primary binary system. However, within the politics of Tawantinsuyu the material of the drinking vessel also expressed a hierarchy within this form of social interaction. All cups were made in pairs but the pairs were made either of gold, silver, wood, or ceramics. The distribution of these objects was not arbitrary; rather the material of the vessel determined to whom the pair was given according to sociopolitical rank within Tawantinsuyu (Cummins 2002: 110–117). Outside of Cusco, these objects were given to curacas at various levels of authority or *quien era*, as Francisco Falcón noted (Falcón 1567: 153–154).[14] Different degrees of authority within the sociopolitical structure of Tawantinsuyu were manifested not only by the object given (queros/aquillas) but also by the material form in which they were made. Of course, the distribution of this vessel type probably extended beyond the rank of curaca. I suspect that ceramic queros were given out to lesser-ranked individuals, but that even the possession of a ceramic pair of these Inka vessels indicated prestige within Tawantinsuyu. After all, we know from archaeological and ethnohistorical evidence that feasting was such a critical element in Inka social policies that the core of any Inka center was given over to the plaza where such celebrations were held (Morris 1982: 153–172). Drinking and the exchange of toasts were the focus of these feasts and drinking vessels were essential items whose value originated before the Inka. Ceramic quero shaped vessels, as far as I can tell, are rarely mentioned in the written sources, a fact that suggests that they were the prerogative of a social group of people whose voice did not enter into the colonial record despite the ample archaeological evidence.[15]

One would also have to say that queros and aquillas not only allowed for the expression of the social relations based on moiety divisions and the demarcation of political hierarchy based on the organization of Tawantinsuyu, but that Andean gender relations were also clearly on display in the way that queros and aquillas were manipulated in Inka rituals. This aspect is much clearer in the colonial visual evidence than in textual descriptions, in part because Spanish authors were not as concerned with describing gender relations as they were with describing social and political relations. If, however, we look at two of several illustrations of Inka rituals by Guaman Poma from his *Nueva Coronica* (fig. 10) and in Murúa's 1590 *Historia del Perú* (fig. 11), in which queros or aquillas appear to be ceremonially used, a female either carries the two vessels to be used or prepares one by pouring corn beer (*aqha*) into it is so as to be used ritually by the male. This relationship is also clearly indicated in Diego de Ocaña's portrait of the Inka in Cusco (fig. 12). He depicts the male frontally, advancing toward the viewer, while the female is shown in profile approaching the male with a painted quero in one hand and a drum in the other. About this image Ocaña writes:

> The dress of elite women Indians is also as the painting shows. They now wear a linen blouse and an underskirt and over this, wrapping the body, something like a tunic without sleeves which

FIG. 10 "June Celebration (Havcai Cusqvi) Drinking with the Sun in the Festival of the Sun," Guaman Poma de Ayala, ink on paper, *Nueva corónica y buen gobierno*, p. 246, The Royal Library, Copenhagen, 1615

FIG. 11 "Celebration after The Inka's and Coya's Wedding," Guaman Poma de Ayala, pink, colorwash on paper, in Martín de Murúa's *Historia del origen y genealogía real de los reyes del, Piru*, folio 82v, private collection, Dublin, 1590–1605

The Composition of Inka Artistic Expression and Power

FIG. 12 "Dress of the Inka King and Queen," colorwash on paper, Fray Diego de Ocaña, *Relación del viaje de fray Diego de Ocaña por el Nuevo Mundo*, folios 332v and 333r, Biblioteca de la Universidad, Oviedo M-215, 1599–1606

they call azú; over this [they wear] a manta over their shoulders which they call llíquica and on their head they wear another small manta that they call llanaca. That cup that she holds in the hand is called cuero [quero], with which they give to men to drink chicha. And in the dances they use that small drum, they wear sandals on their feet in the dance and ordinarily.[16]

Clearly, in Inka festivals, gender roles dictated how queros and aquillas were used. More importantly, perhaps, gender established a transactional relation in which the male assumes a hierarchical position, consuming the drink in a vessel that establishes social intercourse (Cummins 2002). In fact there are descriptions of feasts in which rows of men sit facing each other exchanging toasts while the women sit back to back with the men and pour the aqha that they have not only transported but also produced. At the same time, Ocaña's image and description demonstrate how privileged a role the quero had, such that he had to factor it into his only image of the Inka, an image that was created some seventy years after the Spanish invasion.

Vessels and Textiles

I want to move beyond the immediate use-value of queros and aquillas and suggest that Inka symbolic objects, such as queros, should be thought of not only as discrete entities within some kind of functional paradigm. They also have a kind of syntactical relationship with other seemingly unrelated objects, or at least unrelated in terms of their function and or material.

I therefore want briefly to return to Avila's sermon as it reveals something else about queros and aquillas. When Avila rhetorically asks his Quechua-speaking audience about what had become of the Inka's power and wealth, he couples textiles and queros: "(Maymin) *Toccapuccompincuna, aqquillan, qquerun,* chacran, hatun huacin, huarmincuna?" This is not a hollow phrase, something simply or transparently meant. In this phrasing, Avila, I think, calls upon his deep knowledge of Andean categories of meaning not merely to ask what has become of Inka material wealth by naming these objects. He also calls out their names in Quechua so as to form an Andean set of relationships between the objects and to ask within Andean consciousness what had become of the Inka who had once been so feared: "Maymi cunan ñaupachica manchafcca Yncacuna?" How and why would the listing of these two kinds of diverse things accomplish such a rhetorical goal? How is it that *toccapuccompincuna, aqquillan,* and *qquerun* might conjure up an image of the Inka as being once upon a time so fierce (*tan temidos*), as Avila writes in Spanish.

To begin to answer this question it is important to remember John Murra's pivotal essay on Inka textiles, in which he pointed out that fine *cumbi* cloth was offered by the Inka upon their first approach into a new territory (Murra 1975). This gesture was intended as an act of symbolic generosity, but Murra, following Marcel Mauss, goes on to note that the gift was not innocent. It initiated a cycle of obligatory "reciprocity" by which the new territory symbolically entered, on an unequal basis, into the redistributive economy of Tawantinsuyu (Murra 1975: 170). But what is important to point out here is that the Inka's gift never consisted solely of cumbi textiles. The gift always comprised a set of objects. Unfortunately, however, textiles have always been seen as the principal constituent of Inka gifts. In saying this, I do not wish to deemphasize the critical if not primary role of textiles in Andean society in general and Tawantinsuyu in particular.[17] By misconstruing both the role of textiles and expression of the gift within Inka political economy, however, we miss a critical Inka semiotics based upon the relational position of objects, a kind of phenomenological syntax. Inka scholars have tended instead toward seeing a pristine ontology of the discrete object as the basis of an analytical model.

That is to say, Andean objects cross over or through genres, media, and technologies to perform various meanings in relation to other objects so as to form modalities of expression that become specific by place and arrangement. This is an aspect of *camay* or the vitalizing force that is imbued in every object (Salomon 1991: 16). If we were to look at Inka

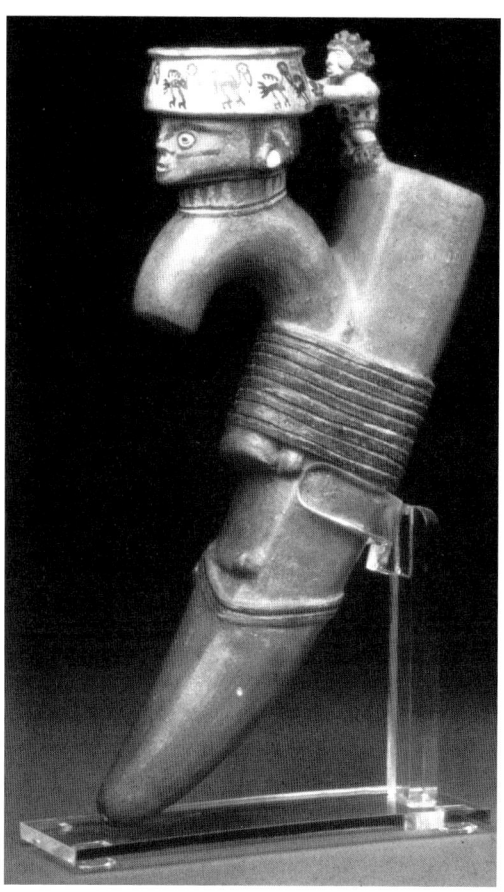

FIG. 13 Paccha in the form of a Chakitaclla, vessel, and human figure, ceramic, ca. 1500

textiles, wooden objects, architecture, and metal working as isolated phenomena, we would miss this crucial point in terms of understanding both mythological narratives and ritual spaces and actions.[18] But it is precisely this conditionality that allows Andean objects to compound one another in a meaningful way, constituting a kind of compositionality in which the field of meaning does not reside in the single object but in a larger spatial relationship. In this larger relationship a number of objects (either two or more of the same type or a collection of different objects) express a more expanded meaning than would each individual object. This in itself moves each object beyond the sphere of functionality, something that so worried Kubler, and inserts a phenomenology among things, a spatialized field of meaning. I shall return to this issue below, but by way of example, it would be as if we were to isolate objects according to their primary use, intrinsic materials, and forming technologies. It would be tantamount to unraveling a *qepi* bundle in a contemporary Andean community, deciding which object is the most significant, analyzing it, and declaring it the essence of the bundle instead of looking at the set of relations between the various things as being a totality spread out on the cloth.[19] Thinking of Inka objects in this way moves beyond context as an interpretive method in terms of the primacy of the object or image with all else being secondary and explanatory. It is to think that there is not a kind of distinction between object and context; rather that they somehow come to constitute each other as what is seen, experienced, and interpreted.

For meaningfulness to take place means that a spatial relationship—a degree of immediacy—between things must occur. This can be done simply by bringing discrete objects of different materials together in proximity, or by forming objects in a single material so as to express their relationship. The latter is best seen in ceramic ritual vessels (*pacchas*) that join the sculptural form of a bowl and a *chakitaclla* (footplow) into a single composition (fig. 13). The offering of *aqha* (corn beer) is thus first poured into the bowl, which then passes through the *chakitaclla* and finally empties into the ground, thereby completing a cycle of planting, harvesting, fermentation, and consumption as understood through these "utilitarian objects" and their quotidian use.[20]

This expressive sense of relationship between things is something that Avila clearly understood in 1648. By calling on the relationship between aquillas and textiles he was able to conjure up an image of the feared Inka in their own terms. This is because when the Sapa Inka appeared with his army at the border of a new territory he did in fact send a gift, but the gift was comprised of "vasos de oro y ropa de Cusco," as Francisco de Santillán recorded in his *Relación del Origen . . . de los Incas* (1563: 46). This same passage appears almost verbatim in the *Relación del Origen* (Anonymous 1580: 58–59) and in other broad metahistories of the Inka. Local histories with specific testimonies corroborate this general impression. For example, Cristóbal Castro and Diego Ortega Morejón, in their *Relación del . . . valle Chincha* (1558: 237), recorded that when the Sapa Inka first appeared on the coast with his army, he told the curacas of the valley that he had not come to take possession of their wealth; that he had more than enough and he had even brought gifts for them. But in exchange, the Sapa Inka wished to be recognized as their sovereign. He then gave them clothes brought from Cusco, golden aquillas, and many other things that the curacas did not have.

FIG. 14 Inka military tunic, tapestry weave, 78 x 96 cm, private collection, ca. 1500

The same kind of testimony comes from the sierras. In 1570, Alonso Poma Guala, the son of the curaca of the Hurin Huancas, testified that his great grandfather, Apu Guala, had told him how the Inka first brought the Jauja region under their authority. He said Tupa Inka Yupanqui brought an army of ten thousand men and camped on a hill. Apu Guala, unsure of the Sapa Inka's intentions, went to speak with Tupa Inka Yupanqui, who assured him that he had come in peace. Apu Guala then pledged himself and his people to the Inka. Alonso Poma Guala added that he was told that "Topa Ynga gave his great grandfather some fine shirts and cloaks and *some cups in which to drink, which among themselves they call aquillas* [emphasis mine]."[21] From what Cristóbal de Albornóz (1989 [1584]: 19) says about rituals in which military feats were recalled in the colonial period, it is likely that at least some of these cumbi tunics were either the checkerboard military tunics (*uncus*) with a key design (figs. 14, 15). It also is important to add that the Inka continued to give similar sets of gifts to curacas on other auspicious occasions. But clearly, as Apu Poma Guala related to his great grandson, the impression of the Inka as tan temido began with the appearance of an army of ten thousand and the offering of a gift of textiles and aquillas.

The Composition of Inka Artistic Expression and Power   279

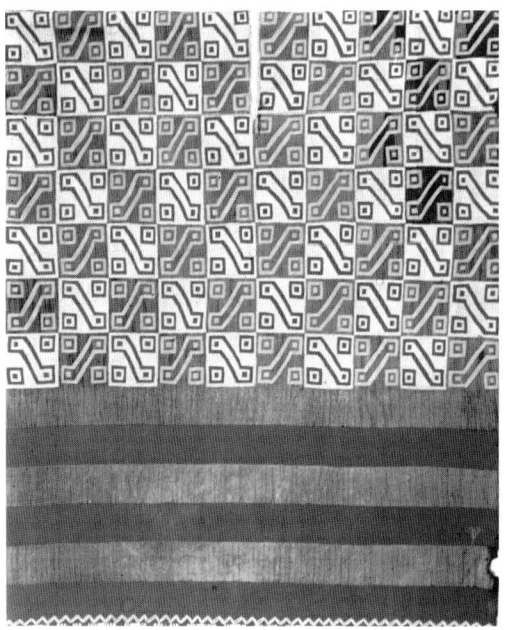

FIG 15 Inka uncu, key design, tapestry weave, the Textile Museum, Washington D.C., 72 x 96 cm, ca. 1500

Aquillas/queros and cumbi textiles formed a constellation of objects, dissimilar in utilitarian function or material production, that not only constituted the Inka's gift, but also conveyed the intention of the gift. In this instance, political power in its most manifest form was conveyed through the presentation of textiles and aquillas. Their acceptance or rejection stood between the restraint or unleashing of Inka military force. Such gifts transcended sociopolitical exchanges and were critical in cosmological interaction. Queros and textiles also constituted objects placed with capachucha sacrifices (Reinhard n.d.).[22] It is therefore not a coincidence, I think, that the principal element of the "key design" in Inka tunics, a diagonal band that shifts at the end to become horizontal, is also the principal element in the most common aquilla design (fig. 16). In fact this type of motif is found on gold, silver, wooden, and ceramic examples (fig. 17). On the queros and aquillas, this element is sometimes clearly part of a schematic representational motif of disarticulated arms and heads. Elsewhere, I have analyzed this motif in relation to Inka acts of suppression of resistance and revolt, and have suggested that the textiles and vessel and their common design elements have a redoubling effect in terms of the intent of the Inka gift through both their presence and appearance in a community (Cummins 2002: 92–95).

Of course, each object, textile and aquilla, carried with it its own set of associations. The aquillas for example stand synecdochically for all past and future Andean feasts and their part in Inka political economy of redistribution and must be given as a pair. The toccapuccompincuna stood for Inka royalty and invention, as Tom Zuidema has noted (1991). Pedro Sarmiento de Gamboa (1572: 84), for example, attributes the invention of the tocapu to Inka Viracocha. In this sense, Kubler was correct; some of the most important imperial expressions were conveyed through utilitarian objects: drinking cups and clothing. Utility is a category of social interaction, however, that can be heightened as an expressive visual means by various transformative processes. One is by heightening the form and perhaps the material so that the object transcends quotidian use and is a kind of a skeuomorph. Another is to call attention to one object through another to produce a set of associations and meanings in which the utility of the thing is one signifying element within a greater relationship, or composition; a kind of metonymy. This is the case with Inka textiles and

FIG. 16 A pair of aquillas, with key design forming human heads and arms, silver, private collection, ca. 1500

aquillas and their relationship, but it is also true for a variety of other imperial objects, including architecture, as will be discussed below.

One can see these principals at work in the designs of one of the most ubiquitous ceramic forms of the Inka, the aryballoid-shaped vessel (*urpu*). Sometimes they are decorated with textile designs (fig. 18) that together seem to evoke a set of ritual offerings in which aqha and cumbi cloth are critical elements. In one of the most elaborate examples coming from near Lake Titicaca, the key design is not only used to reference an uncu design, but the horizontals form a frame, each horizontal a series of twenty-nine

FIG. 17 One of a pair of queros, with key design forming human heads and arms, wood, Museum of the American Indian, Washington D.C., ca. 1500

FIG. 18 Urpu with key design, Basel, Switzerland

17

18

The Composition of Inka Artistic Expression and Power   281

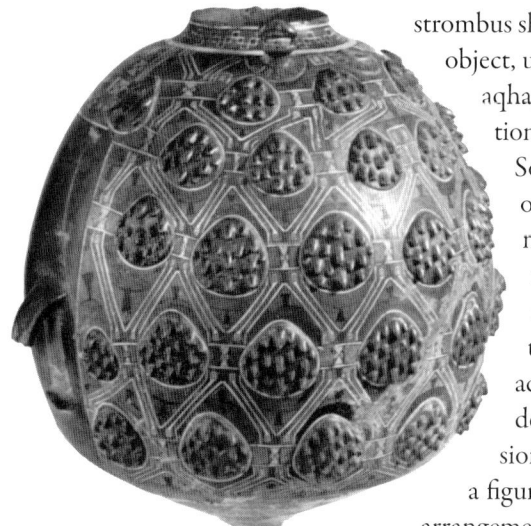

FIG. 19 Urpu with key design and *Spondylus* shells, Musée de l'Homme, ceramic, h: 18.1 in., dia. 24.4 in., ca. 1500

strombus shells (*mullu*) modeled in the round (fig. 19). The object, urpu, by its "utilitarian" function of transporting aqha, two-dimensional design, and sculpted decoration evokes the most important ritual offerings of the Southern Andes. One of the first scholars to report on this vessel already recognized the composite nature of the design as a signifying whole, likening it to European heraldic devices.[23] It is unfortunate that we do not know the context in which this vessel was found nor what other objects, if any, accompanied it. Alone, the elements of the urpu's design imply differing spheres of Andean expression and their interaction, without linking them in a figurative pictorial composition. The compositional arrangement, and by composition I include the vessel as a material form as well as the two-dimensional design, does not seem to require an oral narrative for meaning to be made. Rather, the juxtaposition of elements creates an emergent meaning through their discrete references (raised brown spike forms mimetically suggest *Spondylus*, the key design in green and yellow metonymically suggests a textile, and the vessel shape is in and of itself what it represents) and their compositional unity.[24]

Objects and Designs in Tawantinsuyu

As the first imperial Inka objects received within a newly incorporated territory, sometimes by force, the recursive effect of the aquillas and cumbi textile designs did not only participate in the initial rituals of conquest and incorporation. The Inka designs and forms of the objects, common to almost all Andeans yet slightly different, also initiated Inka visual culture as an imperial phenomenon that was coherent, universal, and distinct from local traditions. Inka designs on these objects were by and large nonpictorial, referring visually more to one another through shared geometric abstract motifs rather than mimetic representation.[25] But even when a tocapu on a toccapuccompi, or cumbi real as Avila calls it, does become representational in an iconic fashion, it refers to itself by depicting another textile.

If one looks at the tocapu design on the Dumbarton Oaks uncu, a toccapuccompi if ever there was one, one tocapu is indexical in that it depicts a miniature military uncu (fig. 20). It is, however, a double indexicality: as a pictorial image it calls attention to a specific genre of Andean uncu while at the same time, as a tocapu, it calls attention to the relation between uncu and tocapu of which it is a part. The tocapu that is recognizable as a miniature military uncu therefore functions doubly in a way that most tocapu do not, or at least not pictorially. Nonetheless,

FIG. 20 Inka uncu with tocapu designs, side B, tapestry weave, wool and cotton, h: 91 cm on one side, w: 76 cm, b-518. PT, Dumbarton Oaks, Washington D.C., ca. 1500.

this doubling suggests the possibility of tocapu to refer simultaneously to the category of toccapuccompi, as a thing in and of itself, and to other phenomena that are a part of the tocapu's larger range of possible placement. The overall design of the tocapu on the uncu brings those references and context together into a larger expression.

But as the tocapu with the military design on the Dumbarton Oaks uncu is set into a relation with other more abstract tocapu, are we to read it only as an iconic sign in a Piercean sense, that is to say as a sign that represents "its object mainly by similarity" (Pierce 1955)? This form of interpretation can only be performed if we look at the tocapu in isolation, in which this tocapu seems merely to mimic a male garment in general and a specific one in particular. If, however, we see it as set into a larger composition and framed by other tocapus that are nonfigural, then it must be interpreted in an expanded sense. All the tocapu in this uncu are composed of abstract geometric motifs, and whatever else they are meant to do, they convey their meaning by convention. The system for producing

FIG. 21 Mummy bundle dressed in military tunic, ca. 1500, Basel, Switzerland

FIG. 22 Engraving of painted chullpa in Palca, in E. George Squier, *Peru; Incidents of Travel and Exploration in the Land of the Incas*, p. 243

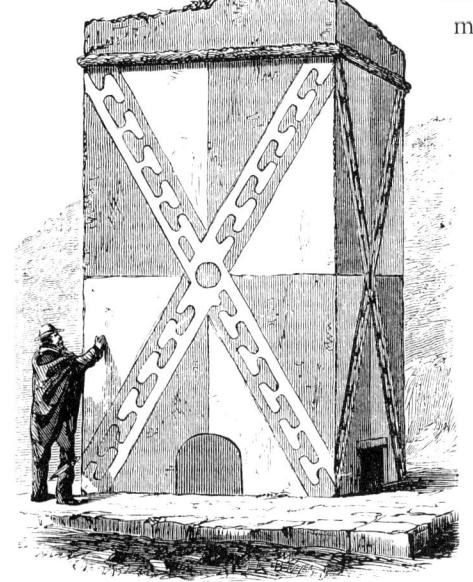

meaning is probably mnemonic, but perhaps associated to words or names of different tocapu (Barthel 1971). That is, the images call up a set of associations and/or categories that may or may not have been nominalized. Should we then think that the miniature image of a military tunic refers through mimicry to the actual tunic and its associations, or should we not think of this image in terms of the associations attached to it as a tocapu and only in relation to the other tocapus, or both?

I will argue that it is both and as such we may be looking at a history of conquests, with the tocapus standing for gifts or battles before the incorporation of a new ethnic group into Tawantinsuyu, clearly a set of associations that Avila called upon in his sermon. On the other hand, we may be looking at a kind of sacred map of *capac hucha* (the ritual of human sacrifice), in which the miniature military uncu stands not for life-sized uncus but for offerings placed within capac hucha, the places being indicated by the other tocapu.[26] Such textiles and pairs of queros were part of the offertory of a capac hucha. At least one mummy bundle was recovered dressed in a military uncu (fig. 21). I am not interested in giving a particular reading of the pattern of this uncu, but rather to suggest that even within the field of Inka abstract design there is the possibility of accumulative meaning just as there is in the association of objects like textiles and queros. In this sense, as with the urpu discussed above, it is important to recognize that the tocapus do not express themselves solely in relation to the larger field of tocapus, as if that field were a discrete system in some form like alphabetic writing and thereby independent of the object on which tocapus appear. The object itself is important. Here, the uncu is both in and of itself what it represents as well as a field of tocapus, one of which references a particular type of uncu. Furthermore, the uncu as uncu either is worn by someone or implies the absent person and the relationship to the tocapus as something displayed through being worn, a point to which I shall return.

In some ways the system I have been describing was also architecturally on display, at least in the southern Andes, on the exterior walls of funerary towers (*chullpas*). E. George Squier first gave notice of painted chullpas in 1877 (fig. 22). He noted that the funerary structures of Palca, a site on the western slopes of the Sierras on the ascent from Tarma to Lake Titicaca, were built with an interior corbel arch and faced with rough stone creating a rectangular structure of some fourteen feet high (Squier 1877: 242–244). The four exterior walls were then stuccoed and painted. The design of each wall was the same. The surface was divided into four quadrants formed by a central vertical and horizontal axis. Each quadrant was intersected by one of two diagonals such that each quarter was divided into two color fields of red and white. More recently, Teresa Gisbert (1996) has reported on the chullpas of the Río Lauca region of Bolivia, where the adobe chullpas of the Aymara-speaking Carangas are still visible. Many of them are painted on the exterior with designs that, like the chullpa recorded by Squier more than one hundred years earlier, are clearly derived from Inka uncu designs. One chullpa (fig. 23) is painted with a design that is very similar to the uncu of Tupac Inka Yupanqui, the Inka who conquered the territory, as depicted in a late-sixteenth-century portrait (fig. 24) (Gisbert et al. 1996: 44–50). Gisbert suggests, correctly, I believe, that the painted designs of the Carangas's chullpas are to be identified with the Aymara lords (*mallcus*) who had accepted Inka rule and who were buried in the structures (ibid.: 49). The abstract designs may have signified, among other things, the political alliance that had been historically forged between the Inka and the ancestors placed within. The structures, therefore, became more than local ethnic burial places. As Tom Abercrombie (1998: 182) suggests, the painted chullpas became perhaps emblematic beacons of the Inka, emblazoned like a patchwork of three-dimensional tocapus on the landscape of Tawantinsuyu. They, and the bodies of the ancestors inside and draped with Inka uncus, helped to recall, or better instantiate, a number of local mythohistoric narratives.

Local mythohistory, however, could be made universal, which we know to have been a part of Inka imperial ideology. For example, all places of local origin (*paqarina*) from which the apical ancestor emerged, were united and superceded by an Inka genesis. This genesis claimed that Viracocha first created all communities at Lake Titicaca and then sent them

FIG. 23 Chullpa with painted checkerboard design similar to Inka textile designs, Lauca River region, Bolivia, Churipatilla, Caranga culture (photo courtesy of Teresa Gisbert), ca. 1500

FIG. 24 Coat-of-arms of the Ejecutoria de Hidalguía for the descendants of Tupac Inka Yupanqui, parchment, gold leaf, and paint, Archivo General de Indias, Sevilla, Mexico 2346, MP, Escudos y Arboles Genealogicos, 78, ca. 1600

out to populate the world after its devastation by flood (Duviols 1973; Sherbondy 1982). As Tom Zuidema has already pointed out in regard to this myth and its rendering in tocapu design on uncus (Zuidema 1982: 447), Viracocha sent each "nation" forth from Tiwanaku wearing the dress that belonged to their sacred place (*huaca*). The Inkas' ability to recognize and respect local traditions and territories while at the same time making them an integral part of Tawantinsuyu, a place of four parts, was critical to political ideology and expression. It, therefore, does not seem to be too much of a stretch to suppose that the designs on the buildings could have been united in a single composition, either on an uncu such as in the Dumbarton Oaks collection or on the painted boards kept in Cusco, producing thereby an "historical map" of conquered territory, ethnic groups, and curacas.[27]

There is a rather solid suggestion that uncus, similar to the one mentioned by Avila, did perform such a representation, a kind of mapping of Tawantinsuyu. The evidence is found in the inventory of Philip II's personal possessions, drawn up after his death in 1599. Among the royal possessions in the monastery of San Lorenzo de El Escorial are listed a number of Inka objects found under the category of *Cosas extrahordinarias*.

Although each entry is brief, many of them give a remarkable amount of historical detail. For example, item number 4.759 lists two wool tassels (*dos borlas de lana*), one red (*encarnada*) and the other yellow (*amarilla*), that had been sent by the viceroy Francisco de Toledo to Philip II. These were *mascaypachas* (Inka "crowns") as indicated by the commentary "that it was said that it [the *borla*] was the insignia with which the Inkas were crowned and the one is that with which was crowned Huayna Capac [*sic*] and the other, Atahuapla, placed in a basket of straw and wool, they have no value."[28] Whether or not these were, in fact, the mascaypacha of the last two Inka kings is not important here. Rather, the understanding of what these objects were and what they signified indicates a careful record keeping of the information that accompanied them from Peru. The comments concerning another Inka object must therefore be considered in regard to how uncus and tocapu might be understood. Item 4.767 lists "another shirt [uncu] of the Indians, that they [the Inka] call cumbi [that is] woven of diverse colors and figures, of which the figures are signs of the coats-of-arms of the provinces [*señales de armas de provincias*] that the Inka possessed, by which he knew them."[29] Unfortunately, the uncu is also described as moth-eaten and full of holes, therefore declared as having no value. Hence, it has not survived. The description, nonetheless, is clear enough. The uncu had a series of woven designs, such as coats-of–arms, that signified the empire in terms of its parts and through which the Sapa Inka recognized them within an organized field of tocapu.[30] And, although the term tocapu is not used in the document, it would seem that this is exactly what these señales de armas de provincias were. Moreover, this once beautiful but now moth-eaten tunic in the Spanish royal collection would have fit Avila's and his audience's understanding of a toccapuc-compi as being one of the few things needed to conjure up Inka power.

If such an uncu could be understood to represent the provinces (*guamani*?) of Tawantinsuyu by means of tocapus (señales),[31] could not then tocapus represent in some fashion the Inka dominion over, or incorporation of such places where tocapu were painted on "public" buildings such as chullpas? It is important to add that pairs of queros are found encrusted just above the lintel of the entrance to these chullpas. Queros and aquillas were, of course, used to feast the dead, as depicted by Guaman Poma and substantiated by archaeology. The queros placed above the lintels were surely linked in some way to this communion with the ancestors (Gisbert, et al. 1996: 47). But as already mentioned, queros and aquillas were often, if not always, given with textiles as gifts by the Inka to compliant curacas. What is striking, then, about these chullpas is that the association between textiles and queros as a mutually signifying set of objects becomes literally incorporated into the structure. That is, the walls are painted as textiles and studded with queros. Just as the body of the ancestor substantiates a set of local socioreligious relationships by its presence, these structures simultaneously house the body and display a part of a larger political and social set of relationships through Inka objects and their design and thereby intersect the local and imperial.

The chullpas painted with Inka designs and studded with queros can be understood as forming a field of meaning that localizes a signifying process of Inka power through two-dimensional designs, architecture, and ritual objects, a process that surely took place throughout Tawantinsuyu. It is not necessary that all chullpas in Tawantinsuyu were painted as the chullpas of Carangas were, nor that queros were embedded above every doorway.[32] It seems that tocapu designs in relation to structures and objects composed a visualization of the Inkas' incorporation of not only territories, but also social relations as exemplified by the bodies of the ancestors placed inside wearing such uncus. Communities as far north as Ecuador were remembered to have had a structure called *cuzcohuasi*, meaning that at the very least there was a specific structure marking Inka presence and dominion.[33]

The expanded form of expression created by the physical interrelatedness/juxtaposition of diverse things and forms also extends to the toccapuccompicuna mentioned by Avila in his sermon. One cannot think abstractly of the uncu as a disassociated textile. The uncu is something intended to be worn by men, so that like the chullpa, the uncu, by what it is, establishes a wider field of gendered relationships (like the quero). In both cases this gendered relationship is centered by the human body in its various Andean states of being. Thus, the central axis of the uncu is predicated on the male figure wearing the piece, orienting the vertical and horizontal of the design as well as establishing a front and a back.[34] The field of tocapu therefore becomes meaningful, or at least more meaningful as it is worn and embodied. The Dumbarton Oaks uncu is an excellent example of how the relationship between the tocapu and the body that wore it might be understood. First, it might be argued that the entire field of tocapu is anchored by one type of tocapu, the one that resembles something else and that resemblance is to another Inka uncu. Moreover, this tocapu seems to be a synecdoche such that each instance of this tocapu refers not just to a military uncu, but to all military uncus and the Inka army that wore them.[35] Moreover, if we take into account the uncu described in the inventory of Philip II as being a field of designs that signified the provinces of Tawantinsuyu, then one may have a history/map of conquests. This map might be of just one of the *suyus*, Collasuyu for example, or of all of the new territories brought into Tawantinsuyu. The relation between the uncu as a garment and the body that wears it is therefore a critical element in this reading in that the field of tocapu (territory) is centered and oriented by its being worn.[36]

FIG. 25 Sapa Inka carried in a litter by representatives of the four suyus, Guaman Poma de Ayala, colorwash on paper, in Martín de Murúa's *Historia de los Incas del Perú*, J. Paul Getty Museum, Ms. Ludwig 13, 84r (67r), 1611–13

Such an interpretation is not as far-fetched as it might first seem. Remember that the first chroniclers confused the spatial center of the empire, Cusco, with its leader. That is, the earliest chronicler of Peru, sometimes identified as Cristóbal de Mena, as well as other early writers called the Inka king Cusco (Pease 1995: 15–22; Houston and Cummins 2004).[37] This, of course, may have been merely a matter of linguistic confusion. Yet, if we look at a late-sixteenth-century representation of the Sapa Inka in one of Murúa's watercolor drawings (fig. 25), the idea of the moveable center of Tawantinsuyu as embodied by the Sapa Inka is represented almost literally. The Inka is seated in a litter that is held

The Composition of Inka Artistic Expression and Power   289

FIG. 26 Inka tunic with chumpi design of repeated diamond tocapus, tapestry-weave wool and cotton, private collection, ca. 1500

aloft by four individuals, each dressed in the representative clothes and headdress of the four suyus. Along three of the litter's arms are written the names of three of the suyus. The fourth says callasaya, perhaps in error. Lettering may have been added some twenty years after the drawing was created.

The illustration of the Inka in his litter was not originally intended for the 1615 Murúa manuscript. The text on the verso of this folio has been crossed out and was papered over with another blank sheet, as are several other illustrations that have been taken from Murúa's early manuscript. This illustration is, I believe, originally described on folio 55r of the 1590 manuscript, which is entitled "Capitulo Tercero, de la manera que fuera, los ingas y la gran Magestad que andaban." In this chapter, Murúa first gives an account of how the Inka was carried in a litter to battle and how he was dressed. He then writes,

> every time that the Inka went out they carried him . . . in very sumptuous and beautifully appointed litters . . . the litters of these kings were always carried by the four most principal lords that existed just as [our king] has in his council Dukes or Marquises . . . and for this were selected those from the four suyus or provinces of collasuyu and chinchasuyu, contesuyu, and antesuyu [and] who always resided with the Inca in his palace.[38]

Murúa's image and text together suggest that the Inka and the court personified the territoriality of Tawantinsuyu. It does not have to be literally the case—and most certainly it was not—that the four lords of the four suyu carried the Sapa Inka's litter. Rather, it needed only to be conceived as such. In this sense, Murúa's colonial illustration performs a double referentiality. At one level, there is the literal or iconic depiction of the Inka's transportation as it is described in the text. At a second level, there is the allegorical representation of the empire. That is, the center (Cusco) of Tawantinsuyu is personified by the figure of the Sapa Inka who sits within a rectangular space that defines the four suyus as personified by the four litter bearers. This drawing is a colonial figuration, relying on the European trope of the personification of territory through figural representation. Nonetheless, the geometry of the overall composition of the Murúa's/Guaman Poma's personification of Tawantinsuyu and its center replicates a common tocapu composition of a four-cornered shape (square, rectangle, diamond) with the center marked (fig. 26). Moreover,

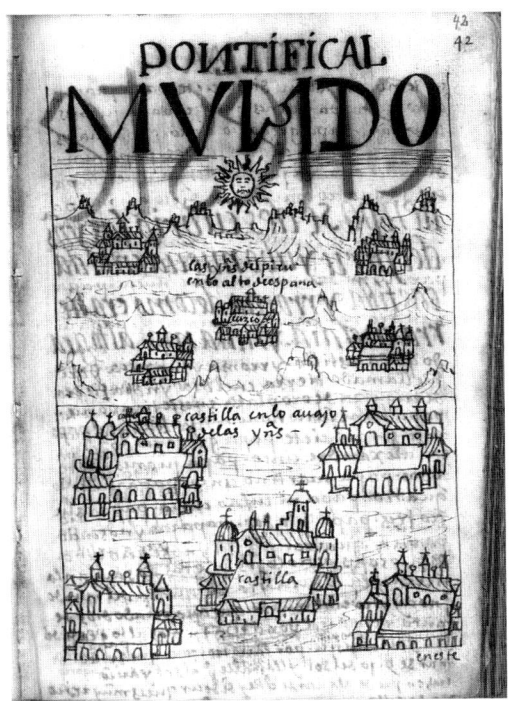 

this configuration forms the design depicted along the baseboard of the litter.

The appearance here of this tocapu motif may be just coincidence, simply a decorative design. But in conjunction with the personification of the four suyu, Murúa's drawing suggests that just as Cusco was imagined in some perhaps geometric form as the geographic center of Tawantinsuyu, the Sapa Inka could be imagined as the embodiment of the political center of Tawantinsuyu. The so-called confusion among early chroniclers between place (Cusco) and person (Cusco) may express, therefore, something much more profound: Andean notions of place and person. More importantly, the litter with the Inka in the center constitutes a composition that comes very close to the "geographical" representation of Tawantinsuyu as depicted in the *Nueva coronica* (Guaman Poma de Ayala 1614: 42; fig. 27) and the 1590 Murúa folio (63v), also both done by Guaman Poma (fig. 28). In both images, the topography of Tawantinsuyu is indicated by a mountainous landscape. Superimposed upon this landscape are five stylized cities arranged in a quincunx configuration. The center in each is identified as Cusco and in the 1590 Murúa illustration the four other cities are identified by the names of the four suyu. A similar quincunx is formed by the five figures in the illustration of the litter, essentially replicating this spatial concept of Tawantinsuyu in a personified form.

The quincunx form is, as already mentioned, a common composition, one that is found on both colonial decorated queros and Inka and colonial

FIG. 27 Mapa del Mundo, Guaman Poma de Ayala, ink on paper, *Nueva corónica y buen gobierno*, The Royal Library, Copenhagen, p. 42, 1614

FIG. 28 Schematic representation of Cusco and the four suyus, colorwash on paper, in Martín de Murúa's *Historia del origen y genealogía real de los reyes del, Piru*, folio 63v, private collection, Dublin, 1590–1605

The Composition of Inka Artistic Expression and Power   291

textiles and ceramics (fig. 29). Its personification in the illustration of the Inka's litter suggests that the graphic two-dimensional design of a tocapu could be conceived of as something three-dimensional and kinetic, an embodied tocapu moving across the very land that it represented socially, culturally, and politically. It could be understood as a geo-numerical sign of the place of power. That is, one sees and experiences as a numerical composition the single entity of the Sapa Inka (Sapa = unique) centering the spatially equidistant but separate entities of Tawantinsuyu (four suyu). What is important here is that place is not represented by topographical features. The geography of Inka myth and history is figured by compositions, embodied and graphic, that are conceptually perceived in relation to social, political, and mythical properties and not mimetic ones.

It might be suggested, therefore, that a different configuration of a tocapu or combinations of tocapus might have represented different concepts of Tawantinsuyu. For example, the mythic place of origin of the Inka is depicted by Pachacuti Yamqui as three hierarchically arranged tocapus (fig. 30). Drawn on a page of paper, they are numerically ordered "the first *Tampottocco*; the second *Marasttoco*, and the third *Suticttoco*." The tocapu of Tampottocco is placed in the center and slightly higher on the page, above the two other tocapus, visualizing its numerical priority. The second tocapu, Marasttoco, is to the right (viewer's left) and the third, Suticttoco, is to the left. The composition thereby spatializes the hierarchy in Andean terms of center right and left, a hierarchy already established in the temporal narrative.[39] The central design is also based upon a quincunx configuration. The center of the tocapu is marked by a circle, with four other circles establishing the four quadrants. These elements are then bounded by a central diamond and three concentric framing rectangles. What is significant, I believe, is that the tocapus are understood to represent place within a mythohistoric narrative context. And although these tocapus are not associated with a textile or any Inka object, it seems very likely that they functioned in some similar capacity as the señales de armas de provincias of the uncu in the Spanish royal collection discussed above. Pachacuti Yamqui may, in fact, have understood that the tocapus he used to demarcate Tampottocco, and the others, were akin to Spanish heraldic imagery. In several Quechua passages in his *Relación*, he employs the noun *unancha* and the verb *unanchani*, the significance of which has been well analyzed by Regina Harrison (1989: 78–81). On one occasion, he uses it specifically to identify the Inka standard, *cacapc unanca*, which glosses as *insignias reales* (Pachacuti Yamqui 1993: 218, 18v; 242, 30v; 244, 31v; 268, 43v). On another, he mentions the return of curacas to their territories after meeting in Cusco with raised banners (*unanchas enarboladas*)

FIG. 29 Detail of an urpu with a set of repeated quincunx forms placed within a vertical band, Museum of the American Indian, Washington D.C., formerly at the Heye Foundation, N.Y., ca. 1500

(ibid.: 247, 33r). *Unanchani* as a verb means "to make signs" (*hazer señales*) and *unancha* is any kind of sign, standard, insignia, or coat-of-arms (*qualquier señal, estandarte, ynsignia, escudo de armas*) (González Holguín 1608: 355).

More importantly, perhaps, the tocapu as a signifying device is not intrinsically bound to any specific medium, as is, for example, the knotted-string recording device (*khipu*), which can only seemingly find expression through constituent elements that are indivisible. The tocapu is multivalent and multimedia, able to cross the cultural border between Inka media and Spanish media. At the same time, representation of Inka objects (uncus, *masciapacha*, clubs, bows and arrows) and not tocapu motifs were used in the formation of heraldic devices granted to Andean nobility almost from the very beginning of the colonial period. That is, there is not a precise equivalency between the forms of Andean tocapu designs and European heraldry. Rather, the congregation of Andean objects within the field of European heraldry seems to hearken to the compositionality of Andean objects as outlined above.

Nonetheless, from other colonial documents, we can surmise that the tocapu represented various categories of information in different media, some traditional and some new, as demonstrated by Pachacuti Yamqui. For example, textiles probably with tocapu or some form of unancha, were conceived as a sort of map, either Pre-Hispanic or colonial. In 1630, Don Fernando Ayra de Arritu, lord (*cacique principal*) and governor of Copotá presented a series of documents of merit in order to achieve rights and privileges based upon his person as a descendent of the ancient curacas of the area. In the second question put to the witnesses concerning his great-great-grandfather, who welcomed the Inka into the area, each was asked if "because of the quality of the lands that he [the Inka] gave him a map woven in cumbi cloth [which] in the native language they called capatira."[40] And each native witness testified that indeed the area had been conquered by "el Ynga Yupanqui of the four provincias of Collasuyu, Antisuyu, Condesuyu and Chinchaysuyu [and] that the said ynga gave him as a sign of it [the quality of the lands] a map woven of cumbi cloth that the Indians call capatira."[41]

The word for the map (*carpatira*) may be a neologism, indicating some specific type of cumbi cloth (*carpa*)[42] on which territory (*tierra/tira*)

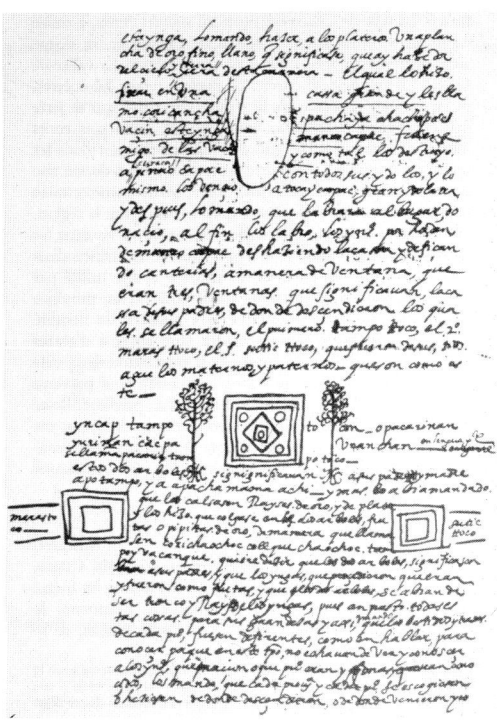

FIG. 30 Pen and ink drawing of the caves of origins of the Inkas, Joan de Santa Cruz Pachacuti Yamqui, *Relación de antigüedades*, Madrid, Biblioteca Nacional, folio 8v, 1613

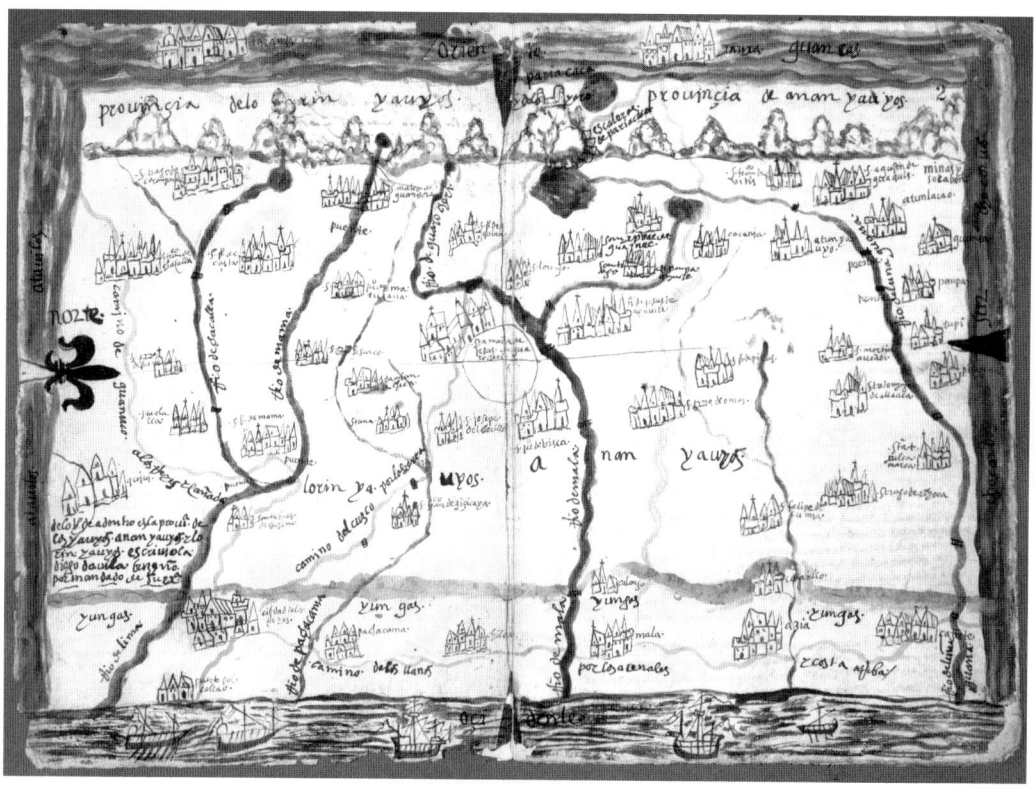

FIG. 31 Map of Huarochiri, ink and color wash on paper, in Diego Dávila Brizeño's *Descripción y relación de la provincia de los Yauyos toda, Anan Yauyos, y Lorin Yauyos*, Real Academia de la Historia, Madrid

was represented. There is no reason, however, to believe that such a cloth pictorially depicted the topography of the lands in either an Albertian or Euclidian manner. Rather, if such a "map" were given by Inka Yupanqui to the great-great-grandfather of Don Fernando, it was within the Inka design of cumbi cloth, upon which political and social topography was represented within the norms of Inka design and most probably within a pattern of tocapus in which there would have been no distinction between ground and figure.

What then is interesting in regard to the images from both the manuscripts of Murúa and Guaman Poma is that one can posit that the composition of topographic elements is taken from an Andean source, probably based on the conventions of "Andean maps" as mentioned or alluded to in Spanish documents, and some form of tocapu. They are placed, however, within a landscape as depicted from a European point of view. That is, not only is the position taken from a bird's-eye point of view, but it is also imagined from the perspective of looking from west to east with the east at the top of the page, or from the ocean toward the mountains. This is a consistent directional orientation in European maps and drawings of Peru and Lima from the sixteenth century, with which Guaman Poma was probably familiar (fig. 31). Hence, what one sees is a synthesis of two cartographic systems that conveys both an Andean conceptual space and a European sense of topography. Here, I think, the tocapu as an expression of the social topography has been translated into a pictorial form without ever losing its compositional/signifying structure, almost as if it were merely superimposed onto the European schema. That is, Murúa's colonial images, executed by Guaman Poma, give a pictorial figural form to one of the fields of expression depicted by tocapu.

Conclusion

Martín de Murúa's and Guaman Poma de Ayala's colonial images give a figural form to the Inka expression of a sociopolitical geography, an expressive system that was based on compositions of a variety of possible relationships. None of these relationships, as far as we know, was conveyed through a pictorial narrative in any Inka medium. Rather, the sociopolitical relationships of Tawantinsuyu were manifested by material objects and their designs, as put together in a compositional relationship, and understood through context, most often centered on the human body within ritual. The tocapu, as one identified form of Inka sociopolitical expression, therefore does not exist as a discrete entity. This is different from the most famous imperial Inka form of representing (recording) information, the khipu. The khipu is simultaneously the object and the sign of Inka sociopolitical accountability, and it is indivisible as far as we know. That is, whereas the information of khipu may be transferred to another medium, oral narrative, or written alphabetic form, the component elements, string and knot, seem integral to each other and are not transferred to another medium. The tocapu, however, is a graphic sign that only comes into being within a greater field of meaning, as it must be placed onto or among other things and into a field of relations, often with other tocapu. As such, the tocapu also partakes in this expanded meaning of compositionality. It is even amenable to being transformed into the drawings of Murúa and Guaman Poma, where it is double languaged in the sense of hybridization as outlined by Mikhail Bakhtin (1981: 356–360), in which one set of forms is being represented by another set that does the actual representing. Here one sees the form of tocapu as represented by the European form of cartography. It seems probable that the commensurability is based upon being associated with conveying information about geography and hence capable of simultaneously conveying very different concepts about it.

It is not only this form of relationship that Avila called upon in his sermon of 1648, but also the fact that queros and aquillas, as Andean things, had a pivotal place expressing materially, ritually, and visibly Inka culture in various ways throughout Tawantinsuyu. Perhaps, even more importantly for Avila, these objects continued to play an important role in the artistic and ritual life of colonial Andeans, manifesting and affirming

FIG. 32 One of a pair of colonial queros on which are depicted a plowing scene in the lower register and an Inka warrior wearing a checkerboard uncu leading a jungle warrior as his prisoner, wood and *barniz de pasto/mopa-mopa*, Brooklyn Museum of Art, 42.149., 7 ½ x 6¼ in., late 17th or early 18th century

social relationships that had precedent in "el tiempo del Inka."[43] Moreover, the power of the Inka became, in the seventeenth and eighteenth centuries, a subject of pictorial representation on a variety of media, and, in particular, painted queros. The scene of the Inka battling with jungle foes (*chunchos*) is, for example, a very common theme on colonial queros (fig. 32). As in colonial heraldry granted to Andeans recognized by the crown, military paraphernalia, such as shields and helmets, also become pictorial motifs on colonial buildings, coats-of-arms (which were sculpted or painted on buildings), queros, and uncus in the colonial period. Inka figures on queros are depicted wearing uncus with checkerboard and tocapu designs in the context of warfare. This colonial iconography on queros, which is coupled with sets of tocapu, was rooted in the compositional relationship between queros/aquillas, uncus, and architecture. How such a relationship was constituted epistemologically is as yet unclear, but it borders on a kind of phenomenology in which the living world is constituted by natural things, cultural objects, creatures, and beings. The juxtaposition as physical relationship of contiguity not only expressed aspects of Inka power in Tawantinsuyu in a material fashion, but this composition was pictorialized in the colonial period just as that power became nothing more than a memory. The political rituals in which the exchange of queros and cumbi textiles marked the exercise of Inka power no longer took place, as that power now was only the subject of memory as marked by those very same objects.

Notes

1   There have been several recent and excellent studies of Inka art and architecture, especially by van de Guchte (n.d.), Paternosto (1996), and Niles (1999). Only van de Guchte addresses the fundamental issues presented by Inka art as an integrated system of representation that is constituent of Inka power. Most studies treat Inka art (textiles, sculpture, ceramics) and architecture as discrete spheres of inquiry. Tom Zuidema's important investigations have considered Inka art; however, his analytical emphasis has been on an interpretation through which other social phenomena can be read.

2   Kubler's argument about Inka art should be read within the larger debate concerning the nature of Inka society in the mid-twentieth century. The Inka became for some scholars the screen upon which were projected the defining twentieth-century political debates about socialism, either utopian or totalitarian. Kubler, of course, sided with the latter camp. But politics makes strange bedfellows and the cultural understanding of Pre-Columbian politics makes even stranger bedfellows. In fact, Kubler's comments were anticipated some forty years earlier by George Batailles. No one could think of a stranger bedfellow for Kubler, yet Bataille wrote in 1928 that

> Cuzco . . . was massive, of a heavy grandeur. . . . The architecture of the Temples which looked down upon the roofs was equally as bare; only the pediment was wholly covered with a plaque of hammered gold. To this gold we must add the brilliantly colored fabrics which clothed the rich and elegant, but nothing could quite dispel the impression of wild seediness and above all, of deadly uniformity. Everything was planned ahead in an airless existence. This organization is not to be confused with that of present-day communism, it was essentially different, since it was based on heredity and on Class hierarchy. Given these conditions, it is not surprising that Inka civilization is relatively dull.
>
> The Aztec people whose extremely powerful confederation had seized almost all present-day Mexico during the fifteenth century, was nonetheless the liveliest, the most seductive even in its mad violence, its trancelike development. (Georges Battaile 1986 [1928]: 3–5)

3   In an otherwise excellent critical reading of the sources on the Inka, Martti Pärssinen interprets the very few chronicles that mention wall paintings as evidence that "many of the important buildings of the Incas seem to have also been painted with narrative motives," and that the painted history boards mentioned by Sarmiento de Gamboa and Cristóbal de Molina were such that

"the method of how the paintings were used was similar to the Aztec system," based on pictorial-glyphic representation (Pärssinen 1992: 26–31). As I have argued elsewhere (Cummins 1994), a comparison of early Mexican and Peruvian chronicles suggests that the Inka and Aztec representational systems were quite different.

4   One need only think of the earthen walls of Chan-Chan, carefully molded in flat relief so that the painted repetitive figures and shapes are set into individual relief by the light and shadow cast by the sun, to understand that the articulated joins of Inka walls in Cusco participate in a pan-Andean (aesthetic?) understanding of a wall in relation to the sun.

This relationship is born out in Andean mythology as recorded in Huarochiri. In explaining the origins of Pariacaca's cult, the paramount divinity of the area, the narrator says:

> Pariacaca began to lay down the rules for his worship. His law was one and the same in all the villages: We are all of one birth [i.e., ayllu].
>
> They say he gave a command to one [particular person in each village]: "Once every year you are to hold a paschal celebration every year celebrating the customs I have established." He said "As for their title of these people they will be called hucasa or huacsa." The huasca will dance three times each year brining coca in an enormous leather bag.
>
> To first become a huacsa, people in fact perform a certain ritual. It is like this: a man of the Caca Sica ayllu functions as the officiant for these ceremonies. From early times these officiants were only one or two people, and, as for their title it was yanca [priest entitled by heredity]. The same title is used in all the villages. This man observes the course of the sun [in the margin in Spanish (esta es la sombra que va haziendo la pared); pirca is the word used in Quechua] from a wall in perfect alignment. When the rays of the sun touch this wall he proclaimed to the people,
>
> "Now we must go." (Anonymous ca. 1607: 71–72)

One of the critical elements here is the constant state of change as light moves through the course of the sun. There is no tangible mimetic sense of surrounding such images found for the Aztec in their personifications of the sun. Of course, there are Inka images of sun, but such images were not significant to this iconography. Rather it is in the shifting state of an essential element (brilliance and shadow) as marked through a wall that one sees the divine command. Here the animate aspect of the sun as both brilliance and shadow is similar to the Nahua concept of *tonalli* (Russo 2002: 232–233).

The social labor embedded literally in walls is well documented by Urton (1988) for the *reducción* of Pacaritambo, but the Pre-Columbian precedent can be seen in the segmental construction of the Moche Huaca el Sol and the retaining walls of the Huari site of Pikillaqta.

5   Andean things are in a real sense different from European things. They are not inert but are embued with a discrete presence and character, both of which are recognized by various qualities, such as *munay munaylla* (*cosa linda* or beautiful thing) (González Holguín 1989: 250). There is no distinction between things and objects, in which an object when it ceases to be functional becomes a thing (see Brown 2001: 4). Thus, I use "thing" and "object" in this essay as interchangeable terms to describe the material world of the Inka.

6   Most Inka lithic sculpture, other than bowls and plates carved into various animal forms, seems to be site specific, carved into the living rock and often at the openings into the earth or other special places in the landscape. See van de Guchte (n.d.) for the most detailed and interpretive analysis of Inka stone sculpture.

7   Frank Salomon (2001) has approached this issue through Nelson Goodman in a provocative and original interpretation of contemporary Andean signs.

8   Except for the words Inka and Tawantinsuyu, I have spelled the Quechua words according to how they most often appear in colonial documents so as to avoid any confusion between their appearance in citations and their use in the essay's text.

9   "Y Luego tras esto todo se acaba, nada permanece. Que es de los Ingas antiguamente tan temidos? Que es de su plata, y oro? Sus vestidos de cumbe real? *Sus vasos de beuer?* Sus chacras? Sus palacios? Sus mujeres? Ya no sabemos ni aun sus nombres."

10 Avila certainly understood the importance of objects as elements in the construction of memory within the European sense of artificial memory and the importance of artificial memory in the evangelization of the Americas. The 1647 inventory of Francisco de Avila's library lists among its content Diego Valades's *Rhetorica christani ad concionandi et orandi usam, ex Indorum maxime,* the most extensive sixteenth-century treatise on artificial memory written by a Spanish author and to which he makes reference in his Latin introduction to the sermons. Valades's book was published in Perugia in 1587 and demonstrates the relationship between images, sermons, and memory in the evangelization of New Spain. For the contents of Avila's library and citation of Valades see Hampe Martínez (1996: 74, 162).

11 The Inka were not the first Andean culture to produce highly charged symbolic objects in different materials. For example, Chimú and Sicán funerary vessels of the same form and size are found in both

ceramic and metal. It is not simply that one copies the other, according to a hierarchy of values, but that they also participate in this hierarchy of value through their form in a shared field of symbolic value. For the Sicán material, see Shimada 1998.

12 "Tuvieron . . . los vasos para bever todos hermanos, de dos en dos: o sean grandes o chicos, han de ser de un tamaño, de una misma hechura, de un mismo metal, de oro o plata, o de madera. Y esto hazian por que huviese igualdad en lo que beviesen" (Garcilaso de la Vega 1943 [1616–17]: bk. 6, chap. 22, 53).

13 Sebastián de Covarrubias (1998 [1611]: 531) first defines *hermanos* as siblings, but immediately goes on to write that "Ermanos suelen lamarse los que están aliados o confederados," which could be understood as Garcilaso de la Vega's use of the term to describe the condition of being paired.

14 This information is copied almost verbatim by Bernabé Cobo (1956 [1653]: bk. 12, chap. 30, 125; see also Diez de San Miguel 1567: 71).

15 Pedro Pizarro (1917 [1571]: 74) mentions a type of drinking vessel that he found in caves just outside Cusco. These were a combination of gold and ceramic that, according to him, were skillfully made. None of these kinds of vessels to my knowledge have survived.

16 "El traje de las indias principales es también el que muestra la pintura. Estas traen ahora camisa de lienzo y faldellín y encima, ceñida al cuerpo, una como tunicela sin mangas la cual se llama azú; encima aquella manta sobre los hombros que se llama llíquica y sobre la cabeza otra manta pequeñita que se llama llanaca. Aquel vaso que tiene en la mano se llama cuero (quero), con que dan a beber la chicha a los indios. Y ellas en los bailes usan de aquel tamborino, traen ojotoso sandalias en los pies y de ordenario" (Ocaña 1969 [1599–1606]: 259).

17 It is important to remember the high value that cloth held for Europeans, who therefore recognized its value in Tawantinsuyu as something commensurable to their sense of worth. The cloth-merchant guilds were extremely powerful throughout Europe. Columbus, himself, came from such a family. Moreover, if one looks at European wills in the Viceroyalty of Peru, objects of clothing are ubiquitous and they are among the most important items listed.

18 The compositionality of Inka objects as creating a field of meaning may echo in some fashion the pan-Andean topos of the revolt of objects found both in Andean iconography and mythology; see Quilter (1990).

19 There may be a corollary to this aggregation of objects to expand and shift meaning in Quechua syntax, which with infixes, prefixes, suffixes to a word constantly alters meaning. See also Mannheim (1998) for a discussion of the formal relationship between textile pattern and song pattern.

20   For a detailed analysis of how such pacchas were made and used see Stone-Miller 2006.

21   "El dicho Topa Ynga, oyo decir este testigo [Alonso Poma Guala], que había dado al dicho su bisagüelo [*sic*] unas camisas y mantas galanas *y unos vasos que bebiese, que llaman entre ellos aquillas*" (Francisco de Toledo 1882 [1570]: 205–206).

22   As far as I am aware, only queros have been recovered from Capahucha burials, whereas cumbi textiles of very high quality have been placed with the sacrificed. This is to say, we do not have a refined understanding of the differences of symbolic value between objects of the same type (queros and aquillas) and objects of a different type (textiles).

23   "Si l'on ne savait qu'il s'agit d'une céramique précolombienne, on se croirait en présence d'un de ces décors à intentions héraldiques dans lesquels les ornemanistes de la Renaissance accompagnaient d'atibuts de fantaisie la pièce principale d'un blason" (Lejeal 1905: 82). The urpu was one of three collected by Count Eugène de Sartiges in the first half of the nineteenth century at the south end of Lake Titicaca at the "hacienda de Cumana" (ibid.: 81).

24   I would like to thank Bill Hanks for discussing compositionality with me as it pertains to linguistics. As usual his comments have been extremely insightful and helpful. By invoking compositionality, I do not want to imply that linguistic analytic terms can be employed in some metaphoric way to describe visual phenomena. Rather, there can be parallel processes and the insights of linguistic analysis can inform visual analysis. This does not mean, however, that the two are always or necessarily commensurable; see Salomon (2001).

25   Abstraction in Andean Pre-Columbian art tends toward a more analytic set of forms that relate to some greater whole and that therefore might have had a synecdochtic role. This certainly seems to be the case for Huari textiles and may be true for Inka tocapu as well.

26   Zuidema (1982: 447–449) has already suggested that uncus such as the Dumbarton Oaks example that have an overall pattern of tocapu may reflect the geographic distribution of huacas and Andean social groups and that they signified within a system that included ceques and quipus.

27   This would account for the numerous references in the chronicles to maps used by the Inka, while there are no colonial maps with strikingly indigenous components. This is very different from Mexico, where many of the maps produced for the *Relaciones Geográficas* combine indigenous and Spanish motifs (see Mundy 1996: 91–133). In Peru, there are in general very few colonial maps and none indicate an indigenous graphic system. For example, the map accompanying Diego Davila Brizeño's 1586 *Descripción y relación de la provincia de los Yauyos toda, Anan Yauyos*

y Lorin Yauyos (fig. 31), was created completely within the cartographic tradition of Spain, even including the social geography of hanan and hurin. Sarmiento de Gamboa (1988 [1572]: 49, 177) twice mentions that Pachacuti Inka Yupanqui collected Inka history and had it recorded on painted boards that were kept in Cusco in a temple. The veracity of Sarmiento's account, however, is in doubt as the translator from Quechua to Spanish, Gonzalo Gómez Jiménez, later noted that information and answers were falsified to the needs of Sarmiento. Moreover, if such boards did exist, they were probably painted with tocapu designs (see Cummins [1994, 2002]).

28 "Dos borlas de lana, la una encarnada y la otra amarilla, que le embió el dicho Vi-Rey don Francisco de Toeldo, que dize que era la ynsignia con que se coronaban los yngas y la una es la con que se coronó Guaynacar [sic] y la otra Atagualpa; metida en una cestilla de paja y lana; son de valor" (Sánchez Cantón 1949 [1599]: 333). The *borla*, or *mascapaycha*, of Atahualpa was seized by Miguel de Este at Cajamarca. How it came into Toledo's possession, enabling him to send it to the royal collection along with that of Huaynacapac's mascapaycha, is unclear. It may be that there were several sets of mascapaycha of which some were kept in Cusco and never worn. González Holguín (1608: 232) gives two definitions for mascapaycha: "borla que era insignia Real, o corona del Rey." According to Sarmiento de Gamboa (1988 [1572]: 65) the panacas, in this case that of Sinchi Roca, were charged with "saber y sustentar las *cosas* y memorias" of the Sapa Inka.

29 Otra camisa de yndios que dicen de cumbi [*sic*] texida de diversos colores y figuras, las quales son señales de armas de provincias que el ynga poseya, por donde las conocía, está apolillada y agugerada y no es de valor (Sánchez Cantón 1949 [1599]: 334).

30 David Rojas y Silvá (1981) has already suggested that tocapu functioned as a kind of coat-of-arms, on the basis of other evidence.

31 The geopolitical dimension implied by the Spanish term *provincias* is unclear in relation to how Tawantinsuyu was organized. I have used the category guamaní as discussed by Pärssinen (1992: 269–272) to translate *provincias*; however, the tocapus may have signified larger or smaller political territories. Moreover, tocapus were used contextually so that the units that they referenced would change either in quality or quantity.

32 The most recent survey of chullpa architectural form (Isbell 1997) does not pay any real heed as to how these buildings may have appeared. We therefore do not have an adequate understanding of chullpas in Tawantinsuyu.

33 In a 1598 will, Curaca Diego Collin left his son a house (casa) "que se llama cuscohuasi" (Collins n.d.: fol. 31v). Clearly this is not a chullpa,

but the name of the structure, *cuscohuasi* (Cusco house), implies that the structure marked some form of sociopolitical relationship between the Inka and the local community.

34 There is the possibility that women were buried/sacrificed wearing uncus. In the museum collection at Basel, a mummy dressed in a checkerboard tunic was x-rayed, revealing that the body was possibly that of a young woman. This, however, does not alter the gender association of the uncu.

35 Francisco Xérez (1534) is the first to describe the Inka army of Atahaulpa as dressed in tunics with a checkerboard design. Cristóbal de Albornóz (1584) says that checkerboard tunics were brought out during ritual ceremonies when past Inka military victories were recounted in song. Called *pilpinto* (butterfly) today, textiles with this design are still kept in communities and are associated with the ancestors (Arze and Medinaceli 1991). The military association of this style of uncu carried through into colonial images in both Andean and Spanish media. For example the coat-of-arms granted to Felipe Guacar Paucar in 1564 includes in the upper-left quarter an uncu with a checkerboard design surrounded by three severed heads and a stone mace (Cummins 1998: 113, fig. 13).

36 The Inka aesthetic concern for the relationship between the human body and an object is most immediately apparent in the design of the urpu or aryballoid-shaped vessel used to transport *aqha*. The design usually is two-sided, with the side that rests on the back, when carried normally, a single field of color whereas the other part, that would be more fully seen, is decorated with one of a number of different patterns, some of which derive from textiles.

37 Anonymous (1534: 34–35) actually calls Huascar Cusco and not Atahualpa: "Then we learned how the cacique (Atahualpa) had captured another ruler called 'El Cuzco' [Huascar] who was a greater leader than himself."

38 "Siempre que el inga salia lo levaban . . . en andas muy ricas y bien aderzadas . . . llevaban siempre las andas de estos reyes quarto señores de los mas principales q en su consejo tenia como entre nosotros duques o marquezes que para el efecto estaban dedicadaos de los quarto suyos que son las quarto provincias de collasuyu y chinchasuyu, contesuyu, y antesuyu los quales residen siempre con el Inca en su palacio" (Murúa n.d.a [1590]: 55r).

39 For an analysis of the symbolic significance of center, right, and left as deployed in colonial Andean compositions see Adorno (1986).

40 "De la calidad de la tierras q le dio un mapa tegido en rropa de cumbi en la lengua de los yndios llaman carpatira" (Audiencia de Charcas n.d.: folio 7r).

41 "El Ynga Yupanqui de las quarto provincias de collasuyu, antesuyu, condesuyu y chinchaysuyu q el dicho ynga le dio en premio dello un mapa tegido en la ropa de cumbe q los yndios la llaman carpatria" (ibid.: 16v).

42 *Carpa* means "carp," but the word may come from *capa*, which Covarrubias (1998 [1611]: 293) defines, in a rather long entry, as "vestidura que se pone todas las demas."

43 See Cummins (1998) for a discussion of and references to the colonial institution and concept of the *El Tiempo del Inca* as manifested in images and objects.

References cited

ABERCROMBIE, THOMAS

1998 *Pathways of Memory and Power: Ethnography and History among an Andean People.* University of Wisconsin Press, Madison.

ADORNO, ROLENA

1986 *Guaman Poma: Writing and Resistance in colonial Peru.* The University of Texas Press, Austin.

ALBORNÓZ, CRISTÓBAL DE

1989 [ca.1584] Instrucción para descubrir todas las huacas del Piru y sus camayos y haziendas. In *Fábulas y mitos de los incas* (Henrique Urbano and Pierre Duviols, eds.): 135–198. Crónicas de las América 48. Historia 16, Madrid.

ANONYMOUS (MENA, CRISTÓBAL DE?)

1929 [1534] *Conquest of Peru: As Recorded by a Member of the Pizarro Expedition* (J. Sinclair trans.). New York Public Library, New York.

ANONYMOUS

1920 [ca. 1580] Relación del origen y gobierno que los Ingas tuvierion. In *Informaciones sobre el antiguo Perú (crónicas de 1533 a 1575): Anotaciones y concordancias con las crónicas de Indias* (Horacio H. Urteaga, ed.): vol. 3, 55–86. Colección de Libros y documentos referentes a la historia del Perú. 2nd series. Sanmartí y ca, Lima.

ANONYMOUS

1991 [ca. 1607] *The Huarochirí Manuscript: A Testament of Ancient and colonial Andean Religion* (Frank Salomon and George L. Urioste, trans.). University of Texas Press, Austin.

ARZE, SILVIA, AND XIMENA MEDINACELI

1991 *Imagenes y presagios el escudo de los Ayaviri, Mallkus de Charcas.* HISPOL, La Paz.

AUDIENCIA DE CHARCAS

n.d. Charcas 56, "Ynformación de Don Fernando Ayra de Arritu, Cacique principal y Gobernador de Copoatá sobre su nobleza," 1634–1639, folios 6r–71v. Archivo General de las Indias, Seville, Spain.

AVILA, FRANCISO DE

1648 *Tratado de los Evangelios que nuestra Madre la iglesia propone en todo el año desde la primera domínica de adviento hasta la última missa de Difuntos, Santos de España y añadidas en el nuevo rezado.* . . . 2 vols. Jerónimo de Contreras, Lima.

BAKHTIN, MIKHAIL M.

1981   *The Dialogic Imagination: Four Essays*. University of Texas Press, Austin.

BARTHEL, THOMAS

1971   Viracochas Prunkgewand (Tokapu-Studien). *Tribus* 20: 63–124.

BATAILLE, GEORGES

1928   Extinct America (A. Michelson, trans.). *October* 36 (Spring 1986): 3–9.

BROWN, BILL

2001   Thing Theory. *Critical Inquiry* 27 (1): 1–23.

CASTRO, CRISTÓBAL, AND DIEGO ORTEGA MOREJÓN

1936 [1558]   Relación y declaración del modo que este valle de Chincha y sus comarcanos se governavan antes que oviese yngas y después q los hobo hasta q los (cristian)os entraron en esta tierra. In *Quellen zur Kulturgeschichte des präkolumbischen Amerika* (Hermann Trimborn ed.): 217–262. Strecker und Schröder, Stuttgart.

CIEZA DE LEÓN, PEDRO DE

1984 [1553]   *Crónica del Perú: Primera parte*. Pontificia Universidad Católica del Perú, Lima.

COBO, BERNABÉ

1956 [1653]   *Historia del Nuevo Mundo*. In *Obras*. Biblioteca de Autores Españoles 91–92. Atlas, Madrid.

COLLIN, DIEGO

n.d.   Testamento de Diego Collin, en caja 7 III–22 1657: Autos de los Indios de Panzaleo contra el Colegio de la Compañía de Jesús, fol. 31v. Archivo Histórico Nacional, Quito, Ecuador, 1598.

CONKLIN, WILLIAM

1986   The Mythic Geometry of the Ancient Southern Sierra. In *The Junius B. Bird Conference on Andean Textiles* (Ann Pollard Rowe, ed.): 123–135. The Textile Museum, Washington D.C.

COVARRUBIAS Y OROZCO, SEBASTÍAN DE

1998 [1611]   *Tesoro de la Lengua Castellana o Española*. Editorial Alta Fulla, Barcelona.

CUMMINS, THOMAS B. F.

1994   Representation in the 16th Century and the colonial Image of the Inca. In *Writing Without Words: Alternative Literacies in Mesoamerica and the Andes* (Walter D. Mignolo and Elizabeth Hill Boone, eds.): 189–219. Duke University Press, Durham, N.C.

All-t'oqapu Inka tunic, PC.B.518. Camelid fiber and cotton. H. 91 cm; W. 76 cm.
© Dumbarton Oaks, Pre-Columbian Collection, Washington, D.C.

1998 Let Me See! Reading Is for Them: colonial Andean Images and Objects "como es costumbre tener los caciques Señores." In *Native Traditions in the Postconquest World* (Elizabeth Hill Boone and Tom Cummins, eds.): 91–148. Dumbarton Oaks Research Library and Collection, Washington D.C.

2002 *Toasts with the Inca: Andean Abstraction and Colonial Images on Kero Vessels*. University of Michigan Press, Ann Arbor.

DAVILA BRIZEÑO, DIEGO

1956 [1586] *Descripción y Relación de la Provincia de Los Yauyos Toda, Anan Yauyos y Lorin Yauyos*. Biblioteca de Autores Españoles 183. Atlas, Madrid.

DIEZ DE SAN MIGUEL, GARCI

1964 [1567] *Visita hecha a la provincia de Chucuito*. Casa de Cultura, Lima.

DUVIOLS, PIERRE

1973 Huari y Llacuaz: Agricultores y pastores: Un dualismo prehispanico de oposición y complementaridad. *Revista de Museo Nacional* 34: 153–191.

ESCOARI DE QUEREJAZU, LAURA

1982 La heráldica incaica y los caciques Cusicanqui de Pacajes. *Arte y arqueología* 56: 163–166.

FALCÓN, FRANCISCO

1918 [1567] *Representación hecha por el licenciado Falcón en concilio provincial sobre los daños y molestias a que se hacen a los indios*. Colección de libros y documentos referentes a la historia del Perú 11. 1st series.

GARCILASO DE LA VEGA, EL INCA

1943 [1616–17] *Comentarios reales de los Incas*. Emece Editores SA., Buenos Aires.

GISBERT, TERESA, J. C. JEMIO, R. MONTERO, E. SALINAS, AND M. SOLEDAD QUIROGA

1996 Los chullpares del Río Lauca y el Parque Sajama. *Revista de la Academia Nacional de Ciencias de Bolivia* 70. Amigos del Libro, La Paz, Bolivia.

GONZÁLEZ HOLGUÍN, DIEGO

1989 [1608] *Vocabulario de la lengua general de todo el Perú llamada lengua Qquichua o del Inca*. Universidad Nacional Mayor de San Marcos, Lima.

GUAMAN POMA DE AYALA, FELIPE

1987 [1614] *Nueva corónica y buen gobierno* (John Murra, Rolena Adorno, and Jorge L. Urioste, eds.). Historia 16, Madrid.

HAMPE MARTÍNEZ, TEODORO
    1996 *Cultura barroca y extirpación de idolatrías: La biblioteca de Francisco de Avila—1648.* Centro de Estudios Andinos. Bartolomé de las Casas, Cusco.

HOUSTON, STEPHEN D., AND TOM CUMMINS
    2005 Body, Presence, and Space in Andean and Mesoamerican Rulership. In *Palaces of the Ancient New World: Form, Function, and Meaning* (Susan Toby Evans and Joanne Pillsbury, eds.): 359–398. Dumbarton Oaks Research Library and Collection, Washington D.C.

ISBELL, WILLIAM
    1997 *Mummies and Mortuary Monuments: A Postprocessual Prehistory of Central Andean Social Organization.* University of Texas Press, Austin.

KUBLER, GEORGE
    1975 *The Art and Architecture of Ancient America: The Mexican, Maya, and Andean Peoples.* 2nd ed. Penguin Books, Baltimore, Md.

LEJEAL, LÉON
    1905 La Collection de M. de Sartiges et les "Aryballes" péruviens du Musée ethnographique du Trocadéro. *International Congress of Americanists: Thirteenth Session Held in New York in 1902*: 75–83. Eschenbach Printing Company, Easton, Pa.

MANNHEIM, BRUCE
    1998 A Nation Surrounded. In *Native Traditions in the Postconquest World* (Elizabeth Hill Boone and Tom Cummins, eds.): 383–420. Dumbarton Oaks Research Library and Collection, Washington D.C.

MORRIS, CRAIG
    1982 The Infrastructure of Inka Control in the Peruvian Central Highlands. In *The Inca and Aztec States 1400–1800: Anthropology and History* (George A. Collier, Renato I. Rosaldo, and John D. Wirth, eds.): 153–172. Academic Press, New York and London.

MUNDY, BARBARA
    1996 *The Mapping of New Spain.* University of Chicago Press, Chicago.

MURRA, JOHN
    1962 Cloth and Its Function in the Inca State. *American Anthropologist* 64: 710–728.
    1975 La función de tejido en varios contextos sociales y políticos. In *Formaciones económicas y políticas del mundo andino*: 145–170. Instituto de Estudios Peruanas, Lima.

MURÚA, MARTÍN DE
    n.d.a   Historia del origen y genealogía real de los reyes del Piru: De sus hechos, costumbres, trajes, maneras de gobierno. Private collection, Ireland, 1590.

    n.d.b [1611–13]   Historia general del Perú. Ms. Ludwig 13. J. Paul Getty Museum, Los Angeles.

NILES, SUSAN
    1999   *The Shape of Inca History: Narrative and Architecture in an Andean Empire.* University of Iowa Press, Iowa City.

OCAÑA, DIEGO DE
    1969 [1599–1606]   *Un viaje fascinante por la América Hispana del siglo XVI, 1599–1606.* Studium, Madrid.

PÄRSSINEN, MARTTI
    1992   *Tawantinsuyu: The Inca State and Its Political Organization.* Studia Historica, 43. SHS, Helsinki.

PATERNOSTO, CÉSAR
    1996   *The Stone and the Thread: Andean Roots of Abstract Art* (Esther Allen, trans.). University of Texas Press, Austin.

PEASE, FRANKLIN G. Y.
    1995   *Las crónicas y los Andes.* Pontificia Universidad Católica del Perú and Fondo de Cultura Económica, S.A. de C.V., Lima.

PIERCE, C. S.
    1955   Logic as Semiotic: A Theory of Signs. In *Philosophical Writings of Pierce* (Justus Buchler, ed.): 98–119. Dover Publications, New York.

PIZARRO, PEDRO
    1917 [1571]   *Relación del descubrimiento y conquista de los reinos del Perú.* Colección de Libros Referentes a la Historia del Perú 6. 1st series. Sanmartí y ca., Lima.

PLATT, TRISTAN
    1978   Symétries en miroir: Le concept de yanantin chez les Macha de Bolivie. *Annales économies, sociétés, civilisations* 33 (5–6): 1081–1107.

QUILTER, JEFFREY
    1990   The Moche Revolt of the Objects. *Latin American Antiquity* 1 (1): 42–65.

REINHARD, JOHAN
    n.d.   Sacred Mountains, Human Sacrifices, and Pilgrimages Among the Inca. Paper presented at Pilgrimage and Ritual Landscape in Pre-Columbian America, Dumbarton Oaks, 7–8 October, 2000.

ROJAS Y SILVÁ, DAVID
    1981 Los Tocapu: Un progama de interpretación. *Arte y arqueología* 7: 119–132.

RUSSO, ALESSANDRA
    2002 Plumes of Sacrifice: Transformation in Sixteenth-Century Mexican Feather Art. *RES* 42: 226–250.

SALOMON, FRANK
    1991 Introduction. In *The Huarochirí Manuscript: A Testament of Ancient and colonial Religion* (Frank Salomon and George L. Urioste, trans. and eds.): 1–38. University of Texas Press, Austin.
    2001 How an Andean "Writing Without Words" Works. *Current Anthropology* 42 (1): 1–27.

SÁNCHEZ CANTÓN, F. J. (ED.)
    1949 [1599] Inventarios reales bienes muebles que pertenecieron a Felipe II. In *Archivo Documental Español*. 2 vols. Real Academia de la Historia, Cusco.

SANTA CRUZ PACHACUTI YAMQUI SALCAMAYGUA, JOAN DE
    1993 [ca. 1613] *Relación de antiqüedadades deste reyno del Perú.* Institut Français D'Etudes Andines, Centro de Estudios Regionales Andinos "Bartolomé de Las Casas," Cusco.

SANTILLÁN, FRANCISCO DE
    1950 [1563] Relación del origen, descendencia, política y gobierno de los Incas. In *Tres relaciones de antigüedades peruanas* (Marcos Jimenéz de la Espada, ed.): 33–133. Editorial Guarania, Asunción del Paraguay.

SARMIENTO DE GAMBOA, PEDRO
    1988 [1572] *Historia de los Incas.* Biblioteca Viajeros Hispánicos, Madrid.

SAWYER, ALAN
    1963 Tiahuanco Tapestry Design. *Textile Museum Journal* 1 (2): 27–38.

SHERBONDY, JEANETTE
    1982 El regadio, los lagos y los mitos de origen. *Allpanchis* 17 (20): 3–53.

SQUIER, E. GEORGE
    1877 *Peru; Incidents of Travel and Exploration in the Land of the Incas.* Macmillan and Co., London.

STONE-MILLER, REBECCA
    2006 Mimesis as Participation: Imagery, Style, and Function of the Michael C. Carlos Museum *Paccha*, an Inka Ritual Watering Device. In *Kay Pacha: Cultivating Earth and Water in the Andes*: 215–224. BAR International Series 1478. Archaeopress, Oxford.

TOLEDO, FRANCISCO DE
  1882 [1570]   Informaciones acerca del señorío y gobierno de los Incas. *Colección de libros españoles raros o curiosos* 16: 179–259.

URTON, GARY
  1988   La arquitectura pública como texto social: La historia de un muro de adobe en Pacariqtambo, Perú (1915–1985). *Revista andina* 6 (1): 225–263.

VAN DE GUCHTE, MAARTEN
  n.d.   Carving the World: Monumental Sculpture and Landscape. Ph.D. dissertation, Department of Anthropology, University of Illinois at Urbana-Champaign, 1990.

XÉREZ, FRANCISCO
  1917 [1534]   *Verdadera relación de la conquista del Perú y provincia del Cuzco...* In *Crónicas iniciales de la conquista del Perú* (A. Salas, M. Guérin, and J. Moure eds.). Plus Ultra, Buenos Aires.

ZUIDEMA, R. TOM
  1982   Bureaucracy and the Systematic Knowledge in Andean Civilization. In *The Inca and Aztec States 1400–1800: Anthropology and History* (George A. Collier, Renato I. Rosaldo, and John D. Wirth eds.): 419–458. Academic Press, New York and London.
  1991   Guaman Poma and the Art of Empire: Toward an Iconography of Inca Royal Dress. In *Transatlantic Encounters: The History of Early colonial Peru* (Rolena Adorno and Ken Andrien, eds.): 151–202. University of California Press, Berkeley.

The Inka, and Andean Metallurgical Tradition

Heather Lechtman

THIS VOLUME EXAMINES EXPRESSIONS OF INKA POWER BY CONCENTRATING on data from archaeological rather than historical research. Its focus is on the material expressions of the Inka state. When it comes to the use of metal for state purposes, archaeology does not serve us well because of the significant part of Inka material culture in metal lost to the Spanish melting pot. If it were not for eyewitness accounts of the first invaders—the Pizarros, Pedro Sancho, Miguel de Estete—who saw the gold- and silver-clad palace and temple walls of Cusco, the life-sized gold and silver figures of royal women with their attendants, and the full-sized gold llamas with their gold shepherds, we would have no idea of the vast quantities of gold and silver mined, processed, and made into objects for use by the state. In Cusco and in temples near the city Estete (1918: 31, f. 11) saw and was impressed by many life-sized gold and silver statues of women, remarking that they "were of the finest that could be made anywhere" and "must have been made in the likeness of some deceased ladies, because each one of them had their retinue of pages and women as if they were alive" (Lothrop 1938: 59).

The Spaniards brought some metal from Cusco to Xauxa where it was melted down (Sancho 1938: 166). The gold and silver objects brought to Cajamarca as Atawalpa's ransom were melted and refined there by Andean founders, whom the Spaniards described as expert in their work. Of this gold, some is described as high karat, some as less fine (Xérez, in Markham 1872: 97–98). One-fifth of the booty was destined for the Spanish crown. In 1535 Charles V issued a document ordering all the gold and silver he received from Peru to be melted in the royal mints at Seville, Toledo, and Segovia (Lothrop 1938). Subsequent shipments were handled in the

FIG. 1 Moche warrior backflaps (in situ) from Tomb 1 at Sipán, Lambayeque Valley, Peru. Heavily corroded backflap made from a silver-copper alloy lies above its counterpart, in gold. Museo Tumbas Reales de Sipán, Lambayeque (photograph courtesy of Christopher B. Donnan).

same way. The archaeology of Inka metallurgy is severely hampered by the near-total disappearance of archaeological evidence, at least in the form of objects.

Even though our studies are severely frustrated by the paucity of Late Horizon gold and silver artifacts, a serious drawback to reliance on the early ethnohistoric documents is precisely their European fixation on gold and silver. The Spaniards scarcely mention objects of copper or its alloys, especially bronze. These items went unnoticed or were unremarkable to Europeans. In consequence, the documents do not present Andean reality with respect to the metals of empire.

Andean Metallurgy as a Three-component System

What the Spaniards failed to notice is what archaeological and laboratory investigation of Andean metallurgy have made plain. Andean metallurgy was a three-component system. The elemental or material components are copper, silver, and gold. The system was set in place as soon as these three metals were identified and used commonly by Andean metalworkers—early in the Early Intermediate period—and the triad remained a physical and cultural reality throughout the Late Horizon.

There is no better example of the physical combinations and cultural associations of these three metals as expressed through artifacts, than the contents of the Moche royal tombs excavated at Sipán, in the Lambayeque Valley of Peru's north coast (Alva and Donnan 1993). Tombs 1 and 2 date to approximately CE 300. The great advantage here is that not only are all the artifacts in context, but we can also observe their spatial relationships to the buried individuals and to one another. Importantly, we can observe their materials relationships to the individuals and to each other.

A striking pattern in the disposition of the Sipán tomb furniture in metals is the occurrence of pairs of objects: one in silver, the other in gold (fig. 1). Frequently, too, single, unpaired objects are constructed partly in silver, partly in gold (figs. 2, 3). The pairing and juxtaposition of these two metals and their consistent relative placement on the right and left side of the male body suggest gender associations: gold/right side/male; silver/left side/female. There is ample ethnohistoric evidence that recalls beliefs among Andean peoples at the time of the European invasion concerning

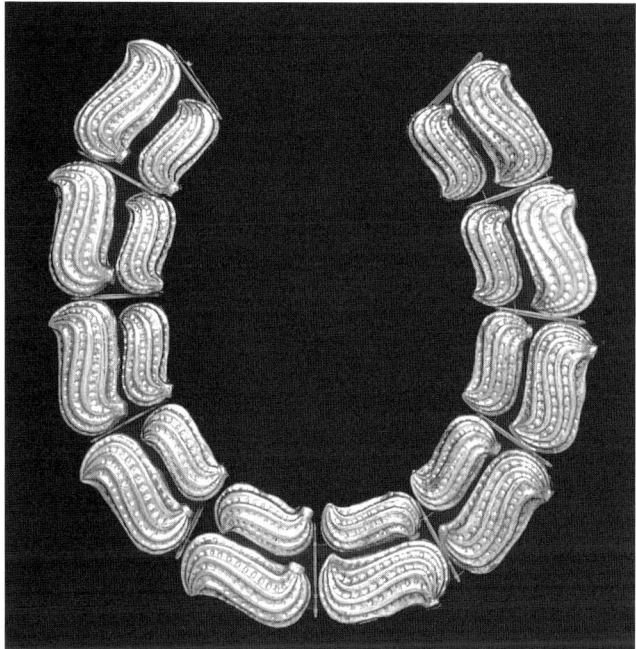
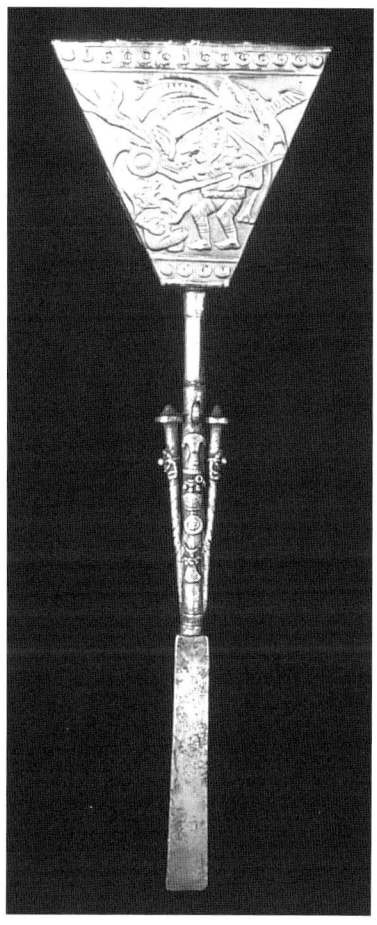

the masculine and feminine aspects of the lateral halves of the body and the association of each half with one of these two metals (Alva and Donnan 1993; Classen 1993). Similar connections between gold, silver, and the human body persist in some highland communities (Money 2004).

In the Sipán royal tombs, copper objects are most frequently associated with women, children, and high-status male attendants to the principal lord. In both Tombs 1 and 2, the women buried with the primary male figure wear elaborate headdresses made of copper. Attendants wear large copper crowns and feathered headdresses supported by long copper shafts; some have large copper discs on their chests. In Tomb 2, the principal burial figure, tentatively identified by Alva and Donnan (1993: 163) as the Bird Priest of the Sacrifice Ceremony, holds a copper bowl in his left hand, wears slippers of copper, and two copper bells at his left side originally hung from an elaborate headdress; circular discs of copper near his head probably formed part of another head ornament. The stout wood planks used to construct the coffin of the warrior priest buried in Tomb 1 were lashed together and secured with thick copper straps (Alva and Donnan 1993: 55–57, figs. 53, 54).

Cobo (1964: vol. 2, bk. 12, chap. 5, 68), in describing the mummy of the Inka king Sinchi Roca, reports that it was found between small bars of copper and woven with cabuya fiber. Gose (1993: 506) sees the close physical connection of the metal bars and the royal mummy as suggesting that, in Andean highland usage, "copper was closely associated with the

FIG. 2 Moche necklace of gold and silver peanut-shaped beads, from Tomb 1 at Sipán. The gold beads hung on the proper right chest of the buried warrior-priest, the silver beads on his left side. Museo Tumbas Reales de Sipán, Lambayeque (photograph courtesy of Christopher B. Donnan).

FIG. 3 Moche scepter-rattle held by the buried warrior-priest in Tomb 1, Sipán. The hollow rattle head of the scepter is made of hammered sheet gold; the stem is a solid casting in silver. Museo Tumbas Reales de Sipán, Lambayeque (photograph courtesy of Christopher B. Donnan).

FIG. 4 Copper burial mask from the cane coffin of a Moche priestess, excavated at the site of San José de Moro, Jequetepeque Valley, Peru. Museo de Sitio de Chan Chan, Moche Valley (see Donnan and Castillo 1994: fig. 13.7).

mallqui complex, in which localized life forms emerge from the underground."[1] At the very least, the passage in Cobo may point to a continuity in burial practice, whether on the coast or in the highlands, in which the body of the paramount lord or king is ultimately secured or enclosed by copper.

At the site of San José de Moro, a major late Moche ceremonial center in the lower Jequetepeque Valley, Christopher Donnan and Luis Jaime Castillo excavated a group of burials of high-status Moche women (Donnan and Castillo 1992, 1994; Alva and Donnan 1993). These burials date to the end of the Moche sequence, approximately CE 550, but are closely related to the Sipán royal tombs through the iconography of their contents. The excavators have identified two of the Moro women as priestesses.

The rectangular coffins of both women were made of cane, covered with a layer of cloth. On the vertical sides of the better-preserved and larger coffin, the cloth was adorned with large, hammered sheet-metal renderings of the woman's head and face, in the form of a mask (fig. 4), her arms and legs (fig. 5), and her distinctive headdress (see Donnan and Castillo 1994: figs. 13.3, 13.7; Alva and Donnan 1993: fig. 247). The mask and limbs are fashioned from copper; the headdress is made of copper or a copper alloy.[2] Both coffins were trimmed with hundreds of copper discs.

The adobe tomb chambers that house the Moro coffins are richly appointed with fine ceramic vessels. *Spondylus princeps* shells and cylindrical lapis lazuli beads were placed in intimate association with the body of the older of the two women. Both women had a copper goblet placed near the right elbow, and both were buried with a representation in sheet metal of their unusual tasseled headdresses. The form of the headdress, the shape of the copper goblets, and the presence in the chambers of certain

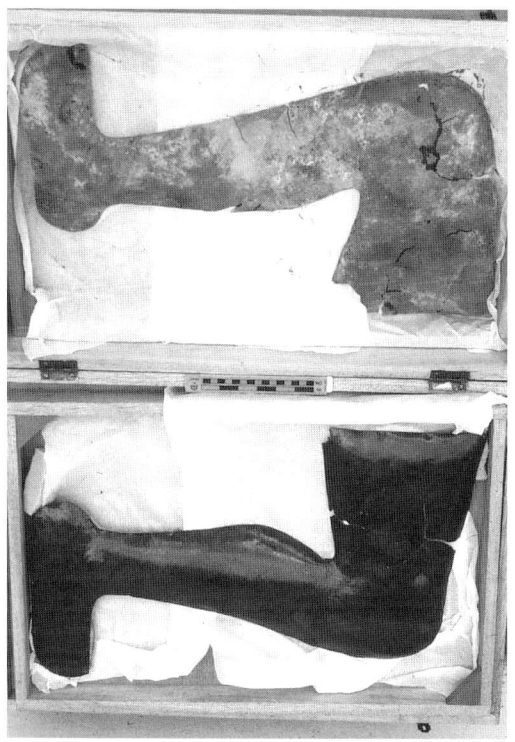
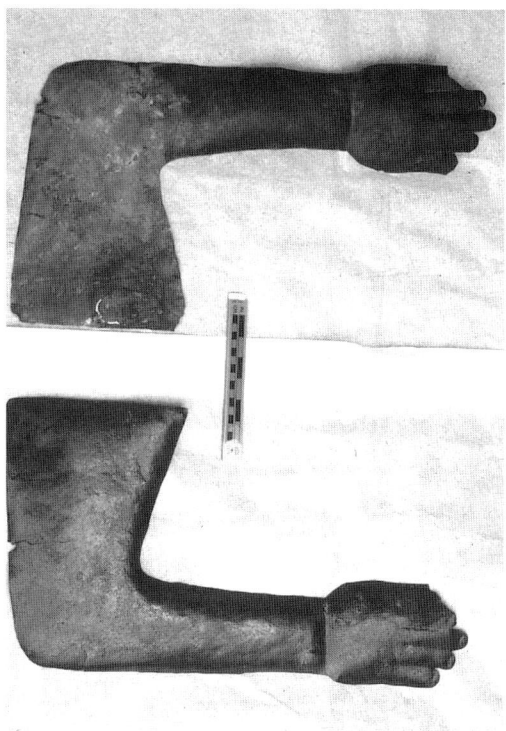

large cup-containing ceramic bowls associated with these female burials identify the tomb inhabitants as elite Moche women (Hocquenghem and Lyon 1980). They are the priestess (figure C) who appears as one of the four main actors in the Moche Presentation Theme, or Sacrifice Ceremony, depicted in fineline drawings on Moche ceramics (Donnan 1978; Donnan and Castillo 1992, 1994; see Quilter 1997 for an alternative interpretation of the iconography of this woman in Moche ceramics). Donnan and Castillo (1992, 1994) point to two of the other prime actors in the Presentation Scene as corresponding to the most prominent men buried in Tombs 1 and 2 at Sipán: Presentation Figure A, a rayed figure, is the warrior-priest of Tomb 1 and Presentation Figure B, part bird-part human, is the individual with elaborate owl headdress who occupies Tomb 2 (Donnan 1978: 158–165; Alva and Donnan 1993: 223–226).

The two excavators of these remarkable late Moche, Moro tombs observe that the more elaborate of the two "is the richest Moche female burial ever scientifically excavated and clearly demonstrates that in Moche society extraordinary wealth and power were not the exclusive domain of males" (Donnan and Castillo 1992: 38). Taken together, the Sipán and Moro elite burials demonstrate that in Moche society extraordinary wealth and power were expressed by objects made of copper. The looted tomb of the Sipán tomb precinct yielded an unique object made of copper[3]: a one-meter-tall staff with a solid cast finial in the form of a

FIG. 5 San José de Moro priestess burial. Hammered, sheet-metal legs and arms were originally affixed to the exterior, vertical sides of the cane coffin. The upper leg and arm in the photograph have not been cleaned; the two lower limbs have been cleaned of external corrosion. The metal sheet appears to be copper.

FIG. 6 Cast, arsenic bronze finial from a staff excavated at the looted tomb, Sipán. The balustrade that surrounds the gabled-roof structure comprises a double row of Moche mace heads. Museo Tumbas Reales de Sipán, Lambayeque (photograph courtesy of Christopher B. Donnan).

gabled architectural structure (fig. 6), perhaps a temple or an elite dwelling (Alva and Donnan 1993: figs. 47, 48). It was "a prized piece of ceremonial paraphernalia, the property of someone of exceedingly high status in Moche society" (Alva and Donnan 1993: 49). Gold and silver were not the exclusive conveyors in metal of high rank and ritual command. In particular, copper was closely associated with elite and powerful women.

Where else is the copper? Laboratory investigations have determined that in a vast majority of the gold- and silver-appearing artifacts from Tomb 1 at Sipán, copper is literally inside the objects, as one constituent of a binary (two element) or a ternary (three element) alloy (Eckmann n.d.; Hörz and Kallfass 2000). The golden objects, such as the peanut necklace beads and the inverted pyramidal head of the warrior priest's rattle-scepter, are made of ternary alloys of gold, silver, and copper. X-ray fluorescence analysis of the enriched surfaces of these objects indicates that the gold concentration varies between 70 and 80 wgt %, the silver is present to between 10 and 12%, and the copper concentration averages about 15 wgt % (Eckmann n.d.; Hörz and Kallfass 2000). Such alloys are approximately equivalent to 17- to 19-karat gold. Since copper was depleted from the surfaces of the artifacts during their manufacture, the copper content of the bulk, unaltered alloys is considerably higher.

Copper is a deliberate addition to these alloys. Native gold in the Andes—or anywhere else for that matter—rarely contains copper in excess of about 3% by weight (Boyle 1979; Lechtman, in Boone 1996: vol. 1, 60). The copper was added for two reasons: to increase the strength, and, more importantly, the toughness of the alloy, and, once the alloy's mechanical properties were improved, to provide the mechanisms by which the golden surface color of the metal could be enhanced by an enrichment process. The gold peanuts, the gold head of the rattle-staff, and the other major, finely wrought golden objects in Tomb 1 are made from what have been referred to as gold-rich *tumbaga*s.[4] The chestplate (Alva and Donnan 1993: fig. 65), located closer to the body of the deceased, is a copper-rich tumbaga, made of a ternary alloy containing approximately 60 wgt % copper, 34% gold, and 6% silver (Eckmann n.d.; Hörz and Kallfass 2000). All these objects have rich golden surfaces as a result of the loss of copper and the subsequent enrichment of gold at the surface during the manufacturing process. Several ingots excavated in Tomb 1 are intermediary in their alloy makeup between the gold-rich and the copper-rich tumbagas, containing 40 to 50 wgt % gold, 15 to 20% silver, and 30 to 40% copper (Eckmann n.d.; Hörz and Kallfass 2000).

Similarly, the silver-colored backflap, the silver-colored handle of the rattle-staff, and the heavily corroded, once-silvery sandals (Alva and Donnan 1993: fig. 111) worn by the warrior-priest are made of binary alloys of silver and copper. Analysis of the sandal bulk metal determined the alloy content to be 50 wgt % silver, 45% copper, 2.55% lead, and 2.5% gold. An ingot from the same tomb was cast from an almost identical alloy: 50% silver, 47% copper, 2.5% gold (Eckmann n.d.; Hörz and Kallfass 2000). The ingot is a pale coppery-pink color; the sandals were richly silver. The surfaces of the sandals, depleted in copper, were enriched in silver and appeared to be of silver as a result of this enrichment.

Unlike the solid cast handle of the gold/silver rattle-staff and the large silver-colored backflap hammered from thick metal plate, many of the other silver-colored metal objects in the Sipán tombs were fashioned from thin silver-copper alloy sheet. Like the low-gold, high-copper tumbagas, these thin sheets were hammered from alloy ingots that were low in silver and high in copper content. For example, a cylindrical bead hammered from an alloy containing 80 wgt % copper, 18% silver, and 1% gold (copper-colored) displays a bright silver surface whose composition has been altered to 13.5% copper, 76% silver, and 8.5% gold (Eckmann n.d.; Hörz and Kallfass 2000).

These objects appeared in various hues of gold and silver as a result of the presence of copper in the alloys from which the objects were made. Copper strengthened; it also transformed metals from one color to another. I have often pointed out that copper was the backbone of Andean metallurgy; that all Andean alloys—except the naturally occurring alloy of gold and silver (electrum)—were alloys of other metals with copper (Lechtman 1980, 1988). Copper was the mother of Andean metals in the sense that it generated the properties Andean peoples sought in metal—most especially the property of color. Copper was the source of those properties, the instrument of transformation (Lechtman 1999a).

Inka Utilization of the Three-component Andean Metallurgical System

To what extent did the Inka provide continuity to the three-component Andean metallurgical system, and in what ways did the system serve the purposes of state? John Rowe (personal communication, 1995, 1997) points out that excavations of Late Intermediate–period or early Inka refuse in the Cusco area almost never yield scraps of metal. Late Inka refuse, on the other hand, is full of metal objects discarded because they no longer functioned. Objects that for centuries had been made from stone, wood, and other materials were suddenly made in metal. In the Cusco region, tin bronze became the material of choice for tools, both utilitarian and symbolic.

The dramatic increase in the volume of metal produced for the crown and the state[5] reflects not only the large labor force, both corvée labor and *mitimaes*, that the Inka committed to mining and processing ores, but also the presence in Cusco of expert smiths who turned copper, gold, silver, and tin into imperial metals. These smiths came from centers of metal production throughout the central Andes, most notably from Chan Chan but also from Pachacamac, Huancavilca, Ica, Chincha (Cieza de León 1967: chap. 59, 195; Rowe 1948; Rostworowski 1977, 1990; Topic 1990; Moseley 1990), and presumably also from the tin-producing region of the altiplano in the south. Rostworowski (1990: 456, fn. 13) reminds us that "the massive exodus of *yunga* artisans should be kept in mind by those studying Inca metallurgy because although . . . [they] followed the artistic patterns imposed by their masters . . . they contributed their North Coast skills and technology." This is patently so: not only in the Inka predilection for sheathing architectural members with sheets of gold, a habit employed by the Chimú at Chan Chan (Rowe 1948; Emmerich 1965) and perhaps foreshadowed by Sicán burial practices (Shimada 1999); or for fashioning drinking vessels of gold or silver in the form of effigies (*vasos retratos*), a tradition begun by Sicán smiths in the Lambayeque valley (Carcedo and Shimada 1985) and continued by the Chimú and by Chincha smiths (Root 1949) on the south coast; but it is also evident in the alloys with which these smiths were accustomed to work and that they continued to make and to use in the imperial setting.

Francisco de Xérez's 1534 account of the Spanish entry into Cusco recounts:

> He saw a well-built house entirely plated with gold, quadrangular, and measuring three hundred and fifty paces from corner to corner. Of these gold plates they took down seven hundred, which together weighed 500 *pesos*. From another house the Indians pulled off a quantity weighing 200,000 *pesos*; but, as it was much alloyed, having but seven or eight carats the *peso*, they would not receive it. (Xérez, in Markham 1872: 95)

The 7- to 8-karat gold sheet corresponds to an alloy containing between about 29 and 33 wgt % gold; the remainder was likely copper with some silver—in other words, low-gold tumbaga. Binary alloys of copper and silver, so prevalent and important in coastal metallurgy (Lechtman 1971; Root 1949), also persisted in Inka manufacture. Pedro Sancho describes the melting down, in Xauxa, of the gold and silver items asssembled as part of Atawalpa's ransom.

And the same smelting was performed for the silver, which was found to contain two hundred and fifteen thousand marks . . . and of them one hundred and seventy thousand or so were fine silver in vessels and plates, pure and good, and the rest was not so because it was in plates and pieces mixed with other metals from which, according, the silver was extracted. (Sancho 1969: 128)

In other words, approximately 20% of the Inka silver melted down in Xauxa was alloyed "with other metals," most certainly with copper. There are few published chemical analyses of Inka gold- and silver-appearing objects that might provide a clearer picture of the range of alloys the Inka used and the correlation between alloy type and object type or object use. Rovira (1990: object no. 7025, fig. 46) discussed one such object, a 13.3 cm high, solid-cast, silver Inka figurine originally inlaid with other materials, most likely metals. He analyzed the head and belly of the female figure (Rovira 1990: 192). It was cast from one or more silver-copper alloys[6] with an average silver content of 61 wgt %, a copper concentration of about 32 wgt %, and minor amounts of tin, antimony, gold, and lead. Linares Málaga (in Dransart 2000) identified a female figurine from the high-altitude shrine of Pichu Pichu in southern Peru as made from a silver-copper alloy.

There is a pervasive continuity in the technological focus of central Andean metallurgy that began during the Early Horizon but was fully elaborated during the Early Intermediate period (Lechtman 1988). It is characterized by an overwhelming commitment to the handling and shaping of metal as a solid material, through plastic deformation, and by an accompanying, equally strong tradition of forming objects in metal from a single or joined assembly of thin metal sheet. Material culture in metal was realized through the management of three metals—copper, silver, and gold—and the alloys they formed with each other and sometimes with other metals. From Moche to Sicán, from Chimú to Inka, the three-component system remained intact. The system was generally abroad and functioned as an Andean technological style in metalworking (Lechtman 1988, 1993, 1999a). It was transmitted directly to the Inka by the smiths they brought to Cusco. Individual objects made from gold plus silver, juxtaposed for their color and symbolic effects, continued to be prized (see fig. 7).

FIG. 7 Inka llama. The head is cast solid in gold, the body in silver. Museo Arqueológico, Universidad Nacional San Antonio Abad del Cusco.

The technical features of the system scarcely varied. What about the cultural features? To posit that there *was* meaning that inhered in the association of these three metals—whether in juxtaposition on a single object or between related objects or as constituents of an object's alloy— we need not claim that meaning remained invariant through time, from one ethnic group to another, or from one polity to another. The claim is simply that the association of the three metals derived from cultural, not merely technical considerations. The metallurgical technology developed in congruence with cultural requirements placed on the materials themselves. Foreign smiths brought to Cusco much more than skills and techniques. They worked with metals that carried gender and with alloys that were transformational, generating colors with political and cosmological import. The Inka tailored the system to their purposes and were successful as much because of the long-standing traditions Andean peoples shared about these metals as for the quantity, size, and quality of metal objects that they displayed publicly.

We have a few hints of the system at work in Inka hands, several from the documents and some from Inka artifacts. During the Late Horizon telling examples of continuity in the deliberate clustering of triad-metal items come from objects that the Inka buried with children who were sacrificed during *capac hucha* rituals. Gordon McEwan and Arminda Gibaja (2004) have excavated a total of seven child burials in an Inka structure at the site of Chokepukio, in the Lucre basin of the Cusco Valley. They suggest that the children were interred during a capac hucha ritual. Six are burials of girls, one is a boy's burial. Closely associated with the burials but lacking any skeletal remains are several offerings of items similar to those that accompany the children. One offering contains an unusual pair of gold and silver plaques in the general shape of the Inka royal tassel (*mascapaycha*) or headdress insignia. Many of the burials include items of gold, silver, and copper or bronze: human (female and male) and llama figurines and *tupu* pins are most common. All the burials and the offerings contain intact *Spondylus princeps* shells or figures carved from *Spondylus*.

THREE METALS, AND THE CONQUEST HIERARCHY

The association of the three core Andean metals figures prominently in a coastal creation myth involving Pachacamac and his brother Vichama, both sons of the Sun, as recounted by Antonio de la Calancha in 1638. The myth was collected twenty years earlier, during the campaigns to extirpate idolatry between 1617 and 1619, by a Jesuit, Luis de Teruel (Duviols 1983). In this myth, Vichama, seeing that the world is without people and that the *huacas* (shrines) and the Sun have no one to worship them, begs his father the Sun to create a new set of human beings. The Sun sends three eggs, one of gold, one of silver, and one of copper. From the golden egg issue the *curacas*, the *caciques*, and the nobles called "second persons (*segunda personas*)" and "principals"; from the silver egg the wives of the latter were born; and from the copper egg the common people, whom we call today *mitayos*, and their wives and their families (Duviols 1983).

Others can discuss the relation between the two creator deities, Viracocha in the sierra and Pachacamac on the coast. For my argument here, I believe it is not a long stretch to suggest that in Tawantinsuyu, the metals of the three-component Andean system were related within an Inkaic structural hierarchy in which each represented or was emblematic of a social group: gold = *collana*; silver = *payan*; copper = *cayao*. Indeed, María Rostworowski made this observation and a similar suggestion in 1983 (Rostworowski 1983: 147, 184). She argued that the tripartite structure given in the myth had both social and gender dimensions: that gold, as collana, was male, specifically referring to the main or principal or oldest man; that silver, as payan, was female; and that copper, as cayao, was also male, specifically referring to younger men or to men situated lower in the social hierarchy.

In Zuidema's (1977) schematic presentation of the Inka *ceque* system, collana signifies principal or first; payan second or middle; cayao origin or source. There is a variety of ways to reckon the membership of these social groupings, though the hierarchical structure remains the same for all reckonings (see Rowe 1985). The king is always collana, his *panaqa* (Inka royal lineage) is payan, and the *ayllu*s who represent all those conquered by the king, are cayao. Alternatively, collana could mean the Inka and Coya, husband and wife; then cayao represents all the rest of humanity, and payan the noble descendents of the king's secondary marriages with members of the cayao social group. Collana could also mean all the Inka nobility, in which case cayao represents all other people, and payan the progeny of the secondary marriages of collana and cayao, or the Inkas of the commoners. John Earls (personal communication, 1979) has pointed out that these terms seem to apply to a conquest hierarchy where collana stands for the conquerors or insiders, cayao for the conquered or outsiders, and payan for the intermarriages of the first two, resulting in those "in the middle."

This scheme was relational and contextual. Like all structural hierarchies, it was historical by nature, built on time-dependent and generative relations. The new structures grow out of changes in the old. The emblems remain constant, however, and I suggest that the Inka appropriated the traditional gender and transformational associations among the three Andean metals and fitted them onto an organizational framework in which each material represented a social segment within the empire (fig. 8). Copper remained the female source or origin metal, which, in combination with the others, retained its primary quality or power of transformation. Cayao

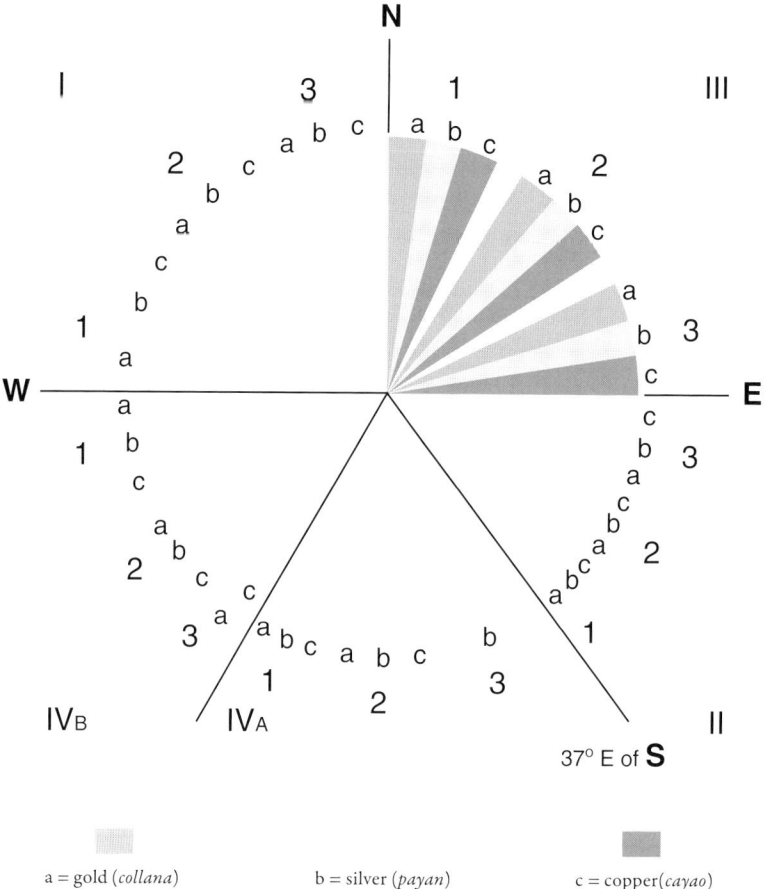

FIG. 8 Schematic diagram of the ceque system of Cusco (after Zuidema 1977: fig. 15.5). Each ceque line in a triad is shown as corresponding to one of the three primary metals in the Andean three-component metallurgical system. Each also corresponds to a social group within the Inka structural hierarchy. The ceque line a always represents gold and collana, b corresponds to silver and payan, and c designates copper and cayao (drawing by Elizabeth Wahle).

a = gold (*collana*)   b = silver (*payan*)   c = copper(*cayao*)

was the social group from which the Inka, collana, took secondary wives. The cayao was the source of the real strength of the empire, for its ranks ensured the vitality and continuity of the royal ayllus. Copper was cayao.

My argument is based not on ethnohistory or linguistic analysis, nor on what people said about these materials and their associations, but rather on archaeology, on what people did, as gleaned from the traditional and deeply cultural ways in which Andean peoples managed these metals and alloys. It is through this kind of understanding that we may suggest the meaning such materials had in relations of power.

Is there any evidence to support my suggestion? There are hints, perhaps none substantial enough to be credited as evidence. In 1570 Inka Titu Cussi Yupangui (1985) described to Lope García de Castro (governor of Peru in the early 1570s, just prior to the viceroyalty of Francisco de Toledo) a Capac Raymi festival in Cusco organized and presided over by Manco Inka in the presence of Gonzalo Pizarro. The document relates that

> Manco appeared with full royal authority... carrying in front of him his royal scepters, and one of these, as it was the principal one, was of solid gold. All those who accompanied him, more than 1000 all together, each one carried his own; half of these were [made] of silver, half of copper.... (Titu Cussi Yupangui 1985: 18, f. 31v; my translation)

The document goes on to describe this group of Manco's followers as *varayoq*s, bearers of staffs of office or insignia—not soldiers. Together with the insignia of the Inka himself, all three metals are represented by the staffs the assembly holds.

There is a similar use of the three metals to distinguish among the ranks of soldiers in the army. Estete, who was present at the disaster in Cajamarca, describes the soldiers who attended Atawalpa there:

> Not one man of the more than 50,000 soldiers was without his well-polished forehead medallion [*patena*] of gold, silver, or copper; which gave them great splendor and it was frightening and awesome to see them. (Estete 1938: 222; my translation)

The shiny head ornaments were made variously of gold, silver, or copper and evidently corresponded to military ranking. Rank within the army was also broadcast by the materials from which certain weapons were made or adorned. Estete, observing events in the plaza at Cajamarca, notes the entry of "the third squadron of [Inka] soldiers, all of them holding their hammers [*martillos*] made of copper and of silver, which is a weapon that they have" (Estete 1918: 24, f. 7v–8; my translation).

It is not certain whether military ranking, as displayed through metal accouterments, had to do with fighting prowess or accomplishment (Rowe 1946), with the organization of soldiers by type of weapon or by strategic position during battle, or, as I am suggesting, recruitment from or affiliation with specific social segments within the imperial hierarchy. Rostworowski made this same suggestion in 1983, observing how frequently Inka military forces were organized in groups of three (Rostworowski 1983: 184). This division, she offered, might have followed the ceque principle: collana, payan, and cayao. On the basis of the metallic color code that seems to have been in place under various circumstances within the military, I would support her supposition.

Another consideration may lend weight to the suggestion offered here that, according to Inka organization of the greater social universe and the ascription of specific materials and their products to units within that organization, copper designated cayao social groupings. This consideration has to do with the proposed long-distance exchange of copper for *mullu*, *Spondylus princeps*. Copper left the central Andes for the north and the sea; *Spondylus* left the sea for the south and for the land (Paulsen 1974; Rostworowski 1970; Gose 1993). Paulsen (1974) has called attention to the frequent association of the shell *Spondylus princeps* with copper in the central and north-central Andes. The long-distance exchange of one for the other, and later the pairing of the two materials in graves and offering contexts, began in the Middle Horizon and was especially prevalent during and after the Late Intermediate period. Paulsen (1974: 603) cites, as one example of that association, a Middle Horizon woven hanging, part of the ritual paraphernalia of a wooden figure that embodied the oracle at Pachacamac: "One side of this hanging was embellished with a series of whole immature *Spondylus* shells, and the reverse with copper ornaments." Menzel (1968: 51–52) describes the Middle Horizon 2 deposit excavated at the site Pikillacta, in the Cusco valley, and published by Valcarcel in 1933. She comments on the close resemblance between corresponding Inka miniature offerings and the Pikillacta Wari–style offering, the latter including forty miniature, stone human figurines, two valves of *Spondylus*, and a copper "bar." Valcarcel (1933: 22) refers to the metal implement as *una makana de champi* (a club made of bronze).[7]

In characterizing Inka miniature offerings, Dransart (2000) specifies that the figures were made of metal alloys (gold, silver, or copper), shell, or stone; in any single offering, all figures were the same sex; and where burial conditions preserved the cloth, they are dressed in miniature Inka garments. She points to *mamacocha*, mother of the lakes (the Pacific Ocean), and to *pachamama*, mother of the earth (the Andes mountains), as providing the raw materials—shell (*Spondylus*) and metal, or stone—for the bodies of the small Inka figures.

In Inka cosmology, the sea was the domain or substance from which all things were created, and it was also the source for all highland lakes and all rivers. The sea, located under and surrounding the earth, wells up to form lakes that feed rivers. Lakes, in turn, are connected to the sea underneath by subterranean channels that the original ancestors used to travel to their points of emergence on earth, the *pacarinas* or dawning points. In a circulatory round, the rivers and all other waters on earth eventually return to the upwelling sea (Earls and Silverblatt 1978; Sherbondy 1992).

Gose (1993) sees the ocean and the Andes—the one signified by the thorny oyster, the other by the copper/silver/gold triad—as domains in an Andean system of cosmological exchanges, not merely human and material exchanges. By the Middle Horizon, he argues, copper had become the primary item shipped from the central Andes to Ecuador, in exchange for *Spondylus*. In this exchange, *Spondylus* and the waters of the ocean were introduced from the outside to the dry highlands, ever in need of rain; and these "waters at the edge of the world could be enticed back [welled up] in toward the center only if they were to lose a certain amount of metallic ancestral substance [copper] to the periphery of the system. This was a sacrificial exchange of ancestral order [represented by the metal copper] for alien vitality [represented by *Spondylus* shell]" (Gose 1993: 508). Though the Inka chose gold and silver to demarcate their celestial status, copper was the third and essential member of a cyclical and dynamic world order in which, at death, *upanis*[8] entered the watery channels of the underworld and travelled along them, following the paths of the ancestors to the final or maximal *pacarina*—the ocean—the ultimate source of water. The copper "traded out" of the Andes "was a powerful ancestral substance" that attracted the upanis to the sea (Gose 1993: 507–508). In this reading, copper is associated with the notion of pacarina and of the primordial—the places from which the original ancestors and life forms in general emerged onto the earth from below ground.

In discussing a possible utility to assigning the categories of "sovereignty," "force," and "fertility," respectively, to the tripartite Inka hierarchical system of social classification—collana, payan, and cayao—Zuidema (1992) stresses his original (1964) interpretation of cayao as signifying origin, in the sense of the primordial. "The pre- and the non-Incas were considered to be of pre-Flood origin" and therefore primordial (Zuidema 1992: 25), while "the material support given by the non-Incas from outside Cuzco might have been classified as Cayao, being derived from Viracocha," or the sea (Zuidema 1992: 25). Cayao, then, represented fertility (Zuidema 1992). For the Inka, copper—from both my laboratory-analytical observations of its generative/transformational aspect and from its association with the emergence of life—was emblematic of cayao.

Gose's formulation of the movement of copper against shell, which allowed the loss of terrestrial substance to gain access to revitalizing ocean water, is a hypothesis that needs exploration and archaeological substantiation. The premise that copper was the resource exchanged for *Spondylus* is weak, as these two materials may have constituted an exchange pair, but to date there is no unequivocal archaeological evidence to support the claim. Hosler, Lechtman, and Holm (1990) discuss and evaluate the available evidence in considerable detail. Copper remains a likely contender as partner to mullu, the "daughters of the sea" (Cobo 1964: bk. 13, chap. 22, 202), but so far there is no evidence that the merchants at Chincha (Rostworowski 1970) or the smiths at Batán Grande (Shimada 1985, 1987) supplied it.

THE TRIAD METALS PLUS IMPERIAL BRONZE: A NEW CONFIGURATION

During the Late Horizon, the close physical association of copper, silver, and gold in individual metal objects occurs principally through the Inka technique of inserting metal inlays into a metal substrate. Figures 9 and 10 illustrate a type of cast-and-inlaid metal figurine, which assumes the posture typical of the more commonly known female and male Inka figurines made of sheet metal (see, for example, Boone 1996: pls. 88, 89). Given

FIG. 9 Inka solid cast silver figurine, with metal inlays said to be of gold, copper, and bronze. Private collection (after de Lavalle 1992: fig. 322).

the similarity of attitudes shared by such objects, whether cast or worked, and the frequency with which archaeologically recovered figures are found fully clothed, it is likely that both figures illustrated here originally wore miniature Inka garments (see Dransart 2000 for a careful analysis of this general class of figures). The Inka also made cast-and-inlaid male figurines in this same genre (see Cuesta Domingo and Rovira 1982: fig. 296).

No chemical analysis is available for either of the solid cast silver (or perhaps silver-copper alloy) figurines shown in figures 9 (private collection) and 10 (collection of the National Museum, Copenhagen). Lapiner (1976: fig. 688), upon visual examination of the intact figure (fig. 9), identified the horizontal bands of metal inlay distributed along the entire length of her head and body as made from gold, copper, and bronze. Many of the inlays on the Copenhagen figure, also cast of solid silver, have been removed. Of those that remain, the shiny, metallic-appearing bands are reported on visual inspection to be made of gold and bronze (Berete Due personal communication, December 1997). At my request, the laboratories of the Department of Ethnography at the National Museum in Copenhagen performed a series of analyses on some of the nonmetallic materials from the dark bands, such as those at mid-calf on the legs. The laboratory determined that the dark material is malachite (copper carbonate) that has formed as a corrosion product in association with a "black amorphous" material "consisting of gold, silver, copper, aluminium, silicon, oxygen, and chlorine— probably a gold, silver, and copper alloy with inclusions" (Berete Due personal communication, March 1998). The inlay alloy that gave rise to the corrosion product is likely to have been a high-copper, low-gold tumbaga. Such tumbagas typically corrode to form a black, porous, and often powdery material. The alloy color of the original inlay was probably a deep pink.

Though we have no verification of the composition of the inlaid metals and alloys on these two and other inlaid figurines, it is notable that both are said to bear bronze (presumably copper-tin) inlays. This comes as no surprise, since tin bronze was the imperial alloy par excellence. The Inka disseminated it widely throughout Tawantinsuyu (Lechtman 1980; Owen n.d.; Costin et al. 1989). High-status objects began to be cast entirely in tin bronze: fancy *tumi*s, finials to staffs, and axes cast complete with their handles. None of these items was meant for utilitarian purposes. Those that were special were highlighted with metal inlays. Figure 11 shows a

FIG. 10 Inka solid cast silver figurine (front and back views), with some metal inlays intact and others missing. The inlays have been identified as gold, bronze, and a copper-silver-gold ternary alloy. Nationalmuseet (no. 0.1417), Copenhagen (photograph courtesy of Berete Due, Etnografisk Samling, Nationalmuseet).

typical Inka tumi with a llama head atop the handle. It was cast and the blade worked from a 10 wgt % tin bronze. The llama head and the handle are decorated with silver and copper inlays (Lechtman, in Boone 1996: pl. 92, fig. 110). The diagram in figure 12 identifies the metal inlays and records their design and location. The panels containing llama figures alternate between inlays of copper and those of silver; one llama is made half of silver, half of copper. The zigzag motifs alternate similarly; one panel in silver, one in copper.

The high-tin bronze handle and blade of the tumi would have been a bright yellow-golden color. From the color alone, the gold-silver-copper combination so characteristic of central Andean metalwork is preserved on this piece. Cuesta Domingo and Rovira (1982: pl. 289) show a tin bronze tumi similarly inlaid with copper and silver feline and geometric designs. Analysis of the bronze determined the tin content as 12 wgt % (Rovira 1990: figs. 259, 260, and analytical table on p. 395); the alloy would have looked bright yellow/golden. Lothrop (1937: pl. 39, object d) and Cuesta Domingo and Rovira (1982: pl. 203) illustrate a tin bronze axe with handle and lashings, all cast in one piece. Lothrop describes the geometric patterns within the panels on the handle as inlaid in silver. Rovira (1990: figs. 47, 48 and analytical table on p. 194) identifies the inlays as made of silver and copper. He further provides two chemical analyses of the blade and handle of this piece. Their average tin content was determined as 13.1 wgt %. The wings and tail of the cast tin bronze (10.3 wgt % tin; Lechtman, in Boone 1996: 311) bird finial in the Dumbarton Oaks collection (Boone 1996: pl. 90) are inlaid with copper and silver bands. Lechtman (in Boone 1996: 311) comments that "their white and red colors were set in a field of gold. The tricolor scheme of this bird is like that of Inca knife B-482 [fig. 11 in this article]; both must have produced a similar visual effect." Note that the Inka tin bronze inlaid objects presented here fall in the composition range of about 10 to 13 wgt % tin, an excellent alloy for casting, working, and ensuring a yellow-golden glow to the objects.

The Inka contribution to Andean metallurgy lay in the large-scale production and widespread distribution of tin bronze. They adopted the alloy from altiplano peoples south of Lake Titicaca who had begun to manufacture tin bronze towards the end of the Middle Horizon (Lechtman 1997, 1999b, 2003a). Until the Inka's heavy exploitation of the rich cassiterite fields of northern Bolivia and northwest Argentina, however, the scale of tin bronze production remained small, even in northwest Argentina (A. González 1979; L. González 2004) where the technology of casting solid items in bronze was highly developed by about CE 650–700. From the archaeological evidence—since there is scant mention of bronze in the ethnohistoric sources—it seems clear that Inka bronze production was destined primarily for making tools, whether lightweight items like sewing needles or heavy-duty ones like crowbars (see Mayer 1994, 1998). Axes and knives were made of bronze, some utilitarian, others representational. Some items, like mace heads, were made of bronze, often for use as symbols of office or status rather than as weapons.

When tin bronze was physically associated with other metals on a single object, whether as an inlay or as the matrix material that carried inlays, the association was always with two or frequently all three of the Andean triad of metals: copper, silver, gold. We do not know the significance of the association when bronze becomes a member of the traditional grouping. It is tempting to contemplate that high-tin bronze, with

FIG. 11 Inka knife (*tumi*), cast and worked in tin bronze (approx. 10 wgt % tin) with inlays of silver and copper. Dumbarton Oaks (no. B-482) (after Boone 1996: fig. 96 and Lechtman, in Boone 1996: 315).

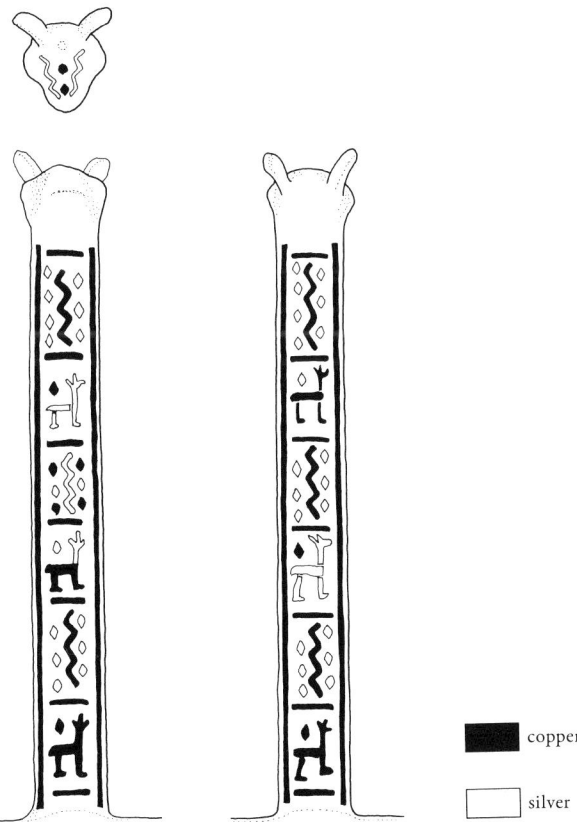

FIG. 12 Drawing of the knife handle reproduced in figure 11. Llama and zig-zag inlays on the handle and head are set in copper and silver. One llama combines a copper body and a silver head (after Lechtman, in Boone 1996: fig. 110; drawing by Elizabeth Wahle).

The Inka, and Andean Metallurgical Tradition

its yellow-golden color, took the part of gold in objects that represent tool-like items (knives, axes, finials), even if they did not function as tools. Hosler (1988, 1994) has shown that smiths in western Mexico made high-tin bronze alloys to produce gold-colored metal, and high-arsenic bronze alloys to produce silver-colored metal, in the manufacture of status items. Perhaps yellow bronze was an Inka stand-in for a gold-appearing metal in objects that required the mechanical and casting properties of a bronze alloy. The meaning accorded to tin bronze as a material and its symbolic and hierarchical position in Inka affairs of state are difficult to address.

FIG. 13 Clothed female figurine of silver, buried to accompany the child sacrificed at the Inka shrine on Cerro el Plomo, Chile. Museo Nacional de Historia Natural, Santiago (photograph courtesy of the museum).

The only metal items we have that represent exclusively women and women's attire are tupus. Although often worn from the onset of adolescence, the tupu was considered an attribute of a married woman, presented as a gift to her by her husband as part of the marriage bond (Money 2004). The Coya, the royal queen and daughter of the Sun, wore a tupu of gold. The archaeological record preserves tupus of gold, silver, and copper or bronze. One could tell where a woman was from by the size and shape of her tupu (fig. 13). In his dictionary of the Aymara language, Bertonio comments that the women of Charcas wore tupus larger than those of Lupaqa women (Money 2004). Presumably the material of which the tupu was made constituted another marker of social hierarchical position.

Bronze

When it comes to Late Horizon bronze, we ought to be on firmer, less speculative ground. I say "ought to be," because despite a substantial number of Inka bronze artifacts in museum collections, some of which issue from controlled excavations, there have been few serious studies of Inka bronze (Mathewson 1915; Gordon 1985; Owen n.d.; Rutledge and Gordon 1987; Gordon and Knopf 2006). We lack compositional and structural analyses of all but a few of these objects. Most of our work on this subject lies ahead.

The Inka are credited with disseminating tin or ingots of the tin-bronze alloy, as well as objects made from tin bronze, throughout Tawantinsuyu. The broad dispersion of tin bronze is understood as a Late Horizon event. But the production of bronze and the technical knowledge about how to make bronze alloys—knowledge that was widespread from Ecuador to northwest Argentina—was a Middle Horizon event (Lechtman 1997, 1998, 1999b, 2003a). We need to use the term "bronze" to reflect a new

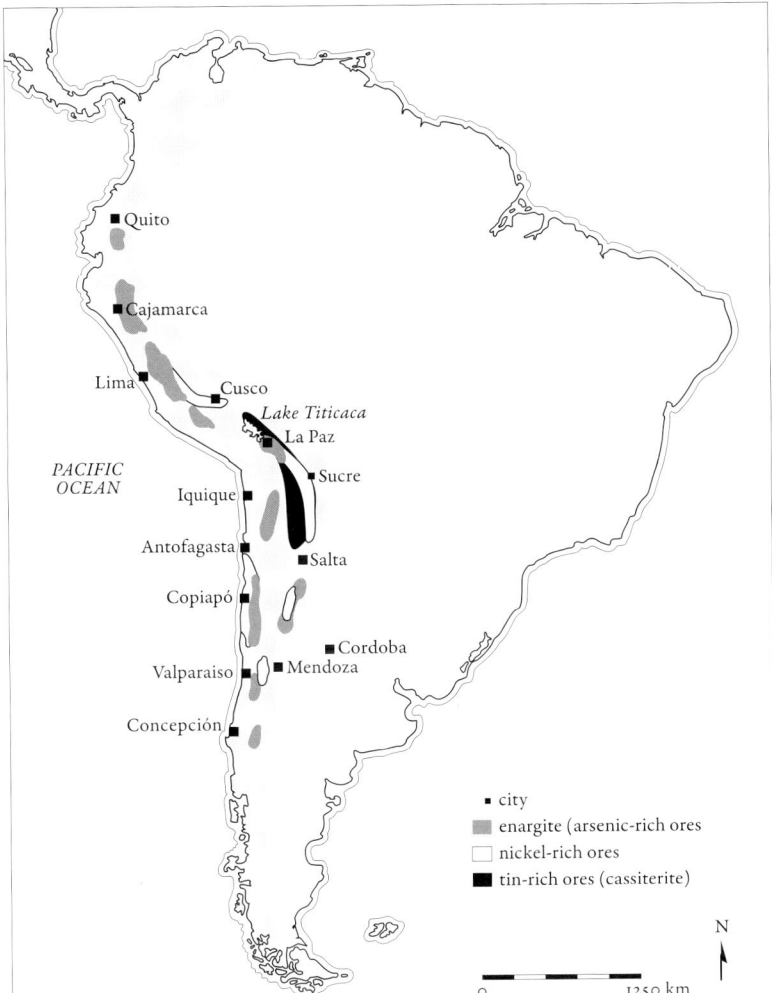

FIG. 14 Map locating the major zones of arsenic-rich, nickel-rich, and tin-rich mineralization in the northern, central, and southern Andes (after Petersen 1989 and Lechtman 1999b).

archaeological reality, namely that during the Middle Horizon at least three primary types of bronze alloy were developed in the Andean culture area: the binary alloy of copper and arsenic, or arsenic bronze; a ternary alloy containing copper, arsenic, and nickel; and the binary alloy of copper and tin, or tin bronze. Each type of bronze alloy was produced and used in those geographic regions where the critical alloying element—arsenic, nickel, or tin—was most abundant (see the ore distribution map in fig. 14). Thus during the Middle Horizon, arsenic bronze production (fig. 15) was characteristic of the north-central and central Andean region with its extensive belt of rich copper sulfarsenide ore deposits (Lechtman 1997, 1999b); the ternary copper-arsenic-nickel bronze alloy (fig. 16) was common to a zone delimited roughly by Lake Titicaca at the north and San Pedro de Atacama, in northern Chile, at the south (Lechtman 2003a, 2003b; Lechtman and Macfarlane 2005); and tin bronze was common to

FIG. 15 Giant axe, cast in arsenic bronze (1.38 wgt % arsenic), from Manabí, Ecuador. Museo de Arte Prehistórico, Casa de la Cultura, Guayaquil (after Hosler, Lechtman, and Holm 1990: fig. 10, table 2).

the south-central Andes, as far south as northwest Argentina (L. González 2004). The type of bronze produced and used was determined for the most part by the location of the closest rich sources of ore. In other words, people exploited the ores in their backyard.

The volume of bronze production was highly variable during the Middle Horizon. On the northern coast of Peru, at centers such as Batán Grande, production of arsenic bronze was high and continued into the Late Horizon. But the quantity of that same alloy used at large Wari centers in the central sierra, such as Pikillacta, was low (Lechtman 2005). In the Titicaca Basin and in the Atacama of northern Chile, production of the ternary bronze alloy was modest in scale throughout the Middle Horizon. In northwest Argentina (A. González 1979, 1992; L. González 2004) the quantity of tin bronze produced was far greater than at Tiwanaku and environs, but it probably did not approach the prodigious output of arsenic bronze manufactured on the far northern coast of Peru. What we do see taking place in the Titicaca Basin is a deliberate change from almost exclusive use of the ternary copper-arsenic-nickel bronze during the early years of the Middle Horizon to a similarly exclusive use of tin bronze toward the end of the Horizon and the beginning of the Late Intermediate period (table 1; Lechtman 1999b, 2003a). Thereafter,

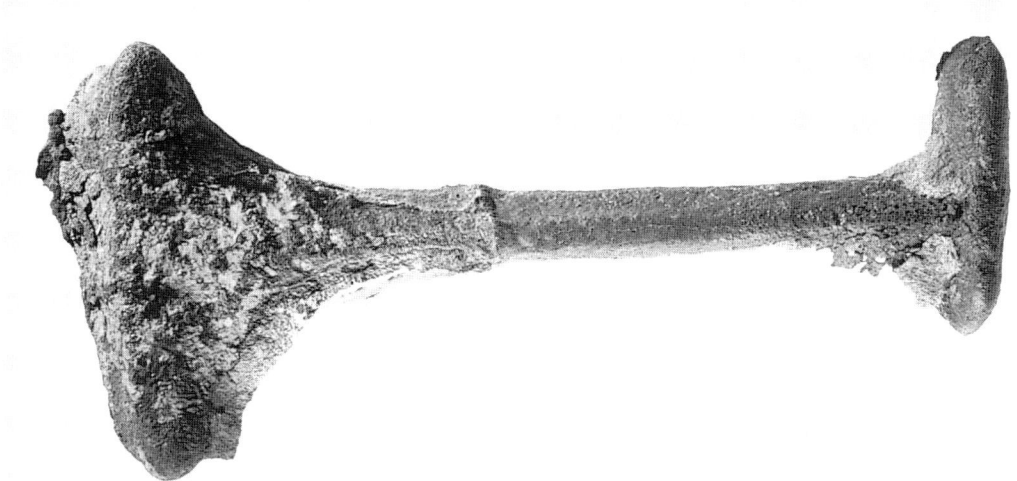

FIG. 16 Intact, cast I-cramp (*grapa*), 19.0 cm long, from the Pumapunku temple mound, Tiwanaku, Bolivia. This view of the underside of the cramp reveals a slight protuberance where molten metal (copper-arsenic-nickel alloy: 6.0 wgt % arsenic, 5.9% nickel) seeped into and solidified at the joint between adjacent stone blocks. Museo Arqueológico de Tiwanaku (after Lechtman 1998: fig. 5b; photograph by Hillel Burger).

tin bronze continued as the alloy of choice in the south-central Andes for a wide range of objects, though production volume remained moderate until the Inka hegemony.

We know little about the overall physical and specific mechanical properties of the copper-arsenic-nickel alloy. In 1995 I discovered that a wide variety of metal artifacts excavated at Tiwanaku are made of this bronze, and at about the same time, Gray Graffam identified a specific type of axe at San Pedro de Atacama, Chile, made of the ternary bronze alloy (Lechtman 1997).[9] Because this alloy has not been used industrially, there is no engineering literature that provides a discussion of its properties.[10] On the other hand, extensive laboratory investigation has demonstrated that for most purposes, arsenic bronzes and tin bronzes behave so similarly as to be interchangeable (Lechtman 1996). Tin bronze can be made slightly harder, but arsenic bronze is far more malleable. The mechanical and physical properties, such as color, of the ternary bronze alloy are likely similar to those of arsenic bronze.

Table 1 Chronology of Titicaca Basin bronze alloys as determined by artifact analyses

		Alloy type								
	No. artifacts analyzed	Cu		Cu-As		Cu-As-Ni		Cu-Sn		Cu-As-Ni-Sn	
Period		No.	% Total	No.	% Total	No.	% Total	No.	% Total	No.	% Total
Late F II–Early TIW IV	11	—	—	1	9.1	9	81.8	1	9.1	—	—
Late TIW IV–Early TIW V	11	1	9.1	—	—	6	54.6	3	27.3	1	9.1
TIW V	6	—	—	—	—	1	16.7	5	83.3	—	—
Post TIW	3	1	33.3	—	—	—	—	2	66.6	—	—

Note: Of the two post-Tiwanaku artifacts classified as Cu-Sn alloys, one contains minor amounts of As, Ni, Sb, and Fe; the other contains a minor amount of As. LF = Late Formative, TIW = Tiwanaku (after Lechtman 2003, table 17.6)

FIG. 17 Inka "standard issue" tin bronze tools, arms, and insignia found widely dispersed throughout Tawantinsuyu, in regions beyond the heartland. Relative distribution of artifact types by geographic location was estimated from E. Mayer (1986, 1992, 1994).

	Tumi	Mace	Axe	Axe-mace
Ecuador	✓	✓	few	✓
Bolivia	✓	✓	✓	✓
Chile	few	few	few	few
Argentina	✓	✓	✓	—

One of the questions before us is: Why did the Inka choose to adopt tin bronze as the imperial alloy when they were based in a region of the central Andes replete with arsenic-bearing copper ores nearby, a region where the metallurgical know-how for producing arsenic bronze from these ores had developed through long-standing and highly successful practice? Why exploit the cassiterite fields far away in the Bolivian or Argentine *puna*, the only such resources within Tawantinsuyu? And what was the impact of that choice?

If we consider only the types of imperial Inka tin bronze objects that were moved around most extensively, they appear to describe categories of tools, perhaps arms, or insignia (fig. 17). The four most common and widely dispersed types are the classic Inka T-shaped axe; the lobed or star-shaped mace head or insignia; a kind of axe-mace that combines the two previous forms; and the fancy Inka tumi. These artifacts share two features: they are made of tin bronze, and they were shaped by casting, though the axes and tumi blades commonly underwent considerable hammering to perfect the form.

Central Andean metallurgy was a technology committed to the plastic deformation of metal in the solid state. Objects of all kinds were produced by hammering metal to shape it. Casting was practiced but remained a seldom used and largely undeveloped technique. In the south-central Andes, however, especially in northwest Argentina, a different tradition had taken hold by the end of the Middle Horizon and was firmly established there in the Late Intermediate period. Large, heavy discs, axes, bells, and insignia were cast solid from copper and copper alloys. Some of those alloys were smelted from local ores, resulting in bronzes with singular compositions characteristic of the ore body (A. González 1979; Fester 1962). Others were made of tin bronze (L. González 2004). In the Bolivian altiplano tin bronze was also regularly used for tools and personal ornaments by the opening of the Late Intermediate period, and some of these were fashioned from cast stock (Lechtman 1997, 1998, 2003a).

The Inka chose to emulate a style of production in copper, which joined a forming technology—casting—with a specific material—tin bronze. The choice of tin bronze allowed the Inka control of the alloy in two respects. There is only one region in all of South America where cassiterite is found. The tin fields of Bolivia and northwest Argentina are among the richest in the world. It was easy for the Inka to manage and circumscribe production of their new alloy. No one else had it—except those altiplano communities that had developed the alloy in the first place. In addition, by using tin bronze instead of arsenic bronze, the Inka controlled the properties of their new alloy with far greater facility. Arsenic bronze is smelted directly from arsenic-bearing copper ores. It is difficult to anticipate, much less regulate, the amount of arsenic that appears in a bronze ingot smelted from such an ore (Lechtman 1996; Lechtman and Klein 1999). But tin bronzes were made by melting together metallic copper and metallic tin; the proportions of tin to copper in the alloy were easy to regulate by weighing out the amount of each to be melted in the crucible. Mathewson's (1915) early metallographic examination of the Inka bronzes from Machu Picchu showed how alloy compositions were carefully controlled and matched to the purpose desired: low-tin bronzes that could be work-hardened were used for tools; high-tin bronzes for fancy tumis, where color rather than strength was the property sought and achieved. Having sole access to the critical raw material—tin—combined with a processing sequence that facilitated uniformity in the bronze alloys, provided the kind of semi-standardized production the Inka required for items that were essentially "state issue." The Inka seem not to have sought or achieved in their bronze alloys a closely standardized product such as is common to *cumbi* cloth, however, or to certain forms of Cusco-style fine pottery.

INKA WARFARE

This volume issues from a symposium that addressed "variations in the expression of Inka power." In that context, an obvious consideration is the effect that availability of tin bronze metal may have had on Inka warfare. I would guess that the impact of bronze on the style of engaging an enemy and on the effectiveness of engagement was small. Imperial Inka tin bronze items that may represent tools of war are the lobed mace head and the so-called halberd, which I take to be the five-pointed axe-mace shown in figure 18. Although both items are known archaeologically throughout Tawantinsuyu, they are present in small numbers in Ecuador, Bolivia, and Argentina, and are all but absent in Chile.

Guaman Poma's (1936) letter to Philip III does not furnish much additional information regarding Inka weaponry in metal. Many of the battle scenes he drew illustrate postinvasion events. They refer to encounters between Andean troops and Spanish soldiers or between groups of Andean soldiers, some of whom fought with, others against, the Europeans. In these scenes Poma tends to show Andean combatants using

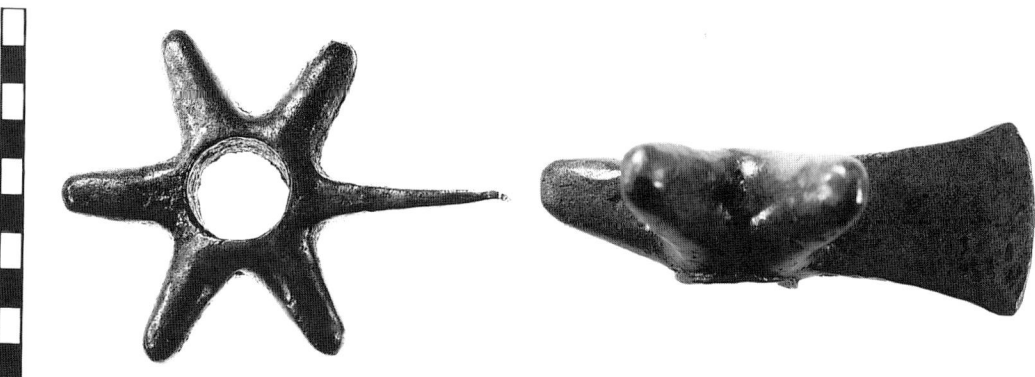

FIG. 18 Top and side views of an Inka tin bronze (10 wgt % tin) axe-mace collected by Adolph Bandelier on the island of Titicaca, Bolivia. American Museum of Natural History, New York (no. B/1846) (after Lechtman 1988, figs. 30.12, 30.13).

what appear to be European weapons, especially the sixteenth-century European iron or steel halberd. The rebel soldiers led by Manco Inka at Vilcabamba outfitted themselves with such Spanish weapons obtained through raiding expeditions (Kubler 1946). Poma's depiction of European-style halberds in the hands of Andean soldiers may, therefore, reflect certain historical circumstances.

Apart from the bronze axe-mace (fig. 18), there has been no published archaeological evidence of Inka metal halberds that predate the European invasion. Spanish eyewitness accounts of Inka military attire describe Inka soldiers as carrying *martillos* (hammers):

> Entrando el segundo escuadrón, entró el tercero, de otra librea, todos con martillos en las manos, de cobre y plata que es un arma que ellos tienen.

> The second squadron having entered, the third entered with a different uniform, all of the men with hammers in their hands made of copper and silver; this is a kind of weapon that they have.
> (Estete 1918[1535]: f. 7v–8; translation mine)

The martillo was a European pole- or staff-arm widespread in military use in the sixteenth century and earlier. It was carried by the foot soldier. Figure 19 illustrates schematically the most common types of pole-arms with which the invading Spanish soldiers were familiar: the halberd, the hammer, and the pole-axe, which combines a hammer with an axe-blade. Figure 19 allows comparison of these European tools of war with Inka counterparts, both arms and insignia: the axe-mace and the *yauri*. Note that the axe-mace (fig. 19d), when viewed in profile (fig. 18), resembles the pole-axe illustrated in figure 19c: the three visible points of the five-point lobed mace at the rear, and the axe blade at the front. It is likely that what Spanish observers described as a hammer was the closest Inka equivalent, the axe-mace. It was not a halberd.

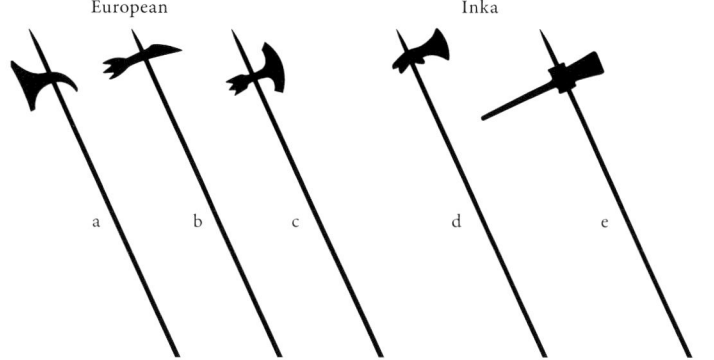

FIG. 19 Schematic drawing of European 15th- and 16th-century pole-arms (a, b, c) and Inka staff arms or insignia (d, e); a = halberd; b = hammer; c = pole-axe; d = axe-mace; e represents an archaeologically known type of Inka tin bronze staff head that Larrea (1960) designates as yauri (a and b are after Harding 1980: 56, items 8, 9; c is modified from Harding, 61, item 8; drawing by Elizabeth Wahle).

In Francisco Xérez's account of the capture of Atawalpa in Cajamarca, he reports stores of Inka arms found in the city by Spanish soldiers:

> Next came men armed with sticks having large knobs at one end, and axes. . . . The axes were the same size or larger. The metal blade was a *palmo* in width, like a halberd. Some of the axes and clubs, used by the chiefs, were of gold and silver. (Xérez, in Markham 1872: 60)

Figures 20 and 21 reproduce Guaman Poma's drawings of events at Cajamarca (Guaman Poma 1936: figs. 382, 384). In his illustration of the encounter between Atawalpa and Hernando Pizarro (fig. 20), Guaman Poma shows the Inka emperor carried in a litter and holding what appears to be a European-style halberd. Guaman Poma may have provided Atawalpa with a halberd deliberately, but we ought also to consider the appearance of Atawalpa's weapon as the result of Guaman Poma's attempt to draw an axe-mace without the skill to render the lobed mace portion of the weapon in foreshortened perspective. The profile view of an Inka bronze axe-mace shown in figures 17 and 18 resembles Guaman Poma's drawing of Atawalpa's weapon in figure 20.

The second of Guaman Poma's Cajamarca scenes (fig. 21) depicts a more formal, nonmilitary setting, with Atawalpa seated on an *usnu* and Francisco Pizarro, in full armor, kneeling before the emperor. Pizarro supports a halberd, but in this setting Atawalpa holds his staff of office. The presumed metal head of the staff resembles the one Atawalpa wields in figure 20, but in the enthroned scene the upper end of the staff is adorned with what may be a bunch of cotton or of grass (see Larrea 1960: 69, quotation from Garcilaso de la Vega).

In other drawings throughout the *Corónica*, Guaman Poma illustrates Inka emperors or members of the royal ayllus carrying their insignia, which resemble axes on long poles. Larrea (1960) argues that the staff heads of these insignia were known as yauri (see fig. 19e).[11] He identifies the imperial scepter, such as the one Guaman Poma shows Viracocha holding (fig. 22), as *tupayauri*. The head was made of solid gold and the

FIG. 20 Atawalpa meets Hernando Pizarro in Caxamarca (from Guaman Poma 1936: fig. 382).

FIG. 21 Atawalpa, enthroned in Caxamarca, receives Francisco Pizarro (from Guaman Poma 1936: fig. 384).

staff terminated in a plume of grasses. Various examples in bronze of what Larrea considers to be yauris[12] have been studied and published (see, for example, Larrea 1960; Rovira 1990; Mayer 1994, 1998). Recently Gordon McEwan and Arminda Gibaja (2004) excavated a copper or bronze yauri in the burial of an Inka child at the Cusco Valley site of Chokepukio. They express surprise at the location of a yauri in a girl's burial, but the association lends weight to the interpretation of these items as Inka badges of office or status rather than as tools or weapons.

All European accounts, eyewitness and later, of Inka pole-type weapons describe the metal heads as made of copper, silver, or gold. Only the bronze axe, mace, and axe-mace are known archaeologically. Clubs and axes or axe-maces of gold or silver would not have served well as impact weapons or cutting and piercing weapons. But the Spanish accounts also describe these metal arms as shiny and highly reflective. We need to keep in mind that an awe-provoking quality of the Inka army was its resplendence (Money 2004). The shininess and brilliance of metal arms and forehead ornaments were meant to frighten and overwhelm an enemy, as were the sounds of rattles and other military instruments (Muelle 1936). In a Mesoamerican context, Hosler (1994) appreciates these sensible properties as "the sounds and colors of power."

The Inka do not appear to have supplied the common foot soldier with bronze weapons. Generals and captains probably had such arms that served as standards or insignia representing state power as much as practical tools of war. Bronze arms were not an important source of power for the Inka during the expansive phase of empire.

IMPERIAL BRONZE

The Inka were responsible for supplying tin or tin bronze in ingot form to metalworkers in regions far from the Bolivian and northwest Argentinian sources of tin ore. People were no longer constrained to use only those metals from their own backyard. The new feature of the state's heavy involvement in the exploitation of metallic ores was the grand scale of that enterprise and the resultant rapid increase in volume of metals produced. This was as true of copper as it was of silver and gold. There was a tin bronze boom in the Bolivian altiplano and in northwest Argentina (L. González 2004) and a dramatic increase in copper-alloy artifacts in the Inka heartland. In the Xauxa region of the central Andes, the onset of the Late Horizon saw a leap in bronze production (Owen n.d.; Costin et al. 1989; Howe and Petersen 1994). In the upper Mantaro, Wanka metalworkers who had been producing objects in arsenic bronze during the Late Intermediate period continued to do so after the arrival of the Inka but gradually began adding tin to their copper or even to the arsenic bronze, producing ternary alloys containing both arsenic and tin. In Cañari territory, in the southern Ecuadorian sierra, some fancy axes previously cast from copper or arsenic bronze were made, without change of style, in tin bronze (Mayer 1992).

FIG. 22 Inka Viracocha with his staff of office, the *tupayauri*. Larrea (1960) argues that the staff head Guaman Poma depicts represents an artifact type known archaeologically in bronze and shown schematically in figure 19e (from Guaman Poma 1936: fig. 106).

Though the volume of all metals produced increased sharply, there were marked differences in the mechanisms through which metal moved within society. Gold and silver circulated primarily as objects through gift exchange from and to the emperor, as in the case of *aquilla*s (see Cummins 2002, and this volume). Such exchanges were carefully controlled. Bronze and tin, on the other hand, were distributed as raw metal to be used locally in fashioning utilitarian items: needles, tumis, tupus, spindle whorls, small chisels, tweezers, axes, and so forth (Escalera and Barriuso 1978; Owen n.d.; Costin et al. 1989; Costin 1998). There was a pronounced increase in the quantity of locally made small metal tools available at the local level. At the same time, the state clearly issued certain standard items, especially tin bronze axes, insignia, and fancy tumis, which saw wide distribution in the sierra (see fig. 18). As John Murra reminded me, the Inka associated craftsmanship in the working of materials with particular ethnic groups. They brought metalworkers to Cusco from Peru's north coast to manufacture items in silver and gold. They brought mullu workers to Cusco from the community of Atico, on the Peruvian south coast, to fashion items from *Spondylus* (Murra 1997; Galdós Rodriguez 1977). If the tin bronze objects I refer to as Inka "standard issue" were made by metalworkers brought to Cusco for the purpose, those craftspeople surely would have come from the south, from the Collao, the Bolivian altiplano, or from northwest Argentina. There is no evidence of state regulation in the types or forms of items made locally from tin bronze (Owen n.d.). Imperial Inka-style objects coexisted with local products.

What was new was the material itself. In the central and northern regions of Tawantinsuyu, tin was available only from state stockpiles. In the south, it is likely that communities continued to mine cassiterite as they had previously (L. González 2004), just as the Inka permitted communities on the northeast shores of Lake Titicaca or at Chuquiabo in La Paz province to continue exploiting their traditional sources of gold (Berthelot 1978) while at the same time providing labor to the large gold mines the state opened at Carabaya and at Chuquiabo.

If tin bronze had an impact on the expression of state power, that impact does not appear to have resulted from any mechanical advantage the Inka gained in their use of bronze. One area in which bronze tools may have made a difference was Inka monumental construction. Long, sturdy crowbars made of this alloy are known from the central Peruvian highlands, including at the site of Machu Picchu (Burger and Salazar 2004; Gordon and Knopf 2006), as well as from Bolivia (Mayer 1994, 1998). These might have provided a mechanical advantage in levering and positioning heavy stone blocks. There is some suggestion in the early documents (Mayer 1998: 89) that such tools were used in mining operations. Since some of them have been found at Tiwanaku, we cannot rule out their use there long before the Inka presence.

Though our data on Inka metallurgy are certainly incomplete, thus far the impression gained from archaeological and ethnohistoric evidence is that metal of all kinds performed for the Inka in much the same way that metal had always performed for Andean peoples. Copper, silver, and gold marked the social and religious status of individuals and groups. In Tawantinsuyu these metals appear to have served a broader role in the state's political agenda by coding features of kinship and gender that the Inka used to define the place of all social units in the conquest hierarchy. These metals provided ideological tools, not mechanical tools, to the state. Even tin bronze, which the Inka clearly intended for widespread distribution, had not seen significant innovative use by the time of the Spanish invasion. It seems to have remained a somewhat "foreign," though imperial alloy.

The impressive engineering achievements by which we know the Inka were accomplished without metal. Their impressive political achievements had metal at the core. In the end, the sweat of the sun and tears of the moon, heavenly instruments though they were, could not protect their progeny from the Spanish onslaught. The irony is overwhelming. The instruments of power in Inka hands, once in the hands of the invader, forsook Tawantinsuyu.

Acknowledgments

John Murra, John Rowe, and R. Tom Zuidema helped guide me through some of the ethnohistoric documents I have cited and in their interpretation. With regard to ethnohistory, I am especially indebted to Pierre Duviols for his unflagging efforts to uncover documentation that might suggest the significance of the metal copper to Andean peoples. Berete Due responded quickly and positively to my request for analysis of some of the inlays on the silver Inka figurine in the collection of the Nationalmuseet, Copenhagen. Christopher Donnan supplied photographs of metal artifacts from the Sipán tombs excavated on the coast of northern Peru. Elizabeth Wahle rendered the careful drawings and diagrams. My sincere thanks to all these colleagues for their patience, instruction, and interest.

Notes

1   Gose refers to the ancient Andean practice of preparing a dead person as a mummy or mallqui, thereby preserving the individual. "There was clearly some sense in which burial was seen as an act of planting and dried, mummified bodies as dormant, desiccated seeds" (Gose 1993: 494).

2   Donnan and Castillo (1992, 1994) and Alva and Donnan (1993) describe these plumed headdresses as made of a copper-silver alloy. Donnan and Castillo (1992) similarly identify the metal of the large mask, illustrated here in figure 4, as a copper-silver alloy. In 1995 I had the opportunity to examine briefly in the field the cleaned mask and partially cleaned arms and legs of the larger burial. I found them to be made of copper and saw no evidence of copper-silver alloy metal. I was not able to see the plumed headdresses, however. It may be that they are made of copper or of a copper alloy.

3   X-ray fluorescence analysis of the finial, carried out at the laboratories of the Römisch-Germanisches Zentralmuseum in Mainz, indicated the presence of about 3 wgt % arsenic in the copper (Eckmann personal communication, December 1994). On the basis of the analysis, the staff should be considered an arsenic bronze.

4   The term tumbaga refers, in a global sense, to Pre-Columbian ternary alloys containing copper, gold, and silver. The proportions in which these three metals were combined varied substantially, resulting in alloys whose color in the cast ingot ranged from pale pink to bright yellow. Objects cast directly from tumbaga alloys often preserved their as-cast color. Those shaped by plastically deforming an ingot, generally through sequences of hammering and annealing the metal, changed color. Tumbaga objects that were worked to shape developed surface color through loss of copper at the surface and consequent enrichment there of the remaining gold and silver components. Processes of color change in alloys through differential surface losses and enrichment have been termed depletion gilding and depletion silvering (Lechtman 1973).

The advantage of using a metallurgical definition for tumbaga—a ternary alloy of copper, gold, and silver capable of color change through surface enrichment and depletion processes—is that the definition embodies the pan-American (Andean, Central American, and Meso-american) utilization of tumbaga alloys and the emphasis placed on their color development properties. At the same time, the inclusiveness of the metallurgical definition masks patterns of alloy use as well as preferences for color and sometimes alloy smell that characterize and may distinguish tumbaga-using societies.

Oliver (2000), in his study of *guanín* (tumbaga) among Taíno (Caribbean) elites, describes the alloy as containing copper, gold, and silver with copper the principal component. The qualities for which Taíno prized objects made of guanín were color, shininess, and their peculiar smell. Oliver stresses that objects made from this alloy type were included by Taíno "in a bounded class of materials [embracing also feathers and shell] that come under the cognitive aegis of gaunín" (Oliver 2000). With respect to Sicán metalworking, Shimada, Griffin, and Gordus (2000) define tumbaga as gold-silver-copper alloys in which the gold content is less than or equal to 40 wgt % (or approximately 10-karat gold), the remainder of the alloy being primarily copper. The authors consider alloys containing more than 40 wgt % gold "high-karat gold alloys" (Shimada, Griffin, and Gordus 2000), but not all contemporary goldsmiths are in agreement. Goldsmith Henry Shawah (Associate of the Worshipful Company of Goldsmiths, England; personal communication, August 1999) refers to alloys in which the concentration of gold is less than 50 wgt % (12 karat) as low-karat gold. He prefers 14-karat alloys (with a gold content of 58 wgt %) as representing an approximate boundary between low- and high-karat gold.

In discussing Sicán material culture in metal, Shimada, Griffin, and Gordus refer to "precious metalworking." They recognize a high "material quality" in metal artifacts "in the sense of proportions of precious metals in the alloy" (2000: fn. 97). They purport to show that the Sicán drew similar distinctions between more or less "precious" metal according to the alloys' gold or gold plus silver content. Yet the large Sicán mummy mask in the Metropolitan Museum of Art, New York, is made of a ternary alloy containing 12 wgt % copper, 40% gold, and 49% silver (Lechtman 1973). The mask alloy corresponds to about a 9.6-karat gold but, by Shimada and Griffin's definition, it is a "precious metal" on the basis of its 89 wgt % gold plus silver content. In the as-cast state, the mask alloy is a pale pink color. The mask developed its rich golden surfaces only through successive stages of the removal of copper, followed by silver (Lechtman 1973). Is the alloy, thereby, a tumbaga? Does it represent a "precious metal," for Sicán smiths or for Shimada and Griffin?

It is time that scholars made an effort to agree upon a working definition of tumbaga and associated metallurgical and cultural designations. We should be able to identify the alloys we encounter in artifacts, to determine the metallurgical/chemical processes by which those alloys and artifacts were produced, and to characterize the cultural content of the materials, the processes, and the artifacts without resort to contemporary classification systems. Oliver's study is a model of excellence in these respects.

5   I follow Murra's (1980) distinction between manufactures for use by the crown (the emperor and members of the royal ayllus) and those for

the state (items produced for purposes of redistribution).

6   The differences in the compositions determined for the head and belly of this figurine suggest to Rovira (1990: 192) that the object was made in two pours, one alloy cast onto another. Both areas analyzed are silver-copper alloys.

7   Mayer's photograph (1998: pl. 289, fig. 4157) of the solid copper or bronze implement from the Pikillacta offering corresponds to the drawing of that item published by Valcarcel (1933: fig. 1). Mayer cites its length as 46 cm (Mayer 1998: 225).

8   The term *upani* refers to the wandering soul of a dead person, which journeys underground in the earth's watery interior (see Gose 1993: 496–499).

9   In 2001 I had the opportunity to sample 36 metal axes from the collections of the R. P. Gustavo Le Paige Museo Arqueológico in San Pedro de Atacama, Chile. Quantitative analyses of these artifacts show that 61% are made from the ternary copper-arsenic-nickel bronze, 19% are made from tin bronze, and 5.6% are made from a quaternary copper-arsenic-nickel-tin alloy. The relative chronological placement of these artifacts remains to be determined, but many undoubtedly are of Middle Horizon manufacture (Lechtman and Macfarlane 2006).

10 Many large stone building blocks in the two pyramid temples at Tiwanku, Bolivia—the Akapana and Pumapunku pyramid mounds—incorporate metal cramps (*grapas*) of copper-arsenic-nickel bronze at joins between abutting faces. Lechtman (1998) discusses the mechanical properties of two of these architectural cramps, one cast, the other worked to shape. Based on the microstructural and chemical data provided by the Pumapunku cramp, Lechtman calculates a series of ternary isotherms, ranging from 1250°C to 500°C, to produce the ternary phase diagram for the entire As-Cu-Ni system (Uhland, Lechtman, and Kaufman 2001).

11 I am indebtred to R. Tom Zuidema for calling my attention to Larrea's long chapter on the *yauri* in his book *Corona Incaica* (1960).

12 Rovira (1990: 303, 304, figs. 168, 169) published the analyses of two tin bronze yauris in the collection of the Museo de América, Madrid. Object no. 7134 contains 10.96 wgt % tin; object no. 7135 contains 10.51 wgt % tin.

References cited

ALVA, WALTER, AND CHRISTOPHER B. DONNAN
1993   *Royal Tombs of Sipán*. Fowler Museum of Cultural History, Los Angeles.

BERTHELOT, JEAN
1978   L'exploitation des métaux précieux au temps des Incas. *Annales. Économies, Sociétés, Civilisations* 33 (5–6): 948–966.

BOONE, ELIZABETH HILL (ED.)
1996   *Andean Art at Dumbarton Oaks*. Dumbarton Oaks Research Library and Collection, Washington, D.C.

BOYLE, ROBERT W.
1979   *The Geochemistry of Gold and Its Deposits*. Geological Survey Bulletin 280. Geological Survey of Canada, Ottawa.

BURGER, RICHARD L., AND LUCY C. SALAZAR (EDS.)
2004   *Machu Picchu: Unveiling the Mystery of the Incas*. Yale University Press, New Haven, Conn.

CARCEDO MORO, PALOMA, AND IZUMI SHIMADA
1985   Behind the Golden Mask: The Sicán Gold Artifacts from Batán Grande, Peru. In *The Art of Precolumbian Gold* (Julie Jones, ed.): 60–75. Little, Brown, Boston, Mass.

CIEZA DE LEÓN, PEDRO DE
1967 [1553]   *El Señorío de los Incas*. Instituto de Estudios Peruanos, Lima.

CLASSEN, CONSTANCE
1993   *Inca Cosmology and the Human Body*. University of Utah Press, Salt Lake City.

COBO, BERNABÉ
1964 [1653]   *Historia del Nuevo Mundo*. In *Obras* (P. Francisco Mateos, ed.). Biblioteca de Autores Españoles 92. Atlas, Madrid.

COSTIN, CATHY LYNNE
1998   Concepts of Property and Access to Nonagricultural Resources in the Inka Empire. In *Property in Economic Context* (Robert C. Hunt and Antonio Gilman, eds.): 119–137. University Press of America, Lanham, Md.

COSTIN, CATHY, TIMOTHY EARLE, BRUCE OWEN, AND GLENN RUSSELL
1989   The Impact of Inca Conquest on Local Technology in the Upper Mantaro Valley. In *What's New? A Closer Look at the Process of Innovation* (Sandor E. van der Leeuw and Robin Torrence, eds.): 107–139. Unwin Hyman, London.

CUESTA DOMINGO, MARIANO, AND SALVADOR ROVIRA LLORENS
1982   *Los trabajos en metal en el área andina*. Ministerio de Cultura, Subdirección General de Museos, Madrid.

CUMMINS, THOMAS B. F.
2002 *Toasts with the Inca*. University of Michigan Press, Ann Arbor.

DE LA VALLE, JOSÉ ANTONIO (ED.)
1992 *Oro del Antiguo Perú*. Banco de Crédito del Perú, Lima.

DONNAN, CHRISTOPHER B.
1978 *Moche Art of Peru*. Museum of Cultural History, University of California, Los Angeles.

DONNAN, CHRISTOPHER B., AND LUIS JAIME CASTILLO B.
1992 Finding the Tomb of a Moche Priestess. *Archaeology* 45 (6): 38–42.

1994 Excavaciones de tumbas de sacerdotistas Moche en San José de Moro, Jequetepeque. In *Moche: Propuestas y Perspectivas* (Santiago Uceda and Elías Mujica, eds.): 415–424. Universidad Nacional de la Libertad, Trujillo, Peru.

DRANSART, PENNY
2000 Clothed Metal and the Iconography of Human Form Among the Incas. In *Precolumbian Gold: Technology, Style and Iconography* (Colin McEwan, ed.): 76–91. The British Museum, London.

DUVIOLS, PIERRE
1983 El *Contra idolatrium* de Luis de Teruel y una versión primeriza del mito de Pachacámac-Vichama. *Revista Andina* 1 (2): 385–392.

EARLS, JOHN, AND IRENE SILVERBLATT
1978 La realidad física y social en la cosmología andina. *Actes du XLIIe Congrès International des Américanistes* (1976) IV: 299–325. Société des américanistes, Paris.

ECKMANN, CHRISTIAN
n.d. Technologische Untersuchungen zu Vergoldungstechniken der Moche Kultur an Objekten aus dem Fürstengrab von Sipan. In *Jahrbuch des Römisch-Germanischen Zentralmuseums Mainz*. Römisch-Germanisches Zentralmuseum, Mainz, Germany (author's manuscript).

EMMERICH, ANDRÉ
1965 *Sweat of the Sun and Tears of the Moon*. University of Washington Press, Seattle.

ESCALERA URENA, ANDRÉS, AND M. ANGELES BARRIUSO P.
1978 Estudio científico de los objetos de metal de Ingapirca (Ecuador). *Revista española de antropología americana* 8: 19–45.

ESTETE, MIGUEL DE
1918 [1535] *El descubrimiento y la conquista del Peru*. Relación inedita (Carlos M. Larrea, intro. and notes). Imprenta de la Universidad Central, Quito.

1938 [1535]   *Noticia del Perú*. In *Los cronistas de la conquista* (Horacio de Urteaga, ed.). Biblioteca de Cultura Peruana 2. 1st series. Desclée, De Brouwer, Paris.

FESTER, G. A.
1962   Copper and Copper Alloys in Ancient Argentina. *Chymia* 8: 21–31.

GALDÓS RODRÍGUEZ, GUILLERMO
1977 [1549]   Visita a Atico y Caravelí. *Revista del Archivo General de la Nación* 4–5: 55–80.

GONZÁLEZ, ALBERTO REX
1979   Pre-Columbian Metallurgy of Northwest Argentina: Historical Development and Cultural Process. In *Pre-Columbian Metallurgy of South America* (Elizabeth P. Benson, ed.): 133–202. Dumbarton Oaks Research Library and Collection, Washington, D.C.

1992   *Las placas metálicas de los Andes del Sur*. Materialien zur allgemeinen und vergleichenden Archäologie 46. Verlag Philipp von Zabern, Mainz, Germany.

GONZÁLEZ, LUIS R.
2004   *Bronces sin nombre: La metalurgia prehispánica en el noroeste argentino*. Ediciones Fundación CEPPA, Buenos Aires.

GORDON, ROBERT B.
1985   Laboratory Evidence of the Use of Metal Tools at Machu Picchu (Peru) and Environs. *Journal of Archaeological Science* 12: 311–327.

GORDON, ROBERT, AND ROBERT KNOPF
2006   Metallurgy of Bronze Used in Tools from Machu Picchu. *Archaeometry* 48 (1): 57–76.

GOSE, PETER
1993   Segmentary State Formation and the Ritual Control of Water Under the Incas. *Comparative Studies in Society and History* 35 (3): 480–514.

GUAMAN POMA DE AYALA, FELIPE
1936 [1615]   *Nueva corónica y buen gobierno*. Université de Paris. Travaux et memoires de l'Institut d'Ethnologie 23. Institut d'Ethnologie, Paris.

HARDING, DAVID (ED.)
1980   *Weapons: An International Encyclopedia from 5000 BC to 2000 AD*. St. Martin's Press, New York.

HOCQUENGHEM, ANNE MARIE, AND PATRICIA J. LYON
1980   A Class of Anthropomorphic Supernatural Females in Moche Iconography. *Ñawpa Pacha* 18: 27–48.

HÖRZ, G., AND M. KALLFASS

2000   The Treasure of Gold and Silver Artifacts from the Royal Tombs of Sipán, Peru: A Study on the Moche Metalworking Techniques. *Materials Characterization* 45: 391–420.

HOSLER, DOROTHY

1988   The Metallurgy of Ancient West Mexico. In *The Beginning of the Use of Metals and Alloys* (Robert Maddin, ed.): 328–343. MIT Press, Cambridge, Mass.

1994   *The Sounds and Colors of Power*. MIT Press, Cambridge, Mass.

HOSLER, DOROTHY, HEATHER LECHTMAN, AND OLAF HOLM

1990   *Axe-monies and Their Relatives*. Studies in Pre-Columbian Art and Archaeology 30. Dumbarton Oaks Research Library and Collection, Washington, D.C.

HOWE, ELLEN G., AND ULRICH PETERSEN

1994   Silver and Lead in the Late Prehistory of the Mantaro Valley, Peru. In *Archaeometry of Pre-Columbian Sites and Artifacts* (David A. Scott and Pieter Meyers, eds.): 183–198. The Getty Conservation Institute, Los Angeles.

KUBLER, GEORGE

1946   The Quechua in the colonial World. In *Handbook of South American Indians* (Julian H. Steward, ed.), vol. 2, *The Andean Civilizations*: 331–410. Government Printing Office, Washington, D.C.

LAPINER, ALAN

1976   *Pre-Columbian Art of South America*. Harry N. Abrams, New York.

LARREA, JUAN

1960   *Corona Incaica*. Facultad de Filosofía y Humanidades, Universidad Nacional de Córdoba, Córdoba, Argentina.

LECHTMAN, HEATHER

1971   Ancient Methods of Gilding Silver—Examples from the Old and the New Worlds. In *Science and Archaeology* (Robert H. Brill, ed.): 2–30. MIT Press, Cambridge, Mass.

1973   The Gilding of Metals in Pre-Columbian Peru. In *Application of Science in Examination of Works of Art* (William J. Young, ed.): 38–52. Museum of Fine Arts, Boston, Mass.

1980   The Central Andes—Metallurgy Without Iron. In *The Coming of the Age of Iron* (Theodore Wertime and James Muhly, eds.): 267–334. Yale University Press, New Haven, Conn.

1988   Traditions and Styles in Central Andean Metalworking. In *The Beginning of the Use of Metals and Alloys* (Robert Maddin, ed.): 344–378. MIT Press, Cambridge, Mass.

1993   Technologies of Power—The Andean Case. In *Configurations of Power: Holistic Anthropology in Theory and Practice* (John S. Henderson and Patricia J. Netherly, eds.): 244–280. Cornell University Press, Ithaca, N.Y.

1996   Arsenic Bronze: Dirty Copper or Chosen Alloy? *Journal of Field Archaeology* 23: 477–514.

1997   El bronce arsenical y el Horizonte Medio. In *Arqueología, Antropología e Historia en los Andes* (Rafael Varón Gabai and Javier Flores Espinoza, eds.): 153–186. Instituto de Estudios Peruanos, Lima, Peru.

1998   Architectural Cramps at Tiwanaku: Copper-Arsenic-Nickel Bronze. In *Metallurgica Antiqua* (Thilo Rehren, Andreas Hauptmann, and James Muhly, eds.). *Der Anschnitt* 8: 77–92.

1999a Afterword. In *The Social Dynamics of Technology* (Marcia-Anne Dobres and Christopher R. Hoffman, eds.): 223–232. Smithsonian Institution Press, Washington, D.C.

1999b [1996] El bronce y el Horizonte Medio. *Boletín, Museo del Oro* 41: 2–25.

2003a Tiwanaku Period (Middle Horizon) Bronze Metallurgy in the Lake Titicaca Basin: A Preliminary Assessment. In *Tiwanaku and Its Hinterland* (Alan L. Kolata, ed.): 404–434. Smithsonian Institution Press, Washington, D.C.

2003b Middle Horizon Bronze: Centers and Outliers. In *Patterns and Process* (Lambertus van Zelst, ed.): 248–268. Smithsonian Center for Materials Research and Education, Suitland, Md.

2005   Arsenic Bronze at Pikillacta. In *Pikillacta: The Wari Occupation of Cuzco* (Gordon McEwan, ed.): 131–146. University of Iowa Press, Iowa City.

LECHTMAN, HEATHER, AND SABINE KLEIN

1999   The Production of Copper-Arsenic Alloys (Arsenic Bronze) by Cosmelting: Modern Experiment, Ancient Practice. *Journal of Archaeological Science* 26 (5): 497–526.

LECHTMAN, HEATHER, AND ANDREW W. MACFARLANE

2005   La metalurgia del bronce en los Andes Sur Centrales: Tiwanaku y San Pedro de Atacama. *Estudios Atacameños* 30: 7–27.

2006   Bronce y redes de intercambio andino durante el Horizonte Medio: Tiwanaku y San Pedro de Atacama. In *Esferas de interacción prehistóricas y fronteras nacionales modernas: Los Andes Sur Centrales* (Heather Lechtman, ed.): 503–539. Instituto de Estudios Peruanos, Lima.

LOTHROP, SAMUEL K.

1937   Gold and Silver from Southern Peru and Bolivia. *Journal of the Royal Anthropological Institute* 67: 305–325.

1938 *Inca Treasure as Depicted by Spanish Historians*. The Southwest Museum, Los Angeles.

MARKHAM, CLEMENTS R.

1872 *Reports on the Discovery of Peru*. The Hakluyt Society, London.

MATHEWSON, CHAMPION H.

1915 A Metallographic Description of Some Ancient Peruvian Bronzes from Machu Picchu. *American Journal of Science* 40: 525–616.

MAYER, EUGEN FRIEDRICH

1986 *Armas y herramientas de metal prehispánicas en Argentina y Chile*. Materialien zur allgemeinen und vergleichenden Archäologie 38. Verlag C. H. Beck, Munich, Germany.

1992 *Armas y herramientas de metal prehispánicas en Ecuador*. Materialien zur allgemeinen und vergleichenden Archäologie 47. Verlag Philipp von Zabern, Mainz, Germany.

1994 *Armas y herramientas de metal prehispánicas en Bolivia*. Materialien zur allgemeinen und vergleichenden Archäologie 53. Verlag Philipp von Zabern, Mainz, Germany.

1998 *Armas y herramientas de metal prehispánicas en Perú*. Materialien zur allgemeinen und vergleichenden Archäologie 55. Verlag Philipp von Zabern, Mainz, Germany.

MCEWAN, GORDON, AND ARMINDA GIBAJA O.

n.d. Report of the Selz Foundation Excavations at Chokepukio, Peru. Unpublished site report, 2004 (author's manuscript).

MENZEL, DOROTHY

1968 New Data on the Huari Empire in Middle Horizon Epoch 2A. *Ñawpa Pacha* 6: 47–114.

MONEY, MARY

2004 *Oro y plata en los Andes*. Colección "Historias Andinas y Amazónicas" 4. Colegio Nacional de Historiadores de Bolivia, La Paz.

MOSELEY, MICHAEL E.

1990 Structure and History in the Dynastic Lore of Chimor. In *The Northern Dynasties: Kingship and Statecraft in Chimor* (Michael E. Moseley and Alana Cordy-Collins, eds.): 1–41. Dumbarton Oaks Research Library and Collection, Washington, D.C.

MUELLE, JORGE C.

1936 Chalchalcha: Un análisis de los dibujos Muchik. *Revista del Museo Nacional* 5 (1): 65–88.

MURRA, JOHN VICTOR

1980 *The Economic Organization of the Inka State*. JAI Press, Greenwich, Conn.

1997 ¿Existieron el tributo y los mercados en los Andes antes de la invasión europea? In *Arqueología, antropología e historia en los Andes* (Rafael Varón Gabai and Javier Flores Espinoza, eds.): 737–748. Instituto de Estudios Peruanos, Lima.

OLIVER, JOSÉ R.

2000 Gold Symbolism Among Caribbean Chiefdoms: Of Feathers, *Çibas*, and *Guanín* Power Among Taíno Elites. In *Precolumbian Gold: Technology, Style and Iconography* (Colin McEwan, ed.): 196–219. The British Museum, London.

OWEN, BRUCE

n.d. The Role of Common Metal Objects in the Inka State. M.A. thesis, University of California, Los Angeles, 1987.

PAULSEN, ALLISON C.

1974 The Thorny Oyster and the Voice of God: *Spondylus* and *Strombus* in Andean Prehistory. *American Antiquity* 39: 597–607.

PETERSEN, ULRICH

1989 Geological Framework of Andean Mineral Resources. In *Geology of the Andes and Its Relation to Hydrocarbon and Mineral Resources* (George E. Ericksen, María Teresa Cañas Pinochet, and John A. Reinemund, eds.): 213–232. Circum-Pacific Council for Energy and Mineral Resources, Tulsa, Okla.

QUILTER, JEFFREY

1997 The Narrative Approach to Moche Iconography. *Latin Americian Antiquity* 8 (2): 113–133.

ROOT, WILLIAM C.

1949 The Metallurgy of the Southern Coast of Peru. *American Antiquity* 15 (1): 10–37.

ROSTWOROWSKI DE DIEZ CANSECO, MARÍA

1970 Mercaderes del valle de Chincha en la época prehispánica. *Revista Española de Antropología Americana* 5: 135–178.

1977 *Etnía y sociedad*. Instituto de Estudios Peruanos, Lima.

1983 *Estructuras andinas del poder*. Historia Andina 10. Instituto de Estudios Peruanos, Lima.

1990 Ethnohistorical Considerations About the Chimor. In *The Northern Dynasties: Kingship and Statecraft in Chimor* (Michael E. Moseley and Alana Cordy-Collins, eds.): 447–460. Dumbarton Oaks Research Library and Collection, Washington, D.C.

ROVIRA LLORENS, SALVADOR

1990 *La metalurgia americana: Análisis tecnológico de materiales prehispánicos y coloniales.* Editorial de la Universidad Complutense de Madrid, Madrid.

ROWE, JOHN HOWLAND

1946 Inca Culture at the Time of the Spanish Conquest. In *Handbook of South American Indians* (Julian H. Steward, ed.), vol. 2, *The Andean Civilizations*: 183–330. Government Printing Office, Washington, D.C.

1948 The Kingdom of Chimor. *Acta Americana* 6 (1–2): 26–59.

1985 Probanza de los incas nietos de conquistadores. *Histórica* 9 (2): 193–245.

RUTLEDGE, JOHN W., AND ROBERT B. GORDON

1987 The Work of Metallurgical Artificers at Machu Picchu, Peru. *American Antiquity* 52 (3): 578–594.

SANCHO DE LA HOZ, PEDRO

1938 [1534] *Relación para S.M. de lo sucedido en la conquista y pacificación de estas provincias de la Nueva Castilla y de la calidad de la tierra . . .* In *Los cronistas de la conquista* (Horacio de Urteaga, ed.). Biblioteca de Cultura Peruana 2. 1st series. Desclée, De Brouwer, Paris.

1969 [1534] *An Account of the Conquest of Peru* (Philip Ainsworth Means, ed. and trans.). Kraus Reprint Co., New York.

SHERBONDY, JEANETTE E.

1992 Water Ideology in Inca Ethnogenesis. In *Andean Cosmologies Through Time* (Robert V. H. Dover, Katharine E. Seibold, and John H. McDowell, eds.): 46–66. Indiana University Press, Bloomington.

SHIMADA, IZUMI

1985 Perception, Procurement, and Management of Resources: Archaeological Perspective. In *Andean Ecology and Civilization* (Shozo Masuda, Izumi Shimada, and Craig Morris, eds.): 357–399. University of Tokyo Press, Tokyo, Japan.

1987 Horizontal and Vertical Dimensions of Prehistoric States in North Peru. In *The Origins and Development of the Andean State* (Jonathan Haas, Sheila Pozorski, and Thomas Pozorski, eds.): 130–144. Cambridge University Press, Cambridge, England.

1999 Sican Metallurgy and Its Cross-craft Relationships. *Boletín, Museo del Oro* 41: 26–61

SHIMADA, IZUMI, JO ANN GRIFFIN, AND ADON GORDUS

2000 The Technology, Iconography and Social Significance of Metals: A Multi-Dimensional Analysis of Middle Sicán

Objects. In *Precolumbian Gold: Technology, Style and Iconography* (Colin McEwan, ed.): 28–61. The British Museum, London.

TITU CUSSI YUPANGUI

1985 [1570] *Ynstruçion del Ynga Don Diego de Castro Titu Cussi Yupangui para el muy ilustre Señor el Licenciado Lope García de Castro . . .* (Luis Millones, intro.). Ediciones El Virrey, Lima.

TOPIC, JOHN

1990 Craft Production in the Kingdom of Chimor. In *The Northern Dynasties: Kingship and Statecraft in Chimor* (Michael E. Moseley and Alana Cordy-Collins, eds.): 145–174. Dumbarton Oaks Research Library and Collection, Washington, D.C.

UHLAND, SCOTT, HEATHER LECHTMAN, AND LARRY KAUFMAN

2001 Assessment of the As-Cu-Ni System: An Example from Archaeology. *CALPHAD* 29: 109–124.

VALCARCEL, LUIS E.

1933 Esculturas de Pikillajta. *Revista del Museo Nacional* 2 (1): 21–35.

XÉREZ, FRANCISCO DE

1872 [1534] *Verdadera relación de la conquista del Perú.* In *Reports on the Discovery of Peru* (Clements R. Markham, trans.). The Hakluyt Society, London.

ZUIDEMA, R. TOM

1964 *The Ceque System of Cuzco: The Social Organization of the Capital of the Inca* (Eva M. Hooykaas, trans.). Brill, Leiden.

1977 The Inca Calendar. In *Native American Astronomy* (Anthony F. Aveni, ed.): 219–259. University of Texas Press, Austin.

1992 Inca Cosmos in Andean Context. In *Andean Cosmologies Through Time* (Robert V. H. Dover, Katharine E. Seibold, and John H. McDowell, eds.): 15–45. Indiana University Press, Bloomington.

Information Control in the Palace of Puruchuco: An Accounting Hierarchy in a Khipu Archive from Coastal Peru

Gary Urton
Carrie J. Brezine

THE CONTROL OF INFORMATION IS ONE OF THE PRINCIPAL WAYS OF exercising power in human societies. This statement was as true for ancient cultures as it is today. There are numerous examples of information control in ancient societies: the hoarding of cuneiform tablets in temple archives, or the production, placement, and occasional defacing of commemorative stelae in Maya sites. There are few explicit examples of such practices from the Pre-Columbian Andes. However, recent research on the khipu, the principal record-keeping device used in the Inka Empire (Ascher and Ascher 1997 [1981]; Quilter and Urton 2002; Urton 2003), is beginning to produce new insights into the highly technical practices and strategies of information collection, control, and manipulation among officials at different levels within the state administrative hierarchy. In this study, we discuss what is perhaps the clearest example encountered to date of the form information may have taken and of how it may have been synthesized and manipulated in its movement between lower- and higher-level accounting centers in the Inka provinces. The corpus of samples discussed in this study makes up what we refer to as a khipu "archive."

In 1949/50, the Italian national, but long-time Peruvian resident, Carlos Radicati di Primeglio published a study of a collection of eight khipus from the Santa Valley, on the north-central coast of Peru (1949–50: 276). In his monograph, Radicati referred to this collection of khipus as an "archive," and went on to deal with them as written archival documents—that is, as records pertaining to the people in some locale who had an interrelated set of interests and common procedures for accounting. Applied to Inka record keeping, the archive paradigm, developed explicitly in a recent publication by Gary Urton (2005), is based on the proposal that khipus with a common provenience or archaeological context should be thought of as accounts produced by either local khipu keepers or Inka accountants resident in that locale. In either circumstance, the records from any narrowly defined region may bear some historical and/or substantive relationship to each other. One possible consequence of such interrelationships is that khipus composing an archive will complement, duplicate, and possibly comment on each other. The sixteenth-century Spanish chronicler Martín de Murúa describes the complex types of information that might have been contained in a khipu archive:

> Thus, the accountants have great heaps (*montones*) of these strings, in the form of registries, just as scribes have in their offices, and there they maintain their archives, and in that way, should anyone want to know something, they have to do no more than go to one of the *Quipucamayo* of these [records] and ask him how much this thing was, or which Inka made this law, [or] who conquered such and such a province, [or] who were his captains, [or] in which years was it dry and which fertile, [or] when were there pestilence and wars, [or] when did certain Indians rebel, [or] when did a certain volcano erupt, [or] when did a certain river flood and destroy the fields? Then, the accountant would take up his cords and give them a reading/interpretation (*daba razón de ello*), without making a single mistake. (Murúa 2001 [1590]: bk. 2, chap. 11, 360–361; translation by Urton)[1]

In addition to the event-based, historical information detailed by Murúa, we have numerous accounts stating that all statistical records concerning the business of the state—censuses, tribute levies, and performance—were retained on khipus stored in archives (Garcilaso de la Vega, 1966 [1609]: 50, 267, 274–275). In this article, we consider the question of the composition and use of khipu archives by focusing on a collection of samples from a single archaeological site and, presumably, accounting context. The site in question is Puruchuco, an Inka-period palace in the lower Rimac Valley, on the central coast of Peru (Jiménez Borja 1956; Villacorta Ostolaza and J. Ávila C. 1998; Wakeham Dasso 1976). We introduce the site of Puruchuco and its Inka khipus after commenting on relevant features of record keeping in the Inka Empire.

The chronicler Garcilaso de la Vega provided an important insight into Inka accounting practices when he noted that the number of khipu keepers in each community was in proportion to the population but that, however small, any given community had no fewer than four *khipukamayuq* ("khipu-makers/keepers"). Garcilaso went on to note that the khipukamayuq "all kept the same records" (1966 [1609]: 331). This suggests a strong element of checks and balances underlying Inka state record keeping, and has been the focus recently of a considerable comparative analysis of various archives by the Khipu Database Project.[2] In the earlier publication on khipu archives, referenced above, Urton described numerous instances of "matching khipus": multiple samples bearing identical or near identical numerical information. It was argued in that study that such matches represent duplicate accounts that may be products of the Inka system of checks and balances.

Inka Decimal Administration and Khipu Accounting

Matching khipus help clarify the sharing of information horizontally, between record keepers at the same level of the Inka decimal administrative hierarchy. However, if this was a true system of checks and balances, we would also expect to find instances of the summation and partition (or subdivision) of information vertically, as information was transferred up and down the linked accounting levels. The horizontal and vertical components of Inka accounting are represented in figure 1, a schematic diagram showing the basic structure of the accounting categories constituting Inka administrative organization.

To a large degree, Inka administration was concerned with accounting for the labor time of state subjects. As has been well documented (D'Altroy 2002: 265–268; Murra 1980), tribute in the Inka state was levied in the form of a labor tax. Each "taxpayer" (i.e., state laborer) was required to work a specified number of days each year on state projects, which included the tending of the Inka's herds of camelids; farming on state agricultural projects; building and maintaining storehouses, roads, and bridges; and performing other duties (for explicit testimony on this point, see Cobo 1983 [1653]: 209; and Garcilaso de la Vega, 1966 [1609]: 271, 273). The best explanation to date of how this labor-based system was implemented is Catherine Julien's article, "How Inca Decimal Administration Worked" (1988). Julien's study, based on a Spanish transcription of an Inka tributary khipu from Chupacho (Huánuco), in the central highlands of Peru, analyzes how Inka accountants assessed tribute levels and assigned tasks to different numbers of local workers. The procedures involved assessing numbers of laborers to perform tasks on the basis of percentages of a standardized accounting unit of four *waranqas* (4,000 tribute payers).

Unfortunately, the Chupacho tributary data are known to us only in the form of a Spanish transcription of the original khipu unaccompanied by its source khipu.[3] Therefore while Julien's study is highly informative, her article cannot inform us how this information might actually have been recorded.[4] To suggest how khipus might record such data, we focus on two issues: How was the administrative system organized? And how did information move within this system?

The first question may be illuminated by examining the hierarchical organization of categories based on decimal groupings of tributaries.

Beginning at the bottom (fig. 1), we see that at the local level, tributaries were grouped into five accounting units of ten members each. One member of each of these groups of ten would have served as Chunka Kamayoq ("organizer of ten"). Five such groupings would make a unit of fifty tribute payers, under the authority of a Pichqa-Chunka Kuraka ("lord of fifty"). Two groups of fifty would be combined into a unit of one hundred tributaries led by a Pachaka Kuraka ("lord of one hundred"), and so on up the hierarchy (see Pärssinen 1992: 370–390 for a discussion of exact versus approximate decimal units in Inka administrative structure and labor [*mit'a*] organization).

Following a line of interconnections up the different levels of figure 1, it becomes clear that the decimal hierarchy was organized such that categories were formed from increasingly higher permutations of dual and quinary organization: 10 x 5 x 2 x 5 x 2, etc. This accords with general Quechua/Inka decimal numerical principles (see Urton 1997: 214–217). Near the top of the decimal administrative hierarchy were the heads of the approximately eighty provinces, officials called T'oqrikoq. Each provincial official was under the direction of a Lord of the Four Quarters, who served directly under the Inka king in Cusco. Cieza de León, the great mid-sixteenth-century traveler and chronicler, gave the following description of the Inkan accounting hierarchy:

> In each provincial seat there were accountants called khipu-keepers who, by their knots, had the record and accounting of what was owed as tribute by the people from that district, including silver, gold, clothing and livestock down to firewood and other, lesser items, and by means of the khipu, arriving at the end of the year, or of ten or twenty years, in the accounting of the one who was commissioned to make the accounting, there would not be lost [from the accounting] even one pair of sandals. . . . And in each valley today they keep such an accounting, and there are always in each place of habitation as many accountants as there are lords and every four months they close out [rectify] their accounts in the aforesaid manner. (Cieza de León, 1967 [1553]: chap. 12, 36–37; translation by Urton)[5]

Garcilaso stated that the governor of each province was required to keep a copy of the khipu account so that "no deception could be practiced by either the Indian tribute payers or the official collectors" (1966 [1609]: 275).

The head official of accounting units up to the level of the Lord of 1,000 could have been the same person. It is likely that the higher-level officials, such as the Hunu Kuraka ("Lord of 10,000") and the provincial governors, the T'oqrikoqs, were appointed by the Inka in consultation with the appropriate Lord of the Four Quarters (Cobo 1983 [1653]: 199).

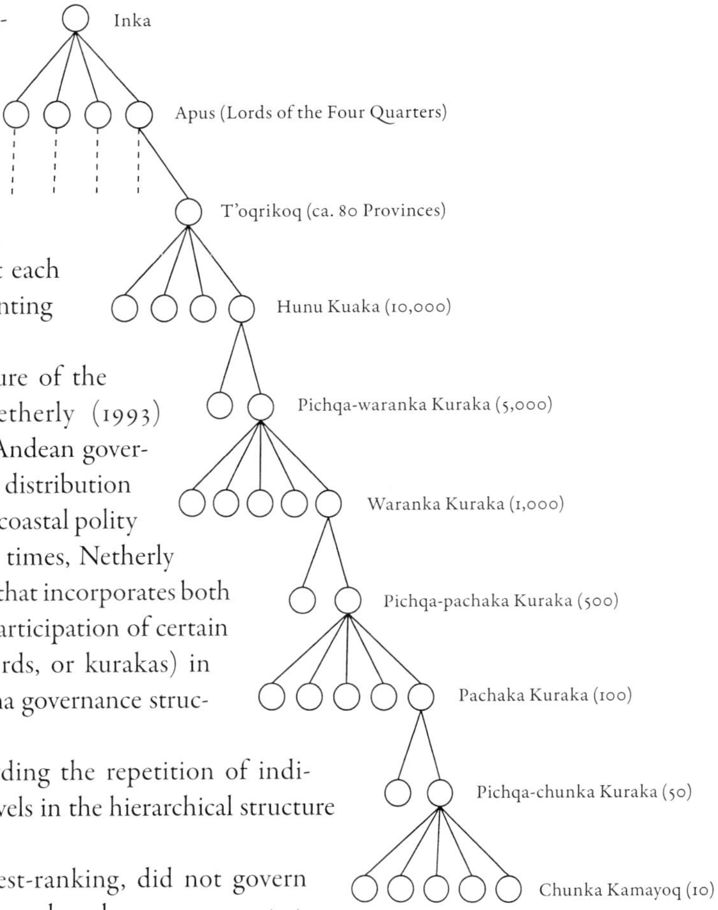

Dualism was a pervasive principle in Inka political organization, and there is good evidence (e.g., Netherly 1993; Urton 2003, 2005) to suppose that dualism would have also been reflected in the sharing of authority at each level of this hierarchy of accounting categories and officials.

In her study, "The Nature of the Andean State," Patricia Netherly (1993) described several features of Andean governance. Through analysis of the distribution of native officials in the north coastal polity of Chicama in early colonial times, Netherly derives an authority structure that incorporates both dualism and the redundant participation of certain individuals (high-ranking lords, or kurakas) in different levels of the Chicama governance structure (see fig. 2).

As Netherly notes regarding the repetition of individuals' names on different levels in the hierarchical structure shown in figure 2,

> [R]ulers, even the highest-ranking, did not govern alone. Though one ruler may have been paramount at any given level, his rule was limited by the fact that he directly controlled only part of the lower levels of the polity. The necessary presence of the lords of the other principal sections of the polity served as a check on unilateral action by the lord of the higher-ranking moiety. (Netherly 1993: 18)

We argue that a hierarchical, dualistic governance structure is compatible with the generalized administrative hierarchy of the Inka state and that it summarizes precisely a parallel structure that we will describe in detail later in this study. We note here Pärssinen's suggestion that the

FIG. 1 Inka decimal administration

FIG. 2 Hierarchy and dualism in the administrative organization of Chicama (16th c.)

Don Juan de Mora							
Don Juan de Mora				Don Pedro Mache			
Don Juan de Mora		Don Alonso Chuchinamo		Don Pedro Mache		Don Gonzalo Sulpinamo	
Don Juan de Mora		Don Alonso Chuchinamo	Don Diego Sancaynamo	Don Pedro Mache	Don Diego Martín Conaman	Don Gonzalo Sulpinamo	

Information Control in the Palace of Puruchuco

parcialidades (*ayllu*-like sociopolitical groups) and waranqa (accounting units of 1,000) in the Rimac Valley were divided in a dualistic manner (Pärssinen 1992: 342; Rostworowski 1978: 49–107). Given the dualistic nature of the administrative structure, it is reasonable to suppose that dualism, in the form of duplicates, or pairs of accounts, would have been a feature of the accounting system too.

The question that is of primary interest to us now with respect to the Inka administrative system is: how did information move between adjacent levels of this hierarchical administration? Figure 1 represents in schematic form the basic organization for the movement of two different, interrelated, types of information that were being passed in opposite vertical directions. The expectations of higher-level officials toward lower-level officials would have moved, via khipus, from the top down. Khipus containing such instructions from the state probably included at least two signing elements: identifiers and numbers. Identifiers would indicate the tasks to be performed, while numbers would represent the quantity of workers to be recruited. Information concerning expectations, moving downward, would be *partitive* in nature; for instance, assignments made to 1,000 tribute payers would be broken down into two groups of 500, the latter of which would be further reduced to five groups of 100, and so on (see Pärssinen 1992: 31–42).

In the reverse direction, we would expect that local accountants would pass data on accomplished tasks upward through the hierarchy. In this direction, information at each level would represent the *summation* of accounts from the level immediately below. These data would eventually arrive in the hands of the Cusco accountants, where the highest level of accounting went on. As Cieza described this situation:

> That which was paid as tribute each period and contributed by the natives of these administrative seats, including gold, silver, clothing and arms, and everything else they gave, was all entered into the accounts of the officials who kept the *khipu*, and who were in all instances responsible for dispensing these items to the troops or distributing them to whomever the Lord ordered or of taking them to Cuzco; but when they came from the city of Cuzco to make the accounting [i.e., the audit], or when they [the local accountants] would go to Cuzco to do it, these same accountants supplied it [the accounting] with their *khipu* in such a way that there could be no fraud, but rather so that all was perfectly accounted for. (Cieza de León 1967 [1553]: chap. 20, 67; translation by Urton)[6]

Cieza's statement attests to the utility of incorporating an element of checks and balances. We have recently described several examples of "matching khipus," which, we believe, represent duplicate accounts from the same level, probably in relation to the checks and balances feature of Inka record keeping. "Close matches" have also been identified; these have close but not matching data. Close matches may represent recounts of census or tribute records at different moments in time, or records made by different accountants who counted items differently, or relationships (often not exactly equivalent) between tribute labor credits and debits (Urton 2003:191–194; and 2005). Until now we had not identified a set of khipus related through summation/partition, such as we would expect to find if information was indeed moving up and down the administrative hierarchy. We believe the Puruchuco khipus that we turn to below embody this kind of reciprocal summing/partitive relationship.[7]

The Archaeological Context of the Puruchuco Khipu

The archaeological site of Puruchuco is located on the south bank of the Rimac River, about 11.5 km northeast of the center of Lima, within the present-day district of Ate (fig. 3). Originally known as Vista Alegre, since it is located on land previously belonging to a hacienda of that name, Puruchuco was excavated and reconstructed by Dr. Arturo Jiménez Borja with Jorge C. Muelle, beginning in 1953 (Jiménez Borja 1973). Excavation took several years. The discovery of the khipu cache occurred on 9 August 1956. The site report from these excavations has not been published to date. Our comments on the archaeological context and disposition of the khipu are based on field notes written at the time of their excavation, and on information from the website of the Museo de Sitio Puruchuco—Arturo Jiménez Borja.[8] The text of this highly informative website was written

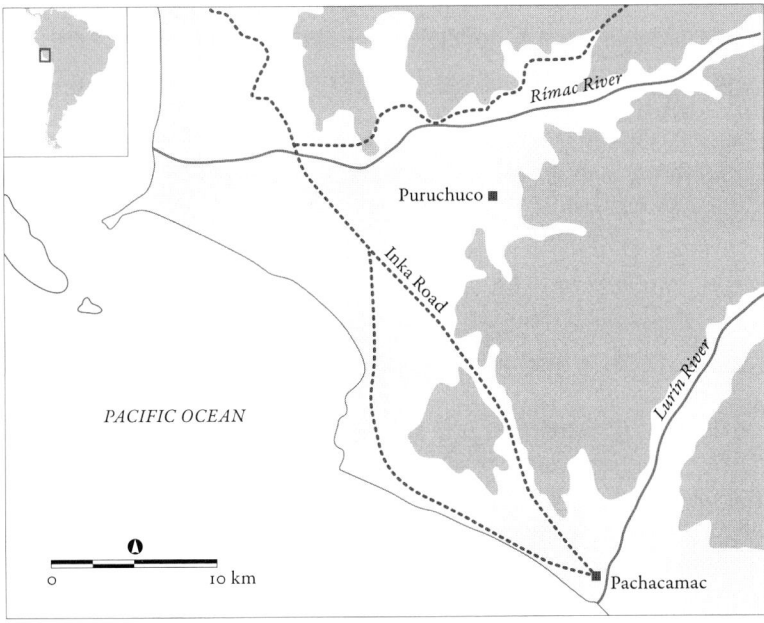

FIG. 3 The location of the site of Puruchuco, Rimac Valley (drawing by Karen Rasmussen, Archeographics, after Villacorta Ostolaza, Vetter Parodi, and Ausejo 2004: 67)

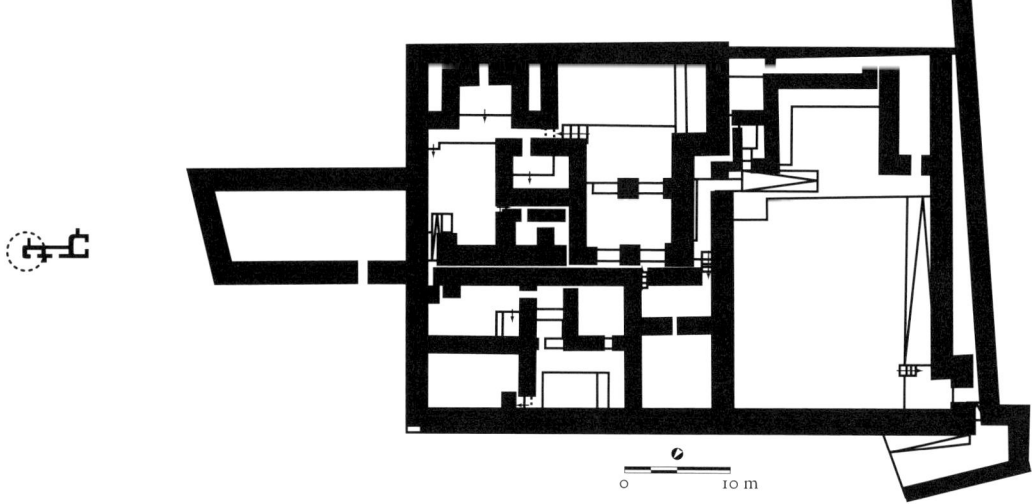

FIG. 4 Site plan of the palace of Puruchuco (drawing by Karen Rasmussen, Archeographics, after Villacorta Ostolaza, Vetter Parodi, and Ausejo 2004: 44)

by our friend and colleague Luis Felipe Villacorta Ostolaza, archaeologist and former director of the Puruchuco Museum (see also Villacorta Ostolaza et al. 2004).

The site is a roughly rectangular compound with high surrounding walls made of tapia (pounded adobe) construction. There is a single, sloping entryway granting access onto a large interior square plaza (fig. 4). A maze of narrow passageways led the occupants through two sectors composed of a mix of residential, administrative, and storage rooms. Villacorta Ostolaza suggests that this large structure was a "palace," as the site seems to have been a center dedicated to the oversight of activities in the surrounding region. The presence of balances and khipus indicates that the site probably functioned as a center of local control and administration.

Around and in some cases abutted to the palace of Puruchuco were several smaller constructions. The cache of khipus was found under the floor of one of these smaller buildings, immediately to the west of the palace (see fig. 4). From its location, Carol Mackey, who first studied the Puruchuco khipus in the late 1960s, surmised that this building was the house of a khipu-keeper who served the lord occupying the palace (1970: 65–66). Fieldnotes from the day the khipus were discovered, written by Victor Salazar, provide a straightforward recounting of what was a highly significant event for khipu studies:[9]

> 9 August, 1956—The work consisted, as over the past three days, in removing "fill," or dirt from the upper part of sector B to fill a pit in Platform A.... In the zone of extraction (Sector B, upper part) of the fill the workman Lizama encountered a narrow-necked urn (*cantaro*), semi-ovoid in form, covered with soot (*hollín*) and with an appliqué on the outer body in the form of

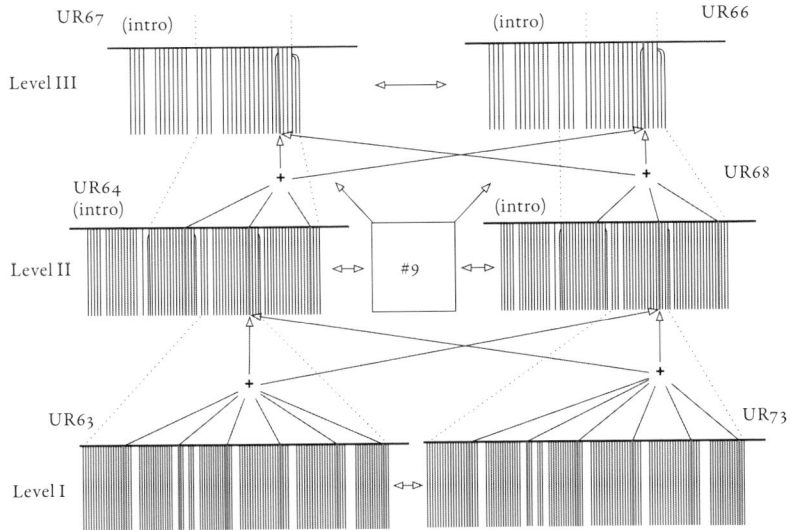

FIG. 5 The accounting hierarchy from the archive of Puruchuco

a serpent; its [i.e., the urn's] mouth was covered by a small lagenaria [bottle gourd], in the interior there were found 10 khipus of regular size, 3 of which had red/orange/yellow tassels, 11 medium-sized ones, and several loose pendant strings, all in a good state of preservation [translation by Urton].[10]

In her discussion of these khipus, Mackey notes that half of the twenty-one khipus found in the urn were in a "rolled condition" (1970: 66). These samples had their primary cords coiled around the pendant strings in the manner of khipus prepared for storage in archives (cf., Conklin 2002: 53–55).

The Puruchuco Accounting Hierarchy

What we term the Puruchuco "accounting hierarchy" pertains to seven of the twenty-one khipu samples found together in the *olla*. Though not included in this analysis, several other khipus may have provided supporting documentation to these seven. The seven khipus are related in a hierarchical arrangement of three interconnected levels, designated levels I, II, and III, as shown in figure 5. Two of the seven khipus (UR63 and UR73) are on level I, the base; three khipus are on the second level (UR64, UR68, and #9 [see below]); and two (UR67 and UR66) are on level III.

Sample #9 was in the Puruchuco museum when Carol Mackey studied this collection in the late 1960s. At that time Mackey recorded numerical, color, and some structural data on the samples represented in figure 5. She labeled the three khipus on the second level as #3 [UR64], #9, and #2 [UR68]. When we restudied the Puruchuco khipu archive in the summer of 2004, the khipu sample designated #9 by Mackey was no longer in the collection. Current museum personnel could not tell us what had become of this sample. We were unable to restudy this khipu and thereby to add observations on spin/ply directions, attachment type(s), and knot directions. (A table containing all numerical and color values recorded by Mackey for what she referred to as samples #2, #9, and #3 appears in Urton 2005.)

The two samples at the top of the hierarchy, UR66 and UR67, are rolled up together into a single bundle. As Mackey first noted (1970: 79), these two khipus bear identical numerical values, and string colors that seem to be a subtle transformation from one to the other. Single knots on khipu UR67 are tied as Z-knots, whereas those on UR66 are tied as S-knots; all other knots on both khipus are tied as Z-knots (see Urton 1994). The possible significance of this is discussed in the interpretation section of this paper.

The Organization and Structure of the Accounting Hierarchy

There are two principal aspects to the accounting hierarchy. First, khipus on the same level match, or closely match; that is, they display identical or very similar numerical sequences and color patterning. Second, values on khipus sum upward, and are subdivided downward. More specifically, the numerical values of certain groupings of strings (to be defined below) on the two khipus on level I sum to values tied onto certain groupings of strings on the three khipus on level II, and the numerical values of certain groupings of strings on the three khipus on level II sum to the values on the two khipus on level III. One can also consider the opposite direction: moving down the hierarchy, values on strings at higher levels are partitioned among groupings of strings on the next lowest level. Though simple in concept, the details of these relationships are complex. Before describing the summation/partitioning in depth, we provide an overview of relevant characteristics of this group of khipus.

Through cord color and spacing, each of the seven khipus is organized into different numbers of subunits. Khipus on level I break down into six subunits; those on level II contain three subunits (plus what we will call "introductory segments"); and the two khipus on level III have only one unit (plus "introductory segments," see below). Inside these subunits, the khipu strings are further subdivided by a combination of spacing between strings and/or by the repetition of color patterning in groups of strings. The general color pattern is a four-string seriation. By seriation, we mean a sequence of colors—e.g., dark brown, medium brown, light brown, white—repeated multiple times (Radicati di Primeglio 1964; see also Salomon 2004: 252–255). The numerical values of the cords vary in magnitude in accordance with the color, with the four strings of each color-seriated set generally increasing in size through the sequence.

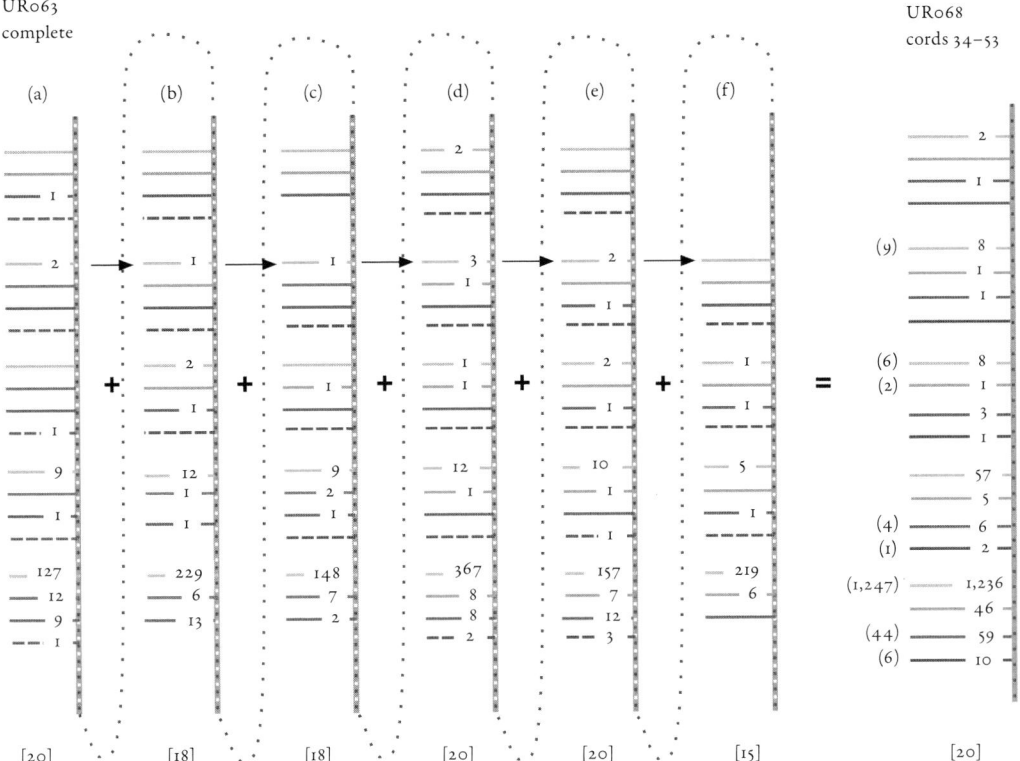

FIG. 6 Numerical and color correlations between khipu UR63 and the central section of UR68

Analysis of the Puruchuco Accounting Hierarchy

To describe more specifically the summation or partitioning between these khipus, we begin by examining an example of summation upward, between levels I and II. We note first that khipu UR73 has been broken; it bears only 69 of what we surmise were originally about 111 pendant strings. The similarity between UR63 and UR73 in color patterning and numeric values is very close; thus we feel confident in assuming that these were originally a matching pair.[11]

Because it is more complete, we choose UR63 as the exemplary khipu from level I; it remains to compare this to UR64 or UR68. In either case, the sums are close rather than exact. We focus on the relationship with UR68, illustrated in figure 6.

UR63 is organized by spacing and color seriation into six pendant string groupings, labeled a–f. The number of strings in each group is shown in brackets at the bottom of the columns. The six columns comprise: a) three sets of (5 × 4 =) 20 strings organized into five groups of four color-seriated strings; b) two sets of (3 × 4 + 2 × 3 =) 18 color-seriated strings; and c) one set of (3 × 4 + 3 =) 15 color-seriated strings. The meandering dotted lines at the tops and bottoms of the columns of UR63, in figure 6, show how this sample is to be reassembled into its proper linear arrangement.

Information Control in the Palace of Puruchuco

The numerical values of string groupings in UR63 sum to values recorded on the middle of the three subunits of UR68. In figure 6, the color-seriated strings of UR63 are aligned across the six segments, and these groupings are aligned with the similarly color-seriated grouping of (5 x 4 =) 20 strings in the central subdivision (strings 34–53) of khipu UR68 (cf., figs. 5, 6). Summing across the aligned strings of UR63 results in totals equal or close to those recorded on the depicted section of UR68. The values knotted into the cords of UR68 are reported on the right; any number between parentheses immediately to the left of these is the actual sum of values on the strings of UR63 at that position. The parenthetical numbers represent values that should have been recorded if the relationship between UR63 and UR68 was a matter of strict addition. The presence of several close, rather than exact, matches suggests that there was some degree of flexibility or variance allowable in the accounting relationship between these two samples, or levels.

Continuing the summing relationship upwards, we next consider khipus UR68 (level II) and UR67 (level III). Their relationship is illustrated in figure 7. In this figure, UR68 is disassembled into its three color-seriated subdivisions (labeled A–C), which are shown aligned with the similarly color-seriated string groupings of khipu UR67. We are confronted in figure 7 with 20 strings in all subunits.

The summations between UR68 and UR67 are more exact than those between UR63 and UR68. Setting aside the broken string in UR67, the values diverge in only two instances, and in each case the discrepancies are small: 2,904 instead of 2,908 and 161 instead of 162. The variance present in the connection between levels I and II has been considerably reduced between level II and III. What is the significance of this?

The explanation may be related to an interesting distinction between values on the six subunits of UR63 (fig. 6) and the three subunits of UR68 (fig. 7). The numerical values on UR63 are relatively homogenous across any given set of aligned strings, while on UR68 the values on subunits (A) and (B) are in general noticeably larger than those on subunit (C). Therefore, on the one hand, considering the values to be the result of summation, it appears that UR68 records two groups of roughly equivalent size and one much smaller group. On the other hand, if UR68 is the result of values on UR67 being partitioned down the hierarchy, it seems that a total sum on UR67 was subdivided with the intent of creating three subgroups, two of which (columns A and B) were intended to be roughly equal, and a third (column C), smaller subgroup. The smaller group could have been subordinate to, or an adjustment of, the larger pair. It is not possible to determine which option is more feasible, because we lack complete information from level I.

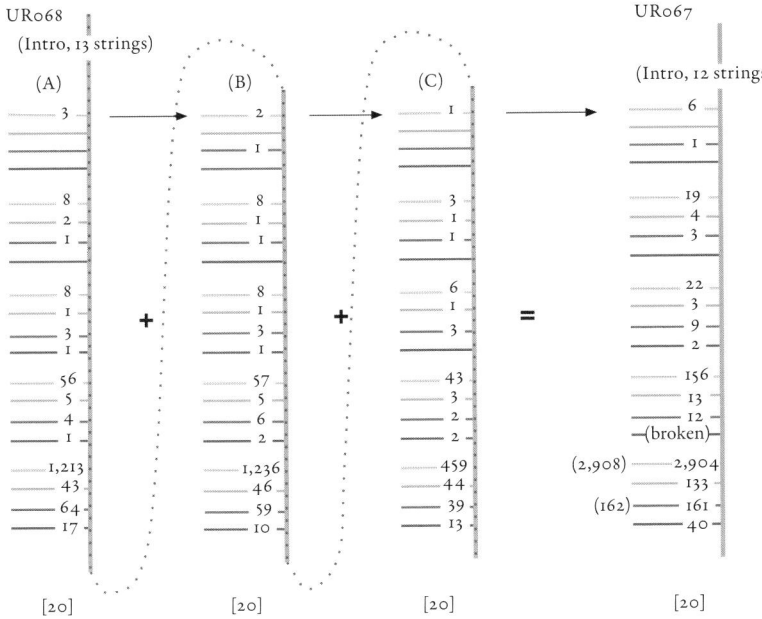

FIG. 7 Numerical and color correlations between khipus UR68 and UR67

The Boundaries of Summation/Partition

It will be noted that pendants between dotted lines in Figure 5 are implicated in the summation/partition relationship. The pendants on level III outside of the dotted lines, and those to the left of the dotted lines that protrude from the tops of the khipus on level IIs, form what we call "introductory segments." We discuss each of these features in turn.

The dotted lines in figure 5 encompass all the pendants on level I khipus but only the middle subunit of level II khipus. That is, complete summation of level I khipu accounts for only a portion of the values recorded on khipus on level II. The other values on level II khipus (subunits A and C in figure 6) are not accounted for by the currently known level I khipus UR63 and UR73. Thus, there may have been four additional level I khipus with the information for these two additional subunits on level II. One pair would have summed to the left-most subunits on level II, while the other would have produced sums recorded on the right subunits. Except for the introductory segments, all strings on level III are involved in the summation relationship.

It appears that the original structure of the Puruchuco accounting hierarchy contained six paired khipus on level I, whose values were summed to produce those on the three subunits of the three khipus on level II, whose subunits, in turn, were summed and recorded on the two khipus on level III. Thus, information was either being funneled and synthesized upward or subdivided and distributed downward among the three levels of khipus.

Information Control in the Palace of Puruchuco

FIG. 8 Puruchuco introductory segments

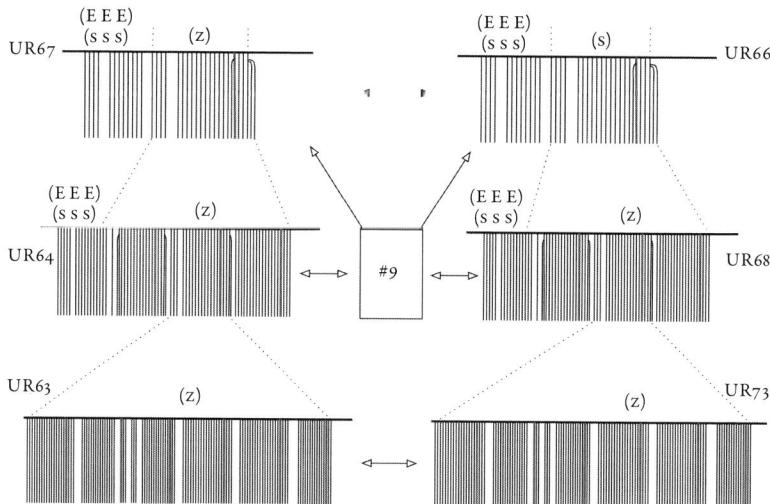

Introductory Segments

We assume that the accounting hierarchy shown in figure 5 was a set of records for use both within and outside Puruchuco. The use of this information at a wider level, perhaps regional or provincial, would have been connected with the reporting function of some or all of these khipus. For example, khipus on level III could represent either a set of instructions issued to the lord of Puruchuco from the provincial governor, or reports on local Puruchuco resources to be sent to the provincial governor. In either of these scenarios, one of the requirements would have been that the khipus bear an indication of their destination or origination. Records consulted wholly within the local community may not have needed to carry a provenience/destination label, although they may have borne labels of local relevance, such as the names of ayllus.

If numerous khipus were coming into a central archive for storage or were being dispersed from that archive to disparate places, it would have been helpful, if not essential, to have place identifiers encoded within each khipu. We suggest that the introductory segments on level II and III khipus represented just such identity labels (see Pärssinen, 1992:39–43).

The numerical values knotted onto strings within the introductory segments on level II and III khipus all contain arrangements of just three figure-eight knots (denoted E) tied onto three separate strings (see fig. 8). Figure-eight knots normally signify the numerical value one (1), however it is important to note that the numeric values on these introductory segments are neither derived from nor implicated in the summation/partition relationship.

The introductory segments in all cases occur near the short, doubled end of the primary cord, which is usually taken to be the beginning of a khipu account. We hypothesize that the arrangement of three figure-eight knots at the start of these khipus represented the place identifier, or toponym, "Puruchuco." Three figure-eight knots tied onto a few of the dozen or so strings is not a lot of information by which to signal a toponym. It is difficult for us to explain otherwise, however, the purpose of these parallel sets of strings, which do not figure in any discernible way into the summation/partition relations. We suggest that any khipu moving within the state administrative system bearing an initial arrangement of three figure-eight knots would have been immediately recognizable to Inka administrators as an account pertaining to the palace of Puruchuco. This implies that there ought to be place identifiers relating to khipus from other archives as well, though we are not prepared to suggest other such labels at this time.

Why don't level I khipus bear introductory segments? Perhaps UR63 and UR73 were not intended to travel away from Puruchuco; instead they were local accounts, drawn up by the resident khipukamayuq for accounting purposes within the palace. If the seven khipus register demands for service received from outside Puruchuco, meaning that if the relationship among them is one of partition, then the level I khipus would have represented the reorganization of the mandate from outside in relation to the availability of resources at the local level. In this scheme, level I khipus would have pertained only to local accounting matters and it would have been unnecessary to attach the place identifier. However, if the overall relationship is one of summation, and these khipus were prepared as a report on local conditions for dispatch outside Puruchuco, then level I khipus would represent the "raw" tables of local information that served as the foundation for constructing level II and III khipus. Level III khipus, the summary reports, would have been sent to a distant administrative center.

Local Accounts or Remote Instructions?

We suggest that khipus may have contrasting number qualities depending on whether they represented instructions coming from the state administration to a local accounting center, or records produced within a local accounting center with regard to existing community resources. In the first circumstance, we suspect that khipu values would have tended to be even decimal values or calculations of values in standard proportional shares.[12] If a khipu account was compiled from within some local administrative center to be sent upward to higher-level officials, counts of resources could be expected to have reflected the vagaries of the natural distribution of items in society. Such numbers are less likely to be whole and rounded or perfectly proportional.[13] This is partly because there are many more "interdecimal" values (e.g., 41, 89, 53) than there are full decimal ones (e.g., 10, 20, 100).

Returning to figures 6 and 7, it seems on the surface that the values on the multiple string segments of UR63 and UR68 are overwhelmingly of the interdecimal, historical, on the ground accounting type. There is not a high incidence of full decimal values, nor do these numbers at first appear to be the products of complex arithmetic calculations aimed at producing standard, proportional values. There are, in fact, some remarkable numerical features on both these khipus, which suggest that they may, in fact, have been produced in a more standardized, calculated manner than is initially apparent.

Each of the six segments (a–f) of UR63 (fig. 6) are organized into four-string, color-seriated sets. The colors are:
1) White (W)
2) Medium Brown (MB)
3) Grey-Green (GG)
4) Grey-Green and White Mottled (GG:W)
[repeat]

The largest numerical values in each set are knotted onto the white, top-most strings. The four-string set with the largest numerical values is in all cases at the bottom of the column. Closer examination reveals an extraordinary numerical relationship between the values on the bottom-most sets of strings and the values on the white strings of all sets: the sum of values on the bottom-most set of strings is roughly equal to the sum of values on all white strings within that column. The sum of all values on the penultimate four-string group is equal to all values knotted onto all the medium brown strings on that column. The same relationship obtains for each four-string group, moving up the four-strings sets and down the seriated colors within each column.

The clearest example of the phenomenon described above occurs in column f, figure 6. The sum of all values in the bottom four-string set is (219+6=) 225; the sum of all white strings is also (1+5+219=) 225. The sum of the next-to-last four-string set is (5+1=) 6, which is also the sum of the one value tied onto a medium brown string. The sum of the third set from the bottom is (1+1=) 2, equal to the sum of values on grey-green strings. However, this relationship does not hold in all cases. In some columns, combinations of more than one four-string set are equal to combinations of values on more than one string color type. For instance, in column b, the sum of the bottom and third from the bottom four-string sets is (248+3=) 251, which is also the sum of values on all white and medium brown strings, (244+7=) 251. In this same column, the sum of the second and fourth four-string sets from the bottom is (14+1=) 15, which is the sum on all grey-green and white mottled strings, (1+1+13=) 15.

How should we interpret this pattern and its variations? We suggest that it may have functioned as a type of internal checking mechanism, but it is not clear exactly how such a verification system would have worked. What is interesting and potentially significant is that the numerical values in UR63 are not entirely random; rather, there is some element of manipulation involved in the arrangements of numbers in the six segments of this sample.

Do similar patterns hold for the three subunits on UR68? At first glance they appear to be similar to those of the six subunits of UR63; the distribution of magnitudes by color and by four-pendant set is roughly the same. However, UR68 does not contain any discernable pattern of matching sums between pendant groups and pendants of the same color. Thus, are the values on UR68 of the historical, local accounting type? Though it is impossible to be certain, we suggest that they are not. The sum of values on all columns on UR68 is 3,498. It seems likely that the accounting value intended here is 3,500, or three and one-half waranqa (1,000s) accounting units. The khipu may be attempting to show a "close match" between columns A and B; column A sums to 1,430 and column B sums to 1,447. Each of these would represent approximately two-fifths of the sum of all values on the khipu, which is 1,400 (i.e., $3,500 \div 5 = 700$; $700 \times 2 = 1,400$). In this interpretation, column C, which sums to 621, could have been intended as an approximation of one-fifth of the total value ($3,500 \div 5 = 700$). However, column C shows evidence of another pattern as well. The sums of each four-pendant set, beginning from the top, are 1, 5, 10, 50, 555: a clear decimal progression. The three subunits of UR68 could represent an ideally matched pair, columns A and B, augmented by corrective or standardized values registered in column C. In either interpretation, the numbers do not appear to have been the result of a natural counting process, but of calculated, proportional values.

The above interpretations of UR63 and UR68 suggest that the most likely direction of action in the Puruchuco accounting hierarchy was partitioning downward from the pair of khipus on level III (received from outside authorities), to a reapportionment achieved in the three khipus of level II to an on-the-ground assignment recorded in the pair of khipus on level I. The six-part organization of UR63 and UR73 could have represented the local assignment of tasks or resources among six groups (e.g., ayllus); the values assigned would have been subject to an internal system of checks and balances by means of the summing of values up the four-string sets and down the color-seriated string groups.

Alternatively, we could argue—although this interpretation seems less compelling to us than the one just given—that figure 5 represents the organization of a bottom-up accounting among six on-the-ground ayllu-like groups. The resources or labor time of these groups are represented on the bottom four-string sets of each column of khipus UR63 and UR73 (perhaps made by two different khipukamayuq). The values recorded on these two khipus are subject to an internal checks and balances regimen as described above. As previously explained, values on the level I khipus are summed to result in the middle subunit of khipus on level II. If this is the case, how does it happen that subunits A, B, and C appear to be organized into 2/5, 2/5, and 1/5 of the total on khipu UR68?

Subunit B, under this scenario, is known to be the result of information passed up from level I. Subunit A could be the product of two other (now lost) khipus that would have been organized like UR63 and UR73 and that would have accounted for some other six-part grouping of ayllu-like accounting units in the Puruchuco area. This implies that level II khipus would have synthesized information from a total of twelve different groups (e.g., ayllus) that were the responsibility of the khipukamayuq at the palace of Puruchuco. The remaining subunit (column C on UR68) could have been from a smaller set of (now lost) khipus, or it may have represented a scaled set of decimal values that were in some way linked to the paired six-part accounts in columns A and B.

In either case, the values in columns A, B, and C are all summarized in level-III khipus UR66 and UR67. These would have been intended as local records for export to the next-highest accounting authority. As the sums registered in the Puruchuco accounting hierarchy are in the thousands (warankas), the next accounting level would have been at a place supporting either a Pichqa-waranka Kuraka ("Lord of 5,000") or a Hunu Kuraka ("Lord of 10,000").

The Link to the Outside

In either of the two scenarios proposed above, the pair of khipus on level III occupy a critical position between the Puruchuco accounting hierarchy and the outside world. Whether information was moving down from level III to level I, or up from level I to level III, UR66 and UR67 would represent the point of contact between the Puruchuco administrative district and the next highest accounting level. The two samples would either have been received from outside, or they would have been prepared to be sent outside. Are there any features of these two khipus that might privilege one over the other? Two such possible markers will be explained in relation to the representations of UR66 and UR67 provided in figure 9.

Figure 9 shows that UR66 and UR67 have their pendant strings laid out in a manner similar to the level I and II khipu discussed earlier (see figs. 7, 8). Pendants on these two samples are organized in groups of four. From left to right, each group is composed of three solid-colored strings followed by a mottled string. This pattern is repeated throughout the khipu with slight variations in one group near the middle, where a mottled pendant is introduced in the third position, and in the final pendant group, which includes subsidiaries. A similar color range is used in both khipus: white,

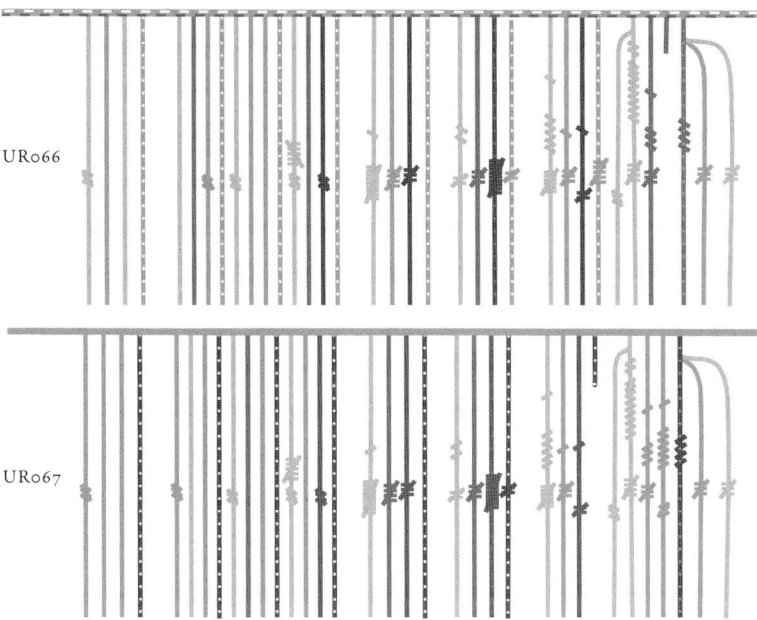

FIG. 9 The paired khipu (UR66 and UR67) from the Puruchuco accounting hierarchy (level III)

light brown, medium brown, and dark brown are the predominant colors. In UR66, dark brown falls on the third pendant of each four-pendant group. In UR67, this color is replaced with grey-green. The same color substitution occurs in UR63 (Level I): final cords of the four-pendant groups in sections b–f are dark brown and white mottled, while cords in correlating positions in section a are grey-green and white mottled.

We argue that the color transformations between UR66 and UR67 were intentional and meaningful. In a distant accounting center, these khipus would be recognized as two distinct records relating to Puruchuco. To return to an example discussed earlier, the two level-III khipus may have differed in the same way that the two upper halves of the local administrative hierarchy in Chicama (see fig. 2) were understood to differ: as a dual, asymmetric (e.g., hanan/upper and hurin/lower) pair. If this was the case, is there any evidence to suggest which of the pair may have been upper and which lower?

There is an interesting pattern of knot-directional variability (see Urton 1994) between the two level-III khipus. On UR67, all knots, with the exception of the three figure-eight knots on the introductory segment, are tied as Z-knots. On khipu UR66, all of the single knots (on the upper portions of the pendants) are tied as S-knots, but the long knots are tied as Z-knots. In earlier studies, Urton (1994 and 2003) demonstrated that Z-knots are about twice as common as S-knots across a sample of 169 khipus. On these grounds, Urton suggested:

> the knot pattern displaying Z-type single, long, and figure-eight
> knots is roughly twice as common as the pattern displaying

Information Control in the Palace of Puruchuco

S-knots in all three positions. Thus, in the surviving khipu samples, Z-knots might have been used to signify unmarked semantic categories, social statuses, symbolic values, or other properties in opposition to their more narrowly specified (marked) counterparts, the latter of which would have been signed by means of S-knots. A relevant datum here (though producing different directional/markedness values), again, is Salomon's material from Tupicocha in which a khipu with predominantly Z-spun/S-plied threads belongs to a senior ayllu of a pair, the junior ayllu of which curates a khipu with predominantly S-spun/Z-plied threads. (Urton2003: 153)

Under this paradigm, khipu UR66, with its greater proportion of S-knots, would have represented the senior (hanan/marked) member of the pair. We think this suggestion is supported by the construction of the primary cord on UR66, which is spun in a distinctive complex arrangement of light brown, white, and grey-green, in contrast to UR67's simple solid-color primary cord. Primary-cord patterning such as that on UR66 is rare outside Puruchuco.

Conclusions

Inka khipu studies began almost a century ago with the seminal research by L. Leland Locke (1912, 1923). Locke provided important insights into the Inka conventions of recording numbers with different types of knots in a hierarchical arrangement. The next major contribution to khipu research was the work of Carlos Radicati di Primeglio (1964, 1979, 1984, and 2006). Working with a collection of eight khipu samples from the north-central coastal Peruvian valley of Santa (1949–50), and other samples in his private collection (Urton 2006), Radicati recorded numerical and structural data and paid particular attention to the analysis of colors. He argued that the key to khipu decipherment lay in samples bearing color-seriated pendant strings, similar to those we have described here from the archive of Puruchuco. Radicati's focus on seriation did not produce a breakthrough, but his work was critical in calling attention to the potential significance of color coding.

The next major advance in khipu studies was the monumental research undertaken by Marcia and Robert Ascher (1997 [1981]). The Aschers recorded detailed information on more than 250 khipu samples in museum and private collections in Europe and North and South America.[14] In addition to producing tabular descriptions of numerical, color, and certain structural features, the Aschers made many valuable observations on numerical and color patterning in the Inka khipus. Their work has taught us that close study of the physical and symbolic characteristics of khipus reveals a wealth of information regarding the logic behind khipu record keeping in the Inka Empire. Like Locke and Radicati, the Aschers focused on numerical and color patterning within individual khipu. A recent heir to the Aschers' primarily numerical-based analyses of khipu is the Peruvian engineer, Hugo Pereyra (1990, 1996, 2001).

The study of khipu structural properties has been advanced in recent years by the research of Bill Conklin (1982, 2002) and Urton (1994, 2003). The focus on structure has heightened awareness of the degree of variability and patterning in spin/ply direction, attachment type, and knot-direction variation (see esp. Urton 2003: 74–88). These studies have recently been augmented by the groundbreaking work of Frank Salomon (2002, 2004), in his careful, inspired ethnographic research on a set of patrimonial khipus in the village of Tupicocha, in the central highlands of Peru. Salomon's studies are of particular interest here because he concluded that color seriation of a type similar to that found in Puruchuco (Salomon 2004: 252–256) is an important strategy in the organization and classification of information in the Tupicochan archive. In this regard, it is important to note that Tupicocha lies within the Andean highland watershed that leads down to the central coast of Peru, in the region of Puruchuco. We suggest that the Tupicocha and Puruchuco khipu archives may have been connected in a highland-coastal accounting tradition in Inka times.

Despite the numerous advances highlighted above, to date we have made very little progress in determining how khipukamayuq signified different objects or categories in these devices. Because previous studies have focussed on individual samples, we have had no evidence about how information was synthesized or partitioned as it moved between accounting levels. The Puruchuco accounting hierarchy is, we believe, the first example indicating how information moved either up or down the Inka administrative hierarchy.

Are the Puruchuco khipus recording a process of data synthesis or data dispersement? There is not sufficient evidence to allow us to give a definitive answer to this question, although we are inclined to see these khipus as related in a partitive manner, as though they represent a set of mandates for local compliance that came to Puruchuco from the outside. Further investigation is needed on this point, however, both of the Puruchuco archive, and of the other archives now recorded in the khipu database at Harvard University. It is hoped that identifying this one, highly complex accounting hierarchy will provide new interpretive insights as well as strategies for identifying similar phemonena in other khipu archives from both the coast and the highlands of Peru.

Careful study of the Puruchuco and other khipu archives may provide the foothold needed for addressing the most difficult question facing students of the Inka khipu: How did the khipu-keepers of the Inka administrative system record the identities of objects—people, animals, produce, manufactured goods, etc.—in the three-dimensional forms of their knotted-string records?

Acknowledgments

We express our deep appreciation to Luis Felipe Villacorta Ostolaza, without whose help, cooperation, and general good will this study would not have been possible. We also express our sincere appreciation to the staff of the Museo de Sitio Puruchuco—Arturo Jiménez Borja—including Patricia Arana Bullón, Jenny Alcántara Díaz, and Julio Tello Solis—who facilitated our research in the khipu collection at the site, in July 2004. For financial support for our research at the Museo de Sitio Puruchuco and our subsequent analysis of the material at Harvard University, we thank the National Science Foundation (BCS-0408324), the Dumbarton Oaks Foundation, and the Faculty of Arts and Sciences, Harvard University. Gary Urton also expresses his deep appreciation to the John D. and Catherine T. MacArthur Foundation for a MacArthur Fellowship, which has supported his research on the Inka khipus since 2001.

Notes

1 "Así tenían los contadores grandes montones destos cordeles, a manera de registros, como los escribanos los tienen en sus escritorios, y allí guardaban sus archivos y de tal manera que el que quería saber algo, no tenía más que hacer sino irse a un Quipucamayo de éstos, y preguntarle cuánto ha que sucedió esto, o cuál Ynga hizo esta ley, quién conquistó tal provincia, quiénes fueron sus capitanes, cuando fue el año seco o abundante, cuándo hubo pestilencias y guerras, cuándo se rebelaron tales indios, cuándo sucedió tal terremoto, en qué tiempo reventó tal volcán, cuándo vino tal río de avenida, destruyendo las chácaras. Luego el contador sacaba sus cuerdas y daba razón de ello, sin faltar un punto" (Murúa 2001 [1590]: 360–361).

2 The Khipu Database Project, which is located in the Department of Anthropology, Harvard University, is described fully at the project website: http://khipukamayuq.fas.harvard.edu/.

3 To date, no such correlation between a khipu transcription and its source khipu has been identified.

4 Ascher and Ascher (1997) have urged the use of what they term "encipherment"—i.e., the construction of hypothetical khipu from textual data—as a possible means for approaching the study of the organizational principles that may have been employed in the actual construction of khipu samples (see also Platt 2002). We are less sanguine about the value of such an approach, as it is based on what we see as the rather dubious proposition that the Inka administrators would have resorted to the same strategies of delineating and organizing various classes of data as the present-day researcher.

5 "En cada cabeza de provincia había contadores a quien llamaban quiposcamayos [sic], y por estos nudos tenían la cuenta y razón de lo que habían de tributar los questaban en aquel distrito, desde la plata, oro, ropa y ganado, hasta la leña y las otras cosas más menudas, y por los mismos quipos se daba a cabo de un año, o de diez o de veinte, razón a quien tenía comisión de tomar la cuenta, tan bien que un par de alpargatas no se podían esconder. . . . Y en cada valle hay esta cuenta hoy día y siempre hay en los aposentos tantos contadores como en él hay señores y de cuatro en cuatro meses fenescen sus cuentan por la manera dicha" (Cieza de León, 1967 [1553, chap. 12]: 36–37).

6 "Lo que tributaba cada término destas cabeceras y contribuían los naturales, así oro como plata y ropa y armas, con todo lo demás que ellos daban, lo entregaban por cuenta a los camayos que tenían los quipos, los cuales hacían en todo lo que por éste les era mandado en lo tocante a despender estas cosas con la gente de guerra o repartillo con quien el Señor mandaba o de llevallo al Cuzco; pero cuando de la ciudad del Cuzco venían a tomar la cuenta, o que la fuesen a dar al Cuzco, los

mesmos contadores con los quipos la daban o venían a la dar a donde no podía haber fraude, sino todo había de estar cabal" (Cieza de León, 1967 [1553, chap. 20]: 67).

7   A shorter version of our description and analysis of the Puruchuco accounting hierarchy appeared in *Science* (Urton and Brezine 2005).

8   The Puruchuco website address is at: http://museopuruchuco.peru-cultural.org.pe/.

9   Thanks to Julio Tello Solis for his transcription (10 July 2004) of the notes from the excavation field reports detailing the discoveries of khipus at Puruchuco.

10   "9 de agosto 1956—El trabajo consistía, desde hacía tres días, en extraer 'desmonte' o tierra de la parte superior del conjunto B para rellenar un pozo de la plataforma A. '... En la zona de extracción (conjunto B, parte superior) de desmonte el obrero Lizama encontró un cántaro de forma semiovoide, cubierto de hollín, con una figura plástica de serpiente, tapado en la boca por una pequeña lagenaria, en su interior contenía 10 quipus de tamaño regular; 3 con borlas rojo, naranja y amarillo; 11 medianos y varias pitas suplementarias sueltas, todas en buen estado de conservación.'"

11   See the tabular data from khipu UR73 at: http://khipukamayuq.fas.harvard.edu/ (click on "Khipu Data Tables").

12   The classic example of a khipu transcription containing predominantly even, proportional numbers is found in Julien's study of the Chupacho khipu transcription (1988).

13   See Murra's study (1975) of the "ethnocategories" of data recorded in a khipu transcription from Xauxa; these data display primarily uneven numbers, detailing the goods given and "stolen" (rancheado) by the Spaniards passing through Xauxa in the mid-sixteenth century.

14   The tabular data recorded from khipu studies by the Aschers since the 1970s may be found online at: http://instruct1.cit.cornell.edu/research/quipu-ascher/.

References cited

ASCHER, MARCIA, AND ROBERT ASCHER
    1997 [1981] *Mathematics of the Incas: Code of the Quipu.* Dover Publications, New York.

CIEZA DE LEÓN, PEDRO DE
    1967 [1553] *El Señorío de los Incas.* Instituto de Estudios Peruanos, Lima.

COBO, BERNABÉ
    1983 [1653] *History of the Inca Empire* (Roland Hamilton, trans. and ed.). University of Texas Press, Austin.

CONKLIN, WILLIAM J.
    1982 The Information System of the Middle Horizon Quipus. In *Ethnoastronomy and Archaeoastronomy in the American Tropics* (Anthony F. Aveni and Gary Urton, eds.): 261–281. Annals of the New York Academy of Sciences 385. New York Academy of Sciences, New York.
    2002 A Khipu Information String Theory. In *Narrative Threads: Accounting and Recounting in Andean Khipu* (Jeffrey Quilter and Gary Urton, eds.): 53–86. University of Texas Press, Austin.

D'ALTROY, TERENCE N.
    2002 *The Incas.* Basil Blackwell, Malden, Mass. and Oxford.

GARCILASO DE LA VEGA, EL INCA
    1966 [1609–1617] *Royal Commentaries of the Incas* (Harold V. Livermore, trans. and ed.). University of Texas Press, Austin.

JIMÉNEZ BORJA, ARTURO
    1956 Puruchuco: Una morada de la Lima prehispánica. *Fanal* 12 (47): 15–18.
    1973 *Puruchuco: Planos, cortes y elevaciones de Mary Jiménez Freeman Morris.* Editorial Jurídica, S.A, Lima.

JULIEN, CATHERINE J.
    1988 How Inca Decimal Administration Worked. *Ethnohistory* 35 (3): 257–279.

LOCKE, L. LELAND
    1912 The Ancient Quipu, A Peruvian Knot Record. *American Anthropologist* (14): 325–332.
    1923 *The Ancient Quipu, or Peruvian Knot Record.* American Museum of Natural History, New York

MACKEY, CAROL
    n.d. Knot Records in Ancient and Modern Perú. Ph.D. dissertation. Department of Anthropology, University of California, Berkeley, 1970.

MURRA, JOHN V.

1975 Las etno-categorías de un khipu estatal. In *Formaciones económicas y políticas en el mundo andino*: 243–254. Instituto de Estudios Andinos, Lima.

1980 *The Economic Organization of the Inka State* [1956]. JAI Press, Greenwich, Conn.

MURÚA, MARTÍN DE

2001 [1590] *Historia general del Perú* (Manuel Ballesteros, ed.). Crónicas de América. Dastin, S.L., Madrid.

NETHERLY, PATRICIA J.

1993 The Nature of the Andean State. In *Configurations of Power: Holistic Anthropology in Theory and Practice* (J. S. Henderson and P. J. Netherly, eds.): 11–35. Cornell University Press, Ithaca and London.

PÄRSSINEN, MARTTI

1992 *Tawantinsuyu: The Inca State and Its Political Organization*. Studia Historica 43. Gummerus Kirjapaino Oy, Helsinki.

PEREYRA S., HUGO

1990 La yupana, complemento operacional del quipu. In *Quipu y Yupana* (Carol Mackey et al., eds.): 235–256. Consejo Nacional de Ciencias y Tecnología, Lima.

1996 Acerca de dos quipus con características numéricas excepcionales. *Bull. Inst. Fr. Études Andines* 25 (2): 187–202.

1997 Los quipus con cuerdas entorchadas. In *Arqueología, antropología e historia en los Andes: Homenaje a María Rostworowski* (Rafael Varón Gabai and Javier Flores Espinoza, eds.): 187–198. Instituto de Estudios Peruanos, Lima.

2001 Notas sobre el descubrimiento de la clave numeral de los quipus incaicos. *Boletín del Museo de Arqueología y Antropología* 4 (5): 115–123.

PLATT, TRISTAN

2002 "Without Deceit and Lies": Variable *Chinu* Readings During a 16th-Century Tribute-Restitution Trial. In *Narrative Threads: Accounting and Recounting in Andean Khipu* (Jeffrey Quilter and Gary Urton, eds.): 225–265. University of Texas Press, Austin.

QUILTER, JEFFREY, AND GARY URTON (EDS.)

2002 *Narrative Threads: Accounting and Recounting in Andean Khipu*. University of Texas Press, Austin.

RADICATI DI PRIMEGLIO, CARLOS

1949–50 *Introducción al Estudio de los Quipos*. Documenta 2. Editorial Lumen S.A., Lima.

1964 *La seriación como posible clave para descifrar los quipus extranumerales*. Biblioteca de la Sociedad Peruana de Historia. Monografías 6. Universidad Nacional Mayor de San Marcos, Lima.

1978 *Señoríos indígenas de Lima y Canta*. Instituto de Estudios Peruanos, Lima.

1979 *El sistema contable de los Incas: Yupana y quipu*. Libreria Studium, Lima.

1984 El secreto de la Quilca. *Revista de Indias* 44 (173): 11–60.

2006 *Estudios sobre los quipus* (Gary Urton, ed. and intro.). Fondo Editorial Universidad Nacional Mayor de San Marcos and COFIDE, Lima.

ROSTWOROWSKI DE DIEZ CANSECO, MARÍA

1978 *Señoríos indígenas de Lima y Canta*. Instituto de Estudios Peruanos, Lima.

SALOMON, FRANK

2002 Patrimonial Khipus in a Modern Peruvian Village: An Introduction to the "Quipocamayos" of Tupicocha, Huarochirí. In *Narrative Threads: Accounting and Recounting in Andean Khipu* (Jeffrey Quilter and Gary Urton, eds.): 293–319. University of Texas Press, Austin.

2004 *The Cord Keepers: Khipus and Cultural Life in a Peruvian Village*. Duke University Press, Durham and London.

URTON, GARY

1994 A New Twist in an Old Yarn: Variation in Knot Directionality in the Inka Khipus. *Baessler-Archiv*, Neue Folge, Band 42: 271–305.

1997 *The Social Life of Numbers: A Quechua Ontology of Numbers and Philosophy of Arithmetic*. University of Texas Press, Austin.

1998 From Knots to Narratives: Reconstructing the Art of Historical Record-Keeping in the Andes from Spanish Transcriptions of Inka Khipus. *Ethnohistory* 45 (3): 409–438.

2001 A Calendrical and Demographic Tomb Text from Northern Peru. *Latin American Antiquity* 12 (2): 127–147.

2002 Recording Signs in Narrative-Accounting Khipus. In *Narrative Threads: Accounting and Recounting in Andean Khipu* (Jeffrey Quilter and Gary Urton, eds): 171–96. University of Texas Press, Austin.

2003 *Signs of the Inka Khipu: Binary Coding in the Andean Knotted-String Records*. University of Texas Press, Austin.

2005 Khipu Archives: Duplicate Accounts and Identity Labels in the Inka Knotted-String Records. *Latin American Antiquity* 16 (2): 147–167.

2006 "Carlos Radicati di Primeglio: Patrocinador de los estudios sobre los quipus." In *Carlos Radicati di Primeglio: Estudios sobre los quipus* (Gary Urton, comp. and intro.): 39–54. Fondo Editorial Universidad Nacional Mayor de San Marcos, COFIDE, and Instituto Italiano di Cultura, Lima.

URTON, GARY, AND CARRIE J. BREZINE

2005 Khipu Accounting in Ancient Peru. *Science* 309: 1065–1067.

VILLACORTA OSTOLAZA, LUIS FELIPE, AND J. ÁVILA C.

1998 *Perspectiva histórica del Distrito de Ate*. Serie Documentos de Trabajo 2. Convenio Municipalidad de Ate, Ministerio de Educación, Lima.

VILLACORTA OSTOLAZA, LUIS FELIPE, LUISA MARÍA VETTER PARODI, AND CARLOS E. AUSEJO CASTILLO

2004 *Puruchuco y la sociedad de Lima: Un homenaje a Arturo Jiménez Borja*. CONCYTEC, Lima.

WAKEHAM DASSO, ROBERTO

1976 *Puruchuco: Investigación arquitectónica*. Departamento de Arquitectura y Urbanismo. Universidad Nacional de Ingeniería, Lima.

ZUIDEMA, R. TOM

1989 A Quipu Calendar from Ica, Peru, with a Comparison to the Ceque Calendar from Cuzco. In *World Archaeoastronomy* (A. F. Aveni, ed.): 341–351. Cambridge University Press, Cambridge, England.

"And All Theirs Different from His":
The Dumbarton Oaks Royal Inka Tunic in Context

Rebecca R. Stone

OVER THE LAST DECADES, SCHOLARS HAVE LOOKED TO THE DRAMATICALLY arduous natural environment to account for uniquely Andean cultural values (Zuidema 1962; Kosok 1965; Murra 1972; Moseley 1992; Burger 1995). Juxtapositions of mountain, desert, and high plain, with their mutually exclusive yet complementary crops, make relative vertical positioning a cultural given, reciprocity a survival mechanism, and hierarchies of unequal but equivalent parts the natural order of things. Completing dualities—the wet and dry seasons, the light and the dark portions of the night sky, upstream and down—define the Andean environment and condition human responses thereto. Movement along continua between such poles constitutes the principle of order, sanctioned by the circling planets but constantly mirrored in wild animal migrations, human transhumance, and many types of economic and aesthetic exchanges of goods. Within such a dynamic system art often serves to echo, create, and perpetuate this endemic restlessness; previously I have characterized the Inka architectural style as prepositional (Stone-Miller 2002: 202).

Prepositional, hierarchical, and relational thinking certainly typify many accomplishments of the Inkas, the crowning empire of the indigenous Pre-Hispanic Andes. It permeates their many ingenious and deceptively simple constructs, such as the *mitimae* colonist program. It helps direct our attention to the intrinsic meanings of the configurations of geometric elements so central to their arts, such as the abstract carving of far-flung boulders or the repetitions of textile patterns. Finally, it places in broader perspective the issues of variation in Inka power highlighted in this volume, by emphasizing the outward-looking orientation of this vast expansionist empire. The present article will consider how such an

FIG. 1 The Dumbarton Oaks All-Tocapu Tunic (Royal Tunic), B-518. Camelid fiber and cotton. H. 91 cm; W. 76 cm. A: "front" side; B: "back" side.

approach was expressed in the well-known, yet perhaps still under-interpreted, royal Inka tunic in the collection of Dumbarton Oaks (fig. 1) and the two nonroyal tunic types it directly incorporates into its *tocapu* array.

First, in order to situate the Dumbarton Oaks royal tunic (*uncu*) within a larger Inka schema, and try to account for its particular formal messages, a brief overview of the underlying nonrepresentational Inka approach to representation is in order. Certain aspects of the Inka approach to representation may be revealed best in practices not primarily aesthetic

in nature. (One must always qualify such a distinction, especially with the Inkas, since the practical and the symbolic, the functional and the beautiful, were so inextricably intertwined in their culture.) For instance, the *ceque* system, a time/space calendar organizing radiating invisible lines of sacred places around Cusco, may best encapsulate Inka thinking style. Anthony Aveni avers "[t]he ceque system was neither image nor representation: it was Tahuantinsuyu itself" (Aveni 1989: 303). Unlike most cultures that utilize maps, diagrams, icons, or effigies to mark time and qualify space, the Inkas sequentially experienced sacred natural and organically cultural places, *huacas*. As far as we know, the information on how to revere the huacas sequentially was learned and transmitted orally. If encoded, it would have been recorded in the positional knot "writing" system of the *khipu*, in a format almost exactly like that of the ceques themselves (Aveni 1989: 279, 283–284; see Urton and Brezine, this volume). In saying that Tawantinsuyu itself—meaning at once the land, the empire, and the social order—*was* the calendar, Aveni characterizes a way of thinking that does not seek removed or arbitrary symbols, but rather assumes the efficacy of direct acts in real places to elucidate and follow natural orders. Writing of the Inkas as an orientation calendar, Aveni describes how "the Inca had converted the landscape into a natural, self-operating calendrical device powered by the movement of the sun, a system with no need of formal writing to articulate it—only the celebrated Inca sun pillars" (ibid.: 289). By means of invisible ceques and standing markers to watch the horizon for geometrical congruences with repeating celestial events, the Inkas measured out space-time accurately by precisely observing nature through a cultural positional framework. Humans shifted relative to their landscape, subtly attuned to *its* self-referential forms—mountains, streams, boulders—as the ultimate markers and arbiters of abstract meaning. This is the opposite of a complex, highly referential iconographic or pictorial system; in our terms the Inkas were deeply structuralist.

In addition, via the ceque lines the Inka took the point of view of the self-proclaimed center looking outward, the ordering center claiming theoretically limitless reach in all directions. I propose to interpret the royal tunic in a very similar fashion. As such, the ceques—and the tunic—represent a dynamic, expansionist system at the core. Such an interaction with the world meant striking a balance between the imposition of cultural order and deep accommodation of natural flexibility. On the side of order, the system's radiating lines constitute above all an organizing idea, since these lines are neither concretely present (not being inscribed on the earth's surface, for example) nor automatically suggested by nature itself (boulders do not themselves obligingly line up). By definition, huacas are contrived, at least in the sense that series of places have been singled out and sequenced, whether literally or conceptually. Their tending likewise followed orderly, if not simple or continuous, patterns that expressed many levels of complicated social relations simultaneously (Zuidema 1964, 1982, 1983). Similarly, the orderliness of centrality was obeyed by positioning the main temple, the Qorikancha, so as to make possible the viewing of the solstices, the most important celestial moments (Aveni 1989: 290). Yet natural flexibility dictated the varied spacing of ceque lines, the unequal numbers of huacas per line, and their different characters. Cobo describes the sixth ceque as consisting of a stone in a niche, a temple, a road, a door, a palace pool, a bath, a root, a hill, a sun pillar, a fountain, and a fortress (ibid: 282–283). This list reflects not only how varied each huaca was from the next, itself a form of flexibility, but that many huacas were human-made frames of nature (a rock in a niche) and acts of containing natural power (the door was the locus of sacrifices to the wind so that it would not do damage). Certainly sun pillars, as positional markers, sanctify cultural framing of natural movement. Further, the accommodating Inka astronomical system also presupposed standing on spots *other* than the Qorikancha for other complementary moments, the equinoxes (ibid.: 292; Zuidema 1982: 434–435).

Architecture as a whole follows the same underlying values as the Inka astronomical system. Passages, steps, and zigzag paths conditioned equally stylized movement; window and door openings framed pieces of mountains; subtly marked boulders echoed the natural forms of the mountains beyond in microcosm; dynamically irregular dressed stone walls formed puzzle-like compositions proclaiming interdependence and reciprocity. All these share a faith in the abstract, nonrepresentational, power-laden messages of juxtapositional and appropriational framing of the vagaries of the world (see Taplin n.d.). The many adjacent treatments of natural and manipulated rock at the base of the Machu Picchu observatory are a case in point (Stone-Miller 2002: 204–205). Throughout that site and the kingdom as a whole, the viewer moved according to an Inka path, whether up to the Intihuatana Stone or along the grand Royal Road, to be stopped and confronted with a piece of the vast landscape that the Inkas visually and ideologically captured, singled out, and probably made geometric as well. Thus, the Inka nonrepresentational aesthetic of flexible framing, far from being a symptom of iconoclasm or a lack of imagination, was a daring, beautiful, and supremely effective expression of an inclusive worldview and its political destination of dominance.

In astronomy, architecture, and other cultural constructs, what assumes importance is the fundamentally Inka juxtaposition of movement and stasis, couched in terms of capturing in frames, such as moving to the door huaca and stopping there for a set of ritual movements directed toward containing the moving wind. Astronomical/calendrical/architectonic practices demonstrate the Inka emphasis on "being here and looking there" as a cultural given. Without dependence on representationalism, the Inka goal was to bring the far near, capture the vagaries of the distant within their ordering frame (such the June solstice sun through the Machu Picchu observatory window). Inescapably, capturing the distant was a political goal as well, one intensely germane to a conquest state. I hope to demonstrate here how Inka textiles participate in this "nonrepresentational," inclusive, hierarchical, relational worldview. They do so through expressive complexity yet apparent minimalism, standardization yet variation, order juxtaposed with its many opponents, and harkening to the land for ultimate, yet still abstract, reference. Given the vastness of the topic, precedence will be given to the royal ideal and only a few observations will be offered about the ethnically diverse.

The eminent scholars honored at this conference and in this volume have all contributed profound insights to any current discussion of how Inka and related textiles shed light on issues of variation in the visual relationships between the Inka and the foreign. John Murra's seminal work firmly places textiles at the core of the Inka program; his thorough research allows us to understand the possible interdigitation of imperial and local through fiber by keeping in mind the strength, longevity, and individuality of the many local fiber traditions encountered, their incorporation into the Inka Empire via conquest, and the potential recirculation of imagery via subsequent tribute paying and gift exchange (Murra 1962, 1975). One of Murra's many specific insights, the linking of the realms of textiles and agriculture in the Inka mind, particularly informs the present discussion (Murra 1962: 715). In turn, John Rowe looks at the Inka state equally in its broad outlines and in the particulars of the important Inka textiles in the Dumbarton Oaks collection (Rowe 1946, 1979, 1996). I will attempt to follow his example of considering both forest and trees, my interpretations of the Inka royal tunic indebted to the groundwork of his careful observations. Tom Zuidema, for his part, generates a rich array of connections between the material and the ritual, using monuments and the chronicles together to interpret thorny questions relevant here (Zuidema 1964, 1982, 1985). María Rostworowski thoughtfully attends to the pivotal highlands-coast relations, crucial for the slippery issues of "related" textiles, the locus of important information for this volume's overarching theme (Rostworowski 1988).

Here I would like to add to the dialogue some observations on Inka choices of forms for their textile statements, particularly the Dumbarton Oaks royal tunic, in hopes of nuancing the ideal and real relationships imperial Inkas established with the diverse ethnicities they absorbed. The most cursory glance at Inka fiber arts reinforces the impression that the Inka placed supreme confidence in the power of geometry to signify, largely without direct references. If we are to let their textiles guide us more surely into the Inka imperial notion of itself in relation to the many other members of, and outsiders to, this supremely complex empire, it behooves us to share their confidence in the meaningfulness of elegant forms and their arrangements. To be politically expedient, designs *had* to speak to a vast array of local constituencies, each with their own deep and distinctive aesthetic traditions; thus, inherent tensions in the expansionist mandate play out in the textile corpus, precisely because textiles played such an important role in the exchanges between the players (see

Murra 1962). These tensions center around maintaining an Inka identity through visual consistency and control, yet asserting dominance over a vast foreign territory, which by definition brings with it newness and otherness. Simultaneous with the Inka attempt to establish a universal abstract vocabulary and one imminently recognizable as their own, it is important to note that Inka textile forms also contain abstract references to imperial ordering of a diverse world, to other designs, and incorporate variations as distinct possibilities. Thus, textiles may have much to tell us about the Inka program to qualify heterogeneity and visually bring the distant near.

The Dumbarton Oaks tunic is a familiar masterpiece, yet new interpretations can be offered, especially in relation to other Inka textiles. I contend that the royal tunic and the other elite tunics that it references directly all participate in the aforementioned Inka strategy of "enframed flexibility"; they frame, contain, and loosely grid the vagaries of the visually non-Inka. Yet the textile corpus achieves this rather obvious strategy of containing otherness in a somewhat counterintuitive fashion. Albeit in a strictly hierarchical visual system, Inka textiles assign *variation itself* to the very top royal level, allow contained diversion as a subtext in the middle administrative level, and finally insist primarily on "pieces of the frame," to borrow John McPhee's phrase, lower down. Interestingly, this sequence challenges a simplistic assumption that the orderly Inka would characterize their ruler as the most orderly and the lower-status as inevitably slipping into its chaotic opposite. It also challenges the stereotype of the Inka as inflexibly, almost mindlessly repetitious, as artistically monodimensional (Jones 1964). I would replace any vestiges of a derogatory view toward Inka formal choices with one that celebrates the multivalence, subtlety, and elegance of Inka textile expressions.

The Evidence of the Chronicles

Before turning to the royal tunic, it is appropriate to review briefly how the Spanish chroniclers characterized textiles in situations involving Inka royalty and foreigners. Mythically, clothing itself defined human ethnic diversity, as in the familiar creation story in which Viracocha painted different patterns on the sculptures of people before they were sent out to populate the earth (Zuidema 1982: 446; Urton 1999: 34–37). Myriad textile patterns have defined the human world in Andean terms for millennia (Stone-Miller 1994; Heckman 2003). During the Inka Empire, its perhaps ten million subjects or more wore thousands of distinctive textile identifiers, and were required to maintain their ethnic dress in all its multiplicity for reasons of political control (Cobo 1993[1653]: 190).

Cosmologically and metaphorically, Pachamama, or Mother Earth, was herself a textile. She was known as Suyrumama, "the long dress that drags over the ground" (Zuidema 1985: 195). The Inka control over dress in general therefore extends to dominion over the earth. It is especially relevant to the present discussion that during the royal accession/marriage ceremony the Sapa Inka and his betrothed walked on multicolored fine textiles arrayed on the ground. Since rugs were not a component of Inka material culture, this act was unprecedented in daily life and therefore fitting for a ruler and a pivotal moment in time. This "red carpet treatment" was not only a special, multiple, textile confirmation of his being above and encompassing everyone else, but also signified his lone right to trample on the earth's own dress. Establishing his right to conquer land and peoples far and wide lies at the symbolic core of the Sapa's acceding to the throne. Thus, it already makes sense that Juan de Betanzos, writing in 1557, described how in exerting his authority over the vanquished Chanca, Yupanqui stepped on their clothing and other accoutrements (1996 [1557]: 88). Yupanqui also won a dispute with his allegedly cowardly father and brother, and won the right to proclaim victory by saying "I step on my enemies" and doing so (Classen 1993: 56). Thus, it is clear that the conquered are interchangeable with their textile patterns, both of which assume lower status and are to be humiliated; both are further analogous to the territory that the Inkas have made their own by walking on it (via the Capac Ñan, the Royal Road). In this way, appropriation of the entire known world is symbolized by textiles/wearers of those textiles placed in a subservient physical relationship to the Sapa's body. Corporeally and metaphorically the ruler was the empire's "head" and the people his body (op cit.: 184). Hence what he wore on his body can be seen to represent the entire empire, a point that will be elaborated below.

More specific kinds of political domination over subject peoples also was expressed through symbolic treatment of clothing: when Yupanqui ritualized his defeat of the Soras he both confiscated their garments and made them wear specially made long red tunics with numerous attached borla fringes, the type that the Sapa normally wore on his forehead (ibid.: 175–176). The defeated lords donned this multiplied symbol of their new lord, then anointed their heads with *asua* (more commonly known to us as *chicha*, maize beer) and maize flour, as if they were an offering of food to him. Obviously being made to wear Inka garb in this context was a symbol of defeat. Then, in a series of coercive complementary gestures, the vanquished were presented with imperial style textiles. Some were made Inka by wearing the army uniform and all those who proved loyal subjects became eligible to win further rewards in the form of Inka-style dress. After having one's own ethnicity trampled upon, the subjects' goal ostensibly became to more closely approximate the Sapa Inka, especially in matters of dress. High status was synonymous with approximating the Sapa through clothing, becoming more visually Inka; indeed, "the tokens most resembling the Inca's were the most honorable and most desirable" (Garcilaso de la Vega 1966 [1609]: 56). One pertinent example is the wearing of the *llautu*, a head wrapping Garcilaso de la Vega calls "a plait of many colors and a finger's breadth wide . . . they wound it four or five times round their heads like a garland . . . the earliest privilege the Inca granted his subjects was to order them to imitate him in all wearing the plait around their heads" (ibid.).

He goes on to comment on the important distinction that was nevertheless made when the would-be Inkas wore the coveted llautu: "though it was not to be of many colors like his own, but of one color only, which was to be black" (ibid.). Repeatedly, the color black was associated with outsiders, as Zuidema has well demonstrated (1992: 22). During Capac Raymi for instance, healthy llamas *of various colors* were sacrificed for the nobility and the ruler, as well as young white camels for Cuzqueños in general. In obvious propagandistic counterpoint, old black llamas had their "ears pierced as if they represented nobility. The honor, however, rings false, because the black llamas were old and in fact represented conquered peoples, who themselves were not allowed to pierce their ears" (ibid.). Thus, the multicolored llamas and the multicolored llautu underscore that polychromy was associated with royalty, a highly relevant theme in relation to the Dumbarton Oaks royal tunic. In general, multiplicity of color was a lordly privilege: "the clothing which was worn by the lords in ancient times was very elegant and of many very fine colors" (Cobo 1990: 187). Certainly the power to command the services of the empire's most skilled dyers to produce the most vibrant colors was implied in the right to wear such gorgeous and hard-won hues. Sumptuary laws ensured that the powerful and inclusive multiplicity of the ruler would be proclaimed by his uniquely and extremely polychromatic garb, likewise others' loyal subjugation was reinforced by their limited monochromatic dress.

The Sapa's rights to everything that was "more" extended to his ability to wear anyone's dress: Betanzos describes how on his tours of inspection Huayna Capac let the locals know he was coming so that they could meet him on the road and give him a garment "like the ones used in that town" (1996 [1557]: 169). Thus, he entered every province already arrayed in local attire, even down to wearing a custom hairpiece so his hairdo matched that of the subjects (ibid.: 168). This extreme "Ich bin ein Berliner" strategy not only made for a good double message of unity and dominance, it demonstrated that the Sapa was not diminished or his identity compromised by wearing others' patterns. His subjects were limited to their local clothing or allowed Inka approximation, according to *Inka* whim. The next and allied privilege of a loyal subject, that of cutting one's hair, shows how distinctions were to be maintained by a balance between approximating the Inka and keeping the ethnic. Garcilaso writes after some time had passed, he granted them the favor of another mark of distinction which they esteemed more highly: this was to order them to have their hair shorn, though in different styles for the various tribes of vassals *and all theirs different from his*, so that there should be no confusion in the distinction he had ordered to be made between each province and tribe and no lessening of the difference between him and them. (Garcilaso de la Vega 1966[1609–17]: 56)

Thus, the Sapa manipulated now-crucial distinctions among different ethnicities and particularly between Inka and non-Inka by altering actual local looks to suit imperial organizational needs.

In sum, the Sapa was presented as the mediator of the foreign through his personal right to extreme multivalency and through his overt manipulation of others' dress. Flexibility, being above the rules that limit one to one's own dress, literally ranked high. These observations from the chronicles set the stage for the messages about variety and control encoded in the transcendent geometry of the Dumbarton Oaks royal tunic.

The Dumbarton Oaks Royal Tunic

Scholars agree that this was indeed a royal tunic. The crux of the argument remains the chronological portraits of the Inka kings by Guaman Poma (figs. 2–13) in which he characterizes their dress in his (admittedly colonial) versions of tocapus (Guaman Poma 1980[ca. 1615]: 61, 63, 69–81). Despite the fact that these renderings are recognized to be less than faithful replicas of actual Pre-Hispanic tunics (see also Stone-Miller 1994: 179, 182), these drawings may yet shed a little more light on the meaning of the all-tocapu format. It seems significant that Guaman Poma not only chose to render all the rulers in some form of the tocapu tunic, but also fairly consistently increased the visual expanse of tocapu in the *imperial* rulers' garb. The first six Sapas wear tunics with only tocapu waistbands (figs. 2–7), perhaps to show retrospectively they were Inka (wearing tocapu) but not as elevated as later kings (figs. 8–12). Rowe has pointed out convincingly that the stepped diamond waistband tunic indicated low-to-middle social status (Rowe 1979: 256–257); it may be that patterned waistbands serve to indicate moderate status in general, after all they are imitation belts, and cost less time and fewer material resources to weave. Huascar, a ruler who never got to rule and is shown dragged away in ropes, also wears the waistband-only tocapu tunics (fig. 13).

Thus, an allied working hypothesis would be that wearing the all-tocapu format tunic is *reserved for individuals and actions in which their full royal role as conqueror is implied or preeminent*. Viracocha Inka sports the first all-tocapu tunic (fig. 9), possibly because in the royal version of history he acts as the fulcrum for the imperial era. Pachakutec wears a

FIG. 2   The first Inka, Manco Capac Inka, from Felipe Guaman Poma de Ayala's *Nueva corónica y buen gobierno*, ca. 1615. The Royal Library, Copenhagen.

FIG. 3   The second Inka, Sinchi Roca Inka, from Felipe Guaman Poma de Ayala's *Nueva corónica y buen gobierno*, ca. 1615. The Royal Library, Copenhagen.

FIG. 4   The third Inka, Lloque Yupanqui Inka, from Felipe Guaman Poma de Ayala's *Nueva corónica y buen gobierno*, ca. 1615. The Royal Library, Copenhagen

FIG. 5   The fourth Inka, Mayta Capac Inka, from Felipe Guaman Poma de Ayala's *Nueva corónica y buen gobierno*, ca. 1615. The Royal Library, Copenhagen.

FIG. 6   The fifth Inka, Capac Yupanqui Inka, from Felipe Guaman Poma de Ayala's *Nueva corónica y buen gobierno*, ca. 1615. The Royal Library, Copenhagen.

FIG. 7   The sixth Inka, Inka Roca, from Felipe Guaman Poma de Ayala's *Nueva corónica y buen gobierno*, ca. 1615. The Royal Library, Copenhagen.

FIG. 8 The seventh Inka, Yahuar Huaca Inka, from Felipe Guaman Poma de Ayala's *Nueva corónica y buen gobierno*, ca. 1615. The Royal Library, Copenhagen.

FIG. 9 The eighth Inka, Viracocha Inka, from Felipe Guaman Poma de Ayala's *Nueva corónica y buen gobierno*, ca. 1615. The Royal Library, Copenhagen.

FIG. 10 The ninth Inka, Pachakutec Inka, from Felipe Guaman Poma de Ayala's *Nueva corónica y buen gobierno*, ca. 1615. The Royal Library, Copenhagen

FIG. 11 The tenth Inka, Topa Inka, from Felipe Guaman Poma de Ayala's *Nueva corónica y buen gobierno*, ca. 1615. The Royal Library, Copenhagen.

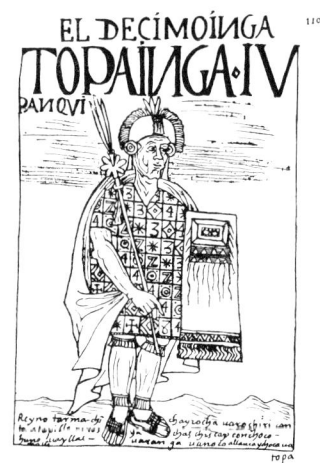

FIG. 12 The eleventh Inka, Huayna Capac Inka, from Felipe Guaman Poma de Ayala's *Nueva corónica y buen gobierno*, ca. 1615. The Royal Library, Copenhagen.

FIG. 13 The twelfth Inka, Tupac Cuchi Hualpa Huascar Inka, from Felipe Guaman Poma de Ayala's *Nueva corónica y buen gobierno*, ca. 1615. The Royal Library, Copenhagen.

simpler, central-column tocapu format (fig. 10), perhaps to be portrayed as fundamentally different, as he was wont to be. Topa Inka and Huayna Capac, the great conquerors, both wear the all-tocapu (figs. 11, 12). Although I might wish Pachakutec's portrait began a run of the all-tocapus, Guaman Poma seldom submits neatly to our linear notions. Nonetheless, for him, the essence of *expansionist* ruling was expressed in tunic compositions featuring more continuous tocapus. Thus, when Guaman Poma chooses to illustrate Pachakutec, Topa Inka, or Huayna Capac performing actual—if ceremonial—tasks, they are be arrayed in other tunic formats, but in their full expansionist glory they alone are completely tocapu covered. Interestingly, the only all-tocapu tunic Guaman Poma renders besides that of these three full-status conquerors is Tupac Amaru, who was the puppet "last" Sapa. While this would seem to negate the theory of conquerors wearing all-tocapu, this illustration may well be one of Guaman Poma's subversively Andean subtextual statements that "the Inka shall rise again."

FIG. 14 Basic patterns of the tocapu in the Dumbarton Oaks Royal Tunic (after J. Rowe 1996: 166). Digitized image courtesy of Hélène Bernier.

Tellingly, Guaman Poma's portraits consistently organize his early colonial versions of tocapu motifs into neat diagonals (figs. 2–5, 7–11, 13). *The royal tunic most decidedly does not* (fig. 1). In fact, ever since Guaman Poma we have searched in vain for an image of ultimate order in the garb of the Sapa Inka. This is understandable, given our cultural assumption that clear linear sequence, i.e., narrative, characterizes the loftiest expressions. Barthel's popularized idea that this tunic constitutes Inka "writing" to me epitomizes such ethnocentrism and has struck other scholars similarly (Barthel 1971).[1] His complex argument of an esoteric order to the motifs, even if true, does not effect the disorderly impression given by the tunics' tocapu arrangement. We cannot expect Inka viewers to have made the king stand still while they diagram such an elaborate system, especially since they were not allowed to look at him directly! Certainly our looking for orderliness to the communication makes sense given the khipu and the many other Inka standardizations. I myself spent time in the trenches obsessively diagramming the welter of the royal tunic's detailed shapes (fig. 14) and magnificent colors. Such analyses and those of John Rowe and Ann Rowe (Rowe and Rowe 1996: 461, 463) *are* relevant here; however, none of us found the key to the visual

FIG. 15 Checkerboard army tunic. Miniaturized as Dumbarton Oaks Royal Tunic pattern 1. Courtesy of the Dallas Museum of Art.

order. It seems rather unproductive to search this composition for messages that it patently does not send. Instead, I hope to suggest here several keys to its particular brand of disorder.

The forms of this spectacular tunic set up a series of juxtapositions that build up layers of relativistic meaning. Meaning located precisely in the relationship of parts is, as suggested above, the quintessence of Inka abstract expressive strategy. Here, the containing grid, an Inka hallmark, and the dominant number of repeats of two long-identified quotations of standard Inka tunics, the checkerboard and the Inka key (figs. 1, 15, 16), tie the Sapa to all things Inka, especially those that subjugate the land into orderliness by conquest and subsequent management. These definite statements of imperial identity juxtapose with the vast majority of the 312 motifs, which are vague rather than literal referents and are arrayed in an apparently disorderly fashion. This unsystematic repetition of generic foreign motifs, among which are interspersed, almost randomly, two specific and recognizable Inka tunic patterns, creates the primary significance of this tunic. At one level this composition embodies the Inka ruler, with his omnipresent "helpers" the army and the administrators, as the mediator of all possible otherness. At another it assigns the creative, ambivalent, and powerful energy of variation and change to the ruler; thus, it represents him as the necessary opposite of the orderliness of the Inka adminstration. Cieza de León claimed "no rich man could deck himself out in more finery than the poor, or wear different clothing, *except the rulers and headmen, who, to maintain their dignity, were allowed great freedom and privilege*" (1960 [1553]: 178). Here I will discuss six ways in which the "great freedom" in the formal choices embraced by the royal tunic are accomplished through color, patterning, juxtapositions, referentiality, overall style, and formal anomalies.

First, in its very visual inclusiveness, its communicative multiplicity, the tunic makes global claims for the Inkas and for the Sapa Inka himself. It exhibits a nearly full range of possible textile colors: cochineal red, white, many shades of gold and tan, plus the challenging and unusual green. The darkest color, the one that reads as black in photographs and upon first glance in the presence of the original, seems in fact to be a very deep purple (Mary Frame personal communication, 1998). Purple implies the use of indigo blue overdyed with red and here also perhaps some intensive mordanting to deepen the resulting color so intensely. There may well have been plain indigo blue portions five hundred years ago, appearing now as tan with grayish residue due to differential fading (ibid.). Thus, the royal tunic in its pristine form included nearly the totality of polychromy available in natural form. Dyes, obviously, come from various ecosystems (cochineal from lower zones supporting the nopal cactus, other colors from higher altitudes [see Antúñez de Mayolo 1976]), and so polychromy in the fiber arts inevitably symbolizes the incorporation and coordination of the foreign in and of itself. For the Inka it may carry an explicitly expansionist message.

Certainly wearing the colorful tunic with the multicolored llautu doubled royal polychromy. Sheer colorfulness also may connote spiritual mediation, a characteristic shared by other multihued phenomena. For instance, multicolored wood was used for sacrificial fires in Cusco; Bernabé Cobo reports that "the fire for the sacrifices that were made in Cuzco . . . was not started and fed with just any wood; it was done with a certain kind of wood which was scented, carefully carved, and very colorful" (1990: 117). Multicolored llamas were sacrificed for the king's health at Capac Raymi (Zuidema 1992: 20). Multicolored textiles adorned the sacred rock in Titicaca:

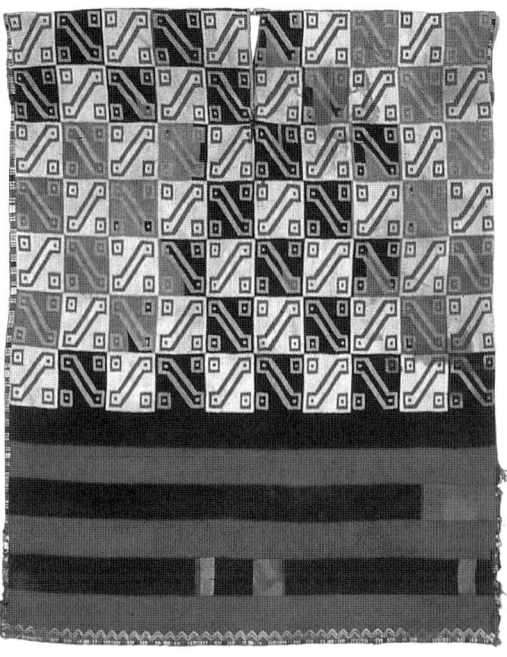

FIG. 16 Inka key tunic. Rotterdam Museum voor Volkenkunde. Quoted as Dumbarton Oaks Royal Tunic pattern 2. Copyright Rotterdam Museum voor Volkenkunde.

> the whole concavity of the rock was covered with plates of gold and silver, and . . . in its various hollows different offerings were placed, according to the festival or the occasion. The offerings were gold, silver, shells, feathers, and rich cloth of cumbi. The entire rock was covered with a rich mantle of this cloth—the finest and most gorgeous in colors of any ever seen in the empire.
> (Squier 1973: 336)

These material examples of polychromy may ultimately echo the colorfulness of the life-giving rainbow, which figured prominently in the Qorikancha (Urton 1999: 10–13) and the fertile earth during the wet season, from whence probably came the visual for the "the long dress that drags over the ground."

In the Dumbarton Oaks tunic, besides the broad range of colors, each individual color area (i.e., shape) is small, so the eye is kept dizzyingly busy. For example, each miniature checkerboard tunic motif tocapu measures a mere 6 cm across, each component black or white square covers less than a square centimeter. There exists no readily apparent way for the eye to organize this welter; it is constantly defeated by the almost randomly placed and supremely complicated motifs that cover the entire tunic. In

The Dumbarton Oaks Royal Inka Tunic in Context

addition, no two similar tocapus are adjacent, nor do tocapus repeat in a logical sequence, at least one that is perceptually available to a viewer. Thus, without careful diagramming it is visually challenging to pick out similar motifs and maintain their locations. John Rowe was able to locate only one instance in which the same sequence of motifs recurred; however, in a total system of 312 tocapus this suggests little more than statistical chance. Finally, variation of colors assigned to the same motifs breaks up the visual field even more. One easily perceptible example is the three color combinations of the Inka key motif: red on gold, gold on red, and green on dark purple. The two red-gold combinations are so close as to be hard to keep separate, the green so different from them that it becomes hard to see the three as a group. More subtle examples of color variation within tocapus abound (see below). In general, it is safe to say that the tunic achieves through color a vision of inchoate multiplicity. It may be argued that such an expressive strategy mirrors the restless mandate of expansionism.

Second, the most salient individual motifs in the Dumbarton Oaks tunic are the miniature checkerboard tunic (a full-size version is seen in fig. 15) and the Inka key tocapus (full-size in fig. 16). These two are more numerous, bolder, and more consistently interpreted than the other motifs. As John Rowe point outs (1996: 461), the checkerboard tunic motif, pattern 1, constitutes the most numerous tocapu with thirty-three occurrences. The Inka key patterns run a close second with thirty altogether.[2] Thus, sixty-three, or twenty percent of the total tunic motifs represent highly recognizable Inka referents. At one extreme, the tiny checkerboards stand out with their small-scale, highly contrastive yet repetitively simple pattern. At the other, the keys are salient as the simplest design, with the largest constituent parts. And even if a viewer were to miss the red and gold Inka key variations among all the other reds and golds, the few green and dark purple keys form the most obvious units of all (they constitute the quick way to distinguish the tunic's "front" from the "back," the former has the six dark keys, the latter only three). While there is still no orderly arrangement for the Inka patterns in the composition as a whole, they nevertheless are the most graspable, recurring images. One easily could interpret this juxtaposition as a statement of stable, recognizable, and dominant Inka presence among the foreign multitudes, the reliable and powerful state insinuated into shifting ethnic variety. Cobo has several perhaps relevant comments about leaving Inka personnel in conquered provinces: "they left the recently conquered provinces well protected by garrisons and fortresses that kept them under control. They also left personnel to instruct the new vassals about the customs, rites and worship of their gods. . . . In order to maintain sufficient well-trained and disciplined troops, the Inkas kept a large number of captains and military officers stationed in the provinces" (Cobo 1990[1653]: 215).

Third, while the two referential motifs directly represent or quote actual Inka tunics, it is the non-Inka patterns that seem most particular to this tunic, in the sense of being distinct from the tocapus on other Inka tunics and distinct from other cultures' exact designs. John Rowe unearthed but one exact recurrence elsewhere of pattern 9 in a tocapu waistband (1996: 463).[3] I have been equally unsuccessful in finding exact matches, which again leads me to believe they may not be the point. I contend that *new* tocapus were to be generated, not ones with a shared referential nature, as part of the Inka imperial conquest mandate. Similarly, the non-Inka tocapus also do not seem to match exactly any known designs from other contemporaneous Andean peoples. (One would think that such geometric patterns as those of the royal tunic, based on only a few variables [diamonds, lines, crosses, etc.], would be unable to avoid similarity to other cultures' motifs. Visual affinity may in some cases be due to the fact that it is difficult to generate totally new patterns after millennia of Andean textile geometric exploration.) While bits and pieces of the motifs here, such as diamonds or steps, can be found in Late Intermediate period and Late Horizon fiber arts, they do not add up to quotations from specific "conquerees." In fact, this avoidance seems to deny the enemies of the Inka a specific voice; for instance, given that there is no recognizably Chimú-motif tocapu, their most formidable combatants were not granted the respect given to checkerboard tunic-wearers.

I further suggest that the unprecedented character of the non-Inka tocapus indicates a symbolic attempt to envision *potential* conquests. The non-Inka patterns worn by the ruler are not to be appropriated from or leased out to other lesser folk, which would tie together various members of the hierarchy through a stable set of foreign patterns. Instead, it is the Inka referents that are made to provide such coherence, as befits an egocentric imperial self-image. Like the reward haircuts, Inkas avoided incorporating real local patterns in favor of creating new imagined ones successfully distinguishable from each other and from the two that are recognizably Inka. This idea diverges from the usual interpretation of tocapus as "heraldic," assuming an analogy with the European tradition of coats of arms and therefore that each pattern stands for a concrete and specific person or people (e.g., Zuidema 1982: 448). If it did, we should have identified some of those one-to-one correlations by now.

Nevertheless, fourth, some of the non-Inka patterns may refer in an appropriative sense to the past of other traditions. It was pointed out to me that pattern 23 echoes—without reproducing—a typical Nasca discontinuous warp-and-weft fret design (fig. 17; Jane Rehl personal communication, 1997). Quotes taken from the Nasca occur in pattern 16, while Wari textile echoes can be heard in the "S" shapes of patterns 12, 13, and 22 (fig. 18a). The Wari/Tiwanaku nested square (fig. 18b) and abstracted

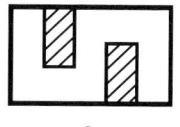  

a b c

FIG. 17 Nasca (AD 300–500) discontinuous warp-and-weft opened-out tunic. Note similarity to pattern 23 in the Dumbarton Oaks Royal Tunic. Courtesy of the Merrin Gallery, New York (photograph by Ken Cohen).

FIG. 18 Motifs from the Dumbarton Oaks Royal Tunic pattern 4 that closely resemble Wari prototypes: a. sideways "S" (denotes feline fangs in Wari examples); b. nested square (used for many elements from staff segments to headdress elements in Wari examples); c. trident motif (used for feet and feathers in Wari examples) (drawing by the author).

back foot motifs (fig. 18c), the latter even down to the white tips, are found in pattern 4. Obviously none of these are exact matches to entire motifs or textile compositions, but they are too detailed to be accidental resemblances. It may be significant that references are made to the *distant* foreign past, perhaps in order to more neutrally coopt the greatness of Early Intermediate period and Middle Horizon states, while denying their actual *current* enemies representation. Certainly the Tiwanaku connection is legitimizing, given the mythic appropriation of human and specifically Inka creation taking place there (Davies 1995: 16–19), the long-distance ceque line connecting Cusco, Huaynacauri, and Tiwanaku (Zuidema 1982: 439–445), and other strong references to Tiwanaku in Inka expressions as a whole (see Stanish and Bauer, this volume).

More generally, by making shadowy reference to others' ancient sacred imagery, by containing links to the ancestors, the royal tunic may visually hold outsiders' huacas hostage. Zuidema calls attention to Cristóbal de Albornoz who states that textiles, the portable "dresses" for rocks and other sculptural huacas, actually were imprisoned in Cusco along with sculpted huacas (1982: 446–447). The deity Viracocha, in creating people, made sure that "each nation was wearing the dress that belonged to their *huaca*" (ibid.). And Viracocha's two sons were named "Imaymana Viracocha, 'Viracocha of all things created' and . . . Tocapu Viracocha,

'Viracocha of the tocapu-designs in ceremonial dresses'" (ibid.: 447). This divine connection strengthens the idea of the ruler wearing his subjects' huacas in a tocapu-covered garment. Huacas of all types were consulted by the ruler about the past, future, and distant places (ibid.: 432): Guaman Poma writes, "[i]n the time of the Inca [King Tupa Yunga Yupanqui] spoke with the huacas and stones and demons and knew because of them the past, the future of them and of the whole world" (1980[ca. 1615]: 263–264). These concepts, of textile-covered huacas and through them omniscience over time, certainly seem embodied in the tocapus of this tunic. Thus, any references to the past worn directly on the Sapa's body itself seek posthumous incorporation of times and peoples we know to have been pre-Inka in reality. Such generic appropriations of others' past glories allowed the ruler to insinuate his control over the past just as he sought to imply his power over future, both in a kind of confident subjunctive.

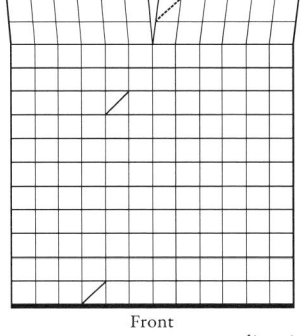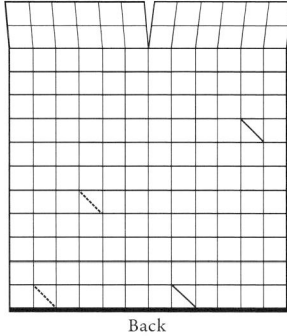

FIG. 19 Diagram of the Dumbarton Oaks Royal Tunic pattern 4, noting direction of the diagonal (drawing by the author)

However, fifth, Inka appropriation means an unmistakable imperial recasting in the interpretation of all the non-Inka motifs, again like the manipulation of hairstyles. Specific examples, such as the Wari-related trident feather element taking a distinctly trapezoidal form (a point unfortunately not conveyed in fig. 18c due to the limitations of computer drawings at the time it was made), are only the tip of the iceberg. The non-Inka patterns are generally and uniformly subjected to the hallmarks of Inka design: the grid format, various framing devices, dominant rectilinearity, and quadripartition. The grid in this composition has no defining lines, no one background color, no strict alternation of red, gold, and dark purple squares; it controls the motifs with an invisible hand. At one edge it is even noticeably compressed (fig. 1, viewer's left side of the "front," right side of the "back"), as John Rowe pointed out (1996: 461). The near-grid organizes with typically Inka "organic geometry." Framing devices, a favorite Inka preoccupation (Taplin n.d.), further divide the grid into a regimented series of individual units: tocapus may have no contrasting-color frame, or one or two; frame types occur in no orderly arrangement. The nonframed tocapus are really ones in which the frame and the background of the motif are the same color. Extra frames diminish the apparent size of the motif, making the grid seem to waver in places. In areas with many frames of almost the same color, that color almost becomes a background color, but the frame-grid takes over again as soon as the eye moves to an adjacent area. Thus, frames are another way in which the visual field visually multiplies and shifts.

Designs are predominantly rectilinear, as in so much of Inka art. One exception, pattern 20 (fig. 14), which makes up less than ten percent of the tocapus, has quite understated curvilinear zigzags. Subdivision is rampant, especially into four parts, suggesting the obvious connection with the four suyus that made up Tawantinsuyu. Unabashedly four-part patterns constitute 11/21 types of motifs and 142/312 instances. Thus, the Inka filter again visually leveled ethnicity, mitigated heterogeneity in an apparent propagandistic message meant to persuade subjects of their potential to fit within Inka dictates.

Sixth, and finally, in the visual subtext of minute details a final distinction is drawn between the Inka and the non-Inka patterns: only the latter contain formal variations. The only possible exceptions to this rule are the two dark purple frames for miniature checkerboard tunic motifs; however, these can be seen as part of the overall variations on framing mentioned above and, in any case, framing vagaries do not affect the motif itself. John Rowe elucidated deviant interpretations in the unusually narrow column, especially the anomalously vertical arrangement of pattern 18 there. He suggested this resulted from artistic misjudgment. This may well be, yet the colors assigned to the vertical pattern 18 are aberrant as well (for instance, the entire background of the square is dark green whereas in other instances it is divided into three color areas). I am inclined to grant that "organic geometry" meant leeway to let the grid expand or contract a bit; this obviously was not a reject tunic, but one that was of the highest status and well worn (ibid.: 457). The empire's most talented weavers, the *acllacuna*, can be seen as creatively interpreting a given motif's shape and color (as did the Wari weavers before them [Stone n.d.]), since there is a great deal of variation and several more anomalies elsewhere in the composition. Some motifs, such as pattern 4, are oriented one way on the front and another on the back of the tunic (fig. 19). Others flip inconsistently throughout, such as the vertical direction of the V's in pattern 11 (fig. 20) and the direction of the diagonals of green x's in pattern 10 (fig. 21). Add color variation and you get an example like pattern 23 (fig. 22), the Nasca reference, which has a complex arrangement to begin with, and four different interpretations: the standard one, its rotation, the standard with color substitutions, and a nonstandard version. Most non-Inka motifs have one or two occurrences that are different from the rest. This definite trend toward artistic variation in the non-Inka motifs suggests that foreignness was equated with unpredictability and anomaly vis-à-vis Inka constancy.

Yet it is important to return to the point that it was the Sapa Inka wearing all this variation, and that even the Inka-referent motifs

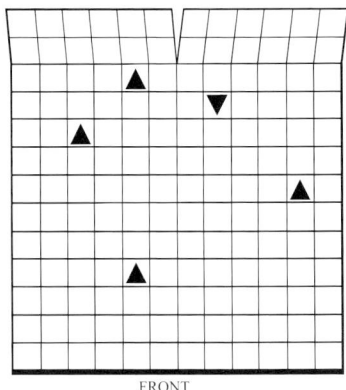 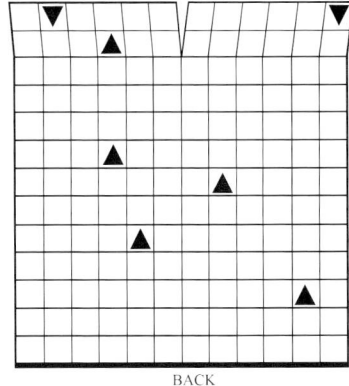

FIG. 20 Diagram of the Dumbarton Oaks Royal Tunic pattern 11 (drawing by the author)

FRONT   BACK

PATTERN 11
MOTIFS

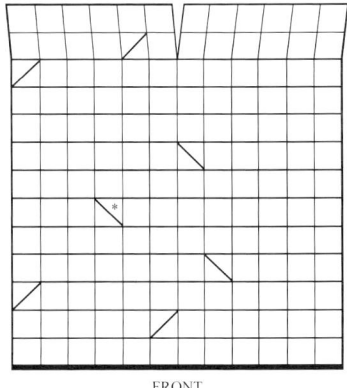 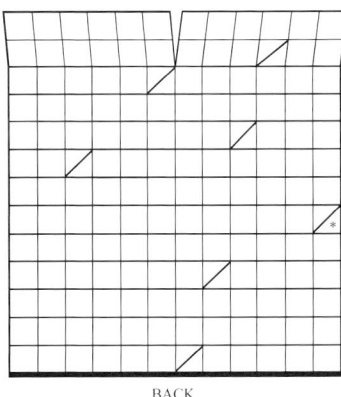

FIG. 21 Diagram of the Dumbarton Oaks Royal Tunic pattern 10 (drawing by the author)

FRONT   BACK

PATTERN 10
DIRECTION OF DIAGONAL
(Formed by two green X's)
*Aberrant Coloration

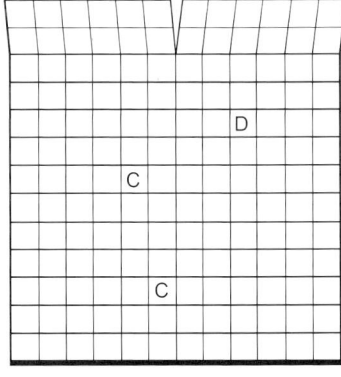 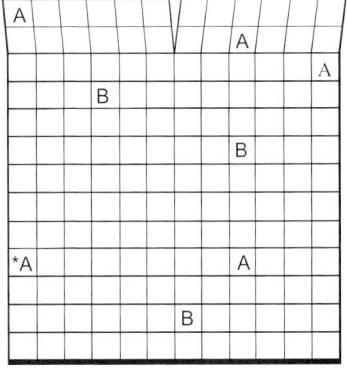

FIG. 22 Diagram of the Dumbarton Oaks Royal Tunic pattern 23 (drawing by the author)

FRONT   BACK

PATTERN 23
A–D Different Interpretations
of Color and Shape Orientation
* Aberrant Coloration

The Dumbarton Oaks Royal Inka Tunic in Context

do not establish a regular checkerboard; in fact, the dark keys unbalance the composition most of all. All the visual upheaval encoded in the composition of his tunic implicitly places the burden of ordering on the wearer himself. To account for this, I contend that at one level his garment characterizes the ruler's essential role as that of a *pachakuti*. The concept pachakuti has been variously defined as the reverser of the world, the turning or change of time, and earthquake (Classen 1993:14; Betanzos 1996[1557]: 159; Sarmiento de Gamboa 1907[1572]: 92). As a concept, pachakuti signals change, cataclysm, inversion, rupture, and the unknown. As a liminal state it forms a crucial part of what Constance Classen calls "the Inca ideological program . . . to transform chaotic, savage bodies into structured, civilized bodies. This program was part of the basic Inca cosmological cycle . . . in which chaos is structured, then degenerates into chaos again, and is restructured" (Classen 1993: 50). Zuidema calls attention to the complex, interrelated Inka concepts of *hucha* and *cama*, which together account for "the primordial stage of 'disorder' or 'secrecy' and 'sin' out of which order was created" (1982: 427). Salomon (1991) likewise explores the idea of *camay*, the manifestation of objective reality from spiritual infusion, in the introduction to the Huarochirí manuscript. It is possible to resolve this tunic's unusual formal juxtapositions as an artistic solution to the problem of encapsulating the Sapa Inka as engaged in necessary upheaval; the tunic visually engages the multitudes of unknown foreigners, structuring them in his grid, intermingling with their shifting potential his stable henchmen, military and administrative.

Certainly any application of this concept is inextricably bound up with the first Inka emperor who took pachakuti as his defining role, Pachakutec (while he is often called Pachakuti, for purposes of clarity I will use Pachakutec when referring to the individual). This tunic may well have actually belonged to the emperor Pachakutec himself; it has considerable evidence of wear and the imperial time span of one hundred years is not too long for textile heirlooms to survive and be used or revered by the descent group (*panaca*). It could even have been worn by his mummified body (*mallqui*) and later saved from Spanish immolation. Be that as it may, whoever wore it was not only personifying the concept but simultaneously referring to the mythicohistorical figure, the ruling nonheir to the throne, Inka Yupanqui, aka Pachakutec. Like Zuidema and most scholars, the objective "truth" of the account of his accession appears less significant than its idealized conceptual claims. The upshot of whatever really did happen was that Inka Yupanqui was credited with irreparably breaking the rules and propelling the Inkas into imperialism. As Zuidema points out, he substantiates his coup d'etat by right of having conquered a group of neighboring foreigners, the Chanca, when his father and the heir apparent evidently balked (Davies 1995: 43–49). In a very significant moment, the deity Viracocha infused him with the necessary confidence by *showing Pachakutec in a mirror all the provinces he was going to conquer* (ibid.: 47). This mythical divinatory act seems conceptually allied to the inclusiveness of the royal tunic's formal patterning; Inka Yupanqui's mirror miracle may even have been understood to be a referent of such a wide-ranging, past- and future-looking garment.

Pachakutec's preternatural success against the Chanca reordered the concept of succession upon merit; it was no less than a wholesale redefinition of the Inka ruler as a conqueror of foreigners rather than a sinchi, or local leader. It is crucial to keep in mind that each of the later emperors confronted new groups of foreigners, reaping no rewards from their predecessor's conquests in terms of tribute income. Pachakutec's political reconstruction of his role as first conqueror may well be central to the multiplicity yet concomitant vagueness of the tunic; if the tunic is like the mirror showing all the potential conquests, the non-Inka motifs cannot mimic the exact patterns of subjects already in the empire. Vague or abstract tocapus intentionally *not* referentially tied to actual non-Inka peoples reflect the capacity of geometric vocabulary to generate variation itself, to approximate those yet-to-be-conquered, ethnically diverse, Viracocha-painted Others. They, like the Sapa himself, represent all that is potential. Indeed, the ruler constantly roamed the realm and directed his armies to conquer beyond its present borders and his administrators to manage the subdued subjects. He could handle the visual and ideological tension of newness in its multiplicity; he had to, if the empire was to expand.

In this way, the Sapa represents what anthropologists term symbolic inversion; the orderer clothes himself in his apparent opposite, a riotous array of other people's patterns. Symbolic inversion denotes the capacity for culture to sustain paradox, to discuss what is not in order to underscore what is. Thus, this tunic may celebrate conquests yet to come and, through visual disorder, confirm the mandate for their ultimate ordering. This symbolic inversion as a dominant interpretation for the composition of the royal tunic not only accounts for highly creative aesthetic patterning, but well serves expansionist political ends (as is true of Inka art as a whole, whose practical, symbolic, and political elements balance one another in elegant ways). Barbara Babcock writes, "[f]ramed disorder in the form of the aesthetic negative is 'variability training,' 'rehearsal for those real situations in which it is vital for our survival to endure cognitive tensions'" (Babcock 1978: 20 [quoting Peckham 1967: 314]). How aptly "framed disorder" describes this tunic, and certainly Inka imperial survival became identified with each heir's ability to pass his "variability training" in the form of continuous campaigns of conquest.

By definition, the role or purpose of symbolic inversion—which, indeed, might well serve as an alternate definition of pachakuti—is to renew an existing system by disputing it, just as Pachakutec renewed Inka power by disputing his family's sense that one small valley was enough. One might say the pre-imperial Inka and the not-yet-conquered foreigners are both uncontrolled situations that the Sapa Inka sees fit to invert. Babcock further clarifies the need for inversion: "through various forms of symbolic inversion . . . culture frees itself from the limitations of 'thou shalt nots,' enriches itself with the subject matter without which it could not work efficiently, and enables itself to speak about itself" (ibid: 20–21). Here "thou shalt nots" might be unruly foreignness, the very subject matter of others that is vitally enriching to a conquest state. Extremely ipseic, "speaking about itself," this tunic intersperses the Inka motifs with the others, setting up the ideal abstract structure to admit and contain variety. Once again, intentionally vague referents help it maintain self-reference.

Certainly the powerful wearer of this anomalous composition was unique, especially in his ability to mediate, to make change, and to channel disorder. Atahualpa's messenger to Huascar addressed him as "Oh unique king" (Betanzos 1996 [1557]: 193). It is important to recall that anomaly, inversion, and liminality follow the ruler from his birth onward.[4] Pachakuti Yamqui's account of the birth of a potential heir to the throne includes all sorts of expressions of oddity, multiplicity, and ambiguity in attendance: hermaphrodites, *multicolored* animals, luminescent stones, dwarves, and hunchbacks.[5] Accompanying Huayna Capac's birth was even a pardoning of sorcerers, those "who worship two gods" (Classen 1993: 61), perhaps to prevent any magical harm to the prince, yet also supporting this theme of multiplicities and ambivalences surrounding royal sons. Multicolored animals/minerals and analogously dualistic people, sorcerers or hermaphrodites, aptly mirror the ambiguous structural position of the heir as in between discrete states of being (part of two ayllus, powerful yet not capable of taking power yet, etc.). (It is interesting to note in this regard that the birth of the heir participates in the definition of sacredness, the overarching term huaca, which includes the concept of split or double, a thing or place or person that is two at once [ibid.: 14].)

If space permitted, a vast number of special symbolic inversions deemed appropriate for the ruler could be offered, such as his lone right to incestuously and polygamously marry (ibid.: 60) or talk directly to the sun. Many rituals he led during his reign likewise underscore his inversion from others as well as the tensions and ambivalences of the Inka vis-à-vis the foreign. In particular, the cleansing ritual *citua* interestingly treats foreigners and the deformed as congruent "unlucky" categories to be excluded, then re-incorporated.[6] All these could be applied to the royal tunic issue: the ruler who could wear the many patterns of Otherness on his body thereby proclaimed his transcendence of any unclean or unlucky aspects of the foreign. The present discussion by no means exhausts the fascinating subject of the Dumbarton Oaks royal tunic.

Non-royal Inka Tunics

True to Inka relativism, royal and nonroyal tunics gain significance in light of one another. Similarities abound among the entire textile corpus to provide necessary Inka commonality: tunic size, shape, proportions; formal structures with checkerboard and partial grid arrangements; and individual pattern rectilinearity, among others. However, the all-tocapu tunic gains in uniqueness when its filled-in grid, its multiplicity, and its lack of regular repetition are discovered to be entirely its own. The controlled, standardized nature of the nonroyal tunics has been long established by John Rowe (1979). It also goes without saying that since the nonroyal examples expressly do *not* represent structural inversion, they must fulfill other imperial needs through their formal appearance. Their appearance is markedly simpler than that of the ruler's, for instance; each motif in any of the non-tocapu tunics is simpler than any motif in the royal one. Certainly such contrasts make necessary distinctions between the director and the directed and do so almost entirely through geometry rather than via referential forms. Minimalistic geometry remains highly communicative of dialectics involving control, conformity, ideal hierarchy distinctions, and territorial organization, on the one hand, and necessary flexibility plus the disorderliness that furthers actual incursions into the foreign, on the other. I contend that expressions lower on the hierarchy reference the *ordered* land—as opposed to the royal symbolic inversion that brings land into the empire in the first place—and yet display formal flexibility, even variety, perhaps in order to elevate the wearer to the prerogatives of the king (as discussed above in the matter of dress and hair-style manipulations).

The principle way that the all-tocapu tunic establishes distinctions among the other tunic types is by singling out and repeating two, the checkerboard and the Inka key, while excluding the rest. It thereby elevates the two roles represented by these particular designs, but not too high. In substantiation of their importance but their secondary nature, Francisco de Xérez mentions that the acllawasi in Caxas wove the army cloth for Atahualpa (Xérez in Markham 1963: 28), which suggests that the provincial outposts of royal weavers were producing checkerboard tunics. This allies royal and military dress but keeps the Cusco acllas sacrosanct, placing that which is military in an appropriately high, royally overseen, but definably lesser position. While no particular mentions are made of the Inka key tunics in the chronicles that I know of, archaeologically checkerboard and key tunics have been found together (J. Rowe 1996: 463, figs. 167, 168) and John Rowe establishes a relative importance from the ceramic effigies interred along with the tunics (to be discussed below). Although deeply allied, we will discuss separately the two nonroyal types found on the royal tunic, as they carry different messages.

CHECKERBOARD TUNICS

First, as an individual tocapu motif the royal tunic contains the checkerboard tunic in its entirety, subjecting its wearer to miniaturization. Such a blatant visual diminution visually projects a message of complete control. From an artistic standpoint one might say that in such a small (six cm) area the checkerboard could not have been characterized otherwise than in encapsulated form. Since its component motifs consist of plain rectangles and a stepped yoke area, neither a plain white or black square as an entire tocapu would convey checkerboard nor would a stepped triangle, which misrepresents the rest of the tunic as plain. Yet the other Inka-referent tocapu, the Inka key, is quoted (one motif pulled out to stand for the whole), while presumably it could have been shrunk to a series of diagonals and dots with the striped area retained below. Thus, the distinction between the miniaturization of the checkerboard and the quotation of the Inka key is intentionally hierarchical in tone, as will be discussed below.

Xérez describes (in Jones 1964: 7) the "red and white chessboard" tunics on Atahualpa's military guards, but this description remains somewhat ambiguous, as is treatment of the checkerboard patterns in Guaman Poma's drawings involving military actions (1980: folios 115, 151). Yet it is still possible to assign this type of pattern to the military, especially the army associated with royalty in some capacity. The account of the royal attendants, whose job it was to sweep the ground in the ruler's path with their hands, described their tunics as red and white; the black squares could have been unnoticed background, as black is perceived as the absence of color. Perhaps the description indeed means that there was a category of only red-and-white checkerboard patterns that were worn by the royal attendants and so far have not been discovered as extant. If so, then the ubiquitous black-and-red-and-white tunics could have been worn by the much more numerous army conscripts (since comparatively many of them survive). Certainly, of all the Inka tunics, this one most elides individuality, a universal aspect of the military strategy.

Either way, when the ruler wore a garment with a tocapu of the miniaturized checkerboard tunic, he claimed control over a lot of lesser-status, army-related personnel. As to status, Cobo writes "the Incas paid much attention to the military and to those who practiced it, since it was the means by which they had achieved such great power and majesty, and through it they maintained this position. Among their vassals, the military profession was the only way to advance to positions of honor, and there was hardly any other way for them to move up and gain importance" (1990 [1653]: 215). Having a prominent place on the royal tunic certainly could represent having moved up in importance. But actual checkerboard tunics do not claim individual importance as does the royal tunic by *looking* different from one another in their woven interpretation (although the addition of beads [*chaquira*] added a "promotion" to the wearer[7]). The relentless consistency of the checkerboards, both in the royal tunic and in reality, the relatively large number of preserved tunics of this type, and the character of their slight variability, all help substantiate their military role (J. Rowe 1979: 245–248).

In fact, the numerous and consistent checkerboard tunics seem to be designed—quite unlike other Inka tunics—to be worn in a group, again highly suitable for the army. Two features that distinguish them are the half-squares at the sides and the minor but recurrent differences in the height of the red yoke at the shoulder and the total number (ten or eleven) of rows of squares included (ibid.). Any deviance from a decimal choice becomes noteworthy in Inka art and both these elements betray such aberrations. The two half-squares at each side, together with the nine full squares in the middle of each row, add up to ten across, at least numerically speaking. However, visually, from the front or back the half-squares remain partial until, from the side, the entire tunic is rendered a continuous checkerboard.[8] By this unusual manipulation of shape, the front and back of the tunic form an uninterrupted patterned cylinder.[9] In addition, and perhaps more significantly, one tunic becomes perceptually and conceptually continuous with its hypothetical neighbor; with their wearers standing in close proximity one tunic completes the next, like a giant puzzle.

This horizontal partiality that embeds the individual within a larger whole is joined by two vertical adjustments to the design that perform a similar communicative task. The slightly variable height of the red yoke at the shoulder and the addition of one extra row of squares are two ways to shift the design within the typical overall tunic dimensions. These adjustments also serve to add actual length to the tunic, which may help contribute to the exact continuity of one wearer to the next. Tall foreigners conscripted into the army could have a regular red area and an extra row of squares, a medium-sized cadet could have a long red area, and a normally small wearer the standard proportions. Since all checkerboards place black squares directly under the red yoke, the black half-squares would line up, no matter how various the individual wearers. Throughout the group, each person standing hip to hip would complete his neighbors' squares, their hemlines remain basically constant, no one exposing thighs or covering ankles. This would not only modify heterogeneity in a practical sense, and preserve dignity, but also promote a visual leveling that is consistent with the regularity, simplicity, and sheer geometry of the pattern itself.

Side by side the plain, uninterrupted expanse of the red yokes would become visual "ground" and the squares a long, jagged zigzag "figure." In this arrangement the person does not maintain visual coherence, since the peaks are formed at people's shoulders. The mountains and valleys of the highlands form an almost unavoidable association, especially the productive, gridded landscape and the rich river valleys of the ideal Inka world. Stepped terraced mountains framing river valleys certainly evoke a utopian visual structure. The army actually traversed this landscape as the instrument for acquiring more orderly land for the empire. In any case, they project an ideal earth's surface, and may thereby abstractly reference "the long dress that drags over the ground."

It is tempting to use the color symbolism mentioned above (Zuidema 1992) to see the black squares as representing foreigners; white, Cusco/Inka nobility, and red royalty (the color of the borla fringe). Such an interpretation would have the checkerboard tunic claim to be conquering the Other for Cusco and the Sapa. In any case, since its color system includes extremes—the darkest, the lightest, and the warmest—it inherently makes a global graphic statement. Worn with the actual stark highlands or monochromatic sandy coast as backdrop, the effect of such contrasting color extremes would be amazing. Red, as is well known, is a perceptually advancing and aggressive color and the stepped yoke arrangement draws the eye by its dynamic outline. The red inverted triangle also serves to emphasize broad, manly shoulders and thus communicate power to dominate. Also, a crowd of checkerboard tunic wearers would seem like many more with the breakup of their seemingly uninterrupted bodies into tiny squares, overwhelming wearer and victims alike with their graphic power. The Sapa's individual multiplicity and the army's multiplied group form a tight complementarity, in which the eye is busied and fooled into seeing more than is really there. Cobo avers that "some [soldiers] painted themselves in a variety of colors and designs to frighten their enemies" (1990: 216). In this, the army would be further leveling its members, adding to the geometric flurry, and attempting to be more Sapa-like in polychromy. This paints a picture of the perfectly Inka balance of individual identity and its constructive loss as a soldier in a group with a higher purpose.

Cobo further adds subtlety to the equation when he claims that the army did not fight in orderly squadrons: "their method of fighting was to attack by all rushing together at their adversaries; they would shout and clamor in order to frighten them; but they would not maintain orderly squadrons" (ibid.: 219). This undulating, pulsing, scattering attack movement adds yet again to the unequivocal visual power of each composition. It does not compromise the hip-to-hip nature of a large army, but does pair the most orderly of designs with the most disorderly of actions, just as in the counterpoint of the very stately and controlled Sapa Inka wearing his nearly random tocapus. Naturally, the army's actual, direct interaction with foreigners requires flexibility in movement, whereas the Sapa's propagandistic statement of his flexible interaction with Others takes place in the conceptual realm. Hence the complementary inversions in their garb reflect the balance between order and disorder (cama and hucha) endemic in the Andean worldview.

INKA KEY TUNICS

In many ways, the Inka key tunics can be placed in an intermediate position between the checkerboard and the royal tunics. It is certainly typical of the Inka strategy to make status distinctions and to reinforce hierarchy even between the two patterns on the royal tunic that represent nonroyal Inkas. Once again the clues afforded by the haircut issue—the importance of distinguishing among others and between the Sapa and everyone else—seem widely applicable; here the role and status distinctions drawn specifically among Inkas are likewise claimed as the bending to the will of the royal wearer. Thus, if the Sapa chose to incorporate your clothing into his, it remained his prerogative. He claimed his right as "Berliner" once again, free to wear you while you were not free to do likewise.

There are inherent indicators of relatively higher status encoded in the Inka key pattern. Rather than being encapsulated in its entirety, as was the checkerboard, the Inka key motif was excerpted on the royal tunic. In other words, individual full-sized squares from the former were transferred basically intact and undiminished into the latter royal context. In a sense the key motif was shared between those who wore it exclusively and the one who directed its wear. Certainly important as well is the inclusive reference that the four dots underlying the key pattern make to the four quarters of Tawantinsuyu. A diagonal line unites two of the four "suyus," which may subtly refer to Viracocha's "diagonal" journey of creation from southeastern Tiwanaku to the northwestern seacoast (Urton 1999: 34–37) as well. These larger meanings aside, on the royal tunic the key motifs are presented in such a way as to suggest that key wearers were more elevated in status than checkerboard ones. Even in its basic shapes and three possible color combinations, the key motif is perceptually more complex and has more flexibility in interpretation than the checkerboard motifs. It is easy to pick out from the welter of the royal tunic, as befits a higher-status pattern.

Within an actual Inka key tunic, the eye is challenged more than with a checkerboard tunic composition, thus approximating more closely the elaboration reserved for royalty. In other words, if visual elaboration increases with social status, since royalty undisputedly wears the most complex, then the key wearer ranks above the black-and-white checkerboard wearer. In key formats more colors are generally involved, diagonals alternate direction to form an overall zigzag, yet the colors change from one square to the next, so that a checkerboard subtext is created (fig. 16). In addition, one can perceive diagonals of the same colors connecting in a basket-weave pattern, or groups of four diagonals creating large diamonds or "X" shapes. Thus, the plain checkerboard idea is overlaid with a complementary color and pattern system that adds considerable depth and visual interest lacking in the black, white, and red format. The shared checkerboard pattern links the two tunics, while further elements distinguish them, as would make sense if they were functionally related. The aforementioned archaeological association of the two tunic types serves to substantiate further the hypothesis that the two types were interrelated but differed in status and role. An additional detail sheds further light: the checkerboard tunic found with the key one has gold beads around the neckline, the *chaquira* that elevate its wearer above the rest. Perhaps this grave shows that a person could be in the military, garner rewards therein, and then later be promoted to an administrative role. This was suggested by Cobo (1990: 215) when he wrote, "the military profession was the only way to advance to positions of honor." (It certainly applies to other military hierarchies, such as our own, in which generals may ultimately administer after emerging from the ranks of enlisted men.) Such a successful individual would likely be buried with the tunics that documented all his accomplishments.

In the absence of more direct evidence of what the key wearer did, one must be vague and suggest that it was an organizational, bureaucratic, and/or administrative role, since the key sums up the empire's four administrative units and interrelates them through the diagonal line so well. Another level of reference may be to the empire, ideally after conquest, fully ordered by the grid and reduced to two color combinations, taking the element of contrast exploited in the black-and-white checkerboard and tempering it somewhat. The ordering of terraces may reverberate in the bold stripes that always lie below the key section of these tunics. Lingering throughout this type of tunic composition are the play of light and shadow on terraces and the many zigzags and steps of Inka stonework (see, for instance, Stone-Miller 2002: 190–207).

Be that as it may, the sense of higher status of the key also comes through in the lower degree of formal standardization that key tunics exhibit vis-à-vis the checkerboard tunics. For instance, although they always have six stripes in the lower portion, key tunics vary as to which color is at the top (the darker or the lighter one). Although they always have ten columns, they may have seven or eight rows of keys.[10] At the top (the shoulder) the rows of keys do not always start with the same color combination or with the same "S" or " Z" direction of the diagonal. Tunics do not even contain the same color scheme consistently or the same number of colors.[11]

Furthermore, a tunic now in the Museum voor Volkenkunde in Rotterdam (fig. 16) displays surprising individual variability in color within the typical shape system. Unmistakably, two different colors are being used in irregular substitution; the black-brown and dark gold-tan threads may interchange within a square, diagonal, or background of a key or in the striped section below. They take turns in no particular order and independently of the highly regular shape system, creating their own subtext of stripes and other shapes. This color variety is particularly obvious in the striped section, which not only displays large areas of gold where black should be, but even sets up a new secondary tone by alternating the colors of adjacent individual wefts in certain areas. Thus, the black-brown and the dark gold-tan meld to make an intermediate mottled brown. In the key motifs area, the usual checkerboard alternation between two colors of motifs would suggest that all the keys should consistently have gold as light and black-brown as dark portions. However, of the thirty-five dark keys on the side of the tunic shown in figure 16, only eleven are all-black, while nine are all-gold, and fifteen have either a little gold in black or vice versa (of which six are predominantly gold with some black and nine are the opposite). All columns and rows exhibit some color interchange, as do most of the bottom stripes; in other words, color aberration is spread throughout the design. For this reason, as well as the stark difference between the black and the gold to begin with, it seems this variation is highly intentional (not the result of running out of the correct dark color and substituting something close to avoid it being noticed). The "back" of the tunic features most of the tan substitutions on one side; however, as on the "front" tan and black are interspersed even in the predominantly tan area. The *different* irregular color distributions of the two sides underscore the asymmetrical use of color in the tunic as a whole.

The weavers of this tunic in particular thus qualified the already qualified orderliness of the key pattern with the dynamism of unexpected color leaps. Perhaps such a distinctive interpretation claims for its wearer some of the higher status assigned to variability, allowing him to be somewhat different. Symbolically, the wearer of an especially idiosyncratic Inka key tunic may communicate that he is less under royal control (as were the key motifs in the royal tunic, with their three color combinations asymmetrically arrayed on the royal tunic's two faces). Such extreme formal dynamism may claim higher status for this particular person than others; he emulated more closely the Sapa, who was the wearer of the most color, the most formal variability, and therefore the most color variability, in the realm. Like the addition of the chaquira to increase the status of the checkerboard tunic wearer in the grave that contained both nonroyal tunic types, the official who wore the Rotterdam key tunic may have been given a "promotion." At least this uncu certainly shows that leeway is acceptable within the strict dictates of such a design, leeway that specifically leans toward the multicolored and the irregular, shown above to be the formal privileges of the ruler.

Conclusions

I hope to have made a case for the important role variation had to play in Inka royal and closely related textiles. As the imperial propaganda of the ruler, tocapu and their variation played the role of a divine mirror that magically foretold the Sapa's future conquests. Patterning visually reinforced the ruler's unique ability to embody the necessary disorder of pachakuti. For the ruler's many minions, lesser degrees of variation modified the individual toward corporate goals, engineering a forceful yet flexible fit within the dictates of uniform and uniformity. Thus, the creative collisions of formal variation encoded in the most valued cumbi nuanced the different worlds coexisting within the Inka Empire. With its formal extremes, the Dumbarton Oaks royal tunic emerges triumphantly as encompassing Other while remaining fundamentally "different from theirs." Thus, submitting to the Inka avoidance of narrative strategies in their aesthetic expressions, the relative polychromy and predictability of textiles carefully delineated an elaborate hierarchy of power. The bold subtleties of Inka geometry created in thread a flexible frame for a complex panoply of imperial power relations.

Acknowledgments

Richard Burger, Craig Morris, and Ramiro Matos offered valuable advice at various stages of this project, for which I am most grateful. I would also like to thank Karen O'Day, Jane Rehl, and Valerie Watkins for research assistance, Anne Dowd for problem-solving ideas, and Sarahh Scher for help with illustrations.

Notes

1   Zuidema is the most receptive to Barthel's argument of a complex, underlying order to the repetition (1982: 448) and yet even he almost immediately contradicts Barthel by commenting on the "more random order" of the non-Inka tocapus; Zuidema's comments reflect my point that a possible mathematical order is not perceptible, nor was it intentionally made perceptible, but rather a random impression was created purposefully. John Rowe and Ann Rowe dismiss Barthel as "guesswork" (1996: 463–464).

2   I am adding all three color combinations together, collapsing John Rowe's patterns 2a, 2b, and 3, which I see as different color combinations rather than as different motifs. Likewise I do not consider patterns 13 and 14 to be separate, because the direction of the four "S" motifs varies, nor 18a and b, which are different color combinations (18c represents the vertically oriented anomaly, but since there are other salient variations in other patterns I am not sure it need be singled out). The same applies to 20a and b, which are somewhat different in shape and color but still represent two of a number of slightly divergent interpretations of the same motif. In sum, I would have the patterns numbered without A's and B's and represented only by one of their typical shape configurations, leaving their many subtle variations in shape and color to more in-depth diagramming, as in figs. 19–22).

3   John Rowe discusses two variants of patterns 6 and 20b elsewhere, yet rather than seeing these as links to other textiles, to my mind the whole idea of the tocapu is to generate variants. His identification of patterns 2 and 20b on a colonial tunic imply the breakdown of sumptuary laws after the Spanish invasions, a matter not relevant to the present discussion.

4   I would say that this is not only because he is so special, his role so elevated, but also because there is particular tension surrounding royal succession; at birth and into adulthood it remains unclear which of the royal sons will actually take power, so any one princeling holds untold potential as an unknown, a future possibility. There may be a number of them uncomfortably occupying the same structural position. Thus, to be an Inka prince is to be inherently dual, maybe a member of his father's lineage (ayllu), yet maybe the future head of a new one of his own. Classen interprets the anomalousness of his birth as an Inka ruler alive at the same time as his father, the Inka ruler [1993: 61]; however, I would qualify this since all the Sapas are technically "alive," in mummy (mallqui) form or otherwise, so there seems to be a wider acceptance that multiple Inka rulers necessarily coexist. In fact, wearing this tunic may claim at least conceptually that Pachakutec and its current wearer are coexistent.

5   These women were generally known as *ancacuna* [Murúa 1987 [1611–1616]: 398). For more on them see Linné 1943; Classen 1993: 14–15; and Guaman Poma (1987 [c. 1615] vol. 1: 98, 112, 196, 224).

6   "All strangers, all whose ears were broken, and all deformed persons were sent out of the city, it being said that they should take no part in the ceremony because they were in that state as a punishment for some fault. Unfortunate people ought not to be present, it was believed, because their ill-luck might drive away some piece of good fortune." (Molina 1873[1576]: 21). On citua see Classen 1993: 82–85. Capac Raymi also required non-Inkas to leave Cusco (Murúa 1987 [1611–1616]: 450).

7   *Chaquira* is the Quechua name for small metal beads sewn around the neck slit of a tunic. It is fairly rare and seems to indicate a special status.

8   Even one aberrant tunic with "twelve" squares across (Rowe's BW-7, Textile Museum 1966.7.172; Rowe 1979: 247, fig. 3) has eleven squares and two half-squares.

9   For the Wari treatment of this half square in the tunic's narrow side column, see Stone n.d.

10   There are about equal numbers of each (i.e., seven rows or eight rows). An exception is one miniature with four columns and six rows (Rowe 1979: 250).

11   Without having seen all the Inka key tunics in color, unfortunately I cannot be more specific.

References cited

ANTUÑEZ DE MAYOLO, KAY

    1976 *Peruvian Natural Dyes and Coloring Sources: An Ethnobotanical Study*. California Polytechnic State University, San Luis Obispo, California.

AVENI, ANTHONY

    1989 *Empires of Time: Calendars, Clocks, and Cultures*. Kodansha International, New York.

BABCOCK, BARBARA

    1978 Introduction. *The Reversible World: Symbolic Inversion in Art and Society* (Barbara Babcock, ed.): 13–36. Cornell University Press, Ithaca.

BARTHEL, THOMAS S.

    1971 Viracochas Prunkgewald. Tocapu Studien 1. *Tribus* (20): 63–124.

BETANZOS, JUAN DE

    1996 [1557] *Narratives of the Incas* (Roland Hamilton and Dana Buchanan, trans.). University of Texas Press, Austin.

BURGER, RICHARD

    1995 *Chavin and the Origins of Andean Civilization*. Thames and Hudson, New York.

CIEZA DE LEÓN, PEDRO DE

    1960 [1553] *The Incas of Pedro de Cieza de León* (Harriet de Onis, trans.). University of Oklahoma Press, Norman.

CLASSEN, CONSTANCE

    1993 *Inca Cosmology and the Human Body*. University of Utah Pess, Salt Lake City.

COBO, BERNABÉ

    1993 [1653] *History of the Inca Empire* (Roland Hamilton, trans.). University of Texas Press, Austin.

    1990 [1653] *Inca Religion and Customs* (Roland Hamilton, trans.). University of Texas Press, Austin.

CONKLIN, WILLIAM J.

    1996 Structure as Meaning in Ancient Andean Textiles. In *Andean Art at Dumbarton Oaks* (Elizabeth Boone, ed.): 321–328. Dumbarton Oaks Research Library and Collection, Washington D.C.

COSTIN, CATHY LYNNE

    1998 Housewives, Chosen Women, and Skilled Men: Cloth Production and Social Identity in the Late Pre-Hispanic Andes. In *Craft and Social Identity* (Cathy Costin and Rita Wright, eds.): 123–141. Archaeological Papers of the American Anthropological Association 8. American Anthropological Association, Arlington, Va.

DAVIES, NIGEL
   1995   *The Incas*. University of Colorado Press, Boulder.

GARCILASO DE LA VEGA, EL INCA
   1966[1609–17]   *Royal Commentaries of the Incas and General History of Peru, Part 1* (Harold V. Livermore, ed.). University of Texas Press, Austin.

GUAMAN POMA DE AYALA, FELIPE
   1980[ca. 1615]   *El Primer Nueva corónica y buen gobierno* (John Murra, Rolena Adorno, and Jorge Urioste, eds.). Historia 16, Madrid.

HECKMAN, ANDREA M.
   2003   *Woven Stories: Andean Textiles and Rituals*. University of New Mexico Press, Albuquerque.

JONES, JULIE
   1964   *Art of Empire*. Metropolitan Museum of Art, New York.

KOSOK, PAUL
   1965   *Life, Land and Water in Ancient Peru*. Long Island University Press, New York.

LAPINER, ALAN C.
   1968   *Art of Ancient Peru and Ecuador*. Arts of the Four Quarters, New York.

LAVALLE, JOSE ANTONIO DE, AND JOSE ALEJANDRO GONZALEZ
   1989   *Arte Textil del Peru*. Industria Textil Piura, Lima.

LINNÉ, SEJOURNÉ
   1943   Humpbacks in Ancient America. *Ethnos* 8 (4): 161–185.

MARKHAM, CLEMENTS R. (ED.)
   1963   *Reports on the Discovery of Peru*, part 1: *Report of Francisco de Xeres, Secretary to Francisco Pizarro*. B. Franklin, New York.

MOLINA, CRISTÓBAL DE
   1963[1576]   *Narratives of the Rites and Laws of the Yncas* (Clement Markham, ed.). B. Franklin, New York.

MOSELEY, MICHAEL
   1992   *The Incas and Their Ancestors*. Thames and Hudson, New York.

MURRA, JOHN
   1962   Cloth and Its Functions in the Inca State. *American Anthropologist* 64 (4): 710–728.
   1972   El control vertical de un máximo de pisos ecológicos en la economia de las sociedades andinas. In *Visita de la provincia de León de Huánuco, Huánuco, Peru en 1562* (Iñigo Ortiz de Zúñiga): 429–476. Universidad Nacional Hermilio Valdizán, Huánuco, Peru.
   1975   *Formaciones Económicos y Políticas del Mundo Andino*. Instituto de Estudios Peruanos, Lima.

MURÚA, MARTÍN DE
    1987[1611–16] *Historia General del Peru* (Manuel Ballesteros, ed.). Historia 16, Madrid.

PECKHAM, MORSE
    1967 *Man's Rage for Chaos: Biology, Behavior and the Arts.* Schocken, New York.

REINHARD, JOHAN
    1996 Peru's Ice Maidens. *National Geographic* (June): 61–81.

ROSTWOROWSKI DE DIEZ CANSECO, MARÍA
    1988 *Historia del Tahuantinsuyu.* Instituto de Estudios Peruanos, Lima.

ROWE, ANN POLLARD
    1984 *Costumes and Featherwork of the Lords of Chimor: Textiles from Peru's North Coast.* The Textile Museum, Washington, D.C.
    1996 Inca Weaving and Costume. *Textile Museum Journal* 34–35: 5–53.

ROWE, JOHN
    1946 Inca Culture at the Time of the Spanish Conquest. In *Handbook of South American Indians*, vol. 2, *The Andean Civilizations* (Julian H. Steward, ed.): 183–330. Bureau of American Ethnology, Bulletin 143. Smithsonian Institution, Washington D.C.
    1979 Standardization in Inca Tapestry Tunics. In *The Junius B. Bird Pre-Columbian Textile Conference* (Ann Pollard Rowe, Elizabeth P. Benson, Anne-Louise Schaffer, eds.): 239–264. The Textile Museum and Dumbarton Oaks, Washington D.C.
    1996 All-T'oqapu Tunic. In *Andean Art at Dumbarton Oaks,* vol. 2 (Elizabeth Boone, ed.) 2: 457–464. Dumbarton Oaks Research Library and Collection, Washington D.C.

ROWE, JOHN, AND ANN ROWE
    1996 Inca Tunics. In *Andean Art at Dumbarton Oaks*, vol. 2 (Elizabeth Boone, ed.): 453–465. Dumbarton Oaks Research Library and Collection, Washington D.C.

SALOMON, FRANK
    1991 Introductory Essay: The Huarochirí Manuscript. In *The Huarochirí Manuscript* (translation from the Quechua by Frank Salomon and George L. Urioste): 1–38. University of Texas Press, Austin.

SALOMON, FRANK, AND GEORGE URIOSTE (TRANS.)
    1991 *The Huarochirí Manuscript.* University of Texas Press, Austin.

SARMIENTO DE GAMBOA, PEDRO
    1907 [1572] *History of the Incas* (Sir Clements Markham, ed.). The Hakluyt Society, Cambridge.

SQUIER, EPHRAIM GEORGE

1973 *Incidents of Travel and Exploration in the Land of the Incas.* Harper and Brothers, New York.

STONE, REBECCA

n.d. Technique and Form in Huari-Style Tapestry Tunics: The Andean Artist, A.D. 500–800. Ph.D. dissertation, Department of Anthropology, Yale University, 1987.

STONE-MILLER, REBECCA

1994 *To Weave for the Sun: Ancient Andean Textiles.* Thames and Hudson, New York (reprinted from *To Weave for the Sun: Andean Textiles in the Museum of Fine Arts, Boston*, 1992).

2002 *Art of the Andes from Chavín to Inca.* Rev. ed., Thames and Hudson, New York and London.

TAPLIN, JESSICA

n.d. The Shape of Power: Inca Thresholds Controlling Cultural and Social Edges. Master's thesis. Emory University, 2000.

TUSHINGHAM, A.D., KENT C. DAY, AND LÉO ROSSHANDLER

1976 *Gold for the Gods.* Royal Ontario Museum, Toronto.

URTON, GARY

1999 *Inca Myths.* University of Texas Press, Austin.

VAN STAN, INA

1966 *The Fabrics of Peru.* F. Lewis, Leigh-on-Sea, England.

ZUIDEMA, R. TOM

1962 The Relationship between Mountains and Coast in Ancient Peru. In *Mededelingen van het Rijksmuseum voor Volkenkunde*: 156-165. Rijksmuseum voor Volkenkunde, Leiden.

1964 *The Ceque System of Cuzco.* International Archives of Ethnography, supplement to vol. 50. E. J. Brill, Leiden.

1982 Bureaucracy and Systematic Knowledge in Andean Civilization. In *The Inka and Aztec States: 1400–1800* (George A. Collier, Renato I. Rosaldo, John D. Wirth, eds.): 419–458. Academic Press, New York and London.

1985 The Lion in the City: Royal Symbols of Transition in Cuzco. In *Animal Myths and Metaphors in South America* (Gary Urton, ed.). University of Utah Press, Salt Lake City (reprinted from *Journal of Latin American Lore* 9 [1]: 39–100).

1992 Inca Cosmos in Andean Context. In *Andean Cosmologies Through Time* (Robert Dover, Katharine Seibold, and John McDowell, eds.): 17–45. Indiana University Press, Bloomington.

The Archaeology of Inka Power: Concluding Thoughts

Richard L. Burger

THE SYMPOSIUM AT DUMBARTON OAKS THAT INSPIRED THIS VOLUME ON the Inka was long overdue. Some thirty annual conferences had been given at this research center on different aspects of Pre-Columbian studies and not one had focused on the Inka. When Ramiro Matos, Craig Morris, and I decided to put together the symposium, we attempted to identify a theme that would unite much of the new archaeological work being done on the Inka. We selected "Variations in the Expression of Inka Power" as more appropriate than any of the alternatives, because so much of the fieldwork on Tawantinsuyu has examined the way in which the Inka state modified existing power relationships and the way in which these changes affected the lifeways of a wide range of societies in the north, central, and southern Andes. The specification of "variations in its expression" signaled the consensus that Tawantinsuyu cannot be viewed productively as a monolithic and homogenous empire, but rather that it must be treated as a mosaic of dissimilar polities and ethnicities that, for a short time, were brought together under the complex expansionist strategies of the Inka conquerors.

Thinking about Inka Power

But why focus on power? The simplest answer might be that it reflects the tendency in U.S. archaeology to dwell on theoretical issues that have been in fashion within sociocultural anthropology but are now out of style. Indeed, power has been in vogue since the early 1970s within sociocultural anthropology, culminating with Eric Wolf's distinguished lecture, at the American Anthropology Association Meetings in Washington, D.C. in 1989, called "Facing Power: Old Insights, New Questions." Although

Wolf (1990) observed that the term power was one of the most loaded and polymorphous terms in our repertoire, he argued that it was impossible to understand the frequent and radical transformations that characterize the long-term history of the world's peoples without it. As with all long-lived trends, a backlash set in (e.g., Brown 1996), but the fundamental insights provided by a concern with power justify its continued popularity as a focus of investigation, particularly as a salutary alternative to other more static frameworks such as structuralism and cultural ecology. The consideration of power has led to a revalorization of human agency long denied or ignored and raised issues that seem increasingly relevant as the world's cultures are transformed at an unprecedented pace.

A concern with the exercise of power has never been alien to Andean archaeology and it has been especially central to the study of the Inkas, as illustrated by classic works such as *L'Empire socialiste des Inka* by Louis Baudin (1928). Since the beginning of the century, radically different notions of Inka power have been entertained. Was Tawantinsuyu a powerful totalitarian dictatorship with complete control or was it a thin veneer over locally autonomous groups? Did the Inkas exercise power for the benefit of the masses or solely for the benefit of the exploitative elite who maintained the fiction of benevolence? Was resistance to Inka power continual and significant or did the Inkas develop a successful strategy to maintain a *pax inkaica* in which resistance was stifled or co-opted? These issues continue to be confronted by ongoing scholarship, but when one compares the syntheses of Inka history by Thomas C. Patterson (1991) and María Rostworowski (1999), it is difficult to avoid wondering whether such radically different characterizations of this civilization are not merely a function of contrasting theoretical orientations. More evidence on Tawantinsuyu is available than ever before, but it has stimulated rather than resolved debates about this remarkable empire.

The four scholars to whom this volume is dedicated have written extensively on the question of Inka power. John Rowe pioneered a consideration of the institutionalized ideological strategies and mechanisms through which the Inka state exercised power, while Tom Zuidema focused on the way in which notions of hierarchy and asymmetry are encoded into the Andean worldview, thereby inserting notions of power into the very structure of Andean thought and its expression in social organization. John Murra's work explored the way the Inka state used its power to modify and transform the traditional economic base upon which Tawantinsuyu had been constructed, while María Rostworowski explored the role of ethnic histories in the shaping of the varying constructions of Inka power in different regions; she also highlighted how its expression may have differed from our preconceptions of imperial power drawn from Old World models. These contributions continue to be of enormous importance and all of the chapters in this volume build upon their insights.

While a concern with power relations has never been far from center stage in Inka studies, attention has traditionally centered on the coercive power that the Inka state was able to wield over its subjects, whether through its powerful army or punitive sanctions against individuals who failed to conform to state norms. This focus has deep roots in Western thought, as exemplified by Voltaire's dictum, "power consists in making others act as I choose" (Carroll n.d.). The threat of force, from this perspective, is used to achieve compliance in order to effect outcomes consistent with the interests of those in authority and was essential where, as among the Inka, the government held monopoly over violent means. Patterson (1991: 160), for example, writes:

> An ideology of *pax incaica* provided little more than an illusion of tranquility, a thin veneer at best, to the core reality of a conflict-ridden society. For all but a few years of the century when it claimed hegemonic powers, the Inca state and the imperial ruling class were forced to engage in armed struggle to suppress the open conflict generated by the contradictions that structured everyday life.

Who can forget the vivid accounts of Inka punishments described by Bernabé Cobo and the illustrations of these punitive measures by Felipe Guaman Poma—the plucking out of the eyes of the military leader who did not follow orders, the hanging by the feet of the youths who did not follow the Inka's puritanical rules about sexual relations, and other gruesome state-sanctioned punishments—stoning, pushing people off cliffs, beating in their heads with a club, imprisoning them with wild animals, and so forth (e.g., Guaman Poma 1980 [ca. 1615]: 277, 280, 282, 284; Rowe 1946: 271–272)?

While the iron hand within the silken glove may have been one aspect of Inka reality, most contemporary students of power would argue that such coercive power can only rarely be exercised—its force is greater as a threat than as an everyday reality. There are simply too many people in an empire to be able to enforce coercion widely; it is not economical. Moreover, the recourse to physical coercion is generally incompatible with efforts to legitimize state authority. Its overuse can undermine government authority and stimulate resistance to it. Machiavelli (2003), who has sometimes been described as having a "realist" perspective on power, argued that power as social control is made the more effective by the averting of conflict and the economizing of the use and threat of sanctions. Power is asymmetrical but need not manifest conflict and resistance.

In this spirit, recent efforts by social scientists have focused on the way in which power was exercised by the Inka without the use of force.

Eric Wolf (1990) discusses a mode of "tactical power," which controls the settings in which people may show their potentialities and interact with others. Another mode of power, which he calls "structural power," controls the distribution and direction of energy. Many of the chapters in this volume focus on these two modes of power. The creation of settings for the exercise of power in places such as those described by Craig Morris and Julián Idilio Santillana at La Centinela or by Susan Niles at Quispiguanga are good examples of the use of tactical power; the restructuring by the Inka of the political economy described by Ramiro Matos and Carmen Arellano for a highland province in central Peru or by D'Altroy, Williams, and Lorandi for the South Andes are vivid examples of structural power in action.

Inka Power: Some Comparative Considerations

In trying to use archaeology to identify the way in which the Inkas exercised structural power, we should temper our expectations with what is known from other empires. This must be done cautiously because some preconceptions of what other empires were like have little foundation. For example, I was shocked that my image of a bureaucratically top-heavy Roman empire was far from accurate. Susan Alcock (1993) has estimated that only one Roman official existed for every 350,000 to 400,000 provincials. In an account of Greece under Roman rule, she illustrates how little formal Roman administrative architecture was created by the incorporation of this area into the empire. At the same time, Alcock shows how spatial organization and reorganization reveal changes in the structure of authority and resources in response to the new world in which Greece now existed (Alcock 1993). Nevertheless, in most of Greece it was a subtle change. This pattern contrasted with the situation along the Roman frontier, where troops created fairly radical changes in the social and economic environment. And even in Greece, where Roman presence was relatively light, the Roman armies sacked Corinth and destroyed many temples.

In some empires, there were massive displacements of people. This was the case in the Assyrian empire, in which large numbers of conquered people from the periphery were forcibly moved toward the center to implement agricultural and other developments (Liverani 2001). This same practice existed among the Inkas, as can be seen in many of the chapters in this volume that are concerned with *mitimaes, yanacona, camayoc,* and other categories of displaced peoples (see, for example, the chapters in this volume by D'Altroy et al., Niles and Batson, Salazar, and Stanish and Bauer). The investigations described in these chapters illustrate how archaeology has independently confirmed this historically known pattern in Tawantinsuyu.

As Eric Wolf (1990) notes, power is dependent on meaning. Since there are infinite versions of the world, dominant groups exercise power by promoting and upholding one version of the many possible ones to be true or faithful to tradition. To make this cultural assertion credible, it must be repeated and enacted, lest it be questioned and denied. The description of the state-controlled pilgrimage to the Islands of the Sun and Moon by Stanish and Bauer underscores the Inka appreciation of the importance of imparting meaning through careful staging and repetition.

The way in which the Inkas used earlier traditions to reinforce their legitimacy is particularly fascinating. It is interesting that the Inka chose to emphasize their links with the sacred places of Tiwanaku, including the Island of the Sun, rather than with Huari and its centers, such as Pikillaqta. The special importance of Tiwanaku as a legitimating tool in Inka ideology is reiterated in Salazar's discussion of the architecture at Machu Picchu. The Inka also showed concern with abandoned older sacred centers, such as Manchay Bajo, Chavín de Huantar, and Pucara, and particular attention to the still-influential oracle center at Pachacamac, but the Islands in Lake Titicaca and the center at Tiwanaku held a unique place in Inka ritual life and in its official myths.

In the spirit of a comparative perspective, it should be noted that the co-opting of local or regional religious centers by an expanding empire is common in world history. The newly formed Japanese state, for example, transformed local sacred places into hierarchically organized networks of shrines under the emperor's control. Worship was reformulated to be consistent with the sun cult, since the Japanese emperor was descended from the sun (Barnes 1988). Co-option, however, is only one possible strategy. In other cases, expanding empires chose to exercise their physical power against sacred places, as in the Roman destruction of the Temple in Jerusalem or Pizarro's desecration of the Pachacamac oracle.

The Problem of Inka Chronology

To study the way in which the Inkas exercised power, we need rigorous diachronic control. A shift in diet from venison to llama meat, for example, that occurs suddenly over a five-year period may be the result of heavy-handed state intervention, but the same change in preferences more likely reflects evolving adaptations to new sociopolitical or environmental contexts if it occurs gradually over a century. Unfortunately, we do not have adequate temporal control for the Inkas, and consensus is lacking even in regard to basic issues, such as when Inka expansion began. The problem of Inka chronology appears often in this book (e.g., Arellano and Matos Mendieta, this volume), and was the focus of heated debate during the Dumbarton Oaks symposium that inspired it. There is widespread skepticism about the continued viability of the Rowe chronological framework (1945) for the Inka dynasty. This "short chronology" was originally proposed over half a century ago, on the basis of a judicious set of inferences drawn from conflicting historical documents. Rowe's working hypothesis has, with time, become reified and taken on more authority than its author originally intended.

One new source of evidence that has raised reservations about the Rowe chronology is the large numbers of radiocarbon dates that appear to be inconsistent with his "short" framework. A longer alternative chronological framework, such as that adopted in the chapter by D'Altroy, Williams, and Lorandi, remains a plausible interpretation of the new radiocarbon evidence. However, with two sigma ranges of some 300 years for many dates and sample contexts of varying quality, the available C14 evidence suggests the importance of keeping an open mind. It is possible to argue that these dates do not yet require the radical revision that many are demanding. For the latter, it would be desirable to obtain a suite of dates collected specifically for the purpose of testing the Rowe hypothesis. Such an analysis should be limited to organic materials of a short life-span to eliminate the "old wood problem," and it should use only high-precision C14 dates with narrow two-sigma ranges. With the availability of AMS dating, such a project is feasible and should be able to resolve the ongoing debate.

Another line of reasoning that has led to skepticism about the Rowe chronological framework, exemplified by Albert Meyers's chapter, is that if stratification of deposits occurs within the Inka occupation and accompanied by visible culture changes, this implies a much longer duration than that contemplated by the Rowe chronology. While this may be the case, it is not necessarily so. There is no reason why a particular feature such as the one at Samaipata might not be leveled or modified and replaced with a building of a different function in twenty or thirty years. There are any number of examples of deep, varied deposits in historic times that were produced in less than a century; this could be true as well for Samaipata.

A final and widespread set of concerns about the Rowe chronological framework for the Inkas is that the four-score and ten years allowed for the Inka Empire's expansion and impact is simply not enough. These reservations seem to be based more on common sense or intuition than any scientific data. It is worth remembering that the expansion of Alexander the Great's empire began in 336 BC, when he succeeded his father Philip II as king of Macedonia. In the preceding twenty-three years, Philip had transformed Macedonia from a backward frontier kingdom on the fringe of Greece to a powerful military state already dominating Greece through the League of Corinth. By 323 BC, in only thirteen years, Alexander had defeated the Persians, dominated the entire Near East, and conquered territory into the Hindu Kush, reaching Punjab in what now is India. Much of the impact of Alexander's conquests resulted from the implementation of new policies by his successors in the provinces; this included the establishment of new patterns of agriculture and urbanism based on the movement of large numbers of foreigners from other parts of the empire. In Egypt, these Ptolemaic transformations were concentrated in a fifty-year period. If we look at Greece, Egypt, or northern India we find radical changes in the societies in question, and these changes were established within ninety years (Walbank 1981).

If profound transformations were possible in less than a century in a well-documented Old-World case, why should we doubt a priori its plausibility for the New-World case of the Inkas? Equally short time spans were recorded for the creation of the Yamato state in Japan and Genghis Khan's expansion across Asia and Europe (Barnes 1988; Barfield 1989). If we have no trouble accepting the dismantling of Tawantinsuyu by a handful of Spaniards in a decade, why is it so hard to accept the creation of this empire in nine or ten decades? The chronological problem for the Inkas cannot be resolved without a better body of evidence, but in the interim we will continue to debate this question using the existing C14 measurements with their inherent limitations and the admittedly imperfect historical records.

The Power of Inka Objects

In current theoretical writings (Appadurai 1986), the exercise of power is often mediated through objects, just as it is shaped by the built environments of political capitals and ceremonial centers. Objects are cultural phenomena, which are historically constructed to function within the symbolics of power and, as Geertz (1983: 124) emphasizes, in studying the processes of power "the easy distinction between the trappings of rule and its substance becomes less sharp, even less real; what counts is the manner in which, a bit like mass and energy, they are transformed into each other." A classic example of this is the way in which the gift of *queros* and *aquillas*, described in the chapter by Tom Cummins, was used by the Inka elite in order to establish hierarchical relations. Through this gift to the curacas, the Inkas initiated an asymmetrical relationship that was reaffirmed every time these ritual drinking vessels were used to entertain, even long after the Inka leaders had departed. This same argument is applicable to the equally distinctive tunics and other clothing distributed by Inka leaders as they advanced through the empire (Murra 1962; Rowe 1979). The role of repetition in maintaining ideologies and relationships is, in a sense, facilitated by these objects, which act as a proxy for the Inka leaders themselves. While a curaca might not be present at a banquet hosted by an Inka leader at the local provincial center each month, he could wear the standardized Inka tunic or drink *chicha* from the silver cups that had been received as gifts.

Khipus offer a particularly interesting case of the power of objects in Tawantinsuyu. In a sense they physically symbolize the control of knowledge by the individuals representing the state and their presence would have shaped the interaction between their keepers and the general populace. There is a large literature, much of it inspired by the work of Michel Foucault, focusing on the special link between knowledge and power, and the way in which knowledge-power strategies shape the social world. Given these insights, it is significant that the khipu, as a class of object, is nearly coterminous with the expansion of the Inka state. As Gary Urton and Carrie Brezine discuss in their chapter, over four-hundred khipus have now been documented in museums throughout the world and almost all of them are thought to be Inka or later in date. Although there is some evidence for a small number of khipu-like objects dating to the Middle Horizon (Conklin 1982), these are very rare and as in the case of the Inka khipu, they appear to be associated with an expansive empire. It may be more significant that there is a dearth of khipu-like devices associated with multivalley states, such as the Kingdom of Chimor, or the small states and chiefdoms (*curacazgos*) that characterized the Central Andes immediately before Tawantinsuyu. While this may be a sampling problem, the extensive excavations of Late Intermediate–period sites along the Peruvian coast, including those of Max Uhle, and the even more extensive looting in search of textiles makes this explanation unlikely.

Thus it can be argued that the emergence of khipus as a widespread phenomenon is a function of the transaction of power during the Inka Empire, just as the Japanese wooden record-keeping tablets known as *mokkan* appear for the first time during the late sixth century in conjunction with Japan's first fully developed state—the Yamato State (Barnes 1988: 24).

The role of khipus in the symbolics of power is well illustrated by the drawings of Felipe Guaman Poma de Ayala, in which the knotted records are held prominently in portraits of the empire's administrators in a manner analogous to the way the Inka emperors are shown holding their staffs and other emblems of authority. Thus, the khipus have a social role that transcends their role as a technology or device; they carry symbolic meaning above and beyond the information encoded in them. Inasmuch as relations are mediated through the khipu, the identity and authority of its keepers are complexly intertwined with these knotted strings; they are, in the sense emphasized by Geertz (1983), inseparable from the charisma of the individual that uses them. In this light, it is perhaps not surprising that khipus are buried with individuals just as rulers in the Andes were usually buried in their royal trappings.

The complex ways in which objects were used to exercise power is explored in the chapter on Inka metallurgy by Heather Lechtman. In it she shows how Inka metal technology was used to code features of kinship, gender, and social hierarchy, thus naturalizing the distinctive cultural system that underpinned Tawantinsuyu. While these metals were primarily ideological tools working at the subconscious level, the selection of tin bronze as the emblematic state copper alloy made it possible for the Inkas to exercise very real state control over metal production through their imperial domination of the rare cassiterite deposits located on the Bolivian puna.

Resistance, Accommodation, and Agency

In contemporary anthropological studies of power, many scholars have tried to refocus attention not on the domination by elites but rather on the resistance by subjects. Much of this literature draws on the work of James Scott (1985), particularly the *Weapons of the Weak*, which sees resistance not only in rebellions but also in less obvious activities such as inefficiency and noncompliance. Patterson (1991), for example, sees everyday forms of passive resistance in patterns like those in which collaborating elite adopt Inka identity through use of Inka pottery style, but commoner peasant kin continue to use materials rooted in pre-Inka tradition, even robbing old tombs to inspire traditional designs. This interpretation, based on the pioneering work of Dorothy Menzel (1959, 1976), points to the limitations of Inka power even in a relatively weak coastal valley.

In another remarkable contribution, Rebecca Stone explores how a single object, the Dumbarton Oaks tocapu tunic, embodies the elaborate ideology that sustained the Inka emperor or Sapac Inka. This textile, believed to be the sole surviving example of a tunic actually worn by an Inka ruler, is covered with hundreds of polychromatic tocapu motifs in a complex fashion that has long defied simple explanation. Stone argues that the tunic expresses the concept of *pachacuti*, reverser of the world, and that it therefore intentionally works against the Inka ideal of imperial order in order to demonstrate the transcendent power of the Sapac Inka. The tunic not only sets the emperor apart as unique, with its nonrepetitive patterns and extreme polychromy, but it also specifically alludes to the emperor's special role as a conqueror of foreign lands. In a particularly subtle argument, Stone demonstrates that the majority of the tunic's symbols suggest a source in non-Inka cultures, some predating Inka expansion, while carefully avoiding copying or quoting from the actual foreign motifs. Thus, the designs can be interpreted as suggesting past and future conquests, including those yet to be fulfilled. Stone argues that the long-sought order of the tunic is intentional disorder and that the key to interpreting the 312 tocapu motifs is that there is no key. Ultimately, it was this concept of pachacuti embodied in the Dumbarton Oaks tunic that provided the ideological basis for the power of the Sapac Inka (Unique Inka).

Considerations of resistance among the nonelite members of Tawantinsuyu have often been frustrated by the lack of attention paid to these people by the Spanish chroniclers. Fortunately, modern archaeologists can sometimes effectively infer objective conditions and cultural forms of the common people overlooked in historical records. This is illustrated in Lucy Salazar's treatment of Machu Picchu's silent majority—the servants, artisans, and other retainers who served the needs of the royal family and its guests (see also Verano 2003). While we may want to know what life was like for the *yanacona* that occupied this country palace on the eastern slopes, the answer will not be found in the numerous Spanish chronicles, all of which focus on the Inka elite and other subjects of special interest to the Spanish crown. Nonetheless, based on the study of Machu Picchu's population, we can not only confirm that they were a multiethnic mix of people drawn from throughout Tawantinsuyu, but also demonstrate that they were a healthy group, well nourished and not involved in heavy labor. We can also show that they had children while at Machu Picchu and that their children formed a small but important part of the population. Moreover, through study of their graves, we can show how the memory of their ethnic homelands was embraced even in death as they buried their dead with heirlooms from their provincial homelands. Many of these everyday objects had been repaired repeatedly at Machu Picchu rather than being discarded.

In his book *The Inka Empire: The Formation and Disintegration of a Pre-capitalist State*, Thomas Patterson (1991) views the state as fragile due to its contradictions among both the rulers and the ruled. The Inkas were continually suppressing civil wars resulting from succession disputes, border wars, and local revolts by people who wished to reassert autonomy. Morris and Santillana's (this volume) radical suggestion that the architecture of La Centinela implies some sort of dual governance by Inka and local Chincha rulers goes beyond the political arrangements usually considered by historians. It is consistent, however, with archaeological evidence for a range of governance strategies reflecting the challenges of the diverse societies and polities incorporated into Tawantinsuyu. After formulating this interpretation based on archaeological evidence, Morris encountered confirmation of this arrangement in a Spanish chronicle (Craig Morris personal communication, 2004).

In studying Inka power, it is hard to trace the tensions and motives crucial to discussion of agency using archaeological methods. Nonetheless, as Susan Niles and Robert Batson's chapter shows, this is not entirely impossible. In this contribution they depart from the usual tendency of seeing Inka monumental complexes as anonymous expressions of the state and instead focus on the attribution of a specific architectural complex to a specific architect, Sinchi Roca, and his patron and half brother, the emperor Huayna Capac. Niles and Batson explain the particular effort to construct Quispiguanca with over 150,000 laborers as a function of Huayna Capac's conscious strategy to convey his legitimacy and publicly assert his control over the resources and powers associated with the position of the Sapa Inka. While this consideration of individual strategy and agency is laudable, it is rare in archaeology.

Some Final Thoughts on Inka Power

The crucial role of archaeology in understanding the Inka Empire cannot be exaggerated. One example referred to in Lucy Salazar's chapter suffices to illustrate this point. The Andean highlands are a unique environment that presents special challenges to domestic plants originating in lower altitudes, and thus it is not surprising that for much of ancient and modern times the main sources of food have been potatoes and other tubers and grains domesticated from wild ancestors native to the high Andes. Despite this, the historical records on the Inkas dwell at length on the cultivation of maize and the many celebrations devoted to it. This focus by Spanish chroniclers led many scholars to view maize as the staple of the Inkas, even in the highlands, and this view was widely held until the distinguished Andeanist, John Murra (1960), concluded from his critical analysis of the documentary evidence that while maize was central to Inka ideology and ceremony, it never displaced traditional Andean staples in the highlands. Analyses of the multiethnic population of yanacona at Machu Picchu, however, confirms that maize was indeed the staple for the entire population, regardless of their point of origin, and in most cases maize constituted sixty to seventy percent of their diets (Salazar this volume; Burger et al. 2003). This finding is consistent with earlier research by Christine Hastorf (1990) on the population of Jauja during Inka times. The mounting evidence against the Murra hypothesis highlights the limitations of the historical record and the importance of complementing it with archaeological research.

While most contemporary scholars have drawn upon a notion of power derived from Hobbesian and Weberian roots, there is a separate tradition of writings that views power as the collective capacity to accomplish. This perspective, associated with Montesquieu, but going back to Plato and Aristotle, does not view power within a zero-sum framework in which the gain of one through the exercise of power is always at the expense of another. Scholars with this perspective, such as Talcott Parsons and Hannah Arendt, believe, rather, that through this collective exercise of power all those involved may gain. Arendt (1970) wrote, for example, that the essence of power does not rely on the command-obedience relationship but instead corresponds to the the human ability to act in concert. Power, from this perspective, can be defined as the capacity to mobilize resources of society for the attainment of goals for which a general public commitment has been made or may be made. In sum, power is exercised with others rather than over others.

Archaeology allows us to follow transformations of Inka power over time and through space without assuming that a single pattern will prevail. Increasing evidence suggests the central role of the Inkas in creating productive terracing systems in distant and dissimilar high valleys, as illustrated by archaeological research in the Jauja Basin in Junín (Hastorf 1990), the Carahuarazo Valley in Ayacucho (Schreiber 1987), and the Colca Valley in Arequipa (Malpass 1987). There are widespread examples of where Inka conquest allowed populations to move off of unproductive and isolated but defensible ridge-tops to locations closer to more productive valley lands. The creation of massive state farms in Cochabamba and the vast storage facilities in Huánuco Pampa and Jauja are now a matter of archaeological record. While many of the romantic notions of Baudin (1928) and others may be seriously flawed, perhaps it is time in Inka studies to balance the contemporary focus on the power to coerce with renewed attention to their power to create.

Acknowledgments

I have chosen to make only modest changes to my spoken remarks at the Dumbarton Oaks symposium, but I thank Jeffrey Quilter and Lucy Salazar for their critical comments and constructive suggestions for improvement.

References cited

ALCOCK, SUSAN
    1993 *Graecia Capta: The Landscape of Roman Greece*. Cambridge University Press, Cambridge, England.

APPADURAI, ARJUN
    1986 *The Social Life of Things*. Cambridge University Press, Cambridge, England.

ARENDT, HANNAH
    1970 *On Violence*. Harcourt Brace and Company, New York.

BARFIELD, THOMAS J.
    1989 *The Perilous Frontier: Nomadic Empires and China*. Blackwell, Cambridge, Mass.

BARNES, GINA LEE
    1988 *Protohistoric Yanamato: Archaeology of the First Japanese State*. Museum of Anthropology, University of Michigan, Ann Arbor.

BAUDIN, LOUIS
    1928 *L'Empire socialiste des Inkas*. Institut d'Ethnologie, Paris.

BROWN, MICHAEL
    1996 On Resisting Resistance. *American Anthropologist* 98 (4): 729–749.

BURGER, RICHARD L., JULIA LEE-THORPE, AND NIKOLAAS VAN DER MERWE
    2003 Rite and Crop Revisited: An Isotopic Perspective from Machu Picchu and Beyond. In *The 1912 Yale Peruvian Scientific Expedition Collections from Machu Picchu: Human and Animal Remains* (Richard L. Burger and Lucy C. Salazar, eds.): 119–137. Yale University Publications in Anthropology 85. Dept. of Anthropology, Yale University Division of Anthropology: Peabody Museum of Natural History, New Haven, Conn.

CARROLL, BERNICE
    n.d. Peace Research: The Cult of Power. Paper read at the annual convention of the American Sociological Association, Denver, Colorado, 1 September 1971.

CONKLIN, WILLIAM
    1982 *The Information System of Middle Horizon Quipus*. Annals of the New York Academy of Sciences 385: 261–281.

GEERTZ, CLIFFORD
    1983 Centers, Kings and Charisma: Reflections on the Symbolics of Power. In *Local Knowledge*: 121–146. Basic Books, New York.

GUAMAN POMA DE AYALA, FELIPE
    1980 *El primer nueva corónica y buen gobierno*. 1st ed. (John Murra, Rolena Adorno, and Jorge Urioste, eds.): Siglo Veintiuno, México, D.F.

HASTORF, CHRISTINE
    1990   The Effect of the Inka State on Sausa Agricultural Production and Crop Consumption. *American Antiquity* 55 (2): 292–301.

LIVERANI, MARIO
    2001   The Fall of the Assyrian Empire: Ancient and Modern Interpretations. In *Empires* (Susan Alcock, Terence D'Altroy, Kathleen Morrison, and Carla Sinopoli, eds.): 374–391. Cambridge University Press, Cambridge, England.

MACHIAVELLI, NÍCCOLÓ
    2003   *The Prince*. Penguin Classics, London.

MALPASS, MICHAEL
    1987   Prehistoric Agricultural Terracing at Chijra in the Colca Valley, Peru. Preliminary Report II. In *Pre-Hispanic Agricultural Fields in the Andean Region* (W. Denevan, K. Mathewson, and G. Knapp, eds.): 45–66. Proceedings of the 45th International Congress of Americanists. Bogota. BAR International Series 359 (i). BAR, Oxford.

MENZEL, DOROTHY
    1959   The Inca Conquest of the South Coast of Peru. *Southwest Journal of Anthropology* 15: 125–142.
    1976   *Pottery Style and Society in Ancient Peru: Art as a Mirror of History in the Ica Valley, 1350–1570*. University of California Press, Berkeley.

MURRA, JOHN
    1960   Rite and Crop in the Inca State. In *Culture in History* (Stanley Diamond, ed.): 393–407. Columbia University Press, New York.
    1962   Cloth and Its Functions in the Inca State. *American Anthropologist* 64 (7): 10–28.

PATTERSON, THOMAS C.
    1991   *The Inca Empire: The Formation and Disintegration of a Precapitalist State*. Berg Publishers, New York.

ROSTWOROWSKI, MARÍA
    1999   *History of the Inca Realm*. Cambridge University Press, Cambridge, England.

ROWE, JOHN HOWLAND
    1945   Absolute Chronology in the Andean Area. *American Antiquity* 10 (3): 265–284.
    1946   Inca Culture at the Time of the Spanish Conquest. In *Handbook of South American Indians* (Julian Steward, ed.), vol. 2, *The Andean Civilizations*: 183–330. Government Printing Office, Washington, D.C.

1979 Standardization in Inca Tapestry Tunics. In *The Junius B. Bird Pre-Columbian Textile Conference* (Ann P. Rowe, Elizabeth P. Benson, and Anne-Louise Shaffer, eds.): 239–264. The Textile Museum, Washington, D.C.

SCHREIBER, KATHARINA
1987 Conquest and Consolidation: A Comparison of the Wari and Inka Occupations of a Highland Peruvian Valley. *American Antiquity* 52 (2): 266–284.

SCOTT, JAMES
1985 *Weapons of the Weak*. Yale University Press, New Haven, Conn.

URTON, GARY
2003 *Signs of the Inka Khipu: Binary Coding in the Andean Knotted-String Records*. University of Texas Press, Austin.

VERANO, JOHN
2003 Human Skeletal Remains from Machu Picchu: A Reexamination of the Peabody Museum's Collections from the Peruvian Expedition of 1912. In *The 1912 Yale Peruvian Scientific Expedition Collections from Machu Picchu: Human and Animal Remains* (Richard L. Burger and Lucy C. Salazar, eds.): 65–117. Yale University Publications in Anthropology 85. Dept. of Anthropology, Yale University Division of Anthropology: Peabody Museum of Natural History, New Haven, Conn.

WALLBANK, FRANK W.
1981 *The Hellenistic World*. Harvester Press, Brighton, Sussex.

WOLF, ERIC
1990 Facing Power: Old Insights, New Questions. *American Anthropologist* 92: 586–596.

Notes on Contributors

CARMEN ARELLANO is currently Director of the National Museum of Archaeology, Anthropology, and History of Peru. As a cultural anthropologist, she is a specialist in Andean colonial indigenous societies and has published a history of the communities of Tarma (Central Highlands of Peru) from the sixteenth through the eighteenth centuries (1988) and a document on the visitation of the first Intendent of Tarma in the eighteenth century (1986). A book about the impact of Inka administration in the Central Highlands is in preparation, co-authored with Ramiro Matos Mendieta.

ROBERT BATSON is an architect in the Dallas, Texas area. He has researched Inka architecture for twenty years and contributed architectural illustrations to *Inca Architecture and Construction at Ollantaytambo* by Jean-Pierre Protzen and *The Shape of Inca History* by Susan A. Niles. He is a member of the Institute of Andean Studies and has presented several papers on Inka architecture to that group.

BRIAN S. BAUER is a professor of anthropology at the University of Illinois at Chicago. He is an anthropological archaeologist who works with contact and prehistoric societies of South America. His scholarly interests are focused on the development of state societies in the Americas. He is the author of numerous books including *Ancient Cuzco* (2004), *Ritual and Pilgrimage in the Ancient Andes* (co-authored with Charles Stanish, 2001), *The Sacred Landscape of the Inca* (1998), *Astronomy and Empire in the Ancient Andes* (co-authored with David Dearborn, 1995), and *The Development of the Inca State* (1992).

CARRIE BREZINE was full-time database administrator for the Harvard Khipu Database Project from 2002 to 2005, and in the summer of 2005 was textile consultant for Frank Salomon's investigation of the Patrimonial Khipu of Rapaz, Peru. A weaver and spinner with a B.A. in mathematics, she has published "Symmetry on the Loom" in the volume *Symmetry Comes of Age* (2004); with Gary Urton, "Khipu Accounting in Ancient Peru" (*Science*, 2005); and with Frank Salomon et al., "Los khipus de Rapaz" (*Revista Andina*, 2006). Ms. Brezine is currently a Ph.D. candidate in archaeology in the Department of Anthropology at Harvard University.

RICHARD L. BURGER is the C. J. MacCurdy Professor of Anthropology and Chairman of the Council on Archaeological Studies at Yale University. An archaeologist specializing in the ancient Andes, he is the author of *Emergencia de la Civilización en los Andes* (1993), *Chavín and the Origins of Andean Civilization* (1995), *Excavaciones en Chavín de Huántar* (1998), and, with Lucy Salazar, *Machu Picchu: Unveiling the Mystery of the Incas* (2004). He is the current president of the Institute of Andean Research.

TOM CUMMINS is the Dumbarton Oaks Professor of the History of Pre-Columbian and Colonial Art and Chair of the Department of the History of Art and Architecture at Harvard University. He has published essays and books on the early Pre-Columbian Ecuadorian ceramics and on colonial art and architecture in Peru, Ecuador, Colombia, and Mexico.

TERENCE N. D'ALTROY is Professor of Anthropology at Columbia University in the city of New York. He is an archaeological anthropologist with a principal interest in the comparative study of early empires. He has published *Provincial Power in the Inka Empire* (1992) and *The Incas* (2002), is first author of *Empire and Domestic Economy* (2001), has co-edited *Empires* (2002), and recorded *The Inkas: Inside an American Empire* (2004).

HEATHER LECHTMAN is Professor of Archaeology and Ancient Technology and Director of the Center for Materials Research in Archaeology and Ethnology at the Massachusetts Institute of Technology. Her research interests lie in understanding the dynamics of technology developed in prehistoric and nonindustrial societies using the combined methods of archaeology and the science and engineering of materials. Her numerous articles on the metallurgies practiced among the prehistoric societies of Andean South America establish that zone as one of few loci for the development of sophisticated metal technologies in the ancient world.

ANA MARÍA LORANDI is Professor of Anthropology at the University of Buenos Aires. An ethnohistorian specializing in the Andean region, she has investigated the Inka Empire and Spanish and indigenous society during the colonial period. She has published *La etnohistoria: Etnogénesis y transformaciones sociales andinas* (1992), *El Tucumán colonial y Charcas* (ed., 1997), *Ni ley, ni rey ni hombre virtuoso: Guerra y sociedad en el virreinato del Perú, siglos XVI y XVII* (2002), and *Spanish King of the Incas: The Epic Life of Pedro Bohórquez* (2005).

RAMIRO MATOS MENDIETA is Associate Curator at the National Museum of the American Indian, Smithsonian Institution. His research concerns the Central Andes, with a focus on the development of indigenous societies from Pre-Ceramic to Inka times. He is co-author (with Jeff Parsons and Charles Hastings) of *Prehispanic Settlement Patterns of the Upper Mantaro and Tarama Drainages, Department of Junín, Peru*, vol. 1: *The Tarma-Chinchaycocha Region* (2000). He is the author of *Pumpu: Centro administrativo Inka de la Puna de Junín* (1994), and is currently preparing a book on Inka culture in the Central Highlands of Peru.

ALBERT MEYERS is a senior lecturer in anthropology and Amerindian studies at the University of Bonn, Germany. His main interests are in the fields of archaeology and ethnohistory of the Andes and in cultural resource management. Among his published books are *Die Inka in Ecuador* (1976, Spanish version 1998), *Las cofradías Perú: en el Région Central* (1981, with O. Celestino), and the co-edited volumes *Manipulating the Saints: Religious Brotherhoods and Social Integration in Postconquest Latin America* (1988, with D. E. Hopkins) and *Religiosidad popular en América Latina* (1990, with K. Kohut).

CRAIG MORRIS was Curator of Anthropology at the American Museum of Natural History in New York until his death on June 14, 2006. He was also Dean of Science there from 1994 through 2004. He specialized in the archaeology of the Inka expansion, and worked in the central highlands and on the south coast of Peru, as well as in the Cochabamba Valley of Bolivia. Among his publications are *Huánuco Pampa: An Inca City and Its Hinterland*, with Donald E. Thompson, and *The Inca Empire and Its Andean Origins*, with Adriana von Hagen. He was a member of the National Academy of Sciences and a Fellow of the American Academy of Arts and Sciences.

MARÍA DE LOS ANGELES MUÑOZ is a researcher at the Instituto de Investigaciones Antropológicas y Museo Arqueológico, Universidad Mayor de San Simon in Cochabamba, Bolivia. After graduate work in Mexico and postgraduate research at the University of Bonn and the Museo de América in Madrid, she carried out archaeological investigations at Samaipata, Chuquisaca, and Cochabamba, and is currently the director of the Proyecto de Investigaciones Arqueológicas Inkallajta. She is the author of numerous publications, including *Gestión participativa del patrimonio: Un caso boliviano* (2006) and *Patrimonio cultural y desarollo local comunitario: El Caso Incallajta* (2007).

SUSAN A. NILES, Professor of Anthropology at Lafayette College, specializes in the architecture and culture history of the Inka and early colonial periods. In addition to articles, she has published *Callachaca: Style and Status in an Inca Community* (1987) and *The Shape of Inca History: Narrative and Architecture in an Andean Empire* (1999). She has also written on North American vernacular architecture in *Dickeyville Grotto: The Vision of Father Mathias Wernerus* (1997).

LUCY C. SALAZAR, Research Associate in the Department of Anthropology and Curatorial Affiliate at the Yale Peabody Museum, was the co-curator for the exhibit *Machu Picchu: Unveiling the Mystery of the Incas*. She is an authority on Inka archaeology and the early prehistory of Peru. She has over two decades of experience in archaeological fieldwork and museum research, and has co-directed numerous excavations in Peru. Salazar has written extensively on daily life at Machu Picchu, and received grant support for her work on the Inkas from the National Endowment for the Humanities, National Science Foundation, and the Josef Albers Fund. She recently co-edited, with Richard Burger, the monograph *The 1912 Yale Peruvian Scientific Expedition Collections from Machu Picchu: Human and Animal Remains* (2003) and *Machu Picchu: Unveiling the Mystery of the Incas* (2004).

JULIÁN I. SANTILLANA is Associate Professor of Andean Archaeology at the Pontificia Universidad Católica del Perú and the Universidad Mayor de San Marcos, both in Lima. He is an archaeologist specializing in agricultural technology, urbanism, and religious systems of Inka culture, and has published "Andenes, canales y paisaje" (1999), "Las Plazas del Cuzco y el Espacio Ceremonial Inca" (2001), and "Chancas e Incas: Un nuevo examen" (2002).

CHARLES STANISH is Lloyd Cotsen Chair in Archaeology and Director of the Cotsen Institute of Archaeology at the University of California, Los Angeles. A specialist in central Andean archaeology, he has published *Ancient Titicaca* (2003), *Ritual and Pilgrimage in the Ancient Andes* (with B. Bauer, 2001), and *Ancient Andean Political Economy* (1992), and co-edited (with J. Marcus) *Agricultural Strategies* (2006).

REBECCA R. STONE is Associate Professor of Art History at Emory University and Faculty Curator of Art of the Ancient Americas at the Michael C. Carlos Museum. A specialist in Andean and Central American art, she has published *To Weave for the Sun: Andean Textiles at the Museum of Fine Arts, Boston* (1992), *Art of the Andes from Chavin to Inca* (1996, 2002), and *Seeing with New Eyes: Highlights of the Michael C. Carlos Museum Collection of Art of the Ancient Americas* (2002).

GARY URTON is Dumbarton Oaks Professor of Pre-Columbian Studies in the Archaeology Program, Department of Anthropology, Harvard University. His books include *At the Crossroads of the Earth and the Sky: An Andean Cosmology* (1981), *The History of a Myth: Pacariqtambo and the Origin of the Inkas* (1990), *The Social Life of Numbers: A Quechua Ontology of Numbers and Philosophy of Arithmetic* (1997), *Inca Myths* (2000), and *Signs of the Inka Khipu: Binary Coding in the Andean Knotted-String Records* (2003). He has also edited or co-edited numerous volumes on Inka civilization and Quechua culture in the Andes. He has been Director of the Khipu Database Project at Harvard University since 2002.

VERÓNICA ISABEL WILLIAMS is a professor of archaeology at the Universidad del Centro de la Provincia de Buenos Aires and Researcher of CONICET (Argentina). An archaeologist specializing in pre-Inka and Inka society, she has published numerous articles about the southern Andes and the archaeology of northwestern Argentina. Her books include *Political Power and Social Stratification in the Calchaquí Valley (Northwest Argentina)* (2006), *Poder estatal y cultura material en el Kollasuyu* (2005), *Nuevos datos sobre la prehistoria local en la quebrada de Tolombón: Pcia de Salta* (2003), *El imperio Inka en la provincia de Catamarca* (2000), and, with Benjamin Alberti, *Gender and Ethnicity in South American Archaeology*.

Index

A

Abaucán Valley, 89
Abrocoma, 172
aclla (aqlla), 3
acllacuna, 404
acllahuasi, 17, 29, 170
Aconcagua, Mt., 111, 113
Acostampu (Acostambo), 11
administrative centers, 11–12; Chakamarka, 31–32; disposition of, 28, 39n. 18; Huánuco Pampa, 11, 14, 16, 96, 144, 145, 148, 149, 156, 267, 434; Pumpu, 33–34; Tarma, 27; Tarmatampu, 28, 29–31; Warawtampu, 34–35
Agua de los Loros, 102
Agua Verde, 91
akllawasi. See acllahuasi
alloys, 177, 314, 316, 318–322, 324, 326, 328, 330, 332–337, 341, 342, 344 n. 2, 344–345n. 4, 346nn. 6, 9, 431. *See also* bronze, Inka metallurgy
Almagro, Diego de 90
Amazona, 16, 22, 32
Ambrosetti, Juan B., 102
Amuesha, 32
ancacuna, 418n. 5
Angashmarca, 23
Apacheta Acay, 100
Apacheta Ingañan, 100
apu, 113
aqha (corn beer), 275, 286, 278
aqlla. See aclla
aqllawasi, 255. *See also acllahuasi, aklla wasi, akllawasi*
aquilla, 270, 271 fig. 8, 272, 273–277, 279–282, 281 fig. 16, 287, 295, 296, 341, 429
arsenic bronze alloy, 333
aryballoid-shaped vessel, 281, *see urpu*
Ascher, Marcia, 376, 379n. 4, 380n. 14
Ascher, Robert, 376, 379n. 4, 380n. 14
Astupampa (Astubamba), 26, 34
asua, 392
Atapillu (Atapillos, Atavillos, Atauillo), 13, 14, 21, 22, 27, 32, 33, 35, 36
Aveni, Anthony, 387
Averías, 118
Avila, Francisco de, 272–273, 329n. 10
"Aviso," 136
ax-mace, 338
Ayaviri, 94
ayllu, 27, 30, 167, 274, 323, 324, 339, 373, 374
Ayra de Arritu, don Fernando, 293

B

Bakhtin, Mikhail, 295
Bandelier, 1
Batista, Father Cícero Romão, 48
Baudin, Louis, 424
beads (*chaquira*), 411
Belén Black-on-Red, 118
Belgrano, 100
Beorchia Nigris, Antonio, 111
Betanzos, Juan de, 23, 99, 117
Bicho Muerto, 108–109
Bingham, Hiram, 1, 167, 169, 170–171, 173, 174, 177, 247n. 3
Black Polished, 118
Bolsón de Andalgalá, 91, 100, 108, 92 fig. 3, 107 fig. 11
Bonbon, 13, 13 fig. 2
Bonbon plateau, 38n. 5
Bowman, Glenn, 47–48
bronze, 332–343
Brumfiel, Elizabeth, 176

C

cabeceras, 14, 15, 16–17
Cabello Valboa, Miguel, 90, 122n. 2
cacap unanca, 292
cacique, 187, 293, 323. See also *curaca*
Cajón Valley, 109
Calahoyo Grande, 109
Calchaquí Valley, 89–106
Calchaquíes, 88, 110
camay, 277, 406
camayoc, 169, 171
camelid pastoralism, 117
Campo de Huasamayo, 109
Campo de Pucará, 99
Cañari. See Kañari
Canas Province, 110
cancha, 214. *See also kancha*
cangahua, 227, 228 fig. 3
Canta, 15
Canziani, Jose, 137
capac hucha, 113, 280, 284, 301n. 22, 322
Capac Raymi, 324–325
Capillas, 100
carpa, 293, 304n. 42
carpatira, 293
Carrasco, Andrés, 165
Casa Morada, 102
Castillo, Luis Jaime, 316
Castro, Cristóbal, 279
Catamarca, 91, 92, 106, 115; major Inka and Inka-era local sites, 10 fig. 10
Caxaconde, 35, 39n. 21
caya, 19
ceque, 111, 387, 388–389

Cerro Amarillo, 99
Cerro Chasquillas, 99
Cerro El Plomo, 113
Cerro El Torro, 113
Cerro Grande del Inga, 98, 99
Cerro Mercedario, 113
Ceruti, María, 111
Chakamarka, 11, 15, 16, 26, 27, 28–35; Inka road, 32 fig. 13; location of Inka settlements, 15 fig. 4
chakitaclla, 278
Challa Bay settlement, 73
Challapampa, 61
champa, 17
Chan Chan, 138
Chancha, 12 fig. 1, 17, 30, 30 fig. 11
Chanchamayo, 16, 18, 22
chaquira (beads), 411, 418n. 7
charki (*charqui*), 19, 58
chicha, 63, 392
Chicoana, 88 fig. 2, 94, 102, 110, 115
Chicón, 188
Chilecito. *See* La Rioja
Chiliques, 113
Chincha, 94, 135–137, 157
Chinchaycamac, 144
Chinchaycocha (Chinchayqocha), 5, 12–27, 35–36
Chinchaysuyu, 12–16, 23–27, 35–36
Chinchero, 212, 217n. 5
Chinkana, 64
"chosen women" (also called Mamacona), 53–54. *See also acllahuasi*
Chucaripupata, 72–73
chullpa, 224, 285
chunchos, 232, 296
Chunka Kamayoq, 360
chuño, 19
Chupacho (Chupaychu), 14, 34
Churumata, 111
Cieza de Leon, Pedro de, 13, 14, 15, 23–26, 28–31, 36, 56, 70, 99, 360, 398, 38n. 7
citua, 408, 418n. 6
ciudadelas, 138
Coati. *See* Island of the Moon
Cobo, Bernabé, 4, 23, 45, 53–54, 399, 425
Cobos, Rafael, 78n. 4
Cocha Sontor, 209
Cochahuasi, 207
Cochas, 30
Cochasquí, 226–230
Coctaca, 114
Collachagua (Collaguas), 25, 35
Collana, 27
colonists (*mitimaes*), 167
comarca, 28
Condorhuasi, 255

Congos, 27
Copacabana, 53–58
Copiapó, 113
copper, 317, 318, 319
Coricancha, 50–51, 62, 268
Corral Blanco, 100, 109
Corralito, 100, 109
corregimiento, 27
Cortaderas, 99, 100, 102, 103 fig. 6, 109
Covey, Alan, 90–91
criados (yanacona), 169, 171
cumbi, 63, 277, 279, 280–281, 282, 287, 293, 294, 296, 301n. 22, 304n. 42, 399, 416
curaca, 94, 273, 323, 430. *See also cacique*
Curatola, Marco, 137
Cusco, 3, 4, 23, 24, 25, 28, 29, 33, 34; Capac Raymi festival in, 324–325; metalworking, evidence of, 319–320; schematic diagram of ceque system of Cusco, 324 fig. 8
Cusco archaeology, 224–225
Cusco polychrome, 118, 118 fig. 14
cuyus manco, 200–201
Cuzco. *See* Cusco
cuzcohuasi, 288, 302–303n. 33

D

Diaguitas, 88
Donnan, Christopher, 316
d'Orbigny, Alcide, 230
Due, Berete, 328

E

Eade, John, 47
Earls, John, 323
Eaton, George, 167, 167 fig. 3
electrum, 319
encomienda, 34
Espinoza Soriano, Waldemar, 110
Estete, Miguel, 29

F

Falcón, Francisco, 274
Famabalasto Black-on-Red, 118
footplow (*chakitaclla*), 278
Fountain of the Inka, 68
Fuerte Quemado settlement, 89, 90, 115

G

galapón, 200
García, Alejo, 90
Garcilaso de la Vega, El Inka, 23, 62, 66, 273, 359
Gasparini, Graziano, 255
Gentile Lafaille, Margarita, 14
Gibaja, Arminda, 322
González Holguín, Diego, 274
Gose, Peter, 315–316, 344n. 1

Graffam, Gray, 335
Guaman Poma de Ayala, Felipe, 26–27, 36, 394, 395–397 figs. 2–13, 425; depiction of Inka palace types, 201 fig. 19; depiction of Manco Inka setting fire to the cuyus manco, 201 fig. 20
guano, 137
Guaraníes, 98
Guarco, 94
Guitián, 102, 104 fig. 7

H

Haenke, Thadäus, 230
hammers (*martillos*), 338
hanan, 274
Harrison, Regina, 292
Hastings, Charles, 38n. 9
Hastorf, Christine, 433
hatun ñan, 17
Hatun Sawsa, 20
Hatunqolla, 109
Haulfín Valley, 89
huacas, 49, 51, 52, 71, 74, 75, 111, 286, 301n. 25, 322, 388–389, 402–403, 408
Huallaga Valley, 13–14, 16, 21, 22, 26
huanta (*guanca*), 205
Huancavelica, 20
Huánuco Pampa, 11, 14, 16, 96, 144, 145, 148, 149, 156, 267, 434
huaquero, 143
Huarautambo, valley of, 16
Huasahuasi, 16, 18
Huayna Capac (Wayna Qhapaq), 25, 26, 29, 56–57, 90, 186–187, 188, 299
hucha, 406
Humboldt, Alexander von, 1
Huno Kuraka, 360
hunting (southern Andes), 116–117
hurin, 274, 300n. 13
Hyslop, John, 4, 17, 34, 58, 224

I

Iñak Uyu, 54, 64 fig. 8
Inca (Inka). *See* Inka
Incarracay, 255
Ingapirca, 17, 27, 32
Inka cemeteries, 165–183
Inka installations, nine largest, 11
Inka metallurgy, 320–346
Inka Paya, 118
Inka period, chronology of, 245 table 1
Inka settlements: administrative centers, 11–12; three types of, 11
Inka weaponry: ax-mace, 338; bronze ax-mace, 338; Inka pole-type weapons, 340; iron or steel halberd, 338; pole-ax, 338; *yauri*, 338

Inka Yupanki, 90
Inkahuasi, 255
Inkallajta, 96, 255, 257
Inkapirka, 255
Intipuncu (Door of the Sun), 62
Island of the Moon, 46, 64–66, 71, 74, 75
Island of the Sun, 60–71

J

Jacahuasi, 16, 30
Jauja (Xauxa), 20 fig. 1, 23, 24
Jiménez Borja, Arturo, 363
Jujuy, 98–99
Juli, 53
Julien, Catherine J., 109, 359
Junín, 11, 13, 15, 16, 17, 18, 20, 24, 33

K

Kachiqocha, 19
kallanka, 17, 29, 38n. 11, 31, 34, 35, 102
Kañari, 94
kancha, 17, 29, 31, 34, 169. *See also* cancha
Kasapata, 61
Kentipuncu (Door of the Hummingbird), 62
kero. See quero
Khipu Database Project, 359, 379n. 2
khipu, 293, 295, 357–359, 376–378, 430; accounting hierarchy, 365–368; archaeological context of, 363–365; decimal groupings of, 359–363; *khipukamayuq* ("khipu-makers/keepers"), 23, 358, 360, 371; khipu-keeper, 364; local or remote, 371–374; structure of, 369–371
Killke ceramic style, 3, 168
Kollasuyu, 85, 94, 100
Kona Bay, 68–69
Kubler, George, 267
kumpi wasi, 29
Kurupata, 70

L

La Centinela, 2, 138–154
La Encrucijada, 100
La Lagunita, 109
La Maravilla, 109
La Oroya, 18
La Rioja (Chilecito), 91, 111
labor tax, 359
Lake Chucuito (Titicaca), 53, 78n. 2
Lake Junín (formerly known as Lake Chinchayqocha), 13, 16, 38n. 14
Lake Titicaca, 16; Island of the Moon, 45; Island of the Sun, 45; Lake Titicaca region, 46 fig. 1
Lake Titicaca origin myth, 54, 55–56
Lake Titicaca pilgrimage complex, 46
Late Horizon, chronology of, 245 table 1, 246

Index 445

Lauricocha, 14, 16
Lerma Valley, 99
Licancabur, 113
Llanos de Mojo, 98
llauta, 393
Llullaillaco, 111
Loca, 58
Locke, L. Leland, 376
Londres de Quinmivil, 107
Los Amarillos, 89
Los Graneros, 100
Lucre ceramic style, 168
Lumbreras, Luis, 137

M

Machu Picchu, 1, 168–175
Mackey, Carol, 364, 365–366
makana de champi, 326
mallqui, 406
mamacocha, 326
Mamacona (*mamakuna*), 53–54, 68, 144
Manchachi, 255
Manco Capac, 54
Mantaro-style pottery, 18–19, 20, 20 figs. 7, 8
Marasttoco, 292
Marcacocha, 19
Marcapunta, 19
Margolies, Luise, 255
Marka-Marka, 29
mascaypacha, 322
Maule River, 99
Mauss, Marcel, 277
McEwan, Gordon F., 322
Medanitos, 115
Mena, Cristóbal de, 289
Mendoza, 91
Menzel, Dorothy, 431
mercaderes, 136
metallurgy. *See* alloys; bronze; Inka metallurgy
military tunic. *See* tunics, *uncu*
mit'a, 3, 30, 95, 167, 214, 360, 385
mitima (mitmaq), 3, 14, 30, 34
Moche, 314–316, 317, 318
Morejón, Diego Ortega, 279
Muelle, Jorge C., 363
mullu (*Spondylus princeps*), 136–137, 282, 316, 322, 325, 327
Murra, John V., 2, 3, 5, 277, 300n. 17, 424, 433
Murúa, Martín de, 145, 215, 267, 275, 289, 290–291, 294, 295, 358

N

Nasca, 402, 428
Netherly, Patricia, 361
Nevados de Aconquija or Pucará de las Pavas, 99

Niles, Susan A., 185–221, 426
Ninaqaqa (Ninacaca), 17, 19, 32
Nordenskiöld, Erland, 230, 260
nucleated villages, 20

O

Ojo de Agua, 100
olla, 19, 171, 226
orejones, 111
origin myths, 54–56
Oroncota, 255

P

Pacarina (*paqarina*), 285–286, 326
Pacariqtambo (Paqaritambo), 54–55, 56, 244
pacchas, 278, 301n. 20
Pachacamac, 2, 51–52, 78n. 1
Pachacuti Yamqui, Joan de Santa Cruz, 23, 25, 35, 56, 215, 273, 292, 293, 293 fig. 30
Pachaka Kuraka, 360
Pachakutec (Pachacuti, Pachakuti, Pachakuteq), 23, 24, 27, 28, 29, 406–407, 431
Pachamama, 23
pachamama, 326, 391–392
Paititi, 98
Palcamayo (Pallqamayu), 16, 17, 18, 21, 22, 24, 30
panaca, 167, 285–286, 406
parcialidades, 362
Pasco, 11, 13, 15, 20
patena (forehead medallion), 325
Patterson, Thomas C., 176, 424, 432
Pereyra, Hugo, 376
Perrin Pando, Alberto, 72
Pichca Chunca Kuraka, 360
Pilco Kayma, 60 fig. 5
pilgrimage, 47–77
pillco or pillku bird, 62, 78n. 5
Pillcopuncu (Door of the Pillco), 62
Pirwa-Pirwa, 29
Pizarro, Hernando, 29, 52
Pizarro, Pedro, 13, 14, 16, 17, 34, 35, 36, 38n. 4, 117, 200
pole-arms, 338
pole-ax, 338
Polo de Ondegardo, 24, 25, 27
Poma Guala, Alonso, 279
Potrero de Payogasta, 91, 92 fig. 3, 92–93 table 1, 100, 105–106, 105 fig. 9
Potrero Valley, 105
Potrero-Chaquiago, 91, 92 fig. 3, 92–93 table 1, 107–108, 107 fig. 11; agricultural production, 115
Pucará de Andalgalá, 98, 99
Pucará de las Pavas or Nevados de Aconquija, 99, 109
Pucará de Palermo, 100

Pucará Morado, 99
Pucará Tres Cruces, 99
Pucher, Leo, 235
Pueblito Calilegua, 99
Puerta de La Paya, 102
Puerta de Zenta, 99
pukara, 70
Pukatampu, 17, 30
Pular, 88, 112, 113, 114, 119–120
Pulares, 110
Pumapunca (Door of the Puma), 62
Pumpu (Pumbo, Bonbon, Bonbom), 11–17, 20–30, 33–36
Puncu, 60, 67 fig. 9
Punrun, 13, 26
Puruchuco, 365–366; accounting hierarchy, 365 fig. 5; description of, 365; museum, 363–364

Q

Qaqas (San Pedro de Cajas), 19, 22, 30
qepi bundle, 278
q'ero. *See* quero
qhapaq ucha. See capac hucha
Qochas, 17
qollqas, 17, 22, 31 fig. 12, 99, 255
Quebrada de Humahuaca Valley, 89, 91, 105, 109, 115
Quebrada de Yocavil, 108–109
Quechua, 99, 111, 38n. 6
quechua (zone), 16
quero (drinking vessel), 74, 270, 272–277, 280, 281 fig. 17, 284, 287–288, 291, 295, 296, 429
Quilmes settlement, 89, 115
Quimal, 113
quipu. *See* khipu
Quiri-Quiri province, 94, 106–107
quispi, 205
Quispiguanca, 192–199, 209–215

R

Radicati di Primeglio, Carlos, 357, 376
Ramos Gavilán, Alonso, 53–54, 56–57, 58, 63–64
Ranchillos, 109
Reinhard, Johan, 72, 111
repartimiento, 1
retainers (*yanaconas*), 167
Río Blanco, 100
Robinson, Martin, 48
Rojas, Diego de, 90
Rostworowski de Diez Canseco, María, 2, 3–4, 5, 136, 323, 424
Rowe, John H., 2–3, 168, 217n. 6, 244, 400, 409–410, 424
royal estate, 167–168
royal tunic. *See* tunics, *uncu*

S

Sacred Rock of Titikala, 45, 53, 62, 63, 63 fig. 6
Sacred Rock settlement, 73
Sacrifice Ceremony or Moche Presentation Theme, 317
Saignes, Thierry, 98
Salazar, Victor, 364
salinas (salt deposits), 19, 30
Sallnow, Michael, 47
Salomon, Frank, 376
Samaipata, 230–265
San Antonio del Cajón, 109
San Blas–style pottery, 17–22
San José de Moro, 316–317
San Juan Pata, 29
San Pedro de Atacama, 335, 346n. 9
Sancho, Pedro, 320–321
Santacruz Pachacuti Yamqui, Joan de. *See* Pachacuti Yamqui, Joan de Santa Cruz
Santa Maria Valley, 89; architectural constructions, distinctive, 109; Bicho Muerto, 108–109; Potrero-Chaquiago, 107–109; Pucará de las Pavas or Nevados de Aconquija, 109; Quebrada de Yocavil, 108–109; Quiri-Quiri, 106–107; Shinkal, 107; Watungasta, 108
Santamariano Bi-Color, 118
Santamariano residential architecture, 102
Santamariano Tri-Color, 118
Santiago de Compostela, cathedral of, 48, 49
Santiago del Estero, 111
Santillán, Francisco de, 279
Santillán, Hernando de, 99
Sapa Inka, 273, 279, 289–290, 291, 292, 392, 397, 413, 432
Sarmiento de Gamboa, Pedro, 24, 55, 117, 178n. 1, 215, 280, 297n. 3, 302nn. 27, 28
Sausa (Junín), 11
saya, 94
Schobinger, Juan, 111
Scott, James, 431
segunda persona, 323
señoríos, 17
Shinkal, 107
shrines: Coricancha, 50–51; *huacas*, 49, 322; Islands of the Sun and Moon, 52–54; Pachacamac, 51–52; shrine worship and regional control, 74–77
sillar, 17
Simbolar River, 107
Sinchi Roca, 212–213
Sipán. *See* Moche
sling stones, 98
spindle whorls, 120
Spondylus shell, 113, 136–137, 157, 282, 316, 322, 325–327, 342. *See also mullu*

Index

Squier, Ephraim George, 1, 58, 60
state farms, 114–116
storehouses. See qollqas
Suticttoco, 292
suyu, 50, 85

T

tambo. *See* tampu
Tambo Colorado, 2, 86, 145
Tampottocco (Tamputoco), 54, 292
tampu: definition of, 11, 38n. 2; location of Inka settlements, 15 fig. 4; types of, 28
Tapraq, 35
Tarapacá, 94
Tarma, valley of, 13–36
Tarma-style pottery, 21 fig. 10; description of, 21
Tarmatampu (Tarmatambo), 11, 15, 16, 21, 22, 26, 28–31, 35
Tarragó, Myriam N., 115
Tastil, 100
Tawantinsuyu, x fig. 1, xiv, 2, 4, 5, 6, 36, 75, 85, 111, 135, 136, 138, 142, 144, 146, 147, 155, 169, 177, 267, 268, 274, 275, 277, 284, 285, 286, 287–292, 295, 296, 299n. 8, 300n. 17, 302nn. 31, 32, 323, 328, 332, 336, 337, 342, 388, 404, 413, 423, 424, 426, 429–432
Telarnioc, 17, 30
Tello, Julio C., 2
Terrazas, Fernando, 260
Thaksi Kala, 45
Thupa Yupanki, 24, 25, 27, 29, 35, 90
Tilcara, 89
tinkuy pata, 33
Titani Peninsula, 68
Titicaca [Lake Chucuito], 16, 53, 78n. 2
Titikala, Sacred Rock of, 45, 53, 62, 63, 63 fig. 6
Titu Cussi Yupangui, 324
Tiwanaku state, 69, 72–74
tocapu, 269, 272, 280, 282–284, 285, 286, 287–288, 290–296, 301nn. 25, 26, 302n. 31, 386, 394, 396, 397, 400–401, 403, 404, 407, 409–410, 413, 417nn. 1, 3, 431
Tolombón settlement, 110
Topa Inka, 56
Torres, Elba, 177
Trimborn, Hermann, 230
Tschudi, Johann Jacob von, 1
Tucumán Province, 94, 99, 109, 111
Tucumanao or Tucumangasta, 111
Tucumanos, 88
tumbaga, 318, 344–345n. 4
tunics, 269 fig. 7, 273, 277, 277 fig. 14, 278, 282, 282 fig. 21, 285, 288 fig. 26, 300nn. 34, 35, 384, 384 fig. 1, 386, 388–389, 390, 391, 392, 395, 396–400, 396 fig. 15, 397 fig. 16, 400 figs. 17, 18, 401 fig. 19, 402, 403 figs. 20–22, 404–405, 406, 407–414, 415nn. 3, 4, 416nn. 7, 8, 9, 11, 427, 428–430. *See also uncu*
tupus, 169, 320, 330
Turner, Victor, 46

U

Uchuy Sawsa, 18
Ucu, 17
Uhle, Max, 2, 50, 142, 155
unancha, 290, 291
uncu, 269 fig. 7, 277, 278 fig. 15, 279, 280–281, 281 fig. 20, 282–286, 290, 291, 294, 299 n. 26, 301nn. 34, 35, 384, 414
upani, 325, 346n. 8
urpu, 281
Urubamba, town of, 185, 186 fig. 1, 187, 188, 201, 207, 212
Urubamba River, 186, 186 fig. 1, 188
Urubamba Valley, 3, 185, 186 fig. 1
Ushkus, 11
ushnu (*usnu*), 17, 30, 31, 241, 339

V

Vaca de Castro, Cristóbal, 36
Valdéz, 119–120
Valdivia, 99
varayoqs, 325
vicuña, 22
Vilcashuaman (Ayacucho), 11
Viracocha, 54, 56
visitas, 188
Vista Alegre. *See* Puruchuco
vizcacha (*Lagidium peruanum*), 173
Volcán, 89
volcanic tuff (*cangahua*), 227, 228 fig. 3

W

wak'a. See huaca
Wakuyu, 72–73
Wallace, Dwight, 137
wamani, 11, 13, 14, 15, 20, 27, 28, 30, 34, 36, 113; definition of, 13, 16
waranqas, 359
Warawtampu, 11, 15, 16, 26, 28, 29, 34–35, description of, 11; location of Inka settlements, 15 fig. 4
Watanabe, Luis, 177
Watungasta, 108
Wayna Qhapaq. *See* Huayna Capac
Wiraqocha Inka, 23
Wolf, Eric, 423–424, 426, 427

X

Xauxa, valley of, 24. *See also* Jauja
Xérez, Francisco de, 320
Xuco Guaman, 28